MEDICAL RECORDS REVIEW

MEDICAL RECORDS REVIEW
Fourth Edition

KRISTYN S. APPLEBY

JOANNE TARVER

76 Ninth Avenue, New York, NY 10011
www.aspenpublishers.com

This publication is designed to provide accurate and authoritative information in regard to the subject matter covered. It is sold with the understanding that the publisher is not engaged in rendering legal, accounting, or other professional services. If legal advice or other professional assistance is required, the services of a competent professional person should be sought.

—From a *Declaration of Principles* jointly adopted
by a Committee of the American Bar Association
and a Committee of Publishers and Associations

Figures 2–3, 3–1 and 6–6 from THE ANATOMY COLORING BOOK by WYNN KAPIT and LAWRENCE M. ELSON. ©1993, 1977 by Wynn Kapit and Lawrence M. Elison.
Reprinted by permission of HarperCollins Publishers, Inc. and Pearson Education, Inc.

©2006, 1999 Aspen Publishers, Inc.
a Wolters Kluwer business
www.aspenpublishers.com

Printed in the United States of America.

1 2 3 4 5 6 7 8 9 0

Library of Congress Cataloging-in-Publication Data

Appleby, Kristyn S.
    Medical records review/Kristyn S. Appleby, Joanne Tarver.—4th ed.
        p. cm.
    Includes bibliographical referecnes and index.
    ISBN 0-7355-6118-4 (casebound : alk. paper)
    1. Medical records—Law and legislation—United States.
    I. Tarver, Joanne.   II. Title.
    [DNLM: 1. Medical records—legislation & Jurisprudence—United States. WX 33 AA1 A648m 2006]

    KF3827.R4A96 2006
    344.7304′1—dc22

                                                                        2006023611

About Aspen Publishers

Aspen Publishers, headquartered in New York City, is a leading information provider for attorneys, business professionals, and law students. Written by pre-eminent authorities, our products consist of analytical and practical information covering both U.S. and international topics. We publish in the full range of formats, including updated manuals, books, periodicals, CDs, and online products.

Our proprietary content is complemented by 2,500 legal databases, containing over 11 million documents, available through our Loislaw division. Aspen Publishers also offers a wide range of topical legal and business databases linked to Loislaw's primary material. Our mission is to provide accurate, timely, and authoritative content in easily accessible formats, supported by unmatched customer care.

To order any Aspen Publishers title, go to *www.aspenpublishers.com* or call 1-800-638-8437.

To reinstate your manual update service, call 1-800-638-8437.

For more information on Loislaw products, go to *www.loislaw.com* or call 1-800-364-2512.

For Customer Care issues, e-mail *CustomerCare@aspenpublishers.com*; call 1-800-234-1600; or fax 1-800-901-9075.

Aspen Publishers
a Wolters Kluwer business

SUBSCRIPTION NOTICE

This Aspen Publishers product is updated on a periodic basis with supplements to reflect important changes in the subject matter. If you purchased this product directly from Aspen Publishers, we have already recorded your subscription for the update service.

If, however, you purchased this product from a bookstore and wish to receive future updates and revised or related volumes billed separately with a 30-day examination review, please contact our Customer Service Department at 1-800-234-1660, or send your name, company name (if applicable), address, and the title of the product to:

ASPEN PUBLISHERS
7201 McKinney Circle
Frederick, MD 21704

ABOUT THE AUTHORS

Kristyn S. Appleby earned her B.A. in anthropology from California State University at Long Beach and her paralegal certification in the attorney assistant program at Sonoma State University, where she is an adjunct faculty member. Ms. Appleby has worked as a paralegal since 1983, specializing in cases involving complex medical and psychological injuries. Together with co-author Joanne Tarver, she has presented nationwide seminars on Medical Records Review for the Legal Professional.

Joanne Tarver received her B.S.N. from Sonoma State University, where she is an adjunct faculty member, and her M.B.A. from San Jose State University. She has had extensive experience in acute care nursing and has worked in clinical resource management for a nationwide integrated health care system. Ms. Tarver has experience as a consultant in medical-legal chart review and has acted as an expert witness in medical malpractice cases.

SUMMARY OF CONTENTS

CONTENTS

xi

CONTENTS

CONTENTS   xvii

CONTENTS

CONTENTS

FOREWORD

Litigation attorneys who serve the insurance industry and self-insured corporations are continually under pressure to reduce costs of litigation. For other reasons, the plaintiff's bar is also faced with reducing the amount of time spent on any particular file. Whoever the law firm is, and whoever it represents, it is expected to deliver the same or a higher level of quality legal representation as it has in the past. One of the more time-consuming review projects is invariably related to medical records. So, it is important to ensure that anyone who sets out to review and understand medical records be able to do so efficiently and effectively.

Personal injury litigation continues to be the largest single arena of litigated matters in the United States. Before any attorney can accurately evaluate the value of a claim, he or she must be able to accurately read and understand the medical records and their significance. This book takes one on a guided tour of the human anatomy while describing terminology and abbreviations used by medical professionals. The authors provide not only the means to obtain and digest the records, but the method to put critical information into a form that is both easily understood and able to be used at trial, arbitration, or mediation.

Making sense of medical records is often difficult even for medical professionals. So, when those individuals who work in litigation are required to review, translate, and understand medical records, the task can be overwhelming. For many years, the "bible" for my law firm and hundreds of other firms has been this publication. Since its initial publication in 1984, this publication has been an invaluable teaching tool and reference source for our paralegals, secretaries, legal assistants, and attorneys over the years. And, the volume occupies a prominent place at the desk of every paralegal and attorney in my office.

BARRY CLIFFORD SNYDER
Snyder Law, a Prof. Corp.
Santa Barbara, CA
www.snyderlaw.com

PREFACE

This book is the product of the friendship of two individuals, one a registered nurse and one a litigation paralegal. The idea began in the course of information discussions concerning issues in our respective disciplines. Gradually it became apparent that the fields of medicine and law had become closely intertwined in many aspects and that professionals from both fields were handling medical records in litigation without adequate background preparation.

As a result of these discussions, the authors developed a course designed to address certain identified information gaps. This course was initially incorporated in 1987 into the curriculum of the Paralegal Program at Sonoma State University and later taken nationwide as a seminar.

However, this fourth edition bears little resemblance to that first publication of 1984, an initial offering that was little more than a rudimentary look at the medical record and its use by paralegals in litigation. This fourth edition, building on the information contained in previous editions and updates, incorporates input from those who use our book in their work and from the authors' respective fields into an intense assessment of the medical record for use by all legal professionals.

One of the primary focus areas for this new edition was to improve the flow of information and so the chapters have been revised, reordered, and reorganized. Rather than just skimming the surface of the topics, this edition offers greatly expanded, in-depth tips and tools on how to translate information in the medical record into a document helpful throughout in the litigation process.

June 2006

KRISTYN S. APPLEBY
Sebastopol, California

JOANNE TARVER
Cambria, California

ACKNOWLEDGMENTS

To my husband Bill, my son James, and my daughter Carlyn for their unfailing support and love. To Diane Petropulos for her support and encouragement in the development of the seminar on which this book was based and ultimately written. To Bonnie Twieg for her support and encouragement in all of my writing endeavors, personal and professional. To all of the excellent attorneys, paralegals, doctors, and nurses with whom I have had the good fortune to work on fascinating cases. And special thanks to all of the legal and medical professionals who use medical records in litigation, purchased this book, and attended our seminars since 1989, for their generous suggestions for improvements and additions.

K.S.A.

To my husband Jim, graphics expert, consultant, mentor, and (most importantly) best friend, and to my daughters Jennifer and Kimberly for their consistent support in this endeavor. To numerous professional colleagues from many disciplines who have enabled me to grow personally and professionally throughout my career. Finally, to the profession of nursing that has given me such great rewards and, hopefully, has enabled me to be an advocate for those in need of health care.

J.T.

Artwork drawn (in part), modified, and compiled by Jim Tarver.

CHAPTER 1

UNDERSTANDING MEDICAL RECORDS

§ 1.1   Introduction

The primary source of information in litigation involving personal injury is the medical record. The law requires that a record be generated when any type of healthcare is given, including all types of diagnostic testing, nursing care, and treatments. Medical records have specific purposes in healthcare delivery and must contain certain types of information. Because information contained in the medical record is crucial in proving (or disproving) allegations involving injury, it is critical that the legal professional understand the universe of medical records and what is required to obtain, and understand, the information contained in the record. This chapter will assist the reader in understanding the purpose, content, and legal requirements of the medical record, and discuss issues concerning confidentiality.

§ 1.2   Purpose

The medical record has several specific purposes, including:

- documentation of all aspects of patient care management
- communication between health care providers
- identification of health patterns and/or problems
- records the effectiveness of interventions (treatments, drug therapy, surgical procedures, special diets)
- provides clinical data for research and education
- legal documentation of care and treatment received by an individual.

§ 1.3   Content

The Joint Commission on Accreditation of Healthcare Organizations (JCAHO) evaluates and accredits more than 15,000 health care organizations and programs in the United States. An independent, not-for-profit organization, the Joint Commission is the nation's predominant standards-setting and accrediting body in health care. Since 1951, the Joint Commission has maintained state-of-the-art standards that focus on improving the quality and safety of care provided by health care organizations. The Joint Commission's comprehensive accreditation process evaluates an organization's compliance with these standards and other accreditation requirements; a healthcare institution which does not meet JCAHO requirements for accreditation, is not eligible for payments from Medicare or Medicaid.

JCAHO language is clear on the medical record standards for acute care hospitals. It states that hospitals must:

- initiate and maintain a medical record for every individual treated
- ensure only authorized individuals make entries in the medical record and that each entry is identifiable by the signature of the individual making it

- contain sufficient information to identify the patient, support the diagnosis, justify treatment, document hospital course and results of treatment, and promote continuity of care among health care providers
- ensure verbal or telephone orders that are given by physicians are accepted and transcribed by authorized individuals identified by title or category in the medical staff bylaws.

JCAHO requires that medical records be reviewed for completeness, accuracy, and timeliness of documentation of pertinent information discussed in the preceding sections. Medical records are considered complete when all information is present and authenticated (signed by the appropriate medical provider). This information must include documentation of all final diagnoses and complications, recorded without the use of symbols or abbreviations. JCAHO requires that the medical record be complete no later than 30 days after discharge. The following is an example of how this content might be documented:

1. **Client's history (past medical history and current complaint)**
   This is a 50-year-old male involved in a motor vehicle accident last night. He was the driver of a car struck broadside and had to be extracted from the vehicle. He enters with obvious deformity of the left femur and multiple cuts and abrasions of his face *(current complaint)*. He has a 5-year history of hypertension for which he takes hydrochlorothiazide daily *(past medical history)*.
2. **Diagnosis of any illness**
   X rays of the left leg reveal a fracture of the middle third of the left femur. X rays of the skull and facial bones are negative.
3. **Treatment/intervention prescribed or provided**
   The patient will be placed in balanced suspension traction with 35 pounds of weight. All facial lacerations and abrasions will be cleaned and sutured.
4. **Client's response/reaction to treatment**
   Follow-up X rays of the left leg reveal good alignment of the fracture of the mid-third femur.

Inadequate documentation in any area of the medical record is problematical, especially in medical malpractice litigation as it can diminish the basis of the medical record in defending the care provided. A common assumption, "if it wasn't charted, it wasn't done," becomes paramount in malpractice cases. In the example above, if the physician had not documented that the patient's fracture was in good alignment (patient's *response* to treatment) after the application of the suspension traction (the *treatment*), the documentation would have been severely inadequate. In the "real world" of medical records, the quality of documentation varies tremendously. Be aware, however, that *quantity* of documentation is not consistent with *quality*. Voluminous documentation can contain little useful information; likewise, brief, concise notes can contain all information necessary to meet content requirements.

§ 1.4   Legal Requirements

Before a medical record may be used as evidence in litigation, the following must be established:

1. **The record is that of the patient in question.** Each page of the record should have the patient clearly identified by both name and medical record number. Healthcare institutions can have thousands of patients, so erroneous filings do occur but should be easy to spot.
2. **The record was compiled in the ordinary course of business (at the time the events occurred).**
3. **The record was prepared by persons who had knowledge of the events being recorded.** Each care provider must enter his or her own chart notes; one nurse cannot chart for another, etc.
4. **The record was prepared before litigation began.**
5. **The record is legible.** (See § **8.39** for a discussion of illegible records.)

Once information has been entered into a medical record, alteration of the content, if necessary, must follow certain protocols. On occasion, medical records are altered intentionally. Signs of questionable valid alterations include the following:

1. Changes in the timing of medical record entries, especially when they are crucial to allegations of malpractice.
2. Excess number of late entries involving circumstances surrounding allegations of malpractice. Late entries, if they are made, should

include both the date and time the chart entry is made and the date and time the actual event occurred.

3. Use of whiteout or similar fluid to redact or cover up any item in the medical record. Obliteration of any entry is not acceptable for correcting erroneous entries. Mistakes in the medical record should be lined out with a single line, marked "error," and the correct notation made.

§ 1.5   Responsibility

The medical record is not "owned" by the patient. Rather, the institutions and healthcare professionals that provide care to an individual own the record. With this ownership comes the responsibility for safeguarding the content against loss, tampering, and unauthorized access. Healthcare providers must adhere to the legal and regulatory requirements that govern the content and retention of records. Regardless of the source of the record (large acute care facility or sole practitioner), many of the requirements are essentially the same.

§ 1.6   Record Retention

The length of time that medical records must be retained by health care providers is defined by law and is usually determined by statutes of limitation. In California, for example, Title 22 of the California Administrative Code requires acute care facilities to retain medical records of adults for seven years and those of children until one year after the eighteenth birthday. In no event may records of a minor be destroyed in less than seven years.

Both the American Medical Association and the American Medical Record Association recommend a 10-year retention period for most parts of the acute care medical record. JCAHO recommends that retention time should depend upon both the need for using the records in continuing patient care and for legal, research, or educational purposes, and on law and regulation. Many health care providers elect to retain records longer than recommended by law; some retain all medical records permanently.

All health care facilities should have policies on record retention that are based on federal and state statutory and regulatory requirements, statutes of limitation, medical research conducted in the institution, and recommendations of applicable healthcare and health information associations.

§ 1.7   Confidentiality

The doctrine of confidentiality is the cornerstone of the physician-patient relationship. Only by being completely candid with a physician concerning his or her health history and present symptoms can a patient be assured of receiving the best medical care. In turn, the patient reasonably expects that all confidential information relayed to the physician will not go beyond the physician's office. The genesis of this doctrine can be traced to Hippocrates, widely acknowledged as the father of medicine. In the fourth century B.C., Hippocrates (or a member of his school) wrote a treatise on the conduct of physicians. A portion of this work, commonly known as the Hippocratic oath, states: ". . . and whatsoever I shall see or hear in the course of my profession . . . if it be what should not be published abroad, I will never divulge, holding such things to be holy secrets. . . ." The American Medical Association reaffirmed this concept in the *Principles of Medical Ethics* § 5.05:

> The information disclosed to a physician during the course of the relationship between physician and patient is confidential to the greatest possible degree. . . . [T]he obligation to safeguard patient confidences is subject to certain exceptions which are ethically and legally justified because of overriding social considerations.

§ 1.8   —State Legislation–Privileges

Despite what would seem to be the universal nature of this doctrine, it was not recognized at common law. New York became the first state to grant a testimonial privilege to physicians in 1828. Since that time, forty-two states have statutorily recognized the physician-patient privilege. See **Table 1–1** at the end of this chapter for a state-by-state reference to specific statutes.

Unlike the physician-patient privilege, 49 states plus the District of Columbia statutorily recognize some form of a psychologist-client privilege. Clearly, the governing bodies in this country recognize the continued need for protection of the confidentiality of psychiatric and psychological communications. See **Table 1–2** at the end of this chapter for a state-by-state reference to specific statutes.

Generally speaking, these statutes provide that an evidentiary privilege may be asserted on behalf of the patient with regard to physician-patient communications in judicial and quasi-judicial proceedings. In some jurisdictions this privilege has been extended to communications between a patient and nurse, psychologist, psychotherapist, or social worker. Conversely, some jurisdictions limit this privilege to psychotherapeutic relationships that involve either a psychiatrist or a psychologist holding a Ph.D.

In a 1996 case, *Jaffee v. Redmond* (518 U.S. 1), the U.S. Supreme Court recognized for the first time a federal psychotherapist-patient privilege and extended the privilege to confidential communications with a licensed social worker in the course of psychotherapy. In states without a privilege statute, some courts have recognized a duty on the part of a physician to remain silent. The duty has variously been interpreted to derive from an implied contract of confidentiality, a patient's constitutional right to privacy, state licensing statutes, and as a matter of public policy.

§ 1.9   Confidentiality in the Age of Computers

The protection of individual privacy was easy to ensure when medical records were kept in paper folders in the physician's office or the medical records department of a hospital. However, a growing reliance on computers, the development of commercial information companies, and the trend toward managed care have in fact created a new commodity. Medical information is now recognized as a business asset that can be bought or sold.

§ 1.10   Medical Information as a Commodity

Data collection from computerized or other patient records for marketing purposes raised serious ethical concerns. In some cases, data collection firms working on behalf of pharmaceutical corporations obtained medical information from physicians in return for computer hardware and software incentives. This information was then turned over to the pharmaceutical company. The American Medical Association stated that these types of agreements may "violate principles of informed consent and patient confidentiality" and harmed the integrity of the physician-patient relationship. (*See* AMA Opinion & Standard 5.075—Disclosure of Records to Data Collection Companies.)

§ 1.11   Health Care Information Technology

For years, paper has been and remains the dominant storage medium for medical information in most clinical settings. In 1993 the General Accounting Office estimated that some 34 million annual hospital admissions and 1.2 billion outpatient visits generated 10 billion pages of clinical records. With the development of computers and highly sophisticated data collection and sharing systems, the concept of a "paperless" medical record inches closer to reality.

Proponents of health care information technology envision a more efficient, smooth-running health care system with better coordination of care, reduced variation in practice patterns, and a lower rate of administrative costs. In a 1997 report released by the National Research Council, it was estimated that deployment of health care information technology was proceeding rapidly, with spending estimated at more than $10 to $15 billion per year.

The Council report identified the following goals of this rapidly expanding system:

- Universal "electronic exchange" of the billions of reimbursement claims made each year and related information for the medical billing and insurance industries
- Management and transport of individual medical information in electronic clinical records for hundreds of millions of U.S. patients
- Use of aggregate data compiled from computer-based clinical and administration databases for utilization review, outcomes research, population-based health studies, and public health surveillance
- Ability of medical practitioners to access real-time decision-support tools (replacing paper-based references and guidelines)
- Remote consultations among practitioners, along with continuing professional education by video- and computer-conferencing, and via computer-based multimedia programs

- Consumer health education, home health care self-management assistance, and remote monitoring via telephone, video, and computer-based tools
- Internet-based data on providers, institutions, and managed care networks.

Institutional and provider responsibility for ensuring the confidentiality of information contained in the medical record includes protection against unauthorized disclosure to personnel, unauthorized disclosure to outsiders, and accidental or malicious errors. Electronic technology widely used today for storing and transmitting medical information challenges existing systems for ensuring confidentiality. The principal advantage of these technologies is rapid access to information, but this benefit must be balanced against its potential impact on confidentiality. Responsibilities for ensuring confidentiality of medical records extend to electronically stored or transmitted medical records. Computerized medical record information systems should have procedures that provide security against unauthorized access to files. Additionally, a plan should be in place that protects files against loss or destruction from system failures (i.e., a disaster recovery system).

§ 1.12 —American Medical Association Guidelines

The American Medical Association issued guidelines for the protection of confidential medical information placed into computers (Opinion & Standard 5.07—Confidentiality: Computers). These guidelines included the following:

- Only authorized personnel should enter confidential medical information into a computer-based medical record. The identity of these individuals should be entered in the record, along with the date and time the entry was made.
- Full disclosure regarding the existence of computerized databases containing medical information about the patient should be made to the patient prior to obtaining informed consent for treatment. This disclosure must include the identification of all individuals and organizations with access to the information.

- Express consent must be given by the patient to any release of patient-identifiable clinical or administrative information to individuals or organizations outside the medical care environment.
- Dissemination of confidential medical data should be limited to those individuals or organizations with a bona fide use for the data. Patient identifiers should be omitted when appropriate. Further release of the data to other individuals or organizations or subsequent use of the data for other purposes is not authorized.
- Procedures for purging the database of inaccurate or archaic data should be established. The patient and physician should be notified prior to any purging of data.
- Individuals and organizations external to the clinical facility should not be provided on-line access to the database. Access to the database should be controlled with security measures, including passwords, encryption or encoding of information, and scannable badges or other types of user identification. Personnel audit procedures should be developed to establish a record in the event of unauthorized disclosure of medical data. Terminated or former employees should have no access to medical record data.
- Backup systems should be in place to prevent data loss as a result of hardware or software failure.
- Upon termination of computer services for a physician, the computer files maintained for that physician should be physically turned over to the physician. No destruction of the files may take place until the physician verifies that a copy of the data exists elsewhere.

§ 1.13   —Federal Legislation Concerning Medical Privacy

Federal legislation was enacted to protect the privacy of a variety of types of information: educational records (1974), bank records (1978), cable television services (1984), electronic communications (1986), employee polygraphs (1988), video rentals (1988), and telemarketing (1988). However, with very few exceptions (see the Privacy Act discussion below) it was not until the year 2000 that the federal government actually took action to protect the confidentiality of medical information.

§ 1.14   —The Privacy Act of 1974

The first federal protection for medical information came with the Privacy Act of 1974, which was enacted to protect individuals against disclosure of information held by *federal agencies* in any "system of records." Hospitals operated by the federal government, such as the Veterans Administration and Indian Health Services, were subject to the Privacy Act, as were a small number of private health care and research facilities that maintained medical records under federal contracts. Under the Privacy Act of 1974, any disclosure of information or data collected must be "relevant and necessary" to the agency's mission. Release of personally identifiable data required consent, unless the disclosure was "compatible" with the purposes for which the data was collected, or if disclosure served a public policy need for which statutory authority exists. In 1988 the Computer Matching and Privacy Protection Act amended the original 1974 Act. This amendment required agencies to develop agreements to control information exchange.

§ 1.15   Health Insurance Portability and Accountability Act (HIPAA)

Recognizing the serious need for a national patient record privacy standard, the Health Insurance Portability and Accountability Act (HIPAA) was signed into law on August 21, 1996. The first part of this legislation, the "portability" aspect, serves to protect the ability of people with current or pre-existing medical conditions to get or maintain health insurance if starting a new job. It also established medical savings accounts and tax deductions for long-term care insurance. The second, and most significant aspect of HIPAA, the Standards for Privacy of Individually Identifiable Health Information (The Privacy Rule), deals with establishing standards for the privacy and security of all individually identifiable health information in any form, electronic or non-electronic, held or transmitted by a health care provider. While the proper designation is the HIPAA Privacy Rule, common usage is to refer to the rules and regulations as HIPAA, the Privacy Rule, or the rule(s). Initially, the proposed legislation only addressed health information found in electronic records and any paper records that had at some point existed in electronic form. Extensive public comment which focused on concerns that the rule would not achieve its intended purpose but would adversely affect the quality of, or create barriers to, patient care. On that basis, the rule was amended to apply to all records in any form. In essence, HIPAA has created a privacy system that covers virtually all health information held by hospitals, providers, health plans and health insurers. The entire Privacy Rule, as well as additional materials, may be located at *www.hhs.gov/ocr/hipaa.*

Under the provisions of HIPAA, healthcare providers and health plans are required to give their clients a clear, written explanation of how they can use, keep, and disclose health information. Healthcare providers who see patients are required to obtain patient *consent* before sharing their information for treatment, payment, and health care operations purposes. Written patient *authorization* to disclose information must be obtained for non-routine uses and most non-healthcare purposes, such as releasing information to financial institutions regarding mortgages and other loans, or selling mailing lists to interested parties such as life insurers. Patients have the right to request restrictions on the uses and disclosures of their information. Providers and health plans generally cannot condition treatment on a patient's agreement to disclose health information for non-routine uses.

§ 1.16   —State Confidentiality Laws May be Preempted by HIPAA

HIPAA provides a federal floor of privacy protection for an individual's health information held by a covered entity (for example, acute care hospital, physician or insurance plan) or by a business associate of the covered entity (for example, copy and record storage services, law firms). However, this federal floor leaves other, stronger protections of state law in place. The protections are cumulative, so that the individual gets the strongest protections and benefits of each law. (45 C.F.R. § 160.203.)

State laws that are contrary to HIPAA are preempted by the federal requirements, unless a specific exception applies. These exceptions include if the state law (1) relates to the privacy of individually identifiable health information and provides *greater* privacy protections or privacy rights with respect to such information, (2) relates to the reporting of disease or injury, child abuse, birth, or death, or for public health surveillance, investigation, or intervention, or (3) requires certain health plan reporting, such as for management or financial audits. In these circumstances, a covered entity is not required to comply with a contrary provision of HIPAA. (45 C.F.R. §§ 160.201 to 160.205.)

For example, a state law that provides individuals the right to inspect and obtain a copy of their medical records in a more timely manner than HIPAA is deemed "more stringent" than HIPAA. In the case where a more stringent provision of state law is contrary to a provision of HIPAA, an exception to preemption is provided for the more stringent provision of state law, and the state law prevails. As defined by HIPAA, "contrary" means that it would be impossible for a covered entity to comply with both the State and Federal requirements, or that the provision of State law is an obstacle to accomplishing the full purposes and objectives of HIPAA. Where the more stringent state law and HIPAA are not contrary, covered entities must comply with both laws. For example, in California, a statute requires that all authorizations for release of medical information be in a 14-point font, although HIPAA has no similar requirement. As a result, authorizations in California must meet all of the HIPAA requirements and be in a 14-point font. (See § 7.14 for a further discussion of HIPAA requirements for authorizations.)

§ 1.17   General HIPAA Concepts & Definitions

At 440,000 words and more than 1,500 printed pages, HIPAA has been described as only a few chapters shy of *War and Peace*. The ramifications of HIPAA for the medical profession as a whole and the average citizen are deep and significant.

Practice Note: What follows is a general discussion of important concepts and definitions in HIPAA; discussions in other chapters will address only those aspects of the rule which in some way affect the use of medical records in litigation.

§ 1.18   —Uses and Disclosures for Treatment, Payment, and Health Care Operations

The intent of HIPAA is to establish a foundation of federal protection for personal health information, while avoiding barriers to the delivery of health care. The primary areas of concern are treatment, payment, and health care operations.

Treatment is defined as the provision, coordination, or management of health care and related services among health care providers, or by a health care provider with a third party, consultation between health care providers regarding a patient, or referral of a patient from one health care provider to another.

Payment covers activities of health care providers to obtain payment or reimbursement for services and of a health plan to obtain premiums, to fulfill coverage responsibilities and provide benefits under the plan, and to obtain or provide reimbursement for the provision of health care.

Health care operations refers to certain administrative, financial, legal, and quality improvement activities of a covered entity that are necessary to run its business and support the core functions of treatment and payment. The rule specifically defines these activities. (45 C.F.R. § 164.506.)

§ 1.19   —Protected Health Information (PHI)

Protected health information is defined as all "individually identifiable health information" held or transmitted by a covered entity or its business associate, in any form or media, where electronic, paper, or oral. (45 C.F.R. § 160.103.) PHI includes the patient's name, Social Security number, telephone number, medical record number, or ZIP code. [*Note:* excluded from PHI are employment, education, and certain other records.]

§ 1.20   —De-Identified Health Information

There are no restrictions on the use or disclosure of de-identified health information (DHI), defined as information which neither identifies nor provides a reasonable basis to identify an individual. (45 C.F.R. §§ 502(d)(2), 164.514(a) and (b).)

§ 1.21   —Consent for the Use or Disclosure of PHI

Providers and health plans are required to give their patients a clear written explanation of how the entity can use, keep, and disclose their health information. Health care providers who see patients are required to obtain patient consent before sharing their information for treatment, payment, and health care operations purposes. Patient authorization to disclose information must be sought and granted for nonroutine uses and most non-healthcare purposes, such as releasing information to financial institutions determining mortgages and other loans or selling mailing lists to interested parties such as life insurers. Patients have the right to request restrictions on the uses and disclosures of their information. Providers and health plans generally cannot condition treatment on a patient's agreement to disclose health information for nonroutine uses.

§ 1.22 —Limitations on Use and Release of PHI

With few exceptions, an individual's health information can be used for health purposes only. This means that patient information can be used or disclosed by a health plan, provider, or clearinghouse only for purposes of health care treatment, payment, and operations. Health information cannot be used for purposes not related to health care—such as use by employers to make personnel decisions, or use by financial institutions—without *explicit authorization* from the individual. Covered entities are required to develop policies and procedures to control and track the use of medical information, and maintain the privacy of that information.
This can be done by:

1. Adopting written privacy procedures. These must include who has access to the protected information, how it will be used within the entity, and when the information would or would not be disclosed to others. They must also take steps to ensure that their business associates protect the privacy of health information.

2. Training employees and designating a privacy officer. Covered entities must provide sufficient training so that their employees understand the new privacy protections procedures, and designate an individual to be responsible for ensuring the procedures are followed.

3. Establishing grievance processes. Covered entities must provide a means for patients to make inquiries or complaints regarding the privacy of their records.

§ 1.23 —Entities Covered by HIPAA

HIPAA covers all health care providers and health plans such as hospitals, medical practices (including solo practitioners), employers, rehabilitation centers, nursing homes, public health authorities, life insurance agencies, billing agencies and some vendors, service organizations, and universities. It also covers health care clearinghouses that generate and electronically transmit medical information such as billing, claims, enrollment, or eligibility verification. Each defined group is known as a "covered entity." (45 C.F.R. §§ 160.102, 160.103).

§ 1.24   —Definition of Business Associate

Typically, covered entities do not provide all services internally, but instead contract with a variety of businesses to provide specific services. In general, "business associate" is defined as a person or organization who, on behalf of a covered entity, performs or assists in the performance of functions or activities that involve the use or disclosure of individually identifiable health information (e.g., claims processing and administration, data analysis, utilization review, quality assurance, billing, benefit, or practice management). A business associate is also an individual or organization who provides legal, actuarial, accounting, consulting, administrative, accreditation or financial services to or for a covered entity (other than in the capacity of a member of the covered entity's workforce). Each business associate must enter into a written contract with the covered medical entity, which requires the business associate to maintain and to follow all of the provisions of HIPAA with regard to privacy of medical information. Further, the business associate itself must enter into contracts with other entities requiring these third parties to follow the provisions of HIPAA. (45 C.F.R. §§ 160.103; for a sample seven page Business Associate Contract, see *www.hhs.gov/ocr/hipaa/contractprov.*)

Practice Note: This provision evidently recognizes that defense counsel providing legal advice or representation to a medical provider are "business associates" under HIPAA. Conceivably, HIPAA would then require the business associate to enter into a contract for services with the provider. Further, defense counsel would be required to obtain appropriate contracts from all of the services utilized during the course of litigation— subpoena services, expert witnesses, document storage facilities, other attorneys, services providing exhibits for trial, the company that destroys documents, etc.

§ 1.25   —Disclosure of PHI to Business Associate Via Written Agreement

HIPAA allows a covered entity to disclose necessary protected health information to its business associates under the following conditions:

- The covered entity receives satisfactory assurances in writing from the business associate in writing, either in the form of a contract or other agreement,
- When the business associate provides assurances that it will safeguard protected health information it receives from the covered entity,
- The covered entity provides the business associate only information necessary to carry out health care functions, and
- The business associate does not use protected health information for its own independent use or purposes. (45 C.F.R. §§ 164.302 *et seq.*).

If a covered entity determines that a breach of the above requirements occurred, the entity must demonstrate that it took reasonable steps to cure the breach, and if unsuccessful in these efforts, it must terminate the contract with the offending business associate.

§ 1.26   —Disclosure of PHI to Business Associate Not Requiring Written Agreement

In some instances, there are exceptions to the business associate standard. (45 C.F.R. § 164.502(e)(i)(ii).) Under the following circumstances, a covered entity is not required to have a business associate contract before protected health information is disclosed:

- Disclosures to a health care provider for treatment of the individual.
- Some (defined) disclosures to a health plan sponsor such as an employer.
- Collection and sharing of information by a health plan that is a public benefits program, such as Medicare, that is required to determine eligibility or enrollment.
- Disclosures by a health care provider to a health plan for payment purposes.

- With persons or organizations whose functions or services do not involve the use of disclosure of protected health information, e.g., janitorial or maintenance services.
- With a person or organization that acts as a conduit for protected health information, such as courier or mail services, or their electronic equivalents.
- To disclose protected health information to a researcher for research purposes, either with patient authorization or pursuant to waiver or as a limited data set (as specifically defined by the Privacy Rule).
- When a financial institution processes consumer initiated financial transactions to facilitate payment for health care or health care premiums.

§ 1.27   —Use of PHI

Generally speaking, a covered entity may use or disclose medical information without the individual's authorization under certain circumstances. (45 C.F.R. § 164.502(c)(1).) Those circumstances include:

- For its own treatment, payment, and health care operations activities,
- For the treatment activities of any health care provider (including providers not covered by the Privacy Rule), e.g., as in a referral to a specialist who needs the information to treat the individual or as in transmission of patient health care instructions to a nursing home,
- To another covered entity or health care provider (including providers not covered by the Privacy Rule) for payment activities of the entity that receives the information, or
- To another covered entity for health care operations of the entity has a relationship with the individual and if the disclosure of the protected health information is pertinent to relationship. For example, a health care provider may disclose protected health information to a health plan for HEDIS purposes, provided the health plan has a relationship with the individual who is the subject of the information. (See § 8.36 for a discussion of HEDIS.)

Faxing.   Faxing medical information is a common practice that, prior to HIPAA, had no official rules or statutory requirements governing it. HIPAA now allows covered health care providers to share protected health information for treatment purposes via facsimile, as long as they use reasonable safeguards when doing so. For example, when faxing protected health information to a telephone number that is not regularly used, a reasonable safeguard may involve a provider first confirming the fax number with the intended recipient. Similarly, a covered entity may pre-program frequently used numbers directly into the fax machine to avoid misdirecting the information.

§ 1.28 —Disclosures of PHI to Others Without Authorization

HIPAA permits certain existing disclosures of health information without individual authorization for certain defined activities and for activities that allow the health care system to operate more smoothly. All of these disclosures have been permitted under existing laws and regulations. (45 C.F.R. §§ 164.512 *et seq.)* Within certain guidelines found in the regulation, covered entities may disclose information for:

- Oversight of the healthcare system, including quality assurance activities;
- Public health matters;
- Research (generally limited to when a waiver of authorization is independently approved by a privacy board or Institutional Review Board);
- Limited law enforcement activities;
- Emergency circumstances;
- For identification of the body of a deceased person, or the cause of death;
- For facility patient directories (patient has right to agree or object);
- For notification and other purposes (admission to hospital, picking up prescriptions for another, Red Cross disaster relief efforts, etc.);
- Victims of abuse, neglect or domestic violence;
- For activities related to national defense and security.
- Judicial and administrative proceedings (45 C.F.R. § 164.512(e); See §§ 7.33—7.41 for a discussion of HIPAA in litigation.)

The rule permits, but does not *require* these types of disclosures. If there is no other law requiring that information be disclosed, physicians and hospitals will still have to make judgments about whether to disclose information, in light of their own policies and ethical principles. Consider the situation in which a hospital patient is medically unable to agree or object to disclosure of information about his or her status to another person. The physicians involved must then make a decision about disclosure of the medical information based on their own professional judgment.

§ 1.29   —Incidental Uses and Disclosures of PHI

General provisions permit incidental uses and disclosures of protected health information that occur as a result of permissible necessary disclosures as long as the entity has applied reasonable safeguards and the "minimum necessary" standard. Reasonable safeguards include administrative, technical, and physical measures as outlined in entity policies. Examples include: speaking quietly when discussing health information with patient or family in public areas, securing medical records in locked areas and providing password protection for computerized information. (45 C.F.R. § 164.510.)

§ 1.30   —Minimum Necessary

This standard focuses on how much medical information is available, to whom, and under what circumstances. However, this provision does not apply to the transfer of medical records for purposes of treatment, since physicians, specialists, and other providers need access to the full record to provide the best quality care. HIPAA gives providers full discretion in determining what personal health information to include when sending patients' medical records to other providers for treatment purposes. (45 C.F.R. § 164.502(b).)

§ 1.31   —Non-Routine Disclosures with Patient Authorization

Disclosures of this type must meet standards that ensure the authorization provided by the patient is truly informed and voluntary. The rule establishes the privacy safeguard standards that covered entities must meet, but it leaves detailed policies and procedures for meeting these standards to the discretion of each covered entity. In this way, implementation of the standards will be flexible, to account for the nature of each entity's business, and its size and resources. (45 C.F.R. § 164.508.) Policies or practices that allow hospital employees to have free access to medical information not necessary to perform job duties are in potential violation of this standard. The minimum necessary rule does not apply to the following disclosures:

- By a health care provider for treatment purposes,
- To the individual who is the subject of the information,
- Pursuant to an individual's authorization,
- As required for compliance with HIPAA Administrative Simplification Rules,
- To HHS when disclosure of the information is required under the Privacy Rule for enforcement purposes, and
- Uses or disclosures required by other law (e.g., statute, regulation, or court orders). (See **§§ 7.13—7.18 and Forms 7–2 and 7–3** for a discussion of HIPAA-compliant authorizations.)

§ 1.32   —Reasonable Reliance

In some cases, it is allowable for the entity to rely on the requesting party as to what is the minimum amount of information needed. This provision, known as reasonable reliance, is permissible when the request is made by a public official or agency, another covered entity, a professional who is a workforce member or a business associate of a covered entity, or researchers with documentation for the Institutional Research Board (IRB). Reasonable reliance is not mandated, however, and the covered entity has the ultimate right to make its own minimum necessary determination.

§ 1.33   —Marketing

This portion of HIPAA gives individuals control over whether and how protected health information is used and disclosed for marketing purposes. (45 C.F.R. § 164.501). With limited exceptions, the rules require an individual's written authorization before a use or disclosure of such information can be made for marketing. To accomplish this objective, the rule distinguishes marketing communications from those communications about goods and services that are essential for quality health care and defines what constitutes marketing as well as exceptions to the rule.

HIPAA defines marketing as making "a communication about a product or service that encourages recipients of the communication to purchase or use the product or service." In all situations meeting this definition, prior authorization must be obtained before protected health information can be released. Specific examples of this include: (1) communication to individuals on new services when the communication is not for the purpose of providing treatment advice; (2) communication from a health insurer promoting a home and casualty insurance product offered by the same company; and (3) health plan selling member lists to companies that sell drugs or equipment and those companies in turn using that information to market goods and services directly to individuals.

The three exceptions to the definition of marketing activities are if communication is made (1) to describe a health related product or service that is provided by, or included in the benefit plan of the covered entity making the communication, (2) for treatment of the individual, and (3) for case management or care coordination of the individual. In all of these exceptions, the activity must otherwise be permissible under HIPAA.

§ 1.34 —Special Protection for Psychotherapy Notes

In HIPAA, psychotherapy notes are held to a higher standard of protection because they are not part of the medical record and never intended to be shared with anyone else. The phrase "psychotherapy notes" refers to those notes documenting or analyzing the conversations occurring in private, family or group counseling sessions. The regulation seems to imply that these type of notes should be kept in a separate part of the chart. The HIPAA definition does not include chart entries concerning medication prescription and monitoring, counseling session start and stop times, modalities and frequencies of treatment furnished, results of clinical tests, and any summary regarding symptoms, functional status, treatment plan, diagnosis, prognosis, and progress to date.

A covered entity must obtain an individual's specific authorization to use or disclose psychotherapy notes except for the following circumstances:

- The notes may be used for treatment by the covered entity who originated them;
- For the covered entity's own training;

- To defend itself in legal proceeding brought by the individual;
- During investigation by HHS to determine covered entity's compliance with HIPAA;
- To avert a serious or imminent threat to public health or safety;
- To a health agency for oversight of the originator of the notes; and
- To the coroner or medical examiner as required by law.

45 C.F.R. § 164.501. (See **Form 7–2** for an example of a HIPAA-compliant release of psychotherapy records.)

Practice Note: All states but one (West Virginia), including those without a specific physician-patient privilege, have some sort of statutory psychotherapist-client privilege. (See **Table 1–2** for a listing of state statutes regarding the Psychologist-Client Privilege.)

§ 1.35   —Accountability for Use and Release of PHI

Individuals have the right to complain to a covered provider or health plan, or to the Secretary of the DHS, concerning violations of the provisions of this rule or the policies and procedures of the covered entity. Penalties for covered entities that misuse personal health information are provided in HIPAA. Health plans, providers, and clearinghouses that violate these standards would be subject to civil liability with civil penalties of $100 per incident, up to $25,000 per person, per year, per standard.

Federal criminal penalties were also enacted for health plans, providers, and clearinghouses that knowingly and improperly disclose information or obtain information under false pretenses. Penalties would be higher for actions designed to generate monetary gain. Criminal penalties up to $50,000 and one year in prison for obtaining or disclosing protected health information; up to $100,000 and up to five years in prison for obtaining protected health information under "false pretenses"; and up to $250,000 and 10 years in prison for obtaining or disclosing protected health information with the intent to sell, transfer or use it for commercial advantage, personal gain, or malicious harm. (45 C.F.R. §§ 160.300 *et seq.*)

§ 1.36   —Unauthorized Use of PHI
for Employment Purposes

Companies that sponsor health plans will not be able to access the personal health information held by the plan for employment-related purposes, without specific written authorization from the individual. However, records that relate to other employee benefits such as life and disability insurance, workers compensation, and long term care are not covered by HIPAA.

§ 1.37   —Equivalent Treatment of Public and Private Sector Health Plans and Providers

The provisions of the Privacy Rule generally apply equally to private sector and public sector entities. For example, both private hospitals and government agency medical units must comply with the full range of requirements, such as providing notice, access rights, requiring consent before disclosure for routine uses, establishing contracts with business associates, among others.

§ 1.38   —Common Myths About HIPAA

For months prior to, during, and after the enactment of HIPAA, rumors abounded about how it would change the practice of medicine, often for the worse. In those states that did not previously recognize a physician-patient privilege, HIPAA requirements for consent to and authorization for release of medical information have no doubt significantly altered the practice of medicine. However, in states with strong patient confidentiality statutes, HIPAA has proven to be less onerous than previously thought with regard to the release of medical information. Much of the disinformation, however, has come from unfamiliarity with the Privacy Rule itself. Below are some of the more common misconceptions and the reality behind them:

Myth: A patient is required to sign a consent form before his doctors, hospitals, or ambulances can share information for treatment purposes.
Truth: Providers can freely share information with other providers where *treatment* is concerned, without getting a signed patient authorization.

Myth: Medical providers must eliminate all "incidental disclosures" of medical information.
Truth: Incidental disclosure is defined as a use or disclosure of protected health information "incidental to" an otherwise permitted use, such as posting patient names on hospital rooms. Incidental disclosures do not

violate HIPAA when providers and other covered entities have common sense policies which reasonably safeguard and appropriately limit how protected health information is used and disclosed. Medical providers can continue to use patient sign-in sheets, place patient charts outside exam rooms, or use whiteboards at nursing stations.

Myth: All communications between medical providers and the families and friends of patients are now forbidden.
Truth: Covered entities can share needed information with family members, friends, or anyone else identified by a patient as being involved in his or her care, as long as the patient does not object. And unless a patient objects, a hospital can share information with callers and visitors about the patient's location and general condition. Even if the patient is incapacitated, a provider can share information with others if he or she believes it is in the best interest of the patient to do so.

Myth: HIPAA prevents calls or visits to hospitals by family, friends, clergy, or anyone else. Hospitals cannot tell a spouse if their husband or wife has been admitted.
Truth: Unless the patient objects, basic information can still appear in the hospital directory, so that when people visit or call for the patient, they can be given the patient's room and phone number, and general health condition. Clergy do not have to ask for patients by name if a religious affiliation was provided by the patient on admission.

Myth: Medical providers can no longer report child abuse.
Truth: Physicians and other health care workers must continue to report suspected child abuse or neglect to appropriate government authorities.

Myth: HIPAA is anti-electronic.
Truth: HIPAA started out life as a means to regulate electronic transmission of medical information. Medical providers can continue to use e-mail, phones, or fax machines to communicate with patients and other providers. However, common sense and appropriate safeguards must be in place to protect patient privacy.

§ 1.39   Areas in Which HIPAA Does Not Apply

Passage of HIPAA was an enormous step forward in protecting the privacy of medical information. However, it is obvious now that with the use of computers, computerized records, and "paperless" medical record systems, sensitive private information will end up in data files. Most certainly, an individual's personal medical information is seen by hundreds of individuals unknown to the patient—insurance claims adjusters, medical office and hospital employees, and businesses associated with healthcare providers, including law firms. The following sections discuss situations in which personal medical information is not protected by HIPAA.

§ 1.40   —Medical Information Bureau

The Medical Information Bureau (MIB) is a voluntary membership association of life insurance companies with approximately 600 members, including virtually every major insurance company issuing individual life, health, and disability insurance in the United States and Canada. Its stated purpose is the prevention of fraud. Because MIB is neither a health care provider, health care, plan, nor health care clearinghouse, it is not a covered entity under HIPAA.

When a member organization accepts an application for insurance, the application is sent to the underwriting department, which estimates the future cost to insure the applicant. This estimate is determined by comparing the applicant's profile as it appears in the application with the company's history in providing coverage for large numbers of other people with similar profiles. The most important pieces of information used in developing these profiles are called *risk factors* (age, health, smoker or nonsmoker, etc.).

If an applicant has a condition the insurance industry has defined as "significant to health or longevity," member companies are required to send a brief, coded report on the applicant to the MIB. The MIB currently categorizes 230 types of significant medical conditions, such as blood pressure, EKG readings, and X rays. Additionally, there are five non-medical codes that refer to an individual's personal behavior or lifestyle—for example, participation in aviation activities, hazardous sports, or an adverse driving record.

In addition to medical information, the MIB maintains an insurance activity index that records the name of any member company that requests information on an individual and the date(s) of inquiry. This information, along with patient identifiers (name, birth date, birth state, occupation, area of current residency) is placed in the MIB data bank, which contains over 15 million files. Social Security numbers, mailing addresses, and telephone numbers are not included. The MIB coded reports are kept for a period of seven years from date of receipt, after which they are automatically eliminated by computer edit. Insurance activity index records are retained for two years.

Any member organization that accepts an application for insurance may request information on the applicant from the MIB. This process serves to deter applicants from omitting or misrepresenting facts on an application. If the information contained in the MIB files is not consistent with the application, further investigation can be made. Information obtained from the MIB may not be used either in whole or in part to determine an applicant's eligibility for insurance. Rather, the MIB maintains that its information is intended as an "alert" to the need for further investigation. Sound underwriting practices require that coverage decisions be based not on unverified MIB reports, but on information obtained from the applicant, medical examinations, physicians, hospitals, or other medical facilities. Individuals may access this information to determine if a personal file exists, obtain a copy of the file, or make corrections to the file. The MIB can accessed at *www.mib.com.*

§ 1.41 —Disclosures Made Outside the Physician-Patient Relationship

Very often physicians interact with individuals for purposes other than diagnosis and/or treatment. The most common example is when a physician is appointed by the court to examine an individual or has been retained by defense counsel to conduct an independent or defense medical examination (IME or DME). (See **Chapter 10, §§ 10.4–10.26** for an in-depth discussion on IMEs.)

A physician who performs an examination solely for the purpose of preparing a party's case for trial, and in anticipation of serving as an expert, functions only in the role of examiner. As such, no treatment is offered or provided. For this reason, any information related to the physician during an examination is separate and distinct from the goals that the confidentiality doctrine seeks to protect, and thus is never really "privileged."

A California case resulted in serious repercussions for this exception. In *Urbaniak v. Newton,* 226 Cal. App. 3d 1128, 277 Cal. Rptr. 354 (1991), the plaintiff was injured in a work-related accident. As a result, he suffered from headaches, back pain, shoulder pain, numbness, and tingling in his right hand. He was sent by the defense to Dr. Newton, a neurologist, for an IME. A portion of Dr. Newton's exam involved performing an electro-myogram (EMG), which studies the electrical activity of muscles at rest and during contractions. During this procedure, reusable metal electrodes were inserted into the plaintiff's skin and drew blood. After the examination, and just before the plaintiff left the office, he called Dr. Newton's nurse aside. Asking the nurse not to place this information in the chart, he stated that he was HIV-positive and felt "morally compelled" to recommend that she sterilize the electrodes before using them on another patient. At no time did the plaintiff relate this information directly to Dr. Newton.

When Dr. Newton prepared his report, he essentially discounted any role the original incident might have had in the plaintiff's injuries, instead focusing on his HIV-positive status. Dr. Newton stated that Urbaniak's "status as an AIDS victim . . . might account for his symptoms." Copies of this report were sent to the defense attorney, the plaintiff's attorney, the workers' compensation insurer, the workers' compensation appeals board, and ultimately to Mr. Urbaniak's chiropractor, apparently to justify termination of payments.

The appellate court noted that the plaintiff "reasonably anticipated privacy" when he spoke with the nurse about his condition. The court inferred that Dr. Newton knew of and ratified the use of information confided to his nurse. It went on to state that the "offending information had limited relevance to the medical examination. It would have been possible to mention the patient's concern over his health as a source of stress without specifically mentioning his HIV-positive status." The court found that enforcing such reasonable expectations of privacy would "simultaneously foster needed disclosures of HIV-positive status and protect against their abuse." In this case, the plaintiff's constitutional right to privacy was deemed to outweigh the exception to the physician-patient privilege.

Practice Note: Only ten states (Alaska, Arizona, California, Florida, Hawaii, Illinois, Louisiana, Montana, South Carolina, and Washington) have *expressly* recognized a constitutional right to privacy.

§ 1.42   —Disclosures Made in the Public Interest

A covered entity may disclose PHI for certain public health activities to certain specified recipients, including public health authorities (such as HRSA, the Centers for Disease Control and Prevention, the Food and Drug

Administration, the Occupational Safety and Health Administration, and state public health agencies, when they are operating as a public health authority), persons subject to the jurisdiction of the Food and Drug Administration, and to persons exposed to a communicable disease (if other laws authorize such notification). (45 C.F.R. § 164.512(b).) Disclosures for public health purposes are subject to the Privacy Rule's minimum necessary requirement.

This situation recognizes that a physician's duty of nondisclosure is superseded in some circumstances by the need for public safety or when a disclosure would be in the public interest. An example would be the information contained on birth and death certificates. Another example would be mandatory medical reports concerning injuries received as a result of child or elder abuse or firearm and knife wounds.

The most controversial aspect of this exception relates to disclosure of information pertaining to infectious, contagious, or communicable diseases. The courts have long held treating physicians to a duty to protect third parties with whom they have no specific relationship, especially when their patient might expose such parties to various diseases as tuberculosis, syphilis, scarlet fever, hepatitis, and meningitis.

§ 1.43   —Disclosure of HIV-Related Information

Currently, one of the most highly charged areas of medicine and law is that concerning the disclosure of information concerning HIV (human immunodeficiency virus) testing and status. HIV is the broad term for the disease complex once referred to as AIDS (acquired immune deficiency syndrome). AIDS was originally thought to be the disease itself but is now recognized as the final stage of HIV infection.

Twenty-four years after the disease made its first appearance, the HIV/AIDS pandemic continues to spread. More than 20 million people have died from AIDS worldwide. An estimated 38 million people currently have HIV, and 4.8 million of them became infected for the first time in 2003. In 2005, approximately 2.9 million people died of AIDS and more than 2 million women with HIV gave birth, passing the infection along to 630,000 infants.

HIV causes death by destroying T-4 helper cells, which the body's immune system uses to structure its defense against viruses and bacteria. Destruction of the T-4 helper cells essentially leaves the patient vulnerable to opportunistic infections and cancers—Pneumocystis carinii pneumonia, Kaposi's sarcoma, and lymphomas such as Hodgkin's disease. It is these infections and cancers that ultimately kill the patient. Full-blown AIDS can develop eight to twelve years after infection by the virus.

New medications known as antiretroviral drugs have had a positive effect on delaying the onset of AIDS. Different classes of antiretroviral drugs act at different stages of the HIV life cycle. A combination of several (typically three or four) of the drugs is currently being offered. However, because of the complexity of selecting and following a regimen, the severity of the side effects, the importance of compliance to prevent viral resistance, and the cost of the drugs, patients should be involved in therapy choices and the risks and potential benefits to patients without symptoms should be fully explored. Additionally, research into an AIDS vaccine continues. HIV/AIDS and the confidentiality issues surrounding these conditions impact the legal field. Litigation has been conducted in various areas of the law—unlawful disclosure of HIV or AIDS status, wrongful termination, employment discrimination based on HIV or AIDS status, negligence, battery, and intentional infliction of emotional distress.

During the early 1980s, the nation's blood supply and blood products became contaminated with HIV. It is estimated that 50 percent of this country's hemophiliacs (and more than 80 percent of people afflicted with severe hemophilia) were infected with HIV. Additionally, approximately 20 percent of the spouses, children, and partners of infected hemophiliacs also became infected. A class action lawsuit was filed against the manufacturers of blood products.

Most states have laws governing the practice of medical confidentiality, especially when it concerns information regarding communicable or sexually transmitted diseases. More than two-thirds of the states currently have laws dealing with HIV disclosure and confidentiality. The federal government requires that all states report frank cases of AIDS, but some states have gone farther by instituting regulations that require reporting of individuals who are HIV-positive but asymptomatic (showing no symptoms). (See **Appendix M** for a survey of state-specific HIV/AIDS citations.)

§ 1.44   —Physician's Duty to Warn

In 1988 the American Medical Association issued physician guidelines regarding HIV and a physician's duty to warn third parties. These guidelines state that if no statute mandates or prohibits reporting of sero-positive individuals to public health authorities, and it is clear to the physician that the seropositive individual is endangering an identified third party, the physician should take the following steps:

1. Attempt to persuade the infected individual to cease endangering the third party
2. If persuasion fails, notify authorities
3. If the authorities take no action, notify and counsel the endangered third party.

§ 1.45 —Workplace Safety

In 1970 Congress passed the Occupational Safety and Health Act (OSHA), requiring employers to meet specified standards in order to provide a safe workplace. The Occupational Safety and Health Administration was established to develop the standards, issue regulations, determine employer compliance with the regulations, investigate accidents, issue citations, and impose penalties on employers. Through the auspices of OSHA, federal and state agencies collect medical information directly from the employer regarding employees who have either received on-the-job injuries or died in the workplace. The information collected must be relevant and necessary to accomplish a lawful purpose, that is, to determine employer compliance with OSHA regulations. (See Occupational Safety and Health Act, 29 U.S.C. § 651 *et seq.* (1970).)

Workers in the health care field are especially concerned about the risk of exposure to bloodborne pathogens. According to OSHA estimates, approximately 5.6 million workers are at risk throughout the United States. *Bloodborne pathogens* are defined as pathogenic microorganisms that can be present in human blood and can cause disease in humans. They include such pathogens as HIV, hepatitis B virus (HBV), and the hepatitis C virus (HCV). Occupational exposure to pathogens can also occur from other potentially infectious materials (OPIM), which include a variety of human body fluids (for example, cerebrospinal, synovial, pericardial, amniotic, and saliva).

Exposure to bloodborne pathogens may occur in many ways. However, the most common means of transmission to health care workers is through a needlestick, when a contaminated needle accidentally punctures the skin.

Other occupations subject to exposure to bloodborne pathogens include blood banks, commercial laundries that service health care facilities, correctional facilities, public safety operations (police, fire, ambulance), funeral service facilities, and medical equipment service and repair operations.

§ 1.46   —Workers' Compensation

When on-the-job injuries occur, claims are made through the state workers' compensation system for medical care, temporary disability, permanent disability, vocational rehabilitation, transportation, and death benefits. These systems are not designed to maintain confidentiality because access to injury reports is important in allowing investigation and maintenance of safety in the workplace. This situation creates a problem for health care workers and others with occupationally acquired HIV who desire access to the compensation system but need to preserve the confidentiality of their medical status and records. The occurrence of occupationally acquired HIV cases will likely increase in the future, as the number of HIV cases increases.

Interestingly enough, HIPAA *does not apply* to entities that are workers' compensation insurers, administrative agencies, or employers, except to the extent they are otherwise covered entities. Generally HIPAA permits disclosure without authorization to the extent necessary to comply with laws relating to workers' compensation or similar programs that provide benefits to injured workers. Information disclosed with authorization must meet HIPAA requirements. Individuals do not have a right to request that a covered entity restrict a disclosure of protected health information about them for workers' compensation purposes when that disclosure is required by law or authorized by, and necessary to comply with, a workers' compensation or similar law. (45 C.F.R. § 164.522.)

§ 1.47   Ethical Considerations for Legal Professionals

On April 7th, a young woman receives a diagnosis of HSV II (herpes simplex virus II—genital herpes) from her physician. The physician discusses preventative measures with the patient and prescribes medication. Three weeks later, the woman is involved in a motor vehicle accident. She is seen the day of the accident for her injuries, which appear to be minor and consist mainly of low back pain. X rays are taken at her request (negative), and she is given pain medication, again at her request. Some months later the young woman sues for her injuries. Does the April 7th visit have anything to do with her low back pain from the motor vehicle accident? At first glance, the answer would probably be "no, it has no relationship." However, what if the plaintiff alleges in her complaint that since the accident, she has no longer been able to enjoy marital relations with her husband? The question of the relationship between the two events in her medical record takes on an entirely new meaning now.

All legal professionals are bound by codes of ethics that prohibit them from revealing any information learned in the course of investigation and subsequent litigation. This duty must be taken one step further when reviewing medical records.

Records reviewed during litigation very often reveal information about the parties that may have little or no relationship to the issues of the lawsuit itself. This may be personal information involving members of the plaintiff's family, or the individual's medical history or social or sexual behavior. During the course of litigation, summaries of medical records are often disclosed to third parties, for example, insurance companies.

How much of this kind of peripheral information can legitimately be included in a summary? It depends on the relationship of the information to the issues of the lawsuit itself. Anything dealing with the physical or emotional injuries as alleged by the party should be included in the summary. If information of a peripheral nature is or conceivably could be significant to the litigation issues, then it should be included. Evidence of past substance abuse, for example, might be relevant peripheral information. Information having no bearing on the litigation, either specifically or peripherally, should generally not be included. However, this decision can be made only on the basis of the reviewer's knowledge of the specific issues of the case. As in all facets of the legal profession, the utmost discretion must be utilized when reviewing medical records and using the information contained therein. While serving the needs of the client, the legal professional must be aware of and guard against breaching the vital doctrine of confidentiality.

Practice Note: If information in the medical record has not been included in the summary but might conceivably be of importance, attach a separate memo concerning this information. In this way, areas of potential concern can be referred to the attorney for a decision.

Table 1–1

States Recognizing Physician-Patient Privilege

State	Statute
Alabama	none
Alaska	Rules of Evid. R. 504; § 9.25.400
Arizona	Rev. Stat. Ann. § 12-2235
Arkansas	Rules of Evid. R. 503
California	Evid. Code §§ 990-1007
Colorado	Rev. Stat. § 13-90-107 (d)
Connecticut	Gen. Stat 52-146(o)
Delaware	Uniform Rules of Evid. R. 503
District of Columbia	Code Ann. § 6-2001
Florida	Stat. 455.241 et seq.
Georgia	Code Ann. § 38-418
Hawaii	Art. V, R. 504
Idaho	Code § 9-203 (4)
Illinois	735 Comp. Stat. 5/8-802
Indiana	Code § 34-46-3-1
Iowa	Code § 622.10
Kansas	Stat. Ann. § 60-427
Kentucky	none
Louisiana	Code of Evid. Art. 510(A), Rev. Stat. Ann. § 13:3734(A)(1)
Maine	R. Rev. R. 503
Maryland	none
Massachusetts	Gen. Laws Ann. ch. 111, § 70E
Michigan	Comp. Laws § 600.2157
Minnesota	Stat. Ann. § 595.02 (1)(d)
Mississippi	Code Ann. § 13-1-21
Missouri	Rev. Stat. § 491.060
Montana	Code Ann. § 26-1-805
Nebraska	Rev. Stat. § 25-504
Nevada	Rev. Stat. § 49.225
New Hampshire	Rev. Stat. Ann. § 329.26
New Jersey	Stat. §§ 2A:84A-22.1 and 22.2
New Mexico	Rules of Evid. 11-504
New York	Civ. Prac. L & R 4504
North Carolina	Gen. Stat. § 8-53
North Dakota	Rules of Evid. R. 503
Ohio	Rev. Code Ann. § 2317.02(B)(1)
Oklahoma	Stat. tit. 12, § 2503
Oregon	Rev. Stat. 40.235 Rule 504-1
Pennsylvania	42 Pa. Cons. Stat. Ann. § 5929
Rhode Island	Gen. L. § 5-37.3-4
South Carolina	none
South Dakota	Codified Laws §§ 19-13-6 and 19-13-7
Tennessee	none
Texas	Rev. Civ. Stat. Ann. art. 4495b, § 5.08
Utah	Code Ann. § 78-24-8 (4)
Vermont	12 Vt. Stat. Ann § 1612, 18 Stat. Ann. § 7101(13)
Virginia	Code Ann. § 8.10-399
Washington	Rev. Code Ann. § 5.60.060
West Virginia	none
Wisconsin	Stat. Ann. § 905.04
Wyoming	Stat. § 1-12-101

Table 1–2

States Recognizing Psychologist-Client Privilege

State	Statute
Alabama	Code §§ 34-26-2, 34-8A-21
Alaska	Stat. §§ 08.29.200, 08.63.200, 08.86.200
Arizona	Rev. Stat. § 32-3085
Arkansas	Rules of Evid. R. 503; Code. Ann. § 17-97-105
California	Evid. Code §§ 1010-1027
Colorado	Rev. Stat. § 13-90-107(g)
Connecticut	Gen. Stat §§ 52-146(d)-52-146(j)
Delaware	Uniform Rules of Evid. R. 503
District of Columbia	Code Ann. § 7-1201.01
Florida	Stat. Ann. §§ 90.503, 456.059
Georgia	Code Ann. § 24-9-21
Hawaii	Rev. Stat. § 626; Art. V, R. 504.1
Idaho	Code § 54-2314
Illinois	735 Comp. Stat. 5/8-802
Indiana	Code § 54-2314
Iowa	Code § 622.10
Kansas	Stat. Ann. §§ 65-5601-65-5603, 74-5323, 74-5372
Kentucky	Rules of Evid. R. 507
Louisiana	Code of Evid. Art. 510(a), Stat. Ann. § 13:3734(A)(1)
Maine	R. Rev. R. 503
Maryland	Code Ann. Cts & Jud. Proc. § 9-109
Massachusetts	Gen. Laws Ann. ch. 233, § 20B
Michigan	Comp. Laws §§ 330.1750, 333.18237
Minnesota	Stat. Ann. § 595.02 (1)
Mississippi	Rules of Evid. R. 503, Code Ann. § 73-31-29
Missouri	Rev. Stat. §§ 337.055, 491.060
Montana	Code Ann. § 26-1-807
Nebraska	Rev. Stat. § 27-504 (Rule 504)
Nevada	Rev. Stat. § 49.209
New Hampshire	Rev. Stat. Ann. § 330-A:32
New Jersey	Stat. Ann. § 45:14B-28
New Mexico	Rules of Evid. 11-504
New York	Civ. Prac. L & R 4507
North Carolina	Gen. Stat. § 8-53.3
North Dakota	Rules of Evid. R. 503
Ohio	Rev. Code Ann. § 4732.19
Oklahoma	Stat. tit. 12, § 2503
Oregon	Rev. Stat 40.230 Rule 504
Pennsylvania	42 Pa. Cons. Stat. Ann. § 5944
Rhode Island	Gen. Laws § 5-37.3-6
South Carolina	Code § 44-22-90
South Dakota	Codified Laws §§ 19-13-7 and 36-27A-38
Tennessee	Code Ann. § 24-1-207
Texas	Health & Safety Code §§ 611.002 and 611.003
Utah	Rules of Evid. R. 506, Code Ann. § 58-60-113
Vermont	18 Stat. Ann. § 7101(13)
Virginia	Code Ann. § 8.01-399
Washington	Rev. Code Ann. § 18.83.110
West Virginia	*no statute*
Wisconsin	Stat. Ann. § 905.04
Wyoming	Stat. § 33-27-123

CHAPTER 2

SOURCES AND COMPONENTS

§ 2.1   Sources of Medical Records

As stated in the previous chapter, all licensed health care institutions and individual practitioners are required by law to maintain a record of the care prescribed and administered to an individual. Documentation of this care is found in the medical record. In litigation, the client can help identify all potential sources of medical information for the claim by providing provider names, location of treatment, and dates of service. It is important that all medical records, from all sources, be obtained and reviewed for applicable information. All potential sources of medical records are discussed in §§ 2.2–2.8 below.

§ 2.2   —Medical Records and the Health Care System

To better understand potential sources of medical records, it may be helpful to understand the health care delivery system in the United States. The system is composed of three major groups of participants: health plans, care delivery institutions, and providers (physicians and allied health care providers). (See **Figure 2–1**, Health care delivery system).

The provision of health care is underwritten by a health plan, which sells insurance policies to individuals or to employer groups providing health care benefits for their employees. (In the case of Medicare and Medicaid, the federal and state governments serve this function). The health plan is then responsible for providing care and covering cost of care as set forth in the terms and conditions of the policy. A health plan does not, however, directly provide care. This is done by health care institutions and individual providers. When care and services are delivered, the institution or provider submits claims to the health plan and/or patient for payment.

Health plan reimbursement of health care providers and institutions has changed dramatically. This change was driven mainly by large-scale purchaser rebellion against runaway premium hikes. Purchasers, primarily employer groups, began to put pressure on health plans to reduce premium

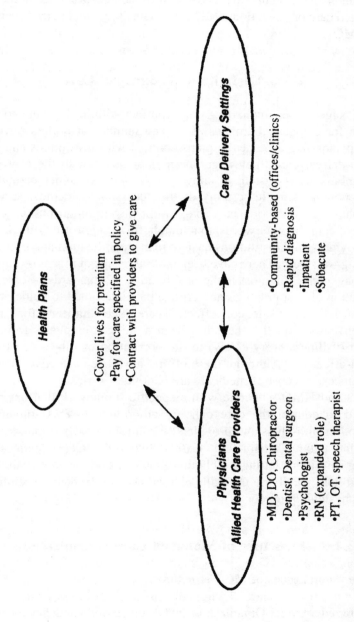

Figure 2–1. Health care delivery system.

prices and demonstrate quality in the care they provided. These demands, in turn, put pressure on health plans to reduce their costs and led to the rise of managed care organizations (MCOs) and health maintenance organizations (HMOs).

§ 2.3   —Definition of Managed Care

Under managed care, employer groups contract with health plans to provide care for company enrollees at a fixed number of dollars for each covered person. Because health plans contract with institutions and providers to deliver care, they negotiate similar terms with these groups. This reimbursement system is known as *capitation*. Under capitation, there is more systematic scrutiny of the necessity of medical services and emphasis on reduction of waste, i.e. having no contribution to the outcome of care. In other words, to maintain financial profitability, health plans, providers, and institutions have to manage utilization and timing of services aggressively. There have been several results of this more aggressive management: foremost is the proliferation of standards of care and identification of best practices and critical paths designed to guide providers in the delivery of safe, cost-effective care. (See **Chapter 9** for further discussion). Additionally, there has been a shift in emphasis from the treatment of illness (very costly) to the prevention of illness (generally very cost-effective). Although these efforts have been effective in some circumstances, the cost of medical care continues to rise.

MCO's and HMO's operate with a specific framework that has been developed to control the care delivery environment. This framework assists both health plans and providers to control cost while maintaining quality and patient satisfaction. Care delivery includes resources for providing care in all settings, including those outside the acute care hospital and relies heavily on the skills of a variety of healthcare disciplines, not just physician providers.

§ 2.4   —Structure of Managed Care Organizations

There are several types of MCO structures:

1.   Preferred Provider Organization (PPO). Employer health benefit plans and insurance carriers contract to provide services from a select group

of providers and institutions. Unlike an HMO, the PPO does not *provide* care itself, but contracts with a group of providers and institutions that form a network to provide care. Generally speaking enrollees may seek care outside the PPO, but typically pay greater out-of-pocket costs.

2. Exclusive Provider Organization (EPO). Variation of PPO, the EPO limits enrollees to providers belonging to one organization.
3. Physician-Hospital Organization (PHO). Physicians and hospitals operate under a joint agreement or contract to deliver care.
4. Health Maintenance Organization (HMO). Administers the health plan and provides care through contracted or employee providers. HMO's differ from fee for service in two key ways: they provide a wide range of comprehensive services at guaranteed reduced cost and their care providers accept reduced compensation for services they provide.

§ 2.5   —Structure of Health Maintenance Organizations

There are also several HMO models, among the most common are:

1. Staff Model. Providers are employed by the HMO and generally receive a set salary. They deliver care out of HMO facilities.
2. Group Model. Care is provided through independent contracts with one or more multispecialty group practices that provide all physician care. Physicians are not employees of the HMO and may provide fee for service care as well.
3. Network Model. HMO contracts either single group practice. Group may or may not contract with more than one HMO.
4. Independent Practice Association (IPA). HMO contracts for services with independent specialty practice or organized association of providers that provides services at a reduced rate.
5. Point of Service (POS). Allows enrollees to choose to go out of plan for care generally pay greater out of pocket costs. POS allows care to be received from HMO, PPO, or fee for service.

§ 2.6   —Medicare and Medicaid Services

The federal government funds health-care benefits to the elderly and disabled through Medicare. Benefits for certain low-income individuals and families are provided through Medicaid, which is jointly funded by the federal government and the states. The Centers for Medicare and Medicaid Services (CMS), an agency within the Department of Health and Human Services, has traditionally overseen administration of benefits for both Medicare and Medicaid. Three new business centers have been formed within CMS: the Center for Beneficiary Choices, the Center for Medicare Management, and the Center for Medicaid and State Operations. The goal of the reorganization is to provide increased responsiveness to beneficiaries and providers, and support health-care quality improvement initiatives. The CMS website (*http://www.cms.gov*) contains many resources on a variety of topics. Medicare can also be contacted at (800) 633–4227 where services to beneficiaries are provided 24 hours a day, 7 days a week.

§ 2.7 —Health Care Institutions

Medical records found in licensed health care institutions (e.g., acute care hospitals, rehabilitation and skilled nursing facilities) and medical providers (e.g., physicians, surgeons, chiropractors) must include documentation of the specific care and services provided to an individual in that setting.

Institutions may offer inpatient or outpatient services or both. Inpatient care involves a stay usually more than 24 hours. Outpatient care can be provided in a community-based setting or in an inpatient setting. Stays can be on a come-and-go basis or for periods of time generally less than 24 hours. Currently, a trend exists to shift care away from some inpatient facilities (e.g., acute hospitals) because of their associated high costs. This has led to a proliferation of community-based agencies in recent years. Some examples of care delivery settings are:

1. **Acute care general hospitals**—usually provide both inpatient and outpatient care; most also offer selected specialty care such as obstetrics, pediatrics, and psychiatry.

2. **Long-term care facilities,** also called skilled nursing facilities, convalescent hospitals, or nursing homes—provide care for clients who no longer need acute care but are unable to care for themselves in the community setting.

3. **Psychiatric facilities**—provide care for mental and emotional conditions; may provide either inpatient or outpatient services, or both.

4. **Rehabilitation facilities**—provide specialized services in both inpatient and outpatient settings; assist in restoring functional losses resulting from catastrophic injury or substance dependence. Examples of rehabilitation specialization are spinal cord injury, head injury, and substance abuse disorders (alcohol, drugs, eating disorders).

5. **Home health agencies**—may be privately owned, for-profit or nonprofit organizations; provide treatment and care to clients in the home setting. These organizations function under the direction of a practitioner licensed to prescribe services and may involve the delivery of either one or several care modalities simultaneously, for example, registered nursing functions, occupational therapy, and so on.

6. **Outpatient surgery centers**—perform surgical procedures that require a limited recovery time and allow same-day discharge. Examples of procedures commonly performed in these settings are hernia repairs, cataract removals, and arthroscopic surgery.

7. **Observation units**—provide short-term care and treatment (usually less than 24 hours) for medical conditions. Examples of care given in these settings include blood transfusions, IV infusions for dehydration, and observation following head injury. (See **Figure 2–2,** Sources of medical records).

§ 2.8   —Health Care Practitioners

Records of private practitioners describe the care and treatment given to an individual by a licensed health care practitioner. Examples of such professionals include:

1. **Physician,** Medical Doctor (M.D.), or **Osteopath,** Doctor of Osteopathy (D.O.). Physicians are licensed (by states in which they practice) to diagnose, treat, and prescribe drugs for health problems. Physicians will frequently limit their practice to a particular area of medical care. The areas of practice of medical specialization are listed in **Chapter 9.**

   A physician may be board-certified in any specialty area. Board certification indicates that the physician has passed oral and written examinations focusing on that particular specialty. A physician who specializes is not necessarily board-certified. A board-certified specialist can be valuable as an expert witness.

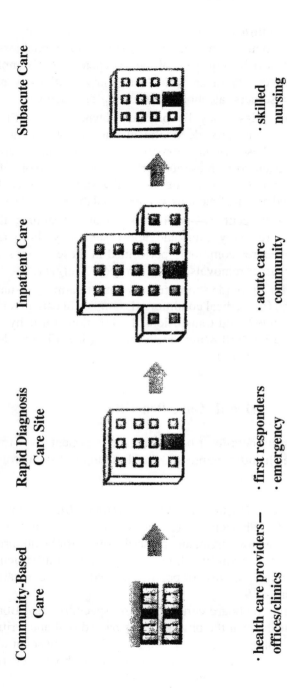

Community-Based Care

· health care providers—
  offices/clinics
· psychiatric
· pharmacies
· home health

Rapid Diagnosis Care Site

· first responders
· emergency
  departments
· outpatient
  surgery centers
· observation units

Inpatient Care

· acute care
  community
  tertiary
  quaternary
· pyschiatric

Subacute Care

· skilled
  nursing
· rehabilitation

Figure 2–2. Sources of medical records.

2. **Chiropractor,** Doctor of Chiropractic (D.C.). Chiropractors provide non-invasive interventions through manipulation and massage for problems associated with bones, joints, and muscles. They are not licensed to prescribe medication or to perform surgical procedures.

3. **Dentist,** Doctor of Dental Surgery (D.D.S.). Like physicians, dentists may specialize in a particular area of practice for problems involving the teeth and gums, face, and jaw. Areas of practice specialization for dentists are listed in **Chapter 9.** Dentists may become board-certified in their particular specialty area.

4. **Dietitian,** Registered Dietitian (R.D.). Dietitians apply the principles of nutrition in both health and disease. In health care settings, practice focuses on maintaining adequate body nutrition in the presence of illness.

5. **Nursing Assistant or Nurse's Aide** (C.N.A. or N.A.). Nursing assistants provide care to patients under the direction and supervision of a licensed health care professional, such as a physician or registered nurse. They are utilized in both inpatient and outpatient settings. Generally, nursing assistants are not licensed, but they can become certified nursing assistants (C.N.A.s) by completing a formal training program.

6. **Optometrist,** Doctor of Optometry (O.D.). The optometrist performs eye examinations and prescribes corrective lenses for vision problems. Optometrists differ from ophthalmologists in education and scope of practice. They focus on diagnosing and measuring vision and prescribing corrective lenses when necessary.

7. **Pharmacist/Pharmacy.** Individuals responsible for providing medications to the patient, both while hospitalized and as an outpatient. A pharmacist can receive either a doctorate in Pharmacology (Pharm.D.) or be a Registered Pharmacist (R.Ph.). Many pharmacies keep client medication data on computers and may be able to supply a printout of the date a prescription was filled, type of medication, and cost.

8. **Physical Therapist,** Registered Physical Therapist (R.P.T.). The physical therapist provides treatment for problems associated with bones, joints, and muscles and rehabilitation care for functional deficiencies. Therapists cannot prescribe treatment for a client, therefore they provide care only under the direction of a health care practitioner licensed to prescribe.

9. **Physician Assistant** (P.A.). Physician assistants are trained and licensed to provide basic medical services under the supervision of a physician.

10. **Podiatrist,** Doctor of Podiatry Medicine (D.P.M.). Podiatrists provide care and treatment for disorders of the feet. They also perform selected surgical procedures involving the feet and are licensed to prescribe medications.

11. **Psychologist,** may be Doctor of Philosophy (Ph.D.), Master of Arts (M.A.), Marriage, Family & Child Counselor (M.F.C.C.). Psychologists provide interventions and therapy for varied mental and emotional problems. They are distinguished from psychiatrists by education and degree earned as well as by scope of practice. They cannot prescribe medication.

12. **Registered Nurse (R.N.), Licensed Vocational/Practical Nurse** (L.V.N./L.P.N.). These two types of nurses provide care and interventions for health care problems under the direction of a physician. R.N.s and L.V.N.s are distinguished by their education and degree earned, as well as by their scope of practice. The scope of practice for nurses varies from state to state and is regulated through a state governing body charged with that responsibility. Many states have Nurse Practice Acts that clearly define their practice scope.

    Family Nurse Practitioner (F.N.P.), **Certified Nurse Midwife** (C.N.M.), **Certified Registered Nurse Anesthetist** (C.R.N.A.). These registered nurses have, through specialized education, assumed expanded nursing roles under the direction of a physician. Although the scope of their practice differs from state to state, examples of such expanded roles could be: performing physical examinations, performing uncomplicated deliveries (C.N.M.), suturing minor lacerations, and administering general anesthesia (C.R.N.A.).

13. **Respiratory Therapist,** Registered Respiratory Therapist (R.R.T. or R.T.). As licensed professionals, respiratory therapists work under the direction of a physician to treat respiratory conditions. Examples of care provided include management of postoperative respiratory care, management of ventilators, and administration of drugs via the respiratory tract.

14. **Social Worker,** Masters in Social Work or Licensed Clinical Social Worker (MSW or LCSW). The scope of social work encompasses a variety of areas related to assisting clients in time of hardship or crisis. In the medical arena, the social worker evaluates the psychosocial

status of the patient and recommends interventions that will assist the patient to regain maximum functionality. Social workers are often case workers; that is, they are assigned to specific patient populations and their families throughout the course of illness.

15. **Speech Therapist and Occupational Therapist** (O.T.). As their names suggest, these therapists provide clients with appropriate rehabilitative treatment prescribed by a licensed provider.

Practice Note: It is critical to obtain all medical records related to a claim. As a legal professional, understanding the health care delivery system, levels of care settings, and various licensed professionals can assist in identifying various sources of records. The client can help identify potential sources of pertinent medical information as well, and the information given can be more comprehensive by asking some educated questions. When determining potential sources, always ask the following questions: *where* was the care provided and *who* provided it? (See **Chapter 7,** Obtaining Medical Records).

§ 2.9   Components of Medical Records

Medical record documentation standards for hospitals are clearly defined by both the Joint Commission for Accreditation of Healthcare Organizations (JCAHO) and by the Centers for Medicare and Medicaid Services (CMS). For both organizations, part of the accreditation process requires meeting documentation standards. Without this accreditation, a health care facility is not eligible for Medicare and Medicaid reimbursement. Consequently, although documentation in medical records differs widely in appearance and format, it must contain information necessary to conform to regulatory requirements.

In addition to documentation of the medical care given to an individual, JCAHO standards also require hospital medical records to document evidence of the following:

- care planning and involvement of the patient and family in care and decision making about care choices
- a mechanism to resolve conflicts that may arise between the organization and a patient or family, and
- a process to address ethical issues when necessary.

Finally, organizations must demonstrate that systems are in place to communicate pertinent health care information across care settings within an organization or facility. There are multiple situations in a twenty-four hour period in which patient information is communicated from one person to another, one department to another, or from one facility to another:

- between ongoing and oncoming shifts
- from the operating room to post-anesthesia recovery
- between an acute care facility discharging a patient to a skilled nursing facility or home health agency, or
- discharge from a skilled nursing facility to an acute care hospital.

These systems must be fully described in the facility's policies and procedures.

§ 2.10   —Acute Care Records

Because of the complexity of the care they deliver, acute care hospitals have the greatest number of medical records components. The main components and the types of information found in them are as follows:

1. **Front Sheet or Face Sheet**—contains all patient demographic information, such as medical record number, name, address and telephone, age, next of kin. The admitting physician is also listed, as well as the date of the last prior admission (if any). An admitting diagnosis is given. Upon discharge, this sheet is updated to include the final diagnoses (principal and secondary), complications, procedures done, and consultants utilized. Finally, medical records personnel assign appropriate ICD-9 codes to all diagnoses, procedures, and complications. ICD-9 codes (International Classification of Diseases) were originally developed by the World Health Organization as a method to classify diseases uniformly. For example, a diagnosis of myocardial infarction will have the same ICD-9 number assigned by all hospital providers, independent of location. (See **Form 2–1**).

2. **History and Physical (H&P)**—contains the patient's current chief complaint, past medical history, review of systems (physical exam), findings (diagnosis), and treatment plan. Medical staff bylaws define who may perform H&Ps. For example, a hospital may allow physicians, interns and residents, medical students, physician assistants, and nurses in advanced practice roles to perform history and physicals. In all cases, the H&P must be completed within 24 hours of admission and signed by the physician responsible for the patient (attending physician). (See **Form 2–2**).

3. **Patient Progress Notes**—contain a chronological narrative of the patient's condition and response to treatment plan. Both objective (clinician's observation) and subjective (patient's perception) information should be included. Notations must be made at least daily in acute care facilities and as indicated by a change in patient condition. The more critically ill a patient is, the more frequently progress notes are made. All notes must be dated and signed. The time of note entry is also desirable, but in practice, is often omitted. (See **Form 2–3**).

4. **Physician Order Sheet**—contains orders for all treatments, tests, medications, and procedures for the patient while in the hospital. Admitting orders usually specify the patient's diagnosis and condition. Orders communicate the care plan to other members of the health care team. Telephone or verbal orders from the physician may be written by designated personnel, but these must be countersigned by the ordering physician within 24 hours. Physician orders may include *standing orders.* Standing orders contain preprinted treatments, medications, tests, and so on that a physician signs at the time of initiation. They are commonly used in intensive care units and in elective surgery cases pre- and post-operatively. (See **Form 2–4**).

5. **Nurses' Notes** (general and special care units)—record the care administered to the client while in the hospital. Nurses' notes reflect implementation of doctors' orders as well as assessment of patient condition and response to treatment. Nurses' notes are made over a 24-hour basis. Initial patient assessments are done at the beginning of each work shift and changes from this baseline condition are noted. Patient treatments, medications given, and other interventions are recorded. Specialized notes are usually made upon admission to, and discharge from, a facility. Nursing note formats differ according to the type of care provided. For example, intensive care units are

organized to allow for more extensive monitoring and observation data than general care units.

A common format that allows for this is the *flowsheet*. Flowsheets permit frequent documentation of critical patient data without the need for extensive narrative charting. The format usually contains preprinted assessment parameters followed by a series of boxes that the nurse uses to document patient-specific data. Flowsheets should always make allowances for narrative charting and should allow the reader to identify which provider delivered the care and in what time period. The full name of the provider, not just his or her initials, should be on each page of the flowsheet.

Another type of nursing documentation sometimes used is *charting by exception*. Charting by exception is based on the premise that all required care was given unless otherwise charted. Many variations of this type of nursing documentation exist; however, their formats are often similar to those seen in flowsheets. If the nursing documentation system of a hospital is not clear, contact the facility for clarification and/or for copies of their documentation policies and procedures.

6. **Graphic Sheets**—contain graph records of the patient's vital signs—temperature, pulse, respiratory rate, and blood pressure—taken at ordered intervals. Graphic sheets may also contain other information such as weight and intake and output (I&O).

7. **Medication Record**—lists all medications administered to a patient while in the hospital. The record should reflect administration of the medications specified on the physician's order sheet and include the medication's name, dose, and route and the time given. If a medicine is not given, the time is circled and the reason indicated.

8. **Nursing Care Plans** (nursing orders)—may or may not be part of the permanent medical record. Nursing care plans contain orders pertaining to the patient's nursing care. They should address individual patient needs based on assessment of current and past problems, including both physical and psychosocial needs. Nursing care plans are accepted in the legal definition of nursing in most nurse practice acts. Recently, however, they have evolved into multidisciplinary care plans, which allow a more integrated approach to patient care. JCAHO standards require care planning, but not nursing care planning per se.

9. **Laboratory, X Rays, Special** Tests—results of all laboratory and X ray studies, pathology reports, and other diagnostic tests ordered while in the hospital.

10. **Surgery, Documents**—consist of consents, records of operation, anesthesia records, operating room nurses' notes, and recovery room records. These documents reflect the care of the patient during the perioperative period. The record of operation should be written or dictated immediately after surgery and should describe findings, technical procedures used, specimens removed, preoperative and postoperative diagnoses, and identify the primary surgeon and assistants. Most operative notes are dictated, although a brief entry of operation is also made in the physicians' progress notes. (See **Form 2–5**).

11. **Emergency Department Records**—describe the care and treatment provided in the emergency department. Records contain both R.N. and M.D. notes, history and physical, orders, disposition of the client, and follow-up instructions. This medical record section may also contain records supplied by paramedics (EMTs) or other rescue personnel.

12. **Consultations**—basically the same information that appears in history and physical, but from the consultant's specialty focus. Consultation requests may be necessary in the case for an obscure diagnosis, a complicated disease condition requiring specialized skill/expertise and risk assessment, or an evaluation for medical/surgical treatment.

13. **Records of Special Disciplines**—reflect care and treatment given by additional health care team members, such as physical therapy, respiratory therapy, nutrition services, and social services. These notes should reflect the implementation of the physician's orders, and document the progress and response to treatment or intervention.

14. **Consents**—contain the patient's written permission for treatment in a facility, for all surgical procedures, and for other specific invasive tests and procedures. A consent should identify the name of the procedure and the physician performing it. It must be signed by the client, dated, timed, and witnessed by an authorized person.

15. **Advance Directives**—allow documentation of the types of medical interventions an individual would choose if he or she were incapacitated. Advance directives also allow designation of specific individuals (e.g., spouse, children) to make ongoing health care decisions for the patient in the event of his or her prolonged incapacitation.

16. **Protocols**—plan for a course of medical treatment. Examples of common protocols include those for anticoagulation therapy, parenteral nutrition, and chemotherapy.

17. **Care Paths**—also referred to as *critical paths, care maps,* or *care tracks.* Care paths establish goals and expected outcomes for patients

associated with specific provider interventions, along with an ideal sequence and timing of interventions to optimally achieve these goals and outcomes. They focus on quality and efficiency of care after treatment decisions are made. For further discussion on the use of care paths in establishing a standard of care. (See **Chapter 9**).

18. **Pharmacy Records**—not included as a component of health care institutions or health care provider medical records. Many pharmacies now computerize a patient drug profile, that is, a history of medications prescribed and filled, with dates and quantity. This may be an important source of information when a client has a history of seeking care from multiple providers (or emergency departments) that prescribe similar drugs.

19. **Unusual Occurrence or Incident Reports**—document deviations from events expected during the course of normal business. Examples of unusual occurrences are slip-and-falls (patients or visitors), medication errors, treatment delays, belligerent behavior by visitors or other staff members, or deviations from expected care standards. Unusual occurrence reports are not part of the medical record per se, but rather an internal risk management tool to document events factually. These reports are tracked and trended and are often used in conjunction with quality assurance/improvement programs.

Practice Note: Unusual occurrence or incident reports are generally not discoverable unless evidence of their existence can be proven (documentation in medical record that incident report was initiated).

20. **Discharge Summary**—provides an overview of the hospital course of treatment. The discharge summary must contain final diagnosis, pertinent laboratory and X-ray data, treatment and client response, plan for follow-up, and client condition at discharge. The report may be dictated by the attending physician or resident physician. If done by a resident, the report must be countersigned by the attending physician. Discharge summaries must be completed within 30 days of discharge. If the patient is transferred to another acute care facility, a transfer summary may be done in lieu of the discharge summary. A transfer summary should contain the same information as the discharge summary. (See **Form 2–6**).

21. **Autopsy Report**—contains the examination findings after death, including the immediate cause(s) of death. Autopsies are usually

done if the cause of death is uncertain or unknown, but are not performed without consent of next of kin. An exception to this procedure is a coroner's examination involving deaths of a suspicious or violent nature. Most states have statutes defining what constitutes a coroner's case.

Information in all medical record components must be written by the person responsible for the actual delivery of care. The accuracy of dictated reports must be verified by the author by handwritten or electronic signature. In teaching institutions, entries made by students are countersigned by the appropriate licensed personnel.

Practice Note: Many of the previously noted types of hospital records are dictated by the physician (or other provider) and eventually transcribed by the medical records department. The dates of dictation and transcription are usually noted somewhere near the bottom of the page, as for example: D:07/25/05 T:07/31/05.

The time frame for the dictation and transcription may vary from institution to institution, but there is a definite hierarchy of importance.

Admission history and physical examinations are extremely important documents and should be dictated, transcribed, and on the chart within 24 hours of admission (also a JCAHCO requirement). Discharge summaries, in contrast, are less important because the patient has already been released from the hospital.

§ 2.11   —Skilled Nursing Facility Records

Nursing home litigation has increased significantly over the past decade, requiring legal professionals to have detailed knowledge not only of medical records in general but also of records unique to skilled nursing or long-term care facilities. A skilled nursing facility (SNF) is a specially qualified health-care provider with the staff and equipment to offer residents skilled nursing care or rehabilitation and other health-related services. *Skilled nursing care* is defined as 24-hour-per-day supervision and medical treatment by a registered nurse under the direction of a physician. Admission to an SNF may be on a short-term basis for rehabilitation following surgery or on a long-term, custodial basis for the elderly or individuals unable to care for themselves. An individual facility may specialize exclusively in the care and treatment of Alzheimer's patients or contain a wing within the facility to house such patients. Each SNF must be state-licensed and in compliance with that state's standards and regulations. If a facility wishes to accept Medicaid and/or MediCare recipients and receive direct reimbursement from the government, it must also be certified, meaning the facility agrees to provide equal care to all residents, regardless of the source of payment, and consistent with the spirit of federal government regulations, which basically represent national community practice standards.

The Omnibus Reconciliation Act of 1987 (OBRA) included Nursing Home Reform Amendments covering a broad range of regulations dealing with care issues in SNFs, from patients' rights to evaluation and treatment of incontinence. The federal agency responsible for enforcing OBRA regulations is the Health Care Financing Administration (HCFA)* of the Department of Health and Human Services. HCFA inspectors conduct inspections of each SNF at least once a year but can visit more often in response to complaints. An inspector can cite a facility for violating OBRA regulations, which may result in penalties ranging from monetary fines to closure of the facility.

HCFA maintains a database containing information on every MediCare- and Medicaid-certified nursing home in the country. This database— Online Survey, Certification, and Reporting (OSCAR)—provides annual profiles of the resident populations of skilled nursing facilities with comparisons to state, regional, and national statistics. The data is compiled by the facility itself and completed at the time of the annual state certification study. Information includes the number or percentage of residents (1) with decubitus (pressure) ulcers, (2) receiving specialized services (occupational, speech, and physical therapy for example), and (3) showing significant weight loss. The OSCAR report also gives information on the facility's history of compliance with MediCare and Medicaid regulations and summarizes particular problems found in that SNF.

OSCAR reports can be obtained from the facility, the state agency in charge of licensing and certification surveys, or online from CMS at *http:// www.medicare.gov/nursing/home.asp*. The Web site offers a link to a directory containing the phone number for each state's long-term-care ombudsmen and survey agency. There is also a directory to each individual state Health Insurance Assistance Program, which provides information about the cost of long-term care. The underlying premise in OBRA is that SNFs must ensure that each resident attains the "highest practicable level of physical, emotional, and psychosocial functioning." This goal is achieved by the initial and continuing comprehensive assessment and planning for all aspects of a resident's needs. The tool developed for this purpose is the Minimum Data Set (MDS).

Minimum Data Set (MDS)

The MDS, a standardized national resident assessment instrument unique to long-term care facilities, is designed to produce a comprehensive, accurate, and reproducible assessment of each resident's functional capacity. The MDS has two basic purposes:

1. Information is collected in a standardized fashion and submitted to the federal government for research and analysis, and individualized care plans are triggered based on the information collected for the MDS.

2. As the MDS is completed, the nursing staff is able to assess the resident's functional capability, needs, and strengths. The assessment findings are then used by an interdisciplinary team to develop individual care plans for each resident.

    The MDS assessment is performed over the first seven days following admission and then at required intervals of 14, 30, 60, and 90 days. A re-assessment is also required after any noticeable change in physical or mental condition. The MDS assists the clinical nursing staff in screening for potential problems, such as wandering, dizziness, falls, risk for pressure ulcers from incontinence, immobility, peripheral vascular disease, or a history of prior pressure (decubitus) ulcers.

The MDS is completed based on information gathered by skilled nurses, nursing aides, social workers, recreational therapists, and dieticians. Interestingly, no components of the MDS require physician input, although medical diagnoses and information are used.

The specific sections included in an MDS are as follows:

Identification and background information—name, gender, date of birth, social security and MediCare numbers, reason for assessment, responsibility/legal guardian, advanced directives.

Demographic information—location admitted from, zip code of primary residence, lifetime occupations, education, language, cycle of daily events, etc.

Cognitive patterns—comatose, memory, recall ability, cognitive skills for daily decision-making, indications of delirium/periodic disordered thinking, change in cognitive status.

Communication/hearing patterns—hearing, communication devices, making self understood, speech clarity, ability to understand others, change in communication/hearing.

Vision patterns—vision, vision limitations/difficulties, appliances.

Mood and behavior patterns—indicators of depression, anxiety, sad mood, mood persistence, change in mood and behavioral symptoms (e.g., wandering, verbally abusive, socially inappropriate).

Psychosocial well-being—sense of initiative/involvement, unsettled relationships, past roles.

Physical functioning and structural problems—ADL self-performance, ADL support provided, bed mobility, transfer, walk-in room, dressing, eating, personal hygiene, bathing, change in ADL function, etc.

Continence in last 14 days—bowel, bladder, bowel elimination pattern, appliances and programs, change in urinary continence.

Disease diagnoses—diseases (e.g., endocrine/metabolic, heart/circulation, musculoskeletal), infections (e.g., methicillin resistant, clostridium difficile, HIV), other current or more detailed diagnoses and ICD-9 codes.

Health conditions—problem conditions (e.g., weight gain or loss, delusions, dizziness, syncope), pain symptoms, pain site, accidents (e.g., fell in past 30 days), stability of conditions.

Oral/Nutritional status—oral problems, height and weight, weight change, nutritional problem and approaches (e.g., parenteral/IV, feeding tube), parenteral or enteral intake.

Oral/Dental status—oral status and disease prevention.

Skin condition—ulcers, type of ulcer, history of resolved ulcers, other skin problems, treatments, foot problems, and care.

Activity pursuit patterns—time awake, average time involved in activities, preferred activity settings, general activity preferences, changes in daily routine.

Medications—number, new medications, injections, days received the following medications (e.g., anti-psychotic, antianxiety).

Special treatments and procedures—special care (e.g., chemotherapy, dialysis, IV medication), programs (alcohol/drug treatment, Alzheimer's/dementia special care, hospice, etc.), therapies (e.g., speech, occupational, physical, respiratory, psychological), intervention programs for mood, nursing rehabilitation/restorative, devices and restraints, hospital stays, ER visits, physician visits or orders, abnormal lab values.

Discharge potential and overall status—discharge potential, overall change in care needs.

(See **Form 2–7**).

Resident Assessment Protocols

Once the MDS is completed, a second form unique to the long-term care environment is prepared. The Resident Assessment Protocol (RAP) is essentially a decision tree based on all information collected in the MDS. In other words, if certain information is contained on the MDS, this will lead to the conclusion that a problem exists, or is likely to develop, and a care plan may need to be formulated. (See **Form 2–8**).

Care Plans

After the MDS assessment has been completed and the RAP prepared, the specific plan for delivery of nursing care to a resident is developed. This is called the care plan. HCFA requires that the care plan, an interdisciplinary document, be developed within seven days of the completion of the MDS.

A care plan is developed for each identified problem and consists of four main elements:

Nursing *diagnosis* (problems, strengths, needs)

Outcomes/goals to be expected with resolution of the diagnosis

Interventions/approaches to be taken in order to help the resident achieve the Outcome

Evaluation of the effectiveness of the intervention.

The nursing notes and flow sheets will provide evidence of how the plan of care was implemented. (See **Form 2–9**).

2-22   SOURCES AND COMPONENTS

Resident Care Conferences

On a periodic basis, the interdisciplinary team will meet to discuss the status of a resident. Typical attendees include licensed nurses, CNAs, dietitians, occupational therapists, physical therapists, psychologists, the resident, and interested family members. Specific care planning notes, signed by all present, may be generated as a result.

Activities of Daily Living

Activities of daily living (ADL) include such tasks as bathing, grooming, eating, ambulating, and dressing. An individual's ability to perform these basic tasks help to assess the need for assistance or placement in a SNF.

The method of documenting these routine aspects of SNF care is the flowsheet. Typical flowsheets have areas for percentage of meals consumed, continence of bladder and bowel, daily hygiene activities, and so on. They may also be used to document behavior, such as wandering. Flowsheets are generally completed by CNAs and can be problematic if the information contained on the flowsheet differs from that given in the licensed nursing notes. (See **Form 2–10**).

§ 2.12   —Health Care Practitioners' Medical Records

The medical records of health care providers vary according to the type of treatment and care provided to the client. Basically, they include progress notes made at the time of each visit, the results of tests, and a record of drugs prescribed. Any minor surgical procedures performed in the office should also be described in detail. Information contained in a health care practitioner's medical records is similar to that found in records from health care institutions. For example, a physician's office progress note should contain information similar to that found in a hospital progress note. Medical records maintained by any practitioner should meet the requirements discussed in **Chapter 1, § 1.2.**

§ 2.13   —Chiropractic Records

Chiropractic records can present a dilemma when they need to be reviewed and summarized. First, the handwriting can be difficult to read. Second, forms utilized by chiropractors to record treatments vary from office to office. Some practitioners use blank paper to record their treatment and observations; others use preprinted forms. No matter which charting format is used, the following information should be included:

1. Date of treatment
2. Patient's subjective symptoms
3. Type of adjustment and other treatment given
4. Reaction to treatment
5. Date of next visit.

More than 45 different types of chiropractic techniques are currently utilized. Some of the more common methods include diversified, Gonstead, SOT, applied kinesiology, and toggle-recoil. The technique chiropractors use depends on a number of factors, including the school where they received training. Generally speaking, unless the lawsuit involves chiropractic malpractice, it is not important to identify the kind of manipulation utilized.

Chiropractic uses standard medical terminology, concentrating on those terms associated with orthopedics, neurology, radiology, and physical therapy. Unfamiliar terms generally relate to specific chiropractic adjustments and maneuvers. (See **Appendix G** for a list of orthopedic and neurologic tests commonly utilized by chiropractors. The terms and abbreviations used may vary, depending on the school or theory to which the chiropractor adheres. Chiropractic records are summarized in the same manner as medical records. See **Chapter 8** for methods of summarizing records and for suggestions on dealing with problem medical records).

§ 2.14   Medical Terminology

As in law, medicine has its own language. Specific terms can be learned easily and will become more familiar with time. Sections 2.15 through 2.17 provide a brief introduction to the composition of medical terms, the language of various specialties, the terminology and meanings of common diagnostic tests, and medical abbreviations. Additional resource material in these areas may be found in the **Bibliography.**

§ 2.15 —Derivation of Medical Terms

At least 50 percent of our general English vocabulary is of Greek and Latin derivation. A conservative estimate states that as much as 75 percent of our scientific vocabulary has its roots in these languages. The majority of medical terms stem from Greek and Latin. A significant number of terms are also derived from other languages:

Arabic—alcohol, alkali, syrup, tartar

Anglo-Saxon—bladder, blood, heart, knee, ache

French—malaise, poison, grand mal, petit mal Italian—influenza, malaria

Dutch—cough

German—Fahrenheit

Other terms are named after the individual who perfected a particular test or procedure or who discovered a scientific fact. For example:

Pasteurization—the process of heating milk to kill harmful bacteria. This procedure was named after Louis Pasteur, the French scientist who discovered the process.

Curie—the unit for measuring the intensity of radioactivity. This measurement was named after French chemist and physicist Marie Curie, the codiscoverer of radium.

Practice Note: If the focus of your practice is in medical malpractice, workers' compensation, or personal injury, formal instruction in medical terminology may be indicated. Such courses are often offered on-line through community or junior colleges. Also, a number of excellent textbooks have been written in a self-learning format.

§ 2.16 —Word Components

Most medical terms are not derived from a single word, but are a combination of two or more word elements. These elements are the root or key word, the prefix, and the suffix. Each of these elements has a distinct meaning and, when combined, they give the word its complete meaning.

Root Words.   The main element of a word is the root. The root contains a definite idea and may be complete in and of itself. Words such as "tendon" and "spasm" are root words whose meaning is complete.

Some root words have combining forms, the purpose of which is to make pronunciation easier. This is usually accomplished by adding a vowel to the root, most often the vowel "o." An example of a root word with a combining form is "osteoarthritis." Osteo is a root meaning "bone," arthro is a root meaning "joint," and -itis is a suffix meaning "inflammation." Translated as a whole, osteoarthritis means "inflammation of the bone joint." Usually the element that gives the key to the word's meaning appears at the beginning of the word. A list of root words and their combining forms that describe body systems and organs can be found in **Appendix A.**

Compound Words.   When two roots are combined and each retains its basic meaning, it is called a compound word. Some common compound words are "headache," "newborn," and "heartbeat."

Prefixes.   A prefix is an element placed at the beginning of another word (such as a root) to modify the meaning of that root or to show various types of relationships. Prefixes can be used to show time and place, position in relation to other parts, type, direction, number, size, amount, and color. Prefixes never stand alone. Note that prefixes can also have combining forms. A list of prefixes commonly used in medical terminology appears in **Appendix B.**

Suffixes.   A suffix is an element added to the end of a word that can change the meaning of the word or make it more specific. Like prefixes, suffixes never stand alone, but must be attached to a root or a root combining form. A list of suffixes can be found in **Appendix C.**

All medical terminology is composed of combinations of the word elements just listed. Each element contributes to the meaning of the whole word. By separating words into their component parts, identifying their meaning becomes easier. As an example, the word "laparohysterosalpingo-oophorectomy" can be broken down in this manner:

Laparo—refers to the loin or flank

Hystero—combining form of the root word meaning uterus

Salpingo—combining form of the root word that refers to the fallopian tube

Oophor—root word referring to the ovary

Ectomy—suffix meaning excising or cutting out.

Thus, laparohysterosalpingo-oophorectomy is the term for the surgical procedure in which the uterus, fallopian tubes, and ovaries are removed, also called a complete or total abdominal hysterectomy. A list of general medical terminology can be found in **Appendix D.**

§ 2.17   Discipline-Specific Medical Terminology

Many medical disciplines use terms unique to their area of practice. Examples of some specialties and their medical terminology follow:

1. **Chiropractic.** Personal injury and professional malpractice cases often contain chiropractic records that must be included in any summary of records. Chiropractic can be defined as a nonsurgical and drugless method of healing, based on the premise that dislocation of the spinal vertebrae can contribute to a variety of ailments. This concept, the relationship between the spine's structure and the function of the nervous system, is fundamental to chiropractic. Spinal manipulative therapy (SMT) is utilized to correct these imbalances and restore health. (See § **5.13**) . A list of chiropractic terminology can be found in **Appendix F.**

2. **Dental.** To a legal professional accustomed to reviewing medical records, dental records may appear to be written in a foreign language. Nevertheless, the terminology follows the same rules of construction used in medical fields (roots, prefixes, suffixes) and many of the words are even identical. If you review dental records on a regular basis, your best ally is a good dental dictionary. (See the **Bibliography**). A list of basic dental terms and their meanings appears in **Appendix H.**

3. **Podiatric.** Doctors of podiatric medicine treat disorders of the feet by both surgical and nonsurgical methods. The concept of biomechanics is significant in podiatry. *Biomechanics* describes the human body as a well-lubricated system of pulleys, levers, and fulcrums that

functions in a very sophisticated manner. An injury to one joint of the body may be the result of an improper function in another part of the body. The relationship of the foot, leg, hip, and upper body unites these parts into one functional whole. With this fundamental concept in mind, the podiatrist not only studies and treats diseases of the feet but also assesses the role the foot plays in causing disease elsewhere in the body. **Appendix I** contains a list of common podiatric terms and their meanings.

4. **Psychiatric.** Reviewing psychiatric or psychological records requires knowledge of psychiatric terminology (a list of common psychiatric terminology can be found in **Appendix J**) and the use of a resource manual that offers definitions of the wide range of human behaviors and disease processes. In May 1994 the American Psychiatric Association published the fourth edition of the *Diagnostic and Statistical Manual of Mental Disorders,* or DSM-IV This book, along with its companion *Quick Reference to the Diagnostic Criteria from DSM-IV,* represents the consensus of current opinion even as the knowledge in the field continues to evolve. As such, it provides access to the multitude of syndromes, symptoms, and signs related to psychiatric illnesses and their diagnoses.

§ 2.18   Understanding the DSM-IV

The *DSM-IV* looks at each patient in terms of five diagnostic axes with a category for conditions "not attributable to a mental disorder," including malingering. As the psychiatric or psychological examination is completed, certain disorders or conditions are identified in the patient and placed in the appropriate axis. When completed, the axes facilitate a comprehensive and systematic evaluation with attention given to various mental and medical conditions, psychosocial and environmental problems, and level of functioning that might have been overlooked if the focus had been on assessment of a single presenting problem.

When an individual has more than one disorder or condition within an axis, all should be reported with the principal diagnosis within that axis listed first. It is assumed that any disorder or condition listed in Axis I is the principal diagnosis or reason for the visit, unless Axis II diagnoses are followed by the qualifying phrase "principal diagnosis" or "reason for visit." The numerical codings found within the axes are ICD-9 codes for billing and reimbursement purposes.

The axes and their principal conditions are as follows:

Axis I—Clinical Disorders; Other Conditions That May Be a Focus of Clinical Attention. Cognitive (e.g., delirium, dementia, amnesia); substance-related; schizophrenia and other psychotic disorders; mood, anxiety, somatoform, and factitious; dissociative; sexual and gender identity, eating and sleep disorders; impulse-control disorders not classified elsewhere; adjustment; other.

Axis II—Personality Disorders; Mental Retardation. Paranoid; schizoid or schizotypal; antisocial; borderline; histrionic; narcissistic; avoidant; dependent; obsessive-compulsive; personality disorder not otherwise specified.

Axis III—General Medical Conditions. Infectious and parasitic diseases; neoplasms; endocrine, nutritional and metabolic diseases and immunity disorders; diseases of the blood and blood-forming organs; diseases of the nervous system and sense organs; diseases of the circulatory system; diseases of the respiratory system; diseases of the digestive system; diseases of the genitourinary system; complications of pregnancy, childbirth, and the puerperium; diseases of the skin and subcutaneous tissue; diseases of the musculoskeletal system and connective tissue; congenital anomalies; conditions originating in the perinatal period; symptoms, signs, and ill-defined conditions; injury and poisoning.

Axis IV—Psychosocial and Environmental Problems. Primary support group (e.g., death of a family member, family health problems, divorce, separation, remarriage, sexual or physical abuse, birth of a sibling, etc.); social environment (e.g., death or loss of friend, living alone, discrimination, retirement, etc.); educational (e.g., illiteracy, academic problems, discord with teachers/classmates, inadequate school environment, etc.); occupational (e.g., unemployment, threat of job loss, stressful work schedule or environment; job change or dissatisfaction; discord with boss/co-workers, etc.); housing (e.g., homelessness, inadequate housing, unsafe conditions, discord with neighbors/landlord, etc.); economic (e.g., extreme poverty, inadequate finances or welfare support, etc.); access to health care (e.g., inadequate services, transportation problems, little or no health insurance, etc.); interaction with legal system (e.g., arrest, incarceration, litigation, victim of crime, etc.); other (e.g., exposure to disease, war, other hostilities, discord with physician/counselor, etc.).

Axis V—Global Assessment of Functioning (GAF). In this axis, the examiner considers the patient's psychological, social, and occupational functioning on a hypothetical continuum of mental health/illness. Impairment in functioning due to physical or environmental limitations is not included. Assessment will be done at the beginning and end of a hospitalization, or periodically throughout the course of treatment.

91–100 Superior functioning in a wide range of activities; life's problems never seem to get out of hand; sought out by others because of positive qualities; no symptoms.

81–90 Absent or minimal symptoms; good functioning in all areas; interested and involved in wide range of activities; socially effective; generally satisfied with life; no more than everyday problems or concerns.

71–80 If symptoms are present they are transient and expectable reactions to psychosocial stressors; no more than slight impairment in social, occupation, or school functioning.

61–70 Some mild symptoms *or* some difficulty in social, occupational, or school functioning, but generally functioning pretty well; has some meaningful interpersonal relationships.

51–60 Moderate symptoms *or* moderate difficulty in social, occupational, or school functioning.

41–50 Serious symptoms *or* any serious impairment in social, occupational, or school functioning

31–40 Some impairment in reality testing or communication *or* major impairment in several areas, such as work or school, family relations, judgment, thinking, or mood.

21–30 Behavior is considerably influenced by delusions or hallucinations *or* serious impairment in communication or judgment *or* inability to function in almost all areas.

11–20 Some danger of hurting self or others *or* occasionally fails to maintain minimal personal hygiene *or* gross impairment in communication.

1–10 Persistent danger of severely hurting self or others *or* persistent inability to maintain minimal personal hygiene *or* serious suicidal act with clear expectation of death.

0 Inadequate information.

§ 2.19 Results of a DSM-IV Multiaxial Evaluation

After the examination is completed, the provider will formulate his findings in terms of the disorders or conditions (if any) found within all of the four axes with the final, fifth axis indicating the examiner's global assessment of the patient's functioning. If the patient has been hospitalized, assessments should be done on admission and at the time of discharge. The following are two examples of how an individual might be classified following a DSM-IV evaluation.

Example One.

Axis I	296.23	Major depressive disorder, single episode, severe without psychotic features
	305.00	Alcohol abuse
Axis II	301.6	Dependent personality disorder; frequent use of denial
Axis III		None
Axis IV		Threat of job loss
Axis V		GAF = 35 (current)

Example Two.

Axis I	293.83	Mood disorder due to hypothyroidism, with depressive features
Axis II	V71.09	No diagnosis; histrionic personality features
Axis III	244.9	Hypothyroidism
	365.23	Chronic angle-closure glaucoma
Axis IV		None
Axis V		GAF = 45 (on admission)
		GAF = 65 (at discharge)

§ 2.20   Medical Abbreviations and Symbols

One of the most frustrating aspects of reviewing medical records can be the liberal use of abbreviations. Some abbreviations are standard and their meanings easily recognized by the general public. For example, "Rx" is widely known to mean a prescription for medication. However, attempting to decipher abbreviations that are discipline-specific or invented by the provider can be frustrating. Looking at the abbreviation in context will often give clues to its possible meanings. If this technique fails, calling the medical provider may be appropriate. If the provider in question is not available, a nurse or office manager can often be helpful. Providing a list of all medical abbreviations would be difficult, if not impossible. However, most of those commonly encountered in medical records can be found in **Appendix K** with further resources listed in the Bibliography.

Medical symbols are also frequently used (and misused) in the medical record. Although many of them are standard and universally recognized, others have meanings known only to the provider using them. Techniques for deciphering the meaning of medical symbols are similar to those used for abbreviations. A list of commonly used medical symbols is found in **Appendix L.**

§ 2.21   JCAHO Standards on Medical Abbreviations and Symbols

JCAHO recommends that health care institutions develop a list of approved abbreviations, acronyms, and symbols that will be used in the facility. The standard is that "[a]bbreviations, acronyms, and symbols are standardized throughout the organization and there is a list of abbreviations, acronyms, and symbols not to use."

In recognition that the most effective means of protecting patients from the effects of miscommunication between health care providers may not be a comprehensive approved list of abbreviations and symbols, JCAHO developed an official "Do Not Use" short list. This list has 15 specific "do not use" abbreviations and symbols, with "potential problem" identified, and "use instead" language given. For example:

- The abbreviation "MS" can mean either morphine sulfate or magnesium sulfate (a major and significant difference). Providers are directed to spell out fully both of these medications.

- The abbreviation "IU" (international unit) has been mistaken for "IV" (intravenous) or the number "10" (ten). Providers must spell out international unit.

The "Do Not Use" list contains seven further abbreviations and symbols for possible future inclusion on the list. For example, the symbol "μg" (micrograms) has been mistaken for "mg" (milligrams), resulting in a one thousand-fold overdose. A facility's list of approved abbreviations must not contain any of the entries on the "Do Not Use" List. The full JCAHO "Do Not Use" list can be accessed at *www.jointcommission.org.*

Practice Note: If a health care institution is a defendant in a lawsuit, be sure to request a copy of the facility's list of approved abbreviations, acronyms, and abbreviations in discovery, along with the applicable policies and procedures governing the list. This is critical in cases involving medication errors.

§ 2.22   Additional Medical Record Documentation Terminology

In addition to understanding body structure and function, it is also essential to be knowledgeable in the language and terms providers use to document assessment and diagnosis information resulting from their examination. Components of this language include body orientation, body planes, anatomical directions and positions, and body movements. This documentation language is standard and used in virtually all medical records by all types of providers.

§ 2.23   Body Orientation

When documenting medical care findings, it is necessary to have consistent points of reference that define body orientation. The anatomical position (of the body) is the standard used when describing the location of physical findings following examination or treatment. This position presents the body as facing the examiner, standing erect, with the palms of the hands facing outward (see **Figure 2–3**). All findings are described in relation to this position. Otherwise, a left lower leg fracture may have different meaning for an examiner and a medical record reader, depending on the orientation of the examiner when describing the injury: Is it on the examiner's left side or the patient's? Is the patient facing toward or away from the examiner?

§ 2.24   —Body Planes

Body planes are a series of imaginary lines drawn through the body as points of reference. These are also shown in **Figure 2–3.**

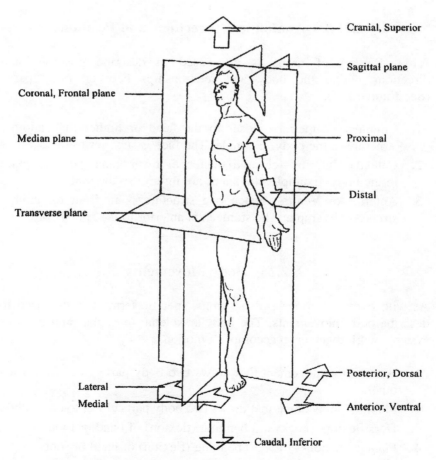

Figure 2–3. Body planes/anatomical positions and directions.

Median Plane—plane that runs top to bottom down the middle of the body, dividing it into equal right and left halves.

Sagittal Plane(s)—any plane that runs top to bottom and divides the body into unequal right and left parts. These planes run parallel to the median plane.

Coronal or Frontal Plane(s)—any plane running top to bottom that divides the body into equal or unequal front and back parts.

Transverse or Cross-Horizontal Plane(s)—any plane that divides the body into upper and lower parts.

§ 2.25 —Anatomical Directions and Positions

A precise set of terms is also used to describe positions and directions within the body and relationships between body parts. (See **Figure 2–3**).

1. Cranial or Superior—closer to the head or higher than another structure in the body. Example: The face is superior to the chest.
2. Caudal or Inferior—closer to the feet or lower than another structure in the body. Example: the knees are inferior to the hips.
3. Anterior or Ventral—when one structure is in front of another structure. Example: The stomach is anterior to the spinal cord.

§ 2.26 Body Movements

As with body directions and positions, specific terms are also used to describe body movements. The body's skeletal, muscular, and nervous systems work together to accomplish motion.

1. Extension—movement that draws two body parts away from each other.
2. Flexion—movement that draws two body parts closer to each other.
3. Dorsiflexion—backward bending (flexion) of hand or foot.
4. Plantar Flexion—forward bending (flexion) of hand or foot.
5. Supination—turning upward of palm of hand.

6.   Pronation—turning palm of hand backward or downward.

7.   Abduction—drawing away from medial plane of the body.

8.   Adduction—drawing toward medial plane of the body.

(See **Figure 2–4** for illustrations of body movements).

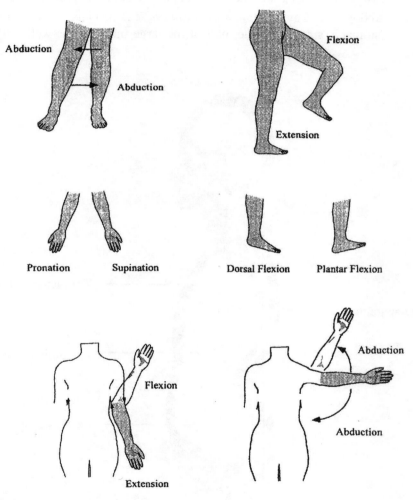

Figure 2–4. Body movements.

Source: Elson & Kapit, The Anatomy Coloring Book (1977). Reprinted with permission.

§ 2.27 Body Cavities

Internally, the body has three cavities:

1. Thoracic or Chest Cavity—contains the lungs, heart, great blood vessels, and the esophagus. The upper boundary of the thoracic cavity is the neck and the lower boundary is the diaphragm.
2. Abdominal Cavity—contains most of the organs of digestion (stomach, small intestine, part of the large intestine) as well as the

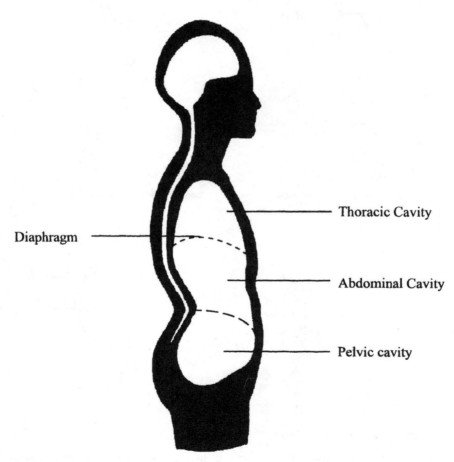

Figure 2–5. Body cavities.

liver, gallbladder, and kidneys. The upper boundary of the abdominal cavity is the diaphragm and the lower boundary is the pelvis.

3. Pelvic Cavity—contains the lower portion of the large intestine, rectum, urinary bladder, and the reproductive organs. There is no distinct boundary separating it from the abdominal cavity.

(See **Figure 2–5**).

§ 2.28   Conclusion

The discussion in this chapter provides an introduction to medical terminology and language norms used in documentation. Chapter 3 will build on this information by addressing body structure and function. Upon completion of a physical examination, the provider documents findings (normal or abnormal) using this language. Understanding these concepts will facilitate medical record review and enable identification of pertinent information for use in medical record summaries.

FORM 2–1
MEDICAL RECORD FACE SHEET

SEX male	PATIENT NAME - Patterson Edward			MR NUMBER 46789	AGE 50		HAPPY AREA
COV	GROUP Prime Coverage	ACCOUNT 1234	SUB GR	HIC#	D.O.B 1/2/35		
				SSN #			
HOME ADDRESS 853 Hamilton Ave Anytown. OH 44513				PHONES 899-7563	EXT EXT		
	PAYMENT P1	SMOKER N		M.S 1	RACE 1	RELIG 1	
LAST ADMISSION - NONE	ON			ADMISSION			
ADMITTING PHYSICIAN - Marshall Medic			TIME	DATE ADMITTED 5/31/95	ADM DAY	TYPE ADM - Emer	OTHER INSURANCE
ATTENDING PHYSICIAN - same							
UNIT	ROOM NO.	BED		DISCHARGE			USUAL PHYSICIAN - J Smith
			TIME	DATE		HOS DAYS	
EMERGENCY CONTACTS - Mirian Edwards, wife							
RELATION NAME - same				PHONES - same			
					EXT EXT		ADMITTING CLERK - JT
ADMITTING DIAGNOSIS - fx left femur							WORK RELATED - no
SURGERY							ON

PRINCIPAL DIAGNOSIS
Fracture left femur

CODE

SECONDARY DIAGNOSIS OR COMPLICATIONS
Facial Lacerations
Pulmonary Emboli

PRINCIPAL PROCEDURE
ORIF left hip

CONSULTANTS
John Smith MD

RESULTS						
DISCHARGED	DISCHARGED AGAINST MEDICAL ADVICE	EXPIRED	AUTOPSY YES NO	CORONER CASE	NO	YES
COMPLETED BY M.D.		ATTENDING PHYSICIAN M.D.				

FORM 2–2
MEMORIAL HOSPITAL HISTORY AND
PHYSICAL EXAMINATION

PATIENT NAME   M.R. NUMBER
Edward Patterson   46789
PHYSICIAN   SERVICE
Marshall Medic   Orthopedics

6/21/2005

This is a 50-year-old male involved in a motor vehicle accident. He was driving a car struck broadside on the passenger side by another vehicle. He had to be extricated from the vehicle. On admission to the emergency room, he was found to have an obvious deformity of the left femur. Subsequent X ray revealed fracture middle third left femur. He also was noted to have 2 lacerations above the left eye with ecchymosis involving the orbital rim on the left. Facial X rays were negative. Although the patient's memory of events surrounding the accident are hazy, he states he did not lose consciousness at any time. Past history: No prior surgeries except an appendectomy 30 years ago. Has mild hypertension for which he takes hydrochlorothiazide 50mg daily. States he has been healthy all his life.

PHYSICAL EXAMINATION
Well-developed, well-nourished male in moderate distress secondary to pain from fractured femur. Vital signs: BP 168/102 P 88 R 24 T 99.2. HEENT: Large ecchymotic area around left eye. There are 2 lacerations above the left orbital rim which have been repaired in the emergency room. Ears, nose, and throat are clear. Chest: Lungs are clear to A&P. Heart tones are regular and without murmur. Abd: Soft, bowel sounds are present. No masses, tenderness, organomegaly. Genital: No burning or frequency. Urinary stream good, has no problems with bladder infections. Testicles descended bilaterally, no hernias. Rectal: No masses. Stool brown in color. Several small hemorrhoids present. Extremities: Fracture of mid-third left femur. Now in balanced suspension traction with 35 pounds weight. Nerve and circulation are intact to all extremities.
Impression: Fracture left femur secondary to motor vehicle accident, facial lacerations, mild hypertension by history. Plan: Balanced suspension traction, possible rodding of femur next week. Cleanse facial lacerations with hydrogen peroxide.

D. 6/21/2005 T. 6/22/2005

FORM 2–3
PATIENT PROGRESS RECORD

PATIENT PROGRESS RECORD

Patient's Name: Edward Patterson

Address

City

(patient ID stamp)

DATE	TIME	ORDERS
6/23/85	900	AP & lat hip port - shows good alignment of femur *(MD signature)*
6/23/85	1000	Doing well, N&C OK. Hct 30.6 - will give 2 units packed RBC's
		Has decided on surgery - will schedule for Tues
		(MD signature)
6/24/85	1000	N&C OK. Discussed surgery, risks, complications
		Plan OR tomorrow, he agrees *(MD signature)*
6/25/85	1200	OP Note
		Closed reduction & nailing left femur under general anesthesia
		16 x 440 rod
		Tolerated well *(MD signature)*

FORM 2–4
PHYSICIAN'S ORDERS

UNLESS SPECIFIED GENERIC ITEMS MAY BE SUPPLIED BY PHARMACY	**PHYSICIANS ORDERS**	DRUG SENSITIVITY 1._____ 2._____ 3._____ 4._____

DATE	TIME		TIME SCREENED
6/21/85	1000	Amit: fx left femur	
		Cond: Stable	
		Diet: NPO except meds	
		Activity: bedrest	
		Rx:Russel's tx w/35# weights	
		ck n&c left leg q 2h	
		Demerol 100mg im q4h prn pain	
		Tylenol tabs ii po w4h pm mild pain	
		CBC in am	
		T&C 2 units blood in am	
		IV D5 0.45S @ 100 cc/hr	
		(MD signature)	

DATE	6/21/85	TIME	DATE	6/21/85	TIME
CLERK SIGNATURE	SL	1020	RN SIGNATURE	KJT	1030

DATE	TIME		TIME SCREENED

DATE	TIME	DATE	TIME
CLERK SIGNATURE		RN SIGNATURE	

DATE	TIME		TIME SCREENED

DATE	TIME	DATE	TIME
CLERK SIGNATURE		RN SIGNATURE	

FORM 2-5
MEMORIAL HOSPITAL OPERATIVE REPORT

PATIENT	M.R. NUMBER
Edward Patterson	46709
SURGEON	PROCEDURE
Marshall Medic	nailing left femur

PREOPERATIVE DIAGNOSIS: Fracture of left femur
POSTOPERATIVE DIAGNOSIS: Same
PROCEDURE: Closed nailing, left femur

The patient was placed on the fracture table under traction, and X rays were taken, which revealed the fracture to be in satisfactory position and alignment. Accordingly, the patient was prepped and draped in the usual fashion. A longitudinal posterior incision was made, beginning at the tip to the greater trochanter, running proximally, splitting the gluteal muscles. The trochanter, base of the neck were identified. Using the awl, the hole was started and this was increased, using the hand reamers. Guide pin was then placed down the shaft and was found to go easily into the distal fragment. The femur was then reamed progressively up to a #15.5 and a nail was placed across the fracture site. This fit securely, giving excellent fixation. The X rays reveal satisfactory position and alignment of the fracture and the rod.
Wounds were thoroughly irrigated and debrided, the subcutaneous tissue repaired with #2-0 Dexon, the skin with staples, sterile compression dressing applied; the traction pin from the tibia was removed, sterile dressing applied. The patient tolerated the procedure well and returned to recovery room in good condition.

                                                      Marshall Medic, MD

D. 6/25/2005 T. 6/27/2005

FORM 2–6
MEMORIAL HOSPITAL DISCHARGE SUMMARY

PATIENT: Edward Patterson
MR NUMBER: 46709
PHYSICIAN: Marshall Medic
ADMITTED: 8/2/2005
DISCHARGED: 8/16/2005

HISTORY: The patient is a 50-year-old white male who underwent closed rodding of his left femur fracture on 6/21/2005 following a motor vehicle accident. Postoperatively, he developed pulmonary emboli, and was begun on heparin. He sustained multiple postsurgical bleeds into the wound, which were treated with aspiration. He was placed on antibiotics. At the time of discharge the surgical wound was still draining and at times had active bleeding. He was followed as an outpatient. Coumadin had been stopped, but the wound has continued to drain and he has intermittent fevers. On admission the wound appeared intact. He was admitted for further treatment.

HOSPITAL COURSE: Significant findings showed a 12 cm. posterior incision with drainage along the skin incision draining salmon-colored fluid. There was no surrounding inflammation. There was minimal pain to palpation. The distal neurovascular was intact. He was afebrile. Cultures obtained from the wound grew Serratia. The department of medicine was consulted. The patient was taken to surgery on 8/5, where incision and drainage of the infected hematoma of the left hip was performed. The patient's blood pressure medicines were stopped because of well-controlled blood pressure. The patient was continued on antibiotics. On 8/8 the patient was returned to surgery, where irrigation and debridement was again carried out and delayed primary closure over two large hemovac suction tubes was performed. The patient was kept on antibiotics. Hemovacs were discontinued on 5/12. He was discharged home with sutures still in and a small amount of drainage each day. He was started on Bactrim 2 tablets q.i.d. and given dressing supplies. He was told not to continue his high blood pressure medicines. He was instructed on crutch walking and weight bearing as tolerated. He was given a follow-up appointment with me on 8/23/2005. His return-to-work date is 12/21/2005.

FINAL DIAGNOSIS: Infected hematoma left hip wound.

D: 9/12/2005 T: 9/19/2005   Marshall Medic

FORM 2-7
MINIMUM DATA SET

numeric Identifier   000U. .CY

MINIMUM DATA SET (MDS) -- VERSION 2.0
FOR NURSING HOME RESIDENT ASSESSMENT AND CARE SCREENING
FULL ASSESSMENT FORM
(Status in last 7 days, unless other time frame indicated)

SECTION A. IDENTIFICATION AND BACKGROUND INFORMATION

1.	RESIDENT NAME			
		a. (First) b. (Middle Initial) c. (Last) d. (Jr/Sr)		
2.	ROOM NUMBER	129		
3.	ASSESSMENT REFERENCE DATE	a. Last day of MDS observation period 09/24/1996		
		b. Original (0) or corrected copy of form (enter number of correction)		0
4a.	DATE OF REENTRY	Date of reentry from most recent temporary discharge to a hospital in last 90 days (or since last assessment or admission if less than 90 days) / /		
5.	MARITAL STATUS	1. Never married 3. Widowed 5. Divorced 2. Married 4. Separated		3
6.	Medical Record No.			
7.	CURRENT PAYMENT SOURCES FOR N.H. STAY	(Billing Office to indicate: check all that apply in last 30 days)		
		Medicaid per diem	a. ✓	VA per diem	f.
		Medicare per diem	b.	Self or family pays for full per diem	g.
		Medicare ancillary Part A	c. ✓	Medicaid resident liability or Medicare co-payment	h.
		Medicare ancillary Part B	d.	Private insurance per diem (including co-payment)	i.
		CHAMPUS per diem	e.	Other per diem	j.
8.	REASONS FOR ASSESSMENT

Note-if this is a discharge or reentry assessment only a limited subset of MDS items need be completed | a. Primary reason for assessment 1. Admission assessment (required by day 14) 2. Annual assessment 3. Significant change in status assessment 4. Significant correction of prior assessment 5. Quarterly review assessment 6. Discharged-return not anticipated 7. Discharged-return anticipated 8. Discharged prior to completing initial assessment 9. Reentry 0. NONE OF ABOVE b. Special codes for use with supplemental assessment types in Case Mix demonstration states or other states where required 1. 5 day assessment 2. 30 day assessment 3. 60 day assessment 4. Quarterly assessment using full MDS form 5. Readmission/return assessment 6. Other state required assessment | | 1 |
9.	RESPONSIBILITY/ LEGAL GUARDIAN	(Check all that apply)		
		Durable power attorney/financial		
		Legal guardian	a.	Family member responsible	e. ✓
		Other legal oversight	b.	Patient responsible for self	f. ✓
		Durable power of attorney/health care	c.	NONE OF ABOVE	g.
10.	ADVANCED DIRECTIVES	(For those items with supporting documentation in the record, check all that apply)		
		Living will	a.	Feeding restriction	f.
		Do not resuscitate	b.	Medication retrictions	g.
		Do not hospitalize	c.	Other treatment restrictions	h.
		Organ donation	d.	NONE OF ABOBE	i. ✓
		Autopsy request	e.		

SECTION B. COGNITIVE PATTERNS

1.	COMATOSE	(Persistent vegetative state/no discernible consciousness) 0. No. 1. Yes (If yes, skip to Section G)	0
2.	MEMORY	(Recall of what was learned or known) a.Short-term memory OK-seems/appears to recall after 5 minutes 0. Memory OK 1. Memory problem	1
		b.Long-term memory OK-seems/appears to recall long past 0. Memory OK 1. Memory problem	1

3.	MEMORY/ RECALL ABILITY	(Check all that resident was normally able to recall during the last 7 days)		
		Current season	a.	That he/she is in a nursing home	d.
		Location of own room	b.		
		Staff names/faces	c.	NONE OF ABOVE are recalled	e. ✓
4.	COGNITIVE SKILLS FOR DAILY DECISION-MAKING	(Made decisions regarding tasks of daily life) 0. INDEPENDENT-decisions consistent/reasonable 1. MODIFIED INDEPENDENCE-some difficulty in new situations only 2. MODERATELY IMPAIRED-decisions poor;cues/supervision required 3. SEVERELY IMPAIRED-never/rarely made decisions		3
5.	INDICATORS OF DELIRIUM-PERIODIC DISORDERED THINKING/ AWARENESS	(Code for behavior in the last 7 days)(Note:Accurate assessment requires conversations with staff and family who have direct knowledge of resident's behavior over this time.) 0. Behavior not present 1. Behavior present, not of recent onset 2. Behavior present,over last 7 days appears different from resident's usual functioning (e.g.,new onset or worsening)		
		a. EASILY DISTRACTED-(e.g.,difficulty paying attention;gets sidetracked)		0
		b. PERIODS OF ALTERED PERCEPTION OR AWARENESS OF SURROUNDINGS-(e.g.,moves lips or talks to someone not present;believes he/she is somewhere else;confuses night and day)		0
		c. EPISODES OF DISORGANIZED SPEECH-(e.g.,speech is incoherent, nonsensical, irrelevant, or rambling from subject to subject; loses train of thought)		0
		d. PERIODS OF RESTLESSNESS-(e.g.,fidgeting or picking at skin, clothing, napkins, etc; frequent position changes; repetitive physical movements or calling out)		0
		e. PERIODS OF LETHARGY-(e.g.,sluggishness;staring into space;difficult to arouse;little body movement)		0
		f. MENTAL FUNCTION VARIES OVER THE COURSE OF THE DAY-(e.g., sometimes better, sometimes worse; behaviors sometimes present, sometimes not)		0
6.	CHANGE IN COGNITIVE STATUS	Resident's cognitive status,or abilities have changed as compared to status of 90 days ago (or since last assessment if less than 90 days) 0.No change 1. Improved 2 Deteriorated		0

SECTION C. COMMUNICATION/HEARING PATTERNS

1.	HEARING	(With hearing appliance, if used) 0. HEARS ADEQUATELY-normal talk, TV, phone 1. MINIMAL DIFFICULTY when not in quiet setting 2. HEARS IN SPECIAL SITUATIONS ONLY-speaker has to adjust tonal quality and speak distinctly 3. HIGHLY IMPAIRED / absence of useful hearing		0
2.	COMMUNICATION DEVICES/ TECHNIQUES	(Check all that apply during last 7 days) Hearing aid. present and used		a.
		Hearing aid. present and not used regularly		b.
		Other receptive comm. techniques used (e.g., lip reading)		c.
		NONE OF ABOVE		d. ✓
3.	MODES OF EXPRESSION	(Check all used by resident to make needs known)		d.
		Speech	a. ✓	Signs/gestures/sounds	
		Writing messages to express or clarify needs	b.	Communication board	e.
		American sign language or Braille	c.	Other	f.
				NONE OF ABOVE	g.
4.	MAKING SELF UNDERSTOOD	(Expressing information content-however able) 0. UNDERSTOOD 1. USUALLY UNDERSTOOD-difficulty finding words or finishing thoughts 2. SOMETIMES UNDERSTOOD-ability is limited to making concrete requests 3. RARELY/NEVER UNDERSTOOD		1
5.	SPEECH CLARITY	(Code for speech in the last 7 days) 0. CLEAR SPEECH - distinct,intelligible words 1. UNCLEAR SPEECH - slurred, mumbled words 2. NO SPEECH - absence of spoken words		0
6.	ABILITY TO UNDERSTAND OTHERS	(Understanding verbal information content-however able) 0. UNDERSTANDS 1. USUALLY UNDERSTANDS - may miss some part/intent of message 2. SOMETIMES UNDERSTANDS - responds adequately to simple,direct communication 3. RARELY/NEVER UNDERSTANDS		1
7.	CHANGE IN COMMUNICATION/ HEARING	Resident's ability to express, understand, or hear information has changed as compared to status of 90 days ago (or since last assessment if less than 90 days) 0. No change 1. Improved 2. Deteriorated		0

FORM 2-7 (continued)

Resident

SECTION D. VISION PATTERNS

1.	VISION	(Ability to see in adequate light and with glasses if used) 0. ADEQUATE - sees fine detail,including regular print in newspapers/books 1. IMPAIRED - sees large print, but not regular print in newspaers/books 2. MODERATELY IMPAIRED - limited vision; not able to see newspaper headlines,but can identify objects. 3. HIGHLY IMPAIRED - object identification in question, but eyes appear to follow objects 4. SEVERELY IMPAIRED - no vision or sees only light, colors,or shapes;eyes do not appear to follow objects	0
2.	VISUAL LIMITAT-IONS/DIFFICULT-IES	Side vision problems - decreased peripheral vision (e.g. leaves food on one side of tray, difficulty traveling,bumps into people and objects,misjudges placement of chair when seating self)	a.
		Experiences any of following: sees halos or rings around lights; sees flashes of light; sees curtains over eyes	b.
		NONE OF ABOVE	c. ✓
3.	VISUAL APPLIANCES	Glasses; contact lenses; magnifying glass 0. No 1. Yes	0

SECTION E. MOOD AND BEHAVIOR PATTERNS

1.	INDICATORS OF DEPRESSION ANXIETY SAD MOOD	(Code for indicators observed in last 30 days, irrespective of the assumed cause) 0. Indicator not exhibited in last 30 days 1. Indicator of this type exhibited up to five days a week 2. Indicator of this type exhibited daily or almost daily (6,7 days a week)	

VERBAL EXPRESSIONS OF DISTRESS

a.	Resident made negat-ive statements-e.g. "Nothing matters; would rather be dead; What's the use; Reg-rets having lived so long; Let me die"	0	h. Repetitive health complaints, e.g. persistently seeks medical attention, obsessive concern with body functions	0
b.	Repetitive questions? e.g. "Where do I go? What do I do?"	0	i. Repetitive anxious complaints/concerns (nonhealth related) e.g. persistently seeks attention/re-assurance regarding schedules, meals, laundry, clothing, relationship issues	0
c.	Repetitive verbaliza-tions - e.g. calling out for help ("God help me")	0	
d.	Persistent anger with self or others - e.g. easily annoyed, anger at placement in nurs-ing home; anger at care received	0	SLEEP CYCLE ISSUES j. Unpleasant mood in morning	0
			k. Insomnia/change in usual sleep pattern	0
e.	Self depreciation - e.g. "I am nothing; I am of no use to anyone"	0	SAD, APATHETIC, ANXIOUS APPEARANCE l. Sad, pained,worried facial expressions- e.g., furrowed brows	0
f.	Expressions of what appear to be unreal-istic fears - e.g. fear of being aband-oned, left alone, being with others	0	m. Crying, tearfulness	0
			n. Repetitive physical movements-e.g.,pac-ing, hand wringing, restlessness, fidge-ting, picking	0
g.	Recurrent statements that something terr-ible is about to hap-pen - e.g. believes he or she is about to die, have a heart attack	0	LOSS OF INTEREST o. Withdrawal from act-ivities of intere-st e.g.,no interest in long standing activities or being with family/friends	0
			p. Reduced social int-eraction	0

2.	MOOD PERSIS-TENCE	One or more indicators of depressed, sad or anxious mood were not easily altered by attempts to "cheer up",console, or reassure the resident over last 7 days 0. No Mood 1. Indicators present. 2. Indicators indicators easily altered present, not easily altered	0
3.	CHANGE IN MOOD	Resident's mood status has changed as compared to status of 90 days ago (or since last assessment if less than) 0. No Changes 1. Improved 2. Deteriorated	0
4.	BEHAVIORAL SYMPTOMS	(A) Behavioral symptom frequency in last 7 days 0. Behavior not exhibited in last 7 days 1. Behavior of this type occurred 1-3 days in last 7 days 2. Behavior of this type occurred 4-6 days but less than daily 3. Behavior of this type occurred daily (B) Behavioral symptom alterability in last 7 days 0. Behavior not present OR behavior was easily altered 1. Behavior was not easily altered	(A)(B)

		(A)	(B)
a.	WANDERING (moved with no rational purpose, seemingly oblivious to needs or safety)	0	0
b.	VERBALLY ABUSIVE BEHAVIORAL SYMPTOMS (others were threatened, screamed at, cursed at)	0	0
c.	PHYSICALLY ABUSIVE BEHAVIORAL SYMPTOMS(others were hit, shoved, scratched, sexually abused)	0	0
d.	SOCIALLY INAPPROPRIATE/DISRUPTIVE BEHAVIORAL SYMPTOMS(made disruptive sounds, noisiness, screaming, self-abusive acts, sexual behavior or disrobing in public,smeared/threw food/feces, hoarding, rummaged through others' belongings)	0	0
e.	RESISTS CARE(resisted taking medications/inject-ions, ADL assistance, or eating)	0	0

SECTION F. PSYCHOSOCIAL WELL-BEING

5.	CHANGE IN BEHAVIORAL SYMPTOMS	Resident's behavior status has changed as compared to status 90 days ago (or since last assessment if less than 90 days) 0. No change 1. Improved 2. Deteriorated	1

1.	SENSE OF INITIATIVE /INVOLVE-MENT	At ease interacting with others	a. ✓
		At ease doing planned or structured activities	b.
		At ease doing self-initiated activities	c.
		Establishes own goals	d.
		Pursues involvement in life of facility (e.g. makes/keeps friends; involved in group activities; responds positively to new activities, assists at religious services)	e. ✓
		Accepts invitations into most group activities	f.
		NONE OF ABOVE	g.
2.	UNSETTLED RELATION-SHIPS	Covert/open conflict with or repeated criticism of staff	a.
		Unhappy with roommate	b.
		Unhappy with residents other than roommate	c.
		Openly expresses conflict/anger with family/friends	d.
		Absence of personal contact with family/friends	e.
		Recent loss of close family member/friend	f.
		Does not adjust easily to change in routines	g.
		NONE OF ABOVE	h. ✓
3.	PAST ROLES	Strong identification with past roles and life status	a.
		Expresses sadness/anger/empty feeling over lost roles/status	b.
		Resident perceives that daily routine (customary routine, activities) is very different from prior pattern in the community	c.
		NONE OF ABOVE	d. ✓

SECTION G. PHYSICAL FUNCTIONING AND STRUCTURAL PROBLEMS

1.	(A)ADL SELF-PERFORMANCE-(Code for resident's PERFORMANCE OVER ALL SHIFTS during last 7 days-Not including setup) 0. INDEPENDENT-No help or oversight-OR-help/oversight provided only 1 or 2 times during last 7 days 1. SUPERVISION-Oversight, encouragement or cueing provided 3 or more times during last 7 days-OR-Supervision (3 or more times) plus physical assistance provided only 1 or 2 times during last 7 days 2. LIMITED ASSISTANCE-Resident highly involved in activity; received physical help in guided maneuvering of limbs or other nonweight bearing assistance 3 or more times-OR-More help provided only 1 or 2 times during last 7 days 3. EXTENSIVE ASSISTANCE-While resident performed part of activity, over last 7-day period, help of following type(s) provided 3 or more times: -Weight-bearing support -Full staff performance during part (but not all) of 7 days 4. TOTAL DEPENDENCE-Full staff performance of activity during entire 7 days 8. ACTIVITY DID NOT OCCUR during entire 7 days		
	(B) ADL SUPPORT PROVIDED-(Code for MOST SUPPORT PROVIDED OVER ALL SHIFTS during last 7 days; code regardless of resident's self-performance classification) 0. No setup or physical help from staff 1. Setup help only 2. One person physical assistance 3. Two persons physical assist 8. ADL activity itself did not occur during entire 7 days	(A)(B)	

			(A)	(B)
a.	BED MOBILITY	How resident moves to and from lying position, turns side to side, and positions body while in bed	3	2
b.	TRANSFER	How resident moves between surfaces-to/from:bed, chair, wheelchair, standing position (EXCLUDE to/from bath/toilet)	3	2
c.	WALK IN ROOM	How resident walks between locations in his/her room	8	8
d.	WALK IN CORRIDOR	How resident walks in corridor on unit	8	8
e.	LOCOMO-TION ON UNIT	How resident moves between locations in his/her room and adjacent corridor on same floor. If in wheelchair, self sufficiency once in chair	8	8
f.	LOCOMO-TION OFF UNIT	How resident moves to and returns from off unit locations (e.g.,areas set aside for dining, activi-ties, or treatments). If facility has only one floor, how resident moves to and from distant areas on the floor. If in wheelchair, self sufficiency once in chair	8	8
g.	DRESSING	How resident puts on, fastens, and takes off all items of street clothing,including donning/removing prosthesis	3	2
h.	EATING	How resident eats and drinks (regardless of skill). Includes intake of nourishment by other means (e.g. tube feeding, total parenteral nutrition)	3	2
i.	TOILET USE	How resident uses the toilet room (or commode, bed-pan, urinal):transfer on/off toilet, cleanses, changes pad, manages ostomy or catheter, adjusts clothes	3	2
j.	PERSONAL HYGIENE	How resident maintains personal hygiene, including combing hair, brushing teeth, shaving, applying makeup, washing/drying face, hands and perineum (EXCLUDE baths and showers)	3	2

FORM 2–8
RESIDENT ASSESSMENT PROTOCOL

INTERDISCIPLINARY TEAM NOTE 09-24 1996 Numeric Identifier: 000000 Resident's Name: Medical Record Number:		PAGE 1

RAP GUIDELINES REVIEW
Including:
- Nature of Condition
- Complications/Risk Factors
- Need for Individualization in Care Plan
- Need for Further Assessment, Referral, Evaluation
Significant Reasons to Proceed/Not Proceed to Care Plan
(Based on review of individualized RAPS) are as follows:

RAP PROBLEM AREA	REASONS BASED ON INDIVIDUALIZED REVIEW OF RAP
COGNITIVE LOSS/ DEMENTIA	REASON TO PROCEED TO CARE PLAN: SHORT TERM MEMORY LOSS. LONG TERM MEMORY LOSS. SEVERELY IMPAIRED SKILLS FOR DAILY DECISION MAKING. USUALLY UNDERSTANDS OTHERS. NEUROLOGIC: DEMENTIA.
COMMUNICATION	REASON TO PROCEED TO CARE PLAN: USUALLY MAKES SELF UNDERSTOOD. USUALLY UNDERSTANDS OTHERS. CHRONIC CONDITION: DEMENTIA. SHORT-TERM MEMORY PROBLEM. LONG-TERM MEMORY PROBLEM. MEMORY RECALL PROBLEM.
ADL FUNCTIONING/ REHAB POTENTIAL	REASON TO PROCEED TO CARE PLAN: NEEDS PHYSICAL HELP TO BALANCE WHEN STANDING. NEEDS PHYSICAL HELP TO BALANCE WHEN SITTING. RESID. BELIEVES THEY COULD BE MORE INDEP. IN SOME ADLS. STAFF BELIEVES THAT RESID. COULD BE MORE INDEP. IN ADLS. REHAB: NOT INDEP. IN TRANSFER. REHAB: NOT INDEP. IN WALKING IN ROOM. REHAB: NOT INDEP. IN WALKING IN CORRIDOR. REHAB: NOT INDEP. IN LOCOMOTION ON THE UNIT. REHAB: NOT INDEP. IN LOCOMOTION OFF THE UNIT. REHAB: NOT INDEP. IN DRESSING. REHAB: NOT INDEP. IN EATING. REHAB: NOT INDEP. IN TOILET USE. REHAB: NOT INDEP. IN PERSONAL HYGIENE. REHAB: NOT INDEP. IN BATHING. REHAB: RESID. BELIEVES CAPABLE OF INCREASED INDEP. IN SOME ADLS. REHAB: STAFF BELIEVES RESID. CAPABLE OF INCREASED INDEP. IN SOME ADLS.
URINARY INCONT & INDWELLING CATHETER	REASON TO PROCEED TO CARE PLAN: OCCASIONALLY INCONTINENT OF BLADDER. USES PADS/BRIEFS. DEFICT IN ABILITY TO WALK IN ROOM. DEFICIT IN ABILITY TO WALK IN CORRIDOR. DEFICIT IN LOCOMOTION ON THE UNIT. DEFICIT IN LOCOMOTION OFF THE UNIT. DEPENDENT IN TRANSFER &.
BEHAVIOR PROBLEM	REASON NOT TO PROCEED TO CARE PLAN: BEHAVIOR HAS IMPROVED.
ACTIVITIES	REASON TO PROCEED TO CARE PLAN: DEFICIT IN WALKING IN CORRIDOR. DEFICIT IN LOCOMOTION ON UNIT. DEFICIT IN WALKING IN ROOM. DEFICIT IN LOCOMOTION OFF UNIT. REVISE PLAN: LESS THAN 1/3 TIME INVOLVED IN ACTIVITIES. REVISE PLAN: DESIRES SLIGHT CHANGE IN TYPE OF ACTIVITIES. REVISE PLAN: DESIRES SLIGHT CHANGE IN EXTENT OF INVOLVEMENT.

FORM 2–8 *(continued)*

INTERDISCIPLINARY TEAM NOTE 09-2-. .996 Numeric Identifier: 000000 Resident's Name: Medical Record Number: <div align="right">PAGE 2</div>	
RAP PROBLEM AREA	REASONS BASED ON INDIVIDUALIZED REVIEW OF RAP
FALLS	REASON TO PROCEED TO CARE PLAN: POTENTIAL FOR ADDITIONAL FALLS: FELL IN PAST 30 DAYS. ADL FUNCTION HAS DECLINED. ARTHRITIS. DEMETIA.
NUTRITIONAL STATUS	REASON TO PROCEED TO CARE PLAN: LEAVES 25% OR MORE FOOD UNEATEN MOST MEALS.AT RISK FOR DEHYDRATION/AT RISK FOR SIGNIFICANT WEIGHT LOSS. MECHANICALLY ALTERED DIET.CHEWING PROBLEM. STAGE 2 PRESSURE ULCER.NUTRITION HELPS IN THE HEALING PROCESS. REDUCED ABILITY TO FEED SELF. DEMENTIA.DX. OF UROSEPSIS,HX. OF DEHYDRATION. DIFFICULTY MAKING SELF UNDERSTOOD. DIFFICULTY UNDERSTANDING OTHERS.(WILL COMBINE WITH DEHYDRATION SUMMARY).
DEHYDRATION/ FLUID MAINTENANCE	REASON TO PROCEED TO CARE PLAN: UTI.DEHYDRATION DIAGNOSIS.RESIDENT LEAVES 25% AND MORE OF FOODS UNEATEN AT MOST MEALS.AT RISK FOR DEHYDRATION AND SIGNIFICANT WEIGHT LOSS.(WILL COMBINE WITH NUTRITIONAL SUMMARY AND CP). MODERATELY/SEVERELY IMPAIRED DECISION MAKING. DEFICIT IN ABILITY TO MAKE SELF UNDERSTOOD. DEFICIT IN ABILITY TO UNDERSTAND. NEEDS PHYSICAL HELP TO BALANCE WHILE STANDING. NEEDS PHYSICAL HELP TO BALANCE WHILE SITTING.
PRESSURE ULCERS	REASON TO PROCEED TO CARE PLAN: AT RISK DUE TO PROBLEM WITH BED MOBILITY.AT RISK FOR FURTHER SKIN BREAKDOWN,RESIDENT HAS IMPAIRED MOBILITY,POOR TO FAIR INTAKE. AT RISK DUE TO BOWEL INCONTINENCE. STAGE TWO PRESSURE ULCER PRESENT. DEMENTIA.DX. OF DEGENERATIVE JOINT DISEASE,ANEMIA. PRESSURE RELIEVING CHAIR. PRESSURE RELIEVING BED. NEEDS TURNING/REPOSITIONING. NUTRITION/HYDRATION PROGRAM. ULCER CARE REQUIRED. DRESSING APPLIED. PREVENTATIVE/PROTECTIVE SKIN CARE.

FORM 2–9
SAMPLE CARE PLAN

```
                              CARE PLAN                           PAGE 1
                        COMMUNICATION IMPAIRED

                    ID#:2719          DATE INITIATED: 11/11/96
```

PROBLEMS/STRENGTHS/NEEDS:

- ALTERATION IN ABILITY TO COMMUNICATE.

- RELATED TO IMPAIRED UNDERSTANDING.

- CONTRIBUTING MEDICAL DIAGNOSIS: DEMENTIA.

- DEFINING CHARACTERISTIC: SHORT-TERM MEMORY PROBLEM; LONG-TERM MEMORY PROBLEM.

- SIGNS OF DISORDERED THINKING: MEMORY RECALL PROBLEM PRESENT.

- MODES OF COMMUNICATION: USES SPEECH TO COMMUNICATE.

- LANGUAGE:. *English*

- DIFFICULTY COMMUNICATING: USUALLY MAKES SELF UNDERSTOOD; USUALLY UNDERSTANDS OTHERS.

- COGNITIVE SKILLS: SEVERELY IMPAIRED, NEVER/RARELY MADE DECISIONS.

GOAL(S):

- ABLE TO COMMUNICATE NEEDS VERBALLY USING SHORT   By: 02/97
  SENTENCES, VERBALLY BY ANSWERING "YES" & "NO"
  QUESTIONS APPROPRIATELY.

- DEMONSTRATES UNDERSTANDING OF VERBAL   By: 02/97
  COMMUNICATION BY RESPONDING APPROPRIATELY.

APPROACHES: Discipline

- OBSERVE FOR DIFFICULTY IN COMMUNICATING. WATCH   N SS A
  FOR GESTURES, WATCH FOR POINTING, WATCH FACIAL
  EXPRESSION.

- ANTICIPATE NEEDS FOR RESIDENT: KEEP SIGNAL CORD   N SS A
  WITHIN REACH AT ALL TIMES, HELP TO FIND THE
  BATHROOM, HELP TO FIND THE DINING ROOM, HELP TO
  FIND OWN ROOM, HELP TO USE TELEPHONE, GUIDE TO
  ACTIVITIES.

FORM 2–9 *(continued)*

```
                        CARE PLAN                              PAGE 2
                  COMMUNICATION IMPAIRED

                      ID#:2719        DATE INITIATED: 11/11/96
```

APPROACHES:	Discipline
· OBSERVE FOR SIGNS OF DISCOMFORT. WATCH FOR FACIAL GRIMACE, WATCH FOR MOANING, WATCH FOR INCREASED AGITATION.	N SS A
· USE GOOD EYE CONTACT WHEN TALKING TO RESIDENT. ALLOW TIME TO RESPOND.	N SS A D
· USE SHORT SIMPLE PHRASES WHEN SPEAKING TO RESIDENT.	N SS A D
· ENCOURAGE TO RESPOND BY NODDING HEAD, TURN TOWARD THE SPEAKER WHEN BEING ADDRESSED.	N SS A
· USE TOUCH THERAPEUTICALLY: HOLD HAND, TOUCH FACE IF WILLING.	N SS A
· PROVIDE SENSORY STIMULATION PER TV, RADIO, 1:1 VISITS.	N SS A
· ALWAYS ANTICIPATE RESIDENT'S NEEDS AT ALL TIMES.	N

EVALUATION:

FORM 2–10
SAMPLE FLOW SHEET: ACTIVITIES OF DAILY LIVING

NIGHT SHIFT — DATE

Positioned q 2 hours as needed (P)	
Fluids offered	
Slept well (S); Restless (R)	
Bladder: Incont. (I); Cont. (C); Foley (F)	
Bowel: Incont. (I); Cont. (C) | # of BMS	
Alert (A); Oriented (O); Confused (C)	
Soft restraints | Postural supports checked q 2 hours	
AM Care: Teeth brushed, dentures in	
Side rails: Up (↑); Down (↓)	
NURSE ASSISTANT'S INITIALS	

DAY SHIFT — DATE

Breakfast — Diet: — % Eaten:	
Eats Indep. (I); Assist (A); Fed	
Pers. Hygiene: Indep. (I); Assist (A); Total (T)	
Dressing: Indep. (I); Assist (A); Total (T)	
Bowel: Incont. (I); Cont. (C) | # of BMS	
Bladder: Incont. (I); Cont. (C); Foley (F)	
Bath: Shower (S); Tub (T); Bed (B)	
Ambulate (I); Assisted (A); Walker (W)	
Wheelchair (W); Chair (C); Bed (B)	
Positioned q 2 hours as needed (P)	
Nourishments given	
Lunch — Diet: — % Eaten:	
Eats Indep. (I); Assist (A); Fed	
Soft restraints | Postural supports checked q 2 hours	
Side rails: Up (↑); Down (↓)	
Participated in activities	
Alert (A); Oriented (O); Confused (C)	
R.O.M. given	
Fluids offered q 2 hours	
NURSE ASSISTANT'S INITIALS	

P.M. SHIFT — DATE

Dinner — Diet: — % Eaten:	
Eats Indep. (I); Assist (A); Fed	
Bowel: Incont. (I); Cont. (C) | # of BMS	
Bladder: Incont. (I); Cont. (C); Foley (F)	
Ambulate (I); Assisted (A); Walker (W)	
Up in Wheelchair (W); Chair (C); Bed Pt. (B)	
Positioned q 2 hours as needed (P)	
Alert (A); Oriented (O); Confused (C)	
R.O.M. given	
Fluids offered q 2 hours	
Soft restraints | Postural supports checked q 2 hours	
HS nourishment offered	
PM Care; Oral Hygiene	
Side rails: Up (↑); Down (↓)	
Participated in activities	
Shower	
NURSE ASSISTANT'S INITIALS	

INITIAL	SIGNATURE	INITIAL	SIGNATURE	INITIAL	SIGNATURE	INITIAL	SIGNATURE
	SD			AJ			
				SS			

LAST NAME	FIRST NAME	ROOM NO.	PATIENT NO.	AGE	MONTH
		124C			Sept. '96

CEN - 18 (4/86)   NURSE ASSISTANT RECORD   000260

CHAPTER 3

BODY STRUCTURE AND FUNCTION

§ 3.1   Introduction

The human body is incredibly complex, yet simple in design and form. It has been studied for centuries in an effort to determine how it functions in both health and disease. Because litigation often involves physical and/ or emotional injury, legal professionals must have a basic understanding of body structures and functions to evaluate client complaints accurately and to summarize medical records concisely. To accomplish this, a basic knowledge of body structure *(anatomy),* the shape and composition of body parts, and body function *(physiology),* the biological processes that enable organs to carry out vital functions that sustain life, is essential. This chapter provides a brief overview of the major body systems and how they function. The material in this chapter is high-level, intending to provide a basic overview of these topics. In general, the information pertains to adults, although some pregnancy and newborn-related information is included. More in-depth information can be obtained from multiple sources, among them the books and websites listed in the **Bibliography.** For information on specific areas, e.g. maternal-child, pediatrics, texts specific to these populations will be needed.

§ 3.2   Body Structure and Function

Body composition begins with simple structures that build into complex systems. All body systems are designed to perform their own functions as well as to work in harmony with other systems to achieve function for the entire body. *Homeostasis* is the term that describes healthy human body function. It is defined as the state of equilibrium or status quo. When homeostasis is upset and the body is unable to correct it, disease results. Body structures involved in this process are hierarchical, building from simple to complex.

Cells

Cells are the basic unit of living material in the body. Their structures are highly specialized, designed to carry out the specific functions they perform. However, despite their specialization, all cells have the same basic components in their structure:

- Membrane—outer covering of the cell that gives it shape and forms the cell wall. The membrane allows nutrients and wastes to pass in and out of the cell.
- Cytoplasm—main substance within the cell wall.
- Nucleus—the control center of the cell; contains DNA, the genetic material that directs cellular reproduction function.
- Protoplasm—the cytoplasm and the nucleus of the cell.

Cells have a finite life. Cell regeneration occurs on a periodic basis, with the length of time to completion depending on the type of cell. New cells are formed through a process known as *mitosis.* During this process, the parent cell divides into two daughter cells. Although some characteristics of the two new cells may differ (e.g., weight), they carry the same genetic instructions that govern their activities and reproduction. These instructions are known as the *genetic code* of the cell. The genetic code of the cell, carried in DNA (deoxyribonucleic acid), is contained in structures called *chromosomes.*

Humans have 46 chromosomes, grouped into 23 pairs. One half of each pair originates from the father, the other from the mother. These chromosomes have approximately 80,000 genes (hereditary units). Genes carry both species and individual-specific information that is transmitted from generation to generation.

The DNA structure itself is a coiled structure of double-stranded DNA molecules (double-helix structure). The strands are linked by hydrogen bonds that are relatively weak. During cell division, a process of immense complexity, the DNA separates at the weak point in the hydrogen bond. Sometimes mistakes are made in copying genetic information before cell division and genes can be lost or can mutate. Mutations may be favorable, unfavorable, or neutral. Unfavorable mutations can result in cell abnormalities that lead to structural and functional problems for the cell that cause heredity diseases such as sickle-cell anemia, hemophilia, cystic fibrosis, and several neurologic diseases.

Tissues

Tissues are groups of cells that work together to perform similar functions. Each type of tissue has a specific composition that enables it to perform designated functions. For example, adipose tissue (fatty tissue) stores nutrients and insulates the body. Connective tissue binds and supports various body structures.

Organs

Organs are groups of tissues working together as a structural unit to perform specialized functions. For example, the stomach is an organ that stores and partially digests food; the heart is an organ that pumps blood.

Body Systems

Body systems are groups of organs working together to perform specific physiologic functions. For example, the circulatory system pumps and circulates blood to all body cells, carrying nutrients and removing waste products. The skeletal system provides rigid support for body structures and offers protection to internal organs. Body systems are discussed in §§ **3.3** through **3.39.** All systems functioning together to achieve a state of homeostasis comprise the human body.

§ 3.3   Cardiovascular System Structure and Function

The cardiovascular system circulates blood to all cells of the body through an intricate network of blood vessels. The blood carries essential nutrients to the cells as it flows away from the heart and carries cellular waste products from the cells as it flows toward the heart.

Structure

The cardiovascular system is made up of the following major organs:

1. Heart—a hollow, muscular organ located to the left of the midline in the thoracic cavity. The heart's primary purpose is to act as a pump, delivering blood into the blood vessels for transportation of nutrients to, and removal of wastes from, all body cells. It accomplishes this through the pumping action of the *myocardium* (heart muscle), along with electrical impulses that are conducted through it. The result is an automatic, rhythmic contraction and relaxation cycle that delivers blood into the peripheral circulation. Contraction and relaxation regulate both heart rate and rhythm.

   The heart is composed of three layers of tissue: the epicardium (surface), the myocardium (middle), and the endocardium (lines the heart chambers). The heart is divided into right and left sides that are divided vertically by the *septum,* each side having two chambers. The upper chamber is called the *atrium,* or collecting chamber; the lower chamber is the *ventricle,* or the pumping chamber.

2. Pericardium—the outside covering of the heart that protects it from injury and infection. The pericardium has two layers:

   • Parietal pericardium—a tough, fibrous outer membrane that provides a protective barrier against infection.

   • Visceral pericardium—a thin, inner layer that closely adheres to the heart itself.

   The space between these two layers is known as the pericardial space. It holds a small amount of fluid that lubricates the two surfaces as they slide over each other when the heart beats. The fluid also protects the heart against external trauma.

3. Myocardium—The myocardium is composed of muscle tissue and is the actual contracting muscle of the heart.

4.   Valves—structures between the atria and ventricles that permit blood to flow through the heart in only one direction: the *tricuspid valve* is located between the right atrium and ventricle; the *bicuspid or mitral valve* is located between the left atrium and ventricle.

5.   Blood Vessels—hollow, tubular structures that carry blood to all parts of the body. The main vessels are attached directly to the heart. These large vessels divide into progressively smaller branches, forming a network that ultimately reaches every cell.

- Arteries—carry blood with oxygen and other nutrients to all cells. The main artery, which connects directly to the heart, is the aorta. The coronary arteries supply the heart muscle itself with blood.

- Capillaries—smallest of the blood vessels, they link arteries to veins. In the capillaries, blood nutrients (for the cell) are exchanged for cellular wastes.

- Veins—carry blood containing carbon dioxide and other cell wastes back to the heart. The main vein leading to the heart is the vena cava. The vena cava has two branches, the inferior and superior venae cavae.

There are two exceptions to this system of circulation: the pulmonary artery, which carries blood with wastes to the lungs for the elimination of carbon dioxide; and the pulmonary vein, which carries blood with oxygen to the heart for distribution throughout the body. See **Figure 3–1.**

Function
Blood Circulation

The right atrium of the heart receives deoxygenated blood from the body via the superior and inferior venae cavae. This blood then flows to the right ventricle, which pumps the blood to the lungs via the pulmonary artery. In the lungs, the blood waste product of carbon dioxide is exchanged for oxygen. Oxygenated blood is then pumped into the left atrium via the four pulmonary veins. Blood flows from the left atrium into the left ventricle, where it is pumped into systemic circulation via the aorta. As blood is pumped into circulation, it exerts a pressure on the arteries receiving this blood. The force of this is measured as blood pressure. See § **4.10** in **Chapter 4** for discussion of blood pressure in physical examinations.

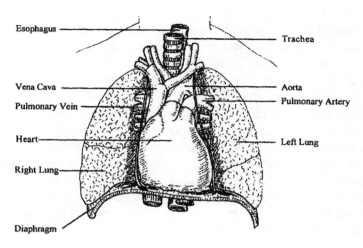

Esophagus

Trachea

Vena Cava

Aorta

Pulmonary Vein

Pulmonary Artery

Heart

Left Lung

Right Lung

Diaphragm

Figure 3–1. Cardiovascular/respiratory systems.

Source: Elson & Kapit, The Anatomy Coloring Book (1977). Reprinted with permission.

Of special note is the blood supply of the heart itself. The heart muscle (myocardium) requires a rich oxygen supply to meet its high metabolic needs. These needs are supplied by the blood delivered through the coronary arteries, which branch off the aorta, encircle the heart, and supply it with blood. The coronary artery has two main branches, the right coronary artery (RCA) and the left coronary artery (LCA). The left coronary artery has two major branches, the left anterior descending (LAD) and the circumflex. The coronary veins return blood from the myocardium to the right atrium.

Heart Electrophysiology

The contraction of the heart that enables circulation of the blood throughout the body is accomplished through electrophysiologic (ability to conduct electrical impulses) properties of the heart muscle itself. These properties regulate the rate (how slow or fast it beats) and the rhythm (intervals between beats) of the heart. Special cells within the cardiac muscle have the ability to conduct electrical impulses very rapidly. These cells initiate impulse conduction and spread their changes in cell membrane excitability, the *action potential,* from one area throughout the whole heart. This spreading stimulates the synchronized contraction of the atria and ventricles, followed by a period of relaxation. This process is referred to as the *cardiac cycle.*

The ability of the heart to circulate blood throughout the body effectively depends on an intact (electrical) conduction system and functional heart muscle (myocardium) that is able to contract in response to stimuli. These stimuli come in waves that occur at regular intervals. The length of time between waves reflects the time for an impulse to travel from one area of the heart to another. Any deviation from the expected times often indicates heart disease. The electrocardiogram measures the heart's conduction efficacy. Heart disease pathology can affect structure and/or function of the heart; these diseases remain a major cause of morbidity and mortality in the United States.

§ 3.4 —Common Problems of the Cardiovascular System

1. Angina Pectoris—chest pain caused by an insufficient oxygen supply to the heart muscle. Narrowed, hardened blood vessel walls that cannot supply adequate blood flow to the heart muscle are the most common cause of angina. Angina is often classified into two categories, stable and unstable angina. Stable angina pain occurs intermittently with the same pattern. Pain is brief in duration (< 5 minutes), rarely occurs at rest, and subsides when precipitating factors (usually exertion) are removed. Unstable angina pain occurs unpredictably, including when at rest.

2. Cardiac Tamponade—result of fluid accumulation in the pericardial cavity, i.e. pus or blood that restricts ventricular filling. This life-threatening condition requires immediate intervention.

3. Cardiogenic Shock—inability of the heart (as a pump) to maintain adequate blood volume to the circulatory system. As a result, tissues cannot receive necessary levels of nutrients and oxygen. This condition requires aggressive medical management and has a high mortality rate.

4. Cardiomyopathy—degenerative disorder of the heart muscle that affects the heart's ability to pump blood effectively. It is diagnosed

based on patient symptoms and by specific diagnostic testing. Cardiomyopathy is categorized into three major classes:

- Dilated cardiomyopathy—most common type, often follows myocarditis

- Hypertrophic cardiomyopathy—most common cause of sudden death in healthy young people, including athletes. May have some genetic basis; some causes are unknown.

- Restrictive cardiomyopathy—least common type, characterized by impaired ventricular filling and ability to stretch. May occur as a result of other diseases.

5. Congestive Heart Failure (CHF)—a condition resulting from impaired cardiac pumping. Heart failure occurs with Coronary Artery Disease (CAD) and longstanding hypertension. There are two main types of heart failure, left sided and right sided.

- *Left sided heart failure* is the most common type of initial heart failure episodes. It is caused by left ventricular impairment that results in back up of blood into the pulmonary veins. This results in symptoms of pulmonary congestion and pulmonary edema.

- *Right sided heart failure* is characterized by backward flow of blood into the right atrium and venous circulation. This results in symptoms of lower extremity edema, enlargement of the spleen and liver and general complaints of fatigue, nausea and diminished appetite

6. Coronary Artery Disease (CAD)—the collective term for disorders causing insufficient blood supply to the myocardium, specifically, angina pectoris, congestive heart failure, and myocardial infarction (see problem-specific information above and below). Coronary artery disease has been widely studied and risk factors for development of associated diseases are well defined. Risk factors can be categorized into those that can be modified, and those that cannot.

- Risk factors that can be modified include blood lipid levels (cholesterol), hypertension, smoking, obesity, physical inactivity, stress in daily living, and control of diabetes (if present).

- Risk factors that cannot be modified include age and gender, ethnicity, genetic disposition, and family history of cardiac disease.

7. Myocardial Infarction (M.I.) or Heart Attack—blockage of one or more of the blood vessels that supply oxygen to the heart muscle. Without oxygen and nutrients that blood supplies, the affected heart

muscle will die. Inadequate cardiac circulation may be treated surgically by open heart surgery (coronary artery bypass graft) or by percutaneous luminar coronary angioplasty (PCTA). Angioplasty utilizes a catheter with an inflatable balloon to dilate narrowed vessels.

8. Myocarditis—inflammation of the myocardial wall. Myocarditis can be caused by infectious agents such as viruses or bacteria, toxic agents such as lead, or drugs such as cocaine.

9. Pericarditis—inflammation of the pericardium. Pericarditis may occur as a primary condition, as a secondary complication of other diseases, or be idiopathic (unknown).

10. Pericarditis with Effusion—results when fluid accumulates in the pericardial sac. If excessive amounts of fluid accumulate, restriction of cardiac contractions can occur, leading to cardiac tamponade.

11. Pulmonary Edema—results from the inability of the left ventricle to pump blood adequately. As a result, fluid from the circulating blood is pushed into the lungs, filling the lungs with fluid. Pulmonary edema is an acute, life-threatening condition that requires immediate intervention.

12. Pulmonary Embolism (P.E.)—one or more blood clots in the arteries supplying the lungs with blood. A common cause of pulmonary embolism is prolonged immobility, e.g. following surgery or injury. P.E. is also seen following myocardial infarction with heart failure and arrythmias.

13. Pulmonary Hypertension—prolonged elevation of the pulmonary artery pressure resulting from increased pulmonary vascular resistance to blood flow. Some causes are unexplained; others are associated with underlying heart or lung disease. Prognosis for severe disease is poor.

14. Rheumatic Heart Disease (RHD)—sequellae of rheumatic fever, a streptococcal bacterial infection that can produce valvular disorders, cardiomegaly (enlarged heart), and congestive heart failure. The disease can result in scarring and deformity of heart valves that impair the flow of blood from atria to ventricles.

15. Heart Arrythmias—abnormal electrical conduction patterns in the heart muscle. There are many different types of rhythm disturbances, ranging from inconsequential to life-threatening. The specific type of arrhythmia(s) are diagnosed through EKG tracings. See § **4.9** in **Chapter 4,** for additional information on EKG testing. Examples of rhythm disturbances are

   • Sinus tachycardia—rapid, regular rhythm with a rate of 100 to 180 beats per minute

- Sinus bradycardia—slow, regular rhythm with a rate below 60 beats per minute
- Atrial flutter
- Atrial fibrillation
- Premature ventricular contractions (PVCs)
- Ventricular fibrillation
- Bundle branch block
- Paroxysmal atrial tachycardia (PAT)
- Premature atrial contractions (PAC)

16. Subacute Bacterial Endocarditis—inflammation of the endocardium of the heart that especially affects heart valves.

17. Valvular Heart Disease—any dysfunction of heart valves that prevents them from fully opening or closing. If a valve cannot fully open (stenosis), the flow of blood from one chamber to the next may be impeded. A valve that does not close completely (insufficient valve) may allow blood to regurgitate back into the chamber from which it is being pumped.

Peripheral Vascular Problems

1. Aortic Aneurysm—a ballooning or out-pouching of the aorta wall. This ballooning weakens the artery wall and may lead to wall rupture and hemorrhage. Aneurysms may affect any portion of the aorta.

2. Aortic Dissection—tear in the inner-most lining of the vessel wall that allows blood to enter between vessel layers. This condition is usually acute and life-threatening.

3. Arterial Occlusion—conditions that involve narrowing of arterial lumen or damage to the arterial lining. Occlusion is classified as acute or chronic and has various causes. May be the result of a thrombosis (blood clot) that occludes the lumen of the vessel.

4. Arteriosclerosis—narrowing of the diameter of an artery, usually caused by build-up of fatty deposits on the arterial wall. This can result in insufficient oxygenation of the tissues supplied by the affected vessels.

5. Atherosclerosis—a form of ateriosclerosis characterized by fatty deposits on the inner walls of the arteries.

6. Buerger's Disease (thromboangiitis obliterans)—inflammation of small- and medium-sized veins and arteries in the extremities of

young adults. Occurrence is relatively rare. Its cause is unknown, although there may be a familial tendency associated with development.

7. Carotid Artery Disease—atherosclerosis of the carotid arteries, the main arteries that supply oxygen and nutrients to the brain.

8. Cerebrovascular Accident (CVA) or Stroke—disruption of a blood vessel in the brain from clot or hemorrhage. Residual effects of strokes range from mild to severe, depending on the location and size of the vessel involved. Effects on the body vary from mild disturbances in coordination and thought processes to disruption of vital functions, leading to coma and death.

9. Chronic Venous Insufficiency—results from dysfunctional valves that reduce venous return. This leads to increased venous pressure and stasis of venous blood. Venous stasis may ultimately lead to open sores, called *stasis ulcers.* Stasis ulcers are also referred to as *venous stasis ulcers.*

10. Hypertension—a sustained elevation of blood pressure (systolic and/or diastolic) over a period of several weeks. See § **4.10** in **Chapter 4** for additional information on blood pressure. This condition can lead to heart attack or stroke. It is classified according to

    • type (diastolic or systolic)
    • cause (primary or secondary)
    • degree of severity (benign or malignant).

    A common cause of hypertension is arteriosclerosis. This condition can lead to development of CAD, CHF, CVA, and renal disease.

11. Hypotension—abnormally low blood pressure. Hypotension has several causes, the most common of which are hemorrhage, severe dehydration and allergic (anaphylactic) reactions. Hypotension can also be *orthostatic,* occurring when changing from lying/sitting to a standing position.

12. Raynaud's Disease—intermittent constriction of small arteries or arterioles in extremities. Episodes cause temporary pallor and cyanosis of digits and changes in skin temperature. It occurs as a response to a variety of stimuli, such as cold temperatures, or stress. Raynaud's is classified as primary or secondary. Primary disease occurs in the absence of other disease, secondary disease occurs in the presence of other autoimmune diseases such as systemic lupus (SLE), rheumatoid arthritis, or scleroderma.

13. Varicose Veins—result from valvular incompetence in the lower extremeties that causes distention and tortuosity of superficial veins.

14. Venous Thrombosis, Thrombophlebitis, Deep Vein Thrombophleblitis (DVT)—the formation of a blood clot in association with inflammation of a vein. There are two types of thrombosis: superficial and deep (DVT). Deep thromboses usually involve the femoral or iliac veins. These clots can migrate to the lung and cause pulmonary embolism.

§ 3.5   Respiratory System Structure and Function

The respiratory system supplies oxygen to, and removes carbon dioxide from, all cells of the body. This is accomplished through the movement of air in and out of the lungs, processes known as *ventilation or respiration.* Once air is inspired into the lungs, gas exchange takes place.

Structure

The following major organs make up the respiratory system:

1. Nose/Nasal Cavity—moistens, filters, cools, or warms inhaled air prior to entering the lungs. Breathing through the nasal passages provides protection for the lungs. Receptors for the sense of smell are located in the nose.

2. Tonsils and adenoids—structures composed of lymphoid tissue located in the naso-pharynx and oro-pharynx respectively. They are thought to serve a protective function in the development of respiratory infection.

3. Sinuses—four pairs of cavities positioned around the nasal cavity. Their main purposes are to make the skull bones lighter and to function in the production of sound.

4. Pharynx—passageway that connects the nose with the mouth.

5. Larynx (voicebox)—located at the end of the pharynx and at the beginning of the trachea. It contains the vocal cords, which produce sound.

6. Epiglottis—small flap of tissue at located at the base of the tongue. During swallowing, the epiglottis closes over the larynx, preventing food or fluid from entering the trachea and lungs.

7. Trachea (windpipe)—cylindrical passageway for air from the larynx into the lungs. The trachea has fibrous rings in its structure that prevent collapse.

8. Bronchi—tubular passageways for air that extend from the trachea to the lungs in a branching fashion. Bronchi decrease in diameter from large to small as they enter the lung. *Bronchioles* are the smallest branches of the bronchi.

9. Alveoli—sac-like cavities (resembling bubbles) at the end of bronchioles. The exchange of oxygen and carbon dioxide takes place in the alveoli. The alveolar surface is composed of cells that provide structure as well as cells that secrete *surfactant.* Surfactant is a substance that reduces the amount of pressure needed to inflate the alveoli and decreases the tendency of the alveoli to collapse.

10. Lungs—two inflatable sac-like organs that surround the bronchioles and alveoli. The right lung has three lobes and the left lung has two lobes. As air is inspired, the lungs inflate, and oxygen is absorbed. When air is exhaled, carbon dioxide is eliminated.

11. Pleurae—serous membranes that cover each lung and line the chest wall. Each pleura has a visceral layer adhering to the lung and a parietal layer covering the inside of the chest wall. The pleural space is the *potential* space between the two layers.

Function
Mechanics of Respiration

The processes of *inspiration* (air intake) and *expiration* (exhalation of air) accomplish respiration. The lungs are located in the thoracic cavity, the bottom boundary of which is the *diaphragm,* a major muscle of respiration. During inspiration, air is taken in through the nasal passages and the diaphragm contracts. Simultaneously, the muscles between the ribs, the *intercostal muscles,* contract as well, causing the size of the thoracic cavity to increase. As a result, the pressure inside the lungs becomes lower than atmospheric pressure, causing air to rush into the lungs. Once inside the lungs, carbon dioxide is exchanged for oxygen. After this has occurred, the chest muscles relax, the lungs recoil, and air moves out of the lungs. Expiration of air is a passive process. The elasticity of lung tissue provides lungs with a natural tendency to return to normal following expansion.

Respiration is governed by the respiratory center in the brain, located in the brainstem medulla. The medulla responds to chemical and mechanical signals from the body. Impulses are then sent from the medulla to the respiratory muscles and inspiration process is initiated. See § **3.14** for additional information on the medulla.

Process of Gas Exchange

Exchange of carbon dioxide and oxygen occurs between air and blood in the alveolar-capillary systems (external respiration) and at the tissue-cellular level (internal respiration). The body tissues are supplied with oxygen for metabolism and release carbon dioxide as a waste product. This exchange process occurs by the process of diffusion. In diffusion, the differences in pressures within the alveoli and the pulmonary capillary bloodstream allow the oxygen and carbon dioxide to move oxygen from alveoli to blood and carbon dioxide from blood to alveoli. Carbon dioxide is then exhaled as a waste product, and oxygen is transported throughout the body by the circulatory system. The oxygen is dissolved in the blood plasma or bound with hemoglobin, a protein in red blood cells (RBCs).

§ 3.6   —Common Problems of the Respiratory System

1. Acute Laryngeal Edema—may be caused by inflammation, injury, or allergic reactions. It results in rapid progressive difficulty breathing that, if not reversed, leads to cardiac arrest.

2. Adult Respiratory Distress Syndrome (ARDS)—sudden, progressive respiratory failure characterized by lung infiltrates and hypoxemia. ARDS usually follows an event that traumatizes lung tissue.

3. Allergy (Allergic Rhinitis)—reaction of the nasal mucosa to a specific allergen. Attacks can be seasonal with allergies related to pollens and grasses, or environmental related to pet dander, spores and molds.

4. Asthma—a chronic inflammatory disorder of the airways, caused by inflammation that causes constriction of the bronchi that can interfere with lung air exchange. Asthma can be mild, moderate, or severe. Attacks are can be triggered by allergies, infection, exercise, and stress. *Status asthmaticus* is a life-threatening complication of asthma, characterized by prolonged bronchospasm. If left untreated, status asthmaticus can result in respiratory and cardiac arrest.

5. Atelectasis—collapse of a segment of the lung secondary to collapsed, airless alveoli. Atelectasis has several causes, among which are infection, trauma, and prolonged immobility.

6. Bronchiectasis—form of obstructive lung disease. It causes permanent, abnormal dilation of bronchi and bronchioles. It most often occurs after recurrent inflammatory conditions.

7. Bronchitis—inflammation of the bronchi and/or bronchioles. Bronchitis can be acute or chronic and be of viral or bacterial origin.

8. Chronic Obstructive Pulmonary Disease (COPD) or Emphysema—enlargement and loss of elasticity of the alveoli that results in an inability to eliminate carbon dioxide from the body properly. One of the most common causes of COPD is smoking; others include infection, heredity and changes that occur with aging.

9. Cystic Fibrosis—congenital disorder of the mucous-producing glands of the body. It commonly affects the lungs by causing overproduction of thick and viscous pulmonary secretions that are difficult to clear.

10. Environmental Lung Disease—lung diseases caused by inhalation and retention of dust particles in the lung. Asbestosis, silicosis, and berylliosis are examples of these types of diseases.

11. Epistaxis—nosebleed. Nosebleeds can vary in severity and result from several different causes including trauma, foreign bodies, nasal spray abuse, or street drug use.

12. Hemothorax—blood in the thoracic cavity, usually caused by trauma.

13. Laryngeal Cancer—malignancy of the larynx. The most common cause is tobacco smoking. Tumors may be removed surgically by laryngectomy, partial or total. With a total laryngectomy, a permanent opening is made into the trachea for breathing and voice is lost.

14. Laryngitis (hoarseness)—inflammation of the larynx that can be caused by an inflammatory process or vocal cord abuse.

15. Lung Cancer—tumors have two major categories: small-cell lung cancers and non-small-cell lung cancers. Treatment may be by surgical removal, radiation therapy, chemotherapy, or a combination of modalities.

16. Nasal Fracture/Deviated Septum—caused by trauma, the tissue that divides the nares is pushed to one side, creating unequal nasal passages. Depending on severity, the deviation can cause obstruction to nasal breathing.

17. Pharyngitis (sore throat)—inflammation of the throat that may be viral or bacterial in origin. A common cause of bacteria pharyngitis is β (beta) streptococcus, commonly known as "strep throat."

18. Pleural Effusion—accumulation of fluid in the pleural space. This condition can be a result of cardiac, renal, infectious, or lymphatic disease.

19. Pleurisy—inflammation of the pleura. Common causes include pneumonia, trauma, tumors or pulmonary embolism.

20. Pneumonia/Pneumonitis—inflammation of the lungs that can be caused by infectious processes such as bacteria or viruses, or by inhalation of chemicals. Pneumonia, if severe enough, can interfere with the lungs' ability to exchange oxygen and carbon dioxide. Pneumonias are commonly classified as

    • community acquired—onset of the disease occurs in the community or <2 days after hospital admission

    • hospital acquired—occurs after 48 hours of admission to the hospital

    • aspiration—caused by entry of food or fluid into the lungs

    • opportunistic—affects those with altered immune response, such as those with HIV infection or undergoing chemotherapy.

21. Pneumonothorax—air in the pleural space. Complete or partial collapse of the lung follows due to the accumulation of air.

22. Pulmonary Tuberculosis—chronic infectious disease characterized by formation of masses of inflamed tissue (granulomas) within the lung. The causative agent is the bacteria *Mycobacterium tuberculosis.*

23. Sarcoidosis—inflammatory condition characterized by formation of granulomatous lesions in the lungs. It can also affect other body systems. The exact causes are unknown but possibilities include genetic, infectious, immunologic, or toxic factors.

24. Sinusitis—inflammation/infection of sinus cavities that occurs seconday to blocked or narrowed exits. The accumulated secretions provide an excellent environment for bacterial growth, which can lead to sinus infection.

25. Sleep Apnea (Obstructive Sleep Apnea)—condition characterized by partial or complete airway obstruction during sleep. This condition can result in *apnea,* a cessation of spontaneous respiration, or *hypopnea,* abnormally slow and shallow respiration.

§ 3.7 Gastrointestinal (GI) System Structure and Function

The gastrointestinal (GI) system, also commonly referred to as the digestive system, has three main functions: the digestion of food, the absorption of nutrients into the bloodstream after digestion, and the elimination of solid waste products after digestion is complete. It is made up of the GI tract and associated organs and innervated by the autonomic nervous system (See § **3.16** for additional autonomic nervous system information). Two types of movement occur in the GI system: mixing (chemical digestive process) and propulsion (peristalsis) movement of digested food through the GI tract.

Structure

As shown in **Figure 3–2**, the GI Tract extends from the mouth to the anus and is made up of the following organs:

1. Oral Cavity (mouth)—contains the tongue, salivary glands, and teeth. Digestion begins in the oral cavity through mechanical action (chewing) and by chemical action (salivary glands secreting digestive juices). The tongue is also essential to speech and taste. Taste receptors are located on the sides and tip of the tongue.

2. Pharynx—connects oral and nasal cavities with the esophagus and trachea. It is the passageway for food as well as air. During swallowing, the *epiglottis* (a piece of tissue) closes over the pharynx to prevent food and fluid from entering the lungs through the trachea and directs them down the esophagus.

3. Esophagus—tube-like, hollow, muscular structure that extends from pharynx to stomach. After food is swallowed, it passes through the esophagus to the stomach.

4. Stomach—pouch-like organ that dilates to accommodate ingested food and acts as a storage reservoir. The stored food is gradually emptied into the small intestine for further digestion. Some digestion occurs in the stomach through action of digestive juices secreted by the stomach.

5. Small Intestine (bowel)—tubular passageway about 20 feet in length that further digests and absorbs food. The small intestine is divided

into three sections: the duodenum, the jejunum, and the ileum. It connects the stomach with the large intestine. The small intestine terminates at the cecum.

6. Large Intestine (bowel)—tubular passageway connecting the small intestine to the outside of the body. The large intestine's main function is to absorb water from the waste products of digestion to form *feces*. The large intestine is divided into the following sections: the ascending colon, the transverse colon, the descending colon, the sigmoid colon, and the rectum. Waste products are propelled through the intestines by wave-like contractions of the intestine called *peristalsis,* feces are formed and stored in the rectum, then are expelled from the body through the anus.

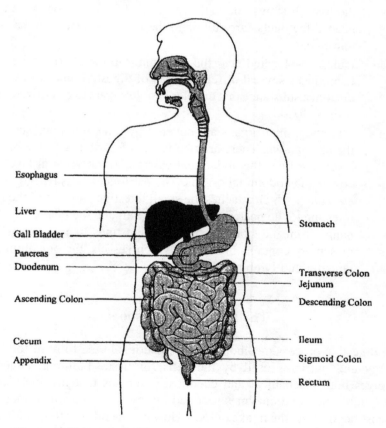

Figure 3–2. Digestive system.

7. Accessory Organs of Digestion—assist in the process of digestion mainly through the production of substances that break down complex foods (fats, carbohydrates, and proteins) into simple sugars. Simple sugars are absorbed into the blood for cell use as food.

    •   Liver—located in the right upper abdominal cavity. The liver has numerous functions that are essential to life. Its main role in digestion is to produce bile, an enzyme that assists in the break-down of fats. It also stores glucose in the form of glycogen and assists in the breakdown of old blood cells.

    •   Biliary Tract—composed of the gallbladder and associated ducts. The gallbladder is a sac-like structure located on the underside of the liver. It stores bile until it is needed for digestion. When it is needed the ducts carry bile into the liver and then into the small intestine.

    •   Pancreas—located near the duodenum in the abdominal cavity. It produces several different types of digestive juices as well as insulin, a substance that enables simple sugars to be utilized in the cells as food.

    •   The abdominal organs are covered by a membranous structure, the *peritoneum*. There are two layers of peritoneum, the parietal layer that lines the abdominal cavity and the visceral layer that covers the abdominal organs. The peritoneum has two folds: the *mesentery* which attaches the small intestine and part of the large intestine to the posterior abdominal wall and the *omentum* which hangs from the stomach over the intestines like an apron. The mesentery contains blood and lymph vessels; the omentum con-tains fat and lymph nodes.

Function
The Process of Digestion

The digestive process metabolizes raw materials in the form of food into energy and nutrients used by the cells for tissue building. Digestion involves both mechanical and chemical processes that involve electro-lytes, hormones, and enzymes secreted by the gastrointestinal tract. The process begins with the intake of food. How much and how frequently food is ingested is determined by appetite, which is governed by the appetite center located in the hypothalamus area of the brain. See § **3.14** for further information on the hypothalamus. Food is swallowed and passes into the esophagus, and then into the GI tract. As food is propelled through the tract, digestive secretions break down food so that it may be absorbed. These secretions, in the forms of electrolytes and enzymes, are produced in the mouth, stomach, duodenum, and jejunum. Accessory organs of digestion also secrete these substances and play an important role in this process. The final phase of digestion occurs in the small intestine. When digestion is complete, nutrients from the intestinal lumen are absorbed into the bloodstream. At the point when nutrients are ready for absorption, the following transformations have occurred:

- Carbohydrates have been changed into simple sugars.
- Proteins have been changed into amino acids.
- Fats have been changed into fatty acids and glycerides.

Remaining products of digestion progress to the large intestine where the absorption of water and electrolytes is completed. The resulting waste products are then moved into the rectum where they are stored until they are expelled from the body in the form of feces.

§ 3.8   —Common Problems of the Digestive System

1. Anorexia Nervosa/Bulemia—eating disorders characterized by self-imposed weight loss. Possible etiologies include concern over body image and distorted attitude towards weight and eating. Voluntary food deprivation continues even in the face of emaciation and starvation. Bulemia (binge/purge) is characterized by bouts of overeating followed by self-induced vomiting and excessive laxative use. These disorders usually affect young women and are treated with psychotherapy and supervised feedings.

2. Appendicitis—inflammation of the appendix. If severe, it may lead to rupture and spilling of bowel contents into the abdominal cavity. Appendicitis is treated by surgical removal.

3. Candidiasis (thrush)—infection of the oral cavity caused by the organism Candida albicans. Candida is normally present in the mouth, and infections from this organism usually occur only in those with altered immune function.

4. Cholecystitis—inflammation of the gallbladder. It can be treated conservatively through diet and medication or by surgical removal of the gallbladder.

5. Cholelithiasis (gallstones)—stones in the gallbladder that can vary in size and number. Symptoms can range from no discomfort to severe pain and blockage of the gallbladder ducts.

6. Cirrhosis—chronic disease of the liver characterized by hardening of the liver cells with resulting decreased function. Causes of cirrhosis are related to chemical exposure, alcohol consumption, and infectious processes.

7. Crohn's Disease (inflammatory bowel disorder or IBD)—inflammatory lesions within distinct bowel segments. The bowel thickens, becomes narrowed and fibrosed, and progressively non-functional. It is chronic, with periods of remission and exacerbation.

8. Diverticulitis—an inflamed sac-like outpouching (diverticula) in the intestine. *Diverticulosis* refers to a condition where multiple diverticula are present but not inflamed. These lesions may rupture, spilling bowel contents into the abdominal cavity. Asymptomatic diverticular disease is managed with diet. Surgical management is indicated when complication such as hemorrhage, perforation, or abscesses occur.

9. Esophageal Varices—dilated (varicose veins) of the esophagus. They occur as a result of hypertension in the venous system that supplies the liver. If severe, rupture of varices may occur, resulting in life-threatening hemorrhage.

10. Food poisoning—acute GI symptoms of nausea, vomiting, diarrhea, and abdominal pain secondary to ingestion of contaminated food. Common bacterial causes of food poisoning include salmonella, shigella, and certain strains of E. coli.

11. Gastric\Duodenal Ulcer—erosion of the lining of the stomach or small intestine that may result in bleeding. Ulcers have many causes, some of which are excess production of digestive juices (see *peptic ulcer disease* below), stress, excessive tobacco, and alcohol use.

12. Gastritis—inflammation of the stomach. Common causes of gastritis are ingestion of corrosive, erosive, or infectious substances (food poisoning). Certain types of drugs, such as aspirin and alcohol, are also common causes. Gastritis can be acute or chronic.

13. Gastroenteritis and Dysentery—*Gastroenteritis* presents as inflammation of the stomach and small bowel with associated nausea and vomiting, diarrhea, and abdominal cramps. *Dysenteries* are inflammatory conditions affecting the colon and are characterized by bloody diarrhea and severe abdominal cramping. Common causes of

gastroenteritis are viruses and bacteria. Amoebas, parasites, and bacteria commonly cause dysenteries.

14. Gastroesophageal Reflux Disease (GERD)—a syndrome characterized by the backward flow of gastric contents into the esophagus. Over a period of time this can lead to esophagitis. GERD is usually treated medically with pharmacologic and dietary management.

15. Gastrointestinal Cancers—can occur in any of the organs of the GI tract, including the oral cavity, esophagus, stomach, liver, pancreas, and intestines.

16. Hemorrhoids—varicose veins of the anus that may be internal and/or external. Hemorrhoids are a common disorder caused by any condition that increases constipation or intra-abdominal pressure, e.g. pregnancy.

17. Hepatitis—inflammation of the liver. Hepatitis can be caused by viruses or by chemicals. Infectious agents causing hepatitis include multiple hepatitis viruses, the most common of which are A, B, and C. Hepatitis may be acute or chronic. Alcohol is a common cause of chemically induced hepatitis.

18. Hernia—abnormal protrusion of organ through defect in the muscular wall. Hiatal hernias are related to muscle weakness in the esophageal support structures that is caused by a variety of conditions such as aging, trauma, or congenital muscle weakness. It is treated in much the same way as GERD.

19. Hiatal Hernia (diaphragmatic hernia)—protrusion of the stomach through the diaphragm into the thoracic cavity.

20. Irritable Bowel Syndrome (IBS)—group of symptoms characterized by intermittent but recurrent alteration in bowel function, either diarrhea or constipation.

21. Malnutrition—excess, deficit or imbalance in the essential components of a balanced diet. *Under-nutrition* can occur with inadequate diet or diseases that interfere with appetite and/or fool absorption. Causes can include socio-economic factors, psychiatric disorders, and medical conditions and treatment. Over-nutrition (obesity) is characterized by abnormally high proportion of fat cells in the body. When body weight is greater than the ideal body weight, the condition is referred to as *morbid obesity.*

22. Pancreatitis—inflammation of the pancreas. The severity of this disease ranges from mild to severe and can be acute or chronic.

The most common cause of pancreatitis is alcoholism, followed by gallbladder disease.

23. Paralytic Ileus—absence of peristalsis that results in lack of food progression through the digestive tract. This condition may occur after abdominal surgery or after trauma.

24. Peptic Ulcer Disease—erosion of the stomach mucous membrane caused by the digestive action of hydrochloric acid and pepsin (digestive enzymes). Although ulcers commonly occur in the stomach, they can occur in other portions of the GI tract, including the esophagus and the duodenum.

25. Peritonitis—inflammation of the peritoneal membrane. It can be primary or secondary, acute or chronic. Examples of common causes are gangrenous cholecystitis, ruptured appendix, colon, or stomach, acute pancreatitis, and septic abortion.

26. Portal Hypertension—increase in pressure of liver's venous system (portal system). Most cases are caused by cirrhosis.

27. Stomatitis—inflammation of the mouth. Stomatitis can be caused by infectious agents or can occur as a side effect of medical treatment (for example, cancer therapy).

28. Ulcerative Colitis (inflammatory bowel disorder or IBD)—inflammatory process that usually affects the entire length of the colon. This disease causes congestion and edema of the bowel mucosa with small lacerations that bleed. Like Crohn's disease, it is chronic, with periods of remission and exacerbation.

§ 3.9   Skeletal System Structure and Function

The skeletal system provides a rigid framework for the body and offers protection for internal organs. See **Figures 3–3** and **3–4.** The bones of the skeletal system also produce blood cells and store minerals. Their shape commonly classifies bones into four types:

- Long—e.g femur, humerus
- Short—e.g. carpal bones of the hand and tarsal bones of the feet
- Flat—e.g. ribs, sternum, skull
- Irregular—e.g. vertebrae, sacrum

Although bones vary widely in size and shape they have similar structures. The outer surface of the bone is the *periosteum* which contains blood vessels and nerves. The inner layer of the periosteum is attached to the bone by collagenous fibers that penetrate into the bone itself. The outer portion of the bone is called the *cortex*. It is compact bone that is dense, hard, and extremely strong. The skeletal system is divided into two major categories: axial and appendicular.

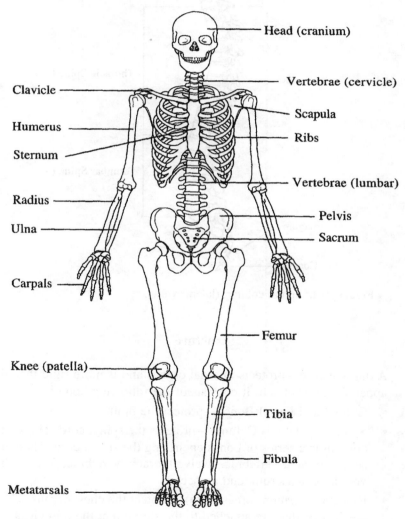

Figure 3–3. Skeletal system.

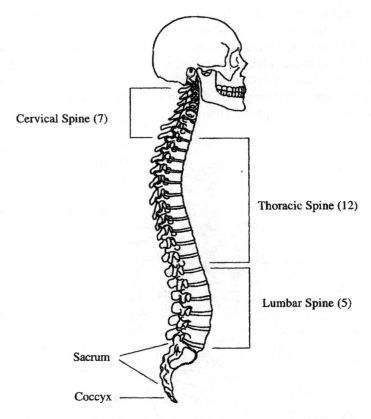

Cervical Spine (7)

Thoracic Spine (12)

Lumbar Spine (5)

Sacrum

Coccyx

Figure 3–4. Spinal column (lateral view).

Structure

1. Axial Skeleton—protects internal organs and is more rigid than the appendicular skeleton. It consists of the following bones:
    *   Cranial and Facial Bones—protect the brain.
    *   Spinal (Vertebral) Column—protects the spinal cord. The spinal column is a series of bones encircling the spinal cord. There are seven cervical vertebrae, twelve thoracic vertebrae, five lumbar vertebrae, a sacrum, and a coccyx.
    *   Ribs and Sternum (breastbone)—protect the chest organs. There are 12 ribs that are attached to the sternum at the mid-chest.

2. Appendicular Skeleton—serves as a movable frame for the arms and legs. The bones provide attachments for muscles and act as levers for muscle movement. It consists of:

   • Pectoral Girdle—includes the bones of the shoulder: clavicle (breastbone) and scapula; the bones of the arms: humerus (upper arm), ulna, and radius (lower arm); and the bones of the hand: carpals, metacarpals, and phalanges (fingers).

   • Pelvic Girdle—includes bones of the pelvis: the ilium, ischium, and pubis; the bones of the legs: femur (upper leg), tibia, and fibula (lower leg); and the bones of the feet: tarsals, metatarsals, and phalanges (toes).

Additional Skeletal System Components

1. Joints—are points where two ends of bone are in proximity and move in relation to each other. Joints are classified by their structure and their degree of movement:

   • Fibrous Joints (synarthroses)—have little or no movement and are tightly attached to each other by fibrous connective tissue. The sutures between the skull bones are examples of fibrous joints.

   • Cartilaginous Joints (amphiarthroses)—have little or no movement. The bones forming the joints are connected by cartilage and connective tissue. The cartilage discs between the spinal vertebrae are examples of cartilaginous joints.

   • Synovial Joints (diarthroses)—freely movable joints. The bones move within a synovial cavity. Synovial joints are classified by how they accomplish movement. Examples of synovial joints are:

   —Ball-and-Socket Joints—the ball-like head of one bone fits into the socket of another bone. Joint movements are flexion, extension, and rotation. The hip joint is an example of a ball-and-socket joint.

   —Hinge Joints—the surface of one bone moves about the rounded surface of another and joint movement is limited to extension and flexion. The elbow is an example of a hinge joint.

   —Pivot Joints—a ring of bone rotates around a protruding piece of another and joint movement is limited to rotation. The skull, rotating on the first cervical vertebra, is an example of a pivot joint.

2. Cartilage—elastic material found between two surfaces of movable joints or between two bones. It is capable of withstanding considerable pressure and tension, and thus serves as a cushion and shock absorber. Cartilage constitutes part of the skeleton in adults and is found in the external ear, nasal septum, and ribs.

3. Ligaments—hold movable joints together. Ligaments are flexible enough to allow free joint movement, yet strong enough to withstand applied force.

4. Tendons—tough bands of fibrous tissue that connect bones to muscles.

5. Fascia—connective tissue sheaths that hold muscle fibers together.

6. Bursae—fluid-filled sacs that prevent friction created by two bony surfaces rubbing together. Bursae can be found over most bony prominences, such as ankles, elbows, and knees.

7. Synovial Cavities—surround all freely movable joints. They contain a fluid that absorbs the heat of friction during movement and lubricates the bone surfaces.

Additional Skeletal System Terms

1. Acetabulum—head of the femur that fits into the socket of the pelvic bone

2. Foramen—holes in bones that allow passage of large vessels and nerves into the bone itself

3. Fossae—bone depressions or hollows

4. Malleolus—protuberance on either side of the ankle

5. Olecranon—elbow.

Function

Bone cortex is organized into structural units called *haversian systems* that contain a central canal. These canals contain nerves and blood vessels that transport nutrients to the bone and carry wastes away. The middle portion of the bone lacks a haversian system and is called *spongy bone*. This bone layer is filled with marrow that forms blood cells. Internal blood supply is connected to the periosteum through channels called *Volkmann's canals*. Bone, like other tissues, is a living organ that constantly changes, with old cells being destroyed and new ones being formed.

§ 3.10   —Common Problems of the Skeletal System

The skeletal, muscular, and nervous systems function closely together and disease or injuries to structures of one system often impact function of the other two. Problems and injures involving the skeletal, muscular, and nervous systems are commonly involved in litigation. Conditions frequently seen are discussed in greater depth in **Chapter 6**, and are noted below.

1. Ankylosing Spondylitis—inflammatory disease of unknown cause affecting joints between the spinal vertebrae. More common in men than in women, the disease is usually progressive, leading to decreased movement and permanent fusion of the spine.

2. Arthritis—inflammation of body joints; a usually a progressive condition characterized by joint pain. There are two types of arthritis:
   - osteoarthritis—non-inflammatory condition of the synovial joints. The exact cause is unknown.
   - rheumatoid arthritis (RA)—systemic disease characterized by inflammation of the connective tissue in synovial joints. RA is considered to be one of the autoimmune diseases. See **§ 3.22** for further discussion of autoimmunity.

3. Bone Tumors—may be benign or malignant. Malignant tumors can be primary or metastatic from another body site. Two major types of bone tumors are chondrogenic (arising from cartilage) and osteogenic (arising from bone).

4. Bunion—painful swelling of the first joint of the big toe. The cause of bunions is not definitely known.

5. Bursititis—inflammation of the bursae.

6. Fasciitis—inflammation of fascia.

7. Fractures—break or crack in a bone. A common cause of fractures is some type of trauma, however they can result from other causes. Types and configurations of fractures, their causes and treatment are discussed extensively in **Chapter 6.** Types of facial fractures are discussed as well.

8. Gout—type of arthritis caused by accumulation of uric acid crystals. Occurs most commonly in the great toe.

9. Kyphosis—excessive backward curvature of the thoracic spine, resulting in a hump (often referred to as dowager's hump).

10. Lordosis—excessive inward curvature of the lumbar spine. May be exaggerated by poor posture, obesity, and weak abdominal muscles.

11. Low back pain—most commonly affects the lumbar spine. Causation can be mechanical or discogenic, that is, related to nerve impingement resulting from a herniated disc. Low back pain can be acute or chronic. Additional information on causes and treatment of low back pain can be found in **Chapter 6.**

12. Osteomalacia—disease that causes bone to become abnormally soft secondary to vitamin deficiency.

13. Osteomyelitis—bone infection. Can occur after orthopedic surgical procedures or following open fracture injuries.

14. Osteoporosis—loss of bone density that results in thin, brittle bones. Occurs in older people, especially in women. Bones with osteoporosis tend to break easily and heal slowly.

15. Paget's Disease—disorder of the bone metabolism, resulting in bone that is weak and prone to fractures. The cause is unknown.

16. Scoliosis—lateral curvature of the thoracic spine. Most commonly seen in children and adolescents.

17. Tendonitis—inflammation of a tendon.

§ 3.11   Muscular System Structure and Function

The muscular system enables movement of the body, facial expression, and allows posture maintenance by contraction (muscle shortening) and relaxation (muscle lengthening). Muscles also give the body form, enable contraction of heart muscle, and internally line many organs.

Muscle Nomenclature

There are hundreds of muscles in the body. See **Figure 3–5.** They are named in four principal ways:

1. By the function they perform: the flexor carpi is the muscle that flexes the wrist.

2. By points of origin and insertion: the sternocleidomastoid muscle has the sternum and clavicle as points of origin and the mastoid bone as a point of insertion.

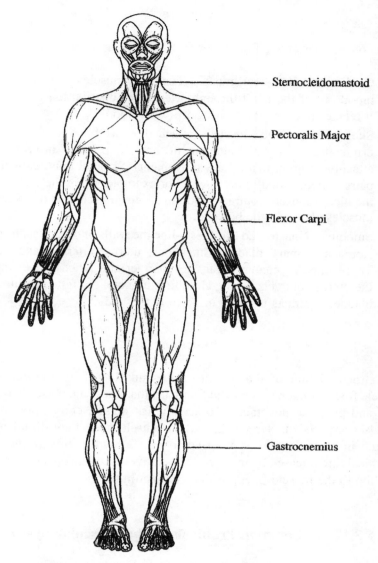

Figure 3–5. Superficial muscles (anterior view).

3. By form or position: the pectoralis minor muscle is the small chest muscle and the pectoralis major is the large chest muscle.
4. By resemblance to an object: the gastrocnemius muscle of the calf is shaped somewhat like the stomach (gastro).

Structure

Types of muscles are as follows:

1. Cardiac Muscle—heart muscle. The heart muscle contracts to force blood out of the heart through arteries for distribution to all cells. It relaxes to allow the heart to fill with blood.
2. Skeletal or Striated Muscles—attached to two bones at the point of origin (the more fixed attachment) and the point of insertion (the attachment point that allows movement). Skeletal muscles work in pairs to permit body movement. For example, when the arm bends, the biceps muscle contracts and the triceps muscle relaxes. Skeletal muscles also give the body form.
3. Smooth or Nonstriated Muscles—line the walls of organs such as the stomach, urinary bladder, intestines, uterus, arteries, and veins. These muscles enable organs to contract and relax. For example, the uterus contracts during childbirth to expel the fetus; the urinary bladder contracts to expel urine from the body.

Function

The structural unit of the muscle is the muscle cell or muscle fiber. Muscle fibers contain specialized filaments that allow the muscles to contract and produce movement. To accomplish muscle contraction, nerve impulses are needed. Nerve cells and the muscle fibers they stimulate are located in close proximity, referred to as *the neuromuscular junction.* Chemicals are released by the nerve cells, travel across the neuromuscular junction to the muscle fibers, which contract in response.

§ 3.12   —Common Problems of the Muscular System

As noted in § 3.10, problems involving the muscular system that may be seen in litigation are discussed further in **Chapter 6;** topics included are noted below.

1. Atrophy—shrinking of a muscle in size and function. Muscle atrophy usually occurs as a result of prolonged disuse.

2. Compartment Syndrome—usually follows orthopedic surgery or trauma. It occurs when fascia that surrounds bones, muscles, nerves, and blood vessels at the injury site swell. Entrapped tissues cannot expand enough to accommodate building pressure. Damage to affected muscles' nerve and blood supply result if this condition is not rapidly treated.

3. Low back pain—most commonly affects the lumbar spine. Causation can be mechanical or discogenic, that is, related to nerve impingement resulting from a herniated disc (See § 3.17). Low back pain can be acute or chronic. Additional information on causes and treatment of both causes of low back pain can be found in **Chapter 6.**

4. Meniscus Injuries—injury to one or both of the two pieces of fibrocartilage tissue that comprise the meniscus, located in the knee between the femur and the tibia. Injury usually occurs as a result of rotation stress on the knee.

5. Muscular Dystrophy—progressive, hereditary, degenerative disease of the skeletal muscles.

6. Myofacial Pain Syndrome—a group of disorders characterized by musculoskeletal tenderness in a specific area of the body. One of the most common disorders seen is *Temporomandibular Joint (TMJ) Syndrome.* See **Chapter 6** for additional information on diagnosis and treatment of these syndromes.

7. Myositis—muscle inflammation.

8. Repetitive stress injuries (RSI)—occur as a result of cumulative trauma resulting from prolonged, forceful, or awkward movements. See **Chapter 6** for additional information on diagnosis and treatment of RSI.

9. Rotator cuff injuries—tear in (any of) the four muscles in the shoulder that make up the rotator cuff. Injuries range in severity, depending of the severity of the tear. See **Chapter 6** for additional information on diagnosis and treatment of these types of injuries.

10. Soft Tissue Injuries—injuries caused by sudden twisting or wrenching of a muscle, usually causing pain and swelling. Types of soft tissue injuries include *dislocation, subluxation, contusion, strain, and sprain.* See **Chapter 6** for additional information on these types of injuries.

11. Whiplash Injuries—occur in the cervical spine as a result of hyperextension and/or hyperflexion of the cervical spine. See **Chapter 6** for additional information on causes, diagnosis and treatment of whiplash injuries.

§ 3.13   Nervous System Structure and Function

The nervous system receives and processes information received by the body from external and internal sources. It is the most complex body system, affecting both physiological and psychological function. The nervous system has three divisions: the central nervous system and the peripheral nervous system, that control the body's voluntary responses to stimuli, and the autonomic nervous system that control involuntary responses. The basic structural and functional unit of the nervous system is the *neuron.*

Structure

§ 3.14   —Central Nervous System

The central nervous system (CNS) contains large numbers of neurons that are arranged to receive and process information encountered in the environment. See **Figure 3–6.** It is composed of the brain and spinal cord.

1. Brain—located within the skull. An incredibly complex structure, the brain is composed of billions of neurons, enabling it to see images and remember them, read, write, reason, and calculate. Most amazingly, it enables humans to laugh, love, and cry. The brain is divided into three major components:

    •   Cerebrum—center of mental activity and voluntary movements. The cerebrum has a right and left hemisphere (side). Both hemispheres are further divided into four lobes: *frontal, temporal, parietal, and occipital.*

    •   Brainstem—includes three areas: the *midbrain, pons, and medulla.* The brainstem is center of vital regulatory functions such as body temperature, cardiac function and respiration; it also contains centers for functions such as swallowing, gagging, coughing, and sneezing. Directly above the brainstem are the *thalamus and the hypothalamus,* structures critical to endocrine and autonomic nervous system function.

    •   Cerebellum—coordination center for the body's motor activities. To accomplish this function, the cerebellum receives information from the cerebrum, muscles, joints, and inner ear.

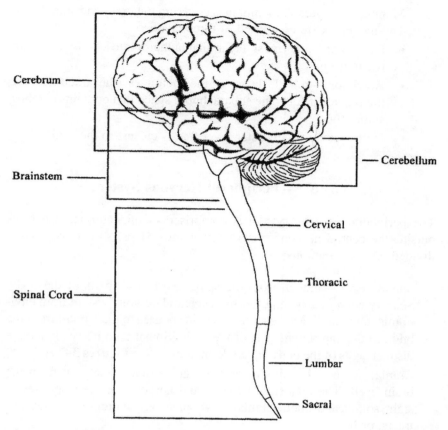

Cerebrum

Brainstem

Spinal Cord

Cerebellum

Cervical

Thoracic

Lumbar

Sacral

Figure 3–6. Central nervous system.

2. Spinal Cord—extension of the brain that runs down the mid-back of the body through the protective bones of the spinal vertebrae. The spinal cord is the main pathway for sensory and motor impulses traveling between the brain and the external and internal environment.

3. Cerebrospinal Fluid (CSF)—fluid that circulates in and around the brain and spinal cord. CSF carries essential nutrients to the central nervous system and serves a protective function.

4. Ventricles—cavities within the brain through which cerebrospinal fluid circulates.

5. Meninges—layers of membranes covering the brain and spinal cord. The meninges are composed of three layers:
   - Pia mater—innermost layer that adheres closely to the brain tissue itself
   - Arachnoid—middle layer of the meninges (the arachnoid and the pia mater form the subarachnoid space that contains cerebrospinal fluid)
   - Dura mater—tough outer layer that is closest to the skull.

§ 3.15   —Peripheral Nervous System

The peripheral nervous system is comprised of all neuronal structures outside the central nervous system. It contains 31 pairs of nerves and is divided into two sections:

- Spinal nerves—branch from the spinal cord to all parts of the body. Sensory nerves carry impulses to the central nervous system from environmental stimuli. Motor nerves carry responses to the stimuli from the brain to the appropriate part of the body. Spinal cord nerves innervate distinct areas of the body called dermatomes. See **Figures 3–7** and **3–8.**
- Cranial nerves—12 pairs of cranial nerves that branch out from the brain itself. The majority of the cranial nerves produce responses to sight, sound, and smell. Cranial nerves have only motor or only sensory tracts, or both.

§ 3.16   —Autonomic Nervous System

The autonomic nervous system is an automatic, self-governing motor system of the body. Its function is to maintain a stable environment within the body by regulating such functions as heart rate, myocardial contractility and conduction strength, and blood vessel constriction and dilation. The autonomic nervous system innervates organs such as the stomach and the heart. It is composed of two subsystems that have opposite effects on the body and balance each other:

- Sympathetic Nervous System—coordinates activities the body uses to handle stress; acts for the whole body for prolonged periods of time

• Parasympathetic Nervous System—conserves and restores the body's energy stores; acts locally for short periods of time.

Function

Neurons are composed of a cell body (nerve cell) and threadlike processes that include one *axon* and several *dendrites*. Axons conduct impulses *away from* the body of the nerve cell, and dendrites conduct impulses from adjacent cells inward *toward* the cell body. Although neurons are the excitable cells of nervous tissue, functionally they cannot carry out typical actions of the nervous system. Actions from simple reflexes to complex thought processes are carried out by nerve nets and circuits made up of

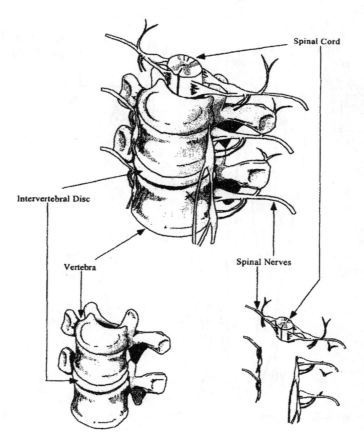

Figure 3–7. Spinal cord and spinal nerves.

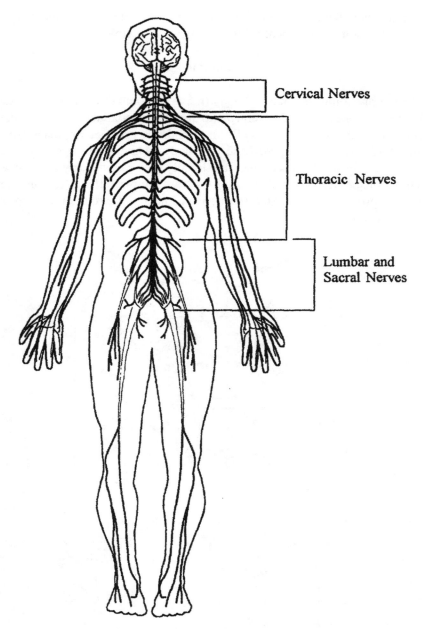

Cervical Nerves

Thoracic Nerves

Lumbar and
Sacral Nerves

Figure 3–8. Anterior view of peripheral nervous system.

multiple neurons that interact with each other through excitatory and inhibitory *synapses.* Synapses are areas of specialized contact between neurons or between neurons and specialized organs. They provide controllable functional connections between neurons and are responsible for integrating and coordinating central nervous system functions. Synapses can be chemical (impulses are transmitted by neurotransmitters released by neurons) or electrical (two cells' electrical nerve impulses cross directly from one cell to another). Once injured, neurons cannot regenerate; however, if the axon alone is damaged, some amount of regeneration is possible.

§ 3.17   —Common Problems of the Nervous System

As noted in § **3.10,** problems affecting the nervous system that may be seen in litigation are discussed further in **Chapter 6;** topics included are noted below.

1. Alzheimer's Disease—form of dementia characterized by progressive impairment of decision-making processes. Types of dementia, along with information on the effect of aging, are discussed in **Chapter 6.**

2. Amytrophic Lateral Sclerosis (ALS)—involves degeneration of motor neurons that progresses relatively rapidly. Death usually results from respiratory compromise. Management is through supportive therapy only.

3. Arteriovenous Malformation (AVM)—congenital malformation of cerebral blood vessels. The affected blood vessels are thin-walled tangles that can leak small amounts of blood or rupture.

4. Bell's Palsy—unilateral paralysis of facial muscles caused by dysfunction of seventh cranial nerve.

5. Carpal Tunnel Syndrome (CTS)—pain and swelling on the thumb side of the hand caused by pressure on the median nerve. This condition can be associated with repetitive stress injury. See **Chapter 6** for additional information on carpal tunnel syndrome.

6. Cerebral Aneurysm—an out-pouching of a cranial blood vessel. The vessel wall may become very weak and rupture, causing bleeding into the brain tissue.

7. Cerebral Tumors—lesions can be primary (develop from central nervous system tissue) or secondary (metastasize from other locations in the body).

8. CVA or Stroke—see § **3.4.**

9. Epilepsy—neurological disorder that causes seizures. It results from malfunction of neurons in the cerebral cortex. Status epilepticus is a condition in which continuous seizures occur. It is a medical emergency as it may lead to inadequate oxygenation of the brain with resulting brain damage.

10. Guillain-Barré Syndrome (GBS)—inflammatory disease of unknown cause that causes degeneration of the myelin sheath of the peripheral nerves. Recovery does occur, although some residual deficits may remain.

11. Head Injuries—conditions involving the skull and/or brain. The most common causes of trauma are motor vehicle accidents; others include assaults, falls, and accidents. Types of head injuries and their treatments are discussed in more detail in **Chapter 6.**

12. Increased Intracranial Pressure—abnormal increase of pressure within the cranium usually caused by a rapidly expanding lesion (bleeding), obstruction of outflow of cerebrospinal fluid (tumor), or increased cerebrospinal fluid formation (cerebral edema). Increased intracranial pressure and its treatment is discussed in more detail in **Chapter 6.**

13. Meningitis—inflammation of the meninges of the brain and spinal cord. The cause of meningitis is often an infectious agent, either bacterial or viral.

14. Migraine Headaches—recurrent, throbbing headaches. The cause of migraines is thought to be due to constriction of intracranial blood vessels with later dilation. Psychosocial factors are also thought to influence migraines.

15. Multiple Sclerosis—progressive, degenerative disease that affects the ability of the nerve cells to conduct impulses.

16. Myasthenia Gravis—autoimmune disease that presents with muscular weakness and fatigue that worsens with exercise. Management is by pharmacologic intervention; there is no cure.

17. Parkinson's Disease—degenerative nerve disease characterized by body tremors and muscle rigidity.

18. Ruptured or Herniated Disc—protrusion of the cartilage disc between two vertebrae. This bulging can cause pressure on the nerves of the spinal cord, causing severe pain. See **Chapter 6** for additional information on herniated discs.

19. Sciatica—compression of the sciatic nerve (major nerve that supplies the leg) from a herniated disc in the spinal column. Sciatica can result in severe leg pain and can also cause nerve dysfunction, depending on the severity of the compression. This condition is discussed in more detail in **Chapter 6.**

20. Spina Bifida/Meningocele—birth defect manifested by incomplete closure of the bones of the spinal column, with or without protrusion of the spinal cord through the skin defect (meningocele).

21. Spinal Cord Injury—injuries occur when the integrity of the spinal cord is disrupted. When disruption occurs, all nerve impulses below the site of the injury cannot be transmitted and paralysis results. Paralysis may be partial or complete, depending on the degree of cord destruction. *Paraplegia* results from cord transection at a level that leaves the functioning of the upper extremities intact. *Quadriplegia,* also termed *tetraplegia,* results in paralysis of all extremities. These injuries and their management are discussed in more detail in **Chapter 6.**

22. Subarachnoid Hemorrhage—bleeding into the subarachnoid space. Hemorrhage may be caused by leaking or rupture of a cerebral aneurysm or be the result of head injury. This condition is discussed in more detail in **Chapter 6.**

23. Transient Ischemic Attack (TIA)—brief, reversible episode of neurologic dysfunction caused by intermittent cerebrovascular insufficiency.

24. Trigeminal Neuralgia (Tic Douloureux)—fifth cranial nerve condition characterized by sudden onset of severe pain along one or more of the nerve branches. Produces some twitching of facial muscles. The true cause of this condition is uncertain.

§ 3.18   Urinary System Structure and Function

The urinary system filters waste products from the blood for excretion from the body in the form of urine. Additionally, it regulates the body's fluid and electrolyte balance and blood pressure. The kidneys perform the above functions; the remaining structures of the urinary system transport urine for excretion. See **Figure 3–9.**

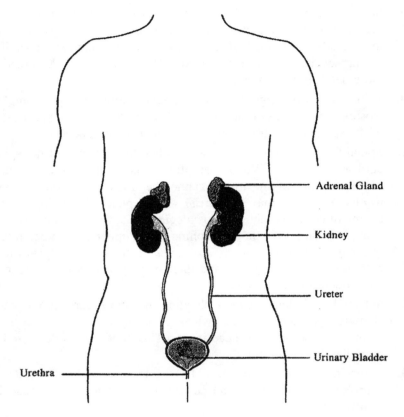

Adrenal Gland

Kidney

Ureter

Urinary Bladder

Urethra

Figure 3–9. Urinary system.

Structure

The urinary system is made up of the following major organs:

1. Kidneys—bean-shaped organs located against the muscles of the back of the abdominal wall about waist level. There are two kidneys, one on each side of the spinal column. Kidneys filter blood of waste products to form urine. Each kidney is divided into three areas: the cortex, the medulla, and the pelvis. The nephron is the functional unit of the kidney. Adrenal glands are located above the kidneys; their function is discussed in **§ 3.20.** The kidneys have two areas: the cortex (outer layer) and the medulla (inner layer). Within the medulla are the structures that filter waste products from the blood to form

urine. Urine collects in the renal pelvis in preparation for transportation to the bladder. See **Figure 3–10.**

2. Glomerulus(i)—performs the actual filtering process of the blood. Glomeruli are microscopic, tubular structures located inside the kidney.

3. Ureters—two thin, tubular structures, one attached to each kidney. Ureters allow urine to flow from the kidneys to the urinary bladder; they have a mechanism that prevents backflow of urine from the ureter into the kidney.

4. Urinary Bladder—muscular, sac-like organ that stores urine. As the bladder fills with urine, it expands. When it reaches a certain capacity, nerves are stimulated, causing the urge to urinate. The bladder then contracts and urine is expelled from the body.

5. Urethra—tube leading from the bladder to the outside of the body. The male urethra also serves as the passageway for semen during sexual intercourse.

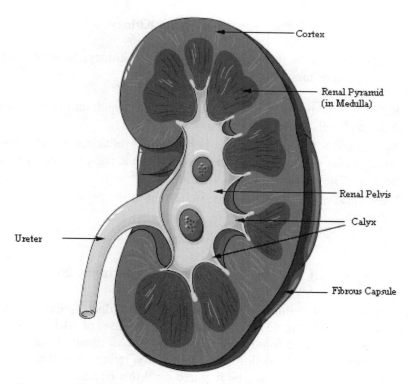

Figure 3–10. Longitudinal section of the kidney.

Function
Formation of Urine

The formation of urine occurs in the nephron by three processes: filtration, reabsorption, and secretion. *Filtration* involves the passage of water and electrolytes in the blood through a semi-permeable membrane in the nephron glomerulus. The end product of this process is called *glomerular filtrate.* The second stage of urine formation involves *reabsorption* of much of the glomerular filtrate back into the body. Finally, the cells *secrete* chemicals that allow transport of substances from the blood into the nephron tubules. This entire process evolves as the forming urine moves through each nephron. It travels through collecting ducts into the renal pyramid, to the calyx, and into the pelvis of the kidney. From the kidney, urine flows down the ureters to the bladder where it is stored until it is *excreted,* that is, expelled from the body through the urethra.

Other Functions of the Kidney

Formation of urine is the major function of the kidney, however other functions deserve mention as well. They include:

- Production of erythropoietin, a substance that stimulates production of red blood cells in the bone marrow.
- Activation of vitamin D. The D vitamin is obtained by the body through diet or exposure to the sun in an inactive form that cannot be used. The kidney activates vitamin D.
- Production of renin, a substance important in the regulation of blood pressure.

§ 3.19 —Common Problems of the Urinary System

1. Acute Renal Failure (ARF)—abrupt loss of kidney function over a period of hours to days. The most common causes of ARF are severe hypotension and hypovolemia or exposure to agents toxic to the kidney. Kidney function may eventually return, however, short-term renal dialysis may be required until this occurs.

2. Chronic Renal Failure (CRF)—progressive decrease in functioning renal tissue. The most common causes of chronic renal failure are chronic pyelonephritis (see **10** below), diabetes, and hypertension. Eventually, CRF progresses to *end stage renal disease (ESRD)*. In ESRD, the remaining kidney tissue becomes unable to form urine; this condition is fatal without treatment. Treatment is by periodic renal dialysis that performs the waste-removing functions of the destroyed nephrons. There are two renal dialysis techniques: hemodialysis and peritoneal dialysis.

3. Cystitis—inflammation of the bladder, usually caused by bacteria that have entered the bladder through the urethra. Cystitis is more common in the female because the urethra is short and because bacteria are normally present in and around the vagina. Symptoms of cystitis are painful and frequent urination. A type of urinary tract infection, see **15** below.

4. Hydronephrosis—distention of the renal pelvis with urine caused by flow obstruction. Causes of occlusion include stones, tumor, or scar tissue in the ureter.

5. Interstitial Cystitis—chronic, painful inflammatory disease of the bladder. Its cause is unknown. Diagnosis is by process of exclusion, considered when symptoms of UTI are present with negative urine tests.

6. Nephritis/Glomerulonephritis—inflammation of the kidney, usually the glomeruli of the kidneys. If not treated, the disease can lead to glomeruli destruction and loss of kidney function. This condition can be a sequella of β-strep infection.

7. Nephrolithiasis—kidney stones. Stones can lodge in the kidney or travel into the ureter. If stones are small, they can be passed with urine. Large stones may cause obstruction of the kidney or ureter and require surgical removal. There is a great deal of pain associated with this condition.

8. Neurogenic Bladder—term encompasses several types of bladder dysfunction, all of which are caused by diseases/injuries of the nervous system. Dysfunction can result in urinary incontinence (uncontrolled urination) or urinary retention (inability to urinate).

9. Polycystic Kidney Disease—hereditary disorder in which grape-like cysts replace normal renal tissue. Eventually, when kidney failure occurs, it is treated with renal dialysis.

10. Pyelonephritis—infection (pus) in the kidneys. Pyelonephritis is usually caused by bacteria that enter the urinary bladder and travel upward through the ureters into the kidney. This condition may be acute or chronic.

11. Reflux—backward flow of urine toward the kidneys. Reflux is usually prevented by protective mechanisms in the ureters that prevent the backward flow of urine.

12. Urethritis—inflammation of the urethra. Infections can be bacterial or viral in nature, including organisms that cause sexually transmitted diseases.

13. Urinary Incontinence—uncontrolled loss of urine in volumes that cause distress for the individual. Incontinence has multiple causes including any disease or structure anomaly that interferes with bladder or urethral sphincter control.

14. Urinary Retention—inability to empty the urinary bladder. This can include incomplete emptying despite urination or inability to urinate at all.

15. Urinary Tract Infection (UTI)—any infection involving the structures of the urinary tract. In infection of the upper urinary tract (kidney), systemic manifestations such as chills and fever commonly occur. Infections of the lower urinary tract. i.e. cystitis produce more localized symptoms.

16. Urosepsis—systemic infection arising from a source within the urinary tract. If not treated promptly and adequately, urosepsis can lead to septic shock.

§ 3.20 Endocrine System Structure and Function

The endocrine system is a complex system of glands located throughout the body. These glands secrete chemical substances known as *hormones* that perform many functions essential to normal body function. The endocrine system, through hormones, and nervous system, through nerve impulses, communicate with each other to coordinate critical body system functions that maintain homeostasis. Hormones travel through the blood to specific *target cells* in the body, which are susceptible only to the action of their specific hormone(s). (See **Figure 3–11.**) It is important to note that not all glands belong to the endocrine system. The body also contains *exocrine* glands that secrete into ducts that empty into body cavities or onto the surface of an organ. In contrast, the glands of the endocrine system secrete directly into the blood.

The endocrine system is incredibly complex and its structure and function are very diverse. In-depth discussion of this system is beyond the scope of this text, however a brief overview is provided below.

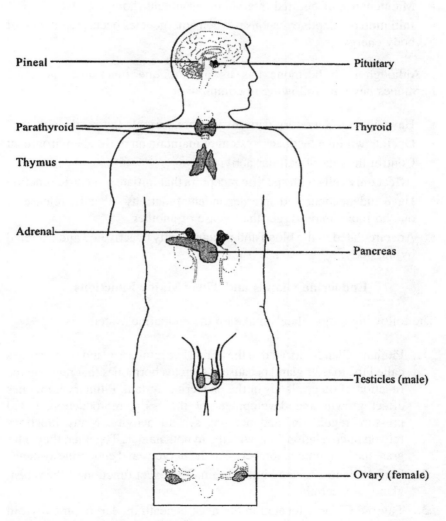

Figure 3–11. Endocrine system.

Through the hormones it secretes, the endocrine system has several functions:

- Differentiation of reproductive and central nervous system tissue in the developing fetus
- Stimulation of sequential growth
- Coordination of reproductive system function
- Maintenance of optimal internal environment (homeostasis)
- Initiation of adaptive responses when emergencies occur; regulation of body energy.

Although each hormone has its own unique functions, endocrine hormones have the following in common:

- Have specific secretory patterns that are variable but predictable
- Operate within a feedback system to maintain an optimal environment
- Control the rate of cellular activity
- Affect only cells with specific receptors that initiate a specific function
- Have independent and interdependent functions—that is, release of one hormone may trigger the release of another
- Are circulated in the blood and are constantly deactivated and excreted by the body.

Endocrine Glands and Their Major Functions

The following major glands make up the endocrine system:

1. Pituitary Gland—located in the brain. The pituitary gland is sometimes called the master gland because it secretes hormones that regulate the function of other glands in the endocrine system. Pituitary hormones affect growth and development of the body, reproduction, blood pressure regulation, and nervous system activity. Many functions rely on inter-relationships with the hypothalamus. Together, they integrate the communication between the nervous and endocrine systems.

2. Pineal Gland—located in the brain. The exact function of the pineal gland is uncertain.

3. Thyroid Gland—located in the neck beneath the larynx, the thyroid gland is composed of two lobes connected by a strip of tissue called the isthmus. The main function of the thyroid gland is to regulate the

body's metabolic activity by controlling the rate at which the body consumes nutrients and oxygen.

4. Parathyroid Glands—small areas of tissue located in the thyroid gland. The main function of the parathyroid glands is the maintenance of body calcium levels. Muscle activity within the body is dependent on calcium.

5. Thymus Gland—located in the chest above the heart, the thymus gland plays a role in the functioning of the body's immune system by protecting the body from tumor cell invasion and bacterial and viral infections. The thymus gland is most active before the onset of puberty and ultimately becomes nonfunctional in adulthood. The role of the thymus gland in the immune system is further discussed in § 3.22.

6. Adrenal Glands—located above the kidneys. The adrenal glands have two main sections, the medulla (inner portion) and the cortex (outer portion). The adrenal cortex secretes cortisol, the hormone that regulates the body's response to stress (the flight-or-fight response). The adrenal glands increase the body's metabolic rate and mobilize energy by releasing stored nutrients in response to stress. They also increase nervous system activity, blood supply to muscle tissue, and respiratory and heart rates.

7. Pancreas—located in the abdominal cavity, the pancreas is also a part of the digestive system. In addition to secreting several digestive enzymes, the pancreas, specifically the Islets of Langerhan, produce insulin. Insulin is necessary to transport simple sugar nutrients in the blood to the cells.

8. Ovaries—located in the pelvic cavity of the female, the ovaries produce hormones responsible for female sex characteristics (for example, breast development), for the production of ova (eggs), and for the maintenance of the menstrual cycle and pregnancy.

9. Testes—located in the scrotum of the male, the testes produce hormones responsible for male sex characteristics (for example, deepening of voice) and for the production of sperm.

§ 3.21   —Common Problems of the Endocrine System

1. Adrenal Insufficiency (Addison's Disease)—deficient production of adrenal gland hormones, resulting in lack of appetite, weakness, and many other symptoms.

2. Diabetes Insipidus—deficiency of antidiuretic hormone (ADH), resulting in excessive excretion of water.

3. Diabetes Mellitus—insufficient or no production of insulin by the pancreas, resulting in the inability of the cells to utilize sugar for food. Over time, multiple complications may occur as a result of diabetes. These include nerve, eye, and kidney damage, heart disease, and circulatory disorders. There are several types of diabetes:

   • Type I Diabetes—occurs predominately in those under 30 years of age. It results from the progressive destruction of the insulin producing cells of the pancreas (β cells) due to an autoimmune process. This destruction occurs over months, but once complete symptoms occur rapidly. Treatment requires injection of insulin.

   • Type II Diabetes—occurs predominately in those over 40 years of age. Contributing factors include obesity, genetics, and family history. The pancreas still produces some insulin, however levels are inadequate to control blood sugar levels. Oral medications are used to enhance insulin production.

   • Gestational Diabetes—develops during pregnancy. Blood sugar levels usually return to normal several weeks after delivery.

4. Hyperparathyroidism—over-activity of one or more of the parathyroid glands. Excessive circulation of the parathyroid hormone leads to demineralization of the bones, high blood calcium, and kidney damage.

5. Hyper-secretion of Adrenals (Cushing's Syndrome)—results in increased depositions of body fat, especially around the facial area (moon face), and serious metabolic deficiencies.

6. Hyperthyroidism (Graves Disease)—excessive secretion of thyroid hormone. Symptoms of hyperthyroidism include weight loss, extreme nervousness, tremors, and increased metabolic rate. The thyroid gland may become so enlarged that it results in a neck protrusion (goiter).

7. Hypothyroidism—decreased secretion of thyroid hormone.

8. Hypoparathyroidism—deficiency of secretion of parathyroid hormone. Causes low blood calcium; severe neuromuscular irritability (tetany) may also occur.

9. Hypothyroidism—inadequate secretion of thyroid hormone. Symptoms of hypothyroidism include weight gain, slow metabolic rate, and decreased mental and physical activity.

10. Syndrome of Inappropriate Antidiuretic Hormone (SIADH)—excessive amounts of antidiuretic hormone (ADH) are secreted, resulting in water imbalance (water intoxication) due to fluid retention.

§ 3.22   Blood and Immune Systems Structure and Function

The blood is a type of connective tissue that has the following functions:

- Transportation of essential gases, nutrients, hormones, and chemicals to all body cells and carries waste products away from the cells.
- Regulation of chemical balance in the body, e.g. fluid and electrolytes and acid-base balance
- Protection of the body in the form of clotting mechanisms and defense against infection

Blood System

Blood consists of two components: plasma and cells. *Plasma* is the liquid in which solid components such as cells, platelets, and nutrients are suspended. Plasma is primarily water, but also contains proteins, electrolytes, gases nutrients and wastes. The blood proteins consist of albumin, globulin, and fibrinogen, all of which are essential to the blood's protective functions. The heart pumps blood throughout the body via the circulatory system. Cells are the solid components of the blood that are suspended in the plasma. They have a limited life span; therefore, new cells must be formed continuously throughout life. The process by which blood cells are formed is known as *hematopoiesis*. This process occurs primarily in the bone marrow. Several types of cells exist in the plasma, all of which have specific functions:

1. Erythrocyte or Red Blood Cell (RBC)—blood cells that contain hemoglobin, the compound that bonds with oxygen and carbon dioxide to serve as a transport mechanism. The majority of RBC's are produced in the bone marrow, although some originate in the spleen. The process of RBC production is known as *erythropoiesis*.
2. Leukocyte or White Blood Cell (WBC)—blood cells that protect the body from infection by ingesting and killing bacteria. There are two

types of leukocytes: *granulocytes (polymorphonuclear leukocytes or PMN's)* that include neutrophil, basophil, and eosinophil cells, and *agranulocytes* that include lymphocytes and monocytes. All types of leukocytes have specific roles in the function of the body's immune system. Their specific roles are discussed in more detail in the text below.

3.   Thrombocyte or Platelet—blood cells that are essential to blood clotting. The clotting process, called *homeostasis,* repairs breaks in blood vessels in order to minimize blood loss after injury. The hemostatic mechanism has three components:

Blood Vessels—constrict in response to injury to slow blood flow

Platelet Plug—cells adhere to damaged vessel's lining, sealing the surface

Blood Coagulation—series of interactions within the blood that result in formation of a fibrin clot.

Major Characteristics of Blood

Color. Arterial blood is bright red because of oxygen within cells; venous blood is dark red because of lower oxygen content.

Viscosity. Viscosity is measured by specific gravity, with normal being 1.048-1.066, three to four times greater than water.

pH. Blood is slightly alkaline, with a normal pH of 7.35–7.45. Neutral pH is 7.0.

Volume. The average adult body contains between four and five liters.

Composition. Plasma (liquid) makes up about 55 percent of the blood, and cells make up the other 45 percent.

Major Functions of the Blood

• Supply oxygen from lungs and nutrients from the GI tract to all body cells
• Remove wastes from tissues to kidneys, lungs, and skin
• Transport hormones
• Protect body from infection
• Control bleeding (through clotting mechanisms)
• Regulate body temperature by heat transfer.

§ 3.23   —Common Problems of the Blood System

Blood disorders are categorized by the components they affect:

- Erythrocytes (red blood cells)
- Leukocytes (white blood cells)
- Platelets
- Clotting mechanisms
- Production of blood cells (hematopoiesis).

1. Acidosis—acidic condition of the blood (normal pH of blood is neutral). Acidosis can occur through malfunction of the respiratory system or faulty body metabolism.

2. Alkalosis—alkaline condition of the blood (normal pH of blood is neutral). Like acidosis, alkalosis arises from respiratory or metabolic causes.

3. Anemia—inadequacy of Hgb and/or packed RBC's (Hct). Anemia is not a disease per se, but a symptom of other pathology. There are multiple causes of anemia, some of which are excessive blood loss, deficiencies and abnormalities of RBC production, and excessive destruction of RBCs.

4. Disseminated Intravascular Coagulation (DIC)—diffuse coagulation (blood clotting) within arterioles and capillaries throughout the body. DIC has many causes, including trauma, shock, and infection. It can be acute and catastrophic or subacute.

5. Hemophilia—hereditary blood disorder in which the clotting mechanism of the blood is deficient. This deficiency causes bleeding into tissues and joints.

6. Hemorrhage—excessive bleeding that results in acute blood loss. Caused by disruption in the integrity of large blood vessels, hemorrhage can lead to death if severe and left untreated.

7. Hyperglycemia—high blood sugar. This condition usually occurs in diabetes mellitus, either as a result of insufficient insulin or oral medication, or because of excessive food intake. Illness may also cause hyperglycemia. If hyperglycemia persists over time without treatment, toxins build up in the blood, causing ketoacidosis or diabetic coma. Symptoms of hyperglycemia are thirst, frequent urination, changes in vision, weight loss, and lethargy.

8. Hypoglycemia—low blood sugar. Hypoglycemia usually occurs with diabetes mellitus if the diabetic receives too much insulin or oral medication, eats too little, or exercises more than normal. Symptoms include headache, sweating, hunger, nervousness, and inappropriate affect (laughing, crying, anger). The onset of hypoglycemia may be rapid, and the immediate intake of high glucose food or drink is required to raise the blood sugar. Without immediate treatment, hypoglycemia may progress to coma and seizures.

9. Leukemia—group of malignancies that affect the blood and blood-forming tissues. There are different classifications of leukemia according to type of cell involved. Leukemia can be acute or chronic.

10. Neutropenia—decrease numbers of total white blood cells.

11. Polycythemia—abnormal increase in red blood cells. There are several different types of polycythemia; effects vary according to type.

12. Purpura—leaking of small amounts of blood into tissues or mucous membranes as a result of either blood vessel damage or platelet deficiency.

13. Septicemia—infection in the blood. Usually results from a primary infection in another part of the body, such as the urinary tract or lungs, that spreads throughout the body.

14. Sickle Cell Disease—group of inherited disorders characterized by an abnormal form of Hgb in the blood. There are several types of this disease and its effect vary greatly with type.

15. Thrombocytopenia—decrease in number of platelets, defined as $<150,000/mm^3$, this disorder can be inherited or acquired. If acquired, the cause can be decreased production or increased destruction of platelets.

The Immune System

The immune system is composed of an intricate network of specialized cells, tissues, and organs that protect the body from invasion of hostile microorganisms. The basis of immunity depends on the immune cells' ability to distinguish self from non-self. All cells contain markers on their surfaces, much like fingerprints; the immune system recognizes these but mounts defense mechanisms to destroy unrecognizable markers. It accomplishes this through several mechanisms. Principal components of the immune system are *leukocytes* and the *lymphoid system.*

Leukocytes

Leukocytes, normally present in circulating blood, increase greatly in numbers in the presence of infection. White cell production in the bone marrow is stimulated, and the volume of circulating cells increases. This condition is known as *leukocytosis.* In contrast, *leukopenia,* a decrease in the circulating WBCs, can occur in conditions marked by bone marrow suppression, such as certain types of leukemia, or from chemotherapeutic agents used to treat cancers. As stated previously, leukocytes are classified as granulocytes or agranulocytes. There are five classes of leukocytes:

1. Granulocytes, also known as polymorphonuclear leukocytes (PMN's)
   - Neutrophils—divided into two types, bands (immature forms) and segmented (mature forms). Their primary function is to ingest harmful microorganisms by a process known as *phagocytosis,* especially in the early stages of infection.
   - Eosinophils—assist in phagocytosis, but their primary role is in dampening the body's allergic reaction responses. During allergic reactions, the number of circulating eosinophils increases, a condition known as *eosinophilia.*
   - Basophils—play a role similar to that of eosinophils in mediating the body's response to allergic reactions.
2. Agranulocytes
   - Monocytes (macrophages)—circulate in the blood, but when they migrate to tissues, they mature into macrophages. *Macrophage* literally means "big eater." Through phagocytosis, macrophages are responsible for removing aged or damaged cells and other cellular debris. Macrophages also participate in defense against tumor cell growth and secrete substances that assist in mounting the body's inflammatory response.
   - Lymphocytes—cells that all originate in the bone marrow and subsequently differentiate into T cells or B cells. T cells undergo differentiation in the thymus gland, where they learn to recognize self from non-self—that is, the cells become able to recognize foreign material such as toxins, bacteria, and cells from transplanted organs. B cells are thought to mature in the bone marrow itself. When stimulated, B cells secrete molecules called *antibodies* into the circulating blood. Both T and B cells continually recirculate between blood, lymph, and lymph nodes.

Lymphoid System

Clear fluid known as *lymph* circulates within a network of vessels similar to blood vessels, and also acts as a drainage system for excess tissue and body fluid. Immune substances are also present in the lymph fluid and are thus able to reach all cells and tissue through circulation. The *bone marrow* and the *thymus* are the primary organs of the lymphoid system.

1. Bone Marrow—present inside long bones, marrow is a major site for production and maturation of immune cells.
2. Thymus—also part of the endocrine system, this gland is the site where T cells (lymphocytes) multiply and become capable of producing an immune response. As noted above, differentiation of lymphocytes into T and B cells occurs in the thymus. T cells are further differentiated into T helper (CD4) cells and T suppressor (CD8) cells. These two types of T cells regulate the immune response to antigens.

Secondary Organs

1. Spleen—organ located in the abdominal cavity. The spleen produces some RBC's, filters old and defective RBC's and removes them from circulation, supports the immune function, and provides storage for platelets until needed.
2. Tonsils and Adenoids—porous clumps of tissue located in the throat and nasal cavity, respectively. The main function of the tonsils and adenoids is to filter harmful bacteria and viruses from the respiratory tract.
3. Lymph Nodes—clumps of tissue located throughout the body. They are most plentiful in the axilla (armpit) and groin as well as in the neck and chest.
4. Clumps of Lymphoid Tissue—located in a organs throughout the body, e.g. gut, genital, bronchial, and skin lymph nodes.

The Immune Response

The immune response involves recognition of, and reaction to, foreign substances that enter the body. These substances, known as *antigens,* are the targets of the immune response. Immunity can be classified as *innate* or *acquired.* Innate immunity exists in an individual without prior contact with an antigen. In contrast, acquired immunity involves prior contact with an antigen. There are two types of acquired immunity:

- Active acquired immunity—results from the invasion of the body by a foreign substance, with subsequent development of antibodies to that substance. This type of immunity may occur naturally, following exposure to the antigen, or artificially through immunization. Immunity is not immediate as the body takes time to develop antibodies, however, once developed, this type of immunity is long lasting.
- Passive acquired immunity—results when antibodies are received by an individual rather than making them. This type of immunity occurs through transfer of antibodies across the placenta from mother to fetus, or through inoculation. This type of immunity is immediate but short-lived.

T cells regulate the immune response to antigens. Helper and suppressor cells occur as a "normal ratio" in a functioning system. In autoimmune diseases, T suppressor cells decrease in proportion to T helper cells, resulting in an overaggressive immune response. When this occurs, the body is unable to distinguish self from non-self and begins attacking normal cells. Resulting diseases can be associated with

- Altered immune response—hypersensitivity reactions, local or systemic
- Allergic disorders—chemical or environmental in origin
- Autoimmune disease—systemic or organ-specific

§ 3.24   —Common Diseases of the Immune System

1. AIDS/HIV Disease—a severe immune system deficiency in previously healthy individuals. Caused by the human immunodeficiency virus that attacks T helper (CD4 cells). Infection may be latent for sometime before illness occurs. AIDS is the last stage in the continuum of HIV infection.

2. Connective Tissue Disorders (collagen diseases)—collective term for several diseases broadly classified as autoimmune disorders. Common examples of these diseases include rheumatoid arthritis, systemic lupus erythematosis, polyarteritis, scleroderma, polymyositis, and

dermatomyositis. There is no cure for collagen diseases, only symptomatic treatment.

3. Hypersensitivity Disorders—also known as allergic responses, these disorders are characterized by an increase in the body's immune response to the presence of an antigen (allergen). Types of hypersensitivity disorders are

    -   Immediate (anaphylactic)—most serious. Anaphylactic reactions can progress rapidly and, if not promptly treated, progress to circulatory collapse and death.

    -   Cytolytic/cytotoxic (blood transfusion reactions)—can occur when donor blood is administered, even with proper typing and crossmatching. Reactions range from mild to severe, the latter of which can result in permanent renal damage, circulatory shock, and death.

    -   Immune complex—causes tissue changes by formation of antigen-antibody complexes in tissues. Inflammation results and leads to acute or chronic disease in specific organ systems. Examples of these diseases include rheumatoid arthritis and systemic lupus erythematosis (SLE).

    -   Cell mediated delayed—induced by chronic infection such as tuberculosis or by contact sensitivities (contact dermatitis). No reaction may occur on first exposure; only with subsequent exposures are hypersensitivities (allergic reactions) manifested.

4. Infectious Mononucleosis—infection of the lymph glands; caused by the Epstein-Barr virus.

5. Lymphadenopathy—abnormal enlargement of the lymph glands; usually indicative of infection or tumor.

6. Lymphedema—swelling due to impaired drainage of lymph fluid. It is classified as primary (by age of onset) or secondary (due to damage or obstruction to lymph system). Common causes are trauma and tumors; it may also result following surgical removal of lymph nodes.

7. Lymphoma—cancer of the lymphatic system; classified as Hodgkin's or non-Hodgkin's lymphomas.

8. Organ Transplant Rejection—part of body's normal response to foreign tissue, but not a desired response after organ transplant. It is treated with the administration of drugs designed to suppress the normal immune response.

9. Splenomegaly—enlargement of the spleen; may be caused by leukemias and other blood disorders.

10. Tonsillitis—infection of the tonsils; usually caused by bacteria or viruses.

§ 3.25   Integumentary System Structure and Function

The integumentary system protects the body and its underlying tissues by serving as a barrier to harmful agents in the external environment. Additionally, it contains organs of sensation (pain, temperature, touch) and regulates evaporation/retention of heat. The integumentary system is composed of two main parts: the skin and skin appendages. The main structures of the integumentary system are as follows:

1. Skin—protects the body from invasion by infectious agents and prevents excessive water loss. Skin cells are replaced with new cells approximately every 30 days. It is composed of the following layers:
    - Epidermis—outer layer of skin composed of two parts: the outer portion that consists of dead cells serving as the protective barrier and a deeper, living portion that folds into the dermis.
    - Dermis—layer of connective tissue located beneath the epidermis, the dermis contains blood vessels, hair follicles, and sweat glands. It also produces the substance collagen that is responsible for the mechanical strength of the skin and plays an important role in wound healing.
    - Subcutaneous Tissue—located beneath the dermis. The subcutaneous tissue although not part of the skin per se, attaches the skin to underlying tissues such as muscle or bone. It contains adipose (fatty tissue) that provides insulation for the body. The amount of subcutaneous tissue varies from individual to individual.

2. Skin appendages include:
    - Hair—protects delicate body structures such as the head and the genital organs.
    - Sebaceous Glands—located in the dermis. The sebaceous glands produce a substance called sebum that helps protect the body from dehydration.
    - Sweat Glands—found in the epidermis, sweat glands assist with regulation of body temperature by excreting sweat in response to

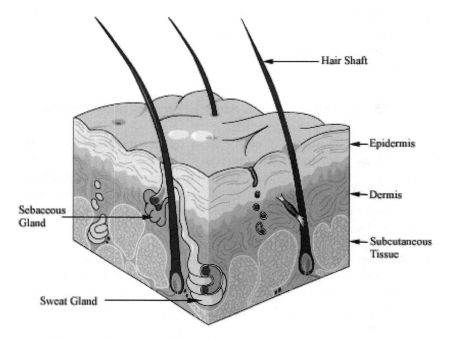

Figure 3–12. Skin layers and appendages.

excessive heat. There are two types of sweat glands: *apocrine glands* located mainly in axillae and anogenital area and *eccrine glands* widely distributed throughout the body.

- Nails—outgrowths of the epidermis. The nails protect the tips of the toes and fingers.

- Sensory Receptors—located in the epidermis and dermis, this network of bodywide sensors informs the central nervous system of events taking place in the external environment. Sensory receptors include those for pressure, pain, touch, heat, and cold.

See **Figure 3–12.**

§ 3.26 —Common Problems of the Integumentary System

1. Acne Vulgaris—common self-limiting condition initiated by androgenic hormones that activate sebaceous glands, causing collection of debris in skin pores.

2. Burns—destruction of one or more layers of skin through exposure to excessive heat, caustic chemicals, or electric shock. Burns are classified according to the depth of skin injury: first-degree burns are the least serious, third-degree burns are the most serious. Additionally, they are classified by causation:

   • Chemical—tissue injury resulting from necrotizing substances. Chemical burns from acids are most common, however alkali burns occur as well.

   • Thermal—tissue injury caused by flames, flash, scald, or contact with hot objects

   • Electrical—tissue necrosis secondary to heat generated for an electrical current. The severity of an electrical burn depends on several factors: voltage, pathway of the current, and the length of time exposed to current flow.

3. Cellulitis—inflammation of the epidermis and subcutaneous tissue, frequently of bacterial origin.

4. Contusions—bruising anywhere in the body, externally or internally. Contusions are caused by the disruption in the integrity of the blood vessels and subsequent bleeding into the surrounding tissues.

5. Decubitus (bedsore or pressure ulcer)—pressure area on the skin resulting from compromised circulation. Decubiti usually develop when there is prolonged pressure on a localized body area, most commonly over bony prominences such as heels, ankles, elbows, and sacral areas. Decubitus ulcers are classified into stages, based on their severity:

   • Stage I—skin is intact, however area may be reddened, and/or tissue consistency altered.

   • Stage II—partial thickness skin involvement of the epidermis and/or epidermis. May appear as a blister or abrasion.

   • Stage III—full thickness skin involvement involving the subcutaneous tissue that may extend down to fascia.

   • Stage IV—full thickness skin involvement with extensive destruction to muscle, bone, or other supporting structures.

6. Dermatitis—irritation or inflammation of the epidermis. Dermatitis can be caused by irritation from chemicals, bites from insects or animals, and allergies.

7. Eczema—not a specific disease, used interchangeably with dermatitis.

8. Esysipelas—acute inflammation of skin, subcutaneous tissue and lymphatics. Usual causative agents are streptococcus or staphylococcus bacteria.

9. Gangrene—tissue death due to compromised blood supply. Gangrene can be caused by arteriosclerosis, trauma, or prolonged pressure on a body area.

10. Herpes simplex—viral infection of the skin or mucous membranes. After initial infection, the virus becomes dormant, living in the body nerve roots. The virus reactivates when exposed to "triggers", e.g. stress, sunlight. The virus has two subtypes that typically infect specific regions of the body, although both types can cause infection in either location. The two virus types are:
    • Herpes Simplex I virus—commonly causes infection on the lips or face. There lesions are commonly referred to as fever blisters or cold sores.
    • Herpes Simplex II virus—commonly causes infection in the perianal and rectal regions.

11. Herpes Zoster (shingles)—infection caused by chickenpox virus. In herpes zoster, clusters of vesicles erupt along cranial or spinal nerve dermatomes.

12. Kaposi's Sarcoma—vascular malignancy that presents as blue or purple macules on the skin. Lesions can also occur in mucous membranes and organs in other parts of the body. The condition severity can range from minor to fulminant with aggressive spread, and is often seen in persons with HIV disease or other immunosuppressed conditions.

13. Psoriasis—chronic, recurrent inflammatory disorder manifested by dry, scaly patches of various sizes. Lesions commonly occur on scalp, elbows, and knees.

14. Rosacea—chronic inflammatory disorder characterized by erythema and rash over face and nose.

15. Skin Cancers—caused by uncontrolled growth of abnormal cells in a layer of skin. The most common cause of these types of cancers is exposure to ultraviolet radiation from the sun. The effects of years of sun exposure are cumulative and damaging and are a primary cause of precancerous and cancerous lesions. Skin cancers are broadly divided into melanoma and non-melanoma lesions:
    • Malignant melanoma—tumors arising in the cells producing the substance melanin. Melanomas have the ability to spread to any

organ in the body and are the most deadly form of skin cancer. Risk factors include UV radiation, genetic, hormonal, and immunologic factors.

- Non-melanoma cancers—all skin cancers not classified as melanomas. Two of the most common types include:
  —Basal cell—locally invasive tumors arising from the epithelial cells in the epidermal basal cells. This type of skin cancer is the most commonly occurring and the least deadly.
  —Squamous cell—frequently occur on sun exposed skin. Pipe, cigar and cigarette smoking are also causes, thus tumors frequently occur on the face and lips. Squamous cell tumors are very aggressive and have the ability to metastasize.

16. Warts—flesh-colored lumps involving the epidermis. Warts are caused by certain strains of the human papillovirus (HPV).

§ 3.27   Reproductive System Structure and Function

The male and female reproductive systems function in the procreation of the species and are responsible for the development of male and female sex characteristics. The primary reproductive organs are referred to as gonads, and are the ovaries in the female and the testes in the male. Their primary function is the production of ova and sperm, respectively. Secondary (accessory) organs are responsible for the transport and nourishment of the ova and sperm and, for the female secondary organs, the preservation and protection of the fertilized egg.

§ 3.28   —Male Reproductive System Structure and Function

The male reproductive system has three specific functions:

- The production and transportation of sperm
- The deposit of sperm into the female
- The secretion of male hormones.

Male Reproductive System

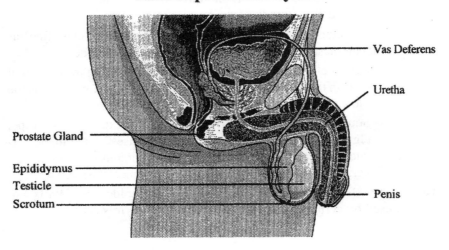

Vas Deferens

Uretha

Prostate Gland

Epididymus

Testicle

Scrotum

Penis

Female Reproductive System

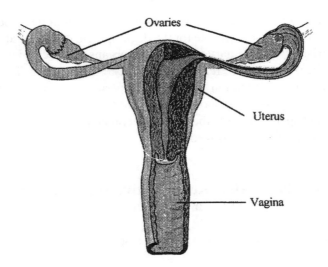

Ovaries

Uterus

Vagina

Figure 3–13. Male and female reproductive systems.

As noted above, the primary male reproductive organs are the testes. They are contained in the *scrotum,* a sac-like structure. Secondary organs of the male reproductive system are as follows:

1. Epididymis—stores sperm cells and transports them into the vas deferens as they mature.

2. Vas Deferens (ductus deferens)—duct system that carries the sperm from the epididymis toward the urethra.

3. Ejaculatory duct—carries sperm from the vas into the urethra.

4. Urethra—duct that carries the semen to the outside of the body. Urine is excreted through the urethra as well.

5. Penis—male organ of copulation. The urethra runs through the penis. When sexually stimulated, tissue in the penis fills with blood and it becomes erect. Semen is deposited in the urethra and expelled, during ejaculation, into the female's vagina.

6. Male Sex Glands—produce and secrete seminal fluid or semen, which surrounds the sperm and forms ejaculate. The glands include the prostate gland, Cowper glands, and the seminal vesicles.

Refer to **Figure 3–13.**

§ 3.29   —Common Diseases of the Male Reproductive Tract

1. Benign Prostatic Hypertrophy—enlargement of the prostate gland. This condition usually occurs in older men and often causes difficulty in urination. The enlarged gland is often reduced surgically by transurethral resection procedure (TURP).

2. Cryptorchidism (undescended testicles)—a congenital condition that may affect one or both testicles. Treatment is by surgical repair before puberty.

3. Epididymitis—inflammation of the epididymis. Epididymitis causes scrotal pain, usually accompanied by fever and testicular swelling. Causes include sexually transmitted diseases, trauma, and has also been associated with prostatitis.

4. Hematocele—collection of blood within the testicle.

5.   Hydrocele—painless collection of clear fluid along the spermatic cord.

6.   Hypospadias—congenital condition in which the urethral meatus opens on the underneath (ventral) side of the penis. This condition is corrected by surgical repair.

7.   Impotence—inability to obtain or maintain an erection. Impotence may have physical or psychological causes.

8.   Infertility—in the male, may result from a defect in sperm production (quantity or quality) that results in the inability to fertilize the female's egg. Infertility is a disorder of a couple, not of one individual. Both male and female need to be evaluated for possible causes of infertility. An individual may elect to become infertile. In the male, infertility is accomplished by vasectomy, an elective surgical procedure that disrupts the passage of sperm along the vas differens, thus resulting in inability to fertilize the female egg.

9.   Orchitis—acute inflammation of the testicles often caused by trauma or infection, e.g. mumps.

10.   Prostate Cancer—malignant tumor of the prostate. Early detection and treatment are critical to controlling tumor growth and preventing spread.

11.   Prostatitis—inflammation of the prostate gland.

12.   Torsion of the Testicle—rotation or twisting of the testicle in the scrotal sac. It is characterized by excruciating pain and, if left untreated, may cause permanent damage to the testicle. Treatment is by surgical repair.

13.   Varicocele (varicose veins)—dilation of the network of veins that drain blood from the testes.

§ 3.30 —Female Reproductive System and Function

The primary organs of the female reproductive tract are the ovaries. The function of the ovaries include:

- The production of eggs
- The secretion of hormones
- The production of the fetus and facilitation of its development.

Secondary organs include the following:

1. Fallopian Tubes—tubes extending from the uterus to the ovaries. The eggs travel into the uterus via the fallopian tubes, the usual site of fertilization.

2. Uterus—muscular, hollow organ located between the bladder and the rectum in the pelvic cavity. It nourishes and protects the fertilized egg during development. The uterus distends as the fetus grows and contracts to expel the child during childbirth. The cervix is the opening of the uterus leading to the vagina. The uterus is divided into three distinct areas:
    • Fundus (dome)—the area between insertion of two fallopian tubes
    • Corpus—body
    • Cervix (neck)—cervix opens into vagina via cervical os (mouth).

3. Vagina—tubular structure leading from the uterus to the outside of the body. The vagina is the structure that receives male sperm during sexual intercourse. It is also the passageway for childbirth.

4. Vulva—external organ covering the opening of the vagina.

5. Mons Pubis—rounded pad of flesh that lies over symphysis pubis bone of the skeleton. It is covered with hair after puberty.

6. Labia Majora—two folds of tissue making up part of the perineum, within which lie the openings of the urethra and vagina.

7. Labia Minora—smaller folds of tissue that lie just within the labia minora.

8. Clitoris—small erectile structure located at the anterior portion of the labia minora. The clitoris is the female organ of sexual arousal.

9. Breasts—develop during puberty in response to hormones. Cyclic hormonal changes affect the breast tissue to prepare it for lactation when fertilization and pregnancy occur.

Refer to **Figure 3–13.**

§ 3.31   —The Menstrual Cycle and Pregnancy

The Menstrual Cycle

The production of eggs and secretion of hormones by the ovaries are accomplished during the monthly menstrual cycle and are controlled by the hormonal activity of several glands. The cycle consists of three phases:

1st phase—proliferative phase during which ovulation occurs.

2nd phase—secretory phase during which hormones are secreted that assist in development of the corpus luteum from the ovum.

3rd phase—menstrual phase which occurs if no fertilization of the ovum occurs, resulting in menstruation.

Pregnancy

If fhe female ovum or egg is fertilized by the male sperm, it implants itself into the lining of the uterus. There it begins to grow into an embryo. When organs are recognizable, usually about the third month, the embryo is termed a fetus. The fetus is nourished through the placenta, a flat, highly vascular structure attached to the lining of the uterus. The umbilical cord connects the placenta to the child at the navel. Nourishment and oxygen travel from mother to child through the cord; wastes are carried for excretion from child to mother through the cord as well. The fluid-filled amniotic sac or membrane (bag of waters) surrounds the fetus and protects the developing child. During the labor process these membranes rupture prior to the delivery of the child.

When the child is mature, the labor process begins. The uterus contracts and eventually expels the child from the uterus through the vagina to the outside of the body. The placenta is then delivered. The umbilical cord is cut and the child's body systems begin functioning independently.

§ 3.32 —Common Problems of the Female Reproductive Tract

1. Abortion—disruption of pregnancy before the fetus is fully developed. Abortion may be spontaneous or induced by artificial means. Spontaneous abortion is also frequently referred to as miscarriage.

2. Amenorrhea—absence of menses, which can be primary or secondary. Primary causes are often chromosomal abnormalities. Other causes can be pregnancy, excessive exercise, hormonal causes, and pharmacologic causes.

3. Breast Cancer—one of the most common malignancies seen in women. There are numerous types of breast cancer, based on cell characteristics and growth patterns.

4. Cervical Cancer—malignancy of the neck (cervix) of the uterus. Although the exact cause is unknown, there is a strong relationship between cervical cancer and the presence of chronic cervical irritation and/or genital warts, caused by specific types of human papillovirus (HPV). Smoking has also been implicated in its development. Virtually all cervical cancer can be cured through early detection by Pap smear and prompt treatment.

5. Cystocele—protrusion of a portion of the uterus into the urethra.

6. Ectopic Pregnancy—implantation of the fertilized egg outside the uterus. The most common site of an ectopic pregnancy is the fallopian tube.

7. Endometrial (Uterine) Cancer—common malignancy of the female reproductive tract. Although its etiology is known to be related to the hormone estrogen, the exact mechanism of malignancy changes in the uterine lining is unknown.

8. Endometriosis—endometrial tissue is located outside the uterus, usually in the pelvic cavity. Severe endometriosis may cause pain on menstruation and infertility.

9. Mastitis—inflammation of the breast tissue, frequently occurring in lactating women.

10. Infertility—in the female, may result from problems with ovulation or tubal obstruction of dysfunction. Fertility is a disorder of a couple, not of one individual. Both male and female need to be evaluated for possible causes of infertility. An individual may elect to become infertile. In the female, infertility is accomplished by tubal ligation, an elective surgical procedure that disrupts the passage of eggs into the fallopian tubes.

11. Ovarian Cancer—leading cause of death from reproductive malignancies. The exact cause is unknown, and symptoms do not occur until the tumor is well established. The mortality rate is high.

12. Ovarian Cyst—fluid-filled sac attached to the ovary. Cysts may be single or multiple and may cause menstrual pain or pain with ovulation. Multiple ovarian cysts are seen in *polycystic ovary disease.*

13. Pelvic Inflammatory Disease (PID)—pelvic infection involving the upper reproductive organs. It is usually caused by sexually transmitted diseases.

14. **Premenstrual Syndrome (PMS)**—a condition still not well understood that manifests itself through a variety of emotional and physical symptoms. Symptoms typically occur within the last few premenstrual days. Common symptoms include altered emotional states, appetite and behavioral changes, fluid retention, and sleep disorders.

15. **Rectocele**—protrusion of a portion of the uterus into the rectum.

16. **Sexually Transmitted Diseases (STDs)**—affect both male and female and arise from a variety of bacterial and viral causes. Some common diseases are
    - Gonorrhea
    - Syphilis
    - Chlamydia
    - Genital herpes
    - AIDS
    - Genital warts
    - Hepatitis B.

17. **Uterine Fibroids**—noncancerous tumors of the uterus. Fibroids can vary in size from very small to quite large. They may cause pain and irregular vaginal bleeding.

18. **Uterine Prolapse**—descent of the uterus into the vaginal canal. It commonly follows multiple childbirth, aging, and lax perineal musculature.

19. **Vaginitis**—condition periodically experienced by most women. It has several causes, including changes in normal bacterial flora, changes in vaginal pH, and mechanical irritation.

Problems Associated with Pregnancy

1. **Abruptio Placenta**—tearing away of the placenta from the uterine wall before the baby is being delivered. Abruptio may result in fetal oxygen deprivation.

2. **Ectopic Pregnancy**—implantation of the fertilized egg outside the uterus. The most common site of an ectopic pregnancy is the fallopian tube.

3. **Placenta Previa**—positioning of the placenta low in the uterus, close to the cervix. Placenta previa may interfere with vaginal delivery.

4. **Toxemia**—condition that may occur in pregnancy, manifested by maternal elevation of blood pressure and fluid retention. If left

untreated, toxemia can lead to kidney failure, seizures, and maternal death.

§ 3.33   —Sensory Organs

In addition to the body systems outlined in the previous material, the body also has sensory organs that allow us to interpret the external environment through sight, sound, smell, taste, and touch. Two of the main sensory organs are the eye and the ear.

§ 3.34   —The Eye: Structure and Function

The eye is the organ of sight. The purpose of the (two) eyes is to connect the human body to the environment. This is done in collaboration with the other sensory organs and the nervous system. The eyes do not actually see, but are the external portion of the visual pathway to the brain.

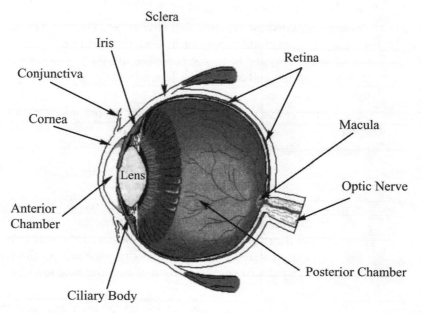

Figure 3–14. The eye.
© *Life*ART, Lippincott Williams & Wilkins, 2002.

Eye Structure

The eyes are composed of groups of structures that include the eyeballs, muscles, nerves, fat, and bones.

1. External eye structures (Ocular adnexa)—function to protect the eyeballs and provide optical clarity. They are composed of:
    *   Ocular muscles—rotate eye in circular movements to allow vision at all angles.
    *   Eyelids—elastic folds of skin that close to protect the eye and distribute film of tears over the eye surface to prevent drying of the eyeball.
    *   Lacrimal apparatus—composed of lacrimal glands and ducts. The glands generate tears, and the ducts direct the flow of tears that are generated.

2. Internal eye—converts light rays and images into neural (nerve) messages that are sent to the brain.
    *   Conjunctiva—transparent layer of mucous membrane that links eyelids and covers eyeballs.
    *   Cornea—transparent structure that covers eye. The cornea is very delicate, has no blood supply of its own (it derives oxygen from the environment) and is very susceptible to injury. The cornea is convex in shape and acts on the lens to bend and direct rays of light to the retina.
    *   Sclera—protective coating of the eye that is continuous with the cornea.
    *   Uveal tract—composed of several structures:
        —Ciliary body—in direct continuity with the iris. It secretes the aqueous humor and supports the lens.
        —Aqueous humor—clear fluid between the iris and the cornea that is secreted by the ciliary body. The aqueous humor circulates from the posterior chamber into the anterior chamber and is eventually filtered into the venous drainage system through Schlemm's canal, a vascular structure near the anterior edge of the sclera.
        —Choroid—posterior segment of the uveal tract between the retina and the sclera.

- Angle structures—angle that is formed where iris and cornea meet. These structures filter the aqueous humor and directs it into the venous drainage system.

- Lens—biconcave, avascular, transparent structure behind the iris. The sole purpose of the lens is to focus light on the retina. The elasticity of the lens allows changes that enable focus on near or far objects.

- Vitreous humor—clear jelly-like structure that occupies space of the vitreous chamber, the largest cavity of the eye. The vitreous humor helps maintain the shape of the eyeball.

- Retina—semi-transparent layer of nerve tissue that forms the innermost lining of the eye. The retina contains all the sensory receptors for light photoreceptors. There are two types of photo-receptors, rods and cones. Rods function best in dim light and damage to them may result in night blindness. Cones are responsible for perception of fine details and color vision. The retina covers most of the eye's interior surface with the exception of two spots:

  —Macula—an area in the center of the retina that appears as a yellowish spot

  —Fovea—depressed area in the center of the macula. Only cones are present in the fovea; it is the point of finest vision.

- Optic nerve—transmits visual impulses from the retina to the brain. The head of this nerve is the optic disk. The optic disk contains no sensory receptors and represents a blind spot in the eye. Half of the visual field of each eye is projected to the other side of the brain, i.e., the right visual field is projected to the left occipital lobe of the brain and vice versa.

Refer to **Figure 3–14.**

Eye Function

The eye forms images that are analyzed by the retina. Receptors in the retina convert the images into neural (nerve) signals that are transmitted to visual centers in the brain. The two eyes collaborate to project at the same point, fuse images, and transmit a single mental image to the brain. This process is referred to as binocular vision.

§ 3.35   —Diseases of the Eye

1. Astigmatism—rays of light are not bent equally in all directions by the cornea. In astigmatism, the cornea is not spherical.

2. Blepharitis—chronic, bilateral inflammation of the eyelid margins.

3. Cataract—thickness and density of lens increases, lens becomes yellow and opaque, affecting vision clarity. Treatment of cataracts is by surgical removal.

4. Chalazion—sterile inflammation of the eyelid gland. There is swelling without redness. If the chalazion is large enough to disrupt vision it may be surgically excised.

5. Conjunctivitis—inflammation of the conjunctiva secondary to bacterial or viral infection, allergy, or irritants, or as a result of systemic or other ocular disease.

6. Corneal abrasion—scratch or defect in the outer layer (epithelium) of the cornea. Abrasions may be caused by foreign bodies or injury.

7. Corneal dystrophies—group of conditions that affect the cornea. These conditions are relatively rare, usually hereditary and may progress to the need for corneal transplant.

8. Diabetic retinopathy—microscopic damage to retinal vessels leads to their occlusion. The occluded vessels cannot supply the retina with blood, which results in death of the retinal tissue and blindness. This stimulates growth of new vessels to supply areas that do not have adequate blood supply. These new vessels are fragile and prone to bleeding into the retinal tissue. Laser therapy is directed to the new vessels to stop growth and thus prevent hemorrhage.

9. Foreign bodies—usually as a result of trauma or injury. Effects from foreign bodies may range from minor to major depending on the type, size, and depth of foreign body penetration.

10. Glaucoma—increase in pressure within the eye (intra-ocular pressure). There several types of glaucoma:

    • Primary open angle—insidious in onset and slow to progress. Symptoms appear late in the disease when vision is impaired by damage to the optic nerve.

    • Angle closure—attacks occur suddenly as a result of anterior angle blockage by the base of the iris. This type of glaucoma requires surgical intervention.

- Low tension—resembles primary open angle glaucoma, however develops in the presence of normal intra-ocular pressures.

- Secondary—occurs as a result of increased intra-ocular pressure secondary to trauma or as a postoperative complication.

- Glaucoma treatment is dependent on the type of glaucoma and may be medical or surgical in nature.

11. Hordeolum (sty)—infection of the eyelid gland, characterized by localized redness and swelling. May resolve spontaneously or need to be surgically incised.

12. Macular degeneration—degenerative process that affects the macula and surrounding tissues. The tissue degeneration results in central vision defects. Macular degeneration may be classified as wet or dry. Wet degeneration can be treated with laser therapy to arrest associated bleeding.

13. Photophobia—an abnormal (painful) sensitivity to light. Photophobia is commonly associated with some eye diseases such as corneal abrasions, acute keratitis, and uveitis.

14. Refractive disorders—light rays are not focused appropriately on the retina. Refractive disorders are broken into three types:

- Myopia or nearsightedness—light rays are focused in front of the retina. In many cases, this is caused by a longer than normal eyeball.

- Hyperopia or farsightedness—light rays are focused in back of the retina. In many cases, this is caused by a shorter than normal eyeball.

- Astigmatism—see **1.**, above.

15. Retinal detachment—tear in retina which allows seepage of vitreous fluid through it. This leads to accumulation of liquid between the retina and the retinal pigment epithelium. This process separates the retina from its blood supply and, if left untreated, can lead to blindness. Retinal detachments are surgically repaired. The goals of surgery are twofold: to place the retina back in contact with the choroids (scleral bucking) and to seal the accompanying holes and breaks (cryopexy or laser photocoagulation).

16. Retinitis pigmentosa—hereditary, degenerative disease of the retina eventually causing loss of vision.

17. Strabismus—abnormal deviation of one eye in relation to other. Strabismus may be convergent (cross-eyed) in which one eye is directed

too far inward, or divergent, in which one eye is directed too for outward.

18. Uveitis—inflammation of uveal tract that can affect one or more of the following structures: iris, ciliary body, or choroid. Commonly arises from hypersensitivity reactions.

§ 3.36 —Evaluation of Eye Function

Eye function is evaluated as a routine part of the history and physical (see **§ 4.10**). Commonly seen in history and physicals is the notation "eyes—PERRLA". This acronym stands for "*p*upils *e*qual, *r*ound, and *r*eactive to *l*ight and *a*ccommodation".

Additional eye function tests are commonly used to assess eye function; some of the most common are:

1. Pupil response—both pupils should be equal and react to light, that is, constrict when light is shone into the pupil and dilate when it is removed. Normal pupil size is between 2 and 6 mm. pupil response to light may be described as brisk or sluggish.

2. Pupil accommodation—ability to adjust focus from near to far. Determined by placing a finger 12–18 inches from the nose and slowly moving toward subject. The eye should follow the finger.

3. Corneal reflex—eye will blink when cornea is touched. This test assesses nerve function of the fifth cranial (trigeminal) nerve.

4. Blink reflex—normally the eye blinks 15–20 times per minute.

5. Ocular motility—evaluates alignment of eyes and movements independently and together. Motility can be impaired by strabismus; neurological conditions, e.g., cranial nerve paralysis; or weakness of the extra-ocular muscles. Three different types of motility tests can be done:

    •   Hirschberg's test—determines presence or absence of strabismus.

    •   Cover, uncover test—determines presence or absence of ocular muscle problems.

    •   Six cardinal positions of gaze—determines ability of eye to look in six directions: right, left, up and right, up and left, down and right, down and left. Muscle weakness will prevent the eye from turning to a particular position.

6.   Visual acuity—assesses macular function using the Snellen eye chart at a distance of 20 feet. Findings are measured relative to how far the average person can see at 20 feet. For example, a reading of 20/40 would indicate that individual can see at 20 feet what the average person can see at 40 feet.

7.   Visual fields—assesses central fields of vision and peripheral vision. Defects can occur in glaucoma, retinal detachment, retinitis pigmentosa, and central nervous system disorders such as brain lesions or strokes.

8.   Direct ophthalmoscopy—done using hand-held ophthalmoscope. Provides a magnified image of the interior portion of the eyeball. The visibility of the eye structures can be enhanced using drops to dilate the pupil and a darkened room.

9.   Indirect ophthalmoscopy—done using a head-mounted light that enables examiner to view a larger area of the retina.

10.   Tonometry—measures intra-ocular pressure used to detect increase in pressures as seen in glaucoma.

11.   Slit lamp evaluation—provides magnified view of external eye structures such as cornea, anterior chamber, iris. A yellow dye (Fluroscein) is applied from a paper strip and is used to detect defects in the cornea.

12.   Refraction—used to quantify optical errors and determine correction needed with glasses or contact lenses. It distinguishes between refractive errors such as myopia, hyperopia, or astigmatism and abnormalities of the visual system itself.

§ 3.37   —The Ear: Structure and Function

The ear is the sensory organ for both hearing and balance. It is divided into three sections: the outer, middle, and inner ear. Sound is transmitted from the external ear through the middle ear (which amplifies the sound) to the inner ear. The inner ear then transforms the sound energy into neural (nervous system) elements that are carried to the brain. Balance organs in the inner ear send impulses to the brain that enables the body to maintain balance.

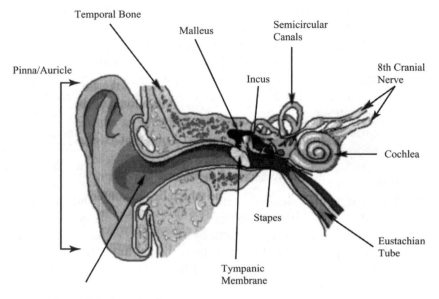

Figure 3–15. The ear.
© *Life*ART, Lippincott Williams & Wilkins, 2002.

Ear Structure

The ear structure is divided into distinct sections:

- External ear has the following components:

    —Pinna/auricle—the most visible part of the ear. The pinna is composed mostly of cartilage and serves to protect the more delicate internal ear structures as well as to amplify sound. The concha is the deepest part of the pinna.

    —External auditory canal (ear canal)—extends from the concha to the tympanic membrane. Its funnel shape collects and directs sound waves to the eardrum.

    —Tympanic membrane—thin, translucent membrane that covers the end of the auditory canal and separates the canal from the middle ear. It conducts sound vibrations from the external ear to the ossicles (bones) in the middle ear.

- Middle ear—contains the three smallest bones in the body, the ossicles. Together the ossicles transmit sound vibrations mechanically. Individually, the ossicles are named are follows:

  —Malleolus (hammer)—the outermost bone that is attached to the tympanic membrane.

  —Incus (anvil)—middle bone of the three.

  —Stapes (stirrup)—innermost bone which lies in contact with the oval window of the inner ear.

- The windows:

  —Round window—opening into the middle ear through which sound vibrations exit the middle ear.

  —Oval window—opens into the inner ear. Sound vibrations enter the inner ear through the oval window. The *footplate* of the stapes bone covers the oval window.

- Eustachian tube—narrow channel connecting the middle ear to the nasopharynx. Its function is to provide air passage from the nasopharynx to the middle ear to equalize pressure from both sides of the eardrum.

- Mastoid—section of the temporal bone of the skull composed of interconnected air-filled cavities and air cells that help middle ears adjust to changes in pressure. The mastoid also helps lighten the skull.

- Inner ear (labyrinth)—located deep within a section of the temporal bone, the inner ear contains the sensory organs for hearing and balance as well as the eighth cranial nerve. The inner ear is composed of two main structures: the bony labyrinth and the membranous labyrinth. The bony labyrinth surrounds and protects the membranous labyrinth. The space between the two structures contains *perilymph fluid*. Main structures of the membranous labyrinth are as follows:

  —Utricle and saccule—position the head as it relates to the pull of gravity.

  —Semicircular canals—sense rotational movements, such as movements or changes in position.

  —Cochlea—a spiral shaped cavity within the inner ear in which a membraneous tube, the cochlear duct is suspended. The cochlear duct is filled with endolymph fluid that transmits impulses responsible for balance to the vestibular portion of the acoustic nerve.

- The organ of Corti—located at the end of the membraneous labyrinth, the organ of Corti is the end organ for hearing. It transforms mechanical sound into different frequencies. Refer to **Figure 3–15.**

Ear Function

Sound vibrations pass through the external ear into the middle ear. From the stapes footplate, they pass through the oval window and move the perilymph. Vibrations of the perilymph are then transmitted through the vestibular membrane to the endolymph that fills the cochlear duct to the organ of Corti. The organ of Corti then transforms the mechanical sound into neural activity and separates sound into different frequencies. Electrochemical impulses then travel from the organ of Corti to the temporal cortex of the brain via the cochlear portion of the eighth cranial (acoustic) nerve. (See § **3.15** for additional information on cranial nerves.) The impulses are decoded from sound to speech in the brain. Impulses responsible for balance are transmitted to the brain via the vestibular portion of the acoustic nerve.

§ 3.38   —Diseases of the Ear

Disorders and disease of the ear can affect external, middle, or inner ear. Some of the most common diseases/disorders affecting the ear are listed below.

1.   Balance disorders—caused by dysfunction of vestibular system and balance reflexes located in the inner ear. Balance disorders may be extremely debilitating and also cause gait problems. They may originate in the central nervous system or the peripheral nervous system. Common disorders are:
    - viral neuronitis—characterized by sudden vertigo without hearing loss. As the name implies, this disorder is caused by viral infection; it is usually self-limiting.
    - viral labyrinthitis—affects both hearing and balance. Balance is usually recovered, however, hearing loss is usually permanent.
    - benign paroxysmal positional vertigo—characterized by short periods of vertigo precipitated by quick head movement or sudden changes in position.

- Meniere's disease—characterized by presence of vertigo, hearing loss, and tinnitus. Recurring episodes of this disease frequently occur.

2. Eustachian tube disorders—usually some type of blockage resulting from middle ear infection, upper respiratory infection, enlarged adenoids in children, or barotraumas.

3. Hearing impairment—can range in severity from difficulty understanding specific words or sounds to total deafness. Many factors influence development of hearing impairment including heredity, trauma, age, noise exposure, infectious disease, arteriosclerosis, drugs potentially toxic to the eighth cranial nerve, and tumors. Hearing loss is categorized by its underlying pathophysiology:

- sensorineural hearing loss—results from disease or trauma to the structures or nerve pathways of the inner ear that lead to the brain stem. Sensorineural hearing loss is usually progressive and is not correctable.

- conductive hearing loss—interference in the conduction of sound impulses through the external auditory canal, the eardrum, or the middle ear. Most conductive hearing loss is correctable by either medical or surgical treatment.

- noise induced hearing loss—diminished hearing occurs in higher frequencies. Treatment is by avoiding noise and/or by wearing ear protection.

- central deafness—central nervous system cannot interpret normal auditory signals.

4. Infections—can affect both external and middle ear:

- External ear infection (external otitis) is caused primarily by bacteria or fungi. The most common external ear infection is swimmer's ear that results from water retained in the external ear canal. Infections can also involve the cartilage of the external ear (see perichondritis below).

- Middle ear infection (otitis media) is caused by various types of bacteria. Causative bacteria depend on age of patient. Infection can be acute or chronic. Chronic infections commonly involve presence of drainage and perforation of the eardrum and, over time, can result in hearing loss. Less commonly, otitis media is seen in conjunction with upper respiratory infections and allergies.

5. Mastoiditis—infection of the mastoid bone. Acute mastoiditis has become rare since the discovery of antibiotics; however

chronic mastoiditis can still occur with repeated middle ear infections.

6. Obstructions:
   - External ear—most common causes are impacted ear wax and foreign bodies. Both can cause decreased hearing, pain, and complaints of "blocked ear." Treatment consists of removal of the blockage through instillation of ear drops and/or ear irrigation.
   - Middle ear—see Eustachian tube disorders below.

7. Otosclerosis—involves excess bone formation around the stapes that prevents normal movement that results in conductive hearing loss.

8. Perichondritis—infection involving the cartilage of the external ear (the pinnal).

9. Presbycusis—hearing impairment resulting from degeneration of the organ of Corti that commonly occurs from age.

10. Tinnitus—commonly referred to ringing in the ears, but may include other noises as well. Tinnitus is not a disease per se, but a symptom. It is often a warning of hearing loss or other problems such as tumor.

11. Trauma:
    - External ear—may be blunt or sharp and should be treated promptly to prevent the development of inflammation in surrounding ear cartilage.
    - Middle ear—can result from a blast or blunt injury. These injuries can dislocate or fracture the ossicles and rupture the tympanic membrane.

12. Tumors or masses—can be malignant or benign.
    - External ear—most benign masses are usually cysts arising from the glands present in the external ear structure. Malignant tumors can occur in the external ear as well.
    - Middle ear—most common benign masses are infectious polyps. Malignant masses involving the middle ear can be primary or as a result of metastasis from a primary in another body location.

13. Tympanosclerosis—hardening of the tympanic membrane as a result of repeated bouts of infection. Tympanosclerosis results in conductive hearing loss secondary to hardening of the membrane around the inner ear ossicles.

14. Tympanic membrane perforation—can be caused by infection or fluid accumulation behind the membrane or from trauma.

§ 3.39   —Evaluation of Ear Function

Hearing testing is not commonly done as part of a routine history and physical. If through the history and physical process, the patient exhibits symptoms of hearing or balance pathophysiology, additional tests may be ordered. Such tests may assess auditory acuity or vestibular acuity. Auditory acuity tests include:

1. Weber test—tuning fork is set into vibration; the rounded tip of the handle is then placed on the center of the nasal bone. The patient is asked whether the tone is heard in the center of the head, the right ear, or the left ear. Normally the sound is heard equally by both ears.

2. Rinne test—vibrating tuning fork is shifted between two positions against the mastoid bone. As the position of the fork is changed, the patients is asked which tone is louder. This test is useful to differentiate between conductive and sensorineural hearing loss.

3. Schwabach test—using the tuning fork, the hearing of the patient is compared to that of the examiner.

    Vestibular acuity tests include:

Romberg test—assesses inner ear for balance. Patient stands with feet together, arms out in front and eyes open, then with eyes closed. Balance should be maintained with minimal amount of swaying.

Test for nystagmus (involuntary movements of the eye)—finger is placed directly in front of patient at eye level. The finger is moved slowly from the midline toward the right ear and left ear, but not more than 30 degrees. The eyes should follow without jerking movements. Nystagmus is associated with vestibular nerve dysfunction.

Practice Note: The information presented in this chapter is intended to provide basic information on body structure and function. It is not necessary to have a medical background to understand it and utilize it in compiling medical record summaries. Understanding how the body works in health is helpful to understand the potential impact of disease or injury on both short-term and long-term functionality and quality of life. In brief, do not be intimidated by body structure and function, medical terminology, diagnostic testing, etc. Invest in a comprehensive medical reference library and use these resources frequently. The internet is an invaluable source for information as well.

CHAPTER 4

DIAGNOSTIC TESTING MODALITIES

§ 4.1   Introduction

Development of the high tech environment during the past several decades has had an enormous impact on the field of diagnostic testing. Diagnostic advancements have reduced unnecessary surgery and facilitated disease treatment by providing more accurate and timely information to health care providers. The correct use of the extensive diagnostic tests available can assist the provider in confirmation or elimination of a diagnosis and information gained from those diagnostic tests can guide health care providers in determining the treatment plan.

While it is not the legal professional's role to interpret test results in most cases, it is important for he/she to have the ability to recognize tests that are pertinent to the client's complaint and issues of litigation. These tests along with their results should be included as part of the medical record summary.

Several types of frequently utilized testing modalities are discussed in the text below, although this discussion is neither all-inclusive nor comprehensive. Because of the rapid changes in the medical field, tests and how they are used can become quickly outmoded. Therefore, it is important to keep abreast of the state-of-the-art treatment for specific diseases. This is best accomplished by utilizing current publications, such as medical texts or published studies, as reference sources. It is essential to have a comprehensive text on laboratory and diagnostic testing as part of your reference library. Several suggestions are listed in the bibliography.

§ 4.2   Blood and Body Fluid Testing

Blood and body fluid tests help the physician to arrive at a diagnosis by confirming or ruling out specific conditions. They are pieces of information that are used along with clinical findings of the physical examination. They are also useful post-diagnosis to monitor the effects of prescribed treatment. There are hundreds of laboratory tests that can be performed. This section lists a few that are commonly ordered by health care providers.

Normal values for blood tests usually accompany reported results and may differ slightly from the normal value ranges listed below. Normal values differ because testing techniques vary among laboratories. When reviewing blood test results, always use the normal value ranges that accompany them as comparators. For some tests discussed below, two sets of normal values are given. Normal values denoted as *"SI units"* refer to *The International System of Units.* This system reports laboratory values in terms of standardized international measures. Not all tests currently have values for SI units and not all laboratories report results using SI unit measurement.

Generally only normal values for adults are referenced in the text below. For some tests, normal values for the newborn and pediatric population may be different from those of adults, as can those for males and females. In addition to age and gender, food ingestion, medication usage, and pregnancy may affect test results.

As stated above, it is important to be able to understand the general indications for a particular test to determine if it is pertinent to a claim. You should always include lab test results in your summary if a test, or the omission of a test, is critical to the case issues. If appropriate, also consider including test results specific to any pre-existing conditions or chronic diseases that exist, for example, blood sugar results for diabetics, blood gas results for individuals with emphysema, that will help establish the client's baseline health. In some cases, showing the trend of a specific lab test result is helpful in "telling a better story." For example, if timely diagnosis of postoperative hemorrhage was a case issue, a breakout summary of several CBC values preceding the diagnosis could demonstrate a falling hematocrit (Hct) and red blood count (RBC) over that time period. When you do include lab values in your case summaries, always include the normal value ranges along with the client's results.

§ 4.3   —Blood Tests

Acid Phosphatase (PAP or TRAP).
Normal value ranges: 0.13–0.63 units/L or 2.2–10.5 units/L (SI units)
Used primarily to diagnose prostate cancer, as well as to monitor the
effectiveness of its treatment.

Activated Clotting Time (ACT).
Normal value ranges: 70–120 seconds
Therapeutic range for anticoagulation: 150–210 seconds
(Normal and therapeutic ranges vary)
This test is used to measure the effect of heparin during anticoagulant
therapy.

Adrenocorticotropic Hormone (ACTH).
Normal value ranges:
     AM: <80 pg/mL or <18 ppmol/L (SI units)
     PM: <50 pg/ml or <11ppmol/L (SI units)
One of the anterior pituitary gland's primary functions is the secretion of
the hormone cortisol. ACTH blood test measures levels of this hormone
and is used to diagnosis Cushing's syndrome (overproduction of cortisol)
or Addison's disease (underproduction of cortisol). In Cushing's syndrome, increased levels may indicate pituitary or nonpituitary tumor. In
Addison's disease, decreased levels of cortisol may indicate primary
adrenal gland failure.

AIDS Serology Testing (AIDS Screen, HIV Antibody, Western Blot, ELISA).
Normal value ranges: negative for HIV antigen or antibodies
These tests are used to diagnose HIV infection and to screen organ donors
for presence of the HIV virus prior to donation.

Alanine Aminotransferase (ALT, formerly SGPT).
Normal value ranges: 4–6 international units/L (SI units)
This test is used to diagnose and follow the progression of liver disease.

Alcohol, Blood (Blood ETOH).
Normal value ranges: <0.05% wt/vol or 50–100 mg/dL

This test measures the amount of alcohol present in the blood to diagnose intoxication or overdose. In most states, blood alcohol results greater than 0.10% indicate legal intoxication.

Alkaline Phosphatase (ALP).
Normal value ranges: Adults: 30–120 units/L or 0.5–2.0 microKat/L (SI units)
This test is performed to detect liver and bone disease. Levels are commonly elevated in obstructive gallbladder disease, cancer of the liver, and Paget's disease, and with healing fractures. Decreased levels are found with diseases such as hypothyroidism, scurvy, and malnutrition.

Ammonia level.
Normal value ranges: Adult: 10 to 80 mcg/dL or 6–47 micromole/L (SI Units)
The liver usually excretes ammonia, produced when the body breaks down protein. Serum ammonia level tests are usually performed to support the diagnosis of liver failure in diseases such as hepatitis or cirrhosis.

Amylase.
Normal value ranges: 60–120 Somogyi units/dL or 30–220 units/L (SI units)
This test is performed to assist in diagnosis of inflammation of the pancreas and other GI tract disorders.

Antidiuretic Hormone (ADH).
Normal value ranges: 1–5 pg/mL or 1–5ng/L (SI units)
ADH, also known as vasopressin, is formed by the hypothalamus and stored in the posterior pituitary gland. Its primary function is to regulate the amount of water reabsorbed by the kidney. This test is used to support the diagnosis of diabetes insipidus (inadequate ADH) or the syndrome of inappropriate ADH secretion (SIADH).

Antinuclear Antibody Test (ANA).
Normal value ranges: Negative at 1:40 dilution
This test is part of the diagnostic workup of autoimmune diseases such as systemic lupus erythematosis and rheumatoid arthritis.

Antistreptolysin O titer (ASO titer).
Normal value ranges:
  Adult: $\leq$ 160 Todd units/ml
An ASO titer is used to determine if a specific disease was caused by a prior streptococcus infection. Principal diseases associated with streptococcal infections are glomerulonephritis, rheumatic fever, bacterial endocarditis, and scarlet fever.

Arterial Blood Gases (ABGs).
Normal value ranges:
  pH: 7.35–7.45
  PCO_2: 35–45 mm Hg
  PO_2: 80–100 mm Hg
  HCO_3: 21–28 mEq/L
  O_2 saturation: 95–100%
This test measures the amount of oxygen and carbon dioxide in the blood, as well as the degrees of alkalinity and acidity. Together, these components measure the adequacy of the body's respiratory and metabolic functions.

Aspartate Aminotransferase (AST, formerly SGOT).
Normal value ranges (age-dependent): 0–35 units/L or 0–0.58 microKat/L (SI units)
AST testing is used to diagnose presence of suspected coronary artery disease or suspected liver disease. It is usually ordered in combination with other related blood testing.

Bilirubin (total, direct, or indirect).
Normal value ranges (age-dependent):
  total bilirubin: 0.3–1.0 mg/dL or 5.1–17 micromole/L (SI units)
  direct bilirubin: 0.1–0.3 mg/dL or 1.7–5.1 micromole/L (SI units)
  indirect bilirubin: 0.2–0.8 mg/dl or 3.4–12.0 micromole/L (SI units)
This test is ordered to assist in diagnosing liver diseases such as hepatitis. Elevated serum bilirubin may also be indicative of gallbladder disease. When serum bilirubin is extremely elevated, the skin and eyes become yellow or jaundiced.

Bleeding Time.
Normal value ranges: 1–9 minutes Ivy method

This test is used to evaluate the adequacy of the blood factors responsible for clotting. It is often used pre-operatively to validate adequacy of blood clotting during and after surgery.

Blood Typing and Crossmatching.
Normal value ranges: compatibility
There are four blood types: A, B, AB, and O. In addition to being one of these blood types, persons are also Rh-positive or Rh-negative. Rh is an antigen carried on the surface of red blood cells. If this antigen is present, a person is Rh-positive; and if the antigen is not present, a person is Rh-negative. Antigens will trigger severe allergic reactions if donor blood is not properly crossmatched with the blood of the recipient. Blood *typing* identifies genetically determined antigens on the surface of the red blood cell. It is the first step in determining recipient/donor *compatibility* and is followed by *crossmatching*.

CA 27.29 and CA 15–3 tumor markers.
Normal value ranges:
    CA 27.29: <38 units/mL or <38 kunits/L (SI units)
    CA 15–3: <22 units/mL or <22 kunits/L (SI units)
These two antigens are used to stage breast cancer and monitor its treatment. Their use as a screening tool is quite limited because of the high incidence of elevated markers in the general population; therefore, they are used most frequently to monitor treatment of metastatic disease.

CA 19–9 tumor marker.
Normal value ranges: <37 units/mL or <37 kunits/L (SI units)
This test is used primarily to evaluate a patient's response to treatment for pancreatic or hepatobiliary cancer and periodically as a post-treatment surveillance tool for tumor recurrence.

CA 125 tumor marker.
Normal value ranges: 0–35 units/mL or <35 kunits/L (SI units)
This marker is used to screen for ovarian cancer and to monitor its treatment. It is an extremely sensitive screening tool.

Calcium, Blood.
Normal value ranges:
    Total calcium: 9.0–10.5 mg/dL or 2.25–2.75 mmol/L (SI units)
    Ionized calcium: 4.5–5.6 mg/dL or 1.05–1.30 mmol/L

The parathyroid gland secretes calcium, which is critical to cardiac function, muscle contraction, nerve function, and blood clotting. Serum calcium is used to monitor patients with renal failure and problems with parathyroid function.

Carcinoembryonic Antigen (CEA).
Normal value ranges: <2ng/ml
Carcinoembryonic antigen is a protein normally produced during the first two trimesters of fetal life. Increased levels in adults may indicate colorectal or other cancers. Although problematic to use as a screening tool, it can be used effectively to monitor the effectiveness of treatment. For example, a rise in CEA can be indicative of cancer recurrence.

Complete Blood Count (CBC).
Normal value ranges (age- and sex-dependent):

RBC (red blood cells): a measure of the number of red blood cells in the circulation. Along with Hgb and Hct, RBC counts are done serially when active bleeding is suspected.
Normal value ranges:
    Male: 4.7–6.1 (RBC $\times$ 10^6/microL) or (RBC $\times$ 10^{12}/L) SI units
    Female: 4.2–5.4 (RBC $\times$ 10^6/microL) or (RBC $\times$ 10^{12}/L) SI units

WBC (white blood cells): a measure of the number of white blood cells in the blood.
This test is helpful in monitoring the status of conditions such as cancer, infection, immunosuppression, and allergy. It is also frequently performed serially at specified intervals, e.g. daily.
Normal value ranges:
    5000–10000/mm^3 or 5–10 $\times$ 10^9/L (SI units)

Differential (WBC) count—quantifies each type of white blood cell in context of what is "normal".
Normal value ranges:

- **Neutrophils:** 55–70%. The primary function of neutrophils is killing and digesting bacteria through the process of *phagocytosis*. They are the first to respond to a site of infection. When infection is severe, immature neutrophils, called *bands,* are released into circulation. This condition is commonly referred to as a *shift to the left* and indicates severe infection.

Neutrophilia (high neutrophil count) occurs mainly in bacterial infections. *Neutropenia* (low neutrophil count) occurs in many viral infections and in overwhelming bacterial infections.

- **Lymphocytes:** 20–40%. Lymphocytes play an important role in the body's immune response. They also fight acute viral infections and chronic bacterial infections. There are two types of lymphocytes, T cells and B cells. *Lymphopenia* (low lymphocyte count) occurs in diseases and conditions affecting the immune system, such as HIV infection. *Lymphocytosis* (high lymphocyte count) occurs in response to viral infections and chronic bacterial infections such as tuberculosis.

- **Monocytes:** 2–8%. Monocytes also kill and digest bacteria and are second to respond to infection, after neutrophils. They stay in circulation only a short time.

- **Eosinophils:** 1–4%. Eosinophils help regulate inflammation and are involved in the allergic reaction, capable of killing the proteins (antigen-antibody complexes) that cause allergic reactions. *Eosinophilia* (high eosinophil count) occurs mainly in infections caused by parasites.

- **Basophils:** 0.5–1%. Along with eosinophils, basophils are involved in the response to allergic reaction and are also capable of killing the proteins (antigen-antibody complexes) that cause allergic reactions.

Hgb (hemoglobin): a measure of the amount of hemoglobin, which carries oxygen to the body, in the blood. Tests are used serially along with RBC and Hct when active bleeding is suspected.
Normal value ranges:
    Male: 14–18 g/dL or 8.7–11.2 mmol/L (SI units)
    Female: 12–16 g/dL or 7.4–9.9 mmol/L (SI units)

Hct (hematocrit or packed cell volume): an indirect measure of RBC number and volume. Along with Hgb and RBC, Hct tests are done serially when active bleeding is suspected
Normal value ranges:
    Male: 42–52% or 0.42–0.52 volume fraction (SI units)
    Female: 37–47% or 0.37–0.47 volume fraction (SI units)

Platelets: used to count the number of platelets in the blood. This test is useful for evaluation of suspected bleeding disorders.
Normal value ranges:
    150,000–400,000 mm^3

Cholesterol.
Normal value ranges (age- and sex-dependent):
    <200 mg/dL or <5.20mmol/L (SI units)
Cholesterol measurement assists in assessment of cardiovascular disease
risk. Elevated levels of cholesterol may indicate cardiovascular disease or
the probability of developing it. Cholesterol is the main lipid associated
with the arteriovascular disease.

Creatinine Kinase (CK) Creatine Phosphokinase (CPK).
Normal value ranges:
    Male: 55–170 units/L or 55–170 units/L (SI units)
    Female: 30–135 units/L or 30–135 units/L (SI units)
This test is used along with several other tests to support a diagnosis of
myocardial injury or infarction. Because CK is present in skeletal muscle
and the brain as well, it is not considered definitive for MI. CK's are also
done to assist in diagnosis of skeletal muscle and neurological diseases.

Creatinine, Blood.
Normal value ranges:
    Male: 0.6–1.2 mg/dL or 53–106 micromole/L (SI units)
    Female: 0.5–1.1 mg/dL or 44–97 micromole/L (SI units)
Blood (serum) creatinine is used to evaluate adequacy of kidney function.
An elevated creatinine level is indicative of decreased kidney function.

Cytomegalovirus (CMV).
Normal value ranges: No virus isolated
This test is used to diagnose CMV infection. CMV is a virus, related to
herpes simplex, herpes zoster viruses, and the Epstein-Barr virus. Infection
is common and often goes undiagnosed in healthy individuals. However,
CMV does have serious implications during pregnancy, when infection
may cause birth defects in the fetus. Immunosuppressed populations may
also suffer serious effects.

Disseminated Intravascular Coagulation (DIC) screening.
Normal value ranges: No evidence of DIC in a panel of tests that includes
bleeding time, platelets, protime, PTT, and coagulation factors.
This test assesses the adequacy of the clotting mechanism. In DIC, the
clotting mechanism is triggered inappropriately, causing small clots to
form in small vessels. Clot formation may eventually lead to anoxic injury
of body organs.

Electrolytes.
Normal value ranges:
   sodium (Na): 135–145 meql/L or 135–145 mmol/L (SI units)
   potassium (K): 3.5–5.5 meq/L or 3.5–5.5 mmol/L (SI units)
   chloride (Cl): 100–110 meql/L or 100–110 mmol/L (SI units)
Electrolyte testing measures the concentration of major mineral substances in the blood, such as sodium (Na), potassium (K), and chloride (Cl). Normal levels of these substances are essential for maintaining homeostasis of body systems. Potassium is especially essential for effective heart function.

Epstein-Barr virus (EBV).
Normal value ranges:
   Titers ≤1:10 nondiagnostic
   Titers 1:10–1:60 indicate infection at some undetermined time
   Titers ≥1:320 may indicate active infection
EBV infection is highly prevalent in the U.S. population. The virus is the causative agent of infectious mononucleosis as well as other types of infections. After active infection, the virus becomes dormant in the body but can become reactivated at a later time.

Gamma-Glutamyl Transpeptidase (GGTP or GGT).
Normal value ranges: 8–38 units/L or 8–38 international units/L (SI units)
This test assists in determining liver function. GGTP will be elevated in liver disease, especially when it results from chronic alcohol ingestion.

Glucose (blood sugar).
Normal value ranges (fasting): <110 mg/dL or <6.1 mmol/L (SI units)
Glucose testing determines the level of sugar in the bloodstream. An abnormally high blood sugar may indicate diabetes. Low values may result from medication or from the condition of hypoglycemia.

Glycosylated Hemoglobin (GHb, GHB, HbA$_{1C}$).
Normal value ranges:
   Nondiabetic Adult: 2.2–4.8%
   Good diabetic control: 2.5–5.9%
   Fair diabetic control: 6.0–8%
   Poor diabetic control: >8%
Glycosylated hemoglobin testing provides information about the level of glucose control of diabetics over the previous three to five weeks. Thus, it

gives the clinician a picture of blood sugar values over time as compared with random (one-time) blood glucose tests, which give a value for one moment.

Hepatitis Virus Studies: Hepatitis A.
Normal value ranges:
> Blood negative for hepatitis A virus (HAV)
> Positive HAV blood test with antibody immunoglobulin G (IgG) indicates past infection.
> Positive HAV blood test with antibody immunoglobulin M (IgM) indicates active infection.

Originally called infectious hepatitis, hepatitis has a short incubation period and is highly contagious. It is transmitted by the fecal oral route and has no carrier state.

Hepatitis Virus Studies: Hepatitis B.
Normal value ranges:
> Blood negative for hepatitis B virus (HBV)
> Positive blood test for hepatitis B surface antigen (HBsAg) indicates active infection or a carrier state.
> Positive blood test for hepatitis B surface antibody (HBsAb) indicates convalescent stage of infection and immunity to HBV.

Hepatitis B, commonly known as *serum hepatitis,* has a longer incubation period than hepatitis A and is transmitted by exposure to blood (including blood transfusions) and other body fluids such as semen and breast milk. HBV infection can become a chronic infection.

Hepatitis Virus Studies: Hepatitis C.
Normal value ranges:
> Blood negative for hepatitis C virus (HCV)

HCV infection, formerly called non-A, non-B hepatitis, is transmitted by blood and body fluids. HCV can also become a chronic infection

Herpes Simplex Virus (HSV) titers.
Normal value ranges: No virus present in the blood.

The herpes simplex virus is classified as Type 1 or Type 2. HSV Type 1 is responsible for oral lesions such as cold sores. HSV Type 2 is transmitted sexually and can cause painful lesions on both male and female genitalia. However, both viruses can cause lesions orally or genitally. Both types of

HSV remain latent in the body and can be reactivated periodically to cause active infection.

Lactic Dehydrogenase (LDH).
Normal value ranges: LDH: 100–190 units/L or 100–190 units/L (SI units)
LDH testing is used to identify injury or disease of many organs, including the heart, liver, kidneys, and skeletal muscle. Because LDH is present in many body tissues, elevated results are not definitive diagnosis for any one disease.

Lipoproteins: High Density Lipids (HDL) and Low Density Lipids (LDL).
Normal value ranges:
   HDL—Male: >45 mg/dL or >0.75 mmol/L (SI units)
        Female: >55mg/dL or >0.91 mmol/L (SI units)
   LDL—Male and female: 60 to 180 mg/dL or <3.37 mmol/L (SI units)
This test is used to assess risk of coronary heart disease. Lipoproteins are blood proteins that transport cholesterol, triglycerides, and other insoluble fats. HDL's carry cholesterol. Known as "good cholesterol," HDL's remove cholesterol from body tissues and transport it to the liver for excretion. LDL's, or "bad cholesterol," deposit cholesterol in the body's arteries. Over time, these deposits may lead to cardiac disease.

Lymphocyte Testing (B cell and T cell counts).
Normal value ranges:
   B cells: 4–25%
   T cells (total): 60–95%
   T helper cells (CD4 cells): 60–75%
   T suppressor cells (CD8 cells): 25–30%
   CD4-CD8 ratio: >1
Both B cells and T cells play a critical role in the normal function of the body's immune system. They help protect the body from invasion by harmful bacteria and viruses and also participate in antibody production. T cell tests are used to monitor the progression of HIV disease. The HIV virus kills T helper cells, resulting in low cell counts and a lower ratio of T helper to T suppressor cells. This leaves the body vulnerable to the opportunistic infections characteristic of HIV disease, although these same infections may be seen in individuals with immunosuppression from any cause.

Magnesium (Mg).
Normal value ranges: Adult: 1.3 to 2.1 mEq/L or 0.65–1.05 mmol/L (SI units)
This test measures levels of magnesium in the blood. Magesium is essential to normal organ functions, including those of neuromuscular tissue. Magnesium levels are frequently tracked in patients with cardiac and renal disease.

Monospot.
Normal value ranges: Negative blood titer (<1:28 titer)
This test is used to diagnose infectious mononucleosis, a disease caused by the Epstein-Barr virus.

Partial Thromboplastin Time, Activated (PTT, APTT).
Normal value ranges:
　　APPT: 30–40 seconds
　　PTT: 60 to 70 seconds
　　Patients receiving anticoagulation therapy: 1.5 to 2.5 times the
　　control value (in seconds).
PTT's assess the body's blood clotting mechanism. Sequential tests are commonly performed routinely when a patient is on anticoagulation therapy such as heparin. When an individual is at risk for developing blood clots, PTTs are kept elevated to prolong blood clotting time.

Prostate Specific Antigen (PSA).
Normal value ranges: <4 ng/mL or <4 mcg/L (SI units)
This test is used to as a screening tool for early detection of prostate cancer. The level of PSA indicates the degree of tumor burden. PSA is also used for monitoring status of tumor after completion of treatment.

Protein Electrophoresis, Serum (SPEP).
Normal value ranges:
　　total protein: 6.4–8.3 g/dL or 64–83 g/L (SI units)
　　albumin: 3.5–5.0 g/dL or 35–50 g/L (SI units)
　　globulin: 2.3–3.4 g/dL
These tests are used to diagnose and monitor disease courses in cancer, immune disorders, liver dysfunction, and malnutrition.

Prothrombin Time (Protime, PT or International Normalized Ratio (INR)).

Normal value ranges: 11.0 to 12.5 seconds; 85% to 100%

Full anticoagulation therapy: 1.5 to 2 times the control value; 20% to 30%

These tests are used to assess the adequacy of the body's clotting system. Factors such as liver disease, gallbladder disease, and the use of certain types of drugs can prolong clotting time. After a heart attack, cardiac surgery, or blood vessel thrombus, medication may be administered to lengthen clotting time and PTT's are done serially to monitor effects of anticoagulation.

Sedimentation Rate, Erythrocyte sedimentation rate (ESR).

Normal value ranges: (age- and sex-dependent):

Female: up to 20 mm/hr

Male: up to 15 mm/hr

Sedimentation rates are used to detect conditions such as infection, auto-immune disease, or malignancy. It is a non-specific test that can detect an inflammatory process, but cannot determine cause. It can also indicate the status of inflammatory conditions, that is, improvement or deterioration.

Serology (VDRL, RPR, FTA).

Normal value ranges: Nonreactive

Positive results may indicate the presence of syphilis, but diagnosis is confirmed by the specific FTA test. Other diseases may cause VDRL and RPR positive results in the absence of syphilis.

Toxicology Screens/Therapeutic Drug Monitoring Screens.

Normal value ranges:

Illegal Substances: negative

Therapeutic ranges for prescription and OTC drugs provided with test results.

Toxicology screens determine the presence of chemical substances such as marijuana, cocaine, and amphetamines in the body. Screens may also be performed for prescription or over-the-counter (OTC) drugs to determine if drug levels are at sub-therapeutic, therapeutic, or toxic. Common drug classes for which therapeutic blood monitoring is done include certain antibiotics, anticonvulsants, cardiac medications, and antipsychotics.

Lab results include therapeutic and toxic ranges along with the individual's result.

Triglycerides.
Normal value ranges:
    Male: 40 to 160 mg/dL or 0.45 to 1.81 mmol/L (SI units)
    Female: 35 to 135 mg/dL or 0.40 to 1.52 mmol/L (SI units)
Triglycerides, a form of fat present in the bloodstream, are produced in the liver. They are carried by low density lipids (LDLs) in the blood, and deposited in tissues. This test is commonly part of a lipid "profile" that includes measurement of cholesterol and lipoproteins.

Troponins.
Normal value ranges:
    Cardiac Troponin T: <2 ng/mL
    Cardiac Troponin I: <0.03 ng/mL
This test is used to determine the origin of chest pain. Cardiac troponins are the most specific indicator of cardiac muscle injury and are commonly used with CK testing in confirming or ruling out MI diagnosis.

Urea Nitrogen, Blood (BUN).
Normal value ranges: 10–20 mg/dL or 3.6–7.1 mmol/L (SI units)
BUN is a rough indicator of kidney function. It can also measure liver function.

Uric Acid, Blood.
Normal value ranges:
    Male: 4.0–8.5 mg/dL or 0.24–0.51 mmol/L (SI units)
    Female: 2.7–7.3 mg/dL or 0.16–0.43 mmol/L (SI units)
This test is used to evaluate gout and renal calculi.

Viral Testing.
Normal value ranges: Varies, depending on specific test.
Viral testing can be performed to determine the presence of a virus itself or the presence of *antibodies* to a virus. Antibody formation is the immune system's protective response to invasion of a potentially harmful agent (the virus). Specimen sources can include blood, throat swabs, urine, tissue, spinal fluid, and skin lesions. Common viral tests include herpes simplex (HSV), cytomegalovirus (CMV), herpes zoster (chicken-pox), and rubella (measles).

§ 4.4 —Tests on Body Fluids and Tissues

In addition to blood testing, numerous tests on body fluids such as urine, joint fluid, sputum, and feces can be performed. Diagnostic testing is also done on body tissues, and specimens are usually obtained through *biopsy* procedures. Once a sample of fluid or tissues is obtained, it is sent to the laboratory for the requested testing. Some of the more commonly requested tests and the procedures for obtaining specimens are discussed below, although many more are available.

1. **Bone Marrow Testing.** Marrow is obtained from the bone via needle aspiration. Typically, the iliac crest is utilized for the aspiration; however, the sternum may also be used. Samples are then microscopically examined for abnormalities in the marrow composition that could indicate presence of diseases affecting the blood system, e.g. leukemia.

2. **Culture and Sensitivity Studies (C&S).** This test can be done on blood and any body fluid, such as stool, urine, sputum, cerebrospinal fluid, and joint fluid. Blood, urine and cerebrospinal fluid are normally sterile and the presence of bacteria may indicate infection; the presence of bacteria not usually found in other body sites may indicate infection as well. To perform a *culture*, a specimen is transferred to a medium that supports bacterial growth (culture medium or agar) and incubated for 24–48 hours. At the end of this time, the bacteria can be identified, e.g., Staphylococcus aureus. The bacterial growth is then tested against a range of antibiotics to determine which inhibit or kill the growth of the organism and which do not. This is *sensitivity* testing. If bacteria are found, the species is identified and testing is done to determine which antibiotics will destroy it. Bacteria that are killed by an antibiotic are said to be *sensitive* to it; bacteria not killed by an antibiotic are said to be *resistant*. C&S studies are crucial to effective management of infections. Often, a *Gram stain* and *smear* are done prior to a culture. Whereas cultures take a minimum or 24–48 hours to grow and identify a specific organism, gram stain and smear results are available within hours. Results of a gram stain identify the organism as gram positive or negative and smear results identify the shape of the bacteria. An example of a smear and gram stain result would be, "many gram positive cocci present."

3. **Cytology.** This technique microscopically examines body fluid to determine the presence of abnormal cells (cancer cells). Cytology

testing is frequently done on sputum, abdominal fluid, and pleural fluid; the results are an important part of cancer diagnosis. Fluids for cytology studies are obtained by various methods, depending on the site from which the sample is needed.

4. **Joint Fluid Studies.** Joint fluid is obtained by inserting a needle into the joint space of concern. Normally clear and colorless, joint fluid is examined for the presence of red blood cells or white cells. Presence of these could indicate hemorrhage or infection (respectively) within the joint space.

5. **Pap Smear.** Cells are taken from the cervix and vagina during a pelvic examination and sent for microscopic study. This test is used as a screening tool for early detection of cervical cancer.

6. **Paracentesis.** Fluid is removed from the abdominal cavity via needle and sent for microscopic study. Fluid secreted by the cells in the abdominal cavity is normally absorbed as it is secreted. Presence of excess fluid may indicate tumor or liver disease.

7. **Periocardiocentesis.** Pericardial fluid is aspirated through a needle that is inserted in the area of the 5th or 6th intercostal space and sent for microscopic examination. Normally pericardial fluid is minimal and periocardiocentesis can help determine the cause of *pericardial effusion* (excess fluid).

8. **Spinal Fluid, Cerebral Spinal Fluid (CSF) Studies.** Also commonly referred to as a *lumbar puncture,* this test is done on cerebrospinal fluid withdrawn via needle from the subarachnoid space of the spinal column. Normally clear and colorless, the spinal fluid is examined for abnormalities in composition. Components tested are:

    • Red blood cells. Normally absent, the presence of red blood cells indicates bleeding within the central nervous system, e.g. stroke, head injury. Red blood cells may also be present as a result of difficulty inserting the needle into the spinal column (traumatic tap).

    • White blood cells. Usually absent or present in minimal quantities, elevated white blood cell levels indicate infection in the central nervous system, e.g. meningitis.

    • Protein and glucose. Present in the spinal fluid in certain quantities, abnormally high or low levels are indicative of disease processes such as infection or tumor.

9. **Stool for Occult Blood (OB).** A sample of stool is collected and examined for the presence of blood. Normally, the stool should be

blood-free. This test is used for early diagnosis of colorectal cancer and for detection of GI bleeding. There are various factors that can result in a *false positive,* that is produce a positive result in the absence of disease.

10. **Stool for Ova and Parasites (O&P).** A sample of stool is collected and examined for the presence of parasites and their eggs. A negative test result is normal. This test is used to diagnose suspected parasitic infections and identify the specific causative agent.

11. **Tissue Specimens for Pathology.** Samples of tissue to be studied are obtained by biopsy and are sent to a pathologist for microscopic examination and diagnosis of abnormalities. *Frozen sections* of tissue can be utilized to determine preliminary findings. In frozen section testing, the surgeon excises suspect tissue, and sends it immediately to a pathologist to be examined for abnormal cells. Frozen section examinations are always followed by standard tissue examinations.

12. **Thoracentesis.** Fluid is removed from the pleural space, typically by needle aspiration, and sent for microscopic study. Fluid secreted by the cells in the chest cavity is normally absorbed as it is secreted. Presence of excess fluid may indicate infection or tumor.

13. **Urinalysis.** A urinalysis (UA) is a commonly used screening test. Normally clear and yellow in appearance, urinalysis can determine the following:

   • Cloudy appearance—presence of bacteria or white blood cells in the urine, indicating possible urinary tract infection.

   • Presence of WBC's—may indicate urinary tract infection.

   • Presence of RBC's—indicator of urinary tract conditions such as tumor, stones, trauma, and infection.

   • Presence of protein—indicator in kidney disease.

   • Presence of casts (clumps of cells)—excessive numbers usually indicate renal disease.

   • Presence of crystals—important predisposing factor in kidney stone formation.

§ 4.5   Diagnostic Radiology

Diagnostic radiology utilizes x-rays in the diagnosis of disease. In simple x-ray studies, short wavelength electromagnetic radiation penetrates tissues and records their densities on film. Because different body tissues have different densities, the images they project on x-ray provide valuable diagnostic information. Radiology procedures vary in complexity from simple x-ray studies to procedures involving intravenous injection of radioactive dyes (contrast media) that enhance imaging of blood vessels, organs, and tissues. In its most sophisticated form, diagnostic radiology utilizes computer technology to visualize body tissues in different slices and along different planes. These studies provide detailed information on abnormalities such as tumors and hemorrhage; they also verify the integrity of body structures.

§ 4.6   —Noninvasive Radiology Procedures

Noninvasive radiology procedures are performed without the intravenous injection of contrast media (dyes) into the body. If contrast media is used, it is usually administered orally. These studies have the lowest risk of complications. Some common noninvasive radiology procedures are discussed below:

1. **Air Contrast Studies.** Air contrast involves the introduction of air into a selected part of the body. This allows better visualization of the tissues because air does not absorb x-rays.

2. **Barium Enema (B.E.) or Lower G.I. Series.** B.E. allows visualization of the colon or lower gastrointestinal tract. Barium is given rectally prior to the examination, and serves as a contrast medium for enhanced visualization.

3. **Bone Densitometry Study.** Densitometry assists in early diagnosis of osteoporosis. It is a noninvasive technique by which a radioisotope is passed underneath the bone (usually the forearm) and the amount of radioisotope absorbed is read by a detector placed above the bone.

4. **Cervical Spine Series.** X-ray of the cervical spine allows visualization of the seven vertebrae located at the top of the spine (cervical vertebrae).

5. **Gallbladder Series (G.B. series).** This test allows visualization and examination of gallbladder function aided by the oral administration of contrast media.

6. **Gastrointestinal Series (G.I. series) or Upper G.I. Series (U.G.I.).** An upper G.I. series visualizes the esophagus, stomach, and part of

the small intestines. Barium is administered orally as a contrast medium to enhance visualization of the organs.

7. **KUB (kidneys, ureters, and bladder or flat plate of abdomen).** Visualizes the abdomen and urinary tract (kidneys, ureters, and bladder). This test is usually performed to identify potential problems in the urinary tract, e.g. urinary calculi. It can also be used to evaluate potential causes of abdominal pain.

8. **Lumbar Spine Series or Lumbosacral Spine X-rays.** A lumbar spine series allows visualization of the lowest five spinal vertebrae (lumbar vertebrae). Lumbosacral spine x-rays visualize the sacrum (tailbone) as well as the lumbar vertebrae.

9. **Mammography.** This test is used for screening and early detection of breast tumors. Mammography visualizes the soft tissue of the breasts.

10. **Thoracic Spine Series.** A thoracic spine series allows visualization of the middle 12 spinal vertebrae (thoracic vertebrae).

11. **Tomography.** This test utilizes oral contrast media to examine tissues or organs, by taking a sequence of films from many angles. This technique allows visualization of tissues that would be obscured using standard x-ray techniques. It is commonly used to diagnose chest pathology such as tumors, abscesses, and hematomas.

12. **Videofluoroscopy.** After barium or a meal containing barium is ingested, X-rays follow the progression of the food or liquid during the swallowing process. Problems with the swallowing mechanism can be identified through this test. It is commonly performed following a stroke when impairment of swallowing is suspected.

§ 4.7   —Invasive Radiology Procedures

Invasive radiology involves the injection of dye contrast media, either intravascular or into a body cavity. Dye injection increases the risk of complications that includes allergic reactions, leakage of the dye from the blood vessels into the body tissues, and introduction of bacteria into the bloodstream via the injection site. Some common invasive radiology procedures are as follows:

1. **Angiography.** A catheter is placed, usually via the femoral artery, into the arteries to be examined. Dye is injected as x-ray films are

obtained. The blood vessel lumens are visualized and provide information on the structure and patency of the vessels.

2. **Arthrogram.** Dye is injected to the joint space to be studied and allows visualization of its structures, e.g. ligaments and tendons.

3. **Cardiac Angiography (cardiac catheterization).** This test visualizes arteries that supply blood to the heart (coronary arteries) and allows assessment of their patency. Such examinations determine the adequacy of the circulation by showing the degree of arteriosclerosis, which causes vessel narrowing.

4. **Bronchogram.** Contrast media is instilled into the bronchia via catheter or bronchoscope. X-ray films are taken, visualizing the trachea and bronchi. Conditions such as obstruction and bronchiectasis can be identified.

5. **Carotid Angiography.** This test visualizes blood vessels in the neck (carotid arteries) that supply blood to the brain and allows assessment of their patency.

6. **Cerebral Angiography.** The integrity of the blood vessels within the brain can be determined by this test. It can identify conditions such as abscesses, aneurysms, hematomas, and some tumors.

7. **Cholangiography (intravenous).** This test visualizes gallbladder and its ducts aided by the administration of a dye contrast media.

8. **Cystography.** This test visualizes the structure and function of urinary bladder before and after voiding. Contrast media is usually injected into the bladder via a urinary catheter inserted prior to the test.

9. **Electrophysiologic Studies (EPS) or Cardiac Mapping.** In cardiac mapping, multiple electrode catheters are placed through a peripheral vein into the right atrium and/or ventricle of the heart. Under close cardiac monitoring, the electrodes are used to pace the heart and potentially induce cardiac arrythmias. Abnormalities in the heart's conduction system can be identified and treated. This test can also assist in the evaluation of syncope, palpitations, and the identification of arrythmia location.

10. **Hysterosalpingography.** After injection of contrast dye through the cervix, the fallopian tubes and uterine cavity are visualized radiographically. Patency of fallopian tubes and abnormalities of the uterine cavity can then be identified.

11. **Intravenous Pyelogram (I.V.P.).** This test visualizes the kidneys and ureters aided by injection of dye contrast media. It provides

better visualization of these structures than does a KUB x-ray (see **7** in § **4.6** above).

12. **Myelography.** This procedure visualizes the spinal cord, subarachnoid space, and spinal nerve roots following injection of media dye into the spinal canal. This examination will detect herniated discs, however CAT and MRI scans are also used for this purpose.

13. **Percutaneous Transhepatic Cholangiography (PTC).** Contrast dye is injected directly into a bile duct through the liver. Bile ducts both inside and outside the liver can be visualized and patency determined. The gallbladder may also be visualized and studied for obstruction due to tumor or gallstones.

14. **Venogram.** After injection of dye contrast media into the venous system, x-rays at timed intervals provide visualization of the venous system. Venograms are used (most commonly) to identify the presence and location of thrombi within lower extremities.

15. **Voiding Cystourethrogram (VCU).** VCU studies evaluate structure and function of the urinary bladder. Dye is inserted into the bladder through a catheter to allow visualization.

§ 4.8   —Computerized Diagnostic Technology

Development of computerized radiology technology has made a monumental contribution to the field of diagnostics by providing fast, accurate information to the health care provider with relatively few patient risks. Although the equipment necessary for performing these procedures is extremely expensive and can potentially become obsolete in a short period of time, this technology has, and will continue to benefit countless patients. It has eliminated unnecessary surgery and shortened the length of surgical procedures through preoperative visualization and diagnosis of pathology.

Until the advent of computerized diagnostic technology, such as the CAT scan, many areas of the body were considered inaccessible. Conventional x-rays provided some information, but procedures involved could either pose potentially serious risks and/or cause considerable discomfort to the patient. The discovery of the CAT scan technique and the resulting improvements in patient care were so significant that it won the 1979 Nobel Prize for medicine and physiology. There were critical developments in technology that made computerized tomography possible, namely, the development of mathematical algorithms used to reconstruct images and development of high-speed computers. The CAT scan (see below) was the first technology of this type. At the time of inception, the principles of CAT scan were unique in the way they approached the processing of radiographic information. This unique approach resulted in two major advantages: (1) the demonstration of subtle differences in soft tissue density, and (2) ability to resolve problems with spatial resolution through use of enhancing contrast between soft tissue structures.

1. **Computerized (axial) Tomography (CT or CAT scan).** This technology examines soft tissues of the body using X-ray beams passing repeatedly (scanning) through a body part. A computer calculates tissue absorption at each point scanned. This technique enables the visualization of normal body structures as well as abnormalities such as tumors, fluid collection, dead tissue, and infection (abscess). CT scans can be performed on any part of the body, with or without contrast media. Body areas with movement, for example, the chest, are best visualized. The use of contrast agents is determined by the provisional diagnosis. For example, suspected tumors visualize better with contrast, but bleeding and edema visualize better without contrast.

2. **Magnetic Resonance Imaging (MRI).** MRI technology utilizes magnetic fields to analyze radio waves (as opposed to x-rays) given off by hydrogen atoms in the body. MRI's scan on any plane. Bone marrow, fat, tendons, and nerves are high in hydrogen nuclei and thus are readily visible. In contrast, bones are very low in hydrogen and, therefore, not as well visualized. MRI's provide excellent visualization of the brain and nervous system. They are also useful in pinpointing disc disease, arteriosclerosis, brain lesions, and soft tissue injuries. MRI's provide information similar to CAT scans, but offer greater soft tissue detail with no radiation exposure. They can be performed with or without contrast.

3. **Positron Emission Tomography (PET scan).** PET scanning is a computerized technology that allows examination of the metabolic function of various tissues, especially those of the brain and heart. Radioactive isotopes are mixed with a natural substance, for example, glucose. This mixture is either injected or inhaled by the patient and subsequently travels throughout the body via circulation. The radioisotopes give off positively charged particles known as positrons that collide with electrons to produce photons. These photons are detected

by the PET scanner and converted through computer analysis into color-coded images that reveal the location of metabolic activity of the organ, that is, the location where chemicals are burned. In other words, PET scan technology provides information on organ *function* as well as *structure*. This capability allows identification of diseases such as dementia in their early stages and can even differentiate between Alzheimer's dementia and dementia from other causes. It can also metabolically distinguish depression from dementia and correlate cognitive abnormalities with specific areas of the brain. In schizophrenia, PET scans show decreased glucose metabolism in the frontal area of the brain. Some studies have shown widespread abnormalities in glucose metabolism following head trauma, e.g. diffuse decrease (of glucose metabolism) throughout the brain in severe head injuries.

PET scans are also used to assess cardiac function. Because both structure and function are studied, PET scanning can combine information about adequacy of myocardial blood perfusion and viability of myocardial cells. Two different radioisotopes (tracers) are injected intravenously. The first tracer travels through the bloodstream to the vessels supplying the myocardium with blood. A computer reconstructs images of the tracer's distribution in the vessels. Next, a glucose tracer is injected that localizes in the myocardium. The uptake level of the glucose tracer is determined by the metabolic activity of the myocardial cells, which gives a picture of cell viability. There is said to be a "match" when a perfusion study shows poor blood flow and the metabolic study shows low levels of glucose uptake, indicating nonviable myocardial cells. A "mismatch" occurs when a perfusion study shows poor blood flow and the metabolic study shows viable myocardial cells.

A less common use of PET scanning is in diagnosing cancers. Because cancer cells burn glucose at a higher rate than normal cells, PET scans can diagnose malignant tissue.

4. **Single Photon Emission Computerized Tomography (SPECT scan).** This technology utilizes a three-dimensional method for observing physiologic (functional) behavior of the brain. It is a two-stage process involving administration of a radiotracer and determination of subsequent radiotracer distribution. Some studies have demonstrated that abnormalities in cerebral blood circulation occur with migraine and cluster headaches. SPECT scans can identify these abnormalities as well as those resulting from head injury. In this

respect, SPECT scans are superior to CAT scans in that they identify abnormalities earlier. Finally, SPECT scans are more advantageous than PET scans in terms of availability and cost-effectiveness.

5. **Digital Subtraction or Venous Angiography.** This computer-assisted X-ray technology subtracts bone and soft tissue images to allow visualization of the cardiovascular system. It is used in diagnosis of, or follow-up for, conditions such as carotid stenosis, brain tumors, and cerebral aneurysm.

§ 4.9   Additional Diagnostic Testing Modalities

In addition to the many types of radiology tests available, other technologies are used alone or in combination with information from, and results of, other tests. Like radiology tests, these diagnostic tests are used to assist in the diagnosis of specific diseases. Types of testing technologies are:

- Electrodiagnostic
- Endoscopic
- Nuclear
- Ultrasound
- Miscellaneous

§ 4.10   —Electrodiagnostic Tests

1. **Electrocardiogram (EKG).** This test records the heart's electrical activity. Transmission of electrical impulses through the heart muscle is necessary for the heart to beat rhythmically and thus pump blood throughout the body. Faulty transmission of these impulses often occurs in heart disease and may produce arrythmias. If arrhythmias are suspected, but do not present on a routine EKG, a *Holter monitor* may attached to the body for 24 hours. Heart rhythms for this period are transmitted to a tape in the monitor and analyzed at the end of the test period. EKG's also can assist in the diagnosis of the extent of heart muscle injury following MI.

2. **Electroencephalogram (EEG).** This test records the brain's electrical activity and can assist in the diagnosis of a variety of neurological

conditions such as epilepsy. Electroencephalograms are also used to diagnose brain injury severity and determine brain death. **See Chapter 6** for additional information on brain injuries and brain death.

3. **Electroencephalographic Brain Mapping and Evoked Potentials.** *EEG brain mapping* is a digital technique that produces color-coded maps of EEG activity, which are used to identify subtle areas of slowing that traditional EEG assessments miss. *Evoked potentials* are a type of EEG in which brain waves are monitored as the patient is exposed to various external stimuli. Evoked potentials map by visual, somatosensory (perception of sensory stimulation), or auditory methods. They are evaluated along the parameters of *latency,* the time between onset of stimulus and any particular point of waveform; *amplitude,* the distance from peak (high point) of one waveform to trough (low point); and *morphology,* the image of the waveform component.

4. **Electromyogram (EMG).** This test measures electrical activity associated with the innervation of skeletal muscle (action potential). Needle electrodes are placed in the muscle to be evaluated. Normally, there is no muscle activity at rest; electrical activity is present with contraction. EMGs can differentiate between primary muscle disease and disease secondary to nerve dysfunction.

5. **Electroneurogram (ENG) or Nerve Conduction Studies.** Nerve conduction studies measure the nerve impulse passage time from point of stimulation to the point of recording. Often performed in conjunction with EMGs, these tests are helpful in diagnosing peripheral nerve injuries.

6. **Stress Test (Treadmill).** A stress test records the heart's electrical activity while exercising. Normally, there are no changes in the EKG rhythm during exercise, but heart rate increases. Heart disease can cause changes in the heart rhythm. A very commonly ordered test, stress testing is used to rule out myocardial infarction in individuals with chest pain. It can also be used to determine the limits of safe exercise and evaluate the impact of cardiac procedures such as heart surgery or angioplasty.

§ 4.11 —Endoscopy

Endoscopy is the general term that refers to the examination of a specific body cavity via a fiberoptic tube, an *endoscope.* In addition to direct visualization of the specific organ(s), tissue samples (biopsies) can be obtained, and minor surgical procedures can be performed. Endoscopic procedures are named for the specific area to be visualized and/or treated. They include:

- Arthroscopy—joint interior, such as knee or elbow
- Bronchoscopy—the larynx, trachea, and bronchi
- Colonoscopy—the rectum, colon, and small bowel
- Colposcopy—the cervix and vagina
- Cystoscopy—the urethra and urinary bladder and the prostate gland in males
- Endoscopic retrograde cholangiopancreatography (ERCP)—the bile and pancreatic ducts (via the duodenum)
- Esophagogastroduodenoscopy—the esophagus, stomach, and duodenum
- Hysteroscopy—the endometrial cavity of the uterus
- Laparoscopy—the abdominal and pelvic organs.
- Sigmoidoscopy—the rectum and sigmoid colon
- Sinusoscopy—the sinus cavities
- Thorascopy—the pleura, lungs and mediastinum

§ 4.12   —Nuclear Imaging

Nuclear scans use radioactive isotopes to identify both structural and functional abnormalities in various parts of the body. Following administration of the radioisotope (usually IV), a scanning device picks up radioactive emissions from body tissues. These tests do not provide information as to the cause of a given abnormality and therefore, are used in conjunction with other diagnostic tests for arriving at a specific diagnosis.

1. **Bone Scan.** The radioisotope (frequently gallium) is injected intravenously and is taken up by bone. It becomes heavily concentrated in abnormal bone and can therefore detect conditions such as malignancies, osteomyelitis, osteoporosis, and fractures.

2. **Brain Scan.** This test can be used to identify abnormalities in the brain, such as tumors or hemorrhage. Because other technology such

as CT scans and MRI's provide more definitive information, these tests may be used in lieu of brain scan for diagnostic purposes.

3. **Cardiac Nuclear Scan.** When cardiac scans are performed, a radio-isotope is injected intravenously and a radiation detector is placed over the heart. An image of the heart is then recorded and photo-graphed to detect conditions such as myocardial ischemia, infarction, and dysfunction of the myocardial wall. It is most frequently used as part of cardiac stress testing and is also known as *heart scan, thallium scan,* or *MUGA scan.*

4. **Gallbladder Nuclear Scan (HIDA Scan).** This test is done to deter-mine patency of the liver and biliary ducts. It can confirm a diagnosis of acute cholecystitis and identify diffuse liver disease.

5. **Gallium Scan.** Gallium is injected intravenously. If any areas of WBC concentration are present in the body, gallium will concentrate there. Through identification of areas of concentration, the location of specific types of tumors and areas of infection in patients with fever of unknown origin can be determined.

6. **Liver-Spleen Scan.** This test visualizes the liver and spleen. It can determine if liver tumor, either primary or metastatic, is present. It is also used to monitor response to liver disease treatment.

7. **Lung Scan.** IV radioisotope is injected and results are read approx-imately 30 minutes afterward. Normally there is diffuse uptake of the nuclear material by the lungs. The test is used to diagnose pulmonary embolus, but false-positives can occur in patients with pneumonia, emphysema, lung tumor, and pleural effusion.

§ 4.13   —Ultrasound

Ultrasound, also known as sonography, projects high frequency waves that are reflected and converted into electrical energy. These waves cannot pass through bone or gas, but provide excellent imaging of fluid-filled organs (pregnant uterus) and soft organs (liver). Doppler ultrasonography mea-sures blood flow within the circulatory system.

1. **Abdominal Ultrasound.** This test visualizes the organs within the abdominal cavity. Specifically, these organs include the kidneys, liver, gallbladder, pancreas, and aorta.

2. **Carotid Artery Duplex Scan.** This test is done to visualize the carotid arteries and their branches. It will identify narrowing (stenosis) and the presence of plaques and register velocity of blood flow.

3. **Echocardiogram.** This test scans the heart utilizing ultrasonic waves to assess motion and function of the heart and heart valves.

4. **Intravascular Ultrasound.** A flexible catheter with miniature transducer at the distal tip is inserted over a guidewire into a coronary artery to provide visual information about the artery's interior. The resulting image is cross-sectional; that is, it depicts the three walls (layers) of the artery: the intima, the media, and the adventitia, as well as the diameter of the vessel lumen. It better depicts plaque distribution and composition and degree of stenosis (closure) of occluded artery. This technique provides more detailed information on the location and type of plaque than older angiography that relies on iodine dyes and x-rays that create two-dimensional pictures.

5. **Transesophageal Echocardiography (TEE).** A transducer is placed via an esophageal endoscope inserted into the esophagus. The transducer provides information on the functionality of the heart and its valves. It is used to evaluate prosthetic valve function and for aneurysm detection.

6. **Transcranial Doppler.** This is noninvasive technique for assessing intra-cranial arteries at the base of the skull. Cerebral blood flow (CBF) can be increased or decreased in relation to the metabolic demand following head injury.

§ 4.14 —Miscellaneous Diagnostic Tests

1. **Audiometry**—measures hearing function. Refer to **Chapter 3, §§ 3.37–3.39** for more information on the ear and additional diagnostic tests available.

2. **Pulmonary Function Tests.** These are a battery of tests that assess the adequacy of the process of respiration (exchange of oxygen and carbon dioxide within the body). Common causes of decreased pulmonary function are emphysema, infection, and tumor.

3. **Pulse Oximetry.** In oximetry testing and monitoring, a sensor is attached to a finger, toe, or earlobe and captures the pulse rate along with the oxygen saturation of the blood. Oximetry decreases

the need for arterial blood gas monitoring and is used frequently in the acute care setting.

4. **Purified Protein Derivative (PPD).** The purified protein derivative from the tuberculosis bacillus is injected under the skin. A positive reaction indicates exposure to tuberculosis. This reaction does not differentiate between past exposure and (current) active tuberculosis infection.

5. **Sleep studies.** These tests are used to diagnose obstructive *sleep apnea,* an obstruction of the upper airway that results in no ventilation for at least 10 seconds. Apneic episodes may result in low oxygen levels in the blood, heart disturbances, muscle spasms, sleep interruption, and insomnia. During sleep studies, airflow adequacy through the nose and mouth are carefully monitored. Additional monitoring is provided through EKG, EMG, and pulse oximetry.

6. **Tonometry**—measures the fluid pressure inside the eye. Pressure will be elevated in glaucoma. Refer to **Chapter 3, §§ 3.34–3.36** for more information on the eye and additional diagnostic tests available.

§ 4.15   Diagnostic Testing During Pregnancy

Fetal testing and monitoring results are critical information to cases involving adverse outcomes to mother or baby during the intra-partum period. Although it is generally beyond the scope of the legal professional (without benefit of medical background and education) to interpret these data, accurate summarization of the data as recorded in the medical records is essential. A variety of diagnostic tests assist with evaluation of both mother and baby during the course of pregnancy. Many of these tests utilize the technologies discussed in the previous sections. The material following presents only a high level discussion of some of the tests that may be performed. In a case involving maternal-child issues, more definitive sources of reference materials should be consulted.

During pregnancy and birth, the goal of medical care and treatment is the prevention of complications to both mother and baby. Maternal complications and deaths associated with pregnancy and delivery arise from three main causes: hypertension, infection, and hemorrhage. Injuries that occur to the newborn during the birth process are most likely to occur when the baby is large, the presentation is breech, or forceful extraction is used. Maternal factors such as uterine dysfunction that lead to precipitous or prolonged labor, preterm or post-term labor can also increase risk to the infant. Many maternal complications and infant birth injuries can be avoided or minimized with comprehensive prenatal care.

§ 4.16 —Ultrasound

Ultrasound (see § 4.13) is a non-invasive test that is useful in assessing many indicators of fetal health during pregnancy. It allows rapid diagnosis of fetal abnormalities so appropriate interventions can be considered. Often during the course of pregnancy an ultrasound is performed routinely in the first trimester to confirm the pregnancy and fetal viability. Some indications for additional testing throughout the course of the pregnancy are

1. To confirm viability. Fetal heart activity can be detected by ultrasound at 6 to 8 weeks. In the case of fetal death, no heart activity would be present. Fetal scalp edema and maceration of the cranial bones may be evident.

2. To confirm gestational age. There is a need to confirm gestational age if the mother is uncertain about the dates of her last menstrual period or if the uterine size does not agree with the date of the last menstrual period. Bleeding during the first trimester and other high-risk conditions can also warrant ultrasound to confirm gestational age.

3. To monitor fetal growth. Concern around the rate of fetal growth can arise if maternal weight gain during pregnancy is poor or if there is history of maternal drug use, hypertension, diabetes mellitus, or previous history of intrauterine growth retardation.

4. To rule out anomalies in fetal anatomy. Ultrasound can visualize all major fetal structures. Therefore, the majority of major anomalies can be identified and appropriate interventions can be planned and executed in a timely manner.

5. To assess placental position, function, and maturity. Determination of placental maturity can be made during the third trimester. Maturity is graded on a scale of 0 (first trimester, least mature) to III (usually after 38 weeks). In post-term pregnancies, mature placentas can experience a decrease in the surface area supplied by maternal blood that may result in decreased oxygen delivery to the fetus.

6. As an adjunct to amniocentesis. The safety of amniocentesis increases if the physician knows the exact position of the fetus and placenta as well as the location of amniotic fluid pockets. See § 4.17 below.

§ 4.17   —Amniocentesis and Amniotic Fluid Volume Determination

Amniocentesis may be done during pregnancy to determine chromosomal, anatomic, and metabolic abnormalities in the developing fetus. It can also determine age and sex. Amniotic fluid is obtained from the uterine cavity by inserting a needle into the mother's abdomen.

Fetal abnormalities have been associated with both increased and decreased amniotic fluid volumes. Oligohydramnios (decreased fluid) is determined by absence of fluid pockets in the uterine cavity and the impression of crowding of fetal parts. Objective determination of oligohydramnios is made when the largest pocket of fluid measured in two perpendicular planes is less than 1 cm. This condition is associated with congenital anomalies of the kidney and growth retardation. Polyhydramnios (increased fluid) is diagnosed by presence of multiple large pockets of fluid, the impression of floating fetus and free movement of fetal limbs. Objective determination of polyhydramnios is made when the largest pocket of fluid measured in two perpendicular planes is greater than 1 cm. Polyhydramnios is associated with neural tube defects, GI tract obstruction, multiple fetuses, and hydrops fetalis. See **Figure 4–1.**

§ 4.18   —Doppler Blood Flow Analysis

Doppler ultrasound can study fetal and placental blood flow non-invasively by visualizing both the uterine and umbilical arteries. Results are reported as systolic/diastolic (S/D) ratios. Ratios should decrease as pregnancy advances with S/D ratios of 3 or less than expected by 30 weeks. Persistently high ratios are associated with intrauterine growth retardation resulting from placental insufficiency.

§ 4.19   —Biophysical Profile

The developing fetus responds to lack of oxygen arising from the central nervous system by changes in body movement, muscle tone, breathing, and heart rate patterns. Biophysical profile (BPP) is a non-invasive dynamic assessment of the fetus and surrounding environment that

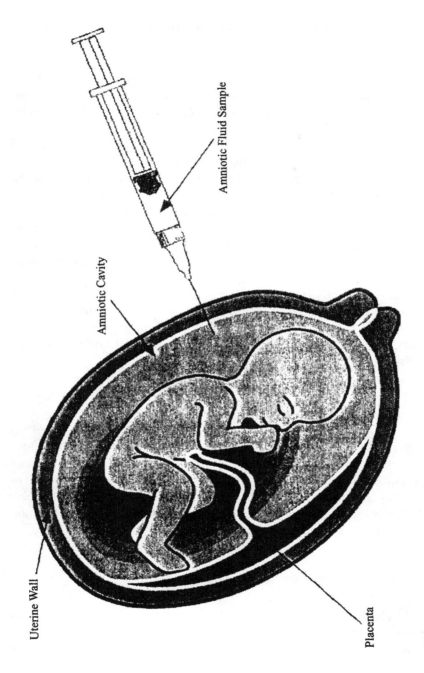

Figure 4–1. Amniocentesis.

evaluates these critical parameters using ultrasound and external fetal monitoring. A fetus with normal biophysical profile indicates a fully functioning central nervous system. Three distinct variables are assessed in biophysical profiling, and absence of any of them is considered significant. These variables should demonstrate:

1. **Fetal breathing movements.** An inward movement of the thorax with descent of the diaphragm, followed by a return to original position should be observed.

2. **Fetal movements.** Single or clusters of activity involving limbs and fetal body should be observed.

3. **Fetal tone.** At least one episode of opening of the hand with finger and thumb extension with a return to closed fist formation should be observed. In absence of hand motion, tone is still recorded as normal if the hand remains in the fist formation for the entire 30 minutes of observation. BPP scoring includes two additional findings: qualitative amniotic fluid volume level with normal recorded as at least 1 cm on two perpendicular planes, and a screening non-stress test. BPP variables are most commonly scored as 0 or 2 points. The biophysical profile is an early predictor of potential fetal problems, and results can be used to plan appropriate interventions and care. See **Table 4–1.**

§ 4.20   —MRI

Like ultrasound, magnetic resonance imaging or MRI (see § 4.8) is a non-invasive tool that provides excellent visualization of soft tissues. It can also provide images in multiple planes without the need for injection of contrast dyes. In pregnancy, MRI can be used to evaluate the following:

1. Fetal structure—central nervous system, thorax, abdomen, GU tract, musculoskeletal system, and overall growth

2. Placenta—position, density, and presence of structural abnormalities

3. Amniotic fluid quantity

4. Maternal structures—pelvis, uterus, cervix, adenexa

5. Biochemical status—pH and ATP content of tissues and organs

6. Soft tissue, metabolic, or functional malformations

Table 4–1

Biophysical Profile Scoring: Technique and Interpretation

Variable	Normal—Score = 2	Abnormal—Score = 0
Fetal Breathing Movement	At least one episode of fetal breathing movement of at least a 30 second duration in a 30 minute observation.	Absent fetal breathing movement or no episode of >30 seconds in 30 minutes.
Gross Body Movement	At least three discrete body or limb movements in 30 minutes. Episodes of active continuous movement are considered as a single movement.	Two or fewer episodes of body or limb movements in 30 minutes.
Fetal Tone	At least one episode of active extension with rturn to flexion of fetal limb(s) or trunk. Opening and closing of hand considered normal tone.	Either slow extension with return to partial flexion or movement of limb in full extension, absent fetal movement.
Reactive Fetal Heart Rate	At least two episodes of fetal heart rate acceleration of >15 beats per min and of at least 15 seconds duration associated with fetal movement in 30 minutes.	Less than two episodes of acceleration of fetal heart rate or acceleration of >15 beats per minute in 30 seconds.
Qualitative Amniotic Fluid Volume	At least one pocket of amniotic fluid that measures at least 1 cm in two perpendicular planes.	Either no amniotic fluid or a pocket of <1 cm in two in two perpendicular planes.

From F. Manning & C. Harman, *The fetal biophysical profile* (R. Eden & F. Boehm eds., 1990), in Assessments and Care of the Fetus: Physiological, Clinical and Medicolegal Principles, Appelton and Lange, 1990. In I. Bobak & M. Jensen, Maternity and gynecologic care, Mosby & Co., St. Louis, Mo, 1993.

§ 4.21   —Daily Fetal Movement Count

In general, the presence of fetal movements during pregnancy is a reassuring sign of fetal health. Counting the number of daily fetal movements is non-invasive and can be easily understood and done at home by the mother with little disruption to daily routine. It is worrisome if fetal movements cease entirely for 12 hours. Generally, less than three fetal movements in one hour warrants further evaluation through non-stress or contraction stress testing, biophysical profile scoring, or both.

§ 4.22   —Biochemical Assessment

Biochemical assessment of the fetus involves the study of components such as genes, exfoliated (cast-off) cells, or chemical composition of tissue, blood, or amniotic fluid. Several procedures are done to perform biochemical assessment during pregnancy.

1. Amniocentesis (see § 4.17). Can be performed after 14 weeks of pregnancy when uterus is sufficiently enlarged and adequate amounts of amniotic fluid are present. Amniocentesis is indicated for prenatal diagnosis of genetic disorders, assessment of pulmonary maturity, and diagnosis of fetal hemolytic disease. Possible maternal complications of amniocentesis include hemorrhage, infection, abruptio placenta, induction of labor, and inadvertent damage to intestines or bladder. Possible fetal complications include infection (amnionitis), injury from needle, preterm labor, and leakage of amniotic fluid.

2. Percutaneous umbilical blood sampling (cordocentesis). Involves insertion of needle into fetal umbilical vessel under ultrasound. It is used for fetal blood sampling and transfusion, prenatal diagnosis of inherited blood disorders, and detection of fetal infection.

3. Chorionic vili sampling. Sampling is done between 10 and 12 weeks of gestation and involves removal of tissue from the fetal side of the placenta under ultrasound guidance. This procedure can diagnose genetic defects earlier than can amniocentesis. Complications arising from chorionic vili sampling include vaginal spotting or bleeding, spontaneous abortion, membrane rupture, and chorioamnioitis.

4. Maternal assays. Samples of maternal serum (blood) are taken and tested for alpha-fetoprotein (AFP) levels to detect neural tube defects such as spina bifida and meningocele.

§ 4.23   —Fetal Heart Rate Patterns

Fetal heart rate is a critical indicator of fetal health at rest and under stressful conditions. Health care providers watch for changes in four basic components of heart rate during the intrapartum period.

1. **Baseline fetal heart rate.** Baseline is defined as the average fetal heart rate when the mother is not in labor or is between contractions. At term, average fetal heart rate is around 135 to 140 beats per minute, with a normal range of between 110 and 160 beats per minute.
2. **Tachycardia.** A baseline fetal heart rate above 160 beats per minute or an increase of more than 30 beats per minute from previous baseline for greater than 10 minutes. Tachycardia can be a sign of fetal hypoxia. Possible causes include maternal or fetal infection, fetal anemia, or drug reactions.
3. **Bradycardia.** A baseline fetal heart rate of below 120 beats per minute or a decrease of more than 30 beats per minute from the previous baseline for greater than 10 minutes. Bradycardia is a later sign of fetal hypoxia and is known to occur prior to fetal death. Possible causes include placental transfer of anesthetics, prolonged compression of the umbilical cord, maternal hypothermia, and maternal hypotension.
4. **Variability.** This is a normal irregularity of fetal cardiac rhythm that is a result of a balancing interaction of the parasympathetic (cardio-deceleration) and sympathetic (cardioacceleration) divisions of the autonomic nervous system.

    See **Chapter 3, § 3.16.** Fetal heart rate variability is described as *short term* (changes in heart rate from one beat to the next) or *long term* variability (rhythmic cycles or waves from baseline, generally 3 to 5 cycles apart). An absence of variability or smooth (flat) baseline is a sign of potential fetal distress. Causes of absence of variability include fetal hypoxia and reaction to drugs causing central nervous system depression.

Periodic changes in fetal heart rate are referred to as accelerations (increased heart rate) or decelerations (decreased heart rate), with decelerations described as *early, late,* or *variable,* depending on timing, shape, and repetitiveness in relation to uterine contractions. *Accelerations* are considered normal if they occur during fetal movement. *Early decelerations* are normal if they are in response to uterine contractions. *Late decelerations* begin after a contraction has been established and consistently persist into the interval after the contraction is over. Late decelerations may indicate fetal hypoxia because of insufficient placental perfusion. They are particularly significant if decreased variability and tachycardia are occurring simultaneously. Finally, *variable decelerations* occur at any time during a uterine contraction phase and are caused by umbilical cord compression. They are a non-reassuring sign if there is a slow return to baseline and a decreasing variability or acceleration below 70 for more than 30 to 45 seconds.

§ 4.24   —Stress Testing

Two types of electric monitoring are done to assess for potential problems, the non-stress test and the contraction stress test. Stress tests can determine if the uterine environment is supportive to the fetus. The non-stress test is the most commonly used test for evaluation of the fetus and fetal activity. The normal fetus will produce characteristic heart rate patterns. Acceleration of fetal heart rate in response to fetal movement is the desired outcome. Non-stress tests are non-invasive, and there are no contraindications to performing them. However, non-stress tests do have some disadvantages, principally high false positive rates as a result of fetal sleep cycles, medications, and fetal immaturity.

Contraction stress tests (CST) identify the fetus in distress that is stable at rest but shows evidence of compromise with introduction of stress. Uterine contractions decrease uterine blood flow and compromise placental perfusion. If the decrease is sufficient to produce hypoxia in the fetus, fetal heart rate deceleration will occur beginning at the peak of contractions and persisting after conclusion (late deceleration). Normally, no late decelerations will occur. Contraction stress testing provides earlier warning of fetal compromise than non-stress testing and fewer false positives; however, there are some associated complications such as ruptured membranes, preterm labor, and bleeding if placenta previa is present. Stress testing is concerned with the assessment of three parameters: accelerations, decelerations (late or early), and variability. See § 4.23 above for definition and explanation of these parameters.

§ 4.25   —Electronic Fetal Monitoring

Electronic monitoring is used during labor to monitor for signs of fetal distress in the intra-partum period. Labor is a stressful time for the fetus, and an adequate supply of oxygen must be maintained throughout the birth process. Electronic monitoring tracks fetal heart rate and detects early signs of oxygen compromise to the fetus. Two methods of monitoring can be utilized, internal and external. Which type is utilized depends on the type of information needed. Both types should include the same types of "normal" parameters that indicate adequate oxygen supply to the fetus: baseline fetal heart rate in the range of 120 to 160 beats per minute with no periodic changes and average baseline variability, and accelerations associated with fetal movement.

External monitoring uses two separate transducers that are applied to the abdomen, one to monitor fetal heart rate and the other to monitor uterine contractions. One of the main limitations of external monitoring is the inability to accurately assess short-term variability and beat-to-beat changes in fetal heart rate.

Internal monitoring can only be utilized after the membranes are ruptured, the cervix is sufficiently dilated, and the presenting part is low enough for electrode placement. Fetal heart rate is monitored by means of a fetal scalp electrode that is attached to the presenting part and gives continuous fetal heart rate documentation on a monitor strip in much the same manner as an EKG. Only internal monitoring can detect short-term variability. Uterine contractions are measured by means of an intrauterine pressure catheter that measures frequency, duration, and intensity of uterine contractions. Both internal and external monitoring print out data electronically, similar in format to EKG data. It is important to note if internal or external monitoring was performed, as the two methods display data differently. It is also important to remember that other parameters of fetal and maternal wellbeing must be evaluated along with fetal heart rate patterns. Medical interventions should be based on careful assessment and interpretation of all data by the clinician.

§ 4.26   Physical Examination and Testing

In many medical malpractice, personal injury, or workers' compensation cases, residual disability must be determined before settlement discussions can begin. Part of this determination is provided from findings of physical examination, done by an appropriate health care provider. In physical examination, the functionality of body systems is assessed and abnormal findings are identified. This information is documented in a *history and physical* exam. Further specific testing deemed necessary, as well as the plan of treatment, is guided by history and physical findings.

§ 4.27   The History and Physical Examination

As stated in **Chapter 2,** documentation required in medical records for inpatient and some outpatient care settings is governed by various regulatory agencies. The History and Physical examination, commonly referred to as the H&P, is a critical component of the medical records, as it documents the baseline status of the individual when first seen by the provider. When reviewing medical records, scrutinize the H&P closely, paying particular attention to past health problems in addition to the current injury/problem. Include in your summary any past health problems that could impact the case. For example, if a client claiming back pain as a result of a recent slip and fall has a history of prior back pain, this would most probably be noted in the H&P and would be important to include in your summary.

The *history* portion of the H&P is obtained through client interview. The information obtained is considered to be *subjective,* that is, not measurable; it is information from the client's perspective. Both medical and psychosocial histories should be obtained. Types of information that should be obtained include:

1. Patient demographics—age, sex, occupation, country of birth, family health history.
2. Past medical history—chronic illnesses, surgeries, past injuries.
3. Current medications—prescription, over the counter drugs, herbal supplements. Alcohol and tobacco consumption (including quantity) should also be documented.
4. Current complaint—the immediate problem, the reason why the individual sought care. If the current complaint arises from an injury, the client's description of the incident should be documented.

The interview process should not be shortchanged. Often, vital information can be overlooked if an examiner does not take a thorough history. Unfortunately, the quality of the history depends, in large part, on the communication skills of the examiner and the time spent building trust with the individual during the interview process.

After the history is completed, the *physical examination* is performed. The physical examination consists of data that can be observed and measured and is, therefore, considered *objective* data. Physical examination uses four basic techniques to obtain data:

1. **Inspection.** A visual examination of the body performed in a deliberate and systematic manner. See examples of information that can be obtained in § **4.28** below.

2. **Palpation or touch.** The examiner applies varying amounts of pressure with his/her hands to determine information such as organ size, tenderness or pain, skin temperature, presence of masses and pulses; e.g., breast examination or pulse palpation.

3. **Percussion.** The hands or an object are used to strike the skin and results in production of sound. The sound emitted allows assessment of the underlying area; for example, lung percussion can identify consolidation in a specific area.

4. **Auscultation or listening.** Internal body sounds, enhanced by a stethoscope, are evaluated and assessed as normal or abnormal; e.g. auscultation of cardiac or bowel sounds.

Vital signs will also be notes as part of the physical exam. Vital signs include:

- Temperature—can be measured in Celsius or Fahrenheit degrees. Temperature can be taken orally, rectally, axillary, or via the tympanic membrane of the ear.

- Pulse (radial and/or apical)—is expressed as number of beats/minute. Radial pulse is measured by palpation of the radial artery and counting the number of beats/minute. Apical pulse is measured by placing a stethoscope over the heart and counting the number of heartbeats per minute.

- Respiration—is measured by observing the number of breaths taken per minute.

- Blood pressure—measures the degree of pressure exerted by the blood against the artery walls. Two pressure measurements are taken: systolic blood pressure (SBP) measures the peak pressure exerted against the arteries when the heart contracts, diastolic blood pressure (DBP) measures the residual pressure in the arteries during ventricular relaxation. These two values are expressed as a ratio, with systolic blood pressure as the top value and diastolic the bottom value, e.g. BP is 120/80.

- Height and weight are also generally included

The physical examination is a systematic assessment of body systems and should include both mental and physical status. Findings from the examination may be either positive or negative and both should be noted if significant. For example, an enlarged liver noted on palpation is a *positive* finding; absence of back/leg pain with straight leg raising is a *negative* finding. Although the system for performing physical examination may vary among practitioners, documented findings should include (in some form) general observations, a review of body systems, including evaluation of motor and sensory function (muscles, joints, and nerves), and assessment of mental status. The review of body systems often includes examination and findings for:

- HEENT—head, eyes, ears, nose, and throat
- Heart or cardiac
- Respiratory or lungs
- GI
- Musculoskeletal
- Neurologic
- Urinary tract
- Reproductive

The most detailed examination will center on the areas involving chief complaints, problems, and injuries as detailed in the history.

§ 4.28   —General Observations

Observation provides the basis for the entire physical examination. Client posture, gait, and movement abnormalities help determine the patient's ability to perform activities essential to daily living and job performance. Other observations may include mental status and mood, speech, and nutritional status.

Postural Characteristics. Observations include how erect a person holds himself in relation to the anatomical position. Changes in stance give clues to further examinations needed. Presence of lordosis, kyphosis, or scoliosis should be noted and evaluated as contributing factors to posture abnormalities.

Gait. Assessment involves observing the client's walk. Normal gait involves a series of rhythmic movements. These combined movements form a gait pattern that propels the body forward smoothly and efficiently. Significant deviations from normal gait patterns indicate alterations in the integrity of the neurologic and musculoskeletal systems. Certain gaits are associated with specific diseases; for example, an *antalgic* gait is associated with hip pain.

Quality of Movement. The quality of movement describes how evenly a person moves. Observations of movement quality help assess the client's degree of mobility and how well activities of daily living can be performed. Pain or neurological dysfunction can alter the quality of movement.

§ 4.29 —Motor Function (Muscles)

Muscles have the functions of contraction (shortening) and relaxation (lengthening). These two motions, working together in muscle groups and joints, enable the body to move. Many causes of joint dysfunction affect surrounding muscles. Conditions that may impair muscle strength result from diseases such as cerebral palsy, polio, Parkinson's disease, and myasthenia gravis. Passive range of motion tests performed on joints demonstrate the tone and strength of surrounding muscles. The ability to perform range of motion under resistance, e.g. with weights on extremities, may also be tested. In addition to muscle strength and tone, muscle coordination should be evaluated.

Muscle Strength. Several different scales for grading muscle strength exist. A common numerical scale is:

- Grade 5 or normal—can hold or move body part against gravity with maximum resistance
- Grade 4 (good)—can hold or move body part against gravity with minimum to moderate resistance
- Grade 3 (fair)—can hold or move body part against gravity only
- Grade 2 (poor)—can move body part through range of motion against gravity with support/assistance

- Grade 1 (trace)—cannot move body part at all, but some muscle contraction can be felt
- Grade 0 (zero)—no evidence of muscle contraction.

Muscle Tone. Muscle tone describes the state of tension of muscles at rest, indicated by their firmness. Major muscle groups of the body are observed for size. Neurological injury, pain, and/or immobility can cause muscle wasting or shrinking that gives the muscle a smaller than normal appearance. The degree of wasting is determined by comparing the affected muscle to its twin counterpart; for example, the quadriceps muscle of the injured leg would be compared to the quadriceps muscle of the uninjured leg.

Muscle Coordination. The examiner may perform maneuvers that test rapid alternating movements, point-to-point ability, and balance maintenance.

If muscle function abnormalities are found during physical examination, additional diagnostic tests may be ordered.

§ 4.30   —Motor Function (Joints)

All body joints have the ability to move by extension (stretching) or by flexion (bending). The degree of movement in joints, called the range of motion, varies a great deal. For example, the elbow has more movement than the spinal vertebrae. Every joint has a unique range of motion although some ranges are similar, for example, the knees and elbows. In addition to demonstrating normal range of motion, joints should be symmetric, without redness, swelling, or deformity. They should glide smoothly when moved, with no crepitus.

Joints require movement to maintain their range of motion. When injury, disease, or elective joint surgery prohibit this, joint function suffers, resulting in decreased ability to flex and/or extend the joint. Conditions that cause impairment in joint function include arthritis, joint immobilization (when a cast is applied for bone fracture), or spinal cord injury. When evaluating joint function, the examiner often tests for both active range of motion (what the client is able to do) and passive range of motion (what the client needs assistance in doing). The examiner also evaluates joint stability, a function dependent on the ligaments supporting the joint.

Several sources have determined values on normal range of motion for body joints. **Table 4–2** contains a partial listing of the values for normal joint motion from the Committee on Joint Motion, American Academy of Orthopedics.

Table 4–2

Normal Joint Motion

Joint	Degrees of Motion
CERVICAL SPINE	
flexion	45
extension	45
lateral bending	45
THORACIC & LUMBAR SPINE	
flexion	80
extension	20–30
lateral bending	35
ELBOW	
flexion	150
hyperextension	0
WRIST	
extension	70
flexion	80
SHOULDER	
forward flexion	180
backward extension	60
abduction	180
adduction	75
HIP	
flexion	120
extension	30
abduction	45
adduction	30
KNEE	
flexion	135
hyperextension	10
ANKLE	
flexion	50
extension	20

§ 4.31   —Sensory Function

Examination of sensory function should include hearing, vision, and taste testing. It should also include testing for discerning pain, touch, vibration, and body position. Sensory organs (eyes, ear, tongue) are supplied by specific cranial nerves and discrete skin areas (dermatomes) are innervated by specific spinal nerves. See **Chapter 6, § 6.18.** Thus, abnormalities in sensory assessment provide valuable information in determining the location of dysfunctional areas.

Sensory function examination involves assessing responses to superficial and mechanical stimuli. *Superficial sensation* testing includes touch and pain. In an unresponsive patient, superficial sensation can only be tested for response to painful stimuli. Responses are elicited through application of *noxious stimuli.* Common forms of stimuli include rubbing the sternum, applying pressure to the bony rim around the eye, and squeezing the clavicle. Responses typically manifested to noxious stimuli are

- Localization—stimulus is pushed away.
- Withdrawal—stimulus is pulled away from.
- Decorticate posturing—fists are pulled up toward the chest and legs are extended. This response is indicative of damage to the brain cortex.
- Decerebrate posturing—arms are extended and outwardly rotated; legs are extended. This response indicates damage to the cerebellum of the brain.
- No response—no visible movement in response to painful stimulus.

§ 4.32   —Reflex Activity

Reflexes are a result of muscles that contract and relax promptly in response to a stimulus. They provide valuable information on the nature and location of nervous system disorders. There are two types of reflexes: superficial or cutaneous, and deep tendon reflexes (DTRs) or muscle stretch.

Superficial Reflexes

Superficial reflexes occur as a result of skin or mucous membrane stimulation. Major cutaneous reflexes are:

1.   Abdominal—skin on the abdomen is scratched and the abdominal muscle in that quadrant contracts.

2. Plantar Reflex—involves stroking the sole of the foot from the heel upward toward the big toe. The normal response is flexion of the toes as illustrated in **Figure 4–2.** Babinski's reflex is an abnormal plantar reflex. Plantar stroking causes the great toe to flex and the remaining toes to fan and indicates some type of brain injury. See **Figure 4–3.**

3. Corneal Reflex—gentle touching of the cornea causes blinking.

4. Pharangeal (gag) Reflex—back of throat is stimulated with an object (tongue blade) and gagging occurs. Superficial reflexes are graded as $0 =$ absent, $\pm =$ slightly present, $+ =$ normal.

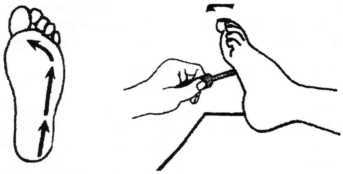

Figure 4–2. Normal plantar reflex.

Figure 4–3. Abnormal plantar reflex (Babinski).

Deep Tendon Reflexes

DTRs result from reflex contraction of a rapidly stretching muscle. These reflexes are located in the ankle, knee (patellar), biceps, and triceps muscles. For example, the patellar reflex (knee-jerk) involves tapping the tendon below the knee with a reflex hammer. The examiner's hand is under the knee, holding the leg in a relaxed position. A normal response will be a jerking outward of the leg. Deep tendon reflexes are graded from 0 through 4+, with 2+ being normal. Often, asymmetrical DTRs are considered more significant than the reflex grade of one limb.

Pupil Reflexes

Because the majority of the cranial nerves innervate the eye, testing of pupil reflexes is an essential component of sensory function assessment. Pupils are tested for reaction to light, accommodation, and extra-ocular movements:

1. Reaction to light—pupils should be equal in size and constrict equally in reaction to light.
2. Accommodation—eyes should deviate toward the nose as the client follows the examiner's finger, which is moving toward the nose.
3. Extra-ocular movements—eyes should follow the examiner's finger as it moves in different directions. Inability of one or both eyes to follow the finger is abnormal.

§ 4.33   —Mental Status

Mental status assessment involves a determination of the baseline level of consciousness, orientation, memory, mood, and speech. In a conscious patient, all can be determined through client interview. It is critical to obtain these baseline functional levels so subsequent findings (of improvement or deterioration) can be measured against them. Many tools exist for evaluating mental status; several common methods follow:

1. Level of Consciousness—one of the most sensitive indicators of changes in neurological status, level of consciousness is assessed by providing specific stimuli and observing the response. The Glasgow

Coma Scale is frequently used to assess the level of consciousness (see § **4.34**), especially following head injury and cranial surgery.

2. Orientation—determines familiarity to person, place, and time; can be determined through appropriate client questioning. Orientation commonly appears in the physical examination as: "Alert and oriented (A&O) × 3".

3. Memory—tests both short- and long-term memory; determined through appropriate client questioning.

4. Mood—should include both *subjective* (what client states) as well as *objective* (what examiner observes). Discrepancies between subjective and objective findings should be noted.

Neuropsychologic Testing

Further mental status evaluation may involve neuropsychological testing. Neuropsychology studies the relationship of brain function to behavior. Assessment tools consist of a battery of tests that can be administered serially to evaluate changes in functional ability. Test results should be compared to any similar tests administered prior to the accident or incident. This type of evaluation is extremely important in determining the client's functional abilities for activities of daily living, employment, and education. Major functional areas tested may include attention and concentration, memory, language, personality, and intellect. The Minnesota Multiphasic Personality Inventory (MMPI) is an example of a common neuropsychological testing tool.

§ 4.34   —Acute Head Injury Assessment

Acute head injuries require close observation and monitoring of both anatomical and functional neurological status. Because neurological changes can occur subtly, these observations must be done frequently and compared to baseline values. Sudden deterioration of neurologic status requires prompt intervention. The seriousness of an acute head injury can be assessed (in part) and quantified by the Glasgow Coma Scale. This instrument consists of three components: eye movements, motor response, and level of consciousness. Each is given a numerical score for best (highest value) and worst (lowest value) responses. Cumulative scores rate the seriousness of the head injury. Generally, a score of 0 to 8 indicates severe injury, 9 to 12 indicates moderate injury, and 13 to 15, mild injury. See **Table 4–3.**

Table 4–3

Glasgow Coma Scale

	Response	Activity	Score
EYES	open	spontaneously	4
		to verbal command	3
		to pain	2
	no response		1
BEST MOTOR RESPONSE	to verbal command	obeys	6
	to painful stimuli	localizes pain	5
		withdrawal	4
		abnormal extremity flexion	3
		extension of extremities	2
		no response	1
BEST VERBAL RESPONSE		oriented	5
		confused conversation	4
		inappropriate words	3
		incomprehensible sounds	2
		no response	1
TOTAL			**RANGE 3–15**

§ 4.35   Newborn Assessment

In the period immediately following birth, rapid assessment of the newborn's ability to adapt to extra-uterine life is critical. The instrument used universally to assess newborn condition is the Apgar Scale. Developed by Dr. Virginia Apgar in the 1950s, this assessment tool is composed of five parameters: heart rate, respiratory effort, muscle tone, reflex irritability, and color. As in the Glasgow Coma Scale, each component is given a numerical score for each possible response. The best response is given the highest value and the worst the lowest value. The Apgar is an excellent tool for predicting the newborn's immediate adjustment to extra-uterine life, but not long-term outcomes. These assessments are routinely done at one and five minutes after birth and until the infant's condition stabilizes. An Apgar score of 0–3 is indicative of severe distress; 4–6, moderate distress; and 7–10, satisfactory. See **Table 4–4.**

Table 4–4

Apgar Scale

	Response	Score
Heart Rate	absent	0
	slow-<100 beats/min.	1
	>100 beats/min.	2
Respiratory Effort	absent	0
	slow or irregular	1
	good; lusty cry	2
Muscle Tone	limp	0
	some flexion of extremities	1
	active motion, well flexed	2
Reflex Irritability	no response	0
	grimaces	1
	coughs, sneezes, cries	2
Color	blue, pale	0
	extremities blue, body pink	1
	completely pink	2
TOTAL		**RANGE 0–10**

§ 4.36   Use of Diagnostic Testing Information in Medical Record Summaries

Following completion of the history and physical, the examiner should document provisional diagnosis(es) and the treatment plan. Multiple sources of both subjective and objective data may exist, for example, findings of physical examinations from other providers. Diagnostic test results are additional examples of objective data. When reviewing medical records from multiple sources, look for discrepancies in both history given by the client physical examination findings and note them in the summary if they are relevant to the case issues. Also look for diagnostic test findings that will or will not substantiate the client's claims. Finally, examine client compliance and follow-up with the treatment plan. A good medical record summary should "tell a story" and chronicle facts surrounding the case issues. Formats for compiling medical record summaries to best present data can be found in **Chapter 8.**

CHAPTER 5

THERAPEUTIC TREATMENT MODALITIES

§ 5.1   Medications

Medications play an important role in the treatment of many diseases and medical conditions. Just as with diagnostic testing, pharmaceutical development has grown at exponential rates during the last several decades. Therapeutic medications are available by prescription from a licensed health care professional or, over-the-counter, referred to as OTCs. Over-the-counter drugs have no legal purchase limit or requirement on who may buy them. They are considered safe when instructions on the label are followed. Both over-the-counter and prescription drugs are sold by brand and generic names. Brand names are protected by patent, but generic or chemical names are not.

For legal professionals reviewing medical records, it is necessary to have a general knowledge of drugs as they relate to case issues so that pertinent information can be included in the summary. If critical case issues surround the administration of a specific drug, e.g. adverse drug reaction, drug-drug interaction, failure to monitor adequately for side effects, etc, detailed research will be necessary. A thorough review of all information related to the medication, its dosage, side effects, contra-indications, and interactions with other drugs should be researched and findings reviewed by a medical expert. To assist in basic understanding of medications and some of the potential problems associated with their administration, the following information provides some overview material. Note that this is an overview *only* and as such, it is essential to have current material on medications as part of your reference library. Be aware that drug information changes rapidly, so be sure that the resource you are using is current and/or applicable to the time period when the issue occurred. For example, if a medication error occurred in 2004, your reference cites should be from that period. There is an abundance of drug-related material available, both printed and web-based. See the **Bibliography** and **Appendix N** (Internet Resources) for some suggestions, as well as websites listed in **§ 5.10** of this chapter.

§ 5.2 —Understanding Prescriptions

Prescriptions are written in a standard format containing the following information: drug name, dose, route of administration, and how often the drug is to be taken. If a prescription is written for a patient not hospitalized, the amount of medication to be dispensed is also indicated. Many symbols and phrases utilized in writing prescriptions are, like other medical terminology, of Latin or Greek origin. Some common symbols and abbreviations used in drug prescriptions are found in **Table 5-1.**

A prescription containing all appropriate information is written in the following manner:

NAME: PHONE NO.:
ADDRESS: DATE:
RX: Tylenol c̄ Codeine 30mg #30
                               Sig: i-ii tabs p.o. q4hrs prn pain
Refills: 3
Signature
DEA #

This sample prescription (RX) directs the patient to take one or two tablets (i-ii tabs) of Tylenol® with Codeine 30mg by mouth (p.o.) every four hours (q4hrs) as needed (prn) for pain. Thirty tablets are to be dispensed (#30) and the prescription may be refilled three times. Additional information/instructions are also included on the prescription label, as appropriate. Medication that causes drowsiness, interacts with food or alcohol, or is to be taken with food or on an empty stomach should be so labeled. Finally, all prescriptions must be signed by the ordering provider.

When drug classes such as narcotics, hypnotics, or tranquilizers are prescribed, health care providers must also list their DEA number following their signature. A *DEA number* is a registration number issued to individuals by the Drug Enforcement Administration (DEA). A Department of Justice agency, the DEA is responsible for regulating the manufacture, distribution, and dispensing of drugs that have abuse potential, that is, physical and psychological dependence. Drugs under the DEA's jurisdiction are divided into five schedules as follows:

• Schedule I (C-I): High abuse potential and no accepted medical use (heroin, LSD).

- Schedule II (C-II): High abuse potential with severe dependence liability (narcotics, amphetamines, and barbiturates).

- Schedule III (C-III): Less abuse potential than schedule II drugs and moderate dependence liability (nonbarbiturate sedatives, non-amphetamine stimulants, limited amounts of certain narcotics).

- Schedule IV (C-IV): Less abuse potential than schedule III and limited dependence liability (some sedatives, antianxiety agents, and nonnarcotic analgesics).

- Schedule V (C-V): Limited abuse potential (small amounts of narcotics used in cough medicines and antidiarrheals).

§ 5.3 —Appropriate Drug Administration

The appropriateness of medication prescription and administration is evaluated, in part, by the *5R Rule,* that is, the *right* drug, in the *right* dose, for the *right* patient, by the *right* route, at the *right* time. Other factors considered when prescribing medication are the patient's medical history (including the presence of any chronic diseases), allergies to food or drugs, potential interactions with other drugs currently being taken, and if the patient is pregnant or breastfeeding. Individual patient drug profiles of what is currently being taken (including OTC medication) should be evaluated before prescribing new drugs. A last important prescribing consideration is age. Generally, the elderly do not tolerate medications as well as younger adults and some drug side effects may be intensified in this population. See **Chapter 6, § 6.35** for further discussion of drug therapy in the elderly. Adjustments in medication prescription and dosage must be made for newborns, pediatric and pregnant individuals, as well as for those with underlying chronic disease.

§ 5.4 —Common Prescription Abbreviations

When prescriptions for drugs are written, abbreviations are commonly used to denote dosage, route and frequency of administration. See **Table 5-1.** Many of these abbreviations have been considered "standard" in medicine for years, however it is now recognized that some are problematic in that they are subject to misinterpretation. See discussion following **Table 5-1.**

Table 5–1

Abbreviations Commonly Used in Prescriptions

Abbreviation	Meaning
a.c.	before meals
a.s.	right ear
a.l.	left ear
a.m.	morning
a.u.	both
c̄	with
cap	capsule
c.c.	cubic centimeters
15 cc	one tablespoon
5 cc	one teaspoon
e.a.	each
gtt.	drops
gt	drop
h	hour
h.s.	at bedtime
m.l.	milliliter
IU	International unit
o.d.	right eye
o.s.	left eye
o.u.	both eyes
p.c.	after meals
p.m.	evening
p.o.	by mouth
prn	as needed
q	every
q.d. or Q.D.	daily
q.i.d.	four times a day
q.o.d. or Q.O.D.	every other day
s̄	without
sig.	take as follows
s.l.	sublingual, under the tongue
sol.	solution
stat	immediately, at once
susp.	suspension
tab.	tablet
t.i.d.	three times a day
U	unit
ung.	ointment
x	times

For the past several years, there has been increased focus on medication errors that occur nationwide. Although several estimates of the magnitude of this problem exist, there is general agreement in both public and private sectors that medication errors cause significant mortality and morbidity in the U.S. In an effort to reduce medication errors, organizations have begun to develop guidelines for safer medication administration. Two of these are The *Joint Commission for Accreditation of Health Care Organizations (JCAHO)* and the *Institute for Safe Medication Practices (ISMP)*. More detailed information on both these organizations, including other aspects of their medication safety guidelines, can be found in **Chapter 9.**

JCAHO has addressed medication safety as part of their Patient Safety Goals. Their medication safety goal has several components that address multiple aspects of drug administration. As a part of this comprehensive approach, JCAHO has published an official "do not use" list of abbreviations that have shown to be easily misinterpreted or misread. It is the expectation that institutions that are JCAHO accredited must demonstrate evidence that there is policy regarding "do not use" abbreviations (that follow JCAHO recommendations) and that there is a system in place to monitor compliance with policy. The JCAHO "Do Not Use" list can be accessed through their website: *http://www.jointcommission.org.*

ISMP has developed a list of *Error-Prone Abbreviations, Symbols and Dose Designations* that includes additional abbreviations (over and above JCAHO recommendations) to be considered for inclusion as "do not use". This list can also be accessed through their website: *http://www.ispm.org.*

§ 5.5   —Routes of Medication Administration

Medications may be prescribed to be given by different routes. The route chosen depends on the medication (most can be given only by specific routes), how fast the medication needs to act (medications given intravenously have the most rapid onset of action), and how the individual can best tolerate it (oral medication given to a patient who is vomiting will not be effective). Common routes of medication administration include:

1. By mouth, orally (po)
2. Under the tongue, sublingually (sl)
3. Under the lip or in the cheek (buccal tablets)
4. Subcutaneously (sc or subque)

5. Intramuscularly (IM)

6. Intravenously (IV).

Additionally, medications may be administered by drops and ointments instilled into the eyes, ears, and nose. Suppositories may be given vaginally and rectally. Solutions, such as antibiotic solutions may be instilled into joints and used as irrigation solutions for body cavities. Ointments and creams may be applied topically to skin areas. A few medications may be administered through the skin (transdermally) via medication-impregnated patches.

In recent years, due to advances in drug delivery technology, additional routes of medication administration have been developed and have gained widespread use in selected situations.

- **Epidural.** A catheter is inserted into the epidural space in the spinal canal. The epidural space lies between the outermost membrane of the spinal cord (dura mater) and the bones and ligaments of the spinal column. Analgesic medications can be administered via this catheter to relieve acute or chronic pain. Because medication is delivered in close proximity to large numbers of pain receptors, pain can be relieved much more effectively than by standard parenteral routes.

- **Patient-Controlled Analgesia (PCA).** PCA allows intravenous narcotics to be self-administered via a computerized pump. The pump is programmed according to physician order to deliver a minimum and maximum dosage range of pain medication at specified time intervals. The medication can then be self-administered to deliver medication as needed within these preset parameters. Because the level of pain is that perceived by the patient, medication delivery is more timely and more adequate pain control is achieved. Efficacy of PCA has been well demonstrated in multiple studies that show PCA patients actually self-administer less medication and recover more quickly than patients in control groups. This method of drug delivery lends itself to use in many settings, for example, home pain control for terminal cancer patients.

§ 5.6   —Medication Side Effects

Virtually all medications have side effects that range from minor and inconsequential to major and lethal. Some side effects are expected and do not necessarily indicate that medication should be discontinued. For example, drowsiness is an expected side effect of antihistamines. Many minor side effects disappear with continued use. Some (potentially serious) side effects can be avoided or minimized by following manufacturer recommended protocols, e.g. periodic blood testing to validate therapeutic levels of a specific drug.

§ 5.7 Medications: Classes, Actions, Indications and Side Effects

It is beyond the scope of this book to provide an in-depth analysis of the pharmacological actions, indications, and side effects of medications. However, **Table 5-2** gives a brief overview of some frequently prescribed drugs classes (as categorized by their principal therapeutic actions). For quick reference, generic and brand names for drugs contained in the tables are listed in **Appendix E.** An excellent on-line source of information is the National Library of Medicine-National Institutes of Health website: *http:// www.nlm.nih.gov/medlineplus.*

Table 5–2

Actions, Indications, and Side Effects of Common Medications

Note: Generic drug name appears first, followed by trade name. All drug trade names can be assumed to be registered trademarks. Indications and side effects noted for drugs are not inclusive.

Drug	Action	Indications	Potential Side Effects
	CARDIOVASCULAR DRUGS		
ANTI-ANGINALS			
Nitrates			
Nitroglycerin (Nitro-Bid, Nitro-Dur, Nitroglyn, Nitrostat, Tridil)	dilates blood vessels that supply heart muscle, improving its blood supply; dilates all body blood vessels	acute angina, angina prophylaxis, hypertension, congestive heart failure	headache, blurred vision, hypotension, nausea and vomiting, skin flushing
Isosorbide dinitrate (Sorbitrate, Isordil, Isonate)		treatment and prevention of angina; not to abort acute angina	
Isosorbide mononitrate (Imdur, Monoket, ISMO)	reduces oxygen demands of heart by decreasing pre-load and after-load	prevention of angina, not to abort acute attacks	headache, orthostatic hypotension, tachycardia, palpitations, ankle edema, flushing, hypersensitivity
Amyl nitrate	reduces oxygen demands of heart by dilating blood vessels and improving myocardial perfusion	relief of angina, antidote for cyanide poisoning	headache, orthostatic hypotension, tachycardia, flushing, hypersensitivity

Table 5–2 (*continued*)

Drug	Action	Indications	Potential Side Effects
Propranolol HCL (Inderal, Inderal LA)	decreases cardiac oxygen demand by blocking catecholamine-induced increases in heart rate, blood pressure, and force of myocardial contraction	treatment of angina and cardiac arrhythmias, and for reduction of mortality following MI	fatigue, lethargy, hypotension, nausea, vomiting, diarrhea, rash, dizziness *Serious side effects:* bradycardia, congestive heart failure, blood disorders
Amlodipine besylate (Norvasc)	decreases myocardial oxygen demand through inhibition of calcium across cardiac and smooth muscle cells; dilates coronary arteries	treatment of chronic, stable angina, vasospastic angina, hypertension	fatigue, dizziness, edema, nausea, abdominal pain, rash, puritis
Nadolol (Corgard)	decreases cardiac oxygen demand by blocking catecholamine-induced increases in heart rate, blood pressure, and force of myocardial contraction	angina, hypertension	fatigue, dizziness, nausea, vomiting, diarrhea, abdominal pain, anorexia, hypotension *Serious side effects:* bradycardia, heart failure

Table 5–2 (*continued*)

Drug	Action	Indications	Potential Side Effects
ANTI-ARRHYTHMICS			
Quinidine preparations (Quinidex Extentabs, Cardioquin, Quinora)	depresses myocardial excitability, conduction velocity and contractility	premature atrial contractions, paroxysmal tachycardia, atrial fibrillation and flutter	ringing in ears, headache, nausea and vomiting, dizziness, blurred vision, rash
Procainamide HCl (Procan SR, Pronestyl, Pronestyl SR)	depresses excitability of heart muscle	premature ventricular contractions, ventricular tachycardia, atrial fibrillation, premature atrial tachycardia	dizziness, mental depression, psychosis with hallucinations, severe hypotension, pericarditis, agranulocytosis with repeated use, fever, muscle and joint pain
Atropine sulfate	inhibits action of acetocholine within the heart's conduction system, enhancing conduction and speeding heart rate inhibits action of acetocholine	treatment of bradycardia, antidote for anticholinesterase insecticide poisoning, pre-operatively to decrease secretions,	headache, restlessness, insomnia, dizziness, bradycardia, blurred vision, dry mouth, constipation, nausea, vomiting, anaphylaxis

Table 5-2 (*continued*)

Drug	Action	Indications	Potential Side Effects
Lidocaine HCl Xylocaine	similar to procainamide and quinidine but with little effect on heart muscle contractility and cardiac output [**must be used with constant cardiac monitoring]	management of acute, life-threatening cardiac arrhythmias that occur during acute myocardial infarction or with cardiac manipulation such as heart surgery	drowsiness, lightheadedness, restlessness, hypotension, bradycardia, tinnitus, blurred vision, nausea and vomiting, excessive perspiration
Calcium Channel Blockers Nifedipine (Procardia, Adalat) Verapamil (Isoptin, Calan) Diltiazem (Cardizem)	slow movement of calcium ions into cells of the heart muscle, which decreases mechanical contraction of myocardial and smooth muscle; decrease myocardial oxygen requirements, dilate coronary arteries	chronic stable angina, essential hypertension, arrhythmias	peripheral edema, hypotension, congestive heart failure, cardiac arrhythmias, dizziness, sleep disturbances, nausea and vomiting, diarrhea
VASOPRESSORS Dobutamine (Dobutrex) Norepinephrine (Levophed) Dopamine HCl (Intropin)	used in shock to treat hypoperfusion of body tissues, increase blood supply to heart and kidneys	as an adjunct to fluid replacement and other drugs and therapies in treatment of cardiogenic, hypovolemic, and septic shock	increased heart rate, increased blood pressure, palpitations, arrhythmias, nausea and vomiting, headache, hypotension, chest pain. Effects are dose-related and dependent on clinical condition of patient

Table 5–2 *(continued)*

Drug	Action	Indications	Potential Side Effects
Tocainide HCl (Tonocard)	depresses excitability of heart muscle	suppression of life-threatening ventricular arrhythmias	drowsiness, lightheadedness, restlessness, hypotension, bradycardia, new or worsened cardiac arrhythmias, congestive heart failure, pulmonary edema, pulmonary fibrosis, tinnitus, blurred vision, nausea and vomiting
Mexiletine HCl (Mexitil)	depresses excitability of heart muscle, shortens duration of action potential	treatment of refractory ventricular arrhythmias, including ventricular tachycardia and premature ventricular contractions	dizziness, new or worsened cardiac arrhythmias, tremor, nausea and vomiting
Bretylium tosylate (Bretylol)	blocks action of adrenergics, prolonging cardiac muscle repolarization and increasing duration of action potential and effective refractory period	treatment of refractory ventricular arrhythmias, including ventricular tachycardia and ventricular fibrillation, unresponsive to other arrhythmias	vertigo, dizziness, lightheadedness and syncope, severe orthostatic hypotension, nausea and vomiting

Table 5–2 *(continued)*

Drug	Action	Indications	Potential Side Effects
Disopyramide phosphate (Norpace)	prolongs action potential of heart muscle	treatment of life-threatening ventricular arrhythmias, ventricular tachycardia	hypotension, heart failure, heart block, new arrhythmias
IONOTROPICS Digitalis (Digoxin, Lanoxin, Digitoxin) Inamrinone lactate (Inocor) Milrinone lactate (Primacor)	strengthens heartbeat and heart rhythm; works directly on heart muscle; amrinone and milrinone are inotropic agents with vasodilator activity	congestive heart failure, atrial fibrillation and flutter, paroxsymal atrial tachycardia, cardiogenic shock; inamrinone and milrinone are used for short-term management of congestive heart failure	cardiac arrythmias, headache, muscle weakness, diarrhea, apathy, depression, anorexia; thrombocytopenia (amrinone)
DIURETICS Thiazides Chlorothiazide (Diuril) Hydrochlorothiazide (Hydrodiuril) Methyclothiazide (Enduron) Polythiazide (Renese)	promote diuresis by inhibiting reabsorption of sodium and other electrolytes and thus promoting excretion of water by the kidneys; anti-hypertensive mechanism is unclear	adjunctive therapy in treatment of edema associated with congestive heart failure, treatment of hypertension alone or in combination with other antihypertensive agents	unusual fatigue, vertigo, headache, irregular heartbeat, orthostatic hypotension, nausea and vomiting, blood disorders, electrolyte imbalances (especially hypokalemia), frequent urination, allergic reaction, especially rash

Table 5-2 (*continued*)

Drug	Action	Indications	Potential Side Effects
Loop Diuretics Furosemide (Lasix) Ethacrynic Acid (Edecrin)	inhibit reabsorption of sodium and chloride in the kidney	edema associated with congestive heart failure, hepatic cirrhosis, and renal disease; oral furosemide for treatment of hypertension	anorexia, nausea and vomiting, headache, vertigo, blurred vision, blood disorders, rash, electrolyte depletion (especially watching for signs of hypokalemia), and hypotension. Careful medical supervision is necessary when these drugs are prescribed.
Potassium-Sparing Diuretics Spironolactone (Aldactone) Amiloride (Midamor) Triamterine (Dyrenium)	interferes with sodium reabsorption in the distal kidney tubules, thus decreasing potassium excretion in the urine	adjunctive treatment with thiazides or loop diuretics in heart failure, primary hyperaldosteronism, cirrhosis of the liver, and nephrotic syndrome	headache, dizziness, nausea, anorexia, diarrhea, abdominal pain, hyperkalemia, weakness, fatigue, muscle cramps, and blood disorders

Table 5-2 (continued)

Drug	Action	Indications	Potential Side Effects
Osmotic Diuretics			
Mannitol (Osmitrol)	hinders reabsorption of water in the kidney tubules, thus inducing diuresis	treatment of acute renal failure and in conditions where glomerular filtration is decreased, i.e., trauma and cardiovascular surgery (mannitol); reduction of increased intracranial pressure, cerebral edema, and reduction of intraocular pressure	nausea, vomiting, diarrhea, fluid and electrolyte imbalance, dehydration, edema, headache, hypotension, hypertension, seizures
Acetazolamide (Diamox)	promotes excretion of fluid and electrolytes by the kidney, thereby decreasing intraocular pressure; cerebral flow, and promotes the release of oxygen from hemoglobin	treatment of glaucoma, seizures, edema in congestive heart failure, mountain sickness	nausea, vomiting, anorexia, drowsiness, blood disorders

Table 5-2 (*continued*)

Drug	Action	Indications	Potential Side Effects
ANTIHYPERTENSIVES			
Methyldopa (Aldomet)	reduces standing blood pressure and supine blood pressure, mechanism of action not conclusively determined	hypertension, hypertensive crisis	transient sedation, headache, dizziness, bradycardia, aggravation of angina, nausea and vomiting, constipation, abnormal liver function tests, bone marrow depression, rash
Clonidine HCl (Catapres)	works on central nervous system to prevent release of chemicals responsible for maintenance of high blood pressure	hypertension	dry mouth, drowsiness, dizziness, sedation and constipation, anorexia, diminished sexual activity, loss of libido, urinary retention
Hydralazine HCl (Apresoline)	exerts peripheral vasodilating effect through direct relaxation of vascular smooth muscle	essential hypertension, alone or in combination with other agents	headache, anorexia, nausea and vomiting, palpitations, tachycardia, angina, toxic reactions, lupus erythematosus

Table 5–2 *(continued)*

Drug	Action	Indications	Potential Side Effects
Nitroprusside Na (Nitropress)	potent IV hypotensive agent that is immediate acting, effect ends when infusion stopped; hypotensive effects are caused by peripheral vasodilation through vessels	hypertensive crisis, uncontrolled hypertension during anesthesia	nausea, diaphoresis, retrosternal discomfort, too rapid reduction in blood pressure
Atenolol (Tenormin)	beta blocker; decreases cardiac output, peripheral resistance, and cardiac oxygen consumption	treatment of hypertension, angina, reduction of mortality and risk of reinfarction following acute MI	fatigue, dizziness, bradycardia, hypotension, congestive heart failure, bronchospasm
Carvedilol (Coreg)	non-selective beta blocker	hypertension, left ventricular dysfunction after MI, mild to severe heart failure, angina, idiopathic cardiomyopathy	asthenia, fatigue, dizziness, hypotension, postural hypotension, diarrhea, hyperglycemia, weight gain, upper respiratory infections, hypersensitivity reactions *Serious side effects:* CVA, bradycardia, AV block, thrombocytopenia, hypoglycemia, hyperkalemia, lung edema

Table 5–2 (*continued*)

Drug	Action	Indications	Potential Side Effects
Doxazosin mesylate (Cardura)	alpha blocker that reduces peripheral vascular resistence and produces vasodilation	essential hypertension	dizziness, asthenia, headache, orthostatic hypotension, *Serious side effects:* arrythmias, leukopenia, neutropenia
ACE Inhibitors Lisinopril (Prinivil, Zestril) Fosinopril (Monopril) Benazepril HCl (Lotensin) Captopril (Capoten) Enalaprilat (Vasotec)	prevent conversion of angiotensin I to angiotensin II (vasoconstrictor) by inhibiting secretion of angiotensin (converting enzyme ACE); results in decreased peripheral arterial resistance	treatment of heart failure, hypertension; treatment of hemodynamically stable patients within 24 hours to improve survival after MI (lisinopril)	headache, dizziness, symptomatic hypotension, angioedema; blood disorders (captopril and enalaprilat)
ANTILIPEMICS Cholestyramine (Questran) Colestipol HCl (Colestid) Lovastatin (Mevacor) Pravastatin sodium (Pravachol) Atorvastatin calcium (Lipitor) Rosuvastatin calcium (Crestor) Simvastatin (Zoxor)	reduce levels of blood cholesterol through a variety of mechanisms	treatment of hypercholesterolemia	constipation, nausea, vomiting, headache, rash, arthralgia, muscle cramps

Table 5–2 *(continued)*

Drug	Action	Indications	Potential Side Effects
MISCELLANEOUS CARDIOVASCULAR DRUGS			
Clopidogrel bisulfate (Plavix)	inhibits binding of ADP chemical to platelet receptor with subsequent decrease in platelet aggregation	reduce incidence of blood clots in persons with atherosclerosis documented by CVA, MI or peripheral vascular disease; also used during cardiac surgery and percutaneous cardiac interventions	headache, dizziness, fatigue, GI hemorrhage, abdominal pain, arthralgia, rash, purpura
Ticlopidine HCl (Ticlid)	unknown; probably inhibits platelet-to-platelet and platelet-to-fibrinogen binding	reduce risk of CVA in patients with prior CVA's; adjunct to aspirin in patients having coronary stent placement	dizziness, diarrhea, nausea, abdominal pain, allergic pneumonitis, rash, post-op bleeding. *Serious side effects:* intracranial bleeding, neutropenia, pancytopenia, agranulocytosis, thrombocytopenic purpura

Table 5–2 (*continued*)

Drug	Action	Indications	Potential Side Effects
RESPIRATORY DRUGS			
BRONCHODILATOR INHALANTS Sympathomimetics Terbutaline (Brethaire, Brethine, Bricanyl) Albuterol (Proventil, Ventolin) Metaproterenol (Alupent, Metaprel) Epinephrine (Primatene, Bronkaid, Adrenalin) Ipratropium (Atrovent)	produce bronchodilation and relieve nasal congestion; relieve bronchospasm by relaxing smooth muscles of bronchioles	asthma, bronchitis, emphysema, bronchiectasis, obstructive airway disease	restlessness, anxiety, fear, insomnia, vertigo, dizziness, pallor, sweating, palpitations, changes in blood pressure, arrhythmias, coughing
Xanthine Derivatives Theophylline (Bronkodyl, Slo-Phyllin, Elixophyllin) Aminophylline (Aminophyllin)	relax smooth muscles of bronchi and pulmonary blood vessels, stimulate central nervous system, induce diuresis	symptomatic relief of bronchial asthma and reversible bronchospasm associated with chronic bronchitis and emphysema	diarrhea, flushing, headache, dizziness, insomnia, irritability, increased urination

Table 5-2 (*continued*)

Drug	Action	Indications	Potential Side Effects
NASAL DECONGESTANTS Pseudoephedrine HCl (Sudafed, Cenafed) Phenylephrine HCl (Neosynephrine, Nostril, Rhinall) Oxymetazoline (Afrin, Dristan)	cause vasoconstriction in nasal mucous membranes, resulting in their shrinkage and thus promoting drainage	nasal congestion, hay fever, allergic rhinitis to promote nasal or sinus drainage; relief of eustachian tube congestion; most are OTC products	fear, anxiety, headache, dizziness, drowsiness, tremor, arrhythmias, palpitations, nausea and vomiting, anorexia
ANTIHISTAMINES Diphenhydramine (Benadryl) Chlorpheniramine (Chlor-Trimeton) Promethazine (Phenergan) Loratadine (Claritin) Fexofenadine HCl (Allegra)	blocks action of histamine (chemical released in the body during allergic reaction); some antiemetic effects; fexofenadine and loratadine are non-sedating	relief of symptoms of allergic rhinitis and conjunctivitis, common cold, urticaria, adjunctive therapy in anaphylactic reactions, relief of motion sickness, many are over-the-counter products	blurred vision, dry nose, mouth, throat; headache, anorexia, nausea, increase in sweating, drowsiness

Table 5–2 (*continued*)

CENTRAL NERVOUS SYSTEM DRUGS

Drug	Action	Indications	Potential Side Effects
NARCOTIC ANALGESICS Morphine Sulfate Meperidine (Demerol) Codeine (phosphate, sulfate) Fentanyl (Sublimaze) Oxycodone with ASA (Percodan) Oxycodone with acetaminophen (Percocet) Hydrocodone with acetominophen (Vicodin) Methadone HCl (Dolophine) Hydromorphone HCl (Dilaudid, Palladone) Pentazocine lactate (Talwin) Propoxyphene (Darvon) Oxycodone HCl (Oxycontin)	bind with pain receptors in the central nervous system to alter perception of pain and emotional response to pain	relief of moderate to severe pain; pre-op medication, analgesic adjuncts during anesthesia (fentanyl); some agents used for antitussive (codeine) and antidiarrheal (paregoric) effects; methadone used for detoxification of narcotic addiction	euphoria, drowsiness, apathy, mental confusion, nausea and vomiting, depressed respiratory rate, peripheral vasodilation, hypotension, constipation [**narcotic analgesics have abuse potential; psychological and physical dependence may occur]

Table 5-2 *(continued)*

Drug	Action	Indications	Potential Side Effects
Butorphanol tartrate (Stadol)	unknown; binds with pain receptors in the central nervous system to alter perception of pain and emotional response to pain	relief of moderate to severe pain, labor pain, pre-op anesthesia	somnolence, dizziness, nasal congestion, insomnia, nausea, vomiting, unpleasant taste *Serious side effects:* increased intracranial pressure, respiratory depression
Tramadol HCl (Ultram)	unknown; not chemically related to opiods, but thought to bind to opiod receptors	moderate to moderately severe pain	dizziness, vertigo, headache, somnolence, nausea, constipation, vomiting *Serious side effects:* seizures, respiratory depression
NON-NARCOTIC ANALGESICS			
Acetominophen (Tylenol)	mechanism of analgesic effect unclear; reduces fever by direct action on hypothalmic heat regulating centers	analgesic, antipyretic in presence of aspirin allergy or aspirin contraindication such as blood clotting disturbances	negligible with recommended dosage; liver impairment with high doses

Table 5-2 (continued)

Drug	Action	Indications	Potential Side Effects
Acetylsalicylic Acid (Aspirin)	lowers increased body temperature through vaso-dilation of peripheral vessels; anti-inflammatory and analgesic effects mediated through inhibition of prostaglandin synthesis	or ulcers mild to moderate pain, fever; various inflammatory conditions such as rheumatoid and osteoarthritis; decreases risk of MIs in patients with previous MIs or unstable angina	minimal with infrequent use; dizziness, ringing in ears, increased risk of bleeding; associated with Reyes syndrome in children, should not be used as antipyretic in children
NON-STEROIDAL ANTI-INFLAMMATORY DRUGS (NSAIDS) Ibuprofen (Advil, Nuprin, Medipren, Motrin, Midol, Pamprin) Naproxen (Naprosyn) Piroxicam (Feldene) Ketorolac tromethamine (Toradol)	anti-inflammatory and antipyretic effects, exact mode of action unknown; NSAIDS do not alter course of underlying disease when used for anti-inflammatory effects	relief of symptoms of rheumatoid and osteoarthritis; mild to moderate pain relief; short term management of moderately severe acute pain (Toradol)	dizziness, GI intolerance; can precipitate acute renal failure in patients with compromised renal function

Table 5–2 (*continued*)

Drug	Action	Indications	Potential Side Effects
ANTIANXIETY DRUGS			
Meprobamate (Equanil, Miltown)	central nervous system depressant, acts on multiple sites within; relieves stress and tension; some skeletal muscle relaxant effects	management of anxiety disorders and short-term relief of symptoms of anxiety	rash, drowsiness, ataxia, dizziness, and vertigo, slurred speech, palpitations, tachycardia, anorexia, nausea and vomiting [**prolonged administration may cause psychological dependence and abuse]
Benzodiazepines Alprazolam (Xanax) Chlordiazepoxide HCl (Librium) Lorazepam (Ativan) Diazepam (Valium)	act in central nervous system at several sites to relieve stress and tension; exert anticonvulsant and skeletal muscle relaxing effects	management of anxiety disorders, also useful as hypnotics, anticonvulsants, and muscle relaxants; used as adjunct in treatment of status epilepticus and recurrent convulsions (diazepam)	drowsiness, fatigue, amnesia, vivid dreams, slurred speech, muscle weakness, blurred vision, constipation and urinary retention

Table 5–2 (*continued*)

Drug	Action	Indications	Potential Side Effects
Hydroxyzine (Atarax, Vistaril)	acts on hypothalmus and brain stem rather than on cortical areas of central nervous system; exerts antiemetic, bronchodilator and antihistaminic activity as well as anti-stress effects	symptomatic relief of anxiety and tension for short-term use; management of itching secondary to allergy; as sedative prior to general anesthesia	drowsiness, sedation, dizziness, dry mouth, headache
Midazolam HCl (Versed)	unknown; thought to depress CNS at limbic and subcortical levels	for pre-op sedation and induction of general anesthesia; most commonly used as conscious sedation before short diagnostic procedures	nausea, hiccups, decreased respiratory rate, headache, over-sedation
ANTIDEPRESSANT DRUGS Tricyclics Amitriptyline HCl (Elavil) Nortriptyline (Aventyl) Imipramine (Tofranil) Doxepin (Sinequan) Amoxapine (Asendin)	act within the central nervous system to increase concentration chemicals necessary for transmission of nerve impulses in the brain	treatment of endogenous depression, migraine or cluster headaches (unlabeled use for amitriptyline)	dizziness, drowsiness, dry mouth, fatigue, loss of appetite, Restlessness [**overdosage will cause serious side effects]

Table 5-2 (*continued*)

Drug	Action	Indications	Potential Side Effects
Fluoxetine HCl (Prozac) Paroxetine HCl (Paxil) Sertraline HCl (Zoloft)	unknown, but presumed to be linked to the inhibition of CNS neuronal uptake of serotonin	treatment of depression, obsessive-compulsive disorder, bulemia (Prozac), and panic disorder (Paxil)	nervousness, anxiety, headache, drowsiness, nausea, diarrhea, dry mouth
Mirtazapine (Remeron)	thought to be caused by enhancement of central noradrenergic and serotonergic activity	treatment of depression	somnolence, increased appetite, dry mouth, constipation, weight gain. *Serious side effects:* suicidal behavior
Bupropion HCl (Wellbutrin)	unknown; weakly inhibits norepinephrine, dopamine, and serotonin uptake	treatment of depression	headache, insomnia, sedation, tremor, agitation, dizziness, tachycardia, auditory disturbances, pharyngitis, nausea, vomiting, anorexia, dry mouth, constipation, weight loss or gain, excessive diaphoresis *Serious side effects:* Suicidal behavior, arrythmias

Table 5–2 (continued)

Drug	Action	Indications	Potential Side Effects
Monoamine Oxidase Inhibitors (MAOIs) Phenelzine sulfate (Nardil) Tranylcypromine sulfate (Parnate)	inhibit specialized enzymes in the central nervous system to cause increases in the concentration of endogenous epinephrine; increase in concentration is basis for antidepressant activity	indicated in cases of atypical (exogenous) depression and when patient is unresponsive to other antidepressant therapy; rarely first drugs of choice	constipation, dry mouth, dizziness, headache; may induce hypertensive crisis, especially when taken with food or beverages containing triamine (e.g., cheese); also interacts with many other drug classes
ANTIPSYCHOTIC DRUGS Chlorpromazine (Thorazine) Thioridazine (Mellaril) Prochlorperazine (Compazine) Thiothixene (Navane) Haloperidol (Haldol)	act in central nervous system by blocking certain chemicals involved with nerve transmission in the brain	management of psychotic disorders, especially manic-depressive illnesses; Tourette's syndrome (Haldol); antiemetic (Compazine)	blurred vision, constipation, decreased sweating, dizziness, fatigue; dose-related: higher doses cause more serious side effects

Table 5-2 (*continued*)

Drug	Action	Indications	Potential Side Effects
Clozapine (Clozaril)	acts in central nervous system by blocking certain chemicals involved with transmission of nerve impulses to the brain	severely ill, schizophrenic patients who fail to respond to conventional courses of antipsychotic therapy	significant risk of agranulocytosis, careful monitoring of WBC while on therapy; also drowsiness, sedation, dizziness, syncope, nausea and vomiting, tachycardia
Olanzapine (Zyprexa)	unknown, may block dopamine receptors	treatment of schizophrenia and bipolar disorders	somnolence, asthenia, insomnia, parkinsonism, dizziness, dry mouth, constipation, dyspepsia, myperglycemia *Serious side effects:* leukopenia, suicide attempt
Quetiapine fumarate (Seroquel)	unknown, may block dopamine and serotonin receptors in the brain	manage symptoms of psychotic disorders, short term treatment of acute manic episodes associated with bipolar disorders	dizziness, somnolence, headache, weight gain, *Serious side effects:* leukopenia, seizures

Table 5–2 *(continued)*

Drug	Action	Indications	Potential Side Effects
Resperidone (Risperdol)	blocks dopamine receptors in the brain	short term treatment of schizophrenia and acute manic episodes associated with bipolar disease	extrapyramidal reactions, headache, insomnia, agitation, anxiety, parkinsonism, pain, rhinitis, constipation, nausea, vomiting, anorexia, weight gain, *Serious side effects:* suicide attempt, TIA or stroke in elderly patients with dementia, hyperglycemia
CNS STIMULANTS Methylphenidate (Ritalin)	central nervous system stimulant that increases mental alertness and decreases fatigue	treatment of narcolepsy, mild depression and abnormal behavior patterns (hyperactivity) in children	abdominal pain, dizziness, drowsiness, loss of appetite, insomnia, nausea
Amphetamine sulfate Dextroamphetamine sulfate (Dexedrine)	unknown; probably promotes nerve impulse transmission by releasing norepinephrine stored in the brain	treatment of attention deficit disorders, narcolepsy; short-term treatment of exogenous obesity	restlessness, hyperactivity, insomnia, tachycardia, palpitations

Table 5-2 *(continued)*

Drug	Action	Indications	Potential Side Effects
Caffeine (NoDoz, Vivarin, Dexitaz)	inhibits enzyme phosphodiesterase	stimulation of CNS	insomnia, restlessness, diuresis palpitations, tachycardia,
SEDATIVES & HYPNOTICS Benzodiazepines Flurazepam (Dalmane) Temazepam (Restoril) Triazolam (Halcion)	act as central nervous system depressant to relieve insomnia; some compounds also used as antianxiety agents	insomnia (prolonged administration not recommended); for conditions requiring restful sleep	headache, palpitations, tachycardia, nervousness, confusion, memory impairment, nightmares
Ethchlorvynol (Placidyl)	unknown; pharmacological effects similar to those produced by barbiturates	treatment of insomnia	dizziness, "hangover," ataxia, hypotension, blurred vision, blood disorders
Zolpidem (Ambien)	exhibits hypnotic activity, but no muscle relaxant or anticonvulsant properties	short-term management of insomnia	daytime drowsiness, dizziness, headache, palpitations, nausea and vomiting, diarrhea

Table 5–2 (*continued*)

Drug	Action	Indications	Potential Side Effects
Barbiturates Phenobarbital Secobarbital (Seconal) Pentobarbital (Nembutal) Amobarbital and secobarbital (Tuinal)	act on central nervous system to produce all levels of mood alteration from excitation to mild sedation, hypnosis, and deep coma; in sufficient doses, barbiturates induce anesthesia; depress respirations; decreases seizure threshold (Phenobarbital) [**drug abuse and dependence on barbiturates may occur with prolonged administration]	sedation, hypnosis, preanesthesia relaxation, long-term anticonvulsant therapy (phenobarbital)	nightmares, "hangover," headache, dizziness, bradycardia, nausea and vomiting, constipation. depressed respirations
ANTICONVULSANTS Barbiturates, Benzodiazepines	see previous text discussion		
Clonazepam (Klonopin)	unknown, probably inhibits effects of exitory neurotransmitters	treatment of akinetic and myoclonic seizures	drowsiness, ataxia, respiratory depression, blood disorders

Table 5–2 *(continued)*

Drug	Action	Indications	Potential Side Effects
Hydantoins Phenytoin (Dilantin)	inhibit spread of seizure activity in the motor cortex of the brain	control of grand mal and psychomotor seizures; prevention and treatment of seizures occurring during or following neurosurgery or following head injury	nystagmus, ataxia, slurred speech, confusion, blood disorders, hyperplasia gums, liver damage, rashes [**appropriate monitoring for side effects must be done with long-term therapy]
Primidone (Mysoline)	mechanism of antiseizure activity is not known	control of grand mal seizures, psychomotor or focal epileptic seizures	ataxia and vertigo, fatigue, irritability, emotional disturbances, nausea and vomiting, anorexia
Carbamazepine (Tegretol)	mechanism of antiseizure activity is not known; chemically related to tricyclic antidepressants	control of seizure activity that has not responded to other anticonvulsant therapy; treatment of trigeminal neuralgia	drowsiness, blurred vision, disturbances in coordination, tinnitus [**aplastic anemia and agranulocytosis may occur with drug administration; platelet and WBC counts should be monitored periodically

Table 5–2 (*continued*)

Drug	Action	Indications	Potential Side Effects
Magnesium Sulfate	prevents or controls convulsions by blocking neuromuscular transmission of impulses, depresses smooth, skeletal, and cardiac muscle function; increases mechanical stimulation of bowel activity when taken by mouth (laxative effect)	seizure prevention and control in severe pre-eclampsia and eclampsia in pregnancy; to treat low blood levels of magnesium (IV use only); as laxative when given orally	flushing, sweating, extreme thirst, hypotension, depressed or no reflexes, hypothermia, depressed cardiac function
Gabapentin (Neurontin)	unknown	adjunct treatment of partial seizures, treatment of postherpetic neuralgia	fatigue, somnolence, dizziness, ataxia, *Serious side effects:* leukopenia
Lamotrigine (Lamictal)	unknown	adjunct treatment of partial seizures, treatment of bipolar disorder	dizziness, headache, ataxia, somnolence, diploplia, blurred vision, rhinitis, nausea, vomiting,

Table 5–2 (*continued*)

Drug	Action	Indications	Potential Side Effects
ANTIPARKINSONIAN DRUGS			
Biperiden HCl (Akineton) Benztropine mesylate (Cogentin)	unknown; thought to block central cholinergic receptors and help balance cholinergic activity in basal ganglia of the brain	treatment of parkinsonism, drug-induced extrapyramidal disorders	confusion and disorientation, depression, tachycardia, blurred vision, constipation
Carbidopa (Sinemet)	exact mechanism unknown; exerts effects on dopamine levels within the brain	Parkinson's disease	dyskinetic movements, involuntary grimacing and head movements, ataxia, orthostatic hypotension, cardiac irregularities, dry mouth, nausea and vomiting, blood disorders
Levodopa (Larodopa)	unknown; thought to exert effect on dopamine, countering depletion in the brain, which is thought to produce parkinsonism	Parkinson's disease	dyskinetic movements, involuntary grimacing and head movements, ataxia, orthostatic hypotension, cardiac irregularities, dry mouth, nausea and vomiting, blood disorders, seizures, psychiatric disturbances, aggressive behavior

Table 5–2 *(continued)*

Drug	Action	Indications	Potential Side Effects
ALZHEIMER'S DISEASE			
Donepezil HCl (Aricept) Galantamine hydrobromide (Razadyne) Rivastigmine tartrate (Exelon)	thought to increase acetylcholine concentration, may improve cognitive function	treatment of mild to moderate Alzheimer's disease	headache, insomnia, dizziness, nausea, diarrhea, vomiting, *Serious side effects:* seizures (Aricept) bradycardia (Razadyne)
Memantine HCl (Namenda)	antagonizes chemical receptors the activation of which seems to increase Alzheimer's symptoms	treatment of moderate to severe Alzheimer's disease	aggressiveness, anxiety, ataxia, dizziness, fatigue, headache, nausea, vomiting, constipation or diarrhea, rash, abnormal gait *Serious side effects:* CVA, heart failure

Table 5–2 (*continued*)

Drug	Action	Indications	Potential Side Effects
MISCELLANEOUS DRUGS			
Lithium Lithotabs Eskalith Lithonate Lithane	deters Na transport in nerve and muscle cells and alters metabolism of certain chemicals in the brain	treatment of manic episodes of manic depressive illness; maintenance therapy prevents or diminishes frequency and intensity of subsequent manic episodes	toxicity is closely related to serum lithium levels; patients must be closely monitored; dizziness, headache, lethargy, drowsiness, slurred speech, fine hand tremors, weight gain, bloating, increased urination and thirst
Sumatriptan succinate (Imitrex)	unknown, but acts on brain receptors to vasoconstrict cerebral vessels	treatment of acute migraine headaches	dizziness, vertigo, atrial fibrillation, ventricular fibrillation, ventricular tachycardia, ME, EKG changes, tingling, warm or burning sensations

Table 5–2 (*continued*)

Drug	Action	Indications	Potential Side Effects
Tacrine HCl (Cognex)	inhibits enzyme cholinesterase in CNS, which temporarily improves cognitive functions in patients with Alzheimer's disease	alleviation of symptoms of Alzheimer's disease	headache, dizziness, nausea and vomiting, increases in transaminases
SKELETAL MUSCLE RELAXANTS Carisoprodol (Soma) Methocarbamol (Robaxin) Chlorzoxazone (Paraflex, Parafon Forte) Cyclobenzaprine (Flexeril) Diazepam (Valium)	produces muscle relaxation by blocking interneural activity in the spinal cord; refer to previous text discussion of diazepam	adjunct to rest, physical therapy, and other measures for the relief of pain associated with acute musculoskeletal conditions	drowsiness, dizziness fatigue, depression or euphoria, increased heart rate, palpitations, nausea and vomiting, anorexia, unpleasant taste in mouth, indigestion
Baclofen (Lioresal)	inhibits reflexes at spinal cord level	relief of spasticity resulting from multiple sclerosis, particularly for relief of flexor spasms	transient drowsiness, dizziness and weakness, confusion, nausea, constipation, urinary frequency

Table 5-2 (*continued*)

Drug	Action	Indications	Potential Side Effects
Dantrolene (Dantrium)	inhibits reflexes at spinal cord level	control spasticity resulting from spinal cord injury, stroke, cerebral palsy or multiple sclerosis; malignant hyperthermia crisis	drowsiness, dizziness, general malaise, diarrhea, speech and visual disturbances, alteration in taste; has great potential for liver toxicity, must monitor liver function closely
GI DRUGS ANTACIDS Maalox Gaviscon Mylanta Riopan Rolaids Alka-Seltzer Bromoseltzer	neutralize gastric acidity, resulting in an increase of stomach pH; inhibit activity of enzyme pepsin	relief of upset stomach associated with hyperacidity, peptic ulcer, gastritis, hiatal hernia	sodium content of antacids may be significant, use cautiously in patients with hypertension, CHF; some preparations cause diarrhea

Table 5–2 (*continued*)

Drug	Action	Indications	Potential Side Effects
ANTICHOLINERGICS Atropine Belladonna Alkaloids Scopolamine Glycopyrrolate (Robinul) Propantheline Bromide (Probanthine)	decrease motility (smooth muscle tone) in the GI, biliary, and urinary tracts; antisecretory and antispasmodic effects	adjunctive therapy for peptic ulcer, functional GI disorders, irritable bowel syndrome, enterocolitis, ulcerative colitis, diverticulitis; treatment of bradycardia (atropine); pre-op medication to decrease respiratory tract and salivary secretions; antidote for poisoning from cholinergic drugs; motion sickness (scopolamine)	headache, ataxia, dizziness restlessness, slurred speech, photophobia, flushed, dry skin, dry mouth
ANTI-ULCER DRUGS Cimetidine (Tagamet) Ranitidine (Zantac) Famotidine (Pepcid) Nizatidine (Axid)	suppresses basal gastric acid secretion, also secretion stimulated physiologically by food, caffeine, and gastric enzymes	short-term treatment of gastric ulcer and duodenal ulcer; prevention of recurrence after ulcer is healed	drowsiness, dizziness, light headedness, depression, cardiac arrhythmias, paranoid psychosis, joint pain

Table 5–2 (*continued*)

Drug	Action	Indications	Potential Side Effects
Omeprazole (Prilosec) Esomeprazole (Nexium)	inhibits activity of acid pump and blocks formation of gastric acid	short term treatment of gastric ulcer (Prilosec), treatment of erosive esophagitis, maintenance of healing erosive esophagitis, treatment of symptomatic gastroesophageal reflux disease (GERD), treatment of *H. pylori* infections	no common side effects; may experience headache, dizziness, nausea, vomiting, diarrhea, rash (Prilosec)
GI ANTIEMETICS Metoclopramide HCl (Reglan, Clopra, Octamide)	stimulate motility of GI tract without stimulating gastric, biliary, or pancreatic secretions; increase tone of gastric contractions	treatment of symptoms associated with diabetic gastroparesis and symptomatic gastroesophageal reflux; prevention/reduction of post-operative nausea and vomiting	mild sedation, fatigue, restlessness, nausea and vomiting, constipation or diarrhea, rash, suicide ideation, seizures, agranulocytosis

Table 5-2 (*continued*)

Drug	Action	Indications	Potential Side Effects
Prochlorperazine (Compazine) Thiethylperazine maleate (Torecan) Dimenhydrinate (Dramamine)	suppresses nausea and vomiting by inhibiting vomiting center in the brain	prevention/treatment of pre- and post-op nausea and vomiting, management of symptoms of psychotic disorders (prochlorperazine); prevention of (motion sickness dimenhydrinate)	extrapyramidal reactions, orthostatic hypotension, blurred vision, dry mouth, constipation, urine retention, transient leukopenia, cholestatic jaundice, mild photosensitivity (prochlorperazine); blurred vision, drowsiness, tachycardia, headache, and dizziness
Meclizine HCl (Antivert)	unknown; may affect neural pathways originating in the labyrinth of the ear	vertigo, motion sickness	drowsiness, hypotension, dry mouth, diplopia, tinnitus, constipation, nausea and vomiting, rash
Ondansetron HCl (Zofran)	selective antagonist of a specific type of serotonin receptor	prevention of nausea and vomiting from chemotherapy or radiation therapy, prevention of post-op nausea and vomiting	headache, malaise, fatigue, dizziness, sedation, diarrhea, constipation

Table 5-2 (*continued*)

Drug	Action	Indications	Potential Side Effects
LAXATIVES			
Milk of Magnesia (MOM)	promote bowel evacuation; OTC laxatives frequently misused	short term treatment of constipation, evacuation of bowel and colon prior to surgery or bowel X-rays	cramping, abdominal discomfort, diarrhea. Regular use of laxatives may cause physiological dependence for bowel function
Fleet Phospho-Soda			
Citrate of Magnesia			
Ex-Lax, Modane			
Dulcolax			
Metamucil			
Correctol			
Serutan			
ANTIDIARRHEALS			
Difenoxin with atropine (Lomotil)	slow intestinal motility; difenoxin is chemically related to demerol, atropine is added to discourage deliberate overdosage	adjunctive therapy of acute nonspecific diarrhea and acute exacerbations of chronic functional diarrhea	headache, sedation, numbness of extremities, flushing, palpitations, nausea and vomiting, dry mouth, abdominal discomfort
Loperamide (Imodium)			
Attapulgite (Kaopectate)			
Opium tincture (Paregoric)			

Table 5–2 *(continued)*

Drug	Action	Indications	Potential Side Effects
HORMONES			
SEX HORMONES			
Estrogens	important in development of female reproductive system and secondary sex characteristics; influence release of other hormones; play an important role in maintaining menstrual cycle	moderate to severe vasomotor symptoms associated with menopause; replacement therapy after removal of ovaries and primary ovarian failure; palliative therapy for prostate cancer in males	acne, bloating, change in sexual desire, dizziness, headache; long-term therapy may increase risk of uterine or breast cancer; increased risk of thromboembolic disease
Progestins (Provera)	primary endogenous pro-gestational hormone, induce change in uterus lining to support pregnancy	amenorrhea, abnormal uterine bleeding, endometriosis	migraine headache, depression, lethargy, increased risk of thromboembolic disease, changes in vision, changes in menstrual cycle, breakthrough bleeding, edema, changes in weight

Table 5–2 (*continued*)

Drug	Action	Indications	Potential Side Effects
Androgens Methyltestosterone (Android, Testred) Nandrolone decanoate (Anabolin, Durabolin)	responsible for growth and development of male organs and maintenance of secondary sex characteristics	replacement therapy in hypogonadism caused by deficiency or absence of testosterone; impotence; treatment of metastatic breast cancer in post-menopausal women	excitation, insomnia, increased libido, hypercalcemia, water retention, skin flushing, nausea; hypoestrogenic effects in women
OVULATION STIMULANTS Clomiphene citrate Clomid Milophene Serophene	induce ovulation in anovulatory women	treatment of ovarian failure	multiple pregnancies, blurred vision, hot flashes, abdominal bloating
Menotropins (Pergonal)	produce ovarian follicular growth in women who do not have primary ovarian failure	induction of ovulation and pregnancy in the infertile patient in whom cause is not due to primary ovarian failure	multiple pregnancies, thromboembolic disease, rupture of ovarian cysts, hyperstimulation of ovaries

Table 5–2 (*continued*)

Drug	Action	Indications	Potential Side Effects
POSTERIOR PITUITARY HORMONES Vasopressin (Pitressin)	possesses antidiuretic effects, increases reabsorption of water in the kidneys; in large doses stimulates smooth muscle contraction, which decreases blood flow	treatment of diabetes insipidus, prevention and treatment of post-operative abdominal distension; IV infusions used to treat bleeding esophageal varices	tremors, sweating, vertigo, pounding head, abdominal pain
Corticotropin ACTH Athcar	naturally secreted by the anterior pituitary, stimulates adrenal gland to produce and secrete its natural steroids	diagnostic tests of adrenal function, hypercalcemia associated with cancer, acute exacerbations of multiple sclerosis and other diseases for which glucocorticoids are indicated (see text below)	euphoria, insomnia, dizziness, headache, nausea and vomiting, abdominal distension, peptic ulcer, hirsutism, amenorrhea, sodium and water retention, potassium and calcium loss, impaired wound healing

Table 5–2 (continued)

Drug	Action	Indications	Potential Side Effects
Oxytocin (Pitocin, Syntocinon)	has uterine stimulation properties, especially on the pregnant uterus	induction of labor; control of postpartum bleeding or hemorrhage	mother: hypersensitivity leading to uterine hypertonicity, uterine rupture, cardiac arrhythmias, post-partum hemorrhage, water intoxication fetus: bradycardia, hypoxia, intercranial hemorrhage
Ergonovine Maleate (Ergotrate)	increases strength and frequency of uterine contractions and decreases uterine bleeding	prevention and treatment of postpartum and post-abortal hemorrhage due to uterine atony	increase in blood pressure, allergic phenomena

Table 5–2 (continued)

Drug	Action	Indications	Potential Side Effects
ADRENAL CORTICOSTEROIDS Glucocorticoids Cortisone Hydrocortisone (Solu-Cortef, Cortef, Hydrocortone) Prednisone Prednisolone Methylprednisolone (Medrol) Dexamethazone (Decadron)	naturally secreted by the cortex of the adrenal glands; varied metabolic effects; modify body's immune responses [**prolonged therapy of endogenous cortisone induces suppression of adrenal secretion; medication cannot be stopped abruptly without severe consequences]	exacerbations and/or maintenance therapy in rheumatoid arthritis, collagen diseases, allergic states, respiratory diseases such as asthma; leukemia and lymphoma palliation, acute exacerbations of Crohn's disease, multiple sclerosis; intra-articular injection for joint inflammation	dose and treatment duration-dependent; mental disturbances, insomnia, thromboembolism, osteoporosis and compression fractures, impaired wound healing, skin thinning, aggravation or masking of infections, ecchymosis, "moon face"

Table 5–2 (continued)

Drug	Action	Indications	Potential Side Effects
ANTIDIABETIC AGENTS Insulins Regular NPH Semilente Ultralente Humulin Novolin	naturally secreted by beta cells of the pancreas; principal hormone required for proper glucose use by the body, allows glucose (cell nutrient) to enter cell membrane; artificial insulin preparations have rapid, intermediate, and long-acting properties; artificial insulins are manufactured from beef, pork, and genetically engineered (human) sources	diabetes mellitus, type I; diabetes mellitus type II not controlled by medication and diet	hypoglycemia: symptoms include sweating, hunger, headache, weakness, progresses to loss of consciousness and seizures if not treated with sugar immediately

Table 5-2 (*continued*)

Drug	Action	Indications	Potential Side Effects
Sulfonylureas Chlorpropamide (Diabinese) Tolbutamide (Orinase) Tolazamide (Tolinase) Glipizide (Glucotrol) Glyburide (DiaBeta, Micronase) Glimepiride (Amaryl)	lower blood sugar by stimulating insulin release from the beta cells of the pancreas; only effective when the body is capable of producing some endogenous insulin	type II diabetes mellitus which cannot be controlled by diet alone	hypoglycemia: symptoms same as those with insulin (see above); GI disturbances, taste alteration, allergic skin reactions, urticaria
Rosiglitazone maleate (Avandia)	lowers glucose level by improving insulin sensitivity	improve glycemic control in type II diabetes, alone or in combination with other antidiabetic agents	no common side effects; may experience headache, fatigue, sinusitis, diarrhea
Metformin (Glucophage)	decreases hepatic glucose production and intestinal absorption of glucose; improves insulin sensitivity	improve glycemic control in type II diabetes, alone or in combination with other antidiabetic agents	diarrhea, nausea, vomiting, anorexia *Serious side effects:* lactic acidosis

Table 5–2 (continued)

Drug	Action	Indications	Potential Side Effects
Glucagon	hormone produced by alpha cells of pancreas, is responsible for the breakdown of glycogen (stored in liver) into glucose	emergency treatment of diabetic patients with low blood sugar who are unconscious or unable to swallow food or liquids	nausea and vomiting, hypersensitivity reactions
THYROID HORMONES Thyroid (Synthroid, Levoxine, Levoxyl)	naturally secreted by thyroid gland; regulates metabolic rate of body tissues; also concerned with growth and differentiation of tissues in the young	replacement of supplemental therapy in hypothyroidism	only with overdosage: staring expression, palpitation, tachycardia, weight loss, leg tremors, abdominal cramps, insomnia, menstrual irregularities
Antagonists Sodium Iodide (I 131)	radioactive iodide that damages and destroys thyroid tissues	treatment of hyperthyroidism (Graves' disease) and some types of thyroid cancer	dose related: large doses, bone marrow depression, blood disorders, radiation sickness

Table 5–2 (*continued*)

Drug	Action	Indications	Potential Side Effects
Potassium iodide, saturated solution (SSKI)	inhibits thyroid hormone formation	preparation for thyroidectomy, treatment of thyrotoxicosis	
ANTIBIOTICS			
PENICILLINS Penicillin G Preparations Bicillin Pentids Crysticillin Wycillin	inhibit bacterial cell wall formation; kill bacteria when adequate drug concentrations are reached; most effective during active multiplication stage of bacteria	treatment of infections caused by bacteria sensitive to killing action of penicillins	allergic reactions ranging from minor itching and rash to anaphylaxis causing death; yeast superinfections; nausea and vomiting, diarrhea
Penicillin V Preparations Penicillin VK Pen-Vee K V-Cillin			

Table 5–2 (*continued*)

Drug	Action	Indications	Potential Side Effects
Penicillinase Resistant Penicillins Methicillin (Staphcillin) Nafcillin (Nafcil, Unipen) Oxacillin (Prostaphlin) Cloxacillin sodium (Tegopen) Dicloxicillin sodium (Dycill, Dynapen, Pathocil)	same as that of penicillins; additionally, effectively neutralize penicillinase (substance secreted by certain strains of bacteria that render regular penicillins ineffective)	treatment of infections caused by penicillinase-producing bacteria (staphylococci)	same as those caused by penicillins
Ampicillin (Omnipen, Principen) Amoxicillin Trihydrate (Amoxil, Trimox)	same as that of penicillins	treatment of infections caused by Shigella, Salmonella, and other infections caused by bacteria sensitive to the drug, such as those caused by Haemophilus influenzae and Neisseria meningitidis	same as those caused by penicillins; Amoxicillin is more completely absorbed by the GI tract than other ampicillin preparations

Table 5-2 (*continued*)

Drug	Action	Indications	Potential Side Effects
Extended Spectrum Penicillins Carbenicillin (Geopen, Pyopen) Ticarcillin (Ticar) Mezlocillin (Mezlin) Piperacillin (Pipracil)	same as that of penicillins	treatment of infections caused by Pseudomonas aeruginosa and other gram-negative bacteria infections; for use in severe systemic infections and used in combination with aminoglycoside antibiotics (see below)	same as those caused by penicillin; also, unpleasant taste in mouth, neutropenia, leukopenia, elevation of liver enzymes
CEPHALOSPORINS First Generation Cephapirin (Cefadyl) Cefazolin (Ancef, Kefzol) Cephalexin (Keflex, Keftab) Cephradine (Velosef) Cefadroxil (Duricef)	inhibit synthesis of bacterial cell wall; most effective against rapidly growing organisms	treatment of infections caused by susceptible organisms; generally: progression from first generation to third generation reveals greater coverage of gram-negative organisms such as Pseudomonas and less coverage of gram-positive organisms such as staphylococcus; progression also shows greater efficacy against resistant organisms	allergic reactions including cross-allergenicity with penicillins, GI disturbances, clotting abnormalities with moxalactam, cefamandole and cefoperazone; yeast superinfections, pseudomembranous colitis

Table 5–2 (*continued*)

Drug	Action	Indications	Potential Side Effects
Second Generation			
Cefaclor (Ceclor)			
Cefamandol (Mandol)			
Cefoxitin (Mefoxin)			
Cefotetan (Cefotan)			
Cefonicid (Monocid)			
Cefuroxime (Zinacef, Kefurox)			
Third Generation			
Cefoperazone (Cefobid)			
Moxalactam (Moxam)			
Cefotaxime (Claforan)			
Ceftriaxone (Rocephin)			
Ceftazidime (Fortaz, Tazidime, Tazicef)			
Ceftizoxime sodium (Cefizox)			

Table 5–2 (*continued*)

Drug	Action	Indications	Potential Side Effects
AMINOGLYCOSIDES Gentamicin (Garamycin) Tobramycin (Nebcin) Amakacin (Amakin) Netilmicin (Netromycin) Streptomycin	kill bacteria through inhibition of bacterial protein synthesis	treatment of severe gram-negative infections of GI tract, skin, bone and soft tissue, sepsis, meningitis; should not be first drug of choice if less toxic antibiotic can be used to treat adequately; treatment of streptococcal endocarditis, enterococcal endocarditis, TB, and tularemia (streptomycin)	significant nephro and ototoxicity; renal function eighth cranial nerve function (hearing) must be closely monitored as well as adequacy of drug blood levels; dosage should be based on weight of patient and drug blood level results; allergic reactions, superinfections
TETRACYCLINES Tetracycline HCL (Achromycin, Tetracap) Doxycycline calcium (Vibramycin) Minocycline HCl (Dynacin, Minocin, Minomycin) Oxytetracycline (Terramycin)	do not kill bacteria, only prevent bacterial multiplication	treatment of uncomplicated infections caused by a wide spectrum of susceptible organisms; treatment of specific infections such as Rocky Mountain spotted fever, mycoplasma pneumonia, plague	GI disturbances, allergic reactions, photosensitivity, renal and hepatic toxicity (IV therapy with high doses); superinfections; should not be taken by pregnant women, nursing mothers, or children under eight because of drug-induced tooth discoloration

Table 5–2 *(continued)*

Drug	Action	Indications	Potential Side Effects
ERYTHROMYCIN E-Mycin Ilosone E.E.S.	may be bacteriostatic or bacteriocidal; suppresses protein synthesis of bacteria	drug of choice for mycoplasma respiratory tract infections, diphtheria, Legionnaires disease, chlamydia infections, whooping cough; alternate drug in penicillin or tetracycline allergy	superinfections, nausea and vomiting, severe abdominal pain, ototoxicity
SULFONAMIDES Sulfasalazine (Azulfidine) Sulfisoxazole (Gantrisin) Trimethoprim Sulfamethoxozole (Bactrim, Septra)	bacteriostatic; interrupt folic acid synthesis of bacteria bacteriocidal activity by inhibiting synthesis of nutrients necessary for bacterial growth; also inhibit vital bacterial enzymes	urinary tract infections, conjunctivitis, malaria, otitis, ulcerative colitis, meningococcal meningitis urinary tract infections caused by susceptible organisms; otitis media in children; acute exacerbations of chronic bronchitis in adults	allergic reactions, blood dyscrasias, photosensitivity, rash, GI disturbances, renal impairment, allergic reactions including rash, agranulocytosis leukopenia

Table 5–2 (*continued*)

Drug	Action	Indications	Potential Side Effects
FLUROQUINOLONES Ciprofloxicin (Cipro) Gatifloxacin (Tequin) Gemifloxacin (Factive) Levofloxacin (Levaquin) Moxifloxacin (Avelox) Norfloxacin (Noroxin)	inhibit bacterial DNA synthesis, mainly by blocking DNA gyrase, bacterialcidal	UTIs, severe bone and joint infections, severe skin infections, lower respiratory tract infections, bacterial prostatitis, sinusitis—caused by susceptible organisms; anthrax	headache, fatigue, drowsiness, confusion, nausea, diarrhea, vomiting, abdominal pain, arthralgia *Serious side effects:* pseudomonas colitis, seizures, leukopenia, neutropenia
MISCELLANEOUS ANTI-INFECTIVES Clindamycin HCl (Cleocin)	inhibits bacterial protein synthesis	treatment of infections caused by susceptible organisms: staphylococcus, streptococcus, and pneumococcus, and other aerobic anaerobic bacteria	thrombophlebitis, nausea, vomiting, abdominal pain, jaundice, rash *Serious side effects:* pseudomembranous colitis, transient leukopenia, thrombocytopenia, anaphylaxis

Table 5-2 *(continued)*

Drug	Action	Indications	Potential Side Effects
Azotrenam (Azactam)	inhibits bacterial cell wall synthesis, causing cell wall destruction	UTIs, septicemia, lower respiratory tract infections, intra-abdominal infections, surgical and Gyn infections caused by susceptible organisms	headache, insomnia, confusion, hypotension, thrombophlebitis nausea, vomiting, diarrhea, rash, hypersensitivity reactions *Serious side effects:* pseudomembranous colitis, seizures, neutropenia, pancytopenia, thrombocytopenia
Nitrofuradantin (Macrdantin)	unknown; may interfere with bacterial enzyme systems and cell wall formation	UTIs caused by susceptible organisms	polyneuropathy with high doses or renal impairment, nausea, vomiting, anorexia, diarrhea *Serious side effects:* hepatitis, hepatic necrosis, agranulocytosis, thrombocytopenia

Table 5–2 (*continued*)

Drug	Action	Indications	Potential Side Effects
Vancomycin (Vancocin)	hinders bacterial wall synthesis damaging bacterial plasma membrane; interferes with RNA synthesis	serious infections when other organisms are ineffective, including methecillin-resistant staph aureus (MRSA), and staph epidermidis; endocarditis, antibiotic-related C. difficile	fever, pain, hypotension, chills *Serious side effects:* pseudomembranous colitis, nephrotoxicity, neutropenia, leukopenia, anaphylaxis
		ANTIVIRAL DRUGS	
Acyclovir sodium (Zovirax)	interferes with DNA synthesis and inhibits viral multiplication	initial and recurrent herpes simplex virus infections, varicella in immunocompetent patients, acute herpes zoster infection in immunocompetent patients, herpes simplex encephalitis	malaise, headache, nausea, vomiting, transient elevation of creatinine and BUN levels. *Serious side effects:* seizures, coma, acute renal failure, thrombocytopenia

Table 5–2 *(continued)*

Drug	Action	Indications	Potential Side Effects
Amantadine hydrochloride (Symmetrel)	unknown; may prevent release of viral nucleic acid into host cell	prophylaxis or treatment of influenza A infection	dizziness, irritability, insomnia, nausea. *Major, but uncommon side effects:* heart failure
Famciclovir (Famvir)	inhibits viral DNA synthesis	acute herpes zoster infections (shingles), recurrent mucocutaneous herpes simplex infections in HIV patients	headache, nausea
Foscarnet sodium (Foscavir)	interferes with viral DNA synthesis	cytomegalovirus (CMV) retinitis in AIDS patients; acyclovir resistant herpes simplex infections	headache, fatigue, malaise, dizziness, neuropathy, hypertension, abnormal EKG, flushing, nausea, vomiting, diarrhea, anorexia abnormal renal function, anemia, granulocytopenia, blood electrolyte abnormalities, rash *Serious side effects:* seizures, pancreatitis, acute renal failure, blood cell disorders, bone marrow suppression, bronchospasm

Table 5–2 (*continued*)

Drug	Action	Indications	Potential Side Effects
Ganciclovir (Cytovene)	inhibits viral DNA synthesis	CMV retinitis in AIDS patients, prevention of CMV disease in patients with advanced HIV infection, prevention of CMV disease in transplant recipients (normal renal function must be present)	nausea, vomiting, diarrhea, anorexia, increased creatinine levels, anemia, rash *Serious side effects:* seizures, coma, blood cell disorders
Oseltamivir phosphate (Tamiflu)	interferes with viral replication	influenza infection in patients with symptoms for < 2 days	no significant common side effects
Ribavirin (Virazole)	unknown, possibly by inhibiting RNA and DNA synthesis	respiratory syncyntial virus in hospitalized infants & children	no significant common side effects *Serious side effects:* cardiac arrest, slow heart rate, apnea
Rimantadine hydrochloride (Flumadine)	unknown, possibly interferes with viral replication	prophylaxis of influenza A	no significant common side effects

Table 5–2 *(continued)*

Drug	Action	Indications	Potential Side Effects
Adefovir dipivoxil (Hepsera)	inhibits virus reverse transcription	chronic hepatitis B infection	asthenia, headache, fever, nausea, vomiting, abdominal pain, rash, hematuria *Serious side effects:* renal failure, hepatic failure, lactic acidosis, hepatomegaly renal insufficiency
Valacyclovir HCl (Valtrex)	terminates DNA chain, inhibits viral replication	herpes zoster (shingles), genital and oral herpes simplex	headache, dizziness, nausea, vomiting, abdominal pain arthralgia

HIV drugs are listed below; often more than one drug is used in treatment. Consult a comprehensive drug text for specific drug indications, side effects, and therapy regimens.

Abacavir sulfate (Ziagen)
Amprenavir (Agenerase)
Atazanavir sulfate (Reytaz)
Delavirdine mesylate (Rescriptor)
Didanosine (Videx)

Table 5–2 (*continued*)

Drug	Action	Indications	Potential Side Effects
Efavirenz (Sustiva)			
Emtricitabine (Emtriva)			
Enfuvirtide (Fuzeon)			
Fosamprenavir (Lexiva)			
Indinavir sulfate (Crixivan)			
Lamivudine (Epivir, Epivir-HBV)			
Lamivudine/zidovudine (Combivir)			
Loprinavir and ritonavir (Kaletra)			
Nelfinavir mesylate (Viracept)			
Nevirapine (Viramune)			
Ritonavir (Norvir)			
Saquinavir (Fortovase)			
Saquinavir mesylate (Invirase)			
Stavudine (Zerit)			
Tenofovir disoproxil fumarate (Virea)			
Zalcitabine (Hivid)			
Zidovidine azidothymidine, AZT (Retrovir)			

Table 5-2 (continued)

ANTI-FUNGAL DRUGS

Drug	Action	Indications	Potential Side Effects
Amphotericin B (Amphocin, Amphotericin B for Injection)	alters cell permeability to allow leakage of intracellular components and eventual fungal cell death	systemic fungal infections such as coccidiomycosis, histoplasmosis, disseminated candidiasis; for GI tract infections caused by candida albicans	headache, malaise, thrombophlebitis, anorexia, nausea, vomiting, abnormal renal function, anemia, weight loss. *Serious side effects:* seizures, arrhythmias, GI bleeding, renal impairment, blood cell disorders, hepatitis, liver failure, bronchospasm
Floconazole (Diflucan)	inhibits fungal cell synthesis and weakens cell walls	oropharyngeal candidiasis, prevention of candidia infections in bone marrow transplant patients	nausea and vomiting. *Serious side effects:* blood cell disorders, anaphylaxis
Grisefulvin (Fulvicin U/F, Fulvicin V, Grisactin 500)	stops fungal cell activity	ringworm infections of skin, hair, or nails	rash, urticaria *Serious side effects:* GI bleeding, blood cell disorders, liver toxicity, hypersensitivity reactions

Table 5-2 (continued)

Drug	Action	Indications	Potential Side Effects
Ketoconazole (Nizoral)	interferes with fungal cell wall synthesis and increases cell wall permeability	candida infections (local and systemic), coccidiomycosis, infections resistant to oral or topical grisefulvin	nausea, vomiting. *Serious side effects:* blood cell disorders, fatal liver toxicity
Nystatin (Mycostatin, Nystat-Rx)	unknown, probably alters cell wall permeability	intestinal, oral, and vaginal candida infections	no significant common side effects
Terbinafine hydrochloride (Lamisil)	inhibits an enzyme critical in cell biosynthesis	nail infection caused by dermatophytes (tinea unguium)	headache. *Serious side effects:* neutropenia, hypersensitivity reactions, anaphylaxis

§ 5.8   The Federal Drug Administration

The Federal Drug Administration (FDA) is *the* authoritative federal agency regulating many facets of the drug industry. The official FDA mission is to protect the American consumer by enforcing the Federal Food, Drug, and Cosmetic Act as well as several related public health laws. To help the agency make sound decisions based on scientific information in the review of regulated products, the FDA works with Advisory Committees comprised of individuals who are recognized as experts in their fields. Experts are from many different sectors in society and include medical professionals, scientists, researchers, industry leaders, and patient and consumer representatives. The FDA website is: *http://www.fda.gov*. additional details on the scope of FDA programs can be accessed from this home page website.

§ 5.9   —Regulatory Activities: Communication

The agency fulfills its mission, in part, through publication of information on regulatory and reinforcement activities, such as:

*   Drug recalls—list actions taken to remove problem drugs from market. The manufacturer can initiate these actions, or they can be initiated by FDA request, or by FDA orders under its statutory authority.
*   Warning letters—issued by FDA to provide information on regulatory matters to companies under their jurisdiction.
*   Enforcement reports—provides weekly reports of FDA regulatory activities.
*   Import alerts—report problem commodities and shippers and provide guidance to FDA field investigators about import coverage.
*   Import detentions—list products detained because of questionable compliance with FDA regulations.
*   On-line sales of medical products—identify information on Web sites with potentially illegal on-line prescription drug sales.
*   Debarment list—names firms or individuals barred from participating in drug industry because of conviction of crimes related to FDA regulations.

- Information on clinical investigators—list disqualified, restricted, or reinstated clinical investigators.
- Public Health Service administrative actions—list researchers with actions imposed against them by the Office of Research Integrity.
- Notices of initiation of disqualification proceedings—contain letters issued to clinical investigators when repeated violation of FDA regulations relating to clinical trials is suspected.
- Investigators reports—publish cases in FDA Consumer magazine that illustrate FDA administrative actions.
- Summaries of court actions—report cases involving seizure, criminal, and injunction proceedings.

The FDA also maintains *MedWatch,* an internet-based resource for safety information on drugs and other medical products regulated by the FDA. *MedWatch* services both health professionals and consumers and covers medical products such as prescription and over the counter (OTC) drugs, biologicals, dietary supplements, and medical devices. *MedWatch* website address is *http://www.fda.gov/medwatch.*

§ 5.10   —Enforcement Activities

When a problem arises with a product under its authority, the FDA can take a number of actions:

1. Initially work with manufacturer to correct a problem voluntarily.
2. If efforts fail, initiate legal actions, including product recalls, product seizure by federal marshals, or detention of imports at port of entry.
3. Request court injunctions against and/or prosecute those that deliberately violate the law. When warranted, criminal penalties, including prison sentences, are sought.

More in-depth information on FDA enforcement activities can be found in their web site *http://www.fda.gov/oc/enforcement.htm.*

In addition to the agency's enforcement activities, it also participates in the 1996 amendment to Freedom of Information Act that mandates publicly accessible electronic reading rooms that also provide agency response materials.

§ 5.11 —Partnerships with Private Sector

To assist the FDA to meet its public health responsibilities, the agency partners with companies in the private sector to develop ideas and proposals that will enhance delivery of mission-related FDA functions, but do not require FDA funding. For example, such a venture could involve contractor or third party development and operation of a system beneficial to FDA as well as to others in the private sector. The developer would then charge a fee for use of the system and the revenue generated would be used to maintain and improve the system. More in-depth information on partnership activities can be found on the FDA website, including an information guide that lists past and present activities and contacts at FDA.

§ 5.12 —Drug Oversite

Some of the most highly visible responsibilities of the FDA involve monitoring drug research, development, and testing in the United States. All drugs, both OTC and prescription, must have FDA approval before they can be prescribed and/or sold. After approval, drug manufacturers are required to provide drug profiles for all medications; they must accompany the drug as a package insert. Drug profiles contain the following information:

1. **Generic name:** chemical name of the drug.
2. **Brand name:** trade name given to a specific manufacturer's generic drug. For example, Valium® is a brand name for the generic drug diazepam.
3. **Type of drug:** classified by chemical composition and pharmacological effects.
4. **Forms and recommended dosages:** form in which drug is manufactured—tablets, liquid, suppositories. Recommended dosages are given, usually for adults and children along with cautions for dose adjustment in presence of certain conditions, e.g compromised kidney function.
5. **Uses of drug:** the most common clinical uses of the drug are listed as well as how the drug acts in the body. Instructions on how to achieve maximum benefit from the drug are also given, for example, taking it either on an empty stomach or with food.

6. **Side effects:** all side effects, major and minor, frequent and uncommon, are listed. The majority of drugs cause minor side effects. If a drug has serious side effects, a warning to that effect is included in the profile, along with a recommended protocol for monitoring patients during therapy.

7. **Interactions:** medications, both prescription and over-the-counter can interact with food and other drugs. Some combinations of medications can cause potentially lethal side effects.

8. **Warnings/precautions:** to emphasize safe use of the drug. Drowsiness, the drug's effect on driving ability or operation of machinery, and the effects of abrupt cessation of therapy may appear as warnings. Any risks during pregnancy and breastfeeding, if known, are also listed. The FDA has established five categories to indicate a systemically absorbed drug's potential for causing birth defects. These categories are summarized in **Table 5–3.**

§ 5.13   —Researching Drug Information

An often-overlooked aspect of medical records review is investigation into the types and quantities of medications used by a plaintiff and any possible relationship to alleged symptoms or injuries involved in the claim. For example, a plaintiff involved in a motor vehicle accident claims subsequent low back pain and sexual dysfunction. An examination of the plaintiff's medical records discloses a history of depression that predates the subject accident. Plaintiff's physician has prescribed Fluoxetine Hcl (Prozac®), as an antidepressant medication. A side effect of this medication is sexual dysfunction. While it is the responsibility of the consultant or expert to relate a condition to injury or medication, it is the legal professional's role to research this information and include it in the medical record summary.

Practice Note: When preparing to research drug information, make certain you have the correct pronunciation and spelling of the drug as there are many, similar-sounding members of a drug class (e.g., Cefazolin Cephalexin, and Cefotetan). Learn both the generic and brand names of the drug. A medication may have many brand names, but only one generic name. For example, within the histamine receptor antagonist category is the generic drug, ranitidine, and different brand names (Zantac, Zantac EFFERdose, Zantac GELdose, Zantac 75).

Table 5–3

Drug Use in Pregnancy

Pregnancy Category	Definition
Category A	Adequate studies in pregnant women have not demonstrated a risk to the fetus in the first trimester of pregnancy and there is no evidence of risk in later trimesters.
Category B	Animal studies have not demonstrated a risk to the fetus but there are no adequate studies in pregnant women . . . or . . . Animal studies have shown an adverse effect, but adequate studies in pregnant women have not demonstrated a risk to the fetus during the first trimester of pregnancy and there is no evidence of risk in later trimesters.
Category C	Animal studies have shown an adverse effect on the fetus but there are no adequate studies in humans; the benefits from the use of the drug in pregnant women may be acceptable despite its potential risks . . . or . . . There are no animal reproduction studies and no adequate studies in humans.
Category D	There is evidence of human fetal risk, but the potential benefits from the use of the drug in pregnant women may be acceptable despite its potential risks.
Category X	Studies in animals or humans or adverse reaction reports or both have demonstrated fetal abnormalities; the risk of use in a pregnant woman clearly outweighs any possible benefit.

§ 5.14 —Drug Information Internet Resources

- Biological Therapies in Psychiatry (*http://www.btpnews.com*). Psychopharmacology newsletter; good resource on new drugs and drug interactions.
- Internet Medical Health (*http://www.mentalhealth.com*). Covers the most used psychiatric medications with links to other drugs not included.
- The Medical Letter on Drugs and Therapeutics (*http://www .medletter.com*) Peer-reviewed publication with critical evaluations of new drugs.

- Pharmaceutical Research and Manufacturers of America (*http://www.Phrma.org*). Information about issues of significances including drugs in development and facts and figures about drugs in current use.
- Pharmacists' Guide to the Internet (*http://www.altimed.com*). Canadian site that is well organized by disease and drug category; other drug information sites are rated; some information in French.
- PharmInfo Net: Pharmaceutical Information Network (*http://www.pharminfo.com*). Database of articles, list of frequently-asked questions (FAQs) about drugs with answers from drug manufacturers, archive of drug-related discussion threads, links to other sites.
- PharmWeb (*http://www.mcc.ac.uk/pharmacy*). Annotated listing of publications, electronic products, journals related to pharmacology, links to pharmacy-related sites, including pharmaceutical companies.
- Rx List—The Internet Drug List (*http://www.rxlist.com*). List of the top 200 most prescribed medications; also includes some foreign drugs.
- U.S. Food and Drug Administration (FDA) (*http://www.fda.gov*). The most important consumer protection agency in the federal government; includes information on new drug approvals, recalls and product alerts, drug evaluations, adverse drug reactions; research programs and approved products.
- Medlineplus from the National Library of Medicine – National Institutes of Health (*http://www.medlineplus.gov*). A wealth of information on both prescription and OTC drugs, herbs and supplements, clinical trials, health topics and multiple links to related sites.

§ 5.15 Chiropractic Care

Lawyers handling personal injury and professional malpractice cases often must evaluate chiropractic records as part of their review of records. Chiropractic can be defined as a nonsurgical and drug-free method of healing that is based on the premise that dislocation of the spinal vertebrae can contribute to a variety of ailments. This concept, the relationship between the spine's structure and the function of the nervous system, is fundamental to chiropractic. Spinal manipulative therapy (SMT) is utilized to correct these imbalances and to restore health. A list of chiropractic terminology appears in **Appendix F.**

§ 5.16 —History and Development of Chiropractic

The concept of manipulating the spine to relieve discomfort and disease has existed for thousands of years. It was practiced by the Chinese, the Greeks, the Egyptians, and some Native American cultures. Prehistoric cave paintings depicting the delivery of spinal manipulations date back to 17,500 B.C.

Chiropractic was founded in Iowa in 1895 by D.D. Palmer, a Canadian immigrant. Palmer was a practitioner of magnetic healing; he had no formal medical training but was well read in both anatomy and physiology. He devoted a great deal of time to the study of the spine and eventually concluded that all disease was the result of abnormal spinal function. Palmer performed his first adjustment in 1895. Subsequent to his initial successes, Palmer's popularity increased and in 1896 he founded the first school of chiropractic in Davenport, Iowa, now known as the Palmer College of chiropractic. One of Palmer's first patients gave the profession its name by combining the Greek words "chiro" (hand) and "praktikos" (done by).

Palmer believed that 95 percent of all human diseases were the result of "slightly displaced vertebrae" and that the remaining 5 percent were due to misaligned joints elsewhere in the body. In his opinion, the chiropractor's role was to adjust any and all displacements of the more than 200 bones in the human body.

In 1906 Palmer's son, B.J. Palmer, took over the school and is credited with the development of the chiropractic profession. By 1910 the Palmer School had courses in X-ray studies and was the first to use this new technology to detect spinal misalignments. In 1935 B.J. Palmer established a research clinic at the school and is credited with developing a prototype of the electroencephalogram or EEG. Although he agreed with his father's philosophy regarding the relationship of skeletal misalignments and disease, he refined chiropractic theory to concentrate only on the spinal vertebrae.

§ 5.17 —Chiropractic Theory

Chiropractic is based on the belief that structure affects function. The spinal cord is the pathway for all sensory nerve impulses that reach the brain and all motor nerve impulses that relay brain impulses to the appropriate muscles. Spinal displacements interfere with the normal transmission of these nerve impulses and blood supply. These displacements are generally known as *subluxations,* but are also referred to as fixations, spinal dysarthrias, or vertebral lesions. Chiropractic believes that when a nerve is irritated by a spinal subluxation, the resulting nerve impulse will be abnormal and disease will result because of the body's inability to adapt and react properly. Correcting these subluxations by spinal manipulative therapy (SMT) removes the interference with the nerve transmission and blood flow, thus allowing the body's natural recuperative powers to restore health.

§ 5.18   —Chiropractic Regulation and Education

The birth of this profession was not an easy one. Based on charges from established medicine that chiropractors were practicing medicine without a license, many early practitioners were arrested, fined, and some jailed. The first legislation to allow the practice of chiropractic was signed in Kansas on March 20, 1913; Massachusetts became the last state to license the profession in 1966. It is now licensed by all the states, the District of Columbia, the U.S. Virgin Islands, and Puerto Rico.

The profession itself is not uniform in its philosophy. Because of basic philosophical differences, a wide variety of theories, procedures, and techniques are practiced in chiropractic. These schools of thought vary as to the types of manipulation utilized, the starting point on the spinal column for manipulation, and the types of ancillary treatments that can be used. The two main schools have been referred to as "straights" and "mixers." The straights represent the conservative side of chiropractic and rely on spinal manipulation of the vertebrae as their primary therapeutic tool. The mixers are more progressive and incorporate a wide range of alternative healing methods with spinal manipulation.

There are 15 colleges of chiropractic in the United States, many of which have been accredited by the Council on Chiropractic Education (CCE). To obtain a Doctor of Chiropractic degree, the prospective candidate must have at least two years of college and four years of resident instruction at a chiropractic college. Most states require candidates to qualify under the same basic science examinations as those required for medical doctors.

Chiropractic colleges offer courses as diverse as philosophy, anatomy and physiology, chemistry and biochemistry, pathology, roentgenology, diagnostic techniques (including orthopedic, neurological, blood, and urine tests), biomechanics, ethics and jurisprudence, neuromusculoskeletal pathology, obstetrics and gynecology, pediatrics, and chiropractic manipulation techniques. The fourth year of chiropractic education includes an internship at one of the college's outpatient clinics, which allows the chiropractic student to treat patients while under the supervision of faculty. The chiropractor's scope of practice is determined by case law and statute. Generally speaking, they are allowed to locate and correct misaligned vertebrae but are prevented from performing surgery, prescribing medication, practicing obstetrics, or reducing major fractures or dislocations. Additional information on chiropractic therapy can be obtained from the American Chiropractic Association website: *http://www .amerchiro.org.*

Practice Note: Consult the local codes to determine the appropriate scope of practice for your jurisdiction. This information can also be obtained from the state Board of Chiropractic Examiners or other appropriate state licensing entity.

§ 5.19   Physical Therapy Treatment Modalities

The history of physical therapy dates back to ancient Greece, where therapeutic exercise and massage were the first modalities to be used consciously to alleviate pain and strengthen injured areas of the body. Hippocrates prescribed therapeutic exercise specifically as a restorative. He also accurately observed causes of muscle wasting, noting that if left unused, muscles become liable to disease, defective in growth, and quick to age.

As a profession, however, physical therapy developed during World War I when many war wounded and disabled needed rehabilitation. These services were provided by the Restorative Aids, who formalized physical therapy as a discipline. In 1921, the American Physical Therapy Association was founded. Currently, two types of professionals provide physical therapy services:

1.   Registered Physical Therapist (RPT). The RPT must complete a curriculum, graduate from an accredited school, and pass a state-administered national examination. Additional requirements may

vary from state to state. Physical therapists may pursue advanced education and experience and become certified as clinical specialists. As of 1996, the American Board of Physical Therapy Specialties recognized seven specialty areas: cardiopulmonary, clinical electrophysiology, geriatrics, neurology, orthopedics, pediatrics, and sports physical therapy.

2. Physical Therapy Assistant. Assistants work under the supervision of the physical therapist. Their duties can include assisting the therapist in implementing planned treatments, training patients in exercises and activities of daily living (ADLs), administering treatments, and using special equipment.

The physical therapist utilizes several different modalities to improve the function of injured or impaired areas of the body. Some of these modalities are also used to prevent injury and optimize efficiency of body function.

§ 5.20   —Therapeutic Exercise

The body is made up of an intricate system of levers (bones) and pulleys (muscles) that allows the body to achieve exceptional levels of mobility. The heart and lungs service the entire body, including muscles and bones, and function more efficiently when the body exercises regularly. The benefits of exercise are realized by all age groups and include increased efficiency of the cardiovascular system, increased respiratory function, and decreased body fat. Therefore, regular exercise is desirable for maintaining optimal body conditioning even in the absence of injury or disease and for preventing injury from occurring or reoccurring. Low back exercise programs are typical examples of injury prevention/reoccurrence through exercise.

Therapeutic exercise programs are often prescribed to restore optimal function after injury or surgery. The programs consist of specific body movements that will improve function affected by injury or disease. In the case of sports injuries, rehabilitation must focus on adapting the individual to the demands that may be made on the body during the athletic performance, that is, strengthening and optimizing functions that are essential to performance. An exercise plan emphasizes components such as establishing a daily routine, mastering pacing, and modifying ADL's. Programs usually initially focus on strengthening exercises and progress to improving endurance.

Exercises may be active (voluntary movements performed by the patient, without resistance) or passive (movements performed for the person by another person or by a mechanical appliance). Continuous passive motion (CPM) is a commonly prescribed passive exercise that utilizes a machine to improve joint range of motion, increase circulation to the extremity, and enhance joint nutrition after knee surgery.

When reviewing medical records, you will encounter many terms descriptive of body movements that are elicited during therapeutic exercise.

1. **Dynamic contraction**—muscle contraction associated with joint movement
2. **Endurance**—ability to persist in physical activity
3. **Isokinetic contraction**—contraction against an accommodating resistance at a preset constant speed
4. **Isometric contraction**—static contraction in which the muscle maintains a constant length
5. **Isotonic contraction**—dynamic contraction against a constant or variable resistance in which there is a change in muscle length, eccentric or concentric. In eccentric contraction, the muscle lengthens while contracting. In concentric contraction, the muscle shortens while contracting.
6. **Static contraction**—muscle contraction not associated with any joint motion
7. **Strength**—maximum force generated by muscle without relation to time
8. **Training effect**—improvement in test performance based solely on familiarity with testing techniques

§ 5.21 —Transcutaneous Electric Nerve Stimulation (TENS)

Electric modalities are occasionally utilized in physical therapy programs. One of the most frequently encountered is transcutaneous electric nerve stimulation (TENS). TENS applies an electrical current through the skin for the control of pain. Electrodes from the TENS apparatus are placed over peripheral nerves, the nerve dermatome, or at pain trigger points. It is thought that the electric current delivered by the TENS blocks transmission of pain impulses to the brain and stimulates the release of the body's natural pain killers (beta-endorphins). This mechanism has also shown ability to increase contractile force of a muscle or recruit more fibers to contract with the stimulus, thereby strengthening weakened muscles or enhancing the strength of normal muscles. TENS therapy is most effective for chronic pain, but its effectiveness varies and is unpredictable. Benefits from TENS therapy are controversial.

§ 5.22   —Cryotherapy (Application of Cold)

Application of cold, or *cryotherapy,* is used for immediate care of soft tissue injuries (within the first 48 hours). It is effective for musculoskeletal injury resulting in hemorrhage, inflammation, edema, muscle spasm, and pain. Cryotherapy may be administered by ice, ice packs, or gel refrigerant products. The effect of cold decreases tissue metabolism, constricts blood vessels, decreases pain sensation, and decreases muscle spasm. Cryotherapy may be contraindicated in Reynaud's disease and in other types of peripheral cardiovascular disease. Note that this type of crythotherapy is distinct and different from that referred to § 5.27, number 2, below.

§ 5.23   —Thermotherapy (Application of Heat)

Application of heat, or *thermotherapy,* has a variety of uses. It can decrease pain and stiffness, increase joint range of motion, decrease muscle spasms and contracture severity, and reduce hematomas. Thermotherapy transfers heat through three mechanisms:

1. **Conduction**—two surfaces are in contact with each other, e.g. application of hot packs
2. **Convection**—air or water molecules move across the body, e.g. whirlpool therapy
3. **Radiation**—heat from a warm source is transferred to a cooler one through a conducting medium, such as air.

Heat therapy can have superficial or deep penetration, depending on how it is applied. Superficial applications include:

1. **Whirlpool**—immersion of affected area into warm water. Therapeutic exercises for the injured area can be done during immersion.
2. **Contrast baths**—alternate immersion of injured part between warm and cold water tanks.
3. **Paraffin wax**—extremity dipped into paraffin bath and allowed to harden for 20 to 30 minutes. Paraffin retains heat, so the risk of burns is greater than with other methods of heat therapy.
4. **Infrared heat**—injured part of the body is positioned under infrared lamp. Superficial skin temperature is increased without heat source coming in contact with skin.
5. **Hydrocollator packs**—commercially available canvas pouches of petroleum distillate that are applied to the injured part for 15 to 20 minutes.

Deep penetration of heat can be accomplished by diathermy. Diathermy uses high frequency electromagnetic currents to induce deep heating in tissues. It is sometimes used to relieve pain of osteo and rheumatoid arthritis, bursitis, tendonitis, strains and sprains, and neuritis. Deeper tissue heat penetration can be accomplished by ultrasound, which is the more frequently used method of administering deep heat therapy.

§ 5.24   —Massage

Massage therapy is accomplished by rubbing and kneading specific areas of the body usually with the hands. It manipulates muscle and connective tissue and which can result in relief of muscle spasms and reduction of swelling in the injured area. It increases blood flow to the affected area, relaxing muscles, and relieving associated pain.

§ 5.25   —Traction

Therapeutic traction is a technique that places a part of the body under tension to correct the alignment of two adjoining structures or to hold them in position. This is accomplished by exerting a pull in two directions, with the pull of traction (often produced by weights) and the pull of counter-traction (produced by the person's body weight or other weights). The main purposes of traction are to reduce fractures or dislocations and maintain alignment, to decrease muscle spasms and relieve pain, to correct or lessen deformities, to promote rest of an injured part, and to promote exercise. Different methods of traction application include manual (pulling of the body part with the hands), mechanical (with ropes and pulleys), internal (devices inserted in casts or into the bone itself), and external (with braces). The type of traction method used depends on the type of injury and for its intended purpose.

§ 5.26   —Use in Medical Record Summaries

Information contained in physical therapy records may be useful to include in your summaries depending on the nature and extent of the client's injuries. If loss of function was evident after the injury, physical therapy may be prescribed to improve function. The effect of therapy on parameters such as range of motion, muscle strength and tone, and endurance may be pertinent information. See **Chapter 4, §§ 4.29** and **4.30** for additional information on range of motion, muscle strength and tone. It may be helpful to track progress or lack of progress in a focused summary. For example, you may want to note the values for the injured joint range of motion over a period of time instead of for one isolated value.

§ 5.27   Additional Therapeutic Modalities

1. **Acupressure**—based on the principles of acupuncture. Pressure or other cutaneous stimulations are applied over acupuncture points.

2. **Acupuncture.** Acupuncture is a method of preventing, diagnosing, and treating pain and disease. Long, thin metal needles are inserted into the body at designated locations and at various depths and angles. It has been used for pain relief in China for many centuries and is now gaining recognition in the United States as an acceptable treatment modality. It has also recently been used as a method of anesthesia during surgery.

3. **Cryotherapy.** This type of therapy involves the use of temperatures below freezing to destroy tissue. It acts rapidly to destroy abnormal tissue with minimal scarring. Some current uses are for removal of tumors of the prostate, cervix, liver, and bowel; removal of skin growths, both benign and malignant; and for removal of birthmarks. Note that this type of crythotherapy is distinct and different from that referred to in § **5.22** above.

4. **Chemotherapy.** A type of drug therapy, chemotherapeutic agents are used to treat malignancies by acting selectively on tumor cells. The drugs may, however, also have effects on normal cells. The type of drugs used and the timing and duration of therapy differ markedly, depending on the type of cancer being treated. Side effects from chemotherapy can be severe and include bone marrow suppression and damage to intestinal lining, hair follicles, and mouth.

5. **Hormone Therapy.** A type of drug therapy, hormone antagonists block the action of male/female hormones. Because certain types of cancers are sensitive to naturally occurring hormones, antagonists slow tumor growth by blocking hormone production. This type of therapy is used to treat cancers such as breast, ovarian, and testicular tumors.

6. **Laser Therapy.** *Laser* is an acronym for light amplification by stimulated emission of radiation. Laser therapy consists of two types: low intensity and high intensity, which have two markedly different types of action. *Low-intensity laser therapy* stimulates tissue healing and decreases pain, inflammation, and swelling. It improves blood and lymph flow and decreases production of the hormone prostaglandin, which can stimulate inflammation and pain. Low intensity laser therapy is also used to treat muscle tears, ligament sprains, and inflamed joints and tendons. *High-intensity laser therapy* destroys cells directly under the laser beam while leaving adjacent cells undamaged. As the beam cuts through tissue, it simultaneously clots blood, making laser a useful surgical tool. High-intensity laser therapy is used in ophthalmology for conditions such as diabetic retinopathy, retinal detachment and tumors of the retina. In gynecology, it is used to unblock fallopian types and destroy abnormal cervical cells; in cardiology, it is now being used to open narrowed cardiac vessels.

7. **Radiation Therapy.** Radiation therapy uses high-energy radiation to kill cancers cells by destroying their ability to reproduce. It is used to

treat specific types of cancer, alone or as an adjunct to other therapies such as surgical excision and chemotherapy. Unlike chemotherapy, radiation therapy causes little or no damage to surrounding healthy tissue. Radiation can be curative or used as a palliative measure to relieve signs and symptoms of advanced cancer.

§ 5.28   Complementary and Alternative Medicine

As individuals live longer, a greater proportion of the population lives with chronic disease. Western medicine often has no cure for these conditions. Additionally, because its philosophy is "disease focused", emotional and psychological support needed for living with chronic conditions may be lacking. As a result, there has been increased consumer interest in care alternatives that are outside of traditional Western medicine.

Many of these alternatives exist, some having little or no scientific evidence of proven benefit and/or safety. Information on risks and benefits of a particular therapy may be confusing both to consumers and to health care providers. To assist in bringing a more systematic approach to providing information on these therapies, the National Center for Complementary and Alternative Medicine (NCCAM) was established. As part of the National Institutes of Health (NIH), NCCAM serves as a clearing house for information and communication on the efficacy and safety of these therapies. It also supports applied clinical research that supports investigation of safety and efficacy. NCCM has developed a classification system for these therapies. Under the umbrella terminology of *Complementary and Alternative Medicine (CAM)*, the classification consists of five categories:

1. **Alternative Medical Systems.** These are complete systems of theory and practice, e.g. Western Medicine. Traditional Chinese medicine is an example of an alternative medical system, as is homeopathic medicine, that has its roots in Western culture.
2. **Mind-Body Interventions.** A core principal of mind-body intervention uses a variety of techniques to assist the mind in influencing body function and symptoms. Some of these techniques include
    * biofeedback
    * cognitive-behavioral therapy
    * hypnosis

- music and art therapy
- prayer and meditation
- patient support groups
- relaxation therapy

See **Chapter 6, § 6.26** for additional detail and use in pain management.

3. **Biologically Based Therapies.** These therapies all use substances found in nature, such as herbs, foods, and vitamins. Examples include aroma therapy and a variety of herbal products, e.g. ginko biloba and echinacea. While some of the herbal therapies have been studied fairly extensively, some have little or no evidence to support their efficacy.

4. **Manipulative and Body-Based Methods.** These modalities are based on manipulation and/or movement of one or more parts of the body. Examples include acupressure and therapeutic massage and chiropractic manipulation.

5. **Energy Therapies.** These therapies focus on the use of energy fields believed to be within the body and those that surround it externally. The existence of the energy fields that surround the body is assumed and has yet to be scientifically proven. These therapies can be categorized into two types:
   - Biofield therapies—intended to manipulate energy fields that surround and penetrate the body.
   - Bioelectromagnetic-based therapies—involve uses of magnetic fields such as pulsed fields or magnetic fields.

In this rapidly evolving arena, changes in and additions to therapies occur frequently. In addition to the NCCAM, many other resources exist as well, many are geared to a type of therapy. In researching complementary and alternative medicine therapies, validate the origin of the material and risk/benefit is supported by clinical research. The National Center for Complementary and Alternative Medicine is an excellent starting point for information. Their website address is: *http://www.nccam.hih.gov.*

CHAPTER 6

SELECTED PROBLEMS: DIAGNOSIS AND TREATMENT

§ 6.1   Treatment of Orthopedic and Neurologic Conditions

Many of the medical conditions seen in personal injury and workers'
compensation litigation involve injury to bones, muscles, and nerves,
either alone or in combination. These injuries often take an extended

time to improve or heal and in some cases, they result in permanent loss of function and associated disability. The likelihood of residual damage must be fully evaluated as it relates to long term implications for the client. §§ **6.16** through **6.31** on nerve, muscle, and bone injuries contain an overview of their causes and treatments, and some potential short- and long-term disabilities that may result.

§ 6.2 —Fractures

Fractures are a break or disruption in the continuity of the bone structure. The incidence of fractures increases with age due to the physiologic changes that occur with aging, osteoporosis, and increased likelihood of falls. In children and younger adults, fractures are almost always the result of traumatic injury that exerts unnatural force on the bone and surrounding structures. There are some exceptions to causation from traumatic injury. *Stress fractures* may occur in normal bone when overuse places repeated stress on it, e.g., from activities such as jogging. Fractures may also occur as a result of tumors that destroy bone tissue and thus weaken its structure. This type of fracture is referred to as a *pathological fracture* and often occurs spontaneously without injury or trauma.

Fractures have varying degrees of severity and are classified in several ways: by presence/absence of bone protrusion through the skin, by degree of fracture stability, and by fracture configuration. See **Figure 6–1** for some examples of fracture types.

Presence/Absence of bone protrusion through the skin:

1. *Simple (closed) Fracture*—broken bone(s) do not protrude through the skin.
2. *Compound (open) Fracture*—broken bone(s) protrude through the skin. The protrusion of normally sterile bone through the unsterile skin increases the risk of infection.

Degree of fracture stability:

1. *Stable*—at least some of the bone's periosteum is intact across the fracture site and an immobilization device has rendered fragments stationary.
2. *Unstable*—bone fragments are grossly displaced during injury, complete disruption of periosteum occurs.

Configuration of fracture:

1. *Transverse Fracture*—runs straight across the bone
2. *Linear Fracture*—runs parallel to the long axis of the bone
3. *Spiral Fracture*—encircles the bone; usually caused by twisting injury
4. *Impacted Fracture*—broken bone edges are wedged together
5. *Comminuted Fracture*—bone is shattered into many pieces
6. *Compression Fracture*—one bony surface is forced against another. This type of fracture most commonly occurs in the vertebrae.

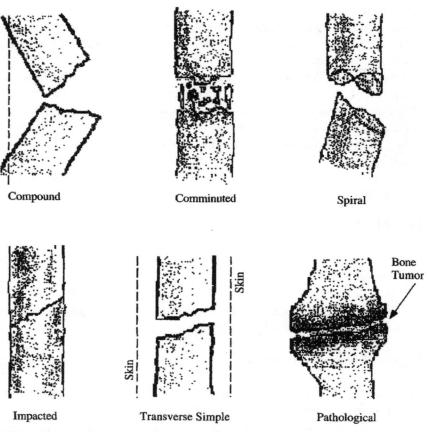

Compound · Comminuted · Spiral

Impacted · Transverse Simple · Pathological

Figure 6–1. Fracture configurations.

No matter the location or type of the fracture, certain diagnostic signs are usually present at the site of injury, including: deformity, swelling/ bruising, pain, muscle spasm, impaired sensation, and/or function. The main goals of treatment are to *realign* the broken bone(s) and *stabilize* the fracture(s). The choice of stabilization mechanism should be one that allows for earliest mobilization and provides the greatest opportunity to achieve the maximum function. Realignment and stabilization are done in several ways, depending on the location and type of fracture.

Realignment of the fracture is accomplished in two ways:

1. **Closed Reduction**—manipulation of bone fragments into alignment without an incision (surgical procedure). After the manipulation is complete, fracture alignment is confirmed by x-ray and stabilized (usually) by casting.

2. **Open Reduction**—commonly referred to as ORIF (open reduction, internal fixation), the fracture alignment and stabilization are accomplished by means of a surgical procedure under anesthesia. The bone fragments are manually aligned and may be stabilized by insertion of hardware, such as metal pins or screws.

Fracture *stabilization* and *immobilization* may be achieved in several ways. The choice of stabilization method is dependent on the location and configuration of the injury: **Figure 6–2** illustrates examples of the following immobilization devices:

1. **Casts/Splints**—external supports to immobilize the fractured bone and promote healing.

2. **Internal Fixation**—metal apparatus such as pins, screws, nails, plates, or joint prosthesis, which are surgically inserted at time of realignment.

3. **External Fixation**—metal devices (pins) are inserted into bone and attached to external rods. This allows increased joint mobility proximal to fracture and easy visualization of the surgical site. This type of immobilization is often used in complex fractures with accompanying soft tissue injuries when development of infection is of concern.

4. **Traction**—mechanical means of applying force to reduce fractures. Traction exerts pull in two directions, the pull of *traction* and the pull of *countertraction.* The traction pull is accomplished by use of weights to pull on the fracture to attain alignment while the countertraction

External Fixation Device

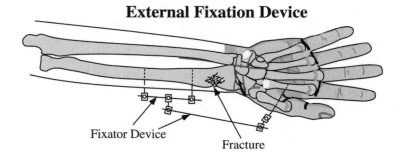

Fixator Device

Fracture

TRACTION: Crutchfield Tongs

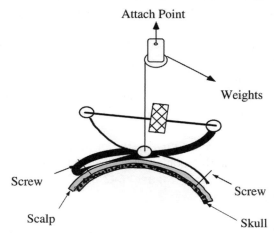

Attach Point

Weights

Screw

Screw

Scalp

Skull

CASTS / SPLINTS   **INTERNAL FIXATION DEVICE: Jewit Nail**

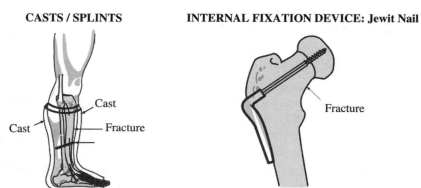

Cast

Cast

Fracture

Fracture

Cast

Figure 6–2. Fracture stabilization methods.

pulls in the opposite direction, usually by the person's body or other weights. There are two main classifications of traction:

- *Skin traction*, which is applied externally to skin via splints or slings. Skin traction is generally for short-term use with weights usually not exceeding 10 pounds, although pelvic or cervical traction may require more weight. Skin traction may be intermittent or continuous.

- *Skeletal traction*, which is accomplished by surgically inserting a pin(s) into bone and then connecting them to traction. This type of traction is indicated when traction will be long-term and continuous. Complications may arise from immobility because of the lengthy time traction must be used to accomplish fracture healing.

Unlike some other body tissues, bone usually regenerates very well and fractures heal completely. New bone formation occurs in stages, usually over six to eight weeks. There are several stages of bone regeneration:

Stage 1: Hematoma forms around the site of the fracture and eventually develops into granulation tissue. This usually occurs within 72 hours of injury.

Stage 2: Cells proliferate around the fracture, with the torn ends of the bone serving as a stimulus for the production of *osteoblasts* (bone cells). Granulation tissue forms and encircles each end of the bone fragments, eventually forming a bridge across the fracture site. The granulation tissue produces the basis for new bone substance called osteoid. This process usually takes place three to fourteen days post-injury.

Stage 3: Minerals are deposited in the osteoid to form *procallus.* Procallus extends beyond the fracture line and forms a temporary splint. This process usually takes place two weeks post-injury.

Stage 4: A permanent callus of true, rigid bone forms, a process called *ossification.* Ossification takes place three weeks to six months after fracture and continues until healing is complete.

Stage 5: Consolidation occurs. During consolidation, the distance between bone fragments diminishes and eventually closes. There is x-ray evidence of bone union.

Stage 6: This is the final stage of healing, during which excess bone tissue is reabsorbed and union is completed.

Common Types of Fractures

Certain types of fractures occur more often than others. Long bones are particularly vulnerable to fractures and therefore fractures in these bones are seen more frequently. Below are several types of fractures commonly seen.

1. **Colles' Fracture.** This type of fracture occurs in the distal radius. It is one of the most common fractures in adults, occurring when attempting to break a fall with an outstretched hand. A Colles' fracture is usually treated with closed manipulation and then immobilizing the lower arm with a splint or a cast.

2. **Fracture of the Humerus.** These fractures involve the shaft of the bone. The treatment (immobilization) depends on the fracture location and presence or absence of displacement. Types of treatments include hanging arm casts and sling and swath for non-displaced fractures.

3. **Pelvic Fracture.** Pelvic fracture severity ranges from benign to life-threatening. Crushing injuries to the pelvis resulting from trauma such as motor vehicle accidents (MVAs) can result in serious intra-abdominal injuries involving laceration of surrounding organs and subsequent internal hemorrhage. If the fracture is stable and non-displaced, treatment may consist of bedrest with earliest possible mobilization Complex pelvic fractures are treated with a variety of modalities, including pelvic sling, skeletal traction, hip spica cast, open reduction, or a combination of these.

4. **Hip Fractures.** These fractures are most common in older adults, more common in women than in men, mirroring the higher incidence of osteoporosis in females vs. men. Hip fractures usually occur as a result of a fall. Types of hip fractures include:

   Intracapsular fractures that occur within the hip joint, i.e., in the femoral head.

   Extracapsular fractures that occur outside the hip joint, usually as a result of a fall. Extracapsular fractures can be *inter-trochanteric* (between the greater and lesser trochanter) or, *subtrochanteric* (the region below the lesser trochanter). These types of fractures are usually treated surgically by open reduction and internal fixation (ORIF) or by total/partial joint prosthesis placement.

5. **Fractures of the Femur.** These fractures occur in the femoral shaft. Fractures of the distal femur are most commonly seen in young adults. Severe, direct blows or rotational force is necessary to produce this type of fracture and damage to surrounding tissues is common. They are initially treated with femoral or tibial pins with skeletal traction such as Russell's traction (see **Figure 6–2**). When some bone union is evident, a hip spica cast is applied.

6. **Fractures of the Tibia.** Like femoral fractures, a strong force is necessary to produce fractures in the tibia. The tibia is more vulnerable to fractures, however, because unlike the femur, it does not have the protection of a strong muscle covering. Tibial fractures also often have surrounding soft tissue damage. Treatment/immobilization of closed fractures is accomplished by closed reduction with cast, or ORIF with rods, screws, and plates for complex fractures with or without soft tissue damage.

7. **Vertebral Fractures.** Vertebral fractures commonly occur as a result of motor vehicle accidents, falls, diving accidents, or athletic injuries. *Compression* fractures may also occur in the vertebrae as a result of degenerative changes caused by osteoporosis. Vertebral fractures are classified as stable or unstable. *Stable fractures* are not likely to cause spinal cord injury as there is no fracture displacement or fracture fragments and the vertebral bodies are held in place by the spinal ligaments. For stable fractures the goal of treatment is to keep the spine in good alignment until union has been accomplished. For cervical fractures this may be done using a cervical collar or halo cast. In *unstable fractures*, the spinal ligaments are disrupted and dislocation of the vertebral structures may occur, resulting in spinal cord injuries. Refer to **§ 6.20** for additional information on spinal cord injuries.

Fracture healing generally occurs more rapidly in children and smaller bones tend to heal faster than large ones. Additionally, the severity of the fracture, i.e., open versus closed, simple versus complex, influence healing time, as do preexisting medical conditions and lifestyle. Examples of some factors that may delay fracture healing include:

- osteoporosis
- hormone deficiencies (e.g., diabetes)
- alcoholism

- nutritional deficiencies
- chronic disease
- cancers
- medications such as steroids.

Fractures that have extended healing times are classified as having:

1. **Delayed Union**—healing does not occur in the expected time. Causes of delayed union can be due to decreased blood supply to the fracture site, inadequate immobilization, or infection. Delayed union is usually resolved with extended treatment and may include use of electrical stimulation to encourage new bone growth.

2. **Non-union**—failure of fracture site to form new bone after six to nine months. Non-union is characterized by excessive motion in the fracture site and can lead to false joint formation *(pseudoarthrosis)*. Non-union of fractures is usually treated by bone grafts. Electrical stimulation may also be used.

3. **Malunion**—fracture heals with angulation or deformity. Malunion may result in deformity and/or compromised functionality of the injured bone. Complications following fractures can be immediate or delayed. Some potentially serious complications that can occur post-injury are:

   - Impairment of motor (movement), sensory (feeling) function, and circulation, particularly distal to the fracture. The cause of these impairments is often swelling of the injured limb that, in turn, causes the cast to become too tight. Excessive pressure, caused by this tightness, may cause permanent loss of motor and sensory function if not treated promptly. Prolonged circulatory impairment can cause tissue death and, in extreme, result in gangrene of the affected area. Frequent checks of nerve and circulatory function are critically important in the immediate post-injury period to prevent these complications or minimize their impact.
   - Skin breakdown and general de-conditioning secondary to prolonged immobility. Frequent position changes, skin checks, and exercise programs are important for prevention/minimization of these complications. Muscle atrophy (decreased muscle mass) may occur at the site of the injury due to disuse following prolonged immobilization. These complications can prolong the rehabilitation period.

- Venous thrombosis and/or pulmonary embolism that can occur secondary to prolonged immobility. Immobility can cause blood circulation in the extremities to become sluggish and thus become prone to clotting (deep venous thrombosis or DVT). In addition to immobility, venous stasis may also be aggravated by inactivity of muscles that normally assist in pumping of venous blood in the extremities. When DVT occurs, danger exists that clots in an extremity will travel to the lung, resulting in a pulmonary embolism (PE). Pulmonary embolism can be life threatening. Prevention measures include anti-embolic compression stockings post-injury and anti-coagulation therapy.

- Post-injury infection at site of fracture. This is of most concern in compound fractures when bone has protruded through the skin. Infections range from superficial skin infections that are easily treated, to severe infections such as osteomyelitis that involve the bone itself and are more difficult to cure.

- *Compartment syndrome* may develop following injury. This condition occurs in muscle groups that are encased in fascia that do not expand. Numerous compartments exist in the upper and lower extremeties. There are two causes of compartment syndrome: decrease in compartment size by restriction with dressings or casts, or increase in compartment contents caused by bleeding, edema, or body response to foreign substance (e.g., snake bite venom). As pressure in the compartment increases, circulation is compromised and damage to muscles and nerves occurs. If compartment syndrome is unrecognized or untreated for more than several hours, irreversible tissue damage may result.

- Fat emboli can be caused when fat globules are forced out of the bone marrow at the fracture site, enter the circulation, and travel to other parts of the body, most commonly the lung. Fat emboli are seen with long bone fractures and can be life threatening.

Some delayed and/or common long-term effects post-fracture may be:

- Arthritis at old fracture or trauma site;
- Restricted range of motion of joints involved in, or near to, the injury;
- Limited function of injured area resulting from permanent neuro-vascular damage to tissues; and
- Limb length discrepancy as a result of injury.

Presence of permanent functional damage as a result of fractures may play an important role in claim settlements. Residual injuries should be carefully noted and progression or deterioration tracked when summarizing the client's medical record. These injuries should be confirmed by examination if necessary.

§ 6.3 —Soft Tissue Injuries

Soft tissue injuries have several classifications. All types may produce similar symptoms initially and are treated with a variety of (similar) modalities. These types of injuries affect principally ligaments, which attach from bone to bone, and tendons, which attach muscles to bone. Both ligaments and tendons have relatively poor blood supply, making post-injury healing a slow process. Types of soft tissue injuries include:

1. **Dislocation**—a severe injury of the ligaments surrounding a joint. The injury results in a complete displacement or separation of the articular surface of the joint.
2. **Subluxation**—a partial or incomplete displacement of the joint surface (less severe than dislocation).
3. **Contusion**—bruising of soft tissue caused by disruption of small blood vessels (capillaries) that supply blood to the tissue.
4. **Sprain**—affects mainly ligaments. Grades of injury are classified by the number of torn ligament fibers and by the resulting degree of joint stability.
   - First degree (Grade I)—a mild injury that involves a small number of fibers. There is overstretching of ligaments but no loss of joint stability.
   - Second degree (Grade II)—a moderate injury, in which there is partial disruption of fibers and some joint instability.
   - Third degree (Grade III)—severe injury in which there is complete tearing of fibers with resulting joint instability. These type of injuries usually require surgical repair.
5. **Strain**—affects mainly tendons. Strains are also classified by degree or grades depending on severity, similar to those of sprain classifications. Often, soft tissue injuries do not occur in isolation, that is, to only one ligament or muscle. Rather, injuries generally involve multiple soft tissues and can occur with or without bone

fractures. Soft tissue injuries are treated with a variety of modalities including activity restriction, ice, medications for pain and muscle spasms, physical therapy, and/or chiropractic treatments. Subluxation and dislocation injuries are reduced as soon as possible and then immobilized to allow ligaments to heal. Although the recovery time for soft tissue injuries may be lengthy, it is usually complete. Severe injuries may result in chronic pain and limited mobility. Symptoms may reoccur with fatigue. Residual effects of soft tissue injuries should be noted in medical records summaries so that their impact on lifestyle and occupation may be evaluated.

§ 6.4 —Whiplash Injuries

Whiplash injuries occur in the cervical spine as a result of hyperextension and/or hyperflexion of the cervical spine, as illustrated in **Figure 6–3.** Such extremes of movement are caused by excessive force that propels the neck to exaggerated backward, forward, or lateral motion, alone or in combination. Common causes of whiplash include motor vehicle accidents, especially rear end collisions, competitive sports such as wrestling, football, and work-related accidents.

Symptoms of whiplash include headache, neck stiffness, and pain that can radiate to the upper shoulder, scapula, or head. Other symptoms that may occur post-injury include:

- Dizziness;
- Ringing or buzzing in the ears;
- Blurry vision;
- Decreased range of motion (ROM) in neck;
- Local swelling and tenderness; or
- Muscle spasms in the paravertebral muscles.

Whiplash injuries are treated with a variety of modalities including neck splints/braces, activity restriction, medication for pain and muscle spasms, physical therapy, and/or chiropractic treatments. Recovery is usually complete, although the recovery period may be several months. Symptoms may reoccur periodically with fatigue, overexertion, or re-injury. In some cases, symptoms may persist for extended periods. A Web-based resource

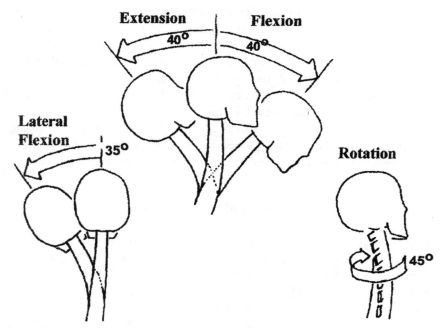

Figure 6–3. Hyperextension/Hyperflexion whiplash injury.

for information on whiplash and other chronic spinal conditions is *http:// www.spinalinjuryfoundation.org*. The Web site contains information for patients and professionals, including publication information for the *Journal of Whiplash and Related Diseases*.

§ 6.5 —Repetitive Stress Injuries

Repetitive stress injuries (RSI) occur as a result of cumulative trauma resulting from prolonged, forceful, or awkward movements. These types of injuries are also known as:

- Repetitive stress trauma;
- Overuse syndrome; or
- Non-traumatic muscular-skeletal disorder.

Repeated movements strain tendons, ligaments, and muscles, which cause tiny tears that become inflamed. If the injury is not given sufficient time to heal, scarring can occur and blood vessels can constrict, depriving the tissues of nutrients. Affected structures can deteriorate and nerve impairment may occur. Injury may occur as a result of poor posture, from activities that are related to occupation and/or workspace ergonomics, or recreation (e.g., sports-related). RSI injuries commonly affect upper extremities and symptoms include aching, burning pain, upper extremity weakness and fatigue, and/or loss of grip strength.

Treatment includes anti-inflammatory medications (NSAIDs), restricted activity, exercise programs, and workspace ergonomic assessment, if indicated.

§ 6.6   —Carpal Tunnel Syndrome

A frequently seen RSI is *carpal tunnel syndrome* (CTS), a disorder arising from compression of the medial nerve as it passes under the carpal ligament at the wrist (see **Figure 6–4**). As the term "syndrome" implies, it is a combination of symptoms affecting the wrist, hands, and fingers and is often occupationally related. Carpal tunnel syndrome is more common in women than in men and often occurs in occupations that require repetitive wrist motion in flexion, extension, or gripping. In addition to occupationally-related CTS, other causes may be:

- Tenosynovitis;
- Neoplasms/ganglia;
- Conditions in which increased fluid retention is likely, such as pregnancy; or
- Hormonal dysfunctions such as thyroid disease and diabetes mellitus.

Symptoms of carpal tunnel syndrome include pain, often worse at night that may radiate to the elbow or shoulder, grip weakness, swelling, pallor, and cooler skin temperature. Tingling and numbness (parathesia) in all fingers, or in all but little finger may also be present.

Diagnosis is made by several methods:

1. **Tinel's Test**—medial nerve is tapped at wrist. Pain is considered a positive sign.

2. **Phalen's Test**—backs of hands are placed together with wrists sharply flexed for one minute. The test is considered positive if tingling in fingers is present.

3. **Two Point Discrimination Test**—is performed using a discrimination caliper or two prongs of a paperclip, which are placed 6mm apart. Tips are placed on the pad of index finger, long finger, and thumb (digits innervated by the medial nerve) until skin is slightly blanched. Test results are abnormal if two points are not discriminated at <6mm.

4. **Electromyogram**—measurement of electrical impulses in muscle. The test is considered positive for carpal tunnel syndrome if weakened muscle response is demonstrated.

5. **Nerve Conduction Studies/Nerve Conduction Velocity (NCV)**—measure the speed at which a stimulus passes between two electrodes. Abnormalities in NCV could be indicative of CTS.

Treatment of carpal tunnel syndrome involves several modalities and may be surgical or nonsurgical in nature. Nonsurgical treatment includes physical therapy, range of motion exercises, elevation of arms to relieve edema, splints to relieve pressure on the nerve, and steroid injections. If relief of symptoms is not accomplished by conservative treatment, endoscopic surgery to release the carpal ligament and tendon to relieve compression may be performed. Recovery from carpal tunnel is usually complete; however, long-term lifestyle or occupation modifications may be necessary.

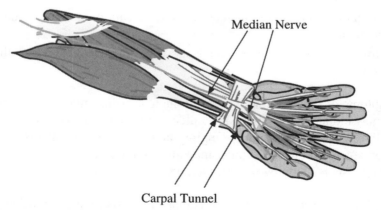

Median Nerve

Carpal Tunnel

Figure 6–4. Median nerve and carpal tunnel.

§ 6.7   —Rotator Cuff Injury

The rotator cuff is a complex of four muscles in the shoulder. Its principal function is to stabilize the head of the humerus in the shoulder joint. The rotator cuff also assists with shoulder joint range of motion and rotation of the humerus. Tears in the rotator cuff may be gradual, occurring as a result of degenerative changes associated with aging or as a result of repetitive stress injury. Injury may also be sudden, occurring when the arm is used to break a fall and the weight of the body causes the arm to collapse while the tendon is under tension. Repetitive overhead motion, such as that occurring in swimming and racquet sports may also cause rotator cuff injuries. Like most soft tissue injuries, there are different degrees of injury, depending on the severity of the tendon tear. Symptoms include shoulder pain that gets worse as swelling occurs and the inability to raise the arm away from the body (abduction). Diagnosis of rotator cuff injury is made principally through MRI and/or by shoulder arthroscopy and arthrography. Non-surgical treatment may consist of rest, ice, heat, NSAIDS, and physical therapy. Surgical treatment may be by direct visualization and surgical repair of the tear via arthroscope. For large tears, an open surgical procedure is required to repair the injury. The shoulder is immobilized post-operatively and an exercise regime is begun immediately to prevent *frozen shoulder*.

§ 6.8   —Meniscus Injuries

The meniscus consists of two pieces of fibro-cartilage, the medial and lateral meniscus that are located in the knee between the femur and the tibia. Two functions of the meniscus are to act as a shock absorber and distribute weight across the knee joint. It also provides secondary stability to the knee along with the knee's ligaments and tendons. Meniscus injury may be acute or chronic. Acute injury occurs in athletes who engage in sports that produce rotational stress on the knee when knee is flexed and foot is planted, such as in basketball. It can also be RSI that is work-related in persons who either frequently work in squatting or kneeling positions or that is a result of repetitive stress over time that occurs as part of the aging process. Symptoms of meniscus injury include pain at joint, swelling, and a sensation of knee instability. Clicking of the knee on flexion may or may not be present. If the meniscus is displaced, it may create a mechanical block to knee motion and result in a "locked knee."

Meniscus injuries are diagnosed by MRI examinations. Treatment may be conservative and include braces or splints, ice, pain medications (NSAIDs), and physical therapy. Surgical repair, if indicated, is done via arthroscopic surgery.

§ 6.9 —Vertebral Fractures and Spinal Cord Injuries

The vertebral column can be thought of as a "bony cage" that provide protection for the spinal cord. Fractures of the vertebrae, if severe, may compromise this protection and result in spinal cord injury. When vertebral fractures are unstable, the spinal ligaments are disrupted and dislocation of the vertebral structures may occur, resulting in spinal cord injury. Spinal cord injuries occur when the integrity of the spinal cord is disrupted. Disruption can occur by:

- Cord compression by bone displacement;
- Interruption of the blood supply to the spinal cord; or
- Traction on the cord from a pulling force.

When disruption occurs, all nerve impulses below the site of the injury cannot be transmitted and paralysis results. Paralysis may be partial or complete, depending on the degree of cord destruction. Classifications of spinal cord injuries are by:

1. **Mechanism of injury.** Cord injury may result from flexion, hyperextension, flexion rotation, extention/rotation, or compression movements.
2. **Level of injury.** Injury can occur in any part of the spine, although the cervical and lumbar spines are most common.
   - Skeletal level—vertebral level where the injury to bones and ligaments occurred.
   - Neurologic level—the lowest segment of the spinal cord with normal motor and sensory function on both sides of the body intact.
3. **Degree of injury**
   - Complete cord involvement—total loss of motor and sensory function below the site of injury. *Tetraplegia* (also termed quadriplegia) is an injury paralyzing all four extremities. *Paraplegia* is an injury that leaves arm function intact.

- Partial cord involvement—mixed loss of motor activity and sensation. The classification of partial cord involvement reflects the specific nerve tracts that are damaged and those that are spared. The initial goal of spinal cord injury treatment is to stabilize the fracture and prevent further cord damage by eliminating damaging motion at the site of injury. This may be done in several ways, depending on the site of the injury. For cervical spine fractures, cervical traction can be applied by means of tongs inserted into the skull or by means of halo traction (see **Figure 6–2**). Additionally, a laminectomy and/or spinal fusion using bone grafts with or without steel rods may be done.

The timing of when surgery should be done may vary, but considerations are based on indications or likelihood of developing cord compression. Clinical conditions of concern are neurological deficit progression, presence of bony fragments, compound fractures, and presence of penetrating wounds of the spinal cord or surrounding tissue

Paralysis resulting from spinal cord injuries requires lengthy rehabilitation at a specialized center and profoundly affects one's quality of life post injury. The American Spinal Injury Association (ASIA) has developed a Standard Neurologic Classification of Spinal Cord Injuries tool to assess the severity of impairment resulting from spinal cord injury (see **Figure 6–5**). The tool combines assessments of motor and sensory function to determine the neurological level and completeness of the injury. It is commonly used to identify changes in status and to identify appropriate rehabilitation goals.

The long-term goal of treatment is to restore the injured person to the highest possible level of function. This is usually accomplished in rehabilitation hospitals that specialize in the care of neurologically impaired individuals. The rehabilitation process is usually lengthy and difficult, involving both emotional and physical issues. Emotional issues surrounding alteration in lifestyle, body image, sexual function, and ability to work must be resolved. Physically, spinal cord injury patients are prone to a myriad of problems, such as urinary tract infection, pneumonia, and pressure sores. Autonomic dysreflexia, a potentially life-threatening response of the sympathetic nervous system to noxious stimuli (for example, full bladder) may also occur in spinal cord injuries above T7.

Living with spinal cord injury is a difficult and complex process requiring access to appropriate care management resources throughout the life

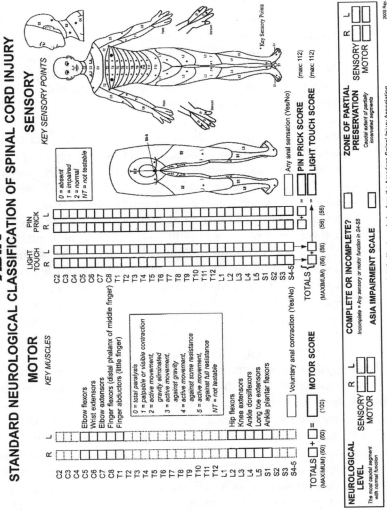

ASIA IMPAIRMENT SCALE

☐ **A = Complete:** No motor or sensory function is preserved in the sacral segments S4-S5.

☐ **B = Incomplete:** Sensory but not motor function is preserved below the neurological level and includes the sacral segments S4-S5.

☐ **C = Incomplete:** Motor function is preserved below the neurological level, and more than half of key muscles below the neurological level have a muscle grade less than 3.

☐ **D = Incomplete:** Motor function is preserved below the neurological level, and at least half of key muscles below the neurological level have a muscle grade of 3 or more.

☐ **E = Normal:** motor and sensory function are normal

CLINICAL SYNDROMES

☐ Central Cord
☐ Brown-Sequard
☐ Anterior Cord
☐ Conus Medullaris
☐ Cauda Equina

Figure 6–5. ASIA Standard Neurologic classification of spinal cord injury.

span of the individual. Care often requires a multidisciplinary approach and total involvement of the injured individual and significant others. There are many Web-based resources for spinal injury. Two resources are:

1. **The American Spinal Injury Association. (ASIA).** Their mission is to:
    *   Promote standards of excellence for all aspects of health care individuals with spinal cord injuries throughout life.
    *   Educate members, health care professionals, patients and their families, and the public on all aspects of spinal cord injury and its consequences.
    *   Foster research aimed at spinal cord injury prevention, improving care, reducing consequent disability, and finding a cure for both acute and chronic spinal cord injury.
    *   Facilitate communication between physicians, allied health care professionals, researchers, and consumers.
    ASIA's website address is *http://www.asia-spinalinjury.org.* Their address is:
    2020 Peachtree Rd, NW,
    Atlanta GA, 30309-1402
    Phone: (404) 355-9772

2. A second resource is the **National Spinal Cord Injury Association (NSCIA).** Their website address is *http://www.spinalcord.org.* The NSCIA provides support for individuals and their significant others living with spinal cord injuries. Both of these websites contain multiple links to additional resources.

    Although medical records of clients with spinal cord injuries are usually voluminous and therefore intimidating to summarize, organizing the information and tracking the client's progress is essential. **Chapter 8** describes some techniques that are useful in organizing information when summarizing voluminous medical records.

§ 6.10 —Low Back Pain

The lumbar spine is most vulnerable to injury that results in low back pain. Low back pain can range from mild to severe, and can be acute or chronic. *Acute low back pain* usually lasts four weeks or less and is often associated with some type of activity that places stress on the muscles of the lower back. Pain may not be immediate, but can increase over several days or can occur secondary to muscle spasm. *Chronic low back pain* lasts longer than three months or is a repeated, incapacitating episode of pain. Low back pain is usually classified by causation into two broad categories: *mechanical* or *discogenic*, the latter related to nerve impingement resulting from a herniated disc. A more detailed discussion of herniated discs follows in § **6.18.**

Mechanical back pain is usually caused by strain to the paraspinal ligaments that run bilaterally along the spinal column. Causes of mechanical back strain can be work-related, due to poor posture, or can occur secondary to recreational activities. Treatment of mechanical back injuries is aimed at relieving symptoms and includes avoiding activities that increase or aggravate pain. Bed rest is usually not necessary, but, if recommended, should only be for one to three days. Prolonged periods of bedrest may contribute to general de-conditioning of the body and prolong the recovery period. Additionally, the treatment plan for mechanical low back pain may include instructions to:

- Avoid sitting;
- Avoid heat in the first 72 hours; use ice packs to reduce inflammation;
- Take pain medication as needed, including NSAIDS and muscle relaxants; and
- Begin and follow a physical therapy exercise program when acute pain subsides.

Individuals with chronic low back pain may present a more complex clinical picture and require additional treatment modalities to successfully manage their pain. Because the mechanism of chronic pain perception is different from that of acute pain, different types of treatment strategies may be utilized. A multidisciplinary approach to management is often used. Refer to §§ **6.25–6.31** below for additional information on chronic pain and its treatment.

§ 6.11   —Herniated (Ruptured) Discs

The spinal cord is the main pathway for both sensory and motor impulses traveling back and forth between the brain and the body's environment.

The bony vertebrae of the spine encase the spinal cord. Between each spinal vertebra lies an *intervertebral* disc composed of cartilage. These discs are composed of tough outer rings (*annular fibers*) that surround a pulpy interior (*nucleus pulposis*) and are named according to their location. For example, L_4–L_5 disc is located between the fourth and fifth lumbar vertebrae. Intervertebral discs act as shock absorbers for the spine, helping to cushion the vertebrae and protect them from the trauma associated with the activities of daily life. Also found between the spinal vertebrae are nerve roots (dermatomes) that emerge from the spinal cord. These dermatomes contain both motor (movement) and sensory (feeling) nerve cells that provide a communication system between the spinal cord and all areas of the body. Branches of each nerve divide into smaller branches as they travel outward from the spinal cord to the body. Each dermatome innervates specific body locations. See **Figure 6–6.**

The sciatic nerve is the largest peripheral nerve in the body. It branches off from the spinal cord roots at vertebrae levels L_4, L_5, S_1, S_2, and S_3 and passes out of the pelvis down the back of the leg and knee. Thus, the sciatic nerve supplies virtually the entire leg with nerve impulses. Injury to this nerve may be caused by external trauma that results in intervertebral disk herniation, or by underlying disease such as spinal tumors or compression fractures of the vertebrae.

When an intervertebral disc herniates or ruptures, it bulges into the vertebral canal and exerts pressure on the spinal nerve. The symptoms, which may range from mild low back discomfort to intense pain that radiates to the affected extremities, are determined by the severity of the disc herniation, as well as its location. See **Figure 6–7.**

Although any intervertebral disc may herniate, the most common locations are those discs between L_4–L_5 and L_5–S_1 vertebrae. The most common symptom is back pain radiating down the buttock and below the knee along the distribution of the sciatic nerve. Specific symptoms may vary depending on exact location of the herniated disc. Physical examination should include assessment of pain, sensation (feeling), motor function, and reflexes.

Both history and physical examination should be meticulous as findings can help determine the level of disc herniation. As shown in **Figure 6–8,** clinical profile of pain, sensation, motor function, and reflexes will help pinpoint the location of the problem. Additional definitive diagnostic studies are also usually done following physical examination and may include CT scan, MRI, or myelogram.

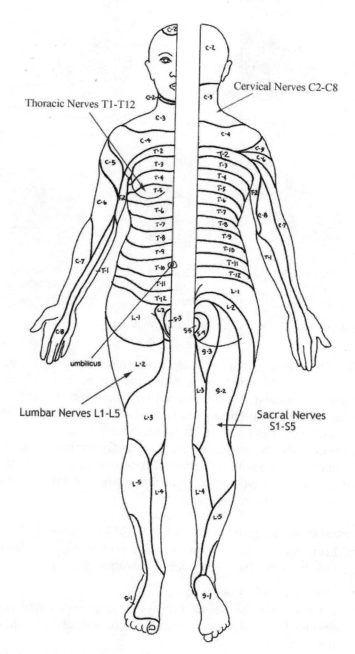

Figure 6–6. Spinal nerve dermatomes.
Source: *The Anatomy Coloring Book.* © 1977 by Wynn Kapit and Lawrence M. Elson. Reprinted by permission of Pearson Education, Inc.

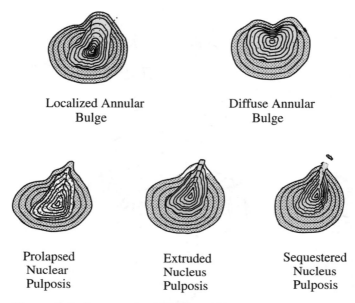

Localized Annular
Bulge

Diffuse Annular
Bulge

Prolapsed
Nuclear
Pulposis

Extruded
Nucleus
Pulposis

Sequestered
Nucleus
Pulposis

Figure 6–7. Intervertebral disc herniations.

Back pain resulting from herniated discs may be treated surgically or nonsurgically. Nonsurgical treatment is usually tried first and includes a combination of bedrest or restricted activity, braces or corsets, traction, heat or ice, pain medication, and drugs to relieve muscle spasms. Physical therapy modalities such as ultrasound and massage, and/or chiropractic treatments may also be prescribed. Surgical treatment may be indicated if pain does not improve with conservative treatment or if neurological deficits are present. The type of surgical procedure performed is based on clinical findings; these include:

1. **Laminectomy**—removal of part or all of the ruptured disc.
2. **Diskectomy**—portion of disc is removed to accomplish decompression of the nerve root. Procedural techniques include:
    *   Microsurgical discectomy
    *   Percutaneous laser discectomy—the desired portion of the disk is removed via tube that is passed into the site of rupture and removed with a laser.
3. **Spinal Fusion**—may be necessary following a laminectomy to stabilize the spine. In a spinal fusion, bone chips are inserted into the

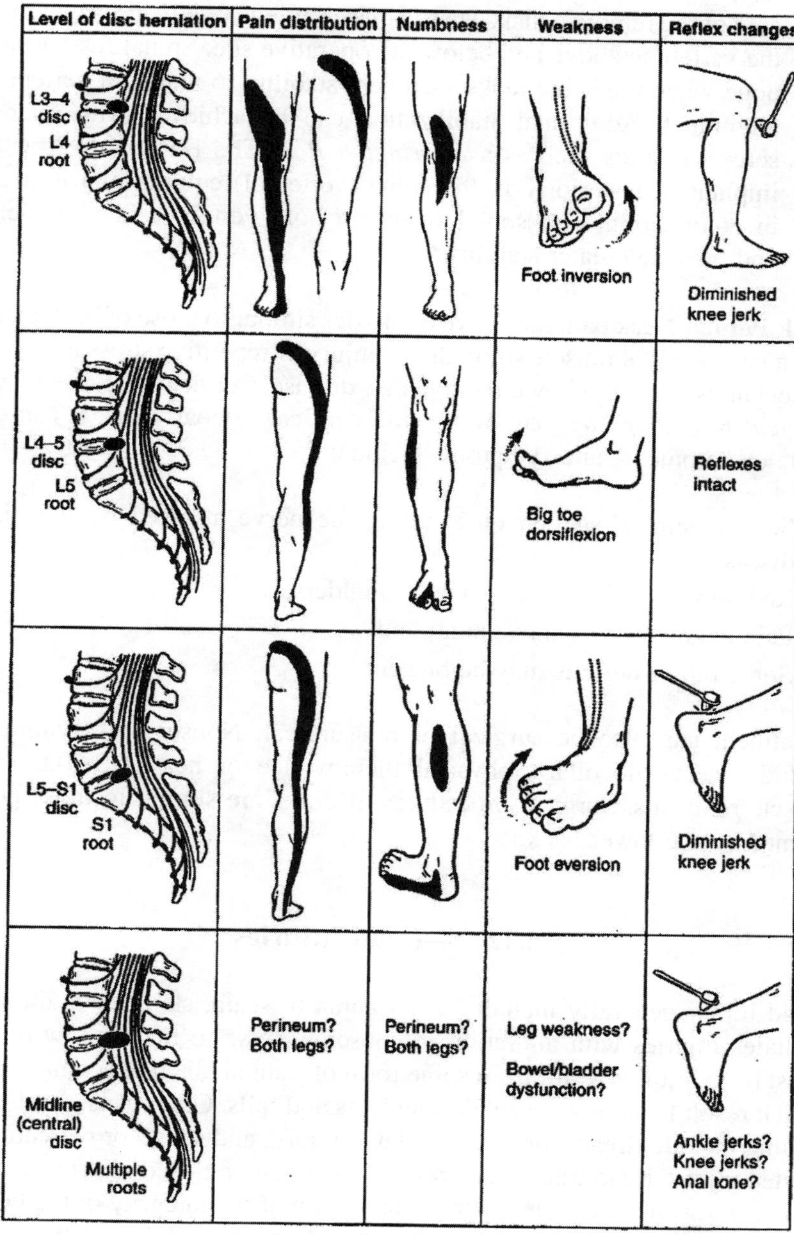

Level of disc herniation	Pain distribution	Numbness	Weakness	Reflex changes
L3–4 disc / L4 root			Foot inversion	Diminished knee jerk
L4–5 disc / L5 root			Big toe dorsiflexion	Reflexes intact
L5–S1 disc / S1 root			Foot eversion	Diminished knee jerk
Midline (central) disc / Multiple roots	Perineum? Both legs?	Perineum? Both legs?	Leg weakness? Bowel/bladder dysfunction?	Ankle jerks? Knee jerks? Anal tone?

Figure 6–8. Common disc syndromes.
Source: Brendan M. Reilly, *Practical Strategies in Outpatient Medicine.* United Kingdom: W.B. Saunders, 1991.

area of the removed disk. These bone chips eventually grow and fuse the vertebrae above and below the operative site. Spinal fusions are done when the spine lacks sufficient stability to maintain vertebral alignment. Additional stabilization can be achieved with plates, screws or rods such as a *Harrington Rod.* The Harrington Rod is implanted posteriorly in the spina (vertebral) column and is used in conjunction with spinal fusion to hold vertebrae in alignment and provide greater stability.

Neck Pain.   Neck pain may have etiologies similar to those of back pain. It can be a result of muscle strain due to injury or repetitive stress injury or can occur as a result of degenerative disc disease. Cervical disc disease or *cervical radiculopathy* may occur with cervical osteoarthritis. It can be acute or chronic. Acute symptoms include:

- Severe pain of sudden onset along the nerve affected by the disc disease;
- Radiation of pain to arms, neck, shoulders;
- Pain aggrevated by movement; and
- Some motor deficits may be present.

Treatment can also be surgical or nonsurgical. Nonsurgical treatment includes cervical collars, physical therapy, ice or heat, NSAIDs and muscle relaxants. Surgical procedures, if done, are similar to those performed on the lower back.

§ 6.12   —Head Injuries

Head injury generally includes any trauma to scalp, skull, or brain and includes injuries with alteration in consciousness, no matter how brief. Most head injuries result from some form of trauma, the most common of which result from motor vehicle accidents and falls. Other causes of head trauma include firearm or assault-related injury, and sports or recreation-related injury. Head trauma can result from open or closed injuries. *Open head injuries* involve some type of disruption of the integrity of the bony skull that occurs with skull fractures. In *closed head injuries*, the skull integrity remains intact but brain concussion or contusion has occurred. Collectively, these types of brain injury are referred to as *traumatic brain injury* (TBI). TBI is a frequent cause of death and disability, although the consequences vary widely depending on the type and extent of the injury. Outcomes range from full recovery to development of persistent vegetative state and/or death. There are several critical periods post-injury that have the greatest potential for poor outcome. These include:

- Immediately after injury—due to the severity of the initial injury that produces massive hemorrhage and shock.
- Several hours post-injury—due to progressive worsening of initial injury or internal bleeding.
- Three weeks post-injury—due to multi-system failure.

In the post-injury period, expert medical/nursing observation and monitoring is key to reducing mortality through early recognition of signs of deterioration. Deterioration is usually a result of increased intra-cranial pressure (ICP). ICP is discussed further in the section below. Some factors that are predictive of poor outcome include:

- Intracranial hematoma;
- Age of patient (elderly have poorer prognosis);
- Abnormal motor responses;
- Impaired/absent eye movements;
- Diminished pupil light reflexes;
- Early and sustained hypotension; and
- Increased intracranial pressure.

§ 6.13   —Skull Fractures

Skull fractures, like fractures in other areas of the body, can be open or closed, and are generally categorized by their configuration and location. (See **Figure 6–9**). Clinical presentation will differ depending on the location of the fracture.

1. **Linear**—single break with no bone fragments or bone displacement.
2. **Comminuted**—multiple adjacent linear fractures.

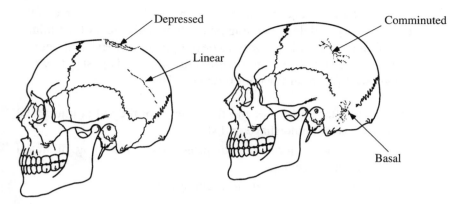

Figure 6–9. Types of skull fractures.

3. **Depressed**—comminuted fracture in which bone fragments are forced downward toward the brain.

4. **Basal**—fracture at the base of the skull; frequently penetrates into sinuses or middle ear, causing cerebral spinal fluid to leak through the fracture site into the external environment.

   Brain laceration can occur with depressed and compound skull fractures and penetrating skull injuries. Lacerations involve actual tearing of the brain tissue and represent severe injury to the brain.

§ 6.14 —Closed Head Injuries

Closed head injuries are usually of two main types: concussion and contusion. These terms are frequently confused even though the injuries and their potential effect upon the brain are completely different. A concussion is the least serious type of head injury, usually classified as *minor* head trauma that causes only transient changes in consciousness, vision, or equilibrium. *Concussion* occurs when an impact to the head jars the brain against the skull, and often results in a mild head injury. A mild head injury is usually characterized by a period of unconsciousness of less than 20 minutes, with a Glasgow Coma Scale of 13 or higher (See **Chapter 4, § 4.34**), a neurological exam with negative findings, and duration of post-trauma amnesia of less than 48 hours. Recovery from the acute episode is usually complete, often within a few hours. However, even mild concussions may have long-term effects. Post-concussion syndrome (PCS) may develop, a condition consisting of headache, fatigue, vertigo, and anxiety. This syndrome may persist for months after the injury, but the intensity of the symptoms usually diminishes with time. Symptoms may include persistent headache, lethargy, behavior, and personality changes that may result in impaired cognitive and behavioral skills and functional deficiencies. Some cases do persist and are highly resistant to treatment and significantly affect a person's ability to perform activities of daily living. The plan of treatment for these cases must be unique to the individual and focus on the alleviation of symptoms.

A *contusion* is the bruising of brain tissue resulting from acceleration/ deceleration motion of the brain within the skull at the time of injury. Along with brain lacerations, contusions are considered *major* head trauma. Contusions involve *coup-contrecoup* motions of the brain caused by mass movement of the brain inside the bony skull. These movements are defined as follows:

- Coup—contusions occurring directly under the injury site.
- Contrecoup—contusions occurring directly opposite the injury site, leading to multiple areas of contusions.

Contusions may produce hemorrhage and edema in the brain, although bleeding may be minimal and absorbed by the body over time. Contusions resulting in hematoma formation require surgical evacuation of the blood clot. Seizures may occur post-injury. As with any type of major head trauma, brain contusions require frequent neurological assessment and monitoring in the post-injury period. Recovery depends on the severity of the injury and whether brain damage exists. Some common complications of major head trauma include:

1. **Hemorrhage or hematoma formation** is caused by disruption of the blood vessels supplying the brain surface. Hematomas and hemorrhages are classified according to their location in the brain:
   - Subdural hematoma—bleeding occurs beneath the outermost protective covering of the brain, the dura mater. Subdural hematomas can be classified as acute (24 to 48 hours after trauma), sub-acute (48 hours to two weeks after trauma), and chronic (weeks to months after minor head injury).
   - Subarachnoid hemorrhage—bleeding occurs between the middle protective lining of the brain, the arachnoid, and the innermost protective lining, the pia mater.

- Intracerebral hemorrhage—occurs in the brain tissue itself; electrical activity in the brain is interrupted and there is a loss of consciousness.

2. **Increased Intracranial Pressure (ICP)**—caused when the brain enlarges due to swelling or hematoma formation but cannot expand because of the rigidity of the skull. Swelling may compromise blood supply to the brain with resulting tissue damage. Early detection and treatment of increasing ICP are critical to minimize brain damage. Symptoms of ICP include change in level of consciousness, changes in vital signs, pupil changes, and changes in motor function.

3. **Cerebral Spinal Fluid Leakage**—occurs from fractures in which bone fragments tear the outer protective covering of the brain, the dura mater. This exposes the brain to the outside environment and increases the risk of infections such as meningitis or brain abscesses.

4. **Neurologic Deficits**—type and severity depend on the nature and location of the injury. Deficits may include problems with hearing, speech, vision, paralysis or paresis, memory problems, or brain damage.

5. **Seizures**—may occur immediately following the acute injury or become a permanent disorder. A variety of diagnostic tests are utilized to diagnose the specificity of head trauma including CT scan, MRI, and PET scans. (See **Chapter 4, § 4.8** for additional information on diagnostic testing). Treatment of head injury depends on the type and location of the trauma. Depressed and comminuted skull fractures require surgical intervention to remove bone fragments and damaged tissue. Of paramount importance in all types of major head injury is frequent observation and neurological assessment that will alert the health care team to increasing intracranial pressure. The assessment should include use of the Glasgow Coma Scale, reflex testing, and pupil responses. The prospect of recovery following head injury is usually positive unless extensive brain damage has occurred. A client experiencing neurologic deficits post-head trauma may require a prolonged rehabilitation period similar to that required for spinal cord injuries and post-injury testing to assess long-term complications of the injury.

§ 6.15   —Irreversible Coma and Brain Death

At times brain damage from head injuries or other causes will be so severe that meaningful recovery is not possible. The *cerebral cortex* controls voluntary movement and actions and is the center for cognitive function. The *brain stem* controls basic body functions such as breathing, vomiting, and eye reflexes on a largely automatic basis, that is, they are not conscious activities of the brain. Severe brain damage may lead to the development of a persistent vegetative state, sometimes referred to as *irreversible coma*, in which only the brainstem functions. In a persistent vegetative state, no conscious activities of the cerebral cortex of the brain are present. With the advent of advanced life support technology, controversy surrounded the definition of brain death as to whether brain death was cessation of cerebral cortex function only or cessation of cerebral cortex function *and* brain stem function. To provide guidance, the Quality Standards Subcommittee of the American Academy of Neurology developed guidelines to determine brain death in adults. These are widely used today. More detailed information is available through the Academy's Web site at *http://www.aan.com.*

§ 6.16 —Facial Injuries

A frequent cause of facial trauma is motor vehicle accidents. Results of such trauma can be both emotionally and cosmetically devastating. Common facial injuries include lacerations and fractures, muscle and soft tissue damage, and eye injuries. Most lacerations and soft tissue injuries to the face bleed profusely and/or produce large amounts of swelling or bruising because of abundant blood supply to the facial tissues. Superficial facial trauma may mask more serious problems, such as head or spinal cord injuries. In evaluating the extent of any facial trauma, head and spinal cord injuries must be ruled out as well.

The primary concern after facial injury is to establish and maintain a patent airway. In evaluating the extent of facial injuries, the coexistence of cervical fractures should also be considered. Stabilization of the cervical spine should be maintained until cervical fracture is ruled out. Concurrent soft tissue injury is also common. Although initially facial fractures can be cosmetically devastating, they usually heal rapidly.

Nasal fractures are the most common type of facial fractures and are usually a result of blunt trauma to the front or side of the nose. Immediate treatment consists of ice packs to reduce swelling, splinting if necessary, and surgical repair if indicated.

Mandibular fractures, those of the lower jaw bone, are the second most common type of facial fractures. They may be simple without bone displacement or complex, involving the loss of tissue and bone. Pain on jaw movement and dental malocclusion are common symptoms of mandibular fractures. Treatment is by surgical intervention consisting of fracture immobilization by jaw wiring. Internal fixation with screws and plates and metal arch bars are used if bone is displaced or teeth are lost. Direct blows to the face are the most common cause of maxillary fractures. Several bones form the maxilla, which combine to form the upper jaw and facial structures. Different types of maxillary fractures can occur, depending on the force and direction of the trauma. These were described by the French physician LeFort, who classified them as follows: (see **Figure 6–10**):

1. **LeFort I**—transverse or horizontal fracture that involves the front teeth up to the nose.
2. **LeFort II**—pyramid-shaped fracture that encompasses the central portion of the maxilla up to the nose.
3. **LeFort III**—separation of facial bones from the cranium (skull). Treatment of facial fractures is by surgical intervention through open reduction and internal fixation. If facial fractures occur in combination with more lifethreatening injuries, such as head or spinal cord trauma, treatment may be postponed until the patient is stable.

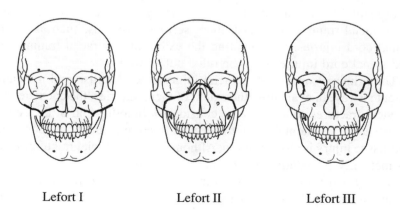

Lefort I   Lefort II   Lefort III

Figure 6–10. Maxillary fractures.

§ 6.17   —Myofacial Pain Syndrome

Myofacial pain syndrome is a group of disorders characterized by musculoskeletal tenderness in a specific area of the body. All syndromes are characterized by presence of pain trigger points that when palpated, create a characteristic pain pattern. Pain is thought to be a result of muscle trauma or chronic strain. Several types of myofacial pain syndromes exist; however, one of the most common is Temporomandibular Joint (TMJ) Syndrome. TMJ syndrome involves dysfunction of the temporomandibular joint (that accomplishes jaw motion) as well as the surrounding cartilage and muscles. It is most common in young women and the syndrome may be acute or chronic. Near the temporomandibular joint are many nerves, blood vessels, and muscles that may be compromised when the joint itself does not function properly. TMJ syndrome symptoms are believed to be the result of the dysfunctional operation of these structures. The hallmark symptom of TMJ is decreased range of motion of the temporomandibular joint, resulting in restricted mouth opening or clicking of the jaw. Pain is often described as dull, worse when chewing hard foods. Often there is spasm of the muscles used for chewing (muscles of mastication). Other symptoms include facial or neck muscle spasm and tenderness, headaches, earaches, dizziness, and depression.

Although the full spectrum of causes is unknown, several known causes of TMJ include jaw malocclusion following dental procedures or orthodontics, hyperextension of muscles secondary to sports injuries, oral surgery, or motor vehicle accidents (whiplash). Facial trauma, arthritis, and stress have also been implicated. Diagnosis is made by findings of decreased range of motion and associated symptoms. MRIs are also used in diagnosis and are favored over CT scans and X rays because they provide better visualization of the soft tissues that may be involved in the disorder. Other causes of pain such as trigeminal neuralgia, sinusitis, temporal arteritis, and dental disease must be ruled out. Treatment of TMJ syndrome consists of a combination of dental and medical therapies and includes the following:

• Dental appliances such as splints.

• Physical therapy modalities such as diathermy and ultrasound.

• Surgery by arthroscopy or open repair.

§ 6.18　Pain

In part because the term "pain" is difficult to define, numerous definitions of pain exist. McCaffrey (1969) defines pain as "Whatever the patient says it is, existing whenever he says it does." The International Association of the Study of Pain describes pain as "an unpleasant sensory and emotional experience associated with actual or potential tissue damage, or described in terms of such damage." All persons experience some type of pain in their lifetime. Pain is a normal physiologic response of the body, a subjective sensation caused by *noxious* (harmful) stimuli that signal the body of actual or potential tissue damage. Pain can be perceived only by the person experiencing it. How pain is interpreted and responded to is unique to that individual and influenced by psychological and cultural factors, e.g., values, beliefs, religion, and customs, that help determine the significance and meaning of pain.

Chronic pain is one of the most costly health care problems in America. Billions of dollars are spent annually on medical expenses, lost income, lost productivity, compensation payments, and legal fees. Many personal injury and worker's compensation cases involve chronic pain as part of their damages. For the legal professional reviewing and summarizing medical records, extracting relevant information on the client's pain history and treatment can be challenging. Understanding some basic concepts about types of pain, and approaches to its assessment, and treatment is helpful to this process.

Theories and Beliefs Relating to Pain

Pain has always been considered a byproduct of injury or disease—that is, if the condition is treated, the pain will stop. Many theories and beliefs have supported this thinking. The specificity of pain theory developed in the 17th century was based on the concept of a fixed, one-to-one relationship between stimulus and sensation: a particular form of therapy administered by all physicians works for all patients and all pain. As recently as the 1980s, it was assumed that infants could not feel or remember pain.

In many cultures, high pain tolerance is valued. Individuals are encouraged not to verbalize their pain characteristics or manifest outward signs of discomfort, especially in the presence of chronic pain. Society encourages stoicism in the presence of pain, yet also widely subscribes to the acute pain model. The acute pain model holds that if someone has pain, some visible signs of discomfort will be present, behavioral or physiologic. Examples of these "appropriate" manifestations of pain could include grimacing, wincing, crying, or guarding the painful area. It is commonly believed that if an individual is laughing, resting comfortably, or conversing or joking with others that he/she cannot be in pain. Contrary to these popular and widespread beliefs, it is now known that over time both behavioral and physiologic adaptation to pain occurs, leading to periods of minimal or no visible signs of pain. Another widely accepted belief is that all causes of pain are identifiable. If its cause is known, pain is more acceptable. Family and friends are more supportive of the individual and clinicians may be more attentive to achieving successful pain management if the cause is known. The term "psychogenic pain" is commonly used to refer to pain for which a physical cause cannot be found. When the cause is unknown or seems insufficient to account for severity of pain, the clinician may attribute it to the individual's anxiety or depression and minimize efforts to treat it. In reality, most pain is a combination of physical and psychological factors; cause and effect between pain and anxiety/depression is unclear as to which comes first.

Common Misconceptions about Pain

Society's beliefs around pain have helped develop many common misconceptions held by both the lay public as well as health professionals. These misconceptions may impede proper assessment of patients with pain by healthcare providers and impact he effectiveness of pain treatment. Some common misconceptions include:

1. Health care providers are the authority on pain, the experts in treating it. In reality, the patient should always be considered the authority on his/her pain.
2. There is a uniform pain threshold, that is, the intensity of the pain experienced from comparable stimuli will be the same from person to person. Not only do different intensities of pain result from comparable stimuli, but the threshold at which pain is perceived differs as well.
3. Patients with low pain tolerance need to make more effort to cope with the pain. Pain tolerance is the duration or intensity of pain the patient is willing to tolerate. This will vary from person to person. Although an individual's coping skills may influence his/her pain

tolerance, other factors affecting pain tolerance are past experience with pain, motivation to endure pain, and energy level.

4. All real pain has an identifiable (physical) cause. Pain is a complex phenomenon with both physiologic and psychological components. As a relatively new science, many aspects of pain are still not fully understood.

5. Persons in pain exhibit visible signs, either physical or behavioral. Because adaptation to pain occurs, lack of expression of pain does not necessarily mean that pain is not present.

6. Pain is not perceived by the very young or the very old. Studies have demonstrated this not to be true. However, how pain is expressed may be altered in these patients.

7. Individuals knowledgeable about opiod (narcotic) analgesia and who regularly request them may be addicted. People who experience pain should be knowledgeable about their pain medications, including opiods, just as persons with diabetes should be knowledgeable about medication and diet that help control blood sugar.

8. Opiods (see definition below) can easily cause addiction and, therefore, should be used sparingly and only for specific diagnoses, e.g., cancer. Numerous studies have demonstrated little risk of addiction associated with opiod administration for pain relief.

As a result of widely accepted beliefs and misconceptions about pain, as well as individual beliefs of health care providers, pain has often been under-treated in the United States. However, newer theories about pain perception and transmission that incorporate both the anatomy *and* physiology of pain transmission have advanced approaches to pain treatment. The Gate Control theory of pain (discussed below) is one of these theories.

§ 6.19 —Physiology of Pain Perception

As previously stated, pain is a complex phenomenon. To understand pain, it is helpful to understand the process of pain transmission, regulation, and perception. The basic process has the following components, also illustrated in **Figure 6–11:**

1. Noxious stimuli are perceived by a specific body part. Stimuli can be thermal, chemical, mechanical, or electrical.

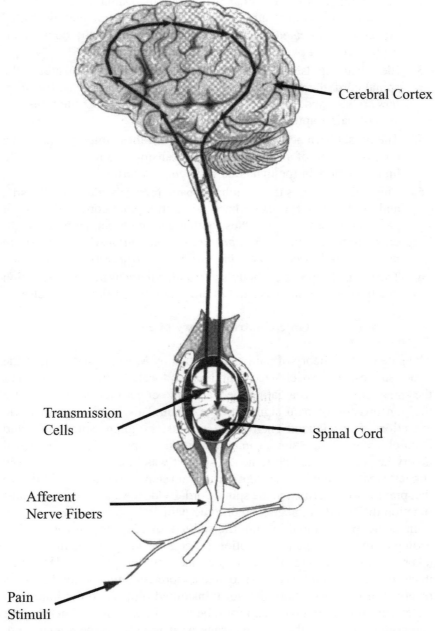

Cerebral Cortex

Transmission
Cells

Spinal Cord

Afferent
Nerve Fibers

Pain
Stimuli

Figure 6–11. Pain perception process.

2. Peripheral tissues are damaged by stimuli. Damage results in the secretion of chemical substances that stimulate nerve endings called *nociceptors*. Located in various tissues throughout the body, nociceptors convert pain stimuli into electrical impulses.

3. Electrical impulses travel along afferent nerve fibers to an area in the spinal cord, the dorsal horn, where chemicals called *neurotransmitters* are secreted. These substances either inhibit or excite transmission of pain impulses.

4. The dorsal horn acts as a clearinghouse for these impulses (see gate control theory of pain, below) and transmits pain information to higher centers in the thalamus and cerebral cortex.

5. The brain identifies the stimulus as pain, precisely identifies the site, and sends this information back down the spinal cord to the site of pain, telling affected muscles to contract and block pain and withdraw from stimulus. *It is important to note that noxious stimuli are not identified as pain until this stage of the transmission process.*

6. The brain also prods the body's autonomic nervous system into action to adjust body functions such as breathing, blood flow, and pulse.

Gate Control Theory of Pain

The gate control theory of pain as described by Melzack and Wall in the 1960s suggests that specialized neural tissue, located in the dorsal horn of the spinal cord, acts as a gating mechanism to either increase or decrease the transmission of pain signals to the brain. This is accomplished via excretion of specialized chemicals, such as serotonin, adrenaline, and endorphins, which are similar in composition to opium. The gate control theory has been revised periodically since it was first described and now suggests that an inhibitory system in the brain stem may exist in addition to that previously described in the spinal cord. Evidence also exists that gates function differently in acute and chronic pain.

In acute pain, impulses are transmitted directly to the brain. For example, the entire pain perception process is complete in the time it takes for a hand to grasp a hot object and withdraw from it. However, in chronic pain, impulses appear to take a more circuitous route. Impulses received in the dorsal horn are not transmitted directly to the brain, but instead are transferred back and forth between interconnected nerves (the gates) that modulate the pain message as it travels up the spinal cord. Eventually, impulses are received in the cerebral cortex, which assesses the damage and sends back down the spinal cord messages that appropriately adjust body junctions. This slower pathway is usually taken by duller, more persistent pain.

In an adult, both acute and chronic pain perception mechanisms are influenced heavily by past experience, culture, and psychological factors, which in turn determine "pain threshold." The pain threshold of an individual, to a large extent, accounts for variations in pain experience from person to person. The following types of thresholds have been described and can be assessed in the person with pain:

- Sensation threshold—lowest stimulus value that produces tingling or warmth.
- Pain perception threshold—lowest stimulus value that produces pain.
- Pain tolerance—lowest stimulus value at which person withdraws or asks to have stimulus withdrawn.
- Encouraged pain tolerance—same as pain tolerance, but person is encouraged to tolerate higher levels of stimulation.

§ 6.20   —Pain Types and Classifications

There are different classifications and descriptions of pain. Obtaining detailed information about pain as described by the patient is important in determining cause. Pain can be described along several parameters:

1. **Onset or time of occurrence.** It is important to determine when the pain began and what the client's situation was at this time. Since the onset, has there been a pattern to the pain—is it cyclical or does its occurrence vary?
2. **Duration.** Is the pain acute or chronic? Refer to the discussion below on the characteristics of acute and chronic pain.
3. **Severity or intensity.** Individuals will use such terms as stabbing, dull, sharp, intermittent, excruciating, burning to describe their pain.
4. **Location.** Is the pain internal or external? Is the pain always in the same location? In chronic pain, an exact location may be difficult for the individual to describe.
5. **Causation.** Is the pain a result of stimulation of nerve pain receptors or nerve damage? See the discussion below for examples of these causes.

Pain is most commonly described in terms of its *duration* and *location.* Pain **duration** is classified as acute, chronic, and psychogenic. *Acute pain* is generally caused by tissue damage. It has a short duration, generally less than six months, an identifiable onset, and a limited/predictable duration. Acute pain diminishes gradually with appropriate interventions and the healing of damaged tissues. *Chronic pain* is of prolonged duration, generally persisting for longer than six months with no identifiable end. Based on certain characteristics, chronic pain can be further subcategorized as:

1. **Recurring acute pain**—recurring episodes of pain that do not have a defined end (e.g., migraine headache pain);
2. **Prolonged time-limited pain**—pain that continues over a fairly lengthy period of time, but has a high probability of ending with appropriate treatment (e.g., burn pain);
3. **Chronic benign pain**—generally due to non-life-threatening causes, but refractory to common treatment modalities (e.g., arthritic pain).

As pain persists and becomes chronic, it no longer becomes a symptom of injury or disease, but a *pain syndrome.* Chronic pain is a medical problem in its own right that requires medical evaluation and treatment. The syndrome can affect social, family, and employment relationships and create a pattern of physical distress and emotional conflict. Major behavioral and affective changes can occur, including:

- anxiety and/or depression and social withdrawal;
- appetite and weight changes—either increased or decreased;
- restricted physical activity leading to decreased work capacity, poor physical tone;
- preoccupation with physical symptoms;
- poor sleep patterns and chronic fatigue.

Pain is often labeled *psychogenic* when no physical cause can be found. It is a common belief that a person experiences psychogenic pain because he or she wants or needs it: to avoid specific tasks, for economic gain, because of drug-related behavior, or to gain attention. This type of pain is also called *pretended pain* or *malingering.* There is evidence however, that chronic pain is the cause of psychogenic pain rather than the result of neurotic symptoms. Even though it does exist, pretended pain should never be assumed.

Pain **location** classifications are as follows:

1. **Cutaneous or superficial pain**—usually well localized on the skin or body surface. The intensity of the pain usually correlates with the intensity of the stimulus. Treatment is relatively uncomplicated because the pain is localized.

2. **Deep somatic pain**—primarily affects muscles, bones, nerves, and blood vessels. Somatic pain is poorly localized because of poor innervation of affected organs. Pain is associated with autonomic central nervous systems symptoms, such as nausea, sweating, and blood pressure changes.

3. **Visceral pain**—affects large internal organs occupying body cavities and may be constant or intermittent in nature. Pain tends to be diffuse, but may become more localized over time.

4. **Referred pain**—occurs in an area of the body remote from the affected organ. For example, a heart attack exhibits no pain in the heart, but pain felt in the left arm, shoulder, or jaw pain.

5. **Radiating pain**—follows dermatome patterns from its site of origin.

The above are examples of *nociceptive pain*, that is pain caused by stimulation of pain receptors. Stimulation can be of chemical, mechanical, or thermal origin. Nociceptive pain should be differentiated from *neuropathic pain*, which is caused by damage to the nervous system when the flow of afferent nerve impulses is partially or completely interrupted.

Neuropathic pain can be central or peripheral in origin. Examples include:

1. **Muscular and bony origin.** Pain can affect ligaments, joints, fascia, tendon, and muscles. It can occur as a result of rupture, sprains, ischemia, inflammation of these structures.

2. **Vascular.** This type of pain is believed to originate from pathology of vessels or surrounding tissues. Pain-producing chemicals in the body also appear to play a role in vascular pain. Examples include migraine headaches and headaches associated with arterial hypertension, brain tumors, and increased intracranial pressure.

3. **Inflammation.** Pain is caused by numerous agents, including chemical agents secreted by the body, e.g., histamine, and external factors such as heat or cold. Symptoms include redness, swelling, heat, pain, inflammation.

4. **Central.** Central pain occurs as a result of central nervous system injury such as infarction or tumor. It is often severe and difficult to treat.

5. **Peripheral pathogenic pain.** This type of pain is caused by changes in nerve structure. This pain may be severe and unrelenting. Although its cause is not fully understood, scarring and degenerative changes in nerves and nervous tissue may play an important role in pain intensity. Manifestations of peripheral pathogenic pain are:

   - **post-herpetic pain**—occurs following infection of the dorsal nerve ganglia, a condition commonly known as shingles. Causative agent is herpes zoster virus (chickenpox virus). Pain is caused by scarring and degenerative changes of affected nerve roots.

   - **causalgia**—result of peripheral nerve injuries. Peripheral nerves of extremities, such as brachial plexus, median, and sciatic nerves are most commonly involved. Nerve injury is usually a result of sprains, bruises, fractures, amputations.

   - **trigeminal neuralgia (tic douloureux)**—occurs along the 5th or 9th cranial nerves. Pain results from a neuritis caused by degenerative changes that injure nerve roots. Trigeminal pain is often triggered by minimal stimuli such as cold air, temperature changes, clothing irritation against affected area.

   - **phantom pain**—perceived in a non-existing body part, e.g., pain in an amputated limb. The mechanism of phantom pain perception is not well understood.

   - **headache**—occurs in pain-sensitive structures in the head and may result from *intracranial* and *extracranial* causes. Causes of intracranial pain include infection, hemorrhage, changes in intracranial pressure. Migraine headaches are the best known example of this type of pain. Extracranial pain results from muscle tension, TMJ, ocular, sinus, dental, or malignant pain such as from cancer. Pain is caused by pressure on or displacement of nerves, interference with blood supply, or blockage within hollow organs.

§ 6.21 —Differences in Types of Pain

It is important to emphasize the differences in nocioceptive and neuropathic pain. Nocioceptive pain results from *normal processing* of sensory input by an intact nervous system. Neuropathic pain is distinctly different in that pain is sustained by *abnormal processing* of sensory input by the peripheral or central nervous system. It becomes critically important to thoroughly assess the underlying pathophysiology of the pain, as pain caused by different mechanisms responds to different treatment modalities. Chronic pain and cancer pain may reflect both types of pain (nociceptive and neuropathic).

§ 6.22   —Harmful Effects of Unrelieved Pain

To counter the belief held by some that individuals with low pain thresholds should learn to live with their pain, numerous potentially harmful effects from unrelieved pain have been observed. Unrelieved pain causes physiological stress responses in the body that affect many body systems. Examples of some system-specific physiologic effects of pain are:

1. **Cardiovascular**—increased heart rate, blood pressure, increased tendency of blood clotting (hypercoagulation). Hypercoagulation may lead to venous thrombosis or pulmonary embolism (blood clots).
2. **Respiratory**—shallow breathing, decreased oxygenation of the lung alveoli, decreased lung capacity. Potential for these effects is increased if source of pain is from the thoracic or chest region. If pain is not adequately treated, complications such as pneumonia and atelectasis may develop.
3. **Endocrine and metabolic**—excessive release of some hormones and decreased release of others. These imbalances have numerous effects on body metabolism. Unrelieved pain prolongs this situation and ultimately can delay recovery from trauma or surgery.
4. **Musculoskeletal**—muscle spasms, impaired musculoskeletal function, fatigue. Especially significant in orthopedic injuries as these effects may interfere with the ability to participate in physical therapy, which may in turn affect return of mobility and functionality of injured area.
5. **Immune system**—depression of the immune response that can cause susceptibility to infection; can predispose to post-operative infections such as pneumonia, wound infections, and sepsis.

In addition to physiological effects of unrelieved pain, behavioral effects are seen as well. Pain may affect the ability to perform daily functions, and may precipitate mental confusion, especially in the elderly.

The resulting impact on quality of life can be significant, with effects noted that range from decreased physical activity to severe depression and suicidal ideation.

§ 6.23   —Pain Assessment

Because pain is a subjective experience, pure objective tests for pain do not exist. As stated previously, an individual's pain response is influenced by many factors, which must be taken into account during the evaluation process. It is impossible to predict how much pain a given stimulus can cause in an individual. Causes of pain can be obscure. Because a physical cause for pain cannot always be found *does not mean that it is not real pain.*

Additionally, health-care provider myths and misconceptions about pain may influence assessment techniques. Personal beliefs about pain can cloud the pain assessment process. Irrespective of all barriers, the key to effective pain *treatment* is accurate *assessment.* As in any type of assessment, the provider must listen to the patient, establish physical findings, and form an objective conclusion. Shortcuts in this process may result in premature conclusions on the part of the provider and lead to less than adequate pain management. Assessment of pain should include both subjective and objective findings; both types of data must be taken into consideration. Summarized information should contain the individual's description of pain as well as the examiner's observation of the person's behavior. As with any type of assessment technique, pain assessment should include both history and physical examination components:

1. **History**—should provide a chronology of events and include factors relevant to determine the location of pain, frequency, extension/radiation, surface versus deep, onset or pattern, duration, character, precipitating or aggravating factors, intensity, and symptoms. Key information includes the effects pain has had on the individual's ADLs and on his or her ability to perform job duties and responsibilities.
2. **Physical examination**—should focus on the objective signs of pain the patient exhibits, which can be divided physiological and behavioral responses. These responses are not diagnostic of pain, but may give clues as to its cause. The information obtained should then be evaluated within the context of cultural and psychological experiences of the individual.

§ 6.24   —Tools for Assessing Pain

More commonly, clinicians whose practice encompasses treatment of patients with pain (acute or chronic) will utilize some type of pain assessment tool. With the development of clinical practice guidelines, patient rights bills, JCAHO pain standards and other regulatory requirements, clinicians must now be able to demonstrate that they assess and actively manage their patients' pain. Several widely accepted tools have been developed to assist the clinician with pain assessment. For initial pain assessment, the *Initial Pain Assessment* tool and the *Brief Pain Inventory Tool* are commonly used. Both of these tools are included in the clinical guidelines for treatment of cancer pain published by the Agency for Health Care Policy and Research (AHPR). The clinician or the patient may complete either tool. The **Initial Pain Assessment** guides the systematic collection of pain history information. It is a 10-point tool that asks the patient to describe the following characteristics of his/her pain:

- location
- intensity
- quality
- onset, duration, variations, rhythms
- manner of expressing pain
- what relieves pain
- what causes or increases pain
- effects of pain
- other comments
- treatment plan.

The **Brief Pain Inventory Tool** focuses on pain experience within the past 24 hours and includes a numeric rating scale along the following dimensions:

- types of pain in the past 24 hours, other than "everyday" types of pain
- identification of the worst area of pain
- numerical rating of the worst pain in the past 24 hours

- numerical rating of the least pain in the past 24 hours
- numerical rating of the average pain in the past 24 hours
- numerical rating of the pain presently
- treatments or medications currently receiving for pain
- maximum pain relief experience in the past 24 hours
- numerical rating of how pain has affected (in the past 24 hours): general activity, mood, walking ability, normal work, relations with other people, sleep, enjoyment of life.

A third tool commonly used for initial pain assessment is the *McGill-Melzack Pain Questionnaire* (see **Figure 6–12**). This tool is complex and time-consuming to use, but it gives the clinician in-depth information about the pain being experienced. The McGill-Melzack test is designed to measure the patient's pain symptoms against five main components:

- Pain Rating Index (PRI)—consists of words describing pain quality.
- Number of Words Chosen (NWC)—a count of the number of words chosen from the 20 total responses in the group.
- Present Pain Intensity (PPI)—selection of the word that most accurately describes pain intensity.
- Line Drawing of the Body—describes the location and frequency of the pain.
- List of Symptoms—individual's description of symptoms experienced. Responses are assigned scores used as a basis for pain treatment. Once treatment is initiated, this tool can be re-administered to assess the efficacy, or lack thereof, of the treatment.

Other pain assessment tools are designed for use in *daily* assessment of pain levels. Many such tools exist and are similar in that they all are used to help the individual describe pain severity. Some commonly used tools include:

- *Visual analog scale with verbal anchors*—individual is asked to rate pain along a horizontal line with a scale of 0 (no pain) to 10 (worst pain).
- *Numeric rating scale*—verbally administered; individual is asked to rate pain on a scale of 0 to 5 or 0 to 10. This type of pain assessment is

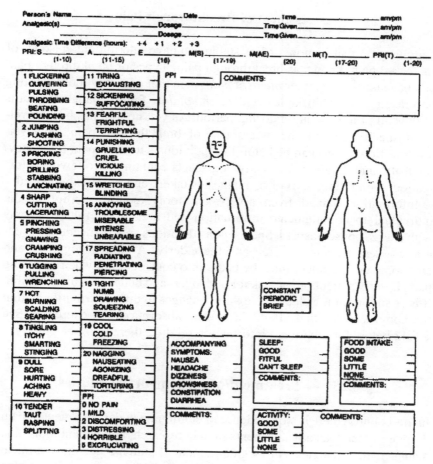

Figure 6–12. McGill-Melzack pain questionnaire.

commonly used post-operatively and response levels are documented in the medical record.

- *Word descriptor scale*—individual is asked to rate pain intensity by using a verbal scale from no pain, slight, moderate, severe, or worst pain.
- *Faces (Wong-Baker)*—a variation of the above tools that describe pain in terms of facial expressions, ranging from a happy face (no pain) to a sad face with tears (worst pain). This tool is used widely to assess pain in children.

Assessment of Breakthrough Pain

Chronic pain that is more or less stable can have intermittent episodes of increased pain, known as breakthrough pain. Types of breakthrough pain can be classified as either *incident pain*, pain that occurs without warning as a result of an identifiable event, or *end of dose failure*, pain that returns at the end of a medication dosing period. As yet, no tool has been developed specifically for the assessment of breakthrough pain; however, 24-hour flow sheets can be helpful to individuals to track pain frequency, intensity, and duration. Typically, log sheets contain the following information: pain rating, activities, analgesics taken, and relief experienced.

Information gained from assessment tools requires ability of the individual to communicate information and are not useful in patients with altered consciousness. Special considerations are also needed to accurately assess pain in children and the elderly. A child's cognitive and emotional development must be taken into consideration when assessing pain. Elderly patients are at risk for both over- and under-treatment of pain. It is common for the elderly to exhibit changes in drug distribution within the body, a factor that affects both drug absorption and excretion. See **§ 6.42** below for additional information on drug therapy in the elderly.

§ 6.25   —Treatment/Management Modalities

In this country, there is still evidence of continuing under-treatment of pain despite tremendous advancements in pain research, assessment tools, and management strategies. Although treatment of pain has become a clinical specialty, it still remains the responsibility of all clinicians to address pain management in the patient's treatment plan. As stated previously, a primary concept in effective pain management is that the individual is the authority on his/her pain. This concept does not require that a clinician totally agrees with what a patient says, only that they accept what the patient says, convey acceptance to the patient, and take appropriate action. Clinicians can have doubts about the validity of the information relayed by the individual, but these should not interfere with the appropriate patient care. Therefore, both objective and subjective data should be used to assess pain levels.

To proactively address some of the issues related to the high incidence of under-treated pain, many professional organizations, federal and state agencies have issued guidelines and standards addressing effective pain management. The Joint Commission of Accreditation of Healthcare Organizations (JCAHO) has had standards relating to pain management since 1992. Over the years, these standards have expanded and as of 2000, JCAHO standards require that healthcare organizations (accredited by JCAHO) develop and implement formal policies and procedures related to appropriate assessment and management of pain. Specific components of the standard require the organization to demonstrate evidence of:

- initial assessment and re-assessment of pain are performed and documented;

- provider education in pain assessment and management is given;

- patient and family education in pain management plan, including limitations and potential side effects of treatment, is given;

- communication of the importance of pain management to family has occurred, with considerations for cultural, personal, and spiritual beliefs.

Clinical practice guidelines for pain management have been developed by several professional organizations worldwide. Some of the more widely referenced clinical practice guidelines include:

1. **Agency for Health Care Policy and Research (AHCPR)**—guidelines for management of acute pain, cancer pain, and lower back problems. Guidelines are free of charge and may be ordered from AHCPR (see **§ 6.24**) or downloaded from their website *http:// www.ahcpr.gov/guide.*

2. **American Pain Society (APS)**—guidelines for acute and cancer pain. For ordering information, visit their website: *http://www .ampainsoc.org* or contact:
   American Pain Society
   4700 W. Lake Avenue
   Glenview, IL 600215-1485
   Phone: (847) 375-4715
   The site also offers regular updates on various topics related to pain research and treatment.

3. **American Society of Anesthesiologists Task Force on Pain Management**—guidelines for chronic pain management. Guidelines

provide decision support to practitioners treating persons with chronic pain. They are intended to optimize pain control, minimize adverse outcomes, and minimize cost, enhance functional abilities and quality of life for individuals with chronic pain. Guidelines may be obtained by contacting:

American Society of Anesthesiologists
520 North Northwest Highway
Park Ridge, IL 60068
Their website address is *http://www.asahq.org*.

Other strategies directed at improving pain management in a variety of settings are:

- Providing greater focus on patient/family and provider education, formally and informally. Provider education programs need to be incorporated into education curricula. The International Association for the Study of Pain (IASP) has published core curriculum for health care professionals. This association also has information on professional medical organizations, outreach groups, and other organizations that provide pain-related information to the general public. Their website address is: *http://www.iasp-pain.org*.

- Incorporating pain assessment as a component of the vital signs record. This raises awareness of the health care professionals and prompts more timely intervention.

- Greater utilization of expertise of professional organizations that focus on pain treatment as well as that of board certified specialists in pain treatment.

A fundamental goal of pain treatment is to identify and remove the cause of pain whenever possible. If this goal is not realistic, the treatment plan should focus on minimizing the adverse effects of pain on the individual's life. This approach is often necessary in treating chronic pain. The use of multiple treatment/management modalities may be necessary to achieve a successful level of pain control. The examiner should include the individual in the development of the plan and listen to what the individual feels will work and what will not. Promoting feelings of control over pain is an important component of successful treatment. A comprehensive pain treatment plan may include noninvasive and/or invasive techniques.

§ 6.26 —Noninvasive Techniques for Pain Control

Noninvasive techniques are often used in combination with pharmacological pain Management. Commonly known as *behavioral techniques*, noninvasive modalities, alone or in combination, can reduce pain in many individuals. To be successful, behavioral techniques require a great deal of participation from the individual. Some common techniques include the following:

1. **Operant conditioning programs**—diminishing frequency of pain-related behavior patterns. The overall goal of these techniques is to reduce pain behaviors by withdrawing positive reinforcement for undesired behaviors and increasing frequency of desired behaviors with positive reinforcement. Operant conditioning does not cure pain, but can reduce associated functional impairment.

2. **Biofeedback**—a variety of techniques that provide an individual with information about changes in body function of which he or she is usually unaware, such as blood pressure changes. Provides a vehicle for distraction and relaxation and a sense of control over one's body and thus, over pain. It has some proven effectiveness in relieving pain associated with tension and stress, low back pain, headaches, and muscle spasms.

3. **Hypnosis**—induction of a trance state during which suggestions to alter the character of the pain may be introduced. In an altered conscious state, the individual becomes more receptive to these suggestions. The mechanism of pain control is not clear.

4. **Acupressure**—based on the principles of acupuncture, is non-invasive. Pressure or other cutaneous stimulations are applied over acupuncture points.

5. **Meditation**—focuses attention away from the pain and can provide a sense of peace and relaxation to the individual. This technique is easily learned and can be practiced anywhere at any time by the individual.

6. **Guided imagery**—uses imagination to create images that focus attention away from the pain. This technique relieves pain through distraction, production of a relaxation response, and subsequent reduction in perceived pain.

7. **Rhythmic breathing**—combines both distraction and relaxation techniques. Rhythmic breathing combines rhythms such as music,

a ticking clock, or a metronome with breathing rhythms and focuses attention on this process and away from the pain.

8. **Relaxation or Progressive Relaxation Therapy (PRT)**—emphasizes the relaxation of voluntary skeletal muscles. PRT reduces anxiety associated with pain, encouraging the individual to first tighten, then relax various muscle groups in the body. The exercise proceeds from one area of the body to another.

9. **Transcutaneous stimulation (TENS)**—See **Chapter 5, § 5.12,** *et seq.*

10. **Cold therapy**—See **Chapter 5, § 5.12,** *et seq.*

11. **Heat therapy**—See **Chapter 5, § 5.12,** *et seq.*

12. **Massage**—involves superficial stimulation of the body by applying pressure to the skin in a patterned fashion using a variety of motions.

13. **Multiple convergent therapy**—combines multiple techniques to enhance effects of single therapy.

§ 6.27 —Invasive Interventions for Pain Control

Invasive interventions include non-surgical procedures that involve the introduction of anesthetic or analgesic agents into the body and surgical procedures designed to interrupt pain pathways. To better understand these procedures, it is helpful to understand the difference between analgesia and anesthesia. An *analgesic* is a pharmacologic substance that diminishes or eliminates pain without producing unconsciousness. An *anesthetic,* in addition to abolishing pain, causes loss of feeling or sensation within the body. There are various types of anesthesia. *General anesthesia* is accompanied by loss of consciousness and amnesia, whereas *local anesthesia* produces pain relief in a specific part of the body without loss of consciousness. Common types of invasive analgesia/anesthesia pain relief interventions include:

1. **Local anesthesia** (nerve block anesthesia)—performed by injecting analgesics close to the nerves, thereby blocking conductivity and transmission of pain impulses. Several types of pharmacologic agents can be used. Nerve blocks are effective in relieving many different types of pain, related to varied conditions such as childbirth, herpes zoster, musculoskeletal problems, and some neuralgias.

2. **Epidural infusions**—deliver analgesia via catheter inserted into epidural space in the spine. See **Chapter 5, § 5.4.**

3. **Intrathecal infusions**—deliver analgesia via catheter inserted into the subarachnoid space.

4. **Patient controlled analgesia**—refers to a method that allows the patient to control pain by using an intravenous drug delivery system. See **Chapter 5, § 5.4.**

5. **Implantable infusion pump**—intra-spinal route for administering narcotics analgesics. Commonly used for cancer patients, who have not experienced adequate pain relief by other methods.

6. **Neurosurgical interventions** (surgical procedures)—include the following procedures:

   • neurectomy—severance of peripheral nerve fibers from the spinal cord, thus blocking the transmission of pain;

   • rhizotomy—resection of a posterior nerve root at the point just before it enters the spinal cord, used to control pain in the upper body;

   • sympathectomy—interruption of afferent visceral nerve fibers of the sympathetic nervous system;

   • cordotomy—accomplishes either bilateral or unilateral interruption of pain pathways, used to control pain in the lower body.

7. **Acupuncture**—requires insertion of needles into specific points of the body, which produces mechanical stimulation to close the gate to pain stimuli. See **Chapter 5, § 5.20.**

§ 6.28   —Pharmacological Management

As stated previously, effective pain treatment is directly related to identification of its underlying cause(s). Once this has been determined, pharmacological intervention is likely to play a role in the treatment plan. For some providers, choosing the most effective drug, along with dosage, and frequency to be taken, is problematic, especially in the treatment of chronic pain. These problems may arise from several sources, e.g., personal beliefs and prejudices about pain treatment or lack of in-depth knowledge about current pain management techniques and treatment options. As a result, pain may be under-treated.

A belief held widely by many clinicians is that the treatment of chronic pain with *opiod* (see definition below) drugs will cause addiction.

While these drugs do have the potential to cause physical dependence, evidence exists that addiction as a result of taking opiods for relief of pain is extremely rare. Additionally, some physicians fear regulatory repercussions from perceived over-prescription of opiod narcotics. To ease concerns, some state medical boards have issued guidelines and policies that clarify the appropriate use of these drugs in pain treatment. Although guidelines have no legal status, they are an official statement by medical boards (which license physicians) and thus have been somewhat effective in addressing MDs' fears. Professional organizations have also included statements on the appropriate role of opiods in pain management. In 1997, American Academy of Pain Medicine and the American Pain Society published a consensus statement on the use of opiods as an essential part of chronic pain treatment.

Analgesics

Analgesics by definition are drugs with pain relieving properties. Commonly analgesics are classified into three main categories: *non-opiods, opiods,* and *adjuvant analgesics.* Within each of these classifications, drugs are further classified into subgroups based on their mechanism of action for pain relief and their effectiveness in relieving specific types of pain. Non-opiods include acetaminophen and non-steriodal anti-inflammatory drugs, commonly referred to as NSAID's. Acetaminophen, e.g., Tylenol®, has fewer side effects than do the NSAID's, e.g., no effect on GI or platelet function. It can, however, cause liver toxicity and should be used with caution in patients consuming large amounts of alcohol. Acetaminophens have little anti-inflammatory effects. In contrast, NSAID's were originally prescribed mainly for their anti-inflammatory properties for conditions such as arthritis. They are now recognized for their effectiveness in a wide variety of painful conditions. Some examples of NSAID's are:

• Ibuprofen (Motrin®, Advil®)
• Naproxen (Naprosyn®)
• Ketorolac (Toradol®)

Non-opiods drugs may be used to treat both nocioceptive and neuropathic pain, especially pain arising in muscles and joints. In higher doses, NSAIDS may be effective for severe pain. Non-opiods can also be used to enhance the effectiveness of opiod drugs as well.

Opiod drugs have two subcategories: morphine-like drugs known as full agonists and a second group known as agonist-antagonist drugs. Drugs within these two subcategories are used very differently in pain management. Examples of full agonist drugs are:

* Hydrocodone (Vicodin®)
* Morphine
* Methadone
* Codeine
* Hydromorphine (Dilaudid®)

Examples of opiod agonist-antagonist drugs are:

* Butorphanol (Stadol®)
* Pentazocaine (Talwin®)

Full agonist opiods are effective in treating moderate to severe pain, both acute and chronic. They are mainstay therapy for acute and cancer pain and are also effective treatment for breakthrough pain. Agonist-antagonists play a more limited role, effective only for certain types of acute pain. Opiods do have numerous side effects, the most common of which are nausea and vomiting, dizziness, confusion, constipation, urinary retention, and respiratory depression. They can cause physical dependence.

Adjuvant analgesics are comprised of several different drug classes, each of which is effective in treatment of different types of pain. Only selected drugs within a class may be effective as adjuvant analgesics. Examples specific drugs by class:

Antidepressants—some chronic pain, especially neuropathic pain.

* Amitriptyline (Elavil®)
* Desipramine (Norpramin®)

Anticonvulsants—some types of chronic neuropathic pain.

* Carbamazepine (Tegretol®)
* Phenytoin (Dilantin®)
* Clonazepan (Klonopin®)

Corticosteriods—some types of cancer-related pain, such as metastatic bone pain.

- Dexamethasone (Decadron®)

Psychostimulants—a variety of painful conditions.

- Dextroamphetamine (Dexidrine®)
- Methylphenidate (Ritalin®)

Side effects caused by adjuvant analgesics differ by drug class. More detailed information on side effects caused by these drugs can be found in **Chapter 5, § 5.7** Key principles of effective pharmacological analgesic therapy require individualizing the drug regimen and optimizing administration, that is dosage, frequency, and route. While the choice of a drug(s) depends on the type of pain being treated, other factors such as age, co-existing medical conditions, incompatibility with other medications being taken, and side effects experienced are also considered. Trials of several different regimens may be necessary before optimal results are obtained.

The World Health Organization (WHO) has developed a three-step approach for the treatment of chronic cancer pain. Originally developed in the 1980's, this model focuses on selecting analgesics or combinations of analgesic groups, based on the severity of the pain. The model has gained wide acceptance in the clinical community and is generally recognized as effective in managing chronic cancer pain. WHO recommendations include the following:

- Mild pain—non-opiod and possibly an adjuvant analgesic.
- Mild to moderate pain, or pain not relieved by non-opiod—addition of opiod to non-opiod and adjuvant.
- Moderate to severe pain—same combinations as recommended for mild to moderate pain, choice of opiod may be different.

§ 6.29   —Pain-Related Litigation

Appropriate pain management is likely to become an escalating area of litigation. In the case of *Bergman v. Chin* (No. 20732, Cal. Super. Ct.

Alameda Cty.), the children of a decedent brought suit against their father's physician for inadequate treatment of his pain. The California case involved an 85-year-old male with metastatic cancer. Days before his death, his daughter alleged that she heard her father moaning in pain frequently over a two day period, apparently obtaining little relief from pain medication that had been prescribed. His daughter called his physician and requested that her father's medication be changed to morphine; the physician refused the request. Finally, the daughter found a physician who did prescribe the morphine and she stated that her father finally obtained relief. He died two days later. In California, survivors cannot seek damages for pain and suffering once an individual is deceased, so the case was tried under an elder abuse law in which reckless negligence must be proven. The jury found in favor of the plaintiffs and awarded $1.5M to the family, though California law caps pain and suffering damages at $250,000. In the judge's final ruling, the judgment was reduced to the $250,000 cap for pain and suffering, but attorneys' fees were also awarded, pushing the total judgment close to $1 million.

Other case law for pain and suffering exists. In a 1989 Georgia case, *State v. McAfee*, the court found in favor of the litigant that pain management was an integral part of medical care. Mr. McAfee was a quadriplegic who was respirator dependent. He sought court approval for discontinuing his respirator (right to refuse medical treatment). In addition, he sought sedation and pain management during this process. The court found in favor of Mr. McAfee, recognizing that in addition to his right to refuse treatment, he also had the right to effective pain management.

The 1990 North Carolina case of *Estate of Henry James v. Hillhaven*, the nursing home was found liable for failure to treat pain appropriately. The complaint alleged that the dying days of Mr. James, who had metastatic cancer, were made intolerable because of inadequate pain relief. In this case, a nurse unilaterally decided that Mr. James had become addicted to the morphine that had been prescribed by the physician. She decided to implement her own pain management plan consisting of a mild tranquilizer and placebos. After death, the family of Mr. James sued the nursing home proving to the jury that the "alternate treatment" failed to meet standard of care. The jury awarded $15 million, and the case was subsequently settled out of court.

If pain management is an issue in litigation, research applicable state laws or guidelines on pain management, any guidelines developed by state medical boards, and examples of pain management guidelines.

Although pain management litigation is relatively new, multiple pain treatment guidelines do exist that can guide the professional in prescribing analgesic medications for pain relief. It is valuable for the legal professional to have a basic understanding of these pain management options, so that pertinent information can be included in the medical record summary. When summarizing drug information related to pain, be sure to research medications with which you are not familiar. Understand a drug's actions, major side effects, adverse reactions, and interactions with other medications. It may also be helpful to do a breakout summary of drug usage if this is an issue in the case. See **Chapter 8** for additional information on using breakout summaries.

It is not the role of a legal professional to interpret the meaning of the information in the medical record, but to summarize that information accurately and highlight discrepancies and conflicting information in the medical record. Information on the client's baseline pain history prior to the current complaint should always be included.

§ 6.30   —Sources of Pain Treatment/Management Information

As more and more Americans live longer and develop chronic diseases, chronic pain is experienced by a greater percentage of the population. This increased incidence of chronic pain, along with the recognition of the needs of individuals with chronic pain has led to the development of a wealth of information on self-management of chronic pain that encompass a wide range of options. Traditional treatment/management modalities have expanded as well. As with virtually all topics of individual concern, the Internet has contributed immensely to both quantity and quality of available information on pain management, including the following:

1. **Alternative nonprescription pain-relieving agents.** In the past several years, there has been an explosion of these medications in the health care market, many of which are marketed as nutritional supplements and are therefore not regulated by the FDA. For example, a popular alternative analgesic medication on the market is *glucosamine*. This drug is used to relieve the pain of osteoarthritis by impeding the breakdown of cartilage and assisting in the regeneration of new cartilage.

2. **Self-help books.** Covering varied methods of chronic pain management, these books include many different approaches, including

dietary and exercise regimens, exacerbation prevention, and techniques for handling psychological issues associated with chronic pain. There are many titles on varied approaches from which to choose that can be researched on line via websites such as *http://www .amazon.com.*

3. **Holistic approaches.** These methods include herbal remedies, chiropractic treatment, acupuncture, tai chi, and others.

For more traditional management of chronic pain, multidisciplinary pain centers offer very comprehensive services. These centers use various treatment modalities to decrease the intensity of pain, minimize the use of potent analgesics, and maximize functionality in the presence of pain. Linkages between pain, emotions, and techniques that enable self-management of pain are also emphasized. Health care disciplines involved in these centers may include physicians from the subspecialties of anesthesiology, neurology, orthopedics, psychiatry, physiatry, and rheumatology. Ancillary disciplines (physical therapy, occupational therapy, social service, nutritional services, nursing and/or case management, osteopathic manipulation, and vocational counseling) may also be involved.

§ 6.31   Genetic Diseases

Genes are the basic units of heredity and carry information for making the proteins required for life by all organisms. A *genome* is all the DNA within a specific organism. Genes are contained within *chromosomes*, structures within the nucleus of all cells. Genes are arranged in linear formation in a specific location, known as a *locus*, along chromosomes. *DNA (dioxyribon nucleic acid)* stores genetic information and records information for protein synthesis. Each DNA molecule has a double stranded formation (double helix). DNA is made up of four chemicals, called *bases*, which are arranged in a specific order for each species. It is this arrangement that determines what an organism will be and how it will look. A change in the DNA sequence that alters the type and amount of protein produced is referred to as *mutation*.

§ 6.32   —Genetic Testing and Gene Therapy

When genes are altered so that their encoded proteins cannot carry out their normal functions, genetic disorders can result. Genetic aspects of certain diseases have been recognized for many years, but detailed information has only recently been made possible as a result of computer technology advances. (See discussion of the Human Genome Project in § **6.33** below.) Because the exact location of many gene defects is now known, this information can be used to develop strategies for prevention and treatment of specific genetic diseases.

To proactively identify susceptibility to genetic disorders, *genetic testing* can be done. Genetic testing provides a reliable method for identifying mutated or defective genes and is used in combination with family history to determine appropriate screening. Based on results of genetic screening, preventive medical or surgical strategies can be employed to prevent disease. Genetic counseling can also be used to help guide reproductive decisions. Currently, genetic tests are available that screen for susceptibility to conditions such as breast and ovarian cancer, cystic fibrosis, cardiovascular disease, blood disorders, and others.

Although treatment of existing genetic disorders is promising, most approaches are still experimental. One such technique currently being tested is *gene therapy*. In gene therapy, "healthy" DNA fragments are injected into damaged cells. These fragments replace the cell's damaged DNA so that the cell can begin to function normally. This is accomplished by use of a carrier, or *vector*, most commonly a virus that has been genetically altered to carry normal human DNA.

Currently, gene therapy is still experimental and the FDA has not approved any human gene therapy product for sale. Several barriers still need to be overcome before gene therapy can be considered effective:

- Short-lived nature of gene therapy as it is currently administered. Newly introduced DNA must remain functional and stable as cells divide.

- Multiple problems associated with viral vectors, including toxicity and the triggering of the body's normal immune and inflammatory responses.

- Immune response of the body which may see the new gene as a "foreign object" and will mount defenses to attack the invader.

- Multigene disorders such as Alzheimer's disease, diabetes and arthritis will be difficult to treat. Conditions resulting from mutations in a single gene are considered the best candidates for gene therapy.

§ 6.33   —The Human Genome Project

The Human Genome Project, an international effort began in 1990. Its goal was to identify all the human genes and determine the complete sequences of the 3 billion DNA chemical bases. This high-level mapping of the human genome, originally a 15 year project, finished two years early in 2003. In the United States, the Department of Energy and the National Institute of Health sponsor Human Genome Project research.

In addition to mapping the human genome and making these findings available for further study, other project goals include developing informational databases for storing information, developing tools for data analysis, and addressing ethical, legal, and social issues (ELSI) that may arise from project findings (See discussion below). Two excellent websites for the Human Genome Project exist that contain information on many aspects of the project. Some of the website's topics include:

- general information, including discussion on ethical, legal, and social issues;
- resources, including an excellent glossary;
- research;
- publications;
- medical applications.

Human Genome Project websites are:

http://www.ornl.gov.hgmis

http://www.nhgri.nih.gov

As the availability of genetic information increases, complex issues will arise regarding its use. Some of these issues, as cited in the Human Genome Project Information, include:

- fairness in use of genetic information by insurers, employers, and others;
- privacy and confidentiality of genetic information; Who owns this information?
- psychological impact and stigmatization due to genetic differences;

- genetic testing for a specific condition due to family history and population screening;
- reproductive issues and the use of genetic information in decision-making and reproductive rights;
- clinical issues including education of healthcare providers, individuals with genetic disorders, and the general public;
- commercialization of products, property rights and accessibility of data.

§ 6.34 —The Ethical, Legal, and Social Implications Research Program (ELSI)

As part of the Human Genome Project, the Ethical, Legal, and Social Implications (ELSI) Research Program was established. The program is organized around four areas:

- Privacy and fairness and use of genetic information
- Clinical integration of new genetic technologies
- Issues surrounding genetics research
- Public and professional education

The program takes the approach of identifying issues of human genetics at the same time the basic science is being studied. ELSI is very aware of the gaps in existing laws and, with other groups, has made recommendations for needed legislation. Their recommendations are based on the premise that information from the Human Genome Project should be used to improve health and not discriminate against workers or their families. Among ELSI's recommendations are:

- Employers should not require genetic testing as a condition of employment, or use genetic information to deprive individuals of employment opportunities.
- Employers can monitor employees for effects of a specific substance found in the workplace that may cause genetic damage. Informed consent of the employee should be required and information gained from monitoring should be kept in medical files, not in personnel files.
- Laws should apply to public and private sector employees. ELSI and its partners have also developed recommendations on legislation needed

to prevent genetic discrimination by insurance companies. The recommendations are that insurance providers should be prohibited from using genetic information or a request for genetic services to deny or limit coverage, and establishing differential rates based on genetic information or a request for genetic services.

Proponents of comprehensive genetic non-discrimination legislation cite many reasons for legislation now rather that later. Among the arguments are:

- Employers fear the potential for increased costs associated with genetic disease/information.
- Economic incentive to discriminate is likely to increase as genetic research advances.
- Genetic information could be used in cases where workers are healthy and unlikely to develop disease or where genetic conditions have no effect on the ability to perform work.
- Insurers can still use genetic information in individual markets to make decisions about coverage, enrollment, and premiums.
- Individuals are not protected from disclosure of genetic information to insurers, employers (who buy health care coverage), and medical information without their consent.
- Insurers can still require individuals to take genetic tests.
- HIPAA protection is not currently extended to individuals.

§ 6.35 —Legislation

The completion of the human genome mapping marked the end of the initial chapter in the genetics work and signaled the beginning of the second, and perhaps more difficult phase, that of tracing the functions of all three billion DNA bases. This work will continue for many decades and drive advances in application for biotechnology as these functions become known. As this work progresses, the implications (many still unknown) for individuals, families, and society will continue to unfold. The potential exists to use information gained from genetic research to discriminate against individuals or groups of individuals. At the time of this writing, no comprehensive anti-discrimination laws pertaining to genetic discrimination have been passed at the federal or state level. The discussion below summarizes the laws that do exist.

Some legislation to prevent genetic discrimination has already been passed and more is pending. Common issues being addressed in legislation include provisions for:

- preventing insurers from denying, canceling, or changing premiums, terms, or conditions of coverage based on genetic information;
- prohibiting insurance companies from requesting or requiring genetic tests;
- requiring written informed consent of the individual when insurer desires third-party disclosure of genetic information;
- explaining risks and benefits of genetic screening tests (testing per se is not harmful; what is done with the information can be).

Federal Laws

No federal legislation has been passed relating to genetic discrimination in individual insurance coverage or genetic discrimination in the workplace. In February 2000, President Clinton signed an executive order prohibiting every federal agency from using genetic information in hiring or promotion. No other legislation is currently pending.

State Laws

States have been more prolific in enacting anti-discrimination laws. However, at best they are a patchwork, and none of them are comprehensive. Some only prohibit discrimination against individuals with genetic disorders, while some regulate the use of genetic testing in employment decisions and the disclosure of genetic test results. The majority of laws generally prohibit employers from requiring genetic testing as a condition of employment. Several states have sponsored genetics reports and have published study findings. Cites for these state reports can be found on the Human Genome Web site at *http://www.ornl.gov.hgmis.*

Additionally, a comprehensive state-by-state survey of statutes related to genetics information and its uses can be found on the National Conference of State Legislatures website which is updated regularly. Their website address is: *http://www/ncsl.org.*

Finally, also refer to the National Institute of Health National Human Genome Research Institute (NIH NHGRI) information (also updated regularly) for all genetics workplace discrimination that has been enacted at the state level. Web site address is *http://www.nhgri.nih.gov/*.

Existing Federal Anti-Discrimination Laws—How They Apply to Genetics

1. Americans with Disabilities Act of 1990 (ADA). This law, enforced by Equal Employment Opportunity Commissions (EEOC), doesn't explicitly address genetic information, but provides some protections against disability-related genetic discrimination in the workplace. In March 1995, the EEOC issued an interpretation of ADA related to genetic discrimination. However, this interpretation is

   limited in scope and effect,

   policy guidance only, and does not have same legal binding effect as statute, and has not been tested in courts.

   There are two main points of the interpretation:
   - Entities that discriminate on basis of genetics are regarding individuals as having impairments. Such individuals are covered by ADA.
   - Unaffected carriers, individuals with late onset genetic disorders who may be identified through genetic testing or family history as being at risk to develop disease are not covered.

2. Health Insurance Portability and Accountability Act of 1996 (HIPAA). This law applies only to employer-based and commercially issued group health insurance and is the only federal law that addresses the issue of genetic discrimination. There are no similar laws protecting individuals seeking to purchase insurance. Genetic discrimination is only one small part of the HIPAA scope. See **Chapter 1** for a more detailed discussion of HIPAA.

3. HIPAA National Standards to Protect Patients' Personal Medical Records, December 2002. This regulation was mandated when Congress failed to pass comprehensive privacy legislation, as required by HIPAA, by 1999. It seeks to protect medical records and personal health information maintained by health-care providers, health plans, health insurers, and health-care clearinghouses. The regulation does

not contain language specific to genetics, but rather has sweeping regulations governing all health information. Scope of Standard:

- Limits non-consensual use and release of private health information.
- Gives patients new rights to access their medical records and to know who else has accessed them.
- Restricts most disclosure of health information to the minimum needed for the intended purpose.
- Establishes new criminal and civil sanctions for improper use of disclosure.
- Establishes new requirements for access to records by researchers and others.

HIPAA final recommendations can be found on the U.S. Department of Health and Human Services (DHHS) web site: *http://www.hhs.gov/ocr/hipaa.*

4. Title VII of Civil Rights Act of 1964. An argument could be made that genetic discrimination based on racially or ethnically linked genetic disorders constitutes unlawful race or ethnic discrimination. This argument would only apply if the discrimination was based on a genetic trait that is substantially related to a particular race or ethnic group. Such relationships have been established for only a few diseases.

Practice Note. Because of this rapidly evolving field, any case involving genetic discrimination must be meticulously researched. Be aware of available resources and utilize them to obtain information pertinent to your case. You should, at a minimum, have a basic understanding of what the Human Genome Project is and its numerous societal implications. The field of genetics is complex and findings from the Human Genome Project will have many impacts, many unknown at this time, for years to come.

When reviewing a client's medical records, note any genetic testing or treatment for genetic diseases. Evaluate the pertinence of the information in regard to the issues of the case and include that information in your summary if appropriate. The websites listed in the sections above are excellent sources for genetic-related legislation and on general issues pertaining to the field of genetics.

§ 6.36 The Aging Process

As the baby boomers age, the percentage of population 65 and over in the United States will increase dramatically. This increase, along with continued longer life expectancy, will have many societal impacts. Families will face decisions on how best to care for elderly family members. Health care and community resources that are available to provide this care will be stretched. It is reasonable to assume that not only more health care services will be needed, but additional resources that support healthy aging will also be required. Care models that focus on illness prevention as well as treatment of illness will be needed for healthy aging of this growing population.

Given the anticipated growth of the elderly population, litigation involving the elderly is likely to increase proportionally. Some current areas of litigation involve cases of elder abuse and neglect, both in community and institutional settings such as skilled nursing or board and care facilities. Common themes in nursing home litigation are medication errors, development of bedsores, falls, and use of restraints. For the legal professional, it is helpful to have some background on physical and mental changes associated with aging process that will help in determining information pertinent to include in the medical record summary.

There are many models that provide a framework for defining the aging process. Most models include characteristics of successful aging, and include abilities to

- stay active
- maintain independence in activities of daily living
- adapt successfully to change, and
- continue to be involved in life

Individuals age differently and at different rates that are influenced by both internal and external factors. Internal factors may include genetics, personality, physical, and psychological response to changes. External factors include environment and lifestyle. In spite of the differences in how individuals age, the elderly have some common concerns, among them are fears of

- inadequate income,
- social isolation,
- acquiring diseases that impact functionality,

- loss of access to support systems, and
- loss of independence.

In fact, maintaining independence becomes a major goal for the elderly; many fear they will become a burden to their family and/or friends. Many of the elderly have some degree of functional impairment that affects their ability to adequately meet their physical needs. Additionally, their ability to maintain a level of function in the community that meets their psycho-social needs is often compromised as well. Body changes experienced during the aging process that contribute to these limitations are both mental and physical and are discussed below.

§ 6.37   —Physiological Changes by System

1. **The cardiovascular system** experiences arteriosclerotic changes to the blood vessel walls. The heart has diminished contractility and filling capacity and becomes less effective pumping the blood into circulation. As a result of these changes there is

   - decreased cardiac output,
   - decreased coronary circulation,
   - increased blood circulation time,
   - reduced circulation to kidneys and brain,
   - increased cardiovascular workload, easily increased by stress and exercise,
   - increased capillary fragility.

   These changes manifest themselves in many conditions to which the elderly are prone. Common are hypertension (a major risk factor for stroke and MI), stroke and MI, heart failure, postural hypotension, susceptibility to bruising, and decrease in energy and endurance.

2. **The respiratory system** undergoes many changes that for the most part occur gradually over time. There is alveolar destruction, loss of chest wall elasticity, calcification of cartilage in rib joints and ver-tebrae, and some wasting of muscles needed for respiration. As a result, there is an increased need for oxygen, especially with exercise

or when under stress, and decreased depth of respiration and oxygen intake. These changes can have significant impact on the strength and depth of coughing and, coupled with any change in mobility such as a fracture and/or exacerbation of chronic respiratory disease, place the elderly at high risk for development of pneumonia.

3. **The musculoskeletal system** changes related to aging all have a direct impact on an individual's mobility, which in turn affects their level of function. The body experiences decrease in muscle mass and strength, skeletal inflexibility, as well as loss of both bone mass and bone density. There is deterioration of joint surfaces that occurs as a result of a lifetime of normal wear; deterioration that can be accelerated by injury, obesity, and/or excessive use. Changes in muscle and bone structure are highly individual and are influenced by both internal and external factors. Changes are associated with age, sex (women are more vulnerable to bone loss than men), and race. Other factors that can accelerate the type and severity of musculoskeletal system changes include alcohol abuse, immobilization, chronic diseases, and sedentary lifestyle. Regular exercise increases musculoskeletal strength immensely and its benefits in the elderly are well known. Characteristic manifestations of age-related changes include:

    *   loss of strength, endurance, agility,
    *   joint stiffness, decreased range of motion,
    *   muscle wasting,
    *   stooped posture,
    *   changes in stance and gait,
    *   difficulty standing and sitting, and
    *   difficulty climbing and descending stairs.
    *   Common musculoskeletal conditions that affect the elderly are arthritis (both osteoarthritis and rheumatoid arthritis), gout, and osteoporosis.

4. **The nervous system** changes are a result of decreased blood supply to the brain and loss of both nerve cells (neurons) and nerve fibers. There is also thought to be a decrease in the chemical substances such as norepinephrine and serotonin that facilitate transmission of nerve impulses. The size of the brain itself decreases and there is thinning of the cortex. Neurological changes affect all voluntary and automatic reflexes, and result in alteration (slowdown) of even

simple motor skills. Additionally, changes in the sensory system diminish perceptions of heat and cold and make the elderly particularly prone to both hypo and hyperthermia.

5. **The GI system** experiences both metabolic and functional changes. These changes result in some of the following conditions:
   - decreased appetite, thirst, caloric needs,
   - difficulty chewing and/or swallowing,
   - digestive disturbances,
   - decreased absorption of vitamins and minerals and other nutrients, and
   - hiatal hernia, intestinal diverticulitis and polyps.

   Malnutrition is common in the elderly. Deficiencies can be caloric, protein, or a mixture of both and can be diagnosed by laboratory tests such as serum protein (an indicator of nutritional status reflected by protein intake) and serum iron, folate and B12 (presence of anemia). Anemia is common in the elderly and often related to nutritional status. Iron deficiency anemia is the most common type. Adequate hydration is also a potential problem; the risk of dehydration in the elderly is high.

   Other factors that can contribute to deficiencies in nutrition include poor dentition, diminished sense of taste and visual acuity, dysphagia, chronic disease processes, confusion, delirium.

   Nutritional status has a direct effect on likelihood of developing pressure sores. Additional risk factors include immobility, weight status, vitamin, protein, and fluid intake.

   Impaired liver function due to decreased circulation may occur. This condition can have significant implications for the elderly. Because the liver metabolizes many drugs, impaired function can cause inadvertent overmedication. See § 6.35 below for more information related to drug administration in the elderly.

6. **The renal (urinary) system** changes that occur in the kidney relate to reduction in kidney size and function. These changes make the kidney less effective at filtering wastes from the blood for excretion in the urine. Kidneys play a crucial role in drug excretion and impaired kidney function, and like impaired liver function, can cause inadvertent overmedication. Changes in the urinary bladder result in decreased urine capacity, impaired emptying, and easier backflow of urine into the kidney. These physiologic changes in urinary tract structures, along with inadequate hydration, make the elderly extremely susceptible to urinary tract infections.

7. **The integumentary system (skin)** undergoes changes in all layers of the skin, as well as in the glands, hair, and nails. Changes are manifested in some of the following ways:
   - wrinkling of skin,
   - dry, cracked, itchy skin due to decreased water content,
   - loss of subcutaneous fat,
   - thin, balding hair,
   - hypo-pigmentation of hair (graying), and
   - atrophy of sweat glands resulting in inadequate sweating mechanism.

8. **The endocrine system** experiences decreased secretion of all hormones. These decreases cause widespread effects on the entire body with specific changes related to each hormone's function. A common example is development of diabetes as a result of decreased secretion of the hormone insulin by the pancreas.

§ 6.38   —Sensory Changes that Occur with Aging

1. **Hearing loss** is very common in elderly, especially the ability to discern high-pitched frequencies and to sort out distractions caused by ambient noise. Impairment can result from several conditions, which are discussed in more detail in **Chapter 3, § 3.38.** Because hearing loss can affect both understanding of speech and maintenance of equilibrium, it may contribute to loss of independence and social isolation. Hearing impairment may also be perceived as dementia because it can result in confusion and impairment of language comprehension.

2. **Loss of vision** also occurs with aging as a result of many physiological changes in the eye. Some results these changes include:
   - increase in the threshold needed for light perception,
   - decreased visual acuity and peripheral vision,
   - decreased ability to adjust to changing amounts of dark and light,
   - decrease in color vision, and
   - loss of accommodation of the lens that compromises focusing ability and results in farsightedness (presbyopia).

   Eye conditions commonly affecting the elderly include:
   - Cataract formation that is caused by increased thickness and density of the lens, resulting in clouding or opacity.

- Glaucoma, which is manifested by increased intra-ocular pressure. The prevalence of glaucoma increases with age.
- Senile macular degeneration caused by decreased blood supply to macula resulting in decreased sharpness of central vision.
- Chronically dry eyes due to decreased tear production or altered composition of the tears.

Visual impairments can impact and influence safety of the living environment and threaten ability to maintain independence.

3. **Loss of taste** may occur gradually over time. Although there is some loss of taste buds during the aging process, loss of taste can result from other causes such as dental problems (tooth loss, dentures), medication, and protein deficiencies. Dry mouth due to decreased saliva production and age-related changes in nervous system also influence perception and processing of taste information.

4. **Loss of smell** is not directly correlated with aging, but taste is highly dependent on smell the acuity of which does diminish with aging. Both play a role in appreciation of foods.

5. **Changes in touch** that diminish sensations of pain, pressure, and vibration occur as part of aging. These diminished sensations can impact ability to perceive pain and temperature extremes.

§ 6.39　—Drug Therapy in the Elderly

The population over 65 accounts for a disproportionate percentage of prescription medications relative to their percentage of the total population. As individuals age, they are more likely to be afflicted with one or more chronic diseases that require prescription medications. The more diseases/conditions an individual has, the more likely multiple medications will be prescribed. The consumption of multiple medications, sometimes referred to as "poly-pharmacy," lends itself to a variety of potential problems, including increased risk for drug-drug interactions. Additionally, physiologic factors related to aging may compound problems that aren't readily identified in drug profiles. In fact, many clinical trials for new drugs lack participants that are over 65, a population segment that in many cases will be primary consumers.

Health care professionals often lack adequate training essential to effectively managing drug therapy in the elderly. Physiological changes associated with the aging process affect how the body utilizes drugs, potentially altering both therapeutic and toxic effects of the drug. Effective drug therapy relies on the effectiveness of four functions: absorption, distribution, metabolism, and elimination. Changes as a result of the aging process can alter one or several of these functions:

1. Drug *absorption* can be delayed or hastened by many factors, including gastric conditions, vascular abnormalities, and decreased liver metabolism.

2. Drug *distribution* throughout the body can be altered by changes in body composition that affects the relationship between a drug's concentration and its distribution in the body. Factors that can affect distribution are a result of changes such as increased total body fat, decreased total body water, and decreased lean body mass. For example, a water-soluble drug with less water to distribute to, can become highly concentrated in the water available. Even after medication is discontinued, toxic effects may be experienced because of decreased rate of elimination in body tissues stores.

3. The liver *metabolizes* many drugs. The rate of metabolism can be influenced by altered blood flow to liver as a result of age related changes in cardiac output (as occurs in heart failure). These conditions result in a decreased first pass metabolism and allow more drug to reach systemic circulation.

4. *Elimination* of drugs is accomplished primarily by the kidney. The rate of elimination can be affected by renal disease and altered blood flow to the kidney. Even in absence of kidney disease, renal clearance is decreased in the elderly. Kidney function is measured by blood tests such as BUN and creatinine. If kidney function is abnormal, drug dosages should be adjusted accordingly to attain therapeutic benefits without toxicity. Direct observation of the individual and obtaining a careful history relating to signs and symptoms of drug toxicity are critical as well. Adverse Drug Reactions (ADRs) can range from minor and insignificant to life-threatening symptoms that require hospitalization. The elderly experience significantly more adverse reactions as compared to their younger counterparts that are related to a variety of causes, including more drug consumption, poor compliance with medication regimens, and physiologic and mental changes such as poor eyesight, poor hearing, and forgetfulness.

Certain drug classes are particularly prone to causing ADRs in the elderly. They include:

1. **Anticoagulants,** such as warfarin, that increase risk of bleeding, especially when taken simultaneously with NSAID's.
2. **Digoxin,** that has high incidence of side effects such as nausea, vomiting, and diarrhea.
3. **Diuretics,** that can cause depletion of body potassium (K+), causing resulting problems such as weakness, muscle cramping, and cardiac problems.
4. **Anti-hypertensives,** that can cause dizziness and fainting. Too rapid lowering of blood pressure can result in decreased blood flow to the brain and may precipitate TIA/stroke.
5. **Steroids,** which can increase fluid retention and cause behavior changes ranging from euphoria to psychotic reactions. Long-term steroids can result in impaired healing and electrolyte imbalance.
6. **Antidepressants and benzodiazepines** can result in excessive sleepiness, drowsiness, and confusion.
7. **Over-the-counter (OTC) medications,** including sleep aids and laxatives.

Various strategies can be employed to minimize the occurrence of adverse drug reactions in the elderly. General principles for prescribing are:

- obtain a thorough drug history (including OTC medications) from patient and/or family to assess the potential for drug-drug or drug-food interaction.
- keep drug regimen as simple as possible.
- start new medication doses low and titrate as needed to reach therapeutic levels; dosage should be based on the individual's age, weight, renal, and hepatic function.
- review all medications frequently and discontinue those not needed.

There should be thorough education of the patient and/or family on medication usage with follow-up evaluation of patient compliance.

In institutionalized patients, the prescription of specific medication classes (e.g., psychotropic drugs) are regulated by both state and federal laws, in large part due to their potential to cause adverse effects in this population. See § 6.38 for further information on use of psychotropic drugs in the elderly.

§ 6.40   —Mental and Emotional Changes Related to Aging

Mental abilities essential to mental health that undergo changes as part of the aging process are *perception* and *cognitive function.* Perception is what a person sees, hears, feels, smells, and tastes. Perception links the individual to the external environment, and depends on the sensory system receiving data and the mind interpreting it. As previously discussed, physical changes associated with the aging process can significantly impair an individual's perception of the environment. Cognitive function (memory) is the ability to process and remember data. It includes ability to pay attention, use judgment, reason and calculate, comprehend, and cope. As aging occurs, there may be increased time needed to process information and to cope with new situations.

Successfully coping with loss is a major contributor to healthy aging. Many losses are experienced as one ages, that can include loss of spouse, friends, family members, employment, health, lifestyle, and independence. A variety of strategies can be used as successful coping mechanisms and those utilized will vary by individual. However, maintaining interpersonal relationships and developing strong support systems appear to be key.

Changes in cognitive function may be manifested in various conditions:

1. **Anxiety** can range from mild to intense. Abnormal levels in the elderly can cause severe distress. Anxiety can be manifested in a variety of behaviors including panic disorder, phobias, generalized anxiety, rituals, and obsessive-compulsive disorders.

2. **Agitation** is a disturbed behavior that may include inappropriate verbal, vocal, or motor activity that is not an obvious expression of need or confusion. It is not a diagnostic term, but a group of signs and symptoms that can result from a variety of medical or psychiatric conditions. Agitation can be verbal or physical.

3. **Depression** is a mood disorder that can occur at any age and be situational or chronic. It may be caused by interaction between

emotional response to stress and physiological changes in the chemical substances that carry impulses between nerve cells. Depression in the elderly can be precipitated by losses associated with aging. The incidence of depression increases dramatically in institutionalized elderly, possibly due to perceived loss of independence. Several tools for the assessment of depression exist; however, one commonly used is the *Geriatric Depression Scale (GDS)*. The GDS has a 30-item scale with a scoring range of 0–10: 10 = normal, 11–20 = mild depression, and 21–30 = severe depression. A short form of this tool also exists with a 15-item scale. Mental symptoms of depression can include feeling discouraged, difficulty concentrating, feelings of inadequacy and pessimism, and loss of interest in activities. Physical signs and symptoms can include sleep disturbances (insomnia or excessive sleepiness), weight gain or loss, decreased energy and endurance, and lack of attention to self-care. Treatment of depression can include counseling and/or medication with antidepressants. However, antidepressants can have major side effects that impair cognitive function and worsen dementia or delirium.

4. **Delirium** is an acute disorder characterized by sudden changes in cognition. The origin of delirium is usually physiologic rather than psychogenic. Common causes are bladder and lung infections, electrolyte imbalances, pain, and dehydration. Additional causes are vitamin deficiencies, medications, (especially sedatives), tranquilizers, and alcohol. Once the cause is identified and successfully treated, the delirium resolves. This characteristic differentiates delirium from dementia, which is a long-term and progressive disease.

5. **Dementia** is an acquired syndrome characterized by progressive deterioration in intellectual faculties that results from organic disease/disorders of the brain. It may be so severe that it interferes with a person's customary occupational, functional, and social performance. Symptoms can include impairment in:

   - abstract thinking,
   - memory and concentration,
   - judgment, and
   - language and motor activities.

   Dementia is often accompanied by emotional disturbances and personality changes and is a long-term, chronic, and progressive disease with no known cure. Because it primarily affects the elderly, the incidence of dementia will increase as the numbers of the elderly population grow. As of May 2004, the Alzheimer's Association estimated that approximately 4 million people in the United States suffer from Alzheimer's Dementia (AD). This number is projected to rise to 14 million by 2050. The economic impact of dementia is huge, as well as is the societal impact on families and their caregivers.

§ 6.41   —Classifications and Stages of Dementia

Although Alzheimer's Dementia (AD) is by far the most common type of dementia, other types of dementia do exist. The main types of dementia include:

1. **Alzheimer's dementia (AD)** is caused by deterioration of nerve cells in the brain. Characteristic of AD is the formation of abnormal numbers of plaques (abnormal proteins) in the neurons. As the neurons degenerate, the brain atrophies primarily in areas that are essential to cognition. AD is most often diagnosed by these characteristic changes as seen on CT or MRI, in conjunction with findings from the history and physical examination.

2. **Vascular (multi-infarct) dementia** occurs as result of interrupted blood supply to the brain due to blood vessel disease. It is the second most common cause of dementia and may occur alone or in combination with AD.

3. **Lewy body dementia** is the third most common type of dementia and is diagnosed based on findings of at least one of three core symptoms: specific visual hallucinations, gait disturbances, and alterations in alertness or attention. It is most likely a spectrum of disorders characterized by a progressive decline in cognitive function, visuo-spatial abnormalities, visual misperceptions and parkinsonism.

Dementia can also be substance induced, result from head trauma, HIV, or progressive neurological diseases such as Creutzfeldt-Jakob (CJ) disease, Huntington's and Parkinson's diseases. Metabolic disorders, such as thyroid or B12 deficiencies, can cause dementia as well. As more and more therapies become available for specific dementia types, it is important to determine the dementia type if possible. Diagnosis is made through physical and neurological examination. Laboratory tests should be done to rule out metabolic causes as well as drugs, nutritional disorders, and psychiatric disorders, especially depression. Additional testing such as CT scan or MRI may also be ordered, if clinically indicated.

Numerous tools for evaluating cognitive impairment and the emphasis can be used for early dementia screening in the primary care setting. Frequently used as an initial screening tool is the *Mini-Cog Evaluation.* Components of the tests are as follows:

- The examiner says three words and asks the patient to repeat them. The patient is given three tries to do this. If unsuccessful, the examiner moves on to the clock drawing exercise.
- Patient is asked to draw a clock face and fill in all the numbers, then show time to be 11:10.
- Patient is then asked to recall and repeat the three words.

Scoring is done as follows:

- Clock: normal = 2 points, abnormal = 0 points
- Word recall: each work correctly recalled = 1 point
- Score of 0, 1 or 2 suggests dementia, score of 3 or higher suggests no dementia.

The *Mini-Mental Status Exam (MMSE)* tests for orientation, memory, attention, and language. It is widely used in dementia screening and at times is administered following the Mini-Cog if results indicate the need for further evaluation. The MMSE maximum score is 30 and scores less than 24 may indicate possibility of dementia.

The stages of dementia have been defined for AD, however, they can be generalized to other types of dementia for the most part. The length of stages (progression of the disease) is individual to the patient:

1. **Stage 1 (early)** is characterized by forgetfulness, mild impairment in language and abstract thinking, orientation, attention, and judgment. Most people in the early stage of Alzheimer's Dementia are fairly functional in their normal environment.
2. **Stage 2 (middle)** is characterized by increasing deterioration in cognitive functioning. Cues are needed for performing normal activities of daily living (ADLs), changes in mood and behavior may emerge,

and individuals may be anxious, depressed, agitated and/or have difficulty sleeping. Safety becomes a major issue in stage 2. Family and/or caregivers are faced with difficult decisions for long term care planning.

3. **Stage 3 (late)** is characterized by profound memory loss which is manifested by
   - confusion of past and present
   - misidentifcation of persons and places
   - mood and behavioral disturbances
4. **Stage 4 (terminal)** is characterized by a lack of name recognition, muteness or garbled speech, and lack of response to surroundings. In the terminal stage the individual is completely dependent on others for survival.

§ 6.42   —Treatment of Dementia

For the most part, the goals of dementia treatment are to maintain maximum functionality and quality of life for as long as possible. Various strategies can be implemented to achieve this goal and include both non-medical and medical interventions.

1. **Non-medical interventions** focus on the provision of a stable day-to-day environment. Changes in noise level, temperature, room, and staff can all have potentially negative impact on the individual suffering from dementia. Specific strategies include:
   - provision of a safe environment
   - reassurance and encouragement
   - supportive communication, don't argue
   - creation of calm, consistent environment
   - use of one-step commands.

   These types of interventions are the first choices for behavior management. Additional strategies may be needed to manage other behaviors, such as socially inappropriate or sexual behaviors, aggression, wandering, and sleep disturbances.
2. **Medical interventions**, specifically medications, help delay progression of dementia in the short term, but offer no cure. The potential benefits offered by these medications must be weighed

against the potential problems, such as over-sedation, drug interactions, and increased risk of falls. The general prescribing principles of geriatric medicine should be followed when prescribing these medications. Several classes of drugs are used to treat dementia, including the following:

- **Cholinesterase inhibitors** are used in the early stage of AD to improve cognition. These medications are effective in the short term only. Individuals receiving them should be evaluated on a regular basis and the medication should be discontinued when no longer effective. Three medications are primarily used, their differences being in side effects experienced and in perceived ease of administration:
  Donepexil (Aricept®)
  Galantamine (Remenyl®)
  Rivastigmine (Exelon®)
- **Antidepressants** are useful if cognitive impairment is a result of depression.
- **Anti-anxiety agents** can be used to treat symptoms caused by anxiety. The most commonly used anti-anxiety drugs are the benzodiazepines, which can produce severe side effects in the elderly and are only recommended for short-term use.
- **Antipsychotic drugs** are useful if there is a psychiatric diagnosis that is a component of the dementia.

The above drug classes are generally referred to as "psychotropic" medications because of their altering effects on perception and/or behavior. Utilization of psychotropics in institutional settings is regulated by *OBRA* because of their potential for overuse. See discussion below.

The *Omnibus Budget Reconciliation Act of 1987 (OBRA)* Nursing Home Reform Amendments was enacted in response to perceived care issues in skilled nursing facilities (SNFs). Although the Centers for Medicare and Medicaid Services (CMS) is responsible for administering this regulation, the provisions in OBRA are used as a basis for state regulations governing nursing homes and by nursing home surveyors who monitor OBRA compliance. Additional discussion of the broad scope of OBRA legislation can be found in **Chapter 2.** Specific OBRA provisions relating to medications mandated that nursing home residents not be prescribed unnecessary drugs. Although this portion of the law has a broad meaning, it generally includes drugs given in "excessive doses" for "extended periods of time in the absence of documented diagnosis or reason." Of particular interest are psychotropic drugs because of the perception of their widespread use to control undesirable behavior. In effect, these drugs cannot be used as "chemical restraints" but can only be prescribed if indications for the drug are clearly documented in the chart. The regulations also address additional requirements for documentation once the psychotropic medication has been initiated. Among the specifics of OBRA:

- Long-acting benzodiazepines should not be prescribed unless shorter-acting drugs have been tried along with non-pharmacological interventions. These rules apply to sedatives as well.
- Specific behaviors which indicate appropriateness of drug prescription must be identified, e.g., biting, kicking. Documentation that patient is "confused" is not acceptable.
- There should be evidence that periodic discontinuation of drugs has been tried to determine if drug is still needed.

§ 6.43   —Medical Record Summaries—Litigation Involving the Elderly

In litigation involving the elderly, it is important to incorporate information related to the mental and physical changes that occur as part of aging if they pertain to the complaint. As in all summaries, any past history, presence of chronic conditions, and level of functioning prior to the litigation should be noted. Where mental status is at issue, it is essential to note related documentation in the medical record, along with any interventions taken. Additionally, pay particular attention to medications such as psychotropic drugs, sedatives, analgesics prescribed and administered. Incorporate the principles of drug prescribing for the elderly into your work and cite regulatory standards as appropriate. For mental conditions such as dementia, the Diagnostic and Statistical Manual of Mental Disorders (DSM-IV) Manual is the definitive guide for coding specific mental diagnoses. The DSM-IV Manual defines criteria for all dementia types including

1. Alzheimer's,
2. Vascular,
3. Lewy Body,

4. Dementia due to Parkinson's, and
5. Other less frequently-seen types.

Access to this valuable resource is a must for cases involving dementia, delirium, or other mental conditions. Also make sure you access regulatory standards and applicable Standard of Care Guidelines specific to the issues of the case. Some suggested resources can be found in **Appendix N** and in the **Bibliography.**

§ 6.44 Infectious Disease: Causes, Treatment and Transmission

When tissue injury occurs, the body responds immediately via a mechanism known as the *inflammatory response.* The inflammatory response is immediate and non-specific, that is, it is triggered by any condition causing tissue injury. Conditions that trigger the immune response include:

- infection
- immune reactions, such as allergic reactions
- thermal injuries, such as frostbite or burns
- chemical injuries from agents such as corrosive chemicals
- tissue death resulting from insufficient blood supply
- traumatic injuries

During this process, the body sends cells and chemical substances to the site of injury to wall off the area, destroy toxins, clean the area of cell debris, and repair damaged tissue. There are three main phases of the inflammatory response:

1. Vascular phase—characterized by an immediate and transitory constriction of blood vessels followed by a lengthier period of vascular dilation and increased vessel permeability. Dilation occurs as a result of the body's release of the chemical histamine, which results in redness and warmth of the affected area. The increase in vessel permeability causes fluid normally in the vascular system to leak into the surrounding tissues, causing edema.
2. Cellular phase—occurs within the first hour of the event. This process involves the migration of neutrophils or polymorphonuclear

leukocytes (referred to in the lab results as PMNs or polys) from the blood vessels into the tissues at the site of injury. Luekocytes comprise approximately 60% of white blood cells and are the first cells to be mobilized in the event of tissue damage. Once in the tissues, the leukocytes engulf and destroy harmful organisms through phagocytosis. The end result of this process is pus formation.

3. Tissue healing phase—begins approximately one day after the event and continues until the tissue is healed. If all compromised tissue cannot be removed, chronic infection results.

In its most severe form, inflammatory response can be systemic. This is a life-threatening condition that can result from massive tissue damage, e.g., sepsis (systemic infection) or severe burns.

As stated previously, the immune system plays a critical role in protecting the body against infection and infectious diseases. Infection has been noted as a cause of serious illness and death from the earliest documentation of medical diseases and their treatment. For hundreds of years, the cause of infection was not known. In the 17th century, microscope-maker Anton van Leeuwenoek reported the existence of microorganisms (germs). However, the significance of his observations was not recognized for nearly 200 years, when three critical discoveries were made:

1. Louis Pasteur discovered the relationship between microorganisms and disease, i.e., that microorganisms caused infection.

2. Dr. Ignaz Semmelwiess pioneered the use of antiseptics in obstetrics and dramatically reduced the incidence of death from infection following childbirth.

3. Joseph Lister demonstrated the efficacy of using antiseptic agents to kill microorganisms on the skin and surgical instruments before surgery. Additionally, in the early part of the 20th century, improvements in environmental sanitation and development of vaccines dramatically reduced morbidity and mortality from infectious disease. The development of antibiotics, hailed as miracle drugs, enabled effective treatment of infections never before possible. History has shown, however, that use of antibiotics has created different problems. Widespread antibiotic use has resulted in changes in bacteria structure and genetic makeup that allows them to survive in the presence of these drugs. Today, some bacteria are resistant to most antibiotics and cause severe illness and death in U.S. hospitals and health care institutions.

Litigation involving infectious disease can be related to prompt diagnosis of infection or infectious disease, as well as the appropriateness of its treatment including choice, dosage, and frequency of antibiotic/anti-infective therapy. In litigation involving trauma and prolonged hospitalization, development of infection in the course of treatment can add another component to damages if it has sequellae that impact recovery. Abundant case law exists for litigation involving HIV, including wrongful termination, issues involving workplace compliance with the Americans with Disabilities laws, and discrimination. It is helpful to have a basic understanding of how infection occurs and effects that may occur as a result of the infection. This knowledge will help you determine pertinent information that should be included in your medical record summary.

§ 6.45 —Infectious Disease Terminology

1. **Agents**—pathogen, organism, microorganism (such as bacteria or virus) that can cause infection. These terms are often used synonymously in describing the process of infection.

2. **Carrier**—a person or animal who harbors an infectious agent without any symptoms of disease. A carrier can transmit the agent to others and result in development of infectious disease

3. **Colonization**—establishment of organisms in or on the body. In a colonized state, organisms do not cause infection, but co-exist within the body without causing disease. This state may continue indefinitely unless the body's defenses become compromised.

4. **Iatrogenic**—term commonly used to refer to an undesirable outcome that develops as a result of a medical treatment or intervention, e.g., an infection acquired in the hospital.

5. **Incubation period**—the time interval between initial contact with an infectious agent and the first appearance of symptoms associated with infection.

6. **Infection**—invasion of body tissues by organisms that produce tissue injury. Infection may progress from mild inflammatory response to severe systemic infection that can cause death.

7. **Infectious disease**—caused by a variety of pathogens. Infectious disease has the potential for transmission to others by a variety of means.

8. **Infectivity**—the ability of a pathogen to invade and replicate in the host.

9. **MRSA (methicillin-resistant staph aureus)**—a strain of staphylococcus aureus that is resistant (not killed) by the antibiotic, methicillin. Methicillin is typically effective in killing this organism even when it is resistant to other antibiotics. MRSA infections are problematic in healthcare institutions such as acute care hospitals, SNF's, etc.

10. **Normal flora**—organisms normally present on body surfaces such as the mouth, skin, gastrointestinal tract, etc. These organisms do not normally cause disease in healthy individuals.

11. **Nosocomial infection**—an infection that develops in a hospital or health care institution that was not present or incubating at admission. Nosocomial infections can occur for many reasons, including use of invasive devices, weakened immune system, use of antibiotics, and chemotherapy or other treatments that weaken the body's immune system.

12. **Pathogenicity**—the ability of an organism to consistently produce disease. For example, the rabies virus always produce disease when introduced into the body, however, the tuberculosis bacteria often does not.

13. **Virulence**—the potency of the pathogen in producing severe disease as measured by case-fatality rates (how often death results).

14. **VRE (vancomycin-resistant enterococcus)**—a strain of enterococcus that is resistant (not killed) by the antibiotic, vancomycin. Vancomycin is typically effective in killing this organism even when it is resistant to other antibiotics. VRE infections are problematic in healthcare institutions such as acute care hospitals, SNF's, etc.

§ 6.46   —Development and Transmission of Infection

Development of an infectious disease begins with *exposure* to the causative agent. Following exposure, three outcomes are possible:

1. **Colonization**—the pathogen can only contaminate body surfaces and not cause disease. A pathogen that colonizes an individual can be transmitted and cause active disease in a new host.

2. **Symptomatic active disease**—body experiences destructive effects of the pathogen or its toxic products. The effects of the pathogen cause symptoms within the body.

3. **Asymptomatic active disease**—body experiences disease that is sub-clinical or without symptoms. Active disease that is asymptomatic can still be transmitted and cause disease in a new host.

If active disease develops, exposure is followed by an *incubation period* in which the pathogen begins to invade the body tissues. Whether colonization or active disease exists, infection can be transmitted to a new host after exposure.

Six elements must be present for infection to be transmitted: a pathogen or agent, a reservoir, a portal of exit, a mode of transmission, a portal of entry, and a susceptible host. This transmission process is commonly referred to as the chain of infection.

1. **Pathogen or agent.** Virus, bacteria, fungus, or other agent capable of causing disease. Pathogens exist in the world around us and most of the time cause no harm to the human body. However, when the balance of pathogen/host symbiosis is upset, infection may result. There are numerous classifications of pathogens that are discussed in more detail in sections below.

2. **Reservoir.** A place where the agent can live and multiply. Reservoirs can be living organisms such as people, animals, or plants, or inanimate substances such as soil, food, or water. A reservoir must provide essentials for the survival of an organism, including its growth and multiplication.

3. **Portal of exit.** A route by which the pathogen can escape the reservoir. This is usually the site of growth for the organism and can correspond to the portal of entry in the new host. For example, if an organism lives in the gastrointestinal tract a common portal of exit is the feces and portal of entry is the mouth of the new host. Common portals of exit from the body include respiratory secretions such as sputum, urine, feces, drainage from open wounds, tears, semen, and vaginal secretions.

4. **Mode of transmission.** Method by which agent or pathogen travels from a reservoir to a new host. Transmission occurs by direct or indirect routes. Direct transmission occurs when there is immediate transfer from one person to another, as occurs in sexually transmitted diseases. Indirect transmission requires a vehicle for transmission such as soil, water, or food. Successful indirect transmission requires that the organism be able to survive until it reaches its new portal of entry.

5. **Portal of entry.** Route by which pathogen gains entrance to a new host. Entry to a new host can be accomplished by:

   - Inhalation—through the respiratory tract by inhalation of infected particles, e.g., tuberculosis
   - Mucous membrane contact—through break in mucous membrane integrity, e.g., sexually transmitted diseases
   - Ingestion—through ingestion of contaminated food or water, e.g., food poisoning
   - Percutaneously—through non-intact skin, e.g., boils, abscesses
   - Transplacentally—from mother to baby through the placenta, e.g., measles

6. **Susceptible host.** A new reservoir for the pathogen to grow and live. Normally, the body successfully defends against disease-causing pathogens through numerous anatomical structures and functions such as skin, mucous membranes, cough reflexes, etc. Many factors alter these defenses and influence the ability of a pathogen to cause disease in a new host. Among these influencing factors are age (the very young and the very old are more susceptible), heredity, general health, nutritional status, presence of concurrent disease (chronic or acute), and lifestyle choices such as drug use and sexual practices. Medical treatments can also increase host susceptibility to infection. Some risk factors include prolonged hospitalization, splenectomy, medication that compromises the body's immune system (e.g., chemotherapy), invasive procedures such as catheters, intravenous lines, and respiratory intubation.

To interrupt the chain of infection transmission, only one of the essential "links" in the chain needs to be disrupted. The most efficient way to break the chain is determined by the type of pathogen, site of infection, and mode of transmission. The Centers for Disease Control and Prevention (CDC) has defined specific techniques known to be effective in preventing the transmission of infection. These are commonly known as Category-Specific Isolation Precautions and are used in hospitals and other health care institutions to control transmission. The choice of the type of isolation category to prevent transmission of an infectious disease should be driven by the causative agent of the disease, its virulence, and the mode of transmission. There are six categories of isolation precautions:

1. **Strict Isolation**—to prevent spread of highly contagious infections that can be transmitted by both air and contact, e.g., chickenpox and plague.

2. **Contact Isolation**—to prevent spread of highly transmissible organisms that do not warrant Strict Isolation. All diseases in this category are spread by direct contact and include anyone with infection or colonization with multiple-resistant bacteria.

3. **Respiratory Isolation**—to prevent transmission of diseases primarily spread over short distances through the air by infected droplets, e.g., measles, whooping cough, meningitis.

4. **Acid fast bacilli Isolation (Tuberculosis Isolation)**—used to prevent spread of *active* pulmonary tuberculosis. Active tuberculosis is commonly defined as an individual with a positive acid fast bacilli (AFB) smear and/or a chest film that strongly suggests active disease.

5. **Enteric Precautions**—to prevent spread of diseases transmitted by direct or indirect contact with feces, e.g., hepatitis A, salmonella, shigella, specific types of E. coli.

6. **Drainage/Secretion Precautions**—to prevent spread of infection transmitted by direct or indirect contact with drainage from an infected body site, e.g., abscesses, surgical wound infections.

In addition to the above category-specific isolation precautions, the CDC has mandated the use of Universal Precautions when contact with blood or body fluids from any individual is anticipated. Universal Precautions are designed to prevent transmission of pathogens such as HIV and hepatitis B and C when infection may not be apparent. They require use of gloves, gowns, and protective eyewear when exposure to blood or body fluids is likely. Although the above isolation guidelines are used principally in hospitals and health care institutions, they are often modified for use in other settings such as the home to prevent transmission to family members or significant others.

§ 6.47   —Human Infectious Agents

The classification and nomenclature of microorganisms (microbiology) is very orderly. Nevertheless, understanding nomenclature can be daunting to those unfamiliar with microbiology. In litigation involving infections or infectious diseases, microbiology or infectious disease reference texts are essential; however, a brief overview of microbiology is provided below.

There are several classifications of pathogenic organisms. The size, shape, and chemical composition of an organism, its growth requirements, its ability to survive under adverse conditions, and its ability to produce toxins determines its classification. Knowledge of pathogens' properties permits specific identification of an organism causing disease and allows initiation of appropriate therapy, including isolation precautions to prevent transmission, if appropriate. The most recognized classifications of organisms that account for the majority of infectious diseases are viruses, bacteria, fungi, and parasites. Lesser known are organisms that include mycoplasma, rickettsiae, and chlamydia. Major characteristics of organism classifications and examples of some of the diseases they cause are discussed below.

1. **Viruses.** The smallest pathogens. Viruses are classified by their composition of a single or double strand of DNA (deoxyribonucleic acid) or RNA (ribonucleic acid) that contains their genetic information. They cause a wide variety of diseases in people. Antibiotics are not effective in the treatment of viral diseases; treatment strategies lie in prevention in the form of vaccines. However, some viral diseases, such as HIV, have no effective vaccines; for these diseases antiviral drugs are available. Common viral diseases are:

   • DNA viruses, such as hepatitis B, herpes simplex, herpes zoster (chickenpox and shingles).

   • RNA viruses, such as influenza, mumps, measles and German measles, HIV.

2. **Bacteria.** Most organisms are extracellular (live outside body cells) and are classified by their shape, their gram stain positivity or negativity, and their oxygen requirements.
   Bacteria shape:

   • round—cocci, diplococci, streptococci, staphylocci

   • spiral shaped—spirochetes

   • rod shaped—bacilli

   Gram stain properties. Bacteria are gram positive or gram negative. Gram staining is done with a dye that is applied to the bacteria. If the bacteria "take" the dye, they are designated as gram positive, if no staining is seen, the bacteria are gram negative. The shape of a bacteria is also determined during this process. For example, you may see gram stain laboratory results noted as "many Gm positive cocci present". Gram stain results are available from the laboratory within hours. This information gives direction to the physician as to the appropriate antibiotic treatment.

Oxygen dependence:

- aerobic—survive in the presence of oxygen
- anaerobic—survive without oxygen
- facultative—can live with or without oxygen

Examples of Bacterial Infections

Common Gm Negative Bacterial Infections & Causative Agents	Common Gm Positive Bacteria Infections & Causative Agents
Urinary tract infections (E. coli, Pseudomonas aeruginosa	Urinary tract infections (Staphyloccus) aureus)
Gonorrhea (Neisseria gonorrhea)	Gas gangrene (Clostridium perfringens)
Whooping cough (Bordetella pertussis)	Tetanus (Clostridium tetani)
Typhoid (Salmonella typhi)	Skin and wound infections (Staphylococci aureus)
Legionnaire's disease (Legionella pneumophilla)	Rheumatic fever (Group A beta hemolytic streptococcus)
Pneumonia (Haemophilus influenza, Pseudomonas aeruginosa)	Pneumonia (Staphyloccus aureus, Streptococcus pneumonia or pneumococcus)

3. **Fungi.** Mainly extracellular organisms (live outside body cells) that resemble plants they grow as branching filaments. Common fungal diseases include vaginal or systemic candia (yeast) infections and coccidiomycosis. Systemic fungal infections, especially in individuals with compromised immune systems, can be extremely serious and are often fatal.

4. **Mycoplasma.** Extracellular organisms (live outside body cells). Mycoplasma organisms cause few diseases in humans. The most common are atypical mycoplasma organisms that cause pneumonia and pelvic inflammatory disease (PID) in women.

5. **Chlamydia.** Intracellular organisms (live inside body cells) that contain both DNA and RNA; like mycoplasma, these organisms can cause pneumonia and cervicitis/PID in women.

6. **Rickettsiae.** Can multiply only within cells. Transmission to humans occurs through bites of ticks, fleas, mites, or lice. Human rickettsial diseases include Rocky Mountain Spotted Fever and typhus.

7. **Protozoa.** Intracellular parasites (live inside body cells) that can move easily from place to place. Parasitic infections in humans include malaria, pneumonia, and toxoplasmosis.

8. **Helminths.** Multi-cellular organisms shaped like worms. Offspring (larvae) are excreted in the urine or feces and transmitted to humans by ingestion or bites that cause breaks in the skin. Helminth infections include trichinosis, schistosomiasis, and enterbiasis.

§ 6.48   —Signs and Symptoms of Infection

The exact signs and symptoms of infection depend on the causative agent, location of infection, and stage of the disease. Manifestations result from direct effect of pathogen or its toxins, the body's inflammatory response, and resultant cell damage.

Organ Specific Effects of Infection

System	Effects
Generalized Effects	Fever, chills, aching muscles
Skin	Inflammation, rash, redness, tenderness
Gastrointestinal	Nausea, vomiting, weight loss, abdominal pain, loss of appetite, jaundice
Respiratory	Sore throat, cough with or without sputum production, foul sputum, lung congestion
Cardiovascular	Rapid heart beat, heart murmurs, alteration in blood pressure and clotting mechanisms
Genitourinary	Frequency/urgency of urination, blood in urine, cloudy or foul smelling urine, flank pain
Musculoskeletal	Muscle weakness aches; joint redness, tenderness or swelling
Nervous	Confusion, headache, seizures, stiff neck

Many diagnostic tests are available to determine the specific sites of infection; they include:

- Gram stain, culture and sensitivity of the suspected infection sites.
- Differential white blood cell (WBC) count
- Erythrocyte sedimentation rate (ESR)
- Urinalysis
- Scans—simple CAT scans or gallium or other dye-enhanced scans

For additional information on these tests refer to **Chapter 4, §§ 4.3–4.8.**

When infection becomes advanced, systemic effects occur. Systemic infection is known as sepsis and often compromises multiple body systems. In life-threatening sepsis, the following abnormalities in systemic functions are often present:

- blood culture positive for the causative infectious agent
- low blood pressure and cardiac output requiring drugs to support circulation
- low white blood cell (WBC) count—initially high in presence of infection, low WBCs indicate an overwhelmed immune system
- abnormalities in blood clotting leading to disseminated intravascular coagulation
- impaired renal function or renal failure

Mortality resulting from overwhelming sepsis is extremely high.

§ 6.49   —Treatment of Infections

Treatment of infection or infectious disease is dependent on the causative agent and the symptoms the infection produces. Anti-infective medications are used as appropriate. Some of these can be toxic to specific body systems such as kidneys, liver, and hearing. Appropriate monitoring must be done if these agents are prescribed. Anti-infectives include antibiotics for bacterial infections, anti-virals for viral infections, and antifungals for fungal infections. For additional information on antibiotic therapy, refer to **Chapter 5, § 5.7.**

§ 6.50   —Infection-Related Litigation

In litigation involving infection or infectious disease, the definitive source for information on diagnosis of infectious disease and transmission prevention is the Centers for Disease Control and Prevention, specifically, the National Center for Infectious Diseases (NCID) branch. The stated mission of the NCID is to prevent illness, disability, and death caused by infectious diseases in the United States and around the world. The agency works in partnership with state and local public health agencies to control and prevent morbidity and mortality from infection and infectious disease. Public health departments have authority to develop requirements for reporting diseases of importance to the health of the general public. This structure exists at many levels:

- County and local public health departments derive authority to require reporting from state health departments.
- State health departments derive authority to require reporting of specific infectious disease through state statutes.
- Nationally, over 50 diseases require reporting to health departments.
- Internationally, agreement has been reached on the following diseases requiring quarantine: plague, cholera, and yellow fever.

Although the CDC has no independent authority to require reporting of infectious diseases, the agency is responsible for collating and publishing health statistics based on infectious diseases required to be reported at the national level. This information is available in their publication, *Mortality and Morbidity Weekly Report.* The CDC website address is *http://www.cdc.gov.*

An additional excellent resource on infectious diseases is a publication of the American Public Health Association, *Control of Communicable Diseases Manual.* The scope and content of this publication includes (for all communicable diseases):

- identification of the disease
- infectious agent
- occurrence
- reservoir
- mode of transmission

- incubation period
- period of communicability
- susceptibility of the host

In litigation involving infections acquired in health care facilities or as a result of medical intervention or treatment, facility policies and procedures relating to infection control should be requested. These represent internal standards of care and it is important to evaluate compliance with these standards in the context of the complaint.

CHAPTER 7

OBTAINING MEDICAL RECORDS

§ 7.1   Determining Which Medical Records to Obtain

A common problem faced by legal teams is determining which medical records to obtain. For plaintiffs, this can be a financial consideration, and the tendency may be to keep costs down by obtaining only those records that concern the subject incident. For the pre-accident medical history, attorneys often depend solely on their client's recollection, which can be a disadvantage. It is essential for the attorney to be aware of and familiar with the client's entire medical status and history prior to the incident in order to understand how the accident or incident impacted the client's life, if at all. It is also vital to identify any prior medical conditions that could affect the allegations made in the case. Deciding not to order prior medical records could initially save money, but in the long run prove costly as defense counsel will always subpoena all medical records and the plaintiff's attorney must then scramble to determine the relationship of a previously unknown pre-existing condition to the subject incident. As a general guideline, plaintiff's counsel should always obtain a complete set of records prior to filing suit.

As soon as the plaintiff's medical providers have been identified (either through depositions or interrogatories, for example), defense counsel should subpoena those records. As the records are reviewed and summarized, additional providers may be revealed. Their records should also be obtained.

§ 7.2   —Initial Client Interview

One of the most useful tools in obtaining a complete medical history is the initial client interview. At the time of the interview, the legal team will identify the client's problem and ultimate goal. The attorney and paralegal should prepare the client for the future conduct of the case, including the anticipated duration of the case, the steps the attorney will take prior to and during litigation, the status and role of the paralegal, and the invasive nature of a lawsuit. A potential plaintiff rarely has any concept of the time and emotional involvement inherent in a lawsuit, nor of the degree of privacy he or she may sacrifice. A client unprepared or unwilling to endure the invasion into his or her personal and business life or the "hurry up and wait" nature of a lawsuit may be advised to reconsider initiating the action. Similarly, early settlement of a matter may be advised in order to avoid the commitment of time or loss of privacy that a party may be unwilling or unable to tolerate.

Cases related to death or significant personal or psychological injuries are especially emotionally charged. Economic damage, loss of physical or mental well-being, and the impact on a marriage and family involve serious stress. A client can be angry and depressed, and may be grieving. Some clients are demanding, abusive, aggressive, absent-minded, or emotional. They may lack normal behavioral constraints due to their losses and stress, and their judgment and concentration may be impaired. The client interview is the time during which the attorney and paralegal can establish trust and focus on the client's problem. Gathering complete information regarding the incident is extremely important, but collecting necessary information can occur over time and during the course of the litigation.

Practice Note: A client is often accompanied to meetings by a relative or friend who may influence the client by their presence, emotional response to the questioning, or contributions to the interview. It is not uncommon, for example, for a spouse or parent to answer questions posed to the client or to interject his/her opinions, thereby preventing the client from telling his or her own story. When this situation occurs, it may be necessary to ask the companion to wait outside the interview room or reschedule the interview for a time when the client is alone.

§ 7.3   Areas of Inquiry at Interview and in Discovery

The areas of inquiry listed in **Form 7-1** are typically used to obtain information during the interview. They also enable the attorney to lay a good foundation for discovery responses when interrogatories are propounded or the client's deposition is taken. Conversely, the categories are good starting points for discovery to be propounded to the plaintiff, and for questioning during deposition. The categories for personal information, incident descriptions, injuries, and damages are applicable to most cases, although the specific questions propounded will vary depending on the client and the basis of the case. The remaining categories relate to particular types of cases and must be combined as appropriate with the more general topic categories.

General Information
Personal
Employment
Incident/Accident (prior/current)
Injuries
Insurance coverage
Medical and related expenses
Loss of income/earning capacity
Other economic damages
Non-economic damages

Special Categories of Inquiry
Animals
Motor vehicle accident
Premises liability
Product liability
Professional malpractice
Toxic tort liability

(See **Form 7-1** for the complete Initial Client Interview outline).

§ 7.4   —Pre-Hospital Care

If the accident required medical treatment at the scene or prior to hospitalization, it will be important to obtain the records related to this pre-hospital care. First responders at the scene may include paramedics, the fire department, police, or ambulance personnel.

Practice Note: Many first responders (typically in small towns) take photographs with their personal cameras of graphic accident scenes or rescues. When interviewing or corresponding with first responders, ask about the existence of any photos.

§ 7.5 —Hospital Records

Obtain the records for any hospitalizations occurring as a result of the incident. This should include records for any hospitalization for physical, rehabilitation, or psychological therapy.

§ 7.6 —Treating Physicians and Specialists

Obtain the records of both the treating physicians who provided the medical care for the particular incident or accident and the plaintiff's personal physician. The records of the family physician are useful for determining the plaintiff's general physical condition prior to the incident. Also obtain the records of specialists to whom the plaintiff has been referred for further examination (neurologists, neurological surgeons, orthopedic surgeons, rehabilitation specialists, and so on).

Mental Health Professionals

If emotional trauma or mental problems are alleged to have arisen from the incident, records from the treating mental health professional must be obtained.

Practice Note: Care must be taken that the authorization or subpoena language be specific as to the type of psychological records being sought.

Ancillary Medical Providers

The plaintiff may have received medical care in addition to that received from physicians and hospitals. This can include chiropractic, physical therapy, occupational therapy, acupuncture, or home health care providers (for example, nursing services or medical supplies).

§ 7.7   —Other Sources of Medical Records

Certain miscellaneous records can also be requested. Employment records obtained to investigate wage loss allegations can be a source of medical information, especially if the employer required a preemployment physical examination.

§ 7.8   —Social Security Administration

Access to Social Security records is severely limited (42 U.S.C. § 1305(a)), and a court order may be required. Disclosure may be made to a claimant, a prospective claimant, or his or her authorized representative regarding matters directly concerning him or her (other than medical information) when consistent with the requirements set forth in 20 C.F.R. 401.3. These matters may also be disclosed to others or to the public, on written authorization by the claimant, prospective claimant, or duly authorized representative.

Medical information can generally only be disclosed to an individual's physician or to a medical facility at which he or she is a patient. This disclosure requires the consent of both the individual and the source of the information. If the source is not available, a physician in the employ of the Social Security department may give consent.

§ 7.9   —Department of Veterans Affairs

The Department of Veterans Affairs maintains a file on every veteran who has filed a claim for hospitalization, compensation, or pension. The file material includes originals or copies of the following:

- Medical care given and examinations made by the service department
- Any statement made by the veteran concerning the nature of the disease or injury for which he or she is making a claim
- Reports of examinations made and treatment given in any regional office, hospital, or clinic
- Information received from the Social Security Administration.

The VA operates the largest health care system in the United States with over 1200 locations at which health care is offered to veterans and their dependents, including 172 medical centers, 650 clinics, 206 counseling centers, 134 nursing homes and other facilities. The VA system has adapted new technology to the needs of its patients, including the use of computerized medical records. In fact, the full medical records of a patient are not transferred from hospital to clinic to the doctor's office as they are available on-line via the VA's computerized patient record system which gives medical providers a complete view of what has been done for a patient and a way to place orders for care and treatment, including the ordering of medications.

§ 7.10 —Confidentiality of VA Records

All files, records, reports, and other papers and documents concerning any claim made to the Department of Veterans Affairs are confidential and privileged and with certain exceptions may not be disclosed (38 U.S.C. § 3301). However, records may be released to the veteran, to his or her surviving spouse or kin, or to the claimant's duly authorized agent or representative as to matters concerning only the claimant, if such disclosure "will not be injurious to the physical or mental health of the person in whose behalf the information is sought or cause repugnance or resentment toward the decedent" (38 C.F.R. 1.503).

Any request for a copy of any record, paper, etc., in the custody of the Department of Veterans Affairs must be in writing. The written application must identify the specific records requested, whether they are to be certified or not, and the reason the records are being requested (38 U.S.C. § 3302). When requested for a lawsuit, an affidavit must accompany the records request giving the character of the pending suit, the date of the alleged injury, the nature of the injuries alleged, and the facts indicating why fraud or other injustice will result unless the records of the Department of Veterans Affairs are produced. If it is determined that fraud or other injustice will result from disclosure of the file, the Department of Veterans Affairs will notify the requesting attorney that the file will be produced before the court at the time of trial and upon receipt of a subpoena.

Practice Note: The confidentiality requirements for VA medical records follow HIPAA; be sure to use a HIPAA-compliant authorization when requesting medical records of a veteran. See **Form 7–2** for a sample form.

§ 7.11 —Military Records

Various military records are available to a requestor, including those concerning medical care and treatment received while on active duty, as a retired or deceased service person, or as a military dependent. Generally speaking, the following must be provided: full name, Social Security number, service number, date of birth, and dates of military service. Most veteran's records are stored at the National Archives and Records Administration's National Personnel Records Center, Miltary Personnel Records (NPRC-MPR). This includes records of veterans who are completely discharged (with no remaining reserve commitment), or who are retired or have died. Records are usually transferred to NPRC-MPR within six months after these events. NPRC-MPR does not have records of members who are still in the active or inactive reserves or in the National Guard. The locations of most personnel records are listed by service branch. Older military personnel records (generally prior to WWI, depending on the service branch) are on file at the National Archives and Records Administration, Old Military and Civil Records Branch (NWCTB), Washington, DC 20408.

- National Personnel Records Center (NPRC), 9700 Page Avenue, St. Louis, MO 63132-5100. Telephone: 314-801-0800; email *MPR .center@nara.gov*; Fax: 314 801-9195. This is the official repository for records of military personnel who have been discharged from the U.S. Air Force, Army, Marine Corps, Navy and Coast Guard. Most official military personnel files at NPRC prior to 1992 contain both personnel and active duty health record. Health records cover outpatient, dental, and mental health treatment which a former member received while in the military service. Health records documents include induction and separation physical examinations, and routine medical care (doctor/dental visits, lab tests, etc.) when the patient was not admitted to a hospital. Clinical (hospital inpatient) records are not filed with the health records but are generally retired to NPRC by the hospital or facility which created them. Other medical records which would not be included are Department of Veterans Affairs (VA) records, or records for service after 1992 when the practice of filing health records with the personnel record portion was discontinued.

To obtain medical records of an individual on active duty, direct the inquiry to the Department of Veterans Affairs, Records Management

Center , St. Louis, MO, which maintains active duty health records or manages their whereabouts when on loan within the VA. Call the VA toll free number at 1-800-827-1000.

Practice Note: Requests for military personnel records or information from them **cannot** be accepted by e-mail. The Privacy Act of 1974 (5 U.S.C. 552a) and Department of Defense directives require a written request, signed and dated, to access information from military personnel records. The email address can be used to request general information (hours of operations, procedures, and forms) or to submit compliments, complaints or concerns.

§ 7.12   Methods of Obtaining Records

As discussed in **Chapter 2**, the medical record is owned by the health care provider who prepared it. The record can be obtained by two methods, either informally by way of authorization (prior to the initiation of litigation) or formally by way of subpoena (after litigation has begun).

§ 7.13   —Disclosures with Authorization (Pre-Litigation)

At any time prior to the initiation of a lawsuit, records can be obtained through a release or authorization that has been signed by the patient or a legal representative. A patient's authorization essentially gives permission to allow copies of any personal medical records or other information (X rays, for example) to be released to a designated individual or group. The term "authorization" can be used interchangeably with "release" or "consent."

Practice Note: Releases can also be used after litigation has begun to update the status of the client's medical treatment or to obtain copies of bills. The adverse party may request a release to bypass the statutory time requirements for obtaining medical records pursuant to subpoena, or when the medical provider is located out of state.

§ 7.14   —HIPAA Requirements

HIPAA permits a covered entity to disclosed protected health information to a third party via use of an authorization. All authorizations must be in plain language, and contain specific core elements. A valid authorization may contain elements or information in addition to those required by HIPAA, as long as the additional information is not inconsistent with HIPAA. 45 C.F.R. § 164.508(a).

The *required core elements* are:

- A description of the information to be used or disclosed that identifies the information in a specific and meaningful fashion.
- The name or other identification of the person or entity who is authorized to make the request.
- The name or other identification of the person or entity to whom the records are to be disclosed.
- A description of the specific purpose of the records to be disclosed. When an individual initiates the request for his or her own records, the statement "at the request of the individual" is sufficient. 45 C.F.R. § 164.508(6).
- An expiration date (e.g., one year) or event (at the end of the research study) after which the request will no longer be valid.
- Signature and date that the authorization was signed. If the requestor is a personal representative, that relationship must be described specifically.
- A statement that the individual has the right to revoke the authorization in writing.

A *defective authorization* is one that has any one of the following defects:

1. The expiration date has passed;
2. The authorization has not been filled out completely;
3. The submitting party has knowledge that the authorization was revoked;
4. The authorization violates any paragraph of this section;
5. Any material contained on the authorization is known to be false.

Compound authorizations are permitted only under certain specific circumstances (for certain research purposes, an authorization for psychotherapy notes may only be combined with another authorization for release of psychotherapy notes, etc.). (45 C.F.R. § 164.508(b)). The sample HIPAA-compliant general authorizations or release forms in **Form 7–**

and **Form 7–3** can be used in a variety of circumstances—to obtain medical records from hospital, private physicians, chiropractors, dentists, and so on—and will be sufficient for most record requests.

Practice Note: As discussed in **Ch. 1 § 1.16**, state law is preempted by HIPAA unless the state law or regulation is more stringent than HIPAA. In any case, authorizations for release of medical records must comply with both state and federal regulations. For example, in California, all releases must be in a 14-point font. The authorization in Form 7–2 is California-specific (14-point font is assumed). If your state law specifically limits the length of time an authorization is valid, that specific time frame must be included in the authorization.

Practice Note: Having the client sign several general authorizations in advance without dating them allows records to be requested without having to contact the client each time a new authorization is needed. In most cases, the original authorization can be copied and the copy used to obtain further records. If the records are voluminous and are to be sent to a copy service for copying, the service does not have to be directly identified because it is acting as the agent for the law firm.

§ 7.15   —Personal Representatives Entitled to Sign Authorizations

Entities are required to treat personal representatives of the individual as they would the individual themselves with respect to disseminating health information. Nothing in HIPAA changes the way in which an individual grants another person power of attorney for health care decisions. State law (or other law) regarding health care powers of attorney continue to apply. The intent of the provisions regarding personal representatives was to implement, not interfere with or change, current practice regarding health care powers of attorney or the designation of other personal representatives. Such designations are formal, legal actions which give others ability to exercise the rights of, or make treatment decisions related to, individual. However, HIPAA does require that covered entities verify personal representative's authority in accordance with 45 C.F.R. § 4(h).

§ 7.16   Categories of Personal Representatives

The following categories are recognized as personal representatives:

Adults or emancipated minors—a person with legal authority to make health care decisions, such as durable power of attorney or a court appointed legal guardian. The scope of access will depend on the authority granted to the personal representative by other law. If the personal representative is authorized to make health care decisions generally, then the personal representative may have access to the individual's protected health information regarding health care in general.

On the other hand, if the authority is limited, the personal representative may have access only to protected health information that may be relevant to making decisions within the personal representative's authority. For example, if a personal representative's authority is limited to authorizing artificial life support, then the personal representative's access to protected health information is limited to that information which may be relevant to decisions about artificial life support.

Practice Note: HIPAA does not require a covered entity to treat a personal representative as the individual if, in the exercise of professional judgment, it believes doing so would not be in the best interest of the individual because of a reasonable belief that the individual has been or may be subject to domestic violence, abuse or neglect by the personal representative, or that doing so would otherwise endanger the individual. This exception applies to adults and both emancipated and unemancipated minors who may be subject to abuse or neglect by their personal representatives.

Deceased individuals—HIPAA requires a covered entity to treat the personal representative as the individual as long as the person has the authority under law to act for the decedent or the estate. The power of attorney would have to be valid after the individual's death to qualify the holder as the personal representative of the decedent.

Unemancipated minors—parent, guardian, or other person acting as parent with legal authority to make decisions. This area of the law identifies circumstances in which the parent is not the personal representative for the child with respect to health information, including: (A) when state or other law doesn't require parental consent before the minor can obtain a specific health care service, such as mental health services; (B) when the court determines or other law authorizes someone other than parent to make treatment decisions for a minor, and (C) when a parent agrees to the confidential relationship between the minor and physician.

Practice Note: HIPAA generally allows a parent to have access to the medical records about his or her child, as his or her minor child's personal representative when such access is not inconsistent with state or other law. However, even in the exceptions listed above, the parent may have access to the medical records of the minor related to this treatment when state or other applicable law requires or permits such parental access. Parental access would be denied when state or other law prohibits such access. If state or other applicable law is silent on a parent's right of access in these cases, the licensed health care provider may exercise his or her professional judgment to the extent allowed by law to grant or deny parental access to the minor's medical information. Finally, as is the case with respect to all personal representatives under HIPAA, a provider may choose not to treat a parent as a personal representative when the provider reasonably believes, in his or her professional judgment, that the child has been or may be subjected to domestic violence, abuse or neglect, or that treating the parent as the child's personal representative could endanger the child.

Practice Note: With the increased level of attention paid to authorizations following HIPAA, it would be advisable to attach a copy of whatever court order or form exists appointing that individual as guardian, conservator, or representative of the person whose records have been requested.

§ 7.17 —Tailoring the Authorization

Within the confines of HIPAA, a release can be tailored to fit various types of records. For example, if copies of an individual's X-ray films are needed, the description of the records requested would read as follows:

> ". . . all X ray studies taken by your office while I was under your observation and treatment and which are currently in your possession."

This authorization can be altered and used when seeking many kinds of medical information, such as laboratory specimen slides, dental study models, and so forth.

Practice Note: Large medical institutions often have client populations that number in the hundreds of thousands. When requesting their records, provide as much identifying information as possible: patient's full name, maiden name, and any other name used if applicable; date of birth; Social Security number; and facility medical number if known.

§ 7.18   —Suggested Language for Authorization

By using specific, well thought out language in your authorizations (and subpoenas) you can avoid ambiguity and resulting problems with your requests.

Medical records (generally)—"Any and all documents, records, and itemized statements of the billing charges pertaining to the care, treatment, and examination of [*name*], for the period [*specify the period requested, e.g., from Jan. 1, 2000, to present, etc.*]. The records requested include but are not limited to all office, emergency room, and hospital inpatient charts, hospital and clinic outpatient charts, admission sheets, history and physical examinations, diagnoses, consultations, lab and X-ray reports, photographs, videotapes, and any other documents or things that may be in your possession or under your control."

Medical records (psychiatric, drug, alcohol, or substance abuse)— "Any and all confidential documents, records, and itemized statements of the billing charges pertaining to the care, treatment, and examination of [*name*], for the period [*specify the period requested, e.g., from Jan. 1, 2000, to present, etc.*]. The records requested are those concerning all [psychiatric or drug, alcohol, or other substance abuse] treatment, counseling or rehabilitation records, and any other documents that may be in your possession or under your control."

Medical records (HIV/AIDS)—"Any and all confidential documents, records, and itemized statements of the billing charges pertaining to the care, treatment, and examination of [*name*], for the period [*specify the period requested, e.g., from Jan. 1, 2000, to present etc.*]. The records requested are those concerning all office, emergency room, and hospital inpatient charts, hospital and clinic outpatient charts, admission sheets, history and physical examinations, diagnoses, consultations, lab and X-ray reports, and any other documents that may be in your possession or under your control concerning treatment received or rendered for HIV (human immunodeficiency virus) or AIDS (acquired immune deficiency syndrome)."

§ 7.19 —Written Request Accompanying Authorization

An authorization for release of medical records should not be sent to a medical provider without a written request from the attorney. See **Form 7–4** for an example of a written request used for records pertaining to the client personally (as opposed to minor children of the client, for example).

§ 7.20 —Requesting Records of a Minor

The content of the written request can be altered as circumstances require. For example, if records concerning a minor are needed, the body of the letter could read: "Enclosed you will find an Authorization for Release of Medical Information directed to your attention and executed by the patient's mother, Mrs._____ [or describe the legal relationship]. Please make a copy of your entire chart and forward it to us at the above address."

§ 7.21 —Requesting Medical Bills

Specific departments of large medical institutions are often responsible for responding to requests for medical records and bills. Or the billing may be done by a separate entity that might contract out to groups of physicians—the emergency or radiology department, for example—to provide on-site services. Consequently, these physician groups do not bill for their work through the medical institution, but through this separate billing service.

Practice Note: The most efficient way of obtaining copies of medical bills is to make the request in a separate letter to the billing department. You must attach a copy of the HIPAA-compliant authorization for release of records directed to that facility. Many jurisdictions are finding that the actual cost of the medical care is not the amount billed, but the amount paid by the insurer (e.g, private insurance, Medicare, Medicaid). Make sure that all billing statements you obtain have actual payment amounts, not just what was billed.

§ 7.22   —Custodian's Response to Request

Generally speaking, the custodian of records must provide all of the records under its custody and control and respond to the request within a reasonable amount of time. Because the medical provider is bound by ethical restraints concerning the patient's right to privacy, and by unfamiliarity with HIPAA, it may attempt to limit the records supplied to those concerning the incident itself. To prevent this from happening, both the release and the letter accompanying it should specifically identify the records in the provider's possession that are being requested.

Practice Note: If you suspect you have not been provided with a complete chart, call the provider's office immediately and request that it comply with your request. HIPAA allows providers to release a complete medical record, including portions that were created by another provider. The "Minimum Necessary" provision [see § **1.30** for discussion] is not imposed when records are obtained pursuant to authorization.

§ 7.23   New Patient Rights Under HIPAA

Unless a person is familiar with the how medical records work and the content of a medical record, the first time they see their own records will no doubt be a revelation. In fact, an individual may read something in her record that she believes was never said or was misinterpreted by the doctor. Under HIPAA, patients have significant new rights to understand and control how their health information is used, including the right to have entries in the medical record amended or corrected.

§ 7.24   —Patient Access to Medical Records

An individual has the right of access to his or her protected health information, and the right to obtain a copy of the record. This request may be in writing but only if the individual is informed in advance of this requirement. The covered entity must act on the individual's request for amendment no later than 60 days after receipt of the amendment. Provided the covered entity gives the individual a written statement of the reason for the delay, and the date by which the amendment will be processed, the covered entity may have a one-time extension of up to 30 days for an amendment request.(45 C.F.R. §§ 164.524 *et seq.*)

Practice Note: This right to access is mainly significant in those states without a statutory right of patients to have access to their medical information. If the entity subsequently grants the request, in whole or in part, it must inform the individual and grant the access requested, including inspection of the record, obtaining a copy of the record, or both. If the requested information is maintained in more than one record set or at more than one location, the entity need only produce the information once in response.

HIPAA permits the covered entity to impose "reasonable, cost-based fees." The fee may include only the cost of copying (including supplies and labor) and postage, if the patient requests that the copy be mailed. If the patient has agreed to receive a summary or explanation of his or her protected health information, the covered entity may also charge a fee for preparation of the summary or explanation. The fee may not include costs associated with searching for and retrieving the requested information. (45 C.F.R. § 164.524(c)(4)).

§ 7.25   —Exceptions to Right of Access

The following are exceptions to the right of access of an individual to their medical record: (1) the records are psychotherapy notes; (2) the information was compiled in anticipation or use in a civil, criminal, or administrative action or proceeding; (3) it is health information protected pursuant to the Clinical Laboratory Improvements Amendments (CLIA) of 1988; and (4) it is health information exempted from CLIA, e.g., information generated by facilities that perform forensic testing, research labs that do not report patient-specific results, and drug testing performed in a lab certified by the National Institute on Drug Abuse (DIDA).(45 C.F.R. § 164.524(a)).

Practice Note: CLIA, 42 U.S.C. § 263a, is the federal law that defines the requirements for certification of clinical laboratories.

§ 7.26   —Non-Reviewable Grounds for Denial of Access to Medical Record

A covered entity may also *deny* an individual access to his or her medical record without providing an opportunity for review when certain conditions exist:

1. The entity is a correctional institution (or healthcare provider acting under the direction of such an institution) and the inmate's request to obtain the information would jeopardize the individual, other inmates, or the safety of any officer, employee, or other person at the institution;

2. The individual agreed to a temporary denial of access when consenting to participate in research that has not yet been completed;

3. The records are subject to the Privacy Act of 1974 and the denial of access meets the requirements of that law;

4. The protected health information was obtained from someone other than a healthcare provider under a promise of confidentiality and access to that information would likely reveal the source of the information. (45 C.F.R. § 164.524(2)).

§ 7.27   —Reviewable Grounds for Denial of Access to Medical Record

Provided that an individual is given the right to have the denial reviewed, under the following circumstances an entity may also deny an individual access to his or her medical record:

1. When a licensed healthcare provider has determined that the access is likely to endanger the life or physical safety of the requesting individual or another person;

2. The protected health information makes reference to another person who is not a healthcare provider, and a licensed healthcare professional has determined that the access requested is likely to cause substantial harm to such other person;

3. The request is made by the individual's personal representative and a licensed healthcare professional has determined that access is likely to cause substantial harm to the individual or another person. (45 C.F.R. § 164.524(3)).

§ 7.28   —Review of Denial of Access

If the request for access is denied, the individual must be given the right to have the denial reviewed. The review will be conducted by a licensed health care professional who has been designated by the entity to act as a reviewing official and who did not participate in the original decision to deny. The designated reviewing official must determine within an undefined "reasonable period of time" whether or not to uphold the denial of access. The entity must then "promptly" provide the individual with written notice of the official determination. (45 C.F.R. § 164.524(4).

§ 7.29   —Request for Amendment of Health Information

Possibly one of the most significant provisions of HIPAA is the right of an individual to request that a covered entity *amend his or her health record if, presumably, that individual feels that certain information is in error* (45 C.F.R. § 164.526(a)). Covered entities may require that a request to amend be in writing and that the individual provide a reason in support of the amendment. The covered entity may deny the request for amendment of the record for various reasons, including:

1. The information was not created by the covered entity, unless the originator is no longer available to act on the request;
2. Is not part of the individual's health record; and,
3. Is accurate and complete.

Practice Note: It remains unknown how this aspect of HIPAA will play out. It is difficult to conceive that a covered entity would make a significant change to a medical record unless the information requested to be changed is obviously erroneous, e.g., right leg instead of left leg, male instead of female, wrong age, sex or marital status. How a covered entity will react to a request to change an entry such as "not wearing seat belt" to "wearing seat belt" based on the individual's sole request, remains to be seen.

The covered entity must act on the individual's request for amendment no later than 60 days after receipt of the amendment. Provided the covered entity gives the individual a written statement of the reason for the delay, and the date by which the amendment will be processed, the covered entity may have a one-time extension of up to 30 days for an amendment request. (45 C.F.R. § 164.526(b)(2)(i)).

§ 7.30   —Amendments to the Medical Record

If the request to amend the record is granted, the covered entity must:

- Insert the amendment or provide a link to the amendment at the site of the information;
- Inform the individual that the amendment is accepted;
- Obtain the individual's identification of and agreement to have the entity notify the relevant persons with whom the amendment needs to be shared;
- Within a reasonable time frame, make reasonable efforts to provide the amendment to persons identified by the individual, and persons, including business associates, that the covered entity knows have the protected health information that is the subject of the amendment and that may have relied on or could foreseeably rely on the information to the detriment of the individual. (45 C.F.R. § 164.526(c)).

§ 7.31   —Denial of Amendments to the Record

If the covered entity denies the requested amendment, it must provide the individual with a timely, written denial in plain language that contains:

- The basis for the denial;
- The individual's right to submit a written statement disagreeing with the denial and the procedure for filing such a statement;
- How the individual's request for amendment and the denial be provided with any future disclosures of the protected health information; and
- A description of how the individual may complain to the covered entity (statement of disagreement) with the name or title, and telephone number of the designated contact person who handles complaints. The covered entity can then file a rebuttal to the statement of disagreement. 45 C.F.R. § 164.526 *et seq.*

The covered entity must identify the record or specific information that is the subject of a disputed amendment and "append or otherwise link" the individual's request for amendment, the denial of the request, the statement of disagreement, and the rebuttal to the specific record. Any subsequent disclosure of the medical record must contain all correspondence related to the request and denial.

§ 7.32 Disclosures Without Authorization Under HIPAA

HIPAA permits certain existing disclosures of health information without individual authorization under various defined situations and for activities that allow the health care system to operate more smoothly. All of these disclosures have been permitted under existing laws and regulations. Within certain guidelines found in the regulation, covered entities may disclose information for:

- Oversight of the healthcare system, including quality assurance activities;
- Public health matters;
- Research (generally limited to when a waiver of authorization is independently approved by a privacy board or Institutional Review Board);
- Limited law enforcement activities;
- Emergency circumstances;
- For identification of the body of a deceased person, or the cause of death;
- For facility patient directories (patient has right to agree or object);
- For notification and other purposes (admission to hospital, picking up prescriptions for another, Red Cross disaster relief efforts, etc.);
- Victims of abuse, neglect or domestic violence;
- For activities related to national defense and security; and
- *Judicial and administrative proceedings. 45 C.F.R. § 164.512(e).*

§ 7.33 —HIPAA in Litigation—Disclosures Pursuant to the Judicial and Administrative Proceedings

When HIPAA was first enacted, one of the many myths prevalent in the health care industry was that it only allowed records to be produced pursuant to authorization. In fact, many health care providers refused to produce medical records pursuant to subpoena in the absence of authorization. This is absolutely not the case. A covered entity may disclose protected health information in the course of any judicial or administrative proceeding under three distinct circumstances—pursuant to a court order, pursuant to a subpoena or discovery request if sufficient notice to the individual has been given, and pursuant to a subpoena or discovery request in the presence of a qualified protective order.

§ 7.34   —Pursuant to Order of Court

The court order must specify the protected health information to be disclosed by the covered entity, and the entity may disclose only that information and no other. (45 C.F.R. § 164.512(e)(1)(i)).

Practice Note: It would be prudent to exhaust the other available remedies discussed below prior to involving the court in a situation in which an order is required. Further, who will make the determination that all of the applicable records, and only the applicable records, have been produced?

§ 7.35   —Pursuant to Subpoena or Discovery Request Not Accompanied by a Court Order

Parties may use the discovery process either through subpoena or request for production of documents if the covered entity receives "satisfactory assurance" from the requesting party that "reasonable efforts" have been made to ensure that the individual whose protected health information has been requested has been given notice of the request.

"Satisfactory assurance" is defined as a written statement and accompanying documentation demonstrating that:

*   A good faith attempt to provide written notice to the individual has been made. (If the individual's location is unknown, the requesting party must mail a notice to the individual's last known address.)

Practice Note: It is unclear whether HIPAA allows notice to be served directly on the plaintiff's attorney. Consider obtaining a declaration from counsel at the outset of litigation that the plaintiff has waived the right to receive this notice directly.

- The notice must contain sufficient information about the litigation or proceeding in which the protected health information is requested to permit the individual to object to the disclosure of the information;
- The time for the individual to raise objections has elapsed;
- No objections were filed; or
- All objections have been resolved by the court. 45 C.F.R. § 164.512(e) (1)(A).

Practice Note: On close reading, these sections mirror what is currently in existence in many states when subpoenaing records (e.g., notice to consumer is required to his/her last known address, and the consumer is then given the chance to raise objections to the subpoena either through a motion to quash or a protective order).

§ 7.36 —Pursuant to a Subpoena or Discovery Request Accompanied by a Stipulation or Qualified Protective Order

Protected health information can be produced by a covered entity in response to a subpoena or discovery request not accompanied by an order of a court if the covered entity receives "satisfactory assurance" from the requesting party that reasonable efforts have been made to secure a qualified protective order. (45 C.F.R § 164.512(e)(B)).

"Satisfactory assurance" means a written statement and accompanying documentation demonstrating that the parties have either stipulated to a qualified protective order and filed it with the court, or the plaintiff's attorney has requested a qualified protective order from the court.

The protective order must contain the following language:

(1) The parties are prohibited from using or disclosing the protected health information for any purpose other than the litigation for which such information was requested *and* "The protected health information must either be returned to the covered entity or destroyed at the end of the litigation."

Practice Note: Plaintiff's counsel should routinely send a Stipulation re Protective Order when the defendant first makes an appearance. The basic sample Stipulation located at **Form 7–5** contains the necessary language requirements and can be easily adapted to Protective Order format.

Practice Note: A area of concern regards the issue of what medical experts and consultants do with the records sent to them for review prior to deposition, in preparation for an IME or testimony at trial. It is apparent that litigators need to now be aware of the status of all medical records sent to consultants during the lifetime of a case. Further, it may be advisable to have an agreement of some type with the consultant at the time (or prior to) sending them for review concerning the ultimate disposition of the records.

§ 7.37   —Obtaining Records Pursuant to a Subpoena

The formal method utilized to procure records is the subpoena process. *Subpoena,* the Latin word for "under penalty," is essentially a court order commanding attendance in court to testify and attaching penalties for failure to do so. This process is utilized to order an individual to appear in court, at a deposition, or other court proceeding. Generally speaking, only independent witnesses must be subpoenaed because parties to an action are produced voluntarily and with proper notice.

When seeking medical or other documentary records, a *subpoena duces tecum* (SDT) or a *deposition subpoena with production of documents* is utilized. The Latin phrase *duces tecum* essentially means "to appear and to bring with you." It is directed to the custodian of records for the medical provider from whom the record is being requested.

Practice Note: Always review records subpoenas as soon as they arrive to determine if the requested records are relevant to the subject action. If not, consider bringing a motion to quash or to modify the subpoena. Additionally, if the records being subpoenaed are from care providers not already in your possession or previously unknown to you, contact the client about their significance. Because subpoenaed records will be used as evidence at trial, plaintiff's counsel should *always* request copies of everything subpoenaed by the defense. Although the time requirements for a subpoena duces tecum vary from state to state, the process is basically the same. Most states follow federal government practice as defined in Federal Rule of Civil Procedure 45. **Table 7–1** contains a list of references to selected state and federal codes governing subpoenas.

Table 7–1

Selected Rules for Records Subpoenas

Jurisdiction	Rule/Code
United States	Federal Rule of Civil Procedure 45
California	Evidence Code § 1158 et seq., Code of Civil Procedure §§ 1985–1986, 2020
District of Columbia	Superior Court Rule of Civil Procedure 45
Florida	Rule of Civil Procedure 1.410; Evidence Code § 92.153
Georgia	Court Rules and Procedure § 24-10-20 et seq.
Illinois	Annotated Statutes, Rule 214
Iowa	Rules of Court—Civil Procedure Rule 155
Maryland	Annotated Code of Public General Laws, Rule 2-411 et seq.
Massachusetts	Massachusetts Annotated Laws § 79
Michigan	Court Rules of 1985, Rules 2.305 and 2.314
Minnesota	Rule of Court 30.02
Missouri	Rules of Court 57.03, 57.09
New York	New York Civil Practice Law and Rules §§ 2301–2306
Ohio	Ohio Revised Code Ann. § 2937.19
Pennsylvania	Rules of Court 234, 1357
Texas	Texas Rules of Civil Procedure Annotated, Rules 177a and 201
Virginia	Code of Virginia Rules 4:5(b), 4:9(c), (c)(1)
Washington	State Court Rules 30(b) and 34(c)

§ 7.38   —General Subpoena Language

The following general terms are used when discussing a subpoena for records. Although these definitions are taken from the California Code of Civil Procedure, they are based on the federal rules and can be considered to be standard terminology:

Personal Records—the original or any copy of books, documents, or other writings pertaining to a consumer and maintained by any witness

Consumer—any individual, partnership of five or fewer persons, associations, and so on, that has used the services of the witness

Witness—a physician, pharmacist, pharmacy, hospital, state or national bank, school, and so forth

Subpoenaing Party—the person(s) causing a subpoena to be issued or served in connection with any civil action.

§ 7.39   —Issuing Subpoenas

Generally speaking, a subpoena is issued in two ways. The clerk of the court in which the action is pending can issue a subpoena embossed with the seal of the court and signed by the clerk. The subpoena is left blank, to be filled in by the requesting attorney prior to service. In addition, as an officer of the court, any attorney of record in a matter can issue a subpoena without the necessity of a clerk's seal.

Practice Note: Always check the applicable federal and state codes for your state's requirements.

§ 7.40   —Requirements for a Subpoena

The subpoena must contain certain basic kinds of information:

_____ A specific description of the item or category of items to be produced. (See **§ 7.16** above for sample language to use in subpoenas.)

_____ The date and time for the production of the records.

_____ A notice to the consumer that personal records about the consumer are being sought. The consumer has the right to object to the production of these records by filing a motion to quash or to modify the terms of the subpoena. Once this objection is formally filed, the witness is not required to produce the records until the objection is heard in court and ruled upon.

_____ The records to be produced must be delivered to the deposition officer (often a professional copy service) by mail or in person and shall be a true and legible copy of the original, as stated in an affidavit signed by the custodian of record. The deposition officer may also copy the records on the premises. The records are produced, along with a signed affidavit or certificate stating that they represent a true and correct copy of the original documents and were maintained in the course and scope of business. (See **Forms 7–6** and **7–7** for sample subpoenas).

§ 7.41   —Certificate of No Records

If a custodian has conducted a thorough search for the subpoenaed records and is unable to locate them, a Certificate or Affidavit of No Records (CNR) is signed. This indicates that, based on the information provided in the subpoena, no such records were identified.

Practice Note: When a Certificate of No Records is received, do not simply file it away, especially if there is strong reason to believe that the records do exist. For instance, in an urban acute care hospital with a patient base of over 250,000, mistakes could easily be made, for example, in the spelling of a name (Smyth instead of Smith, Williams instead of Willems). If you suspect that the records do exist, contact the custodian personally to pursue the search further. Large facilities generally designate one person to respond to subpoenas and other records requests.

In many hospital facilities, individual departments (emergency, radiology, laboratory) keep a separate daily log of patients seen in a 24-hour period. This log is an internal housekeeping device and as such is not a part of any one individual's medical record. If you believe that a person was seen at a facility but no records have been located, verify with the custodian that a log exists for the specific department you are interested in, and then request that the log be checked for the patient's name.

§ 7.42   —Use of Subpoenaed Records

Subpoenaed records need to be summarized in order to provide a succinct and objective account of the injuries involved. The record will be used to determine the extent of those injuries and to evaluate the merit of a case. The process of summarizing the record is discussed in detail in **Chapter 8.**

Practice Note: It is not advisable to alter a subpoenaed document (change the order, add comments to the record, and so on). These records may ultimately be used as exhibits to depositions or motions or as evidence at trial. Any alterations of the record after it was produced pursuant to subpoena can compromise the record's integrity. Instead, make a clean copy of the subpoenaed document and make any changes or notations on that copy. Many jurisdictions have held that copies of a record are admissible as evidence, and the original need not be produced at trial. However, check the applicable code for your state to determine what is required or what can be stipulated to by counsel.

§ 7.43   —Treating Physician's Report

Either before or after litigation has begun, a report prepared by one of the client's providers may be required. The report generally contains an analysis of that provider's examination and treatment of the client, the client's response to the treatment, and the prognosis. The sample in **Form 7–8** is a very specific example of how a medical report request can be worded. Depending on the experience of the provider, it may not be necessary to be this detailed.

§ 7.44   Other Records of Interest in Medical Malpractice Litigation

While the medical record is the primary source of information in medical malpractice litigation, there are other potentially rich sources to be explored. Certain information is required to be reported to national data banks including settlement of malpractice claims, and actions taken by Quality Assurance and Peer Review committees, state boards, professional organizations concerning the license of health care provider. Much of this information is not available to the public, but pertinent information can be accessed and obtained for use in litigation.

§ 7.45   Quality Assurance and Peer Review

Every medical facility maintains multiple committees to facilitate the examination of patient medical information without that patient's knowledge or consent. This helps maintain quality review procedures: to monitor and evaluate the quality and appropriateness of patient care; to review each department's work performance; and to comply with accreditation, regulatory, and licensing standards. It also assists in research or education programs.

One of the most significant committees is medical peer review, a committee of physicians that examines the performance of staff members to monitor, correct, and upgrade patient care activities. The frequency of peer review activities depends on the size of the institution, but generally occurs at least monthly. This time is noncompensated for most committee members.

Hospital bylaws dictate the requirements for committee participation by active staff members. Involvement in one or more committees is a function of staff appointment and, in order to stay active, staff members must attend a certain number of committee meetings.

§ 7.46 —How Cases Are Chosen for Review

Cases are submitted to peer review for a number of reasons. Specialty physicians, with the support of the facility's quality assurance staff, establish the criteria by which cases are reviewed, based on standards of care as they relate to current literature, community practice, and facility experience. Generally speaking, standards of care are becoming less regional in scope and more national. See **Chapter 8** for a discussion of standards of care. Some common examples of referral for peer review are:

1. Readmission within 48 hours of a discharge
2. Unanticipated death within the hospital
3. Adverse drug reaction that may or may not result in harm to the patient
4. Hospital-acquired infection
5. Unplanned transfer to intensive care units
6. Unplanned return to the operating room following surgery
7. Maternal death; hemorrhage; or unplanned surgery.

The quality of medical care provided in any facility depends heavily on how committee members utilize the review criteria and objectively evaluate the medical skills of their colleagues. The courts have generally held that these requirements for candor and objectivity are based on a strong public interest in improving the quality of medical care, which overrides a plaintiff's right to gain access to this information. Although these holdings do not deter plaintiffs' counsel from attempting to obtain peer review reports, information gathered in this manner is not discoverable.

When a peer review committee makes an adverse finding concerning a fellow physician (or dentist), the bylaws dictate what actions are taken. These actions can range from placement of a report in the physician's credential file to modification or even suspension of hospital privileges. Any finding that adversely affects a physician's staff privileges must be reported to the state medical board and to the National Practitioner Data Bank. (See § 7.47 for a discussion of this data bank).

§ 7.47   —Multidisciplinary Peer Review

Cases are also referred for multidisciplinary peer review to determine if the facility as a whole is following its "critical path." Critical paths impose objective criteria on the management of specific illnesses or diseases and are based on standards of care. Participation in this committee comes from all disciplines including medicine, nursing, infection control, physical therapy, dietary, and respiratory therapy. As an example, a facility might monitor all emergency department admissions in which a diagnosis of myocardial infarction has been made. The committee will evaluate the timeliness of interventions and treatment as determined by the facility standard for that condition.

§ 7.48   State Boards and Professional Organizations

Various professional medical organizations have been compiling disciplinary data on their members for years. Among these are state medical and nursing boards, the National Council of State Boards of Nursing, the Federation of State Medical Boards, and the American Medical Association.

State medical and nursing boards maintain records of licensure actions against physicians and nurses. Most state medical boards require that malpractice claims, payments, and settlements against physicians be reported. Some state boards require that malpractice claims, payments, and settlements against nurses be reported. Investigations and complaints to these boards are not matters of public record, but formal board actions are.

The **National Council of State Boards of Nursing, Inc.** (*www.ncsbn .org*) is a not-for-profit organization whose membership comprises the boards of nursing in the 50 states, the District of Columbia, and five United States territories—American Samoa, Guam, Northern Mariana Islands, Puerto Rico, and the Virgin Islands. NCSBN maintains a database containing information about nurses, including licensing verification and disciplinary actions taken against them known as Nur*sys*® (Nurse System). Information provided by member boards includes nurses personal (name, address, etc.), license, and license discipline. All boards of nursing, including non-participating boards, have access to information within Nur*sys*®, and are able to enter and edit discipline information. The purpose of Nur*sys*® is to provide centralized license information to boards of nursing for use in verifying applicant license information, enter and review disciplinary actions, and to send communications between boards of nursing for information requests.

Practice Note: Board of Nursing disciplinary actions are considered public information. Many Boards have determined that it is in the public interest to publicize actions against a nurse's license, including actions that reinstate a nurse's license. Boards use a variety of methods to communicate this information, e.g., newsletters and web sites. The national board website at *www.ncsbn.org* has links to all of the state and territorial board sites. Check with your Board of Nursing regarding access to information about Board actions. If the litigation involves nursing malpractice, make sure to determine the status of the subject nurse's license as soon as possible.

The **Federation of State Medical Boards** (*www.fsmb.org*) is a not-for-profit organization serving as a clearinghouse, forum and representative body for the 70 state medical boards of the United States, the District of Columbia, Puerto Rico, Guam and the Virgin Islands. Since 1912, the FSMB has collected and reported disciplinary actions taken against physicians. Through the Federation Physician Data Center, we provide comprehensive information on disciplinary actions taken and reported against physicians by regulatory and licensing entities throughout the United States and a growing number of international locations. Information concerning disciplinary information on U.S. licensed physicians is available to the public through *www.Docinfo.org*, a Web site operated by FSMB.

Once a user completes the online physician search process, he will receive a Disciplinary Search Report, which provides detailed information on disciplinary actions taken against a physician. This report provides the name of the state medical board or licensing agency that initiated the action, what type of disciplinary action was taken (such as a license revocation, probation, suspension, etc.,) the date of the action and the basis or reason(s) for the action. The Disciplinary Search Report does not include information on medical malpractice settlements or claims.

Practice Note: There is a minimal fee for this service. For access to free disciplinary information you must contact each state medical board individually.

The **American Medical Association** (*www.ama-assn.org*) has compiled a master file of physician members, including office location, areas of practice, speciality licenses, and information on credentials, education, and licensure as provided by the FSMB. The AMA data bank (DoctorFinder) receives over 500,000 annual requests for information.

§ 7.49   Revocation or Suspension of Medical License

State medical examining boards hold the primary responsibility for the evaluation, issuance, supervision, and revocation of physician licenses. Medical licenses can be revoked or suspended for a number of reasons:

1.   Criminal activities such as fraud involving Medicare, Medicaid, or insurance companies
2.   Sexual advances toward or involvement with patients
3.   False and inaccurate medical records
4.   Misrepresentation of hospital status to patients
5.   Revocation of hospital privileges
6.   Conviction of certain crimes such as sexual assault, possession of an unlicensed firearm, accepting a bribe, or violation of a state or federal law
7.   Malpractice, patient neglect, or unprofessional or dishonorable conduct.

§ 7.50   National Practitioner Data Bank (NPDB)

In 1989 the United States Department of Health and Human Services authorized the creation of the National Practitioner Data Bank (NPDB) in order to collect information about the professional competence and conduct of physicians, dentists, and other health care practitioners. Regulations establishing the data bank required hospitals to begin requesting information from September 1, 1990 on. The reporting requirements were not applied retroactively. The NPDB can be accessed at *www.npdb-hipdb.gov.*

§ 7.51 —Reporting Requirements and Information Sources

Information in the data bank comes from several sources, in varying percentages of the total number of reports. The numbers of reports give with each category listed below come from 2004, the last year data was available.

- Health care entities (e.g., hospitals, HMOs, group practices, professional societies) must report adverse peer review actions relating to the professional competency and conduct of physicians and dentists within 15 days of final action. This includes any action that adversely affects clinical privileges for more than 30 days, and the voluntary surrender of clinical privileges or acceptance of restricted privileges while under investigation for possible incompetence or improper professional conduct. At present, reporting of adverse actions concerning other types of health care practitioners (for example, nurses) is voluntary.

- Licensing boards must report within 30 days any actions based on incompetence or professional misconduct, including those that revoke, suspend, or otherwise restrict the license of a physician, dentist, or nurse. (0.6% of total reports)

- When the Drug Enforcement Agency (DEA) revokes or receives voluntary surrenders by practitioners of DEA registration "numbers." (0.8% of total reports)

- When HHS excludes a practitioner from participation in Medicare or Medicaid programs.

- Within 30 days of the date of payment, the insurer or individual payor (physician, dentist, or other health care provider) must report settlements of malpractice claims. This includes settlements made in court, before an arbitration board, or alternative dispute resolution service. Payments of claims against nurses are reported only if the nurse was sued individually. Failure to report such payments can subject the payor to civil penalties of up to $10,000 for each payment involved. Recognizing that settlements are often made for expedience and not on the basis of actual malpractice, the Department of Health and Human Services added a provision stating that payment in settlement of a malpractice action or claim "shall not be construed as creating a presumption that medical malpractice has occurred." (Note: malpractice payments represent 73.6% 2004 total reports; physicians were responsible 78.6%, dentists for 13.3%, and all other types of practitioners for 8.1%)

Practice Note: Self-insured practitioners who settled claims out of his or her personal funds were originally required to report their malpractice payments to NPDB. However, on August 27, 1993, the U.S. Court of Appeals for the D.C. Circuit reversed a prior Federal District Court ruling in *American Dental Association, et al., v. Donna E. Shalala*, No. 92-5038, and held that self-insured individuals were not "entities" under the *HCQIA* and did not have to report payments made from personal funds. All such reports have been removed from the NPDB.

§ 7.52   —Confidentiality of Data

Information obtained in the NPDB is confidential. Defense attorneys, medical malpractice insurers, and the general public are specifically prohibited from obtaining information from the data bank.

Information can be released only to the following entities or individuals:

1. Hospitals requesting information on a practitioner seeking medical staff appointment or clinical privileges
2. Individuals wishing to review information about themselves
3. State licensing boards
4. Health care entities entering into an employment or affiliation relationship with a health care practitioner
5. Professional societies screening applicants for membership or for any other professional review activity
6. Researchers seeking anonymous statistical information

7. Plaintiff attorneys or plaintiffs who can show that a hospital failed to request information regarding a health care professional named in an active malpractice suit against the hospital and the subject health care professional.

§ 7.53 —Requesting Information From (Querying) the NPDB

Federal regulations require that all hospitals *must* request information from the NPDB (make a query) under the following circumstances:

- When a physician, dentist, or other health care practitioner applies for medical staff appointments (courtesy or otherwise) or for clinical privileges at the hospital; and
- Every 2 years (biennially) on all physicians, dentists, and other health care practitioners who are on its medical staff (courtesy or otherwise) or who hold clinical privileges at the hospital.

Other eligible entities *may* request information as follows:

- Boards of medical or dental examiners or other State licensing boards may query at any time.
- Other health care entities, including professional societies, may query when entering an employment or affiliation relationship with a practitioner or in conjunction with professional review activities.

The NPDB also may be queried in two other circumstances:

- Physicians, dentists, or other health care practitioners may "self-query" the NPDB about themselves at any time. Practitioners may not query to obtain records of other practitioners.
- A plaintiff or an attorney for a plaintiff in a malpractice action against a hospital may query and receive information from the NPDB about a specific practitioner in limited circumstances. This is possible only when independently obtained evidence submitted to HHS discloses that the hospital did not make a required query to the NPDB on the practitioner. If the attorney or plaintiff specifically demonstrated the hospital failed to query as required, the attorney or plaintiff will be

provided with information the hospital would have received had it queried.

Practice Note: Defense attorneys are not permitted access to the NPDB because the defendant practitioner is permitted to self-query the Data Bank. Specific procedures for attorney requests are identified in the Fact Sheet for Attorneys on the website located at *www.npdb-hipdb.gov.*

Practice Note: Malpractice payment reporting may be affected by use of the "corporate shield" in which the name of a health care organization (e.g., a hospital or group practice) is substituted for the name of the practitioner, who would otherwise be reported to the NPDB. This is most common when the health care organization is responsible for the malpractice coverage of the practitioner. Under current NPDB regulations, if a practitioner is named in the claim but not in the settlement, no report about the practitioner is filed with the NPDB unless the practitioner is excluded from the settlement as a condition of the settlement. The concept of the "Corporate Shield" may well serve to mask the extent of substandard care and diminish the data bank's usefulness.

§ 7.54   —Types of Actions Reported

In addition to malpractice settlements, various types of actions are reported to NPDB. For example, from November 2005 to January 2006, the following medical providers were reported to NPDB:

- A registered nurse in Arkansas criminally convicted of stealing morphine from a resident of a facility.
- A licensed professional nurse in Michigan pleaded no contest to forging timecards and not providing proper care to an unresponsive diabetic patient, who subsequently died.
- A pharmacist in New York criminally convicted of selling medications without prescriptions. He was the supervising pharmacist in the pharmacy.
- A nurse aide in Iowa criminally convicted of striking a patient.
- A nurse aide in California criminally convicted of sexually abusing a dependent adult in a residential facility.

- A pharmacist in New York criminally convicted of submitting false reimbursement claims to Medicaid for expensive medications he did not dispense.
- A licensed practical nurse in Washington criminally convicted of sexually molesting a resident at a nursing home.
- A registered nurse in Texas criminally convicted of using methamphetamine on multiple occasions, which could affect his patient care.
- An osteopathic physician in Michigan criminally convicted of billing Medicaid and Blue Cross Blue Shield for two sleep studies when only one study was performed.
- A home health aide in Washington criminally convicted for billing DSHS for in-home care services three months after the Medicaid recipient had died.
- A home health aide in Pennsylvania criminally convicted of taking money from a patient's checking account without his knowledge or permission.
- A nurse aide in Iowa criminally convicted for pushing an 83-year-old patient as he attempted to stand in the shower. The patient missed his chair and fell, re-wounding his buttocks and causing bleeding.
- A dentist in Maryland criminally convicted of routinely billing Medicaid for services that were not performed. The dentist billed for hundreds of x-rays that were not taken and for complex dental procedures when simple ones were really performed.
- A physician in Alaska criminally convicted of theft, misconduct involving controlled substances, and sexual assault.
- A registered nurse in Arkansas criminally convicted of taking and using a patient's narcotic medications.

§ 7.55 Healthcare Integrity and Protection Data Bank (HIPDB)

The National Healthcare Integrity and Protection Data Bank was established by the Health Insurance Portability and Accountability Act of 1996 (HIPAA) to combat fraud and abuse in health insurance and health care delivery. The HIPDB contains information regarding civil judgments, criminal convictions, or actions by federal or state licensing agencies against a health care provider, supplier, or practitioner related to the delivery of a health care item or service. Reporting began on

November 22, 1999. Both the HIPDB and the NPDB are operated by the same governmental agency and share a joint Web site (*www.npdb-hipdb.gov*).

§ 7.56   —Reporting Requirements and Information Sources

Information in the HIPDB consists of the following:

- Civil judgments (with the exception of malpractice judgments) against health care providers, suppliers, and practitioners in federal or state courts related to the delivery of a health care item or service
- Federal or state criminal convictions against health care providers, suppliers, and practitioners in federal or state courts related to the delivery of a health care item or service
- Actions by federal or state agencies responsible for the licensing and certification of health care providers, suppliers, and practitioners
- Exclusion of health care providers, suppliers, and practitioners from participation in federal or state health care programs
- Adverse licensure actions from August 21, 1996 through present.

Information in this data bank originates from several sources:

- State and federal law enforcement organizations
- State and federal agencies responsible for licensing or certifying any type of health care practitioner, provider, or supplier
- Federal agencies that administer or provide payment for health care
- Private health plan (any group, organization, or company providing health benefits whether directly or indirectly through insurance, reimbursements, or otherwise. This includes insurance agents, brokers, solicitors, consultants and reinsurance intermediaries, insurance companies, self-insured employers, and health care purchasing groups).

§ 7.57   —Access is Limited

Access to this information is strictly limited by the statute and, as with the NPDB, the general public is precluded from accessing the data bank information. Only the governmental agencies and private health plans that are required to report to the data bank are authorized to obtain data bank information. Subjects of reports may obtain access to their own report. Information in the HIPDB is confidential and must be provided and used in a manner consistent with protecting confidentiality. Persons and organizations receiving data bank information, either directly or indirectly, must use it "solely" for the purpose for which it was disclosed. HIPDB information may be requested for privileging and employment, professional review, licensing, certification or registration, fraud and abuse investigations, certification to participate in a government program, and civil and administrative actions. Because the HIPDB does not contain information pertaining to medical malpractice payments, this Data Bank does not meet the conditions outlined above and may not be accessed by plaintiffs' attorneys.

Defense attorneys are not permitted access to the NPDB under Title IV or to the HIPDB because the defendant practitioner is permitted to self-query the Data Banks. Specific procedures for attorney requests are identified in the Fact Sheet for Attorneys.

FORM 7-1
FORMAT FOR INITIAL CLIENT INTERVIEW
General Information
Personal

- Full name
- Other names used and when
- Address (current and past five years)
- Telephone number, facsimile, email
- Name of parent or guardian (if minor)
- Name and address of conservator (if incapacitated person)
- Marital status
- Spouse's name(s) and date(s) of marriage
- Children's name(s) and age(s)
- Name, address, phone number of person who will always know client's location
- Social Security number
- Date and place of birth
- Driver's license number and restrictions
- Felony or misdemeanor conviction(s)
- Education—high school through graduate or technical training
- Prior claims and lawsuits—circumstances, names of parties, names of attorneys, case names and numbers, resolution

Employment

- Military service and dates, type of discharge received
- Current employer, address, and phone number
- Date employment started
- Position, job description, responsibilities, and duties
- Employer information for five years prior to incident
- Wages and benefits
- Supervisor identification

Accident or incident (act or omission)

- When incident occurred
- Identification of each party involved (including address and phone number)
- Content of conversations with parties
- Location of incident
- Description of incident or conduct

- Identification of each medication (prescription or otherwise), drug, or alcohol consumed in 24 hours prior to incident
- Identification of each witness (name, address, phone, and specific location at site)
- Content of conversations with witnesses
- Comments made by any party or witness at scene
- Location and description of any statements, incident reports, photographs, videotapes, diagrams
- Connection of accident, if any, to employment
- Contact with insurance company regarding accident
- Contact with investigator regarding incident
- Identification of any statements given
- Media reports

Injuries

- Loss of consciousness or shock
- Immediate first aid administered
- Description of injuries sustained and treatment (chronological)
- Complete description of all health-care providers: name; address; phone number; dates and type of service provided, i.e. ambulance; physician; hospital; clinic; psychologist; dentist; radiologic or other diagnostic service; nursing; physical, speech, or occupational therapy, vocational rehabilitation; pharmacy; skilled nursing facility
- Diagnostic testing (laboratory work, x-rays, CT scans, MRI, etc.)
- Medications taken since accident
- Psychological or psychiatric counseling
- Home care required (name, address, and phone number; dates of service; types of service)
- Length of time bedridden
- Medical equipment (description, provider, and costs)
- Period of disability
- Current physical and mental condition
- Description of permanent disability, disfigurement, or psychological disability
- Necessary structural changes to residence to accommodate disability (description, name of contractor, cost)
- Prognosis
- Future health-care/treatment required (name of provider recommending care, approximate time frame and cost)
- Prior health-care providers (at least 10 years prior to incident)
- Prior accidents or industrial injuries
- Prior complaints of a similar nature

Insurance coverage

- Type of policy (homeowners, business, automobile, umbrella, errors and omissions)
- For each applicable policy: insurance company, address, policy number, policy limits, location of policy
- Knowledge of reservation or rights or policy dispute
- For health or disability policies: insurance company, policy number, right of reimbursement, current location of policy

Medical and related expenses

- All medical expenses incurred (ambulance, physician, hospital, clinic, diagnostic studies, medication, durable medical equipment, etc.)
- Copies of medical bills
- Use of Medicare or Medicaid benefits
- Incidental costs related to medical care (travel, hotel, car rental, mileage, parking, tolls)
- Home care costs
- Assistance required for household (cleaning, shopping, childcare, other): type of assistance, name and address of provider, type of service provided, length of time services required, total costs, receipts

Loss of income/earning capacity

- Employer at time of incident
- Name of supervisor
- Position at time of incident
- Duties
- Date employment began
- Special education or training required for position
- Length of time with company
- Salary and benefits at time of incident
- Salary and benefit changes since incident
- Number of hours worked per week (regular and overtime) at time of incident
- Overtime hours during year prior to incident
- Expectations regarding promotion
- If terminated, date and reason for termination
- Dates off work due to incident
- Impact on job, if any, from incident including accommodations made to work place and hours of work
- Employment history for at least five years prior to incident
- Eligibility for disability or unemployment benefits
- Disability or unemployment benefits applied for and received

Other economic damages

- Consequential damages: repair, replacement, or cleaning costs; rental expenses
- Loss in real or personal property value
- Fees for and description of services
- Vocational rehabilitation expenses

Non-economic damages

- Description of damage to personal or business reputation; humiliation suffered; loss of consortium
- Loss of use and enjoyment of property
- Potential future health risks (identify physician or other medical provider with knowledge)
- Fear related to future health risks

Special Categories

Animals

- Description of animal
- Name and address of owner of animal
- Where incident occurred
- Description of incident including any provocation, whether animal was on leash, enclosed in a cage or fence, or under control of a person
- Previous incidents and warnings
- Status of vaccinations

Motor vehicle accident

- Date, day of week, time of accident
- Police on scene, accident report prepared, citations issued, police opinion as to fault and reason for fault
- Name, address, and phone number of each driver involved
- If driver not registered owner, identify person giving permission to driver, including address and phone number
- Name, address, and phone number of each registered owner of each vehicle involved
- License plate numbers for all vehicles involved
- Name, address, and phone number of pedestrian or bicyclist involved
- Insurance information for each involved party (and vehicle owner, if different)
- Identification of all passengers in each vehicle; name, address, and phone number; location in vehicle

- Whether vehicle use was personal or related to employment
- Injuries sustained by all other persons involved
- Alcohol or drug use during 24 hours prior to accident
- Physical or mental disabilities at time of accident
- Use of seat belts while operating or riding in vehicle; presence of bruising or abrasions from seat belt use
- Deployment of air bags, injuries as a result of deployment
- Use of cellular phone while operating or riding in vehicle
- Description of each vehicle involved
- Modifications to standard vehicle equipment (prior to incident) with identification of specific modification, dates completed, person(s) completing modification
- Recent repairs to vehicle and name of repair service; location of operation and repair records, service and repair records
- Use of headlights or turn signals
- Observation of brake lights
- Defects or malfunctions in any of the involved vehicles
- Previous motor vehicle accidents
- Weather and road conditions
- Lighting (natural light, streetlights, lights from surrounding buildings)
- Traffic conditions
- Traffic controls and speed limit
- Street construction, repair work, or obstruction in immediate area
- Description of scene at the time of the accident, including: number of traffic lanes; type of lane markers; traffic signs and signals; warning or caution signs, markers, barriers; road condition signs; pedestrian crosswalks and signals; pavement surface; terrain, curves; sight distance limitations; type of area—rural, residential, business, etc.; buildings in immediate area
- When other party first sighted (vehicle, pedestrian, cyclist)
- Intended destination and route taken
- Activities in vehicle just prior to incident (talking on phone, viewing videos, argument, changing CD or radio station, etc.)
- Direction each party traveling
- Evasive action taken by any party
- Estimated speed of each vehicle
- Point of impact
- Point of rest of each vehicle, person, or bicycle
- Skid marks, gouges, and debris
- Damage to each vehicle involved, repairs performed, total cost of repairs, estimates and receipts
- Current location of each vehicle involved
- Repair of vehicles: estimates, cost, location of documentation

- Personal property damaged, value of property
- Payments received from any insurance carrier

Premises liability

- Owner of subject property
- Rental or lease agreement
- Current monthly rent
- Date moved in
- Name and address of property manager
- Description of unsafe or defective condition
- Date unsafe or defective condition first noticed
- Complaints made regarding subject condition
- Person/entity to whom each complaint made
- Date of each complaint
- Response to each complaint; maintenance or repairs performed as a result
- Exterior incident: weather, lighting, physical conditions
- Slip or trip and fall: shoes worn, clothing, lighting, physical conditions, foreign substance or object on surface, familiarity with location, route taken
- Construction site incident: name and address of contractor, name and address of each subcontractor, description of construction site, OSHA inspections and citations

Product liability

- Description of product involved: model, year, serial number, size
- Description of how and where product was used
- Purpose of product
- Where and when product obtained
- Manufacturer of product
- Current location of product
- Description of product defect
- Training received on use of product
- Prior use and problems with product
- Prior maintenance or repair of product: identification of repair, warranty, cost
- Warnings on product: labels, brochure, consumer use information
- Safety standards associated with product
- Location of: maintenance and repair records, warranties, use and repair manuals, brochures or advertisements, warnings
- Photographs of product

Professional malpractice

- Description of relationship
- Dates of relationship, chronology of relationship
- Agreements involved
- Identification of parties to each agreement
- Location of written contract
- Services performed
- Identity and location of any executed release or consent form
- Identity and location of pertinent files
- Arbitration or mediation agreement
- License, board certification, registration held by professional

Professional malpractice—medical

- Condition for which the medical practitioner was seen
- Treatment given for condition
- Procedures performed by the medical practitioner
- Facility in which treatment was provided
- Discussions regarding consent for treatment
- Discussions regarding risks of procedure, side effects of medication
- Staff members or employees on duty at the time consent for subject treatment was obtained, subject treatment given or procedure performed, follow-up care that was provided
- How often seen by the medical practitioner
- Length of each visit
- All health or psychological care providers involved in treatment at time malpractice committed and subsequent to injury
- Recommendations of any other health-care provider seen before the incident regarding the same condition
- Statement(s) made as to possible malpractice: date, identification of speaker, content of statement(s)
- Opinions expressed by any medical practitioner as to: whether or not correct procedures used, prognosis, future medical treatment
- Names and addresses of authorities in the field
- All collateral source benefits for which eligible: health insurance, workers compensation
- Social Security or state disability, veterans' benefits, private disability insurance

Toxic tort liability

- Address of real property involved
- Name, address, and phone number of each owner

- Business involved
- Identification of each prior owner
- Description of current property use
- History of property use
- Current permits or licenses
- Clean-up or abatement orders, citations or cease and desist orders
- Type of contamination
- Duration of problem
- Public agencies involved
- Estimated clean-up costs
- Anticipated duration of clean-up and required date of completion
- Injuries: current physical injuries, anticipated future health problems
- Agreements involved and parties to agreements

FORM 7–2
**SAMPLE HIPAA-COMPLIANT AUTHORIZATION FOR
DISCLOSURE OF PATIENT HEALTH INFORMATION**

I hereby authorize:

NAME OF DISCLOSING PARTY (*e.g., medical provider*)

_____

_____

ADDRESS

_____

_____

CITY _____ STATE _____ ZIP _____

To disclose to:

NAME OF RECEIVING PARTY (*e.g., attorney*)

_____

_____

ADDRESS

_____

_____

CITY _____ STATE _____ ZIP _____

Records and information pertaining to:

NAME OF PATIENT   DOB

_____   _____

SSN   MEDICAL RECORD NUMBER

_____   _____

DURATION: This authorization shall become effective immediately and shall remain in effect for one year from the date of signature.

REVOCATION: This authorization is also subject to written revocation by the undersigned at any time between now and the disclosure of information by the disclosing party. The written revocation will be effective upon receipt, but will not be effective to the extent that the requester or others have acted in reliance upon this authorization.

REDISCLOSURE: I understand that the requester may not lawfully further use or disclose the health information unless another authorization is obtained from me or unless such use of disclosure is specifically required or permitted by law.

SPECIFY RECORDS: Check the box and initial to specify which type of information is to be disclosed.

_____ Medical information _____ Psychiatric/psychological information

_____ Drug/Alcohol information _____ Results of an HIV blood test

_____ Other health information (specify below)

The requester may use the health information authorized on this form for the following purposes only:

_____

Date:_____   Signature: _____

                               Print Name: _____

Relationship to Patient: _____

Practice Note: Suggested language is given below for use in describing the requested records:

Medical records (generally): "Any and all documents and records, and itemized statements of all billing charges pertaining to the medical and nursing care, treatment, and examination of _____ for the period _____. The records requested include but are not limited to all pre-hospital emergency records, office charts, emergency room and hospital inpatient charts, hospital and clinic outpatient charts, admission sheets, history and physical examinations, diagnoses, consultations, laboratory and radiology reports, photographs, videotapes, and any other documents or things that may be in your possession or under your control.

Medical records (psychiatric, drug, alcohol or substance abuse treatment): Any and all confidential documents, records, and itemized statements of all billing charges pertaining to the care, treatment and examination of _____ for the period _____. The records requested are those concerning all [psychiatric, drug, alcohol or substance abuse] treatment, counseling or rehabilitation records that may be in your possession or under your control.

Medical records (HIV/AIDS): Any and all documents and records, and itemized statements of all billing charges pertaining to the medical and nursing care, treatment, and examination of _____ for the period _____.

The records requested include but are not limited to all pre-hospital emergency records, office charts, emergency room and hospital inpatient charts, hospital and clinic outpatient charts, admission sheets, history and physical examinations, diagnoses, consultations, laboratory and radiology reports, photographs, videotapes, and any other documents or things that may be in your possession or under your control concerning treatment rendered for HIV (human immunodeficiency virus) or AIDS (acquired immune deficiency syndrome).

FORM 7–3
CERTIFICATE OF HIPAA-SATISFACTORY ASSURANCES

(This Certification must by completed fully and signed by an attorney to be valid)

_____	_____
(Case Name)	(Docket Number)
_____	_____
(Patient Name)	(Patient medical record/account number)

CERTIFICATION

I hereby certify that the representations below are true and correct based upon my personal knowledge; that I have reviewed the applicable privacy regulations of the Health Insurance Portability and Accountability Act of 1996 (HIPAA), 45 C.F.R. Parts 160 and 164; that I have complied with the regulations and its requirements to obtain patient health information; and that I will comply with State and Federal privacy laws as to any patient health information that I receive. I further certify the following:

1. I have used reasonable efforts and made a good faith attempt to notify the patient or his/her personal representative in writing by serving written notice of my intent to obtain the patient's health information to the patient or his/her personal representative at this address: _____ (Or if patient's location is unknown, to mail a notice to the patient's last known address listed above) by (Delivery Method—mail, fax, etc.) on _____ (Date).
2. This written notice provided sufficient information about this litigation or proceeding in which the patient health information is requested to permit the patient or his/her personal representative to raise objections in the appropriate court or administrative tribunal within the required time under Fla. R. Civ. P. 1.351 or other applicable rule from the date of service of the notice of intent.
3. The deadline for the patient or his/her personal representative to object to the notice of intent under Fla. R. Civ. P. 1.351 or other applicable rule was set forth in the notice, which indicated that the deadline expired on _____ (Date).
4. Objections (must initial one):
_____ A. Patient or his/her personal representative did not file any objections.
OR
_____ B. Patient or his/her personal representative filed objections with the court or administrative tribunal; the objections have been resolved by the court or administrative tribunal; there are no further objections pending or

requiring resolution; and the disclosures of patient health information being sought are consistent with such resolution(s).

5. This certification is not being submitted to obtain mental health records, HIV test results, or substance abuse records.

6. I have attached the subpoena or other lawful process, and the notice of intent, with this certification.

_____   _____   _____
Signature of Attorney   State Bar Number   Date

(Must bear signature of attorney only)

_____   _____   _____
Print Name of Attorney   Attorney Phone Number   Party Represented

Practice Note: The Authorization example in **Form 7–3** is based on Florida law, and illustrates how one state has taken HIPAA requirements and blended them with Florida law, illustrating one of the many state-specific forms that have been developed since HIPAA came on the scene. Always check your own state's requirements for authorizations and release requirements.

FORM 7–4
SAMPLE WRITTEN REQUEST FOR MEDICAL RECORDS

[date]

Custodian of Records
[name of hospital or provider]
[address of provider]

      Re: [full name of patient]
      Date of Birth: _____
      Medical Records Number: (*if known*)
      SSN: _____

Dear Custodian of Records:

    Enclosed you will find a HIPAA-Compliant Authorization for Release of Medical Information directed to your attention and executed by our client [name of client]. Please make a copy of your entire chart, including billing information, and forward it to us at the above address.

    If you will enclose a bill for your reasonable expenses in providing these copies, we will be happy to forward that sum promptly. Thank you in advance for your prompt attention to this request.

                      Sincerely,
                      [signature of requester]

cc: client
encl: Authorization

FORM 7–5
SAMPLE STIPULATION FOR PROTECTED HEALTH INFORMATION

DAVID F. BEACH (SBN 127135)
LAW OFFICES OF DAVID F. BEACH, P.C.
100 Stony Point Road, Suite 185
Santa Rosa, California 95401
Telephone (707) 547-1690
Facsimile (707) 547-1694

Attorneys for Plaintiff

SUPERIOR COURT OF CALIFORNIA, COUNTY OF SAN FRANCISCO

JOHN Q. PUBLIC,	Case Number: 1234567
Plaintiff,	**STIPULATION RE PROTECTED HEALTH INFORMATION**
vs.	45 C.F.R § 164.512(e)(B)
MARY DOE, and ROES 1 through 50, inclusive,	
Defendants.	

_____/

The parties to this action, through their respective counsel of record, do hereby stipulate to the following:

1. The medical records [*Protected health information*] concerning plaintiff John Q. Public will be produced pursuant to [*subpoena*] [*request for production*] [*other discovery device*] on or before _____ [*date*] from the following covered entities:

First Responder Ambulance Company

County Hospital

William Intensivist, M.D.

James Neurologist, M.D.

Feel Good Chiropractic Office

2. The records to be produced concern treatment rendered to Plaintiff John Q. Public as a result of the motor vehicle accident which occurred on August 1, 2006, and which is the subject of this litigation.

3. Medical records will be produced for the time period of August 1, 2000 to present.

4. The parties agree that they are prohibited from using or disclosing the protected health information for any purpose other than the litigation for which such information is being requested.

5. The parties further agree that the protected health information must either be returned to the covered entity or destroyed at the end of the litigation.

SO STIPULATED.

Dated _____   LAW OFFICERS OF DAVID F. BEACH, P.C.

                           By:_____
                                   DAVID F. BEACH
                                 Attorneys for Plaintiff

Dated _____   LAW OFFICERS OF PERRY MASON, L.L.C.

                           By:_____
                                   PERRY MASON
                                 Attorneys for Defendant

FORM 7–6
SAMPLE FEDERAL SUBPOENA
United States District Court

_____ **District of** _____

DEPOSITION SUBPOENA

PLAINTIFF V. DEFENDANT(S)

CASE NUMBER: 0000000

TYPE OF CASE	SUBPOENA FOR
☒ CIVIL ☐ CRIMINAL	☐ PERSON ☒ DOCUMENT(S) or OBJECT(S)

TO: [NAME AND ADDRESS OF DEPONENT]

YOU ARE HEREBY COMMANDED to appear at the place, date, and time specified below to testify at the taking of a deposition in the above case.

PLACE	DATE AND TIME
[NAME OF DEPOSITION OFFICER, USUALLY A COPY SERVICE]	[DATE AND TIME RECORDS ARE TO BE PRODUCED TO DEPOSITION OFFICER

YOU ARE ALSO COMMANDED to bring with you the following document(s) or object(s):*

[FOR EXAMPLE: All medical records, papers, files, examination notes, including but not limited to x-ray reports, consultation, inpatient and outpatient hospitalization, or emergency room records, medical billings and statements for any and all times whatsoever pertaining to:

NAME OF PATIENT WITH IDENTIFYING INFORMATION]

☐ _Please see additional information on reverse_

Any subpoenaed organization not a party to this suit is hereby admonished pursuant to Rule 30(b)(6), Federal Rules of Civil Procedure, to file a designation with the court specifying one or more officers, directors, or managing agents, or other persons who consent to testify on its behalf, and setting forth, for each person designated, the matters on which he will testify or produce documents or things. The persons so designated shall testify as to matters known or reasonably available to the organization.

U.S. MAGISTRATE OR CLERK OF COURT	DATE
[NAME OF ISSUING CLERK]	
(BY) DEPUTY CLERK	
[SEAL OF THE COURT IMPRINTED HERE]	

This subpoena is issued upon application of the:	QUESTIONS MAY BE ADDRESSED TO:
☐ Plaintiff ☐ Defendant ☐ U.S. Attorney [INDICATE REQUESTING ATTORNEY]	[NAME, ADDRESS, AND PHONE NUMBER OF REQUESTING ATTORNEY] ATTORNEY'S NAME, ADDRESS, AND PHONE NUMBER

*If not applicable, enter "none."

FORM 7-7
SAMPLE CALIFORNIA SUBPOENA

The California subpoena *duces tecum* in **Form 7-7** differs from the federal form only in that it can be issued by an attorney of record as well as by the clerk of the court.

ATTORNEY OR PARTY WITHOUT ATTORNEY *(Name and Address):* TELEPHONE NO.:	CASE NUMBER:
[NAME OF FIRM ISSUING SUBPOENA] ATTORNEY FOR *(Name):* [NAME OF CLIENT]	
NAME OF COURT: POST OFFICE and STREET ADDRESS:	**DEPOSITION SUBPOENA**
PLAINTIFF/PETITIONER: DEFENDANT/RESPONDENT:	**For Production of Business Records**

THE PEOPLE OF THE STATE OF CALIFORNIA, TO *(name)*:

[NAME OF DEPONENT (ENTITY FROM WHOM RECORDS ARE BEING REQUESTED)]

1. **YOU ARE ORDERED TO PRODUCE THE BUSINESS RECORDS described in item 3 as follows:**

Deposition Officer *(name):* [NAME OF DEPOSITION OFFICER, USUALLY A COPY SERVICE]
Date: [MUST BE GIVEN]   Time: [MUST BE GIVEN]
Address:

    a. ☐ by delivering a true, legible, and durable copy of the business records described in item 3, enclosed in a sealed inner wrapper with the title and number of the action, name of witness, and date of subpoena clearly written on it. The inner wrapper shall then be enclosed in an outer envelope or wrapper, sealed, and mailed to the deposition officer at the address in item 1.

    b. ☐ by delivering a true, legible, and durable copy of the business records described in item 3 to the deposition officer at the witness's address, on receipt of payment in cash or by check of the reasonable costs of preparing the copy, as determined under Evidence Code section 1563(b).

   c. ☐ by making the original business records described in item 3 available for inspection at your business address by the attorney's representative and permitting copying at your business address under reasonable conditions during normal business hours.

2. *The records are to be produced by the date and time shown in item 1 but not sooner than 20 days after the issuance of the deposition subpoena, or 15 days after service, whichever date is later. Reasonable costs of locating records, making them available or copying them, and postage, if any, are recoverable as set forth in Evidence Code section 1563(b). The records shall be accompanied by an affidavit of the custodian or other qualified witness pursuant to Evidence Code section 1561.*

3. The records to be produced are described as follows:

   [FOR EXAMPLE: All medical records, papers, files, examination notes, including but not limited to x-ray reports, consultation, inpatient or outpatient hospitalization, or emergency room records, medical billings, and statements for any and all times whatsoever pertaining to:

   NAME OF PATIENT (ONE OF THE PARTIES TO THE LAWSUIT)]

   ☐ Continued on attachment 3.

DISOBEDIENCE OF THIS SUBPOENA MAY BE PUNISHED AS CONTEMPT BY THIS COURT. YOU WILL ALSO BE LIABLE FOR THE SUM OF FIVE HUNDRED DOLLARS AND ALL DAMAGES RESULTING FROM YOUR FAILURE TO OBEY.

Date issued:

NAME OF ATTORNEY ISSUING SUBPOENA
(TYPE OR PRINT NAME)   ▶ _____
            (SIGNATURE OF PERSON ISSUING SUBPOENA)

           _____
               (TITLE)
    (See reverse for proof of service)

FORM 7–8
SAMPLE REQUEST FOR REPORT BY TREATING PHYSICIAN

[Date]

Name & Address of Physician

    Re: Name of client/patient
         ID litigation if appropriate

Dear Dr. _____:

    We represent [name of client] for injuries sustained in a [type of accident] which occurred on [date of loss]. My client has advised me that you have been treating [him/her] for these injuries.

    Please prepare a report (billing me, of course, for the cost) setting forth the following:

1. When did you first see the client?
2. What history was given to you at that time?
3. Was there any significant past history?
4. What were your findings at the time of the first examination?
5. What was your plan of treatment at that time?
6. Did you prescribe (or suggest) that the client be off work for a period of time? If so, for how long?
7. When was the last time you examined the client and what was the client's condition at that time?
8. What was your prognosis at the time of the first visit and the last?
9. Do you anticipate that the client will need additional medical care and/or possible surgery?
10. Is the current condition permanent and stationary?
11. Is this condition related in whole or in part to the accident of [date]?

    I am enclosing a HIPAA-compliant authorization signed by my client, which authorizes you to furnish me with this information. I look forward to hearing from you soon.

                      Very truly yours,
                      [signature of attorney]

cc: client
encl: authorization

CHAPTER 8

SUMMARIZING MEDICAL RECORDS

§ 8.1   Purpose of Medical Record Summaries

The primary reason for summarizing medical records is to provide a succinct and objective account of injuries suffered and/or the events surrounding an act or accident as documented in the injured party's medical records. It is much simpler to utilize well-prepared summaries of a record than to wade through pages and pages of medical documentation in order to locate the key information needed to prepare the case.

In addition to this most obvious purpose, there are other, equally important ones. Because the medical record is the cornerstone in medical malpractice and personal injury cases, it will be used by both the plaintiff and the defense throughout the course of litigation. The plaintiff will use the medical record to gather evidence to substantiate claims of damage and malpractice. The defense will use the same record to refute these claims. The medical record will also be reviewed (hopefully by both sides) for evidence of other, prior injuries or conditions or to locate evidence of alternative causation for the subject injuries.

Another significant purpose for a well thought out medical record summary is to educate the reader about the nature of the injuries, the treatment proposed and completed, the residuals of any treatment, and the prognosis or future course of recovery. While specific in-depth discussions of the injury and/or disease, and the potential outcomes are generated by consultants and expert witnesses, the medical record summary is an excellent forum for educating both the attorney who will use the information found in the medical records and ultimately anyone who will take part in the resolution of the case (e.g., insurance adjustors, mediators, opposing counsel, jury members, and judges).

§ 8.2   Use of Summaries

Medical record summaries are used in a variety of ways. Initially, they are used to evaluate a potential client's claim or to determine the extent of a plaintiff's injuries. At a later point in time, they can be used to prove or disprove claims made by the litigant.

The medical record summaries will provide the plaintiff's attorney with a road map to chart the extent of the client's injury and recovery progress. When used by defense counsel, record summaries are often forwarded to the insurance carrier, which also monitors the progress and/or status of a claimant. It is more economical and much simpler to provide succinct accounts of the records' contents than to send a copy of the entire record itself.

§ 8.3   Role of Legal Professionals in Reviewing Records

The medical record reviewer's role is akin to that of an historian. As the records are reviewed, the most significant portions are presented in the summary, based upon the reviewer's knowledge of the facts and issues of a case. As each record is summarized, a history of the injured party's pre-accident and post-accident medical status is revealed. This history will then be used throughout the duration of the litigation.

Practice Note: It is important to remember that unless you have specific medical training, your role is not to interpret the quality of medical care received by the injured party. As a reviewer, you are only documenting the information as it appears in the record.

§ 8.4   Paralegals as Reviewers

The economic advantages of using a paralegal to review medical records are evident. Although attorneys can and do review and summarize medical records, it makes better economic sense for the attorney to allow a paralegal, well-trained in medical records review, to perform this vital function (at a lower hourly rate) than to spend the many hours needed to review the record firsthand. A paralegal well-versed in the intricacies of the medical record provides an invaluable service this way, by allowing the attorney to concentrate on other aspects of the case, a service that becomes more essential with the increased skill and competency of the paralegal.

§ 8.5   Preparing to Review Records

It is important to ensure that the summary contains all significant data from the record. Determining what is significant should be based upon the issues involved in the case.

It is possible to pick up a set of records, review them, and provide adequate summaries without knowing the issues. However, it is also possible to miss the most significant information contained in the record or to include superfluous and ultimately unimportant data. Therefore, the reviewer should have a good understanding of the specific issues of the case. What injuries are alleged by plaintiff? What claims are being made? With this information, the reviewer will be able to distill the most significant information from the records.

In preparation, reviewing the file material before starting the review of the medical records. Read the complaint and any discovery that has been completed. It is very important for the paralegal to spend some time discussing the case with the attorney. The attorney can summarize the background of the case and will indicate if certain information is significant.

Practice Note: As part of the preparation of a case, plaintiff's counsel should have a solid understanding of their client's preexisting medical history. This should be obtained in the initial and subsequent client interviews. (See **Chapter 7, §§ 7.2–7.3,** and **Form 7–1** for a discussion of the initial client interview process.) If the client has been involved in prior accidents or suffers from a preexisting medical condition, all relevant records must be obtained. Be assured that the defense will subpoena these records. The costs involved in litigation are an important factor to consider, but even more important are the costs to counsel down the road when defense obtains the medical history that the plaintiff should have gotten initially!

§ 8.6 Initial Steps

Stating the obvious, don't start the review process until all of the known records have been obtained, either through authorization or subpoena. Working through the records piecemeal as they arrive takes one of the most important tools out of your toolbox; the ability to see and make connections from one provider to another, from one incident to another, from one action to another.

One of the most frequently asked questions is, "Is it necessary to read the entire record in order to summarize it?" The answer simply is "yes." Although much of the record may not be germane to the case (for example, reviewing lab reports, intake and output charts, and so on for a simple slip and fall), significant evidence can be located in obscure portions of the record, evidence that might have an impact on the case. For example, evidence of a patient's blood alcohol level is considered to be privileged information in many states. The custodian of records will often redact (remove or edit) this data from the chart prior to producing it. However, if the custodian fails to read the entire chart, the information will probably be repeated in the lab results section, in the nurses' notes, and often in consultations by other physicians. In other words, it pays for the reviewer to be thorough.

As the record is reviewed, use Post-Its® or other self-sticking notes to mark significant entries that should appear in the summary, indicating the date of the entry. After the entire record has been reviewed, these marked notations can be organized into the actual summary. Prepare summaries in chronological order, even if the records are not. The goal is to provide a readable document and to be as orderly as possible.

For voluminous records, it may be advisable to prepare an index of the records prior to beginning the summary. Often, information from different parts of the chart will be brought together to form the summary for a particular period of time. If you are working from an index of the records, it will be much easier to go directly to the location in the record when preparing the summary.

§ 8.7 Contents of a Summary

A record summary should always contain certain basic categories of information, as discussed below. Cases involving complex medical or psychological issues are never cut and dried. Issues that were thought to be inconsequential when the records were first reviewed can take on great importance after a deposition or other discovery is completed. Conversely, issues that were thought to be most important can fade as the case moves through discovery. Be prepared to revisit and revise your summaries in complex cases.

The summary should include, among other things, the following categories of information concerning the injured party (plaintiff):

_____ Subjective description of the incident
_____ Subjective description of current condition
_____ Medical provider's visual assessment of the injured party
_____ Medical history of the injured party
_____ Medical provider's physical examination
_____ Medical provider's assessment, clinical impression, or diagnosis
_____ Course of treatment prescribed, further treatment, surgery, medication, etc.
_____ Injured party's response to treatment
_____ Evidence of noncompliance
_____ Medical provider's prognosis
_____ Knowledge of malpractice
_____ Any information supporting or refuting plaintiff's allegations.

Practice Note: When reviewing records, "keep your antennae out." Be aware of inconsistencies in the complaints made by your client (or the plaintiff) and the medical records and examination as performed by the physician or other medical professional. For example, the plaintiff states that he is unable to turn his neck completely to the left, yet the orthopedic examination shows him to have, full and complete cervical range of motion. This inconsistency should be noted and investigated. The ability to spot inconsistencies in the record or to pick up on areas that should be investigated more fully is further reason why your summary should not begin until you have all (or as many as possible) of the known records in your possession.

§ 8.8 —Subjective Description of the Incident

Information regarding the incident is often given to and recorded by first responders and emergency department personnel when taking the patient's medical history. The information can often be found on a patient history or information form that is filled out at a private practitioner's office during the first visit.

Subjective accounts can be important when the specifics of the incident are in question. For example, if the medical record shows that an individual offered a different version of the incident to each provider, list those statements as they appear in the records. This information can, and will be, used during deposition by the defense to impeach a plaintiff's credibility. Better the client's attorney have this information in hand, than to be surprised at deposition.

§ 8.9 —Subjective Description of Current Condition

When a physician performs a complete examination of a patient, a portion of the exam will cover the individual's opinion of his or her current state of health. This description can reveal how the illness or injury has affected the person's lifestyle and ability to function on a day-to-day basis.

§ 8.10 —Provider's Visual Assessment

Visual assessment is an extremely important part of the examination. Physicians can make observations regarding the patient based on their experience and training. Watching the patient climb on the examining table, walk across the room, sit down, or stand up offers clues as to the physical condition of the patient. Physicians are also alert to body language that may indicate the presence (or absence) of pain—facial grimace, specific types of gait, and so forth.

§ 8.11 —Medical History

During the course of the interview, the provider will explore the patient's medical history. Have there been previous complaints or conditions similar to this one? Has the patient been hospitalized or undergone surgery of any kind? What is the patient's family history regarding disease, inherited conditions, and so on? Has the patient been involved in any automobile accidents? Is the individual allergic to any medications or using drugs or alcohol? This type of information allows the provider to make an informed diagnosis and plan further care, and assists the attorney in evaluating a case.

§ 8.12   —Current Complaints

How has this illness or accident affected the patient's lifestyle and ability to function on a daily basis? Is there pain and discomfort with only certain activities or in all phases of day-to-day life? How has the individual's life changed to meet any physical restrictions? This type of information is significant both to the health care provider and the legal professional reviewing the records.

§ 8.13   —Physical Examination

The physical examination portion of the record usually consists of a complete review of the patient's body systems. A review of these systems might be recorded as follows, with normal or abnormal findings documented:

General: Description of the patient, for example, "WDWNWM" (well-developed, well-nourished white male).

HEENT: Examination of the head, eyes, ears, nose, and throat.

Neck: Examined for suppleness, restrictions in range of motion (ROM), presence and strength of carotid pulse, and size of thyroid.

Chest: Examination of the cardiovascular and pulmonary systems, noting the presence or absence of murmurs, gallops, and rubs, breath sounds and chronic cough.

Abdomen: Examination of the gastrointestinal system and the presence or absence of pain or tenderness.

Musculoskeletal and extremities: Back, neck, and upper and lower extremities are all examined thoroughly. Restrictions in the range of motion, flexion, extension, and lateral movement are noted, along with abnormalities in function and size. Muscle spasms, swelling or tenderness to palpation are indicated.

Skin: Examined for color, warmth, and turgor (normal tension), and the presence of distension, swelling, redness, bruising, ulceration.

Neurology: The nerves are tested for function and response.

Mental status: Remarks are entered if abnormal or questionable thought processes are observed during the examination.

Practice Note: Providers often use the acronym *SOAP* to outline the physical examination. This medical shorthand refers to the patient's subjective description of his or her condition *(S)*, the provider's objective observation and examination *(O)*, assessment or diagnosis *(A)*, and plan for treatment *(P)*.

§ 8.14   —Diagnosis or Impression

In this section of the examination, the provider sets forth all of his or her diagnostic conclusions or impressions, based upon the complete examination of the patient and results from any accessory clinical data such as X rays, laboratory work, and so on, that have been obtained. This section will also contain what is known as the "differential" diagnosis (sometimes abbreviated DDx or △△) in which the physician lists the most likely causes of the illness. The physician performs tests to eliminate possibilities until he or she is satisfied that the single most likely cause has been identified. Once a working diagnosis is reached, the physician prescribes a therapy. The term differential diagnosis also refers to medical information specially organized to aid in diagnosis, particularly a list of the most common causes of a given symptom.

§ 8.15   —Treatment Plan

The plan for treating the patient can involve laboratory tests, X rays or other forms of diagnostic radiology, medication, physical therapy, surgery, or referral to other providers for consultation. The provider should also note limitations in the patient's activities; for example, one week off work, no lifting objects over 10 pounds, or no weight on affected limb. The patient's follow-up appointments will also be scheduled.

§ 8.16   —Patient Compliance

One overlooked aspect of reviewing medical records revolves around the issue of patient compliance or noncompliance with physician's orders. An individual who has been injured has the duty to mitigate her damages by following the instructions issued by her physician or other medical provider. Failure to comply with treatment orders can severely impact a plaintiff's recovery, in both the physical and legal sense. In a malpractice action for failure to diagnose breast cancer, the plaintiff was found to be 30 percent contributorily negligent for not following her physician's orders. After she first consulted the physician about a lump in her breast, the physician told her to return in six months. She did not return for 15 months at which time the tumor had doubled in size and was found to be malignant. The nine-month delay in returning for follow-up care resulted in a 75 percent loss of her survival expectancy. (*Roers v. Engebretson,* 479 N.W.2d 422 (Minn. Ct. App. 1992.))

When reviewing records, certain areas relating to the patient's treatment can become the focus of questions concerning compliance. Common areas include:

1. Attending all scheduled physician or other medical provider appointments
2. Attending all scheduled treatments (e.g., physical therapy, hospitalizations, occupational therapy, psychiatric sessions)
3. Taking medication(s) as prescribed (e.g., taking all of the medication for the prescribed time)
4. Adhering to dietary restrictions
5. Adhering to orders to stop smoking or drinking
6. Following work restriction recommendations
7. Adhering to home exercise programs
8. Maintaining rest schedule

Look for this information in a treating physician's office charts, records from physical therapists, occupational therapists, and psychologists. Determine what treatment was ordered, the degree to which the patient did or did not follow the provider's orders, and the result of any noncompliance. Results of noncompliance can be shown through objective testing (e.g., physiologic measurements), development of complications, exacerbation of symptoms, or failure to progress.

The reasons for noncompliance *can* be complex, ranging from the patient's spiritual values, health beliefs, and cultural influences to fear or anxiety surrounding the treatment, lack of adequate transportation, or lack of adequate medical insurance. Plaintiff's counsel should explore all of these areas thoroughly with the client.

§ 8.17   —Prognosis

The prognosis is the provider's judgment in advance as to the probable course of the disease or injury, the individual's chances for recovery, and the degree of recovery that can be expected.

§ 8.18   —Knowledge of Malpractice

This is a significant area of the record in medical malpractice cases. Generally speaking, the statute of limitations begin as of the date the plaintiff knew, or "should have known", about the malpractice act or occurrence. Review the record for any indications that the plaintiff was told specifically about the malpractice, or that it was discussed in general terms. This may take the form of subtle comments from the provider about the "unfortunate error" or the recall of a product, etc.

§ 8.19   —Information Supporting/Refuting Allegations

Allegations made in a complaint should be supported by the record. This may not be the case, however, and it is important to determine this. For example, in a skilled nursing facility (SNF) case, the plaintiff may allege actions taken or not taken by the staff which constitute elder abuse, which result in the development of weight loss, dehydration, pressure sores, and physical abuse. Although these allegations appear in many, if not most, SNF litigation cases and may seem to be "boilerplate" in nature, it is imperative that the SNF record be reviewed completely so as to prove or disprove these allegations. For example, the issue of weight loss can be addressed by tracking all of the known weights of the plaintiff, including those taken prior to, during, and after admission to the SNF admission, during, and after. While this information will be included in the summary, it may be useful to "break out" the weights and present them separately. See § 8:29 for a discussion of breakout summaries.

§ 8.20   Types of Summaries

There are as many ways of summarizing medical records as there are types of records. There is no right way to summarize and no wrong way, no defense way and no plaintiff way—there is only the method that works best for the type of case and for the person using the summary. In fact, the way in which the information is presented is limited only by the imagination of the reviewer. However, there are two basic summary formats—narrative and chronological.

Narrative Method

In the *narrative method,* the information from the record is extracted, paraphrased, and placed in a layout that is easy to read; only material crucial to the fact situation appears in the summary. Narrative summaries are often imported wholesale into demand letters, arbitration or mediation briefs, and trial briefs. The summary can be as detailed as necessary, depending on the requirements of the case and the attorney's needs.

Litigation rarely involves only one or two medical providers. As is often the case, the plaintiff has been seen by multiple providers. In a motor vehicle accident, for example, records can be obtained from the first responder/paramedic, emergency room, acute hospital, treating physicians, chiropractor(s), physical therapy, occupational therapy, etc. A true narrative summary would combine all of these records together, starting with the earliest and ending with the most recent treatment. However, some prefer to summarize the records of each provider individually. Again, there is no right way and no wrong way, only the way that works for you. See **Forms 8–1** and **8–2** for examples of narrative summaries.

Chronological Method

A *chronology,* as the name implies, takes the significant medical treatments or events and places them in chronological order within the summary. The information included can be as detailed or as brief as needed. A limited chronology is often prepared after all the individual records have been summarized in detail. This type of chronology can be used when drafting demand letters or in preparation for deposition or trial.

Other Types of Summaries

Working from these basics, the type of summary used can be expanded. Alternative types of summaries include chronological narratives, break-outs, charts, tables, and graphs.

- A *chronological narrative* combines the format of a narrative and a chronology in an expanded fashion.
- *Breakout* summaries are prepared after the initial, formal summary is completed. This type of summary consists of a focused, issue-specific review, and is presented as a chart, table, or chronology.
- Presenting medical information in a *chart* format is a very visual way of highlighting the main points of medical treatment.

§ 8.21   Narrative Summary Method

When using this method, information from the record is paraphrased and presented as a narration. The summary can be as detailed as necessary, depending on the facts of the case and the desires of the attorney.

§ 8.22   —Sample Narrative Summary

SUMMARY OF MEDICAL RECORDS—JOHN DOE
(Current as of September 30, 2005)

COMMUNITY HOSPITAL
(Records current as of 02/15/05)

Plaintiff John Doe was transported via ambulance on **05/23/04** to this facility where he was seen in the E.D. at 6:53 P.M. by Dr. Ben Casey. Dr. Casey noted that Doe was a 28-year-old male riding in the right front seat of an automobile involved in a head-on collision. He was not wearing a seat belt. Doe admitted to cocaine and alcohol use earlier that day and exhibited "bizarre behavior" while being examined, including refusing to answer questions and insisting that he be allowed to wear his sunglasses.

Doe complained of pain in the right hip area with some mild pain in his neck and low back. On examination, no facial or cranial trauma was noted. Minimal tenderness was found over the right lateral cervical spine and the right anterior rib cage and the lumbosacral area generally. Compression of the right pelvis was extremely painful, and he refused to move his right leg due to the pain.

X rays of the pelvis revealed a fracture of the right sacrum. Lumbar spine x rays showed the presence of spondylolisthesis [forward displacement of a vertebra over a lower segment, usually the 4th or 5th, due to a congenital defect]. A drug screen obtained in the E.D. was positive for amphetamine and cocaine. Diagnoses were right sacral fracture, multiple contusions, and drug abuse. After consultation with Dr. Jane Roe, orthopedic surgeon, Doe was admitted to the hospital for observation and treatment. [17–19]

Practice Note: In this example, the words "bizarre behavior" have been put in quotation marks. This is a highly subjective characterization of the individual's behavior and one that was made by the physician, not the reviewer. You must be careful that you do not *interpret* or put your own spin on the record being reviewed.

§ 8.23   —Use of "Current As Of" Date

The notation—"current as of"—on the sample summary in § 8.22 has two separate meanings:

- Placed under the title of the document (or alternatively, as a footnote) it refers to the last time the summary was updated. See discussion in § 8.7 above.
- Placed under the provider's name it refers to the date the records were obtained, either by subpoena or by authorization. If a significant length of time has passed since records were obtained, they may need to be updated to reflect subsequent visits or treatments;

§ 8.24   —Defining Medical Terms

Depending on the medical experience of the individual for whom the summary has been prepared, it may be necessary to define medical terms within the summary. In the sample narrative summary in § 8.22, a definition has been provided for the medical term "spondylolisthesis." Definitions can be placed directly following the term, within the body of the summary, or as a footnote at the bottom of the page.

§ 8.25 —Reference to Page Numbers

Copy services often number the pages of a medical record after it has been copied; a process often referred to as paginating, pagination, or most commonly in the legal field, Bates® numbering. Named after the Bates® automatic numbering machine, numbers are assigned for each page in a document, usually numeric, though they could be alphanumeric, too.

This simple process is invaluable in summarizing medical records, as it allows the reader or person summarizing the record to locate an original entry as referred to in the summary, literally, everyone can be on the same page. Use these page numbers; insert them in brackets following the entry in the summary, as illustrated in § 8.22. In this way, information in the summary can be immediately located in the original record, and most importantly, will never be lost.

Practice Note: If the medical record is received directly from the medical provider, it will generally not be paginated. If there are no prohibitions to the contrary, paginate the record yourself. This can be done by various methods, ranging from the archaic (use of a manual, hand-held numerical stamper) to computerized labels to computer programs that allow you to add pagination to PDF documents.

§ 8.26 Chronological Method

A chronology is simply a list of dates and events placed in order, usually earliest entry to latest. The entries can be less detailed, essentially presenting a description of the event (surgery, treatment, complication, further injury, and so on) or as detailed as might appear in a narrative. It can be prepared as the initial summary, or essentially as a "summary of the summary" after the records have reviewed and summarized in a narrative format.

§ 8.27 —Sample Chronology (limited information)

This sample contains a portion of a four-page chronology that was prepared in a case in which the plaintiff was severely injured in an automobile accident and suffered several setbacks over a two-year recuperation period. This chronology was prepared after all of the medical records had been summarized in a narrative format; the entries are brief and a quotation from the record is used as it is significant.

CHRONOLOGY OF MEDICAL TREATMENT—JOHN DOE

06/21/05	Admitted to Memorial Hospital. Dx: left femur fracture, cerebral concussion syndrome, left facial contusions. [13–17]
06/22/05	Transferred to Community Hospital. [25]
06/25/05	Surgery—ORIF (open reduction and internal fixation) of left femur fracture. [57–62]
06/27/05	PE (pulmonary embolus) in left lung; Coumadin therapy begins. [122–123, 223]
06/29/05	Transfused with 2 units of packed blood cells; hematoma in surgical wound. [125]
07/05/05	Dr. P.: "I am concerned about patient having another bleeding episode, this could certainly lead to a wound infection"; 100 cc's of clotted blood removed from hematoma; receives 2 more units of packed blood cells. [127]
07/12/05	Discharged to home. [135]
07/19/05	Outpatient visit—bleeding at surgery site [2]
07/22/05	Outpatient visit—continued bleeding, Coumadin discontinued. [3]
08/02/05	Readmitted to Community Hospital—diagnosis: infected surgical wound. [198–203]
08/05/05	Surgery—incision, drainage and debridement of surgical wound. [229–235]
08/08/05	Surgery—second incision and drainage of wound. [241–245]
08/16/05	Discharged to home. [2–5]

§ 8.28   —Sample Chronological Narrative (detailed information)

A chronological narrative is most helpful in medical malpractice cases, allowing the reader to skim the entries without having always to read the entire narrative.

The following example gives both pre- and post-incident medical information. This was a medical malpractice case involving premature removal of surgical staples. The original summary was edited for this sample, and several days of entries were removed.

SUMMARY OF RECORDS—JOHN DOE

05/30/06   **Discharge Summary by Dr. Jane Roe:** Surgery performed due to patient's complaints of increased pain from the incision that required narcotic analgesia and development of severe depression due to the pain and his inability to lead his formerly active lifestyle. Hospital course uneventful with no complications. Advised to resume usual diet and medications with activity as tolerated but mainly limited to walking. Follow up in office on June 2, 2006, for removal of drains. [MC 197–198]

Appointment changed from June 2nd to June 5th while patient still in hospital. [MC 206]

POST-INCIDENT MEDICAL RECORDS

06/05/06   **Seen at Dr. Moe's office by his nurse, Ms. Toe, RN.** "On arrival patient complained of constant pain in left abdomen and requested Tylenol #4. An area 2–3 inches along edge of incision was dark red, no swelling. Otherwise, incision looks good. **Drain and staples removed, steri-strips applied**. Pain in left side better after drain removal. Appears in good spirits. Appointment to return on July 12, 1996. To phone if incision reddens." [Doe 60]

06/12/06   **Seen by Dr. Moe.** Complains of a fair amount of pain around the incision. **"The patient had his staples removed during my vacation last week."** Moderate degree of skin separation involving the lower aspect of the incision, approximately 3-4 cms. Greenish eschar is present, along with some redness. The patient "probably has a very superficial wound infection involving the lower aspect of the incision, and therefore, will put him on a course of antibiotics empirically." [Doe 63]

06/20/06   **Initial visit by Home Health Agency.** "Abdominal wound 7 cm × 4.5 cm × 3 cm deep. Small intestine tissue visibly evident. Moderate amount of yellow drainage; wound very painful to patient, who does not tolerate wound care well. Instructed to take pain medications 45 minutes before arrival of nurse. Patient and spouse cannot look at wound, stating it makes them sick and nauseated." [HHA 3]

Practice Note: The review and summary of medical records should not be done in a vacuum. In other words, the reviewer should always be aware of what allegations are being made or need to be proven so as to best determine what further evidence should be sought. In this sample, the plaintiff stated at his deposition that he refused to give the nurse permission to remove the staples, but she did so anyway, despite his protests. Additionally, he stated (as did his wife in her deposition) that they called Dr. Doe's office two to three times a day to report that the surgical incision had opened, was getting larger, and looked infected. Supportive evidence for these allegations was found in the plaintiff's telephone records, which showed that several calls per day were placed to the physician's office, although there were no notes made in Dr. Doe's chart regarding any of these calls.

§ 8.29   —Breakout Format

This is a very simple type of summary, and yet can be very powerful. For example, one of the allegations made by a plaintiff is that while she was a resident at a skilled nursing facility (SNF) she was not fed and lost 33 pounds over her 7 month stay. After her complete medical records have been summarized, the reviewer could go back and take a look at discrete issues such as this one, and prepare a breakout summary on the plaintiff's weight loss, which might look something like this:

DATE	WEIGHT	LOSS/GAIN	COMMENTS
03/03/01	235 lbs.		First weight located in records; Dr. Smith [3]
07/09/02	267 lbs.	+32 lbs.	Dr. Smith [5]
09/01/03	252 lbs.	−14 lbs.	Dr. Smith [14]
01/03/04	278 lbs.	+26 lbs.	Community Hospital [23]
01/15/04	277 lbs.	−1 lbs.	Community Hospital [23]
01/20/04	273 lbs.	−4 lbs.	Weight on admission to SNF [5]
01/21/04			Dietary consult; resident is 167% of ideal body weight, resident agrees to calorie-restricted diet; weekly weights [8]

DATE	WEIGHT	LOSS/GAIN	COMMENTS
01/28/04	271 lbs.	−2 lbs.	Complains about food quality and taste; snacks hidden in bedside table [130]
02/15/04	270 lbs.	+1 lb.	Family bringing in outside fast food; counseled re importance of keeping to diet [132]
02/23/04	267 lbs.	−3 lbs.	6 lb. weight loss since admission; continue diet [223]
05/01/04	250 lbs.	−17 lbs.	Weight loss continues; resident states "feels good" [157]
07/01/04	240 lbs.	−10 lbs.	Has lost 33 lbs since admission [177]

A breakout summary can be as detailed as required. The issues raised in this breakout revolve around plaintiff's allegations that she was not fed and lost weight, seemingly against her will. However, the records show involvement of the dietary department and nursing in an agreed-upon weight loss program that, despite the resident's best efforts, seems to be working.

§ 8.30   —Chart Format

The chart at **Form 8–1** was prepared for litigation involving polyurethane-covered breast implants. It combines many aspects of the types of summaries previously discussed, including the chronology and narrative. This specific chart was formatted on WordPerfect® and can be revised to add as many columns and rows as are needed to accommodate the required information. It can also be presented in a landscape format as opposed to the portrait used here. This type of summary is very visual and can be easily scanned to pick out specific information. When preparing this summary, the author was looking at certain areas of interest:

- Pre-implant medical history (mostly benign)
- Pre-implant psychological/social history
- The implant process itself and immediate post-implant period
- Any information given to the client to indicate a potential problem with the implants (statute of limitations)
- Post-implant medical history (significant).

Areas of concern that needed to be brought to the attorney's attention were put in boldface type.

§ 8.31   Use of Computers in Summarizing

No matter which type of summary format is utilized, computers are a invaluable tool in organizing the information in easily visualized formats. Although custom software programs are available most generic programs can be effectively adapted to the majority of the legal professional's needs. Keep in mind that while computers can make the job of summarizing medical records easier, it still takes the conscious brain of a reviewer to make sense of the information, to see connections between entries, and to recognize and act upon inconsistencies or strength areas. Three basic types of applications may be useful.

Word-Processing Programs.   These programs allow the creation of text materials and editing, printing, and storing of work product. Common editing functions include spell and grammar check, thesaurus, sort, and cutting and pasting of words, sentences, or blocks of text. Cut-and-paste functions are extremely useful when summarizing multiple sets of medical records and arranging information in chronological order. Most word-processing programs also have table functions that allow the creation of simple charts as demonstrated in the tables in **Forms 8–3** and **8–4.**

Spreadsheet Programs.   Although used primarily for financial calculations, most second-generation programs contain graphics and elementary (flat file) database capabilities. In summarizing medical records, spreadsheets may be used for calculation of medical specials. Charts such as the example in **Form 8–1** can also be created in spreadsheet programs.

Database Programs.   These programs allow the creation of sets of interrelated files. Data fall within a hierarchy, each having a specific purpose. Lowest to highest data hierarchy elements are as follows:

- Field—alphabetic, numeric, or alphanumeric. Social Security numbers, medical record numbers, court locations, defendants, and litigation numbers are examples of fields.
- Record—set of one or more fields concerning one person or case.

- File—set of related records. Depositions and medical records for one case are examples of files.
- Database—set of related files. A database could contain all case files within a law firm—that is, all information related to cases necessary to conduct business.

Relational databases allow linking of all related data items in tables; *flat databases* do not have this capability. Databases can be generic or highly specialized to an industry or profession, such as law. The degree of computer use for medical record summaries may be largely determined by the work environment. However, computer use gives individuals greater flexibility in data presentation and use.

The database in **Form 8–2** is an example of one prepared for breast implant litigation. The fields can be expanded as needed to show multiple implant and explant surgeries, for example. The field type refers to the type of data to be entered, either text up to a certain number of keystrokes, multi or note (which allows entry of narrative information), and date entries.

§ 8.32   Reviewing Medical Records in Malpractice Actions

Experts and consultants will review the medical record and may prepare a summary for their own use. As discussed more extensively in **Chapter 9,** the expert will focus on and address certain questions of liability, such as determining the standard of care applicable to the incident or occurrence at the time; whether a breach of the standard occurred; whether the breach resulted in an injury to the plaintiff; and the extent of the damage. For the legal professional, medical malpractice cases often require more focused summaries. Although multiple defendants may be named in the action (e.g., physicians, hospitals, nurses), the allegations against each party will be very specific. It is extremely important for the legal professional to be as familiar as possible with the issues before the review and summary begins.

Consider the following case history:

Mr. S. was a 42-year-old male who presented to community Hospital ED (in a small, rural town) with complaints of headache, fever, nausea, sweating, and lethargy of one day's duration. A minimal history and physical were done by the ED physician. Findings noted were clear lungs, temperature 102.5. Past medical history was negative, patient had been essentially healthy. A urinalysis was ordered and results were normal. A chest x-ray was not ordered. The examining physician's diagnosis was "viral illness." He discharged Mr. S. to home, advised him to take Tylenol for pain and to drink fluids. In addition, the physician advised Mr. S. to see his regular physician the following day if his symptoms did not improve.

Mr. S's symptoms did not improve and he followed up with his regular physician (Dr. Z) the following day. Dr. Z described the patient as appearing "quite toxic" and, after a rapid physical examination, ordered Mr. S. to be admitted to Community Hospital. Diagnosis on admission was "probable bacterial pneumonia," with a strong possibility of atypical pneumonia such as legionnaire's or mycoplasma. Mr. S. was admitted and antibiotics and supportive care were ordered.

Despite aggressive therapy, his condition deteriorated and Mr. S. developed respiratory failure, massive systemic sepsis, and gangrene of both legs. Eleven weeks after his initial admission, Mr. S. was transferred to a regional medical in the capital for further care and rehabilitation. His left leg was eventually amputated below the knee. Ultimately, blood tests revealed that the etiology of the pneumonia was legionella.

Some six months later, Mr. S. sued Community Hospital, specifically the nurses who cared for him, and Dr. Z. Mr. S.'s allegations included the following:

- Failure of Dr. Z and other consulting physicians to diagnose his illness and prescribe appropriate antibiotics in a timely manner
- Failure of Dr. Z to obtain timely and appropriate physician consultation with out-of-area experts
- Failure of the nursing staff to follow hospital policies and procedures. This allegation was specific to skin care. At the time of his transfer, Mr. S. had numerous pressure sores as well as impending gangrene of both legs.

Mr. S.'s medical records were approximately 1,000 pages in length for Community Hospital alone. Preparation of an index was essential before beginning summarization. In addition to a basic narrative summary of his hospital course, several **breakout summaries** could also be prepared. As the actions of Dr. Z were at issue, all orders for antibiotics and other treatments, along with consultations requested and received, could be placed in a table format such as that in **Form 8–3.** The table format enables easy visualization of the chronology of these events. With regard to nurses' actions, specific information on skin condition, circulatory monitoring, and turning can be similarly displayed. See **Form 8–4.**

§ 8.33 —Plaintiff's Preexisting Medical History

A good understanding of the plaintiff's state of health prior to the alleged act of malpractice is essential. Preexisting injuries and conditions do not excuse substandard medical care. However, the defense may argue that the same injury would have occurred regardless of the defendant's act(s) (no damages have resulted), or that the plaintiff's injury was the result of a cause unrelated to the alleged malpractice.

§ 8.34 Medical Specials

One of the more important functions in reviewing medical records is to keep an accurate accounting of the cost of medical care resulting from an incident or injury. This is done by periodically compiling the various medical charges throughout the course of a lawsuit in a form that can be easily scanned.

Charges incurred during the course of medical care are known as *medical specials* and are a component of special damages. Although the language may vary from state to state, the courts have generally held that a plaintiff's damages can include the reasonable cost of his or her medical care. These "reasonable costs" may include the following:

1. The costs of examination, surgery, care, treatment, or evaluation by physicians, dentists, chiropractors, osteopaths, hospitals, extended care facilities, psychologists, or physical therapists. (This does not include examinations performed at the request of a party's attorney or the cost of any reports generated as a result of these examinations.)

2. Medications as prescribed by a licensed practitioner.

3. The purchase or rental of equipment including commodes, wheelchairs, hospital beds, special automobile equipment, or other items as prescribed or recommended by the medical provider. (In cases involving back or other orthopedic injuries, this might include items such as a hot tub, jacuzzi, or whirlpool, if purchased pursuant to a physician's prescription.)

4. Nonprescription, injury-related items including heating pads, hearing aids, batteries, ointments, vitamins, lotions, disposable gloves, sanitary pads, waterproof pants, shields, and sheets for the incontinent patient.

5. Orthopedic appliances, including crutches, braces, trusses, and special shoes.

6. Prosthetic devices, including artificial limbs and eyes.

7. The cost of skilled attendants (nursing assistants, licensed vocational nurses, registered nurses, physical therapists) if the patient is non-ambulatory or requires specialized care.

8. Mileage to and from all medical facilities at the rate recognized by the IRS.

Practice Note: Remember that not all of a plaintiff's medical bills incurred during the period of time of the lawsuit may be related to that action. For example, in one matter a diabetic male was suing his primary care physician for failure to adequately treat a foot ulcer and included medical bills for laser argon treatments for his severe diabetic retinopathy and for problems related to his inability to maintain an erection. While these medical conditions were clearly related to his diabetes, they were *not* related to any allegations he was raising concerning failure to treat the ulcer. In another personal injury matter, an elderly gentleman who slipped and fell in a market alleged that the cost of installing an electric wheelchair lift at his home was a related medical cost. During his deposition, the plaintiff stated that it actually was his wife who was wheelchair-bound, but he used the lift when bringing groceries home from the store. Examples such as these may be self-explanatory, but each medical charge must be reviewed to determine its accuracy. Printouts of prescription medication should be scanned and only those medications clearly related to the injuries alleged should be claimed by the plaintiff.

§ 8.35   —Obtaining Medical Bills

The first and foremost source of medical specials is the plaintiff, who should have copies of all medical bills. If the bills are not available from the client, obtain them from the medical provider by submitting an authorization signed by the client; request a copy of the bills and a copy of the client's medical records at the same time. Instruct the client to save all receipts when purchasing items such as appliances and prescription drugs.

Medical bills are often supplied to defense counsel by the plaintiff's attorney. Otherwise, they may be obtained when the medical records are subpoenaed. If the medical provider uses outside billing services, the bills may arrive separately from the records. This can result in delays in the production of bills, often requiring follow-up letters or calls to the copy-service or to the provider.

Practice Note: When requesting medical records and bills from a large hospital or other medical institution, use separate letters for each type of request. Many of these institutions use offsite billing services, so your single request for records and bills may go directly to the medical records department but never make it to the billing department. To be assured of getting copies of the bills you need, request them separately. Be sure to always enclose a copy of your HIPAA-compliant authorization as medical bills are considered confidential.

§ 8.36   —Summarizing Medical Specials

Once the medical billings have been obtained, it is important to put them in a usable format. It is also important to update the information on the list of medical specials periodically throughout the course of the lawsuit. In this way an accurate account of the client's or plaintiff's medical expenses is documented in a timely and efficient manner.

The samples summary in **Form 8–5** illustrates a possible format. At a glance, the summary tells the reader:

1.   The amount of medical charges from each provider
2.   The total amount of charges
3.   The identity of all medical providers
4.   The dates of service
5.   The type of services provided.
6.   The portion of each bill that was paid by the insurance carrier
7.   The portion paid by the individual
8.   The amount and date of any liens.

If the charges are entered in chronological order, this long-form summary can also serve as a time line of the individual's treatment.

Practice Note: For every visit or treatment, there should be a corres-ponding bill, and for every bill there should be a notation of treatment.

One method that can be used to track the accuracy of medical billings and visits is to arrange the bills individually in chronological order. One of the authors was involved in a case in which the plaintiff was receiving chiropractic and other medical treatment from providers in both northern and southern California. When the bills were reviewed chronologically, they showed that treatment was apparently received simultaneously on at least seven different dates in both ends of the state. It was later determined that this plaintiff had become associated with a group of health care practitioners in southern California who were fraudulently billing the insurance industry for treatment not rendered. Another reason to always "keep your antennae out" while reviewing records!

§ 8.37   —Medical Liens

Any health care provider (e.g., physician, governmental agency, hospital, insurance company) who expends resources treating a patient with a traumatic injury due to the negligence of a third party can seek repayment through the enforcement of statutory liens. However, federal Medicaid law prohibits providers from "balance billing" – that is, seeking money from patients in additional to what Medi-Cal pays. (*See* 42 C.F.R. § 447.15.)

Medicare Liens.
The federal government has a statutory lien for medical benefits paid under the Medicare Act. 42 U.S.C. § 1395y(b)(2)(B)(ii). The lien, sometimes called a "super lien," gives the government a right of recovery superior to that of all other persons and entities. U.S., Department of Health and Human Services, Centers for Medicare and Medicaid Services, Medicare Intermediary Manual § 3418.6; United States v. Geier, 816 F. Supp. 1332, 1334 (W.D. Wis. 1993). The government has a direct-action right of recovery against benefit recipients, their attorneys, and third-party payers, possibly including a settling defendant. If one is aware or "should be aware" of the lien, then it is perfected in the eyes of Medicare, even when no notice of the lien is given. 42 C.F.R. § 411.24(l)(2).

Settlement documents cannot avoid a Medicare lien by stating that the money is being paid for categories such as loss of consortium or pain and suffering or loss of consortium, as opposed to medical expenses. U.S., Department of Health and Human Services, Centers for Medicare and

Medicaid Services, Medicare Intermediary Manual § 3418.6. Medicare only recognizes allocation of a portion of a recovery to non-medical losses when the court or jury designates the amount of the recovery as such. Id. Although a Medicare lien is superior to attorney fee claims, Medicare will reduce its recovery to allow for the cost of procuring a judgment or settlement. 42 C.F.R. § 411.37.

Medicaid Liens.
Medicaid is a state-administered, federal program designed to provide medical care to the needy. 42 U.S.C. § 1396k(a)(2). A state's Medicaid administrator may enforce the lien even without intervening in the injured person's case.

Identifying Liens.
By way of discovery, the defense attorney should request the source of all benefits paid on the plaintiff's behalf as a result of the injury (e.g., Medicare, Medicaid, insurance), including all documents provided to or received from any lien holder. The plaintiff's attorney should obtain this same information, on an informal basis, from his client.

After potential liens have been identified, verify their existence and amount. With regard to Medicare and Medicaid liens, call or write the administrators and ask for the amount of benefits paid, if any. When requested, the administrators will generally provide written confirmation of the existence and amount of a lien. The administrators will also generally provide written confirmation that they have no record of benefits being paid on behalf of a particular person if no lien exists. At or before the time the case is resolved, an agreement should be reached with all lien holders concerning satisfaction of the liens.

§ 8.38 —Payment of Medical Specials

One of the most controversial areas of litigation revolves around the true value of medical specials. Should a plaintiff be allowed to recover the full amount of the bills rather than the lesser amount accepted by the medical provider from private insurance, Medicare or Medicaid? Or should a plaintiff's recovery be limited to the amount actually paid by the insurer, Medicare or Medicaid and accepted by the provider as payment in full?

Those arguing that the injured person should be allowed to recover the full amount of the bills base their arguments around five distinct issues:

- A plaintiff should receive the benefit of his or her bargain with the insurance company (premiums paid in return for medical care).
- Not allowing a plaintiff to recover the amounts written-off by an insurer (private, Medicare, Medicaid) would benefit the tortfeasor for the plaintiff's efforts and expenditures in procuring the insurance in the first place.
- The collateral source rule main purpose is to not allow a tortfeasor to benefit from assistance provided by the injured party's sources.
- If either side is to get a windfall, it is better to give it to the innocent victim rather than to the tortfeasor.
- The liability of similarly situated defendants should not depend on the fortuity of how a plaintiff's medical expenses are financed.

Arthur v. Catour, 345 Ill. App. 3d 804, 803 N.E.2d 647, 281 Ill. Dec. 243 (3rd Dist. 2004), appeal allowed by Illinois Supreme Court, 5/26/04, Doc. Nos. 97920 and 97946 (private insurance); *Rose v. Via Christi Health System, Inc.,* 276 Kan. 539, 78 P.3d 798 (2003) (Medicare); *Calva-Cerqueira v. U.S.,* 281 F. Supp. 2d 279 (D.D.C. 2003) (private insurance)

Those who argue that a plaintiff's recovery should be limited to the amount paid, and accepted by the provider as payment in full argue that:

- Damages for medical expenses are a form of compensatory damages to make the plaintiff "whole." But to award plaintiff the full amount billed is to make the plaintiff more than whole by awarding him a windfall.
- A plaintiff is allowed to recover the reasonable value of medical care necessary because of the accident; the reasonable value of medical care is what the provider accepts as payment in full.
- A plaintiff cannot recover the amount written off by a provider, because the plaintiff was never liable for that amount.
- The plaintiff does not stand in privity of contract with the health insurer and the health care provider as it relates to charges for services provided; the reduced amount is paid pursuant to a contract between the insurer and the provider.

• The collateral source rule should not be applied to create a benefit that is dependent on the occurrence of a tort; a plaintiff would not get the written-off amount if the injury was not the result of a tort.

Hanif v. Housing Authority, 200 Cal. App. 3d 635, 246 Cal. Rptr. 192 (3d Dist. 1988) (Medi-Cal); *Cooperative Leasing, Inc. v. Johnson,* 872 So.2d 956 (Fla. App. 2nd Dist. 2004) (Medicare); *Moorhead v. Crozer Chester Medical Center,* 564 Pa. 156, 765 A.2d 786 (2001) (Medicare and private insurance)

Court Rulings Regarding Medical Specials

In a 2004 Illinois case, the appellate court held that "plaintiff's damages are not limited to the amount paid by her insurer, but may extend to the entire amount billed, provided those charges are reasonable expenses of necessary medical care." *Arthur v. Catour,* 345 Ill. App. 3d 804, 808, 803 N.E.2d 647 (3d Dist. 2004).

However, in two California cases, *McMeans* and *Nishihama,* the courts both opined that a personal injury plaintiff's claim against a tortfeasor for medical special damages was limited to amounts actually paid by the plaintiff's private insurer, regardless of the reasonable *value* of the medical services received. This determination—which flies in the face of the collateral source rule—was the predicate to the courts' conclusions in both cases: the hospitals had no lien rights because the plaintiffs themselves could seek no more than the discounted payments made by their insurers to the hospitals. *McMeans v. Scripps Health,* 100 Cal. App. 4th 507 (2002); *Nishihama v. City & County of San Francisco,* 93 Cal. App. 4th 298 (2001).

Practice Note: This area of the law remains unsettled. Be aware of what your jurisdiction's holdings are in this regard, but always make sure you obtain medical billings that contain both the amount billed and the amount actually paid.

§ 8.39 Problems with Medical Records

Not all records are clear, legible, and complete. In fact, more often than not at least one of the problems in §§ 8.39 through 8.50 will be encountered when summarizing a record.

§ 8.40 —Illegible Writing

Although most large hospitals (and some sole practitioners' offices) have dictated and typewritten chart entries, this is not true of all providers. One of the most frequent obstacles to reviewing records is attempting to decipher what has been handwritten. Doctors, pharmacists, physical therapists, and chiropractors may write in a style only they can recognize. What can be done in this situation? Reviewing the document several times, comparing other entries by the author, and reading the illegible word or phrase in context can help familiarize the reviewer with that person's individual style of writing. If necessary, show the entry to a colleague. Someone else may pick out words and phrases that you are unable to read.

Practice Note: For plaintiff attorneys, it is acceptable to call the provider and ask for help. If the physician is not available, ask the office staff for assistance. Because office personnel see the doctor's handwriting every day, they should be familiar with it. For defense counsel, there can be strict prohibitions against ex parte contacts with the plaintiff's treating physicians. If the record in question is or could be significant, the content can be explored by deposing the provider. Finally, it is important to remember that a document that cannot be read, even by its author, is not admissible.

§ 8.41 —Poor Copies

Poor-quality copies can be difficult to deal with. If the records have been provided by a copy service, the inferior copy is probably the best possible. Attempting to copy older records from microfilm, certain kinds of slick paper, or existing copies often yields poor results. Contact the provider to see if a more legible copy can be obtained. If a more acceptable copy cannot be obtained and if the document in question is essential, it may be necessary to make arrangements to review the originals in person. For plaintiffs, this can be accomplished with the custodian of records of the facility or provider and carried out according to the in-house procedures.

It is becoming increasingly common for plaintiff's attorneys to request color copies of a medical chart, particularly if the case involves allegations of medical malpractice or nursing home litigation. Anyone who has reviewed a medical record knows that the original is far from the clean, black-and-white set of records provided by a copy machine. Inks of all colors may be used when charting. Originals may be pink, yellow, or green. Highlighting of entries, often found on the original, may not show up on copies. Color copies of medical records are expensive, ranging from $1 to $1.50 per page. However, the clarity achieved using this technology is often superior to that from standard photocopies or records photographed and then copied from film.

Practice Note: Many copy services will now provide scanning technology which produces not only a clearer image, but a disc containing all of the documents.

§ 8.42   —Unfamiliar Terminology

It is extremely important to be as familiar as possible with medical terminology. Use a good medical dictionary to assist with definitions. It is likely that if the word is unfamiliar to you, it will also be unfamiliar to who ever else may be using the summary. Include in the summary a short definition of any word, procedure, or medication that may be unfamiliar. See **Chapter 2, §§ 2.14–2.21** for an in-depth discussion of medical terminology.

§ 8.43   —Chiropractic Records

For many reasons, chiropractic records can present a dilemma to the reviewer. For one thing, the handwriting can be difficult to read. In addition, the type of form the chiropractor uses to record treatments varies from office to office. Some practitioners use blank paper and others use preprinted forms. No matter which form is used, certain information should appear:

1. Date of treatment
2. Patient's subjective complaints
3. Type of adjustment given and other treatment given
4. Reaction to treatment
5. Date of next visit.

There are over 45 different types of chiropractic techniques. Some of the more common include diversified, Gonstead, SOT, applied kinesiology, and toggle-recoil. Which technique chiropractors use depends on a number of factors, including where they were trained. Generally speaking, unless the lawsuit involves chiropractic malpractice, it is not important to know which kinds of manipulation are being utilized.

Chiropractic primarily utilizes standard medical terminology, concentrating on those terms associated with orthopedics, neurology, radiology, and physical therapy. See **Chapter 2, § 2.13** for a discussion of terminology, and **Appendix G** for a list of orthopedic and neurological tests commonly utilized by chiropractors. Unfamiliar terms generally relate to specific chiropractic adjustments and maneuvers. Chiropractic terms and abbreviations vary from practitioner to practitioner and often depend on their training. Chiropractic records are summarized in the same manner as medical records.

§ 8.44   —Chart Out of Sequence

If a requested set of records arrives and is out of chronological order, a few options can be considered. Records obtained by authorization should be paginated, and then placed in chronological order prior to review. Records obtained by subpoena are generally paginated so that they too can be placed in chronological order. However, if they have not been paginated, consider doing so immediately. While it is inadvisable to alter subpoenaed records in any way, the benefit of pagination far outweighs the risk that any party will consider this to be alteration. As subpoenaed records may be used as exhibits to depositions or motions or as evidence at trial, the ability to locate specific records is essential. If, however, you consider (or your state law holds) that pagination of a subpoenaed record after it was produced constitutes alteration and compromises its integrity, copy the record as produced, and place the original in a marked file. Then, paginate the copied set and put it in chronological order for your use.

§ 8.45   —Missing Records

Missing records can be relatively easy to solve but difficult to detect in the first place. How can you determine if parts of a record are missing? If you discover that the third page of a five-page report is missing, it is easy to remedy by contacting the provider and asking for a copy of the missing page. Discovering that portions of a 365-page hospital chart are missing will be more difficult. **Chapter 5, §§ 5.10 to 5.13** discusses the main kinds of information that appear in a chart. For example, if there is no discharge summary for a hospital admission (all admissions require a discharge note), it is easy to contact the medical records department and request a copy of the missing document. Only by knowing what should be in the record can it be determined whether it is complete.

§ 8.46   Alteration of Medical Records

Medical records are the cornerstone of a medical malpractice case, relied on by the parties and their experts to prove or disprove the existence of negligence. When key records are altered or destroyed, the plaintiff's ability to make a prima facie case for negligence is greatly hampered or disappears altogether. Alteration or destruction of records can have disastrous results for the defendant too. An individual who alters records in an attempt to control the outcome of a proceeding will often find those actions ultimately determined in the plaintiff's favor, despite other evidence that might have supported the defendant's legal defense absent the altered records.

§ 8.47   —The Spoliation Doctrine

The spoliation of or attempt to suppress material evidence by a party provides sufficient reason for an inference of guilt or negligence by that party. Courts will not allow parties to benefit from their own misconduct. As far back as 1722 this concept was recognized *(Armory v. Delamirie,* 93 Eng. Rep. 664: *"omnia praesumuntur contra spoliatorem"*—all things are presumed against the destroyer).

The evidentiary presumption against a party acting in a deceitful manner is called the *spoliation doctrine.* The destruction must be shown to be the result of negative intent or bad faith; negligence alone will not justify the inference that the defendant knew his or her case was weak and could not be won otherwise. Alteration of a patient's record for the purpose of overcoming a real or perceived malpractice claim "is reprehensible and evidences a moral deficiency and disregard for the rights of others that [courts] regard as odious and repugnant." *Paris v. Michael Kreitz, Jr., P.A.,* 75 N.C. App. 365, 331 S.E.2d 234 (1985).

One of the first cases to deal with spoliation as it applied to "lost" medical records was the California case of *Thor v. Boska,* 38 Cal. App. 3d 558, 113 Cal. Rptr. 296 (1974). This case involved a plaintiff who notified her doctor, a general practitioner, about a lump in her breast. Over the next 16 months, the defendant physician performed no tests, did not refer her to or suggest that she see a specialist, and essentially told her there was nothing to worry about. When the plaintiff finally consulted other doctors, cancer was found and she underwent a radical mastectomy with indications that the cancer had metastasized.

During discovery, the defendant was unable to produce the plaintiff's original medical records. These records were crucial to the plaintiff's ability to prove that her cancer went undiagnosed and untreated for more than a year and a half. The defendant "could only assume" that he had thrown away the original records, but only after copying them in a "more legible form." He did this when he learned that the plaintiff had consulted a specialist and thought that the new doctor might want to review the records.

The plaintiff testified that the defendant had drawn a diagram in her original records that showed the location of the lump; this drawing did not appear in the copied chart. The trial court would not allow any reference to the unavailability of the original records as this would be unduly prejudicial to the defendant. The jury found on behalf of the defendant.

On appeal, the court noted that the defendant's failure to produce the original medical record concerning his treatment of the plaintiff after he found that she had consulted another physician created a strong inference that he felt guilty. The appellate court found that "at one time he may have panicked or thought it expedient to lose any written record of the occasion." If the defendant had destroyed the records under a consciousness of guilt, such consciousness would be relevant to causation. Finally, the court noted that when a defendant's negligence makes it impossible for the plaintiff to prove proximate cause, it is more appropriate to hold the defendant liable than to deny an innocent plaintiff recovery.

§ 8.48   —Legal Theories and Consequences of Spoliation

In addition to California, Alaska, Florida, Illinois, and Kansas recognize a tort for intentional spoliation of evidence. *Smith v. Superior Court of Los Angeles,* 151 Cal. App. 3d 491, 198 Cal. Rptr. 829 (1984); *Hazen v. Municipality of Anchorage,* 718 P.2d 456, 463-64 (Alaska 1986); *Bondu v. Gurvich,* 473 So. 2d 1307, 1313 (Fla. 1984); *Rodgers v. St. Mary's Hospital of Decatur,* 149 Ill. 2d 302, 597 N.E.2d 616, 620 (1992); *Foster v. Lawrence Memorial Hospital,* 809 F. Supp. 831, 838 (Kan. 1992). This tort requires that several conditions be met.

1. Pending or probable litigation involving the plaintiff
2. Knowledge by the defendant of the pending litigation
3. Intentional acts of spoliation by the defendant designed to disrupt plaintiff's case
4. Actual disruption of plaintiff's case
5. Damages to the plaintiff proximately caused by the defendant's acts or actions

Ohio and New Jersey recognize the tort of fraudulent destruction of evidence, comparable to the intentional spoliation of evidence. *Smith v. Howard Johnson Co.,* 67 Ohio St. 3d 28, 615 N.E.2d 1037, 1038 (1993); *Hirsch v. General Motors Corp.,* 266 N.J. Super. 22, 628 A.2d 1108, 1115 (1993); *Viviano v. CBS, Inc.,* 251 N.J. Super. 113, 597 A.2d 543, 548-49 (1991).

North Carolina recognizes a cause of action for plaintiff's increased costs of investigation stemming from alteration of medical records by defendants. *Henry v. Deen,* 310 N.C. 75, 310 S.E.2d 326, 334-35 (1984). The tort of intentional spoliation of evidence is *not* recognized in New York or Texas. *Weigl v. Quincy Specialties Co.,* 158 Misc. 2d 753, 601 N.Y.S.2d 774 (N.Y. 1993); *Brewer v. Dowling,* 862 S.W.2d 156 (Tex. 1993).

In most states, the alteration of medical records is a crime generally treated as a misdemeanor but may also qualify as a felony if the health care provider is shown to have acted intentionally and willfully. *See, e.g.,* Cal. Bus. & Prof. Code § 2262. In addition to criminal penalties, health care providers can face professional disciplinary actions and civil penalties including denial of a medical license. Nev. Rev. Stat. Ann. § 630.3067. In *Jimenez v. Department of Professional Regulation, Board of Medicine,* 556 So. 2d 1219 (Fla. 1990), a physician was sued for malpractice by a deceased patient's wife, who also filed a complaint with the Department of Professional Regulation. One year after the complaint was filed, the physician made additions to his chart concerning the patient. These additional notes indicated that he had advised the patient to undergo a cardiac stress test and an angiogram but that the patient had refused to do so. In fact, the defendant had failed to make these recommendations at any time. A hearing officer for the state board of medicine ordered the physician placed on probation for one year and to pay a $5,000 fine. The physician appealed this finding to the full board who confirmed the findings and increased the penalty to two years probation following a one year suspension of the physician's license to practice medicine. The physician then appealed directly to the state court of appeal, who also affirmed the board's order and agreed with its statement that "alteration of records is a basic act of dishonesty and is very serious in light of the importance of a physician's need to keep accurate and honest medical records." *Id.* at 1220.

In a medical malpractice case against a physician who was found to have acted with actual malice in altering, falsifying, and destroying records relating to an allegedly unnecessary amputation, the jury awarded a punitive damage award of $3 million. This amount was later found to be excessive to the extent that it exceeded $1 million, where the defendant had a net worth of $2.1 million to $3 million. *Moskovitz v. Mt. Sinai Medical Center,* 69 Ohio St. 3d 638, 635 N.E.2d 331 (1994).

In addition to civil penalties and the possibility of loss of medical privileges a health care provider who has fraudulently altered a patient's medical records may have his or her malpractice insurance canceled. *Mirkin v. Medical Mutual Liability Insurance Society,* 82 Md. App. 540, 572 A.2d 1126 (1990).

If an organization such as a skilled nursing facility is shown to have altered its medical records, renewal of its business license may be denied along with the imposition of costly civil fines. *Colonial Gardens Nursing Home, Inc. v. Pennsylvania Department of Health,* 34 Pa. Commw. 131, 382 A.2d 1273 (1978); *People v. Casa Blanca Convalescent Homes, Inc.,* 159 Cal. App. 3d 509, 206 Cal. Rptr. 164 (1984).

§ 8.49   —Events That May Trigger Alteration

Several types of events can cause a provider to alter a medical record:

- Immediately following a surgery, birth, or other hospital procedure with unexpected or unplanned events or occurrences
- After another provider has assumed care of the patient
- After the patient's death
- At the time of discharge when a provider may review the records and make "corrections" or deletions

- When a provider learns that a plaintiff attorney is seeking a copy of the medical record

Most hospitals and other large medical facilities have a risk management department that investigates and monitors the progress of claims and lawsuits. At the first hint of a poor outcome (e.g., surgical mishap, bad birth, negative reaction to medication) the risk manager will generally confiscate the entire medical record and anything associated with it (e.g., x-rays, pharmacy records, fetal monitoring strips, pathology slides) and keep this evidence locked up. In this way, the facility will better protect itself from accusations that the records or other evidence was altered or tampered with.

In *May v. Moore,* 424 So. 2d 596 (Ala. 1982), the hospital record of an infant was lost following that infant's death. At the defendant physician's deposition, he produced two copies of the infant's chart. Interestingly enough, these copies differed significantly from a copy of original record that had been produced by the hospital administrator at his deposition. The administrator testified that the hospital had become aware of a pattern of "missing charts" involving only patients of the defendant physician. As a result, the administrator had begun making copies of the defendant physician's medical charts and had copied the chart in question prior to its disappearance. The Alabama Supreme Court eventually upheld the admission of evidence at trial that the defendant physician had purposely destroyed records concerning the infant's death. The court found that this evidence could form a sufficient basis for inferring the defendant physician's negligence.

§ 8.50 —Signs of Alteration

An alteration to a record can take many forms:

- Expansion of an original entry
- Changing the content of the record by altering numbers, symbols, or other information
- Overwriting the entry
- Obliterating the original entry by use of a correction fluid or other abrasive or chemical erasure material
- Adding or removing whole pages

When reviewing records, look for possible signs of alteration, such as:

- Changes in the time of entering providers' notes, especially around dates crucial to the issues of the lawsuit
- Inconsistently dated entries
- An excessive number of late entries or "addenda," especially involving circumstances surrounding the act or injury in question. Late entries are appropriate if they include the date and time they were entered as well as the date and time the event actually occurred.
- The use of correction fluid or any other concealing substances that obliterates any portion of the records. This may not be apparent in photocopies of the record; the original documents should be reviewed if a question exists.

In *Ahrens v. Katz,* 595 F. Supp. 1108 (Ga. 1984), portions of original nursing notes had been concealed with correction fluid. A forensic document examiner examined the original record and determined the content of the original entries. The nurse who altered the record testified that the procedure was not in accordance with correct nursing standards and claimed that she could not recall why she had not merely lined out the erroneous material and marked it "error." Although the court found the procedure to be improper, it was unable to infer a fraudulent or guilt motive by the nurse.

Errors in charting should be lined out with a single line, marked "error," and replaced with the correct entry. If large sections of information have been entered incorrectly (for example, into the wrong chart), the section should be marked with a large "X," plus a signed and dated note indicating that the information was inserted into the wrong records. Information should never be obliterated from the record completely.

Another source of altered records might be the opposing party's attorney. For example, when copies of records are provided by a plaintiff's attorney, documents that are considered "unrelated" to the subject accident or incident may have been removed. This may be done with the honest intention of protecting the client's privacy, but generally defense counsel would like to make that determination and will obtain a complete set of the records themselves, either by authorization or subpoena.

If alterations to a record are suspected, arrangements should be made to review the original in person. Plaintiff's counsel will do this by making an appointment with the custodian of records. The records will be available for review only in the presence of the custodian or other designee.

Practice Note: Keep in mind that the original chart might bear little resemblance to the copies in your possession. Pages with writing on the front and back might be copied as two separate pages, or you might discover documents that do not appear in your set. It may be that providers may have an in-house policy as to which documents will be copied in response to a request, regardless of what was asked for. One large health maintenance organization routinely does not copy documents not generated by its own staff, e.g., outside consultant reports. This same provider keeps separate medical charts for in-patient hospitalization, out-patient care, and psychiatric treatment. Before requesting the records, determine the facility's specific method of maintaining their records.

Remember to take your copy of the records with you when reviewing the original records. Use self-sticking tabs or notes to indicate which documents need to be copied or examined further. Always make a list of records that you have requested further copies of so that you will be sure of getting all requested.

Indications that records have been altered can come to light when reviewing an entire set of documents on a patient. An obstetrician/gynecologist who specialized in late second trimester abortions was found guilty of practicing medicine fraudulently as a result of an entry in a patient's office chart that she had "no bleeding at all." This was controverted by testimony of the first responders/EMTs and their records that showed a drop in the patient's hematocrit and the presence of vaginal packing. *In re Hachamovitch v. State Board for Professional Medical Conduct,* 206 A.D.2d 637, 614 N.Y.S.2d 608 (1994).

§ 8.51   —Use of a Document Examiner

If a medical record is suspect, retain a forensic or questioned document examiner to examine the record and determine whether any alteration has occurred. Review a document examiner's credentials closely. Professional organizations offer certification and information on locating and using document examiners. (Association of Forensic Document Examiners, *www.afde.org;* American Society of Questioned Document Examiners, *www.asqde.org.*)

A document examiner can provide various services to the legal field including general consultation, laboratory examination and analysis, on-site examination, destructive testing, preparation of expert reports, and testifying at deposition and trial.

While a document examiner can work with photocopies on a limited basis for the preliminary examination (e.g., to study a writer's punctuation, writing style, or manner of making corrections), the original record must be examined at some point prior to the final report. This is because copies do not reproduce details such as ink color, pressure, and beginning and ending strokes. A document examiner will look at a handwritten record with an eye to the author's style—each individual's handwriting is unique and each act of writing is never repeated exactly.

The examination and comparison of inks and pens can form an important part of the document examiner's work. Ballpoint pens can be distinguished from one another by differences such as the degree of ink glossiness, differences in ink color, the size of the writing ball, and defects common to that type of pen (e.g., "gooping"—small globular deposits of ink found at directional changes).

When a document is written on, underlying sheets of paper may retain an impression or indentation of the writing. A document examiner can bring out the indented writing by use of photographic techniques, infrared examination, or a latent-image developer or electrostatic detection apparatus.

Typewritten or computer-generated records will be examined for certain areas unique to this technology, including type style and pitch, spacing, and misalignment in horizontal and vertical placement of the characters. In this way it can be determined if all of the typewriting was done on the same machine and element, if all portions of the document were typed at one time, and if a number of documents were produced by the same machine.

A document examiner may start by subjecting the subject document to nondestructive testing, initially by examining the ink in the record with the unaided eye. Following this, more sophisticated techniques will be utilized such as a magnification stereomicroscope, dichroic filters, ultraviolet, infrared, infrared luminescent, and laser lights. A video spectroscanning system can show that inks appearing to the naked eye to be the same are in fact different in that their chemical properties will respond differently to various types of lights.

On occasion, a document examiner may have to conduct destructive testing of a record if it is necessary to date the ink, identify the ink manufacturer, or determine how long the ink has been on the paper. A court order is generally required to perform this type of testing. One examination method involves the use of thin-layer chromatography, which allows individual components of a substance to be visually separated, compared to other samples, and identified.

§ 8.52   Medical Research

One of the more important functions legal professionals can perform is medical research involving injuries, illnesses, medications, and treatment regimens. This information is essential in providing the background needed to be knowledgeable about the client's injuries, to take depositions, and to interview treating physicians about the injuries (or preexisting conditions that might have been affected by the incident) or the individual's recovery.

In addition, medical research tools can be used to investigate the opposing party's expert witnesses. When expert witnesses are disclosed, carefully review the curriculum vitae (if provided). Look for journal articles or other publications (e.g., texts, chapters in texts) that deal with the same or similar issues to those that exist in your case. This can easily be done by performing an on-line search via GoogleTM (i.e., "Googling" the expert). Very often, journal articles, seminar appearances, and other publications are identified and available for downloading. These can then be used as background information, and when preparing for and taking the expert's deposition—look for contradictions between the expert's current opinions and testimony in deposition and those expressed in the published article(s).

Legal professionals who consistently work with medical records will find that the most essential support system is the Internet, followed by your office's library. Although it does not have to be extensive, the office library should contain some basic medical texts. Refer to the **Bibliography** for a complete list of suggested library resources.

§ 8.53   —Office-Based Research

A good starting point for medical research is to find the injury or condition in a basic medical book such as one of the *Merck Manuals*. The *Merck Manual of Diagnosis and Therapy,* now in its seventeenth edition, provides concise descriptions and definitions of several hundred diseases and a brief summation of the progression of the disease. All 308 chapters of this manual can be accessed on-line at *www.merck.com/pubs*. Other valuable Merck publications include the *Merck Manual of Geriatrics* (2005, all chapters available on-line), *Merck Manual of Health and Aging* (2005, not all chapters were available on-line at time of publication of this update), *Merck Manual—Second Home Edition* (2005, written for the lay public), and the *Merck Veterinary Manual* (2003, available at *www.merckvetmanual.com*).

As an alternative to the *Merck Manuals*, you might consider *Current Medical Diagnosis and Treatment,* which was first published in the 1950s and revised in 2005. Written in a concise, easy-to-read style, the text covers all aspects of outpatient and inpatient care as well as authoritative descriptions of new developments in medicine. It includes information on over 1,000 diseases and disorders with an emphasis on prevention and cost-effective treatments. It provides easy access to drug dosages, updated prices, and trade names, plus evaluations of new therapies in alternative and complementary medicine. It includes an excellent discussion of HIV and AIDS-related topics.

A basic knowledge of terminology is essential, as is the availability of a good medical dictionary. *Dorland's Illustrated Medical Dictionary,* the grandfather of medical dictionaries, is an absolute must for any legal desk. It also comes in a compact, unillustrated volume known as *Dorland's Pocket Medical Dictionary*. It is also available on-line at *www.mercksource.com*. (See §§ 2.14–2.20 for an extensive discussion of medical terminology.

A brief and concise guide to laboratory tests is essential. Choose one that defines a variety of medical tests, procedures, and terms in one line or less. Multiple on-line resources exist, including Lab Tests OnLine (*www. labtestsonline.org*) a peer-reviewed, non-commercial, and patient-centered site which is the result of a collaboration of professional societies representing the lab community. This public resource on clinical lab testing describes in lay terminology the "how and why" of hundreds of lab tests. The lab test section found in Medline (*www.nlm.nih.gov*) has links to multiple articles and other resources concerning lab tests. Another valuable site is ARUP Laboratories (*www.arup-lab.com*) where you will find its Guide to Clinical Laboratory Testing which lists the methodology for testing, clinical significance, values, and references for thousands of lab tests.

As an introduction to the intricacies of the human body, the *Anatomy Coloring Book* is highly recommended. It covers, among other topics, the skeletal, muscular, and nervous systems. For an on-line, interactive resource, see Human Anatomy on-line (*www.innerbody.com*), which offers a highly educational tour of body systems.

§ 8.54 —Physicians' Desk Reference®

In addition to basic medical texts and dictionaries, it is essential to have a resource for information on drugs. The *Physicians' Desk Reference* (PDR®) is a listing of almost all of the prescription medications currently in use in the United States. It includes a brief chemical analysis, description of the drug's usages, applications, and known side effects. This is a useful reference tool when determining the nature of medications that have been prescribed for a patient and the possible side effects. Drug manufacturers pay to have their products included in the PDR. These drug listings are reprints of the original package insert. The most current or newly discovered side effects of interactions may not be included.

The most commonly used sections of the PDR are:

1. Product Name Index: Medications are listed in alphabetical order by brand name or generic name. If a detailed description of the drug appears in PDR, a page number will follow.

2. Product Category Index: Medications are listed according to their appropriate classification—analgesics, anti-inflammatory agents, central nervous system stimulants, tranquilizers, and so on. This section contains both a quick-reference and detailed list.

3. Generic and Chemical Name Index: Medications are listed according to the principal ingredient, for example, acetaminophen, hydrocortisone, tetracycline, and so on.

4. Product Identification Section: Medications are identified with actual size, full-color illustrations.

5. Product Information Section: Medications are fully described in terms of indications and usage, dosages, routes, methods, frequency and duration of administration, contraindications, adverse reactions, potential for drug abuse and dependence, overdosage, and precautions. Companion volumes are the *PDR for Nonprescription Drugs®* and the *PDR for Ophthalmology®*. Supplements to the main PDR are published in the spring and fall, listing changes and new releases. Because new medications appear on the market constantly, this

publication is revised annually. For research purposes, it is preferable to use an edition that is no more than one or two years old. See the **Bibliography** for other suggested drug resources.

§ 8.55   —Hospital Medical Libraries

When your medical research project requires more extensive resources than the ones available in your law firm, a good medical library is essential. All teaching hospitals and most large hospitals have libraries with on-staff medical librarians. They are generally open to the public for research purposes but do not offer checkout privileges. Medical librarians are usually very approachable and willing to assist with specific research questions. Call in advance to determine the facility's policies.

Universities with schools of medicine and nursing will have extensive holdings in their libraries. More often than not, these libraries offer members of the general public the ability to use the library (usually for a fee). This allows the public access to the holdings, librarians, and on-line research facilities.

Smaller hospitals may also have libraries, but they are generally not open to the public and have a limited selection of books.

§ 8.56   —Regional Medical Libraries

The National Library of Medicine is this country's principal medical library. Many of its resources are made available through the National Network of Libraries of Medicine and NLM's eight regional libraries listed below.

If the local medical library does not have the article or book you are searching for, either you or the librarian can request it from the appropriate regional library. Keep in mind, however, that loans of books are not made directly to individuals but rather through the interlibrary loan program. The regional library should be able to provide you with reprints of journal articles or refer you to appropriate databases. If the publication is not available through the regional system, it can be requested from the National Library of Medicine. Charges for this service vary according to the type of article requested, the difficulty in retrieving the article, and your status (member of the general public, physician or other medical professional, etc.). A charge will be made to local libraries for each interlibrary loan. If the requested article is faxed to you, there will be an additional surcharge.

The following is a list of the eight regional medical libraries in the United States. Please note that each library has the same 800 number; this is a truncated line and will automatically connect you to the appropriate regional library for your area.

GREATER MIDWEST REGION (Iowa, Illinois, Indiana, Kentucky, Michigan, Minnesota, North Dakota, Ohio, South Dakota, Wisconsin); University of Illinois at Chicago, Library of the Health Sciences, 1750 Polk Street, Room 126 (M/C 763), Chicago, IL 60612; Telephone: (312) 996-2464 or (800) 338-7657; Fax: (312) 996-2226; *http://www. nnlm.gov/gmr/*

MIDCONTINENTAL REGION (Colorado, Kansas, Missouri, Nebraska, Utah, Wyoming) University of Utah; Spencer S. Eccles Health Sciences Library, 10 North 1900 East, Salt Lake City, UT 84112-5890; Telephone: (800) 338-7657 or (801) 587-3412; Fax: (801) 581-3632; *http://www.nnlm.gov/mcr/*

MIDDLE ATLANTIC REGION (Delaware, New Jersey, New York, Pennsylvania) The New York Academy of Medicine; 1216 Fifth Avenue, New York, NY 10029; Telephone: (212) 876-8763 or (800) 338-7657; Fax: (212) 534-7042; *http://www.nnlm.gov/mar/*

NEW ENGLAND REGION (Connecticut, Maine, Massachusetts, New Hampshire, Rhode Island, Vermont); University of Connecticut Health Center, Lyman Maynard Stowe Library, 263 Farmington Avenue, Farmington, CT 06030-5370; Telephone: (860) 679-4500 or (800) 338-7657; Fax: (860) 679-1305; *http://www.nnlm.gov/ner/.*

PACIFIC NORTHWEST REGION (Alaska, Idaho, Montana, Oregon, Washington) University of Washington; Health Sciences Center Library, Box 357155, Seattle, WA 98195 Telephone: (206) 543-8262 or (800) 338-7657; Fax: (206) 543-2469; *http://www.nnlm.gov/pnr/.*

PACIFIC SOUTHWEST REGION (Arizona, California, Hawaii, Nevada, U.S. Territories in the Pacific Basin); University of California at Los Angeles, Louise M. Darling Biomedical Library, 12-077 Center for Health Sciences, P.O. Box 951798, Los Angeles, CA 90095-1798; Telephone: (310) 825-1200 or (800) 338-7657; Fax: (310) 825-5389; *http://www.nnlm.gov/psr/.*

SOUTH CENTRAL REGION (Arkansas, Louisiana, New Mexico, Oklahoma, Texas); Houston Academy of Medicine, Texas Medical Center Library, 1133 John Freeman Boulevard, Houston, TX 77030-2809; Telephone: (713) 799-7880 or (800) 338-7657; Fax: (713) 790-7030; *http://www.nnlm.gov/scr/.*

SOUTHEASTERN ATLANTIC REGION (Alabama, Florida, Georgia, Maryland, Mississippi, North Carolina, South Carolina, Tennessee, Virginia, West Virginia, District of Columbia, Puerto Rico, U.S. Virgin Islands); University of Maryland at Baltimore, Health Sciences Library, 601 W. Lombard Street, Baltimore, MD 21201; Telephone: (410) 706-2855 or (800) 338-7657; Fax: (410) 706-0099; *http://www.nnlm.gov/sar/.*

§ 8.57   On-Line Research

If your firm is involved with medical malpractice, product liability, or personal injury cases involving complex medical or psychological issues, access to medical databases through the Internet is essential.

§ 8.58   —The Internet

By now, most people are familiar with and use the Internet (the "Net")—a world-wide broadcast system, a mechanism for information dissemination, and a medium for collaboration and interaction between individuals and their computers without regard to geographic location. The Internet is a worldwide network of networks that interconnects computers ranging from desktop PCs to the largest government and education supercomputers. It is composed of over 60,000 independent networks and millions of individual users (some estimate as high as 50 million users). No one individual or organization is in charge of or controls the Internet. It began in 1969 as a basic text project of the Department of Defense.

The World Wide Web (www, the Web) is a system of interconnected documents and other information and is accessible via the Internet.

It began in 1989 and introduced multimedia format (text, graphics, and sound) to the Internet. See **Form 8–6** for a listing of some of the most common abbreviations, concepts, and terms utilized on the Internet. For a more complete listing of Internet terms, see the list compiled by Internet Literacy ConsultantsTM and found at *www.matisse.net.*

§ 8.59 —Tips for Intelligent Web Surfing

Eventually, it will become all too apparent to frequent surfers that quackery abounds in medical sites on the Web. It is essential, therefore, that the sources you use for your litigation and medical research purposes be reliable and high quality.

Use Recognized Authorities.
Who is responsible for the content of the site and who runs it? Is information about them readily available to the user? Always look for an "about us" page which will identify the site's authors—for example, a branch of the Federal or State government, a non-profit institution, an educational institution, a professional society, a for-profit or commercial organization, or an individual.

Quality Should Be a Focus.
The *quality* of a Web site is increased when oversight of the content is provided by an editorial board and is subject to peer review. For example, Virtual Hospital (*http://www.vh.org*) is a digital health sciences library created in 1992 at the University of Iowa to help meet the information needs of health care providers and patients. The goal of the Virtual Hospital digital library is to make the Internet a useful medical reference and health promotion tool for health care providers and patients. The Virtual Hospital digital library contains thousands of textbooks and booklets for health care providers and patients alike. Content on this site comes from faculty and staff affiliated with University of Iowa Health Care, which includes the University of Iowa Carver College of Medicine and University of Iowa Hospitals and Clinics. Many of the faculty and staff are physician-teachers who prepare doctors and other health care professionals at both a medical school level and residency and fellowship training levels. Content is also provided by clinicians who treat patients in the fields about which they have written, as well as by researchers. All articles

appearing on this site have been peer reviewed, either internally by one or more members of the author's academic department, or externally by outside experts in the field.

Does the site carry the Health On the Net Foundation (HON) accreditation? HON (*www.hon.ch*) was created in 1995 and is a nongovernmental organization whose mission is to guide lay persons or nonmedical users and medical practitioners to useful and reliable online medical and health information. HON provides leadership in setting ethical standards for Web site developers. Web sites must formally apply for accreditation, and it is not automatically given to them. Before beginning research on a site, click on the Web site's HONcode accreditation, which should be displayed prominently. Not all medical research Web sites carry HON accreditation, but this is a good indicator of quality.

Opinion Is Not Evidence.

Always rely on evidence-based medical and scientific research ("This site was developed under the guidance of an Editorial Board of clinicians and researchers from medical institutions who are experts in cerebrovascular accidents"), not testimonials and statements from individuals ("I developed this site after my stroke").

Medical facts and figures should have references (such as citations to articles in medical journals). Also, opinions or advice should be clearly set apart from information that is "evidence-based" (that is, based on research results).

Is the Information Current?

A valid Web site will be updated on a regular basis, often daily. If you click on a few links on the site and they are "broken" or unable to be accessed, the site is probably not kept up to date. It is particularly important that medical information be current, and that the most recent update or review date be clearly posted. Even if the information has not changed, it is helpful to know that the site owners have reviewed it recently to ensure that the information is still valid.

Avoid Bias—Who Is Funding the Site?

Funding for medical research sites can come from various areas—public funds, donations, or commercial advertising. All advertisements should be clearly labeled as "advertisement" or "from our sponsor." Be wary of sites that promote one specific drug as treatment for a condition such as depression, as the drug's manufacturer may be supporting that site. The source of funding can affect what content is presented, how the content is presented, and what the owners want to accomplish on the site.

§ 8.60　—Designing Your Search

As with any kind of research, you should spend a few moments at the outset thinking about what it is you need to accomplish. Your best friend in any on-line research will be the **Search Engine** you choose. Search engines use software called spiders, which comb the Internet looking for documents and their Web addresses. The documents and Web addresses are collected and sent to the search engine's indexing software. The indexing software extracts information from the documents, storing it in a database. The kind of information indexed depends on the particular search engine. Some index every word in a document, others index the title only. When you perform a search by entering key words, the database of that engine is searched for documents that match. The search engine then assembles a Web page that lists the results as hypertext links. Search engines come in two basis types—those that continually sift through the links in its database adding new and updated pages to its database (e.g., *www.google.com*) and those that contain manually added links or reviews of Web sites (e.g., *www.Yahoo.com*). Other search engines are Alta Vista (*www.altavista.com*), Answers.com™ (*www.answers.com*), and HotBot (*www.hotbot.com*).

Initially, you may want to consider conducting a **MetaSearch.** Every time a query is entered, a series of other search and content sites are searched at the same time. The engine culls the results and presents them on a single screen, either by source or by integration in a uniform manner. Duplicates are eliminated and the results are re-sorted according to relevance. A MetaSearch engine produces a snapshot of the top results from a variety of search engines, resulting in a broad range of information. MetaSearch engines are tolerant of imprecise search terms or inexpert operators. Although they tend to return fewer results, there is a greater degree of relevance to the search terms. MetaSearch engines also allow the user to compare the kinds of results available on different search engine types (e.g., indexes, directories, pay-for-placement, etc.), or to verify that a great resource provided by another site has not been missed. Metasearch engines to consider include Dogpile (*www.dogpile.com*); Mamma (*www. mamma.com*); Metacrawler (*www.metacrawler.com*); and ProFusion (*www.profusion.com*).

§ 8.61   —National Library of Medicine and MEDLARS®

The National Library of Medicine (NLM), located on the campus of the National Institutes of Health in Bethesda, Maryland, is the world's largest medical library. The Library collects materials in all areas of biomedicine and health care, as well as works on biomedical aspects of technology, the humanities, and the physical, life, and social sciences. As of 2005, the collections number more than 7 million items, and include books, journals, technical reports, manuscripts, microfilms, photographs, and images.

The computer files of the National Library of Medicine (NLM) contain about 15 million records covering its holdings of books, journal articles, abstracts, and more. This system is known as MEDLARS® (MEDical Literature Analysis and Retrieval System). Among the many databases available through MEDLARS® is MEDLINE®.

§ 8.62   —MEDLINE®

MEDLINE® (Medical Literature Analysis and Retrieval System Online) can be found at *http://www.ncbi.nlm.nih.gov/entrez.* It is a bibliographic database of 180 more than 13 million references to journal articles dating back to 1966. Bibliographic citations and author abstracts are included from more than 4,800 biomedical journals published in the United States and 70 other countries. In addition to the basic citations, it contains abstracts to approximately 60 percent of the articles that are referenced. Since 2002, between 1,500 to 3,500 completed references have been added each day, with over 571,000 total references added during 2004.

The subject scope of MEDLINE is biomedicine and health, broadly defined to encompass those areas of the life sciences, behavioral sciences, chemical sciences, and bioengineering needed by health professionals and others engaged in basic research and clinical care, public health, health policy development, or related educational activities. MEDLINE also covers life sciences that are vital to biomedical practitioners, researchers, and educators, including aspects of biology, environmental science, marine biology, plant, and animal science, as well as biophysics and chemistry.

Increased coverage of life sciences began in 2000. The majority of the publications covered in MEDLINE are scholarly journals; a small number of newspapers, magazines, and newsletters considered useful to particular segments of NLM's broad user community are also included. For citations added during 1995–2003: about 48 percent are for cited articles published in the U.S., about 88 percent are published in English, and about 76 percent have English abstracts that are written by authors of the articles.

MEDLINE is the primary component of PubMed (*http://pubmed.gov*); a link to PubMed is found on the NLM home page at *http://www.nlm.nih. gov*. The result of a MEDLINE/PubMed search is a list of citations (including authors, title, source, and often an abstract) to journal articles and an indication of free electronic full text availability. Searching is free of charge and does not require registration. MEDLINE in PubMed may also be searched using the NLM Gateway, a single Web interface that searches multiple NLM retrieval systems.

Initially, MEDLINE was a bibliographic source only; the full text was not provided. However, a growing number of MEDLINE citations contain a link to the free full text of the article archived in PubMed Central® or to other sites. For articles not available on the web, the "Loansome Doc®" feature in PubMed provides an easy way to place an electronic order through the National Network of Libraries of Medicine® (NN/LM®) for the full-text copy of an article cited in MEDLINE. Registration is required and local fees may apply for this service.

For about 4,500 journals (and the number continues to increase) you can also link from a MEDLINE reference to the publisher's Web site to request or view the full article, depending upon the publisher's access requirements. Services/products providing access to MEDLINE data are also developed and made available from the NLM database. Access to various MEDLINE services is often available from medical libraries, many public libraries, and commercial sources. MedlinePlus®, another service offered by the NLM, provides consumer oriented health information. Health consumers are encouraged to discuss search results with their health care provider.

§ 8.63   Access to MEDLINE®

Free access to MEDLINE® is available through Entrez PubMed (*www. ncbi.nlm.nih.gov/entrez*). PubMed includes links to many sites providing full text articles and other related resources, access to Loansome Doc®

delivery service (charges apply), access to sets of related articles precomputed for each article cited, and access to a Medical Subject Heading (MeSH®) Browser; searches using simple key words or advanced Boolean expressions; and links to publishers' sites for approximately 100 full-text journals.

- **Infotrieve** (*http://www.infotrieve.com*) is a library services company offering free access to MEDLINE® and 65,000 journal titles with full-service document delivery. No account is required. Charges are $12.00 per article, plus any copyright, royalty, or purchase costs. Delivery by first-class mail or on the Internet is free; there is a $1 per page charge for fax delivery, and additional $10 charge per article for rush service and $20 for panic service.

- **Medscape** (*http://www.medscape.com*) A Web site for physicians and allied health care professionals, open to nonprofessionals as well. Medscape is a service of WebMD, Inc., and provides peer-reviewed articles, reference tools, medical and clinical information and resources, medical news, medical conference coverage, treatment updates, and certified continuing education for healthcare professionals. Contents include thousands of full-text, prereviewed clinical journal articles, all of which may be downloaded, as well as a clinical discussion forum, free drug information search, medical news, conference calendar, and bookstore. It allows unlimited free access to MEDLINE®, Aidsline, and Toxline. A one-time, free membership registration is required.

- **Paper***Chase* (*http://www.paperchase.com*) This proprietary site is a service of Beth Israel Deaconess Medical Center of Harvard Medical School. It offers a combined search of MEDLINE®, Aidsline, Cancerlit, HealthSTAR, and OLDMEDLINE. Delivery of full-text articles is by fax, courier, or first-class mail. For individuals, the cost is $19.95 for 30 days or $150 for one year. Copies of documents range from $20 to $28, depending on mode of service.

§ 8.64 —Internet Resources

It would be impossible in this section to list all of the thousands of medical and legal resources available on the Internet. However, the following are some common, well-known, and useful sites that can be utilized as starting points for Internet research.

Practice Note: The following addresses have been verified as of the date of publication. However, readers are cautioned that addresses and individual sites on the Web change frequently.

Aids/HIV

- **AIDS.Com** (*http://www.aids.com*) Published by the American International AIDS Foundation, which is a nonprofit charitable organization committed to providing timely, accurate, and easy-to-understand information about AIDS and HIV to a global lay audience. This site contains fact sheets, clinical trials, latest information on treatment options, and links to related sites.
- **HIV InSite** (*www.hivinsite.org*) developed and maintained by the Center for HIV Information (CHI) at the University of California San Francisco (UCSF), one of the world's leading health sciences institutions. This gateway site presents up-to-date scientific information on AIDS treatment, prevention, and policy. This site has been named one of the Medical Library Association's "Top Ten" most useful Web sites.

Anatomy

- **MEDTropolis** (*http://www.medtropolis.com*) is where you will find the Virtual BodySM, an in-depth, anatomical review of the human body. This site also contains educational materials related to cancer, diabetes, bariatric surgery, etc.

Anesthesia

- **Anesthesia Doc** (*http://www.anesthesiadoc.net*) is a gateway site with links to anesthesia-related practice guidelines, literature search, journals, medical news, e-books, and societies.

Cardiology

- **American Heart Association** (*http://www.americanheart.org*). This site contains information on heart diseases, symptoms, and treatment with links to multiple other related sites.

Family Practice

- **American Academy of Family Physicians** (*http://www.aafp.org*) includes full access to the journals *Annals of Family Medicine* and *American Family Physician.*

General Medicine and Medical Research

- **Advanced Medical Technology Association** (*http://www.himanet. com*) links to topics such as FDA reform, industry topics, current topics, and other categories of interest to this medical technology association whose members include medical device manufacturers, producers of diagnostic products, and medical information systems.
- **American Medical Association** (*http://www.ama-assn.org*) This site contains articles from the *Journal of the American Medical Association*; archived journals on specialties, including general psychiatry, internal medicine, dermatology, neurology, ophthalmology, otolaryngology, facial plastic surgery, and surgery; links to other sites; on-line doctor locator; and free access to whole text MEDLINE® articles.
- **Centers for Disease Control** (*http://www.cdc.gov*) contains information on health and safety topics with an "A to Z" index of short discussions (for example, areas of concern from anthrax and antibiotic resistance to bird flu, youth suicide and zoster); publications; data and statistics; and information about the Centers.
- **eMedicine** (*http://www.emedicine.com*) contains articles on 7,000 diseases and disorders. The evidence-based content, updated 24/7, provides the latest practice guidelines in 59 medical specialties, recent recalls and alerts, news headlines, and specialty home pages. eMedicine's professional content undergoes four levels of physician peer review plus an additional review by a PharmD. The consumer health site, *http://www.eMedicineHealth.com*, contains more than 5,500 pages of health content, and articles written by physicians for patients and consumers. Each article is reviewed by two physicians and a PharmD. Current medical information is available in the Health Resource, First Aid and Emergencies, and Lifestyle and Wellness Centers. Registration is required.
- **EurekAlert!** (*http://www.eurekalert.org*) is produced by the American Association for the Advancement of Science and Stanford University. This site provides access to information about scientific and medical

research, as well as technological developments. It has links to other relevant sites.

- **Food and Drug Administration** (*http://www.fda.gov*) contains information about FDA activities, recalls, product safety, and product approvals, with links to the Code of Federal Regulations and Federal Register and to MedWatch (*www.fda.gov/medwatch*), the FDA Safety Information and Adverse Event Reporting Program.

- **Hardin MD** (*http://www.lib.uiowa.edu*) was first launched in 1996, as a source to find directories of information in health and medicine. The name comes from Hardin Meta Directory, since the site was conceived as a "directory of directories," and contains a listing of, and links to, medical and health sciences libraries on the Web, free full-text PubMed articles, and multiple links to other sites.

- **Health on the Net Foundation** (*http://www.hon.ch*) is a nonprofit organization headquartered in Geneva. Its site includes distribution lists, FAQs, a media gallery with a searchable database of medical images and movies, a library, and health care-related conferences. The site has both French and English access.

- **Healthfinder** (*http://www.healthfinder.org*) is a gateway Web site developed by the National Health Information Center of the U.S. Department of Health and Human Services with links to information and Web sites from over 1,500 health-related organizations, and multiple on-line medical journals (including *American Journal of Epidemiology, Annals of Emergency Medicine, Annals of Internal Medicine, CHEST, Science,* and the *New England Journal of Medicine,* for example). This Web site subscribes to the HONcode principles and has been named one of the Medical Library Association's "Top Ten" most useful Web sites.

- **Mayo Clinic Health Oasis** (*http://www.mayohealth.org*) is a health information site utilizing the expertise of over 2,000 clinical specialists from the Mayo Clinic. This site contains sections on diseases and conditions, treatment options, drugs and supplements, healthy living, etc. There are no links to outside sites. This Web site has been named one of the Medical Library Association's "Top Ten" most useful Web Sites.

- **Medical Matrix** (*http://www.medmatrix.org*) is a proprietary site which requires registration and yearly subscription ($99 for individual). It lists over 6,000 medical Web sites and links to over 1.5 million documents.

- **Medicine Net, Inc.** (*http://www.medicinenet.com*) is an on-line, healthcare media publishing company with a consumer-oriented Web site. It is produced by a network of U.S. board certified physicians and includes sections on diseases and conditions, symptoms and signs, procedures and tests, medications, MedTerms medical dictionary, and multiple links to other sites.

- **National Institutes of Health** (*http://www.nih.gov*) links to all nineteen Institutes, including the oldest, the National Cancer Institute (established in 1937), and the newest, the National Institute of Bioimaging and Biomedical Engineering (established in 2000), and the nine Centers (e.g., National Center on Minority Health and Health Disparities). The site includes links to several databases (Clinical Trials, MEDLINEplus, Healthfinder, PubMed and several federal health agencies. As well, this site contains an "A to Z" health information section.

- *New England Journal of Medicine* (*http://www.nejm.org*) allows on-line subscription for $99 per year (per individual, U.S.) and $149 for online and print. The user is able to search archived issues (back to 1975) and sign up for e-mail summaries.

- **Virtual Hospital**® (*http://www.vh.org*) is a digital health sciences library created in 1992 at the University of Iowa to help meet the information needs of health care providers and patients. The goal of the Virtual Hospital digital library is to make the Internet a useful medical reference and health promotion tool for health care providers and patients. The Virtual Hospital digital library contains thousands of textbooks and booklets for health care providers and patients, as well as links to digital libraries and other components of the University of Iowa's Health Sciences Center.

Law & Regulatory Sites

- **EMTALA Online** (*http://www.medlaw.com*) is a resource center for information on the Consolidated Omnibus Budget Reconciliation Act (COBRA) and Emergency Medical Treatment and Active Labor Act (EMTALA), regulations issued under these statutes, and new court decisions concerning medical malpractice issues.

- **FirstGov for Consumers** (*http://www.consumer.gov*) includes information from the FDA, the CPSC, the National Highway Traffic Safety Administration, and other federal agencies with links to the agency sites.

• **Federation of State Medical Boards** (*http://www.fsmb.org*) is the parent organization to all state disciplinary boards, with direct link access to all 50 state boards. Additionally, at *http://www.docinfo.org*, access to the FSMB database is now open to the public for a per-query charge of $9.95, which results in a Disciplinary Search Report outlining the disciplinary actions that have been taken against this physician. If no disciplinary actions have been reported, you will receive a report stating "No Reported Actions Found."

Oncology

• **American Cancer Society** (*http://www.cancer.org*) offers interactive tools designed to help patients make informed treatment decisions, full disclosure of treatment options, side effects, and outcomes, personalized reports with pros and cons of treatment, questions to ask your physician, and access to relevant abstracts of medical studies.

• **Association of Cancer Online Resources** (*http://www.acor.org*) is a nonprofit organization designed to provide information and support to cancer patients and caregivers through the creation and maintenance of cancer-related Internet mailing lists and Web-based resources. Offers information on types of cancer, treatment options, and clinical trials.

• **National Cancer Institute** (*http://www.cancer.gov*) offers information on types of cancer, causes, genetics, treatment options, prevention, clinical trials, and coping. This site links to PDQ® (Physician Data Query), NCI's comprehensive cancer database which contains peer-reviewed summaries on cancer treatment, screening, prevention, genetics, and supportive care, and complementary and alternative medicine; a registry of approximately 2,000 open and 13,000 closed cancer clinical trials from around the world; and directories of physicians, professionals who provide genetics services, and organizations that provide cancer care.

• **OncoLink** (*http://www.oncolink.upenn.edu*) was founded in 1994 by cancer specialists at the University of Pennsylvania Abramson Cancer Center. OncoLink contains comprehensive information about specific types of cancer, updates on cancer treatments, and news about research advances. The information is updated daily and aimed at all levels, from introductory to in-depth.

Orthopedics

* **Orthopaedic Web Links,** or OWL (*http://www.orthopaedicweblinks. com*) is a gateway site to over 7,100 links/resources for orthopedic surgery and trauma including bibliographies, case presentations, CME, e-mail lists, evidence-based orthopaedics, general resources, multimedia presentations, international resources, organizations and associations, industry, topics, patient information, publications, surgeons and clinics, teaching resources, universities and academic centers.

Pain

* **International Association for the Study of Pain** (*http://www. iasp-pain.org*) was founded in 1973, and is a nonprofit professional organization dedicated to furthering research on pain and improving the care of patients with pain. Among other resources, the site contains archived issues of *Pain Clinical Updates,* which is published four times a year.

Pharmacology

* **Pharmaceutical Information Network** (*http://www.pharmweb.net*) contains a database of articles, a list of FAQs about drugs with answers from drug manufacturers, an archive of drug-related discussion threads, and links to other sites.
* **Pharmaceutical Research and Manufacturers of America** (*http:// www.phrma.org*) has information about issues of significance, including drugs in development, and contains facts and figures about drugs in current use.
* **Internet Drug Index** (*http://www.rxlist.com*) lists top 200 drugs by sales year, drug interactions and side effects for 1,450 + products, and the on-line version of *Taber's Medical Encyclopedia.*

Psychiatry & Psychology

* **American Academy of Child and Adolescent Psychiatry** (*http:// www.aacap.org*) official Web site offers information on child and

adolescent psychiatry, clinical trials, ongoing research, and links to multiple related sites.

- **Internet Mental Health** (*http://www.mentalhealth.com*) is an encyclopedia of mental health information created by a Canadian psychiatrist, Dr. Phillip Long, with information on mental disorders, treatment, research, diagnosis, psychiatric medications, *Mental Health* magazine, links to over 25 mental health-related medical and scientific journals.

- **National Institute of Mental Health** (*http://www.nimh.nih.gov*) uses the Google™ search engine to search for text on a variety of mental health issues, including the signs and symptoms, diagnosis and treatment of disorders (generalized anxiety, attention deficit, obsessive-compulsive, post-traumatic stress, etc.). Additional categories include specific information concerning children and adolescents, women, men, older adults, bibliographic citations, clinical trials, suicide prevention, research and funding, and medication. MedlinePlus® and ClinicalTrials.gov are services of the National Library of Medicine, which provides listings of federally and privately supported research using human volunteers.

Radiology

- **RadiologyInfo™** (*http://www.radiologyinfo.org*) is the public information Web site developed and funded by the American College of Radiology and the Radiological Society of North America, established to inform and educate about radiologic procedures and the role of radiologists in healthcare, and to improve communications between physicians and their patients. The site explains how various x-ray, CT, MRI, ultrasound, radiation therapy, and other procedures are performed, addresses what may be experienced, and how to prepare for the exams.

- **The Visible Human Project®** (*http://www.nlm.nih.gov*), as completed by the National Library of Medicine, consists of complete, anatomically-detailed, three-dimensional representations of the normal male and female human bodies. Transverse CT, MR, and cryosection images of representative male and female cadavers are available, and are designed to serve, among other applications, as a reference for the study of human anatomy.

FORM 8–1
Sample Chart Summary of Medical Records Patient Jane Doe
(current as of June 27, 1996)

DATE	PROVIDER	COMMENTS
01/23/89	Dr. W	Right ankle sprain. [2]
06/14/89	Dr. M	Upper respiratory infection with pharyngitis. **Under a great deal of mental strain, stating that she is undergoing a divorce. [4]**
11/13/89	Dr. P	Initial consult re augmentation; doesn't know anyone who has had breast enlargement but has been considering the procedure for several years; present bra size is 34A, padded, wants B cup range; employed as an aerobics instructor; healthy but bruises easily; nonsmoker. Impression: bilateral mammary hypoplasia. Options discussed—capsule contracture felt to be lessened with polyurethane foam-covered implants. [2]
01/22/90	Dr. P	Bilateral augmentation mammoplasty with 255 cc Replicon, placed in subpectoral location via inframammary incision. **Replicon catalog #RE7-255, control #9141364 (right) and #9141365 (left). [10, 12]**
01/26/90	Dr. P	Seen for suture removal; slight swelling and redness. [4]
02/08/90	Dr. P	Complains of continued soreness and swelling in both breasts with skin rash. [4]
03/06/90	Dr. P	Doing very well; soreness and rash have almost totally resolved; pleased with the result . . . [5]
11/12/91	Dr. P	**"She is thinking she may wish larger implants and that is also discussed with her. I indicated that the Replicon implant is no longer available and brought her up to date on that issue." [5]**
11/05/92	Dr. W	Non-suicidal depression, in counseling, psychologist requested medication. Assessment—major depression, prescribed Prozac. [2]

DATE	PROVIDER	COMMENTS
01/07/94	Dr. S	Meme implants placed 4 years, having no problems but **"is concerned about polyurethane implants. We discussed this in detail."** [1]
01/22/94	Dr. W	HIV test—negative. [22]
04/08/94	Dr. C	Initial rheumatological evaluation: concerned re Meme implants; 6 months ago developed joint aches and problems with joint pain during exercise; on-and-off fatigue; definite Raynaud's syndrome with numbness and tingling of feet and hands for 2 years; photosensitive; dry mouth and eyes; anxiety and depression for past 18 months . . . Exam: purplish discoloration of hands, feet; dermatographia; malar rash; slightly increased adenopathy and thyromegaly; slight hardening of right implant . . . swelling in joints; knees slightly puffy. Impression: arthritis, malar rash, and Raynaud's "fit into category of possible Lupus." Polyurethane implants "must be removed due to the breakdown products of the polyurethane." [5-8]
05/01/96	Dr. B	Consultation for concern over silicone implants and polyurethane coating. Implants appear to be intact but encapsulated. **"Of significance . . . is the fact that the polyurethane coating has already been broken down by her body, almost certainly."** . . . discussed removal and replacement with saline implants . . . [1-2]

FORM 8–2
Sample Database Form Database Medical Information—
Breast Implant Clients

Field	Field Type	Description
NM	TEXT-20	NAME
ADD	MULTI	ADDRESS
DOB	DATE-8	DATE OF BIRTH
SSN	TEXT-9	SOCIAL SECURITY NUMBER
PMD	MULTI	NAME/ADDRESS PRIMARY MEDICAL DOCTOR
1IMPLDT	DATE-8	DATE OF FIRST IMPLANT
1 REASON	NOTE	REASON FOR FIRST IMPLANT
1IMPSURG	MULTI	SURGEON FOR FIRST IMPLANT
1IMPHOS	MULTI	HOSPITAL FOR FIRST IMPLANT
1IMPSUP	MULTI	SUPPLIER OF FIRST IMPLANT
1IMPMFG	MULTI	MANUFACTURER OF FIRST IMPLANT
1MODEL#	MULTI	MANUFACTURER MODEL NAME/NUMBER
1SERIAL#	TEXT-15	MANUFACTURER SERIAL NUMBER
1LOT#L	TEXT-15	MANUFACTURER LOT NUMBER FOR LEFT BREAST
1LOT#R	TEXT-15	MANUFACTURER LOT NUMBER FOR RIGHT BREAST
1SZIMPL	TEXT-8	SIZE OF LEFT IMPLANT
1SZIMPR	TEXT-8	SIZE OF RIGHT IMPLANT
1EXPDT	DATE-8	DATE OF FIRST EXPLANT
1EXPSURG	MULTI	SURGEON OF FIRST EXPLANT
1EXPHOS	MULTI	HOSPITAL OF FIRST EXPLANT
1EXPCOND	MULTI	CONDITION OF IMPLANT ON REMOVAL
1EXPCUST	NOTE	LOCATION OF IMPLANTS SINCE REMOVAL

Field	Field Type	Description
BIRTH#	TEXT-3	NUMBER OF LIVE BIRTHS POST-IMPLANT
CHLDDOB	NOTE	NAME AND DATE OF BIRTH OF CHILDREN
BRSTFED	NOTE	NAMES OF CHILDREN BREAST-FED POST-IMPLANT
CHLDHLTH	NOTE	INFORMATION RE EACH CHILD'S HEALTH, INCLUDING ANY SUBSTANCE USE BY MOTHER DURING PREGNANCY
MEDICTN	MULTI*	PRIOR OR CURRENT MEDICATION USED
SUBABUSE	NOTE	ANY AND ALL ALCOHOL, DRUG, SMOKING, NARCOTIC HISTORY
PREMEDHX	NOTE	ILLNESSES AND HOSPITALIZATIONS PRIOR TO 1ST IMPLANT
PSTMEDHX	NOTE	ILLNESSES AND HOSPITALIZATIONS AFTER 1ST IMPLANT
COMPLCTN	NOTE	COMPLICATIONS AFTER IMPLANT
CAPSUL	NOTE	CLOSED CAPSULOTOMIES
MAMMO	NOTE	MAMMOGRAMS WITH IMPLANTS
MRI	NOTE	MRI OF IMPLANTS
US	NOTE	ULTRASOUND OF IMPLANTS
EXP	MULTI	NAME/DATE OF EXPERT CONSULTATION
EXPRPT	TEXT-3	REPORT RECEIVED—Y OR N
SXS	MULTI*	SYMPTOMS AND DATE OF ONSET
CONFDX	MULTI*	CONFIRMED DIAGNOSES
FAMHX	NOTE	FAMILY HISTORY OF CONFIRMED DIAGNOSES
LASTUPDT	DATE-8	DATE LAST UPDATE TO DATABASE
USER	TEXT-4	INITIALS OF PERSON UPDATING DATABASE

FORM 8–3
Sample Breakout Summary (Medical Care)

Nov. 2005	3	4	5	6	7	8	9	10	11	12
Physician & Actions	ER - sent home	MD: admit to acute	None	Infectious Disease; transfer to ICU; intubate	University MD	None	None	None	None	University MD
Clinical course		DX: pneumonia, cannot exclude legionella or mycoplasma			cyanosis hands & feet, pulses present	increased cyanosis, radial pulse palp., pedal by doppler only		mottled to knees, no pulses		
Antibiotic treatment		Cephazolin & Tobramycin started		Erythromycin ordered 0600, begun 1200						

FORM 8-4
Sample Breakout Summary (Nursing Care)

Nov. 2005	3	4	5	6	7	8	9	10
Weight	not charted	173.5	not charted	174.4	177	184	187.7	190.6
Temp (highest)	102.5	105.2	103	104.2	104	102	101.8	102
Turning	not charted	MD orders every 2 hours	turned 10am, 2 pm, 8 pm	not charted	turned every 2 hours	turned every 2 hours	not charted	turned every 2 hours, nights only
Skin	not charted	not charted	not charted	hands and feet cool	not charted	hands & feet cyanotic	increased cyanosis	mottled to knees
Pulses	not charted	not charted	bilateral radial & pedal pulses present	bilateral radial & pedal pulses present	bilateral radial & pedal pulses present	radial pulses present bilaterally, pedal pulses only by Doppler	radial pulses present bilaterally, pedal pulses only by Doppler	no left pedal, right pedal to Doppler only

FORM 8–5
SAMPLE SUMMARY OF MEDICAL SPECIALS

Medical Specials – Plaintiff
(Current as of March 4, 2005)

PROVIDER	DATE	CHARGES	ADJ-W/O[1]	
REACH Air Ambulance	09/24/03	$7,479.86	$5,357.86	$2,152.00
MEDIC Ambulance	09/24/03	872.00		
JM Medical Center	09/25/03-11/06/03	527,357.45	416,696.87	110,660.58
K Acute Care Hospital	11/06/03-11/26/03	67,964.07	45,955.05	22,009.02 (Pt. A)
Skilled Nursing & Rehabilitation Center[2]	11/26/03-01/01/04	19,039.80	3,780.00	15,259.80 (Pt.A)
	01/06/04-01/17/04	3,400.80	1,314.00	2,086.80 (A)
	01/19/04-01/20/04	238.99	47.81	191.18 (Pt. B)
	05/01/04-10/31/04	2,157.26	150.09	2,006.36 (B)
	11/01/04-02/28/05	19,080.00[3]	6,360.00	12,720.00 (B)
DMER[4]	01/06/04-08/11/04	7,287.33	2,894.91	4,392.42 (B)
Various physicians	09/25/03-10/28/04	39,796.57	27,454.50	12,338.07 (B)
Subtotal		*$ 675,594.13*	*$503,453.19*	*$ 171,096.23*

1. Includes MediCare adjustments and hospital/provider write-offs.
2. Paid by MediCare, Parts A and B.
3. This figure *assumes* monthly charge of $4,770 with approx. 2/3 MediCare Part B payment
4. "DMER": charges found on Medicaid Application, possibly durable medical equipment.

FORM 8–6
COMMON ABBREVIATIONS, CONCEPTS, AND TERMS
UTILIZED ON THE INTERNET

ASCII—(American Standard Code for Information Interchange) This is the *de facto* world-wide standard for the code numbers used by computers to represent all the upper and lower-case Latin letters, numbers, punctuation, etc. There are 128 standard ASCII codes, each of which can be represented by a seven-digit binary number: 0000000 through 1111111.

BBS (Bulletin Board System)—meeting and announcement system that allows people to carry on discussions, upload and download files, and make announcements.

BLOG— a Web site that contains dated entries in reverse chronological order (most recent first) about a particular topic. Functioning as an online newsletter, blogs can be written by one person or a group of contributors. Entries contain commentary and links to other Web sites, and images as well as a search facility may also be included. A blog with video clip entries instead of text is a "video Weblog" (vlog).

Browser—a client program (software) that is used to look at various kinds of Internet resources.

Crawling, crawler—also known as a "Web crawler," "spider," "ant," "robot" (bot) and "intelligent agent," a crawler is a program that searches for information on the Web. Crawlers are widely used by Web search engines to index all the pages on a site by following the links from page to page. The search engine then summarizes the content and adds the links to their indexes. They are also used to locate Web pages that sell a particular product or to find blogs that have opinions about a product.

Cyberspace—the term used to describe the whole range of information resources available through computer networks.

FAQ (Frequently Asked Questions)—a document that lists and answers the most common inquiries about Web sites, software, etc.

FTP (File Transfer Protocol)—a method of moving files between two Net sites.

Gateway—site that serves as an entrance to multiple other sites and links.

HTML (HyperText Markup Language)—a collection of style information used to define the components of a Web document (e.g., layout, font, font size, etc.).

HTTP (HyperText Transfer/Transport Protocol)—a standard computer protocol for moving hypertext files across the Internet.

Hypertext/Hyperlink—a powerful search tool that highlights keywords within text displayed on the computer screen. By selecting the particular hypertext/hyperlink, you are immediately routed to a source containing information regarding that word(s). Frequently, the source is located at another site. Links are usually underlined and in a different color from the rest of the text (i.e., *www.google.com*).

IRC (Internet Relay Chat)—a protocol that allows real-time conversation in Internet chat rooms.

ISP (Internet Service Provider)—an entity that provides your computer with a connection to the Internet, usually through telephone or cable lines. Some of the larger on-line services (AOL, CompuServe) offer their own access to the Net.

Listserv—an Internet mailing list.

MetaSearch—a metasearch is a search engine that sends user requests to several other search engines and/or databases and returns the results from each one. They allow users to enter their search criteria only one time and access several search engines simultaneously. See discussion in **§ 8.59.**

PDF (Portable Document Format)—A file format designed to enable printing and viewing of documents with all their formatting (e.g., typefaces, images, layout, etc.) appearing the same regardless of what operating system is used, so a PDF document should look the same on Windows, Macintosh, linux, OS/2, etc. The PDF format requires use of Adobe Acrobat Reader software to download. This is available on the Internet free of charge.

PPP (Point-to-Point Protocol)—specific software that allows your computer to connect to your ISP through the telephone or cable line.

Search Engine—a software program that searches a database and gathers and reports information that contains or is related to specified terms; a website whose primary function is providing a search engine for gathering and reporting information available on the Internet or a portion of the Internet. See discussion in **§ 8.59.**

SMTP (Simple Mail Transport Protocol)—the main way in which e-mail is sent on the Internet.

Surfing the Web—the act of moving between Web pages or Web sites.

URL (Uniform Resource Locater)—the electronic address for Web pages that identifies where a site can be found. Most URLs begin with "http://www" and end with an extension that indicates whether it is a business (.com), governmental (.gov), educational (.edu), or nonprofit site (.org).

WYSIWYG (What You See Is What You Get)—indicating that what you see on your computer screen closely resembles what you will get when you print.

CHAPTER 9

USE OF MEDICAL CONSULTANTS

§ 9.1   Need for Expert/Consultant Services

An essential attorney-client service is accomplished when medical records are reviewed and summarized. Through the medical record summary, important events in the individual's medical treatment are tracked and documented. Because the choice of a consultant depends on the type and complexity of the injury sustained, a comprehensive and concise medical record summary also helps the attorney clarify important points in a case and make an informed decision on if and what type of consultants are needed.

Cases that deal with personal injury, medical malpractice, product liability, workers' compensation, and toxic exposure may all involve complex medical issues. In these complex cases, it is usually beneficial to request an initial overall case review from a consultant with good general medical knowledge who can help determine potential areas of investigation and the type of expert(s) needed. In some instances, registered nurses, as legal nurse-consultants, are performing this function. Although the roles and functions of consultants and experts may overlap in the evaluation process, they differ in a few fundamental ways. See §§ 9.2 and 9.3 below.

A comprehensive evaluation of the short- and long-term effects of injuries requires the services of a medical professional familiar with the specific type of injury in question. Non-medical professionals (e.g. engineers, environmental and product safety professionals) knowledge-able in their respective fields should be used to address non-medical issues.

§ 9.2   Role of Consultant

A consultant usually reviews the case globally and renders a general opinion based on the findings of that review. Properly used, a consultant can save the attorney time and money. Consultants are able to:

1. Evaluate the case and advise the attorney on its' relative merits. This can include assistance in the decision to pursue litigation.

2. Help develop the potential theories of liability and identify possible defendants and weak areas of the case. For example, if a client's injury is not defensible against the particular strategy outlined by the attorney, it may be defensible against another.

3. Help the attorney understand the nature and extent of any alleged injuries, the possible need for future treatment, and potential for residual disabilities. This assessment places a value on the client's injuries, which in turn helps validate the settlement demand.

4. Prepare reports based upon review of the medical records and examination of the client, and review reports generated by opposing counsel's experts. See § **9.30** for a discussion of medical examinations.

5. Assist during discovery by suggesting areas of investigation through interrogatories and depositions, and help prepare for the depositions of the opposition's experts.

6. Review depositions associated with the case.

7. Conduct literature searches, (e.g., professional texts and articles, case law) for information concerning the injury or medical condition.

8. Assist at trial with testimony and preparation of medical documentary evidence.

The selection of a consultant depends upon the nature and type of injury and the degree of residual damage (if any). Several professionals from related fields such as medicine, nursing, and physical therapy often review cases involving complex injuries. This multidisciplinary approach allows case assessment from different professional perspectives.

§ 9.3   —Identification of Consultants

Parties are not required to identify experts acting solely as consulting or non-testifying experts. Their identities, reports, and facts known or opinions held are discoverable only under exceptional circumstances. These circumstances are generally identified as situations under which it is impracticable for the party seeking discovery to obtain the acts or opinions on the same subject by any other means (Fed. R. Civ. P. 26(b)(4)(B)).

§ 9.4   Role of Expert

An expert witness' role is considerably narrower than that of consultant. As the name implies, an expert has education, experience, and expertise in a specific field and is retained to give an opinion on the facts of a case based on this specialized knowledge. For example, a physician does not provide expert testimony on the competence of nursing practice because medicine and nursing are two separate disciplines. Likewise, a physician who practices as a general surgeon may not testify as an expert on orthopedic surgery because the two are distinct subspecialties within the field of medicine.

An expert utilizes published standards of care (see § **9.31** *et seq.*), current literature, and community practice as foundations for forming an opinion. Experts may initially assist the attorney by acting as a consultant, but when called upon to testify in deposition or at trial, they may address only their particular field of specialization.

§ 9.5   —Identification of Experts

Each expert who may be called to give opinion evidence at trial under the federal rules must be identified (Fed. R. Civ. P. 26(a)(2)). Disclosures concerning expert witnesses must be made at the times and in the sequence directed by the court. In the absence of court direction or stipulation, the disclosure must be made at least 90 days before trial or the date the case is to be ready for trial.

Disclosure is not limited to experts to be called on direct examination but also includes those who may be called to rebut or impeach opposing experts with the qualification that rebuttal experts may be identified 30 days after the opposing part has made its disclosure (Fed. R. Civ. P. 26(a)(2)(C)).

§ 9.6　Basis for Expert Testimony

From 1923 to the mid-1970s, the landmark decision for determining the admissibility of expert testimony on scientific evidence was *Frye v. United States,* 293 F. 1013 (D.C. Cir. 1923). In *Frye,* the court held that the appropriate test for the admission of expert testimony was whether it was "sufficiently established to have gained general acceptance in the particular field in which it belongs." Based on this holding, experts giving testimony had to establish three things:

* The status of the scientific principle and its appropriate field
* The technique of applying the principle
* The application of the technique in a particular case (relevant to expert testimony).

Even though it was felt that the *Frye* decision was deferential to defense, the "general acceptance" standard remained unchallenged until the adoption of the Federal Rules of Evidence, in 1975. See §§ **9.7** *et seq.* The Federal Rules diminished the rigid general acceptance test used by most courts to judge the propriety of expert testimony on "novel" or "unorthodox" techniques. Admissibility of expert scientific testimony could now be permitted if an individual's specialized knowledge would assist the trier of fact. Evidence was to be evaluated on several factors:

* Whether the expert's proposition had been tested and subjected to peer review and publication
* Whether the methodology or technique had a known error rate
* Whether there were standards for applying the methodology
* Whether the methodology was generally accepted in the scientific community.

§ 9.7　—Federal Rule of Evidence 702

Rule 702 of the Federal Rules of Evidence states that "if scientific, technical, or other specialized knowledge will assist the trier of fact to understand the evidence or to determine a fact in issue, a witness qualified as an expert by knowledge, skill, experience, training, or education, may testify thereto in the form of an opinion or otherwise." Because of this specialized degree of knowledge, the medical expert is able to render an opinion at trial based upon the facts of the case, an opinion that otherwise could not be offered. In contrast, lay witnesses can testify only to those facts within their knowledge but may not offer an opinion or conclusion based on those facts.

In a significant number of personal injury cases (and in most medical malpractice cases), expert testimony is required. The role of the expert is to educate and assist the jury in understanding issues and matters that are outside the common experience of a layperson. This testimony is the most important function of an expert.

§ 9.8   —Federal Rule of Evidence 703

This rule provides that the facts or data in a particular case upon which the expert bases an opinion or inference may be perceived by or made known to the expert at or before the trial. If the facts or data are of a type reasonably relied upon by experts in that particular field in forming opinions or inference on a subject, the facts or data need not be admissible in evidence. This rule recognizes that facts and data upon which expert opinions are based may be derived from three possible sources.

1. The first source is firsthand observation of the witness, e.g., opinion testimony offered by a treating physician.

2. The second source refers to information presented at trial, either in the form of a hypothetical question posed to and answered by the expert, or the expert's attendance at trial so that the testimony establishing the facts is heard.

3. The third source refers to the use of data presented to the expert outside of court and other than his or her own perception. A physician bases a diagnosis on information from various sources (e.g., statements by the patient, reports or opinions from other medical providers, medical records, radiology studies). Most of these are admissible in evidence but only after spending time and money to obtain and authenticate them. A physician/expert's validation of these sources in court (subject to cross-examination) as being of a type reasonably relied upon by experts in that particular field in forming opinions or inference on a subject will be adequate.

§ 9.9　—Federal Rule of Evidence 705

This rule provides that an expert may offer his or her opinion first, without initially disclosing the underlying facts or data relied upon. This rule tends to shorten the presentation by the expert at trial in that initial presentation of the data is often complex and time-consuming. In any event, the expert may be required to disclose this information initially by the court and certainly on cross-examination.

§ 9.10　—Evaluating Admissibility of Scientific Evidence: The *Daubert* Decision

In a 1993 decision, the Supreme Court sought to clarify the Federal Rules of Evidence standards for evaluating admissibility of scientific evidence. The case of *Daubert v. Merrell Dow Pharmaceuticals, Inc.,* 113 S. Ct. 2786 (1993) involved two mothers who alleged that their children had suffered birth defects because of the mothers' ingestion of Bendectin®, a medication to reduce nausea, during pregnancy. The plaintiffs' experts' conclusions were based on in vitro research and animal studies. The district court granted a motion for summary judgment on the ground that the plaintiffs' experts were not testifying to subject matter generally accepted within the scientific community. The appellate court affirmed the decision and held that peer review and publication are "hallmarks of reliable scientific investigation." *Id.* at 1131 n.3.

The *Daubert* decision dealt with the admissibility of expert opinion on evidence firmly based on scientific knowledge. It did not apply to expert opinion based on education and experience. In this interpretation of the Federal Rules, the court plainly obligated judges to make determinations as to the validity of scientific evidence. Some jurisdictions have interpreted *Daubert* as a license to completely exclude expert scientific testimony based on empirical analysis alone.

When the *Daubert* decision was handed down in 1993, many questions on its practical application arose. Court interpretations of what was admissible as expert testimony varied widely. Over time, however, a significant body of case law has become available that both plaintiff and defense can draw on to argue admissibility of evidence under *Daubert*. Two of these cases, whose rulings served as a basis for some subsequent court decisions, are discussed below.

§ 9.11 —Evaluating Admissibility of Scientific Evidence: Post-*Daubert*

In *General Electric Co. v. Joiner,* 522 U.S. 136 (1997), the United States Supreme Court determined the abuse of discretion standard was the appropriate standard for Courts to apply in decisions to admit or exclude "scientific expert testimony under *Daubert*." This standard, usually applied to review evidentiary rulings, should extend to scientific testimony as well.

The Case

Robert Joiner was an electrician with Water and Light Department of Thomasville, Georgia in 1973. As part of his job, he worked with and around city's transformers that used a fluid containing PCBs, furans, and dioxins as a coolant. In his testimony, Joiner stated he often had exposure to this fluid either by direct hand contact or even by occasional splashes into his eyes and mouth. In 1991, Joiner was diagnosed with small cell lung cancer and filed suit against the manufacturers of the PCBs, General Electric and Monsanto, the following year. The complaint alleged that the development of Joiner's cancer was linked to his exposure to PCBs. Joiner was at heightened risk for developing cancer as he had been a smoker for about eight years, his parents had been smokers, and there was a history of lung cancer in his family. Even in the presence of these risk factors, the complaint alleged, the exposure to PCBs "promoted" the development of his cancer and if it had not been for this exposure, his lung cancer may not have developed at all.

The defendants removed the case to federal court and once there, moved for summary judgment because:

- There was no evidence that Joiner suffered exposure to PCBs.
- There was no admissible scientific evidence that PCBs promoted Joiner's cancer.

The latter point revolved around expert testimony that Joiner sought to admit. The testimony was based on animal studies in mice that demonstrated development of cancer when the mice were exposed to PCBs. The defendants contended that study findings (in mice) failed to show a link between PCB exposure and the development of cancer in adult humans and moved to exclude the testimony. In other words, the findings of the animal study could not be applied to the facts at issue in the case.

Using *Daubert* principles and the abuse of discretion standard to evaluate the testimony, the federal district court agreed and granted the defendants a summary judgment.

The Court of Appeals for the Eleventh Circuit reversed (*see* 78 F.3d 524 (1996)). The federal appeals court contended that the Federal Rules of Evidence governing expert testimony displayed a preference for admissibility and applied stringent standards for review before exclusion of expert testimony. The appeals Court concluded that the district court had made two errors:

1. It incorrectly excluded the testimony because it drew different conclusions from the research than did the experts
2. It was incorrect in holding that Joiner had not been exposed to PCBs.

The U.S. Supreme Court reversed the Fourth Circuit Court of Appeals decision upon review, holding that abuse of discretion was the appropriate standard to apply in deciding whether to admit or exclude scientific evidence expert testimony. In properly applying this standard, the district court did not abuse its discretion in excluding the testimony. The U.S. Supreme Court also held that these conclusions did not dispose of entire case. It reversed the district court's conclusion that Joiner had not been exposed to furans and dioxins because it was never considered as to whether or not there was admissible evidence on this question. The question as to whether the exposure contributed to Joiner's cancer was left open.

In *Kumho Tire Co. v. Carmichael,* 526 U.S. 137, 141 (1999) the United States Supreme Court addressed how *Daubert* applied to expert testimony that was based not on "scientific" knowledge, but on "technical" or "other specialized" knowledge.

The Case
In July 1993, Patrick Carmichael was driving his minivan when a tire blew out, causing an accident that killed one person and severely injured several others. In October 1993, Carmichael brought suit against the tire maker, claiming the tire was defective. The case utilized deposition testimony provided by an expert in tire failure analysis, who concluded that the accident was caused by a defect in the tire's design or manufacture. The testimony relied on features of tire technology that were not in dispute. Also not disputed was background information on the age and mileage of the tire. The tire, when new, had a tread of 11/32 of an inch. At the time of

the blow out, the tread was 3/32 on some parts of the tire and in some places, had no tread at all. Despite this evidence, the expert witness concluded that the tire was defective. At issue for the defense was the methodology that the expert used to arrive at this conclusion. The methodology relied heavily on visual and tactile inspection of the tire and the application of the expert's theory that in the absence of at least two of four specific factors indicating tire abuse, the tire failure was caused by a defect. Kumho Tire moved to exclude the expert testimony on the grounds that the methodology did not meet Rule 702's requirement for reliability. The federal district court agreed with the defense and also agreed to apply *Daubert's* "gatekeeper" principles to determine admissibility of the testimony, even though this was not scientific knowledge. The court then applied the four *Daubert* factors of

- peer review
- known error rate
- standards of applying methodology
- general acceptance of methodology

The court found that the expert's methodology did not meet the reliability test and excluded the testimony. The plaintiffs moved to reconsider, arguing that *Daubert* should be applied liberally and other factors could argue in favor of admissibility. The court granted the motion and reheard additional arguments for admissibility. However, the court reaffirmed its previous decision and granted summary judgment to the defendants.

On appeal, the Eleventh Circuit Court of appeals reversed the decision, holding that the district court had erred in applying *Daubert* to exclude the experts' testimony. It argued that *Daubert's* "gatekeeping" function was limited to "scientific" knowledge and did not apply to the Kumho Tire expert testimony, which was "skill" or "experience" based.

Kumho petitioned the United States Supreme Court for *centiorari*. In delivering its opinion, the U.S. Supreme Court held that *Daubert's* general principles applied to all expert matters described in Rule 702. It held that:

1. The *Daubert* factors may apply to the testimony of others who are not scientists.
    - *Daubert* made no relevant distinction on the type of knowledge under consideration and thus the factors may apply to testimony of experts who are not scientists.

- There was no evidentiary rationale that *Daubert* "gatekeeping" was limited to "scientific" knowledge. The Court pointed out that in *Daubert,* the latitude given under Federal Rules 702 and 703 is granted to all experts, not just to "scientific" ones.
- It would prove to be difficult for judges to administer evidentiary rules under a gatekeeping obligation that distinguished between "scientific," "technical," or "other specialized" knowledge.
- The Court reaffirmed that the trial judge *may* consider one or more of specific *Daubert* factors when determining admissibility of expert testimony.
- The emphasis on *may* reflects *Daubert*'s interpretation of Rule 702 as a flexible one, allowing application of specific factors that are pertinent to the issues of the case
- The court of appeals must apply the abuse of discretion standard when reviewing trial court's decision to admit or exclude expert testimony

2. For the district's court not to admit testimony was lawful because it didn't question qualifications of the expert, but his methodology. The admissibility of testimony should focus on the expert's principles and methodology, not on the conclusions they generate.

Admissibility of expert testimony (of any type) continues to be at issue in many cases. If your case is relying on such testimony, be sure to thoroughly research case law decisions that are similar. An excellent resource for *Daubert* decisions can be found on the web at *http://www.Daubert OnTheWeb.com.*

§ 9.12   —Common Knowledge Doctrine

Issues in litigation that fall under "the common knowledge doctrine" generally do not require the services of an expert witness. For example, when a health care provider's acts or omissions fall within the general knowledge or experience of a layperson, or so obviously depart from a definition of reasonable conduct, the jury needs no expert guidance to conclude that negligence occurred. Some examples of layperson common knowledge: surgical instruments left inside a patient's body or surgery performed on the wrong body site.

§ 9.13   —Production of Expert Reports

Pursuant to Fed. R. Civ. P. 26(a)(2)(B), reports must be provided for all experts who have been retained or specially employed to provide expert testimony at the trial of the action, or have been employed by a party and whose duties regularly involve giving expert testimony. The latter category would include in-house experts such as a medical researcher on staff at a pharmaceutical company.

The report must be prepared by the expert and not by the attorney who has retained and disclosed the expert. The report must be in writing and signed by the expert, effectively ending the practice in which attorneys instructed their experts to give their findings orally in order to prevent discovery by opposing counsel.

The expert's report must contain a complete statement of the following:

- All opinions to be expressed
- The bases for each opinion
- The data or other information considered in forming the opinion
- Any exhibits to be used as a summary of or support for the opinions
- The qualifications of the witness
- All publications authored by the expert within the past 10 years
- The compensation paid to the expert
- A listing of all other cases in which the witness has testified as an expert, either at trial or in deposition, in the past 4 years (Fed. R. Civ. P. 26(a)(2)(B)).

Practice Note: The broad disclosure required by Fed. R. Civ. P. 26(a) may make it unnecessary to depose experts in every case.

§ 9.14   —Consultant or Expert?

Some experts are initially retained in a consulting capacity, with the understanding that they may later be declared an expert witness. Generally speaking, a consultant's work product and identity are not discoverable until the consultant is declared an expert witness. Reports made by a consultant prior to being named an expert do not automatically lose their status as protected work product. Check local codes for applicable state statutes and case law.

Practice Note: Keep written correspondence with the expert to a minimum. Additionally, direct the expert not to submit or prepare any written reports (including marking or making notations in the medical record) or communications, including opinions, until requested to do so.

§ 9.15 Role of Economists and Actuaries

In addition to obtaining medical evaluations of injuries by consultants and experts, economists or actuaries may be used to determine the value or worth of a case. A worth determination is generally accomplished by utilizing probabilities in calculations based on statistics of previous occurrences. Acting in this capacity, economists and actuaries can help determine the following aspects of a claim:

1. The dollar amount assigned to an injury or death
2. The present value of future income losses (based on earning capacity)
3. Other past and/or future losses
4. Options for structure of the financial settlement (for example, annuities and trusts).

§ 9.16 Evaluating Injuries and Causes

The focus of a consultant or expert's medical record review depends on the type of litigation and the injuries involved. Although medical consultants and experts are expected to form an opinion on the extent and consequences of the injury, they might also be asked to establish a causal relationship between the injury and the surrounding circumstances.

§ 9.17 Product Liability

Under the law of strict liability, companies have an obligation to make products at least as safe as state of the art technology. Consumers must then be informed of potential risks and hazards associated with use of the product, so they may make informed decisions on purchase and use. A non-medical consultant or expert may be called upon to evaluate the technical aspects of product liability. Additionally, medical consultants and experts may be needed to evaluate the cause-and-effect relationship between the product and the injury/illness. Important issues in product liability cases are

- Defective design—the product was not reasonably safe for its intended purpose or use
- Defect in manufacture processes—the defect existed when the product left the manufacturer
- Failure to warn—reasonable attempts were not made to warn consumers of associated dangers of the product.

Product liability litigation has included motor vehicle gas tank designs, intrauterine devices, and silicone breast implants.

§ 9.18   Toxic Exposure

Modern technology has increased the number of toxic substances to which people are exposed, and thus the likelihood of exposure (intentional or unintentional) associated with everyday life has increased. Industries that use toxic materials in their operations are obligated to inform their employees and customers of associated exposure hazards. Protection that reduces potential exposure must be made available to employees. As of 1989, OSHA had set permissible exposure limits (PELs) for approximately 500 hazardous chemicals. Additionally, the American Conference of Governmental Industrial Hygienists (ACGIH) has made a similar set of recommendations. In some cases, ACGIH permissible exposure limits are lower than OSHA's. It is important when evaluating toxic exposure cases to determine which organization's PEL values were relied on at the time of the exposure in question. As in product liability cases, the consultant or expert focuses on relating the injury or illness to the toxic exposure and may also be asked to evaluate working conditions under which the injury occurred. Military personnel exposed to Agent Orange and construction workers' or plant employees' exposure to asbestos are two examples of physical injury and disease linked to toxic substance exposure.

§ 9.19 Workers' Compensation

The workers' compensation system is designed to handle claims for injuries suffered in the workplace. For a claim to be valid, the claimant must demonstrate that injuries are work-related and occurred within the scope of employment duties. The focus of the workers' compensation expert or consultant is to establish a causal relationship between the claimant's injury and his or her job duties. Usually, medical consultants and experts are not asked to evaluate the circumstances surrounding the injuries.

§ 9.20 Personal Injury

Personal injury (PI) encompasses a wide range of causes and circumstances. The PI consultant or expert focuses on the occurrence (slip and fall, motor vehicle accident) and resulting injuries. The expert then determines if the injuries were caused by the accident and if residual damage or potential residual damage exists.

§ 9.21 Medical Malpractice

The medical malpractice consultant or expert focuses on the medical professional's act or failure to act and determines if such conduct resulted in injury. The expert will also be asked to conclude if treatment was within the accepted standards of care. In evaluating medical malpractice liability, the *standard of care* is one of the most important criterion for determining professional negligence. See § **9.31** *et seq.* for additional information on standards of care.

Allegations against medical professionals can be based on many theories: negligence (the most common), consent issues (battery, failure to inform, lack of informed consent), abandonment, and breach of confidentiality.

§ 9.22 —Negligence

Briefly, *negligence* in medical malpractice is the failure of a medical professional to perform his or her duties according to the accepted standard of care, which results in harm to another. Negligence is composed of several elements. The first is the existence of a *duty* on the part of the medical professional to possess and use that degree of knowledge, skill, and care exercised by other reasonable and prudent practitioners under similar circumstances. This duty is generally known as the *standard of care.*

A *breach* of that duty must be established. This breach, or failure to follow the minimum standard, can be caused by something done (commission) or not done (omission). The plaintiff must also prove *causation,* that is, that the breach of the standard of care was the direct cause of the plaintiff's injuries. Finally, the plaintiff must show that the breach resulted in injury or *damages.* If the plaintiff suffers no damages, there can be no recovery.

§ 9.23   —Consent Issues

Causes of action concerning consent issues revolve around three separate areas: battery, failure to inform, and lack of informed consent. *Battery* is the tort of intentional, contact without consent, or application of force to the body of another. In the context of medical malpractice, this can refer to sexual contact by a health care provider with a client without consent, or the performance of medical treatment without consent. Competent adults who clearly express their desire not to undergo a blood transfusion or surgical procedure, or who limit treatment alternatives due to religious beliefs, should not be forced to undergo these unwanted treatments. If a medical professional deliberately ignores these wishes, a battery has been committed.

Prior to performing a medical procedure or treatment, a physician must obtain the patient's consent to do so. *Consent* can be defined as the voluntary agreement by a client to allow touching, examination, or treatment by medically authorized personnel. *Informed consent* is the client's right to know and understand all facets of a procedure before agreeing to it. Generally speaking, informed consent should consist of the following types of information:

- A description of the problem to be treated or the symptom to be diagnosed
- The proposed diagnostic test, procedure, or medication
- The known risks, complications, side effects, and consequences of the treatment

- The reasons or indications that this choice has been made
- The expected results or goals to be achieved after the test or procedure has been performed
- Reasonable alternative treatment methods and their costs
- The consequences to the patient of not performing the test or procedure

The adequacy of the consent will be measured against certain legal standards. These standards vary from jurisdiction to jurisdiction, but generally include:

- What a reasonably prudent physician would tell a patient under the same or similar circumstances.
- What a reasonably prudent patient, parent, or guardian would want to know under the same or similar circumstances in order to decide among several alternatives.
- The complications and results for each medical or surgical procedure that have been determined to be reasonably common that patients need to be informed about.

Consent to surgical or diagnostic procedures should be obtained in writing on preprinted forms. If this is not possible, it is acceptable for the provider to list the known complications and risk factors of a particular procedure with the statement: "The patient has been fully informed and understands the risks involved and consents to [the procedure]."

§ 9.24   —Abandonment

The cause of action for abandonment recognizes that a physician (or other healthcare professional) who consents to advise, diagnose, or treat a person within their scope of practice accepts the duty to provide continuity of care until that person is stabilized, cured, or formally released from the their care. Backup physicians can provide the continuity of care when the original treating physician is not available. The duty to provide care ceases with the death or recovery of the patient, or when the patient is notified in writing of the intention to discontinue care. Notification should be in writing and should allow the patient sufficient time to locate and establish a relationship with a new physician or healthcare professional.

§ 9.25   —Breach of Confidentiality

As discussed extensively in **Chapter 1**, physicians and other medical professionals have a duty to respect the privacy interests of their patients. Absent written consent to release patient medical information, or any of the other exceptions discussed in that chapter, health care professionals may not breach the confidentiality of their relationship with a patient.

§ 9.26   —Scope of Liability

Medical malpractice liability exists at many levels, and is commensurate with individual or entity scope of practice and responsibility. Individuals are held accountable for acts of negligence they personally commit. Management can be held liable for inappropriate assignment or delegation of duties and there can be additional liability for not providing adequate supervision for employees. At the corporate level, liability can potentially exist for hiring incompetent personnel, for not providing adequate employee education, resources, equipment and supplies, and for not adequately training managers. Both managerial and corporate liability have received increased attention in recent years as a result of institutional "downsizing" and replacement of higher skilled employees (such as registered nurses) with unlicensed assistive personnel.

§ 9.27   —Liability Questions in Medical Malpractice

When reviewing the medical treatment, the expert/consultant formulates an opinion on the extent of liability that exists. Before this can be done, however, four main elements must be addressed and weighed:

1. The standard of care applicable to the incident or situation that caused the injury must be determined.
2. Once the standard is determined, the expert/consultant must ascertain if a breach in the standard occurred. A breach can occur by omission or commission.
3. If a breach of the standard occurred, the expert/consultant must determine if the breach resulted in an injury.
4. Finally, if an injury resulted from the breach, the expert/consultant must determine the extent of the damage.

The burden is on the plaintiff to prove that a breach of the applicable standard of care occurred and that the breach resulted in the injuries alleged. *Punitive damages* are awarded to a plaintiff to punish grossly negligent or intentional conduct of a professional. Actions that may be considered for punitive damages must have been committed with intentions of malice or fraud. In establishing the amount of punitive damages, several factors are usually considered:

- Seriousness of the harm incurred from the action
- The duration of time over which the acts were committed
- Attempts to conceal the action
- Profitability as a result of the action.

§ 9.28 —Malpractice Defenses

In cases involving alleged medical malpractice, several defense strategies are commonly used: contributory or comparative negligence, statute of limitations, sovereign immunity, and Good Samaritan laws. *Contributory or comparative negligence* theory examines the acts of the plaintiff to determine if they contributed to the injury. Traditionally, legal doctrine barred a plaintiff's right to recovery if the plaintiff's acts could be shown to have contributed to the injury. Today, however, many courts are allowing such cases to be heard, and modifying damage awards based on the percentage of fault apportioned to the plaintiff. *Statute of limitations* defenses center on the appropriate time frame for filing complaints. In medical practice, the statute begins tolling from the date the malpractice act was known or should have been known by the plaintiff. When reviewing records for medical malpractice cases, it is critical to include any information that could raise the question of contributory negligence and plaintiff knowledge of statute of limitations. Less frequently used defenses are (1) *common law doctrine* that establishes governmental immunity from suits, and (2) *Good Samaritan laws* stating that no legal duty to render care exists in the absence of a provider-patient relationship.

§ 9.29 Future Problems Resulting from Incident

Both consultants and experts consider present and future losses when determining the extent of an injury. Physical and psychological function as well as alteration in lifestyle, present and future loss of wages, and potential future complications resulting from the injury are all to be considered when evaluating a case. These findings will form the basis for possible settlement

§ 9.30   Physical and Mental Examinations

Federal Rule of Civil Procedure 34 allows for physical or mental examinations when either of these aspects of a plaintiff's condition is in controversy. Often referred to as independent medical examinations (IME), they are, in reality, defense medical examinations. The defendant requests that a professional other than one of the plaintiff's treating physicians make an independent examination. The defense attorney locates the physician, schedules the examination, pays the applicable fees, and receives the report generated by the physician. In workers' compensation law, a physician agreed upon by both parties conducts medical examinations.

Generally speaking, these examinations are conducted only by a licensed physician or, in the case of mental examinations, a licensed clinical psychologist or psychiatrist.

Rule 34 states that the order for examination may be made on good cause and with proper notice provisions (that is, time, place, manner, scope of investigation, and identity of person making the examination). In most jurisdictions, these arrangements are made informally by stipulation between parties. A detailed written report, made by the examining physician or psychologist, that sets forth the examination findings (including the results of any tests performed) is provided to the requesting party.

Many jurisdictions limit the scope of IMEs, with prohibitions against performing certain specific tests (for example, X ray, blood work, EMG, CT scan, MRI). This is especially true if the plaintiff's treating doctors have already performed procedures or if procedures are intrusive or painful in nature. Check the code sections in your state for specific requirements for medical examinations.

Practice Note: If your client has been scheduled for a defense medical examination, prepare them in advance for the procedure. Review your client's recollection of medical history and treatment received to date, the mechanics of the injury, and any prior testimony. Caution the client about offering information to the examiner that may be outside the scope of the examination, such as the course of the litigation or facts regarding the incident.

§ 9.31   Medical Standards of Care

Standard of care in the medical profession is defined as the minimal level of care administered by a licensed professional with similar education and training under the same or similar circumstances. Standards of care arise from many different sources. They can be found in

- statutes and regulations (e.g., reporting requirements for child and elder abuse)
- authoritative textbooks
- state practice acts and guidelines
- facility/organization policies and procedures
- equipment manuals
- job descriptions
- accreditation agencies
- court decisions and administrative rulings.

The standard of care applies to the date when the health care provider acted or failed to act. When reviewing medical treatment, therefore, it is essential to determine the standard of care for the time period the actual injury occurred. For example, a total joint procedure done in 1995 should not be evaluated by 2000 standards because standards of care have changed in that interval.

The majority of states recognize a national minimum standard of care; there is less emphasis on community practice as standard of care. Standards are flexible and constantly changing; they should reflect advancements in medicine. When researching standards, include both internal and external standards.

§ 9.32   —Internal Medical Standards of Care

Internal standards are usually established by individual health care facilities and frequently more specifically define and individualize external standards. Examples of internal standards are job descriptions, policies and procedures, protocols, and critical paths. It is important to note that if an internal standard of a facility is higher than the minimum external standard, the institution will be held accountable to their (higher) internal standard. Therefore, when facilities establish internal standards, care is usually taken that they reflect current practice, not some desired or "ideal" state. If appropriate to case issues, it is extremely important to obtain copies of any relevant documents that may represent internal standard of care for the institution.

§ 9.33   —External Medical Standards of Care

External standards come from numerous sources. Many that deal with the appropriateness of medical care are promulgated by professional organizations of specific provider disciplines. Additionally, there are numerous regulatory and accreditation agencies that publish standards for health plans and health care institutions. For example, both government-sponsored and private organizations are developing and publishing clinical practice guidelines or practice parameters that focus on appropriate treatment of specific diagnoses.

§ 9.34   Health Plan Standards

In most states, specific public agencies are charged with the development of regulations that govern the business practices of health plans. At the national level, Title XIII of the Public Health Services Act defines HMO/MCO requirements for organization structure, health service areas, provider contracts, marketing strategies, information systems, quality improvement activities, and grievance and appeal systems. In addition to these government agencies, at least two private agencies publish comprehensive standards that govern multiple aspects of health plan operations.

§ 9.35   —National Committee for Quality Assurance

The National Committee for Quality Assurance (NCQA) is a private, nonprofit organization dedicated to assessing and reporting the quality of managed care plans. The NCQA efforts are organized around two activities: accreditation and performance measurement. *Accreditation* examines a health plan's structures and systems *and performance measurement* looks at the results a health plan actually achieves. NCQA began accreditation activities in 1991 in response to the need for standardized, objective information about the quality of care provided by HMOs and MCOs. As of 2006, the accreditation process encompassed the following categories:

- **Quality improvement.** Includes standards in areas of quality program structure and operations, availability of practitioners, accessibility of services, member satisfaction, and standards for medical record documentation. Additionally, clinical quality improvement is evaluated, looking at areas such as clinical practice guidelines, coordination across health care settings, and chronic condition management.
- **Reviewing and authorizing medical care.** This standard examines multiple aspects of utilization including the structure and processes for making utilization management (UM) decisions, including handling of denials and appeals.
- **Quality of provider network.** Focuses on policies related to practitioner credentialing, as well as sanctioning, complaints and quality issues, and practitioner appeal rights.
- **Members' rights and responsibilities.** Addresses areas of member communication, policies for complaints and appeals, and privacy and confidentiality.
- **Preventive health activities**. HEDIS measures, see § **9.36.**

NCQA accreditation programs encompass the following areas:

- Managed care organizations
- Managed behavior healthcare organizations
- Proferred provider organizations
- Disease management accreditation/certification
- New health plan accreditation

Successful completion of the process results in a one- to three-year accreditation award. Achievement has assumed greater importance in recent years because many employer groups may require NCQA accreditation before offering a health plan as a choice for their employees. This accreditation ensures a defined level of quality in a health plan's service and care delivery. NCQA can be contacted at

2000 L St. N.W., Suite 500
Washington DC 20036
Telephone: (202) 955-3500 Fax: (202) 955-3599
Web: *http://www.ncqa.com*

§ 9.36   —HEDIS Indicators

The performance measurement activities of NCQA are managed through the Health Plan Employer Data and Information Set (HEDIS) indicators. These indicators are a standardized set of performance measures intended to provide purchasers and consumers with comparative information about managed care plans. Currently, these measures only apply to health plan managed care plans, however data is collected by Medicare, Medicaid, and commercial product lines. Key assumptions of indicators such as HEDIS are that HMOs are responsible for integrating members' health care services and improving or maintaining the quality of services members receive. 2006 HEDIS indicators focus on eight areas:

- **Effectiveness of care.** This area has 32 measures in areas of disease prevention, healthy lifestyle habits, disease screening, chronic disease care, and care of selected acute conditions.
- **Access/availability of care.** Measures include access to both ambulatory and primary care providers as well as the timeliness of claims resolution and call answer.
- **Satisfaction with care experience.** This is measured using the CAHPS survey instrument for adults and children, including children with chronic conditions.
- **Health plan stability.** Practitioner turnover and years in business are measured.
- **Use of services.** Measures the areas of pre-natal, well baby, and adolescent visits. Also measured are utilization for inpatient care, mental health, chemical dependency, outpatient drugs and antibiotics.
- **Cost of care.** No measures currently in use.
- **Informed health care choices.** No measures currently in use.
- **Health plan descriptive information.** Measure include information for board certification, enrollment demographics, including race/ethnicity and language diversity of membership.

HEDIS indicators are revised frequently; data collection methodology changes, new indicators are developed, and some existing indicators are deleted. Although indicators may differ slightly according to product line (Medicare, commercial, or Medicaid), many are common to all. Current HEDIS information is on-line and can be accessed through the NCQA website. See **§ 9.35.**

§ 9.37 —Foundation for Accountability (FACCT)

The Foundation for Accountability (FACCT) is also a nonprofit organization that strives to improve the type of information consumers and employer purchasers receive, to enable informed decisions about their health care. The organization is composed of consumer, purchaser, and government representatives, and its core work consists of (1) creating state-of-the-art quality measurement sets and (2) researching what consumers want and need in the way of quality information and how best to convey that quality information to the consumer. Issues or conditions to measure are based on their prevalence, cost, variations in care, and opportunities to improve care. The choice of indicators is also influenced by input from FACCTs Consumer Advisory Council; the type of condition under consideration (acute, chronic, preventive); age and sex of consumers affected (women or men, children, young adults, middle age, or elderly); and type of measure involved (population-based, condition-based, life-stage based). FACCT indicators are considered an alternative to HEDIS.

FACCT evaluates the utility of their indicators and measurement tools on an ongoing basis. As of 2003, FACCT has organized current measurement tools on their website in the Consumer Information Framework. The framework contains five categories that reflect how consumers think about their care. Comparative information is contained within each category. The five categories and information they contain are:

1. The basics—access to care, customer service, and satisfaction.
2. Staying healthy—preventative care, reduction of health risks, early detection of illness, and education.
3. Getting better—recovery through appropriate treatment and follow-up.
4. Living with illness—for ongoing, chronic conditions: self-care, symptom control, complication avoidance, and maintenance of activities of daily living. Information is available on the following conditions: asthma, diabetes, heart care, and HIV.
5. Changing needs—coping skills needed as a result of dramatic changes in lifestyle due to disability or terminal illness.

Child and Adolescent Health Measurement Initiative

FACCT is also coordinating the work of the Child and Adolescent Health Measurement Initiative (CAHMI). This group's goal is to improve healthcare and quality measurement for children and adolescents. It is a collaborative effort among consumer and health-care provider organizations, public and private sector purchasers, and policymakers.

Clearinghouse for Consumer-Centered Health

The FACCT website also contains a page for the *Clearinghouse for Consumer-Centered Health Care.* The page has five icons representing the following different interest groups:

* Consumers
* Health-care providers
* Health-care purchasers
* Health plans and insurers
* Policymakers and researchers

Within each section is a wealth of resources including additional websites, tools, and other resources. The site is very user-friendly and easy to navigate. More detailed information on all FACCT activities is available on their website: *http://www.facct.org.*

§ 9.38   —The Leapfrog Group

The Leapfrog Group is a non-profit coalition of public and private organizations that provide health-care benefits. The group began in 2000, with the backing of many large employer groups that were concerned about the safety of health care delivery in hospitals and the impact of medical mistakes on employee health. This concern was driven by the findings in a 1999 Institute of Medicine publication, "To Err is Human: Building a Safer Health System," on hospital safety in America. This comprehensive study found that many medical mistakes made in hospitals were preventable. The study also included a series of recommendations designed to minimize the occurrence of mistakes. See **§ 9.48** for a more detailed summary of study findings.

The Leapfrog group's purpose is to help consumers make more informed decisions about their health care, with a major emphasis on choosing hospitals utilizing three practices that have demonstrated reduction in *preventable* mistakes. The three identified hospital practices are:

1. Use of computerized physician order entry system.
2. Have proven outcomes or extensive experience with specific procedures.
3. Have adequately staffed Intensive Care Units by MDs and other staff trained in critical care.

Although there are many additional practices that can reduce preventable mistakes, Leapfrog has chosen the above three as their initial areas of focus. The group estimates that these three steps together could prevent approximately 60,000 hospital deaths and more than half a million serious medication errors annually. The Leapfrog Group website has developed a toolkit for Leapfrog Group members to use in the marketing of healthcare services to prospective purchasers. Use of the toolkit materials is voluntary and designed to assist group members in their communications with potential healthcare purchasers. Information for consumers is available as well and provides information on quality and safety practices that have been shown to reduce injuries in hospitals. The Leapfrog Group website is: *http://www.leapfroggroup.org*

§ 9.39 —Utilization Review Accreditation Commission/ American Accreditation Healthcare Commission

The Utilization Review Accreditation Commission (URAC) is a nonprofit organization founded in 1990. Initially, its purpose was to establish accreditation standards for managed health care organizations using Utilization Review (UR) programs for determining medical necessity of care. In later years, URAC's program expanded to cover a broader range of services in various healthcare settings. Their membership constituencies are diverse and independent of any stakeholder group. Membership includes representatives from industry, purchasers, consumers, providers, and regulators. The organization offers accreditation in areas such as utilization review and case management, disease management, health care practitioner credentialing, claims processing, and workers' compensation utilization management. It also offers accreditation in areas such as consumer education and support and HIPAA privacy and security. URACs website contains information on a variety of topics, including consumer information.

URAC can be contacted at
1220 L St. N.W., Suite 400
Washington, DC 20005
Telephone: (202) 216-9010
Fax: (202) 216-9006
Website: *http://www.urac.org*

§ 9.40   Health Plan Litigation

The rise of managed care organizations (MCOs) and health maintenance
organizations (HMOs) brought a marked increase in liability claims
against these organizations. The Employee Retirement Income Security
Act of 1974 (29 U.S.C. §§ 1001-1461), commonly known as ERISA, has
historically provided protection to health plans against most liability
claims. However, in recent years this protection has diminished somewhat
as a result of diverse legal opinions on the statute's application.

§ 9.41   —ERISA

ERISA was enacted in 1974 as a comprehensive law governing both
employee benefit plans and the persons who manage them. Among its
many provisions, ERISA established benefit plan regulation (including
those provided by health plans) as a federal concern. Therefore, ERISA
provided its own set of remedies for claims relating to benefit plans, and as
federal law, preempted similar state law and statutes.

The claim of preemption by ERISA has historically provided a defense
to most liability claims involving managed care. The defensive advantages
of preemption are well known. Under preemption, punitive and extra-
contractual damages are not allowed; participants are not entitled to a
jury trial; and claim decisions by plan administrators can be challenged
as arbitrary or capricious if a plan gives the administrator discretionary
authority to determine eligibility or interpret plan terms.

State-law claims can be subject to preemption in one of two ways: by
complete or conflict preemption. *Complete preemption* can occur when a
civil action is brought for any of five reasons:

1. For an administrator's refusal to supply information
2. To recover benefits due or to enforce rights

3. To clarify rights to future benefits

4. To sue for breach of fiduciary duty

5. To prohibit an act in violation of ERISA or the plan terms, and to redress violations.

A state claim not falling within this scope, however, can still be preempted under the *conflict preemption* portion of ERISA. Unlike complete preemption, conflict preemption does not create federal question jurisdiction. Thus, when the question of conflict preemption arises, the district court cannot resolve state versus federal jurisdiction of the claim. United States circuit courts have disagreed about which state claims are and are not preempted by ERISA provisions. State medical malpractice cases are also subject to this division.

§ 9.42 —ERISA-Related Litigation

Since ERISA was passed, some courts have consistently supported plan regulation as a federal concern and have ruled in favor of preemption. The Supreme Court supported the concept of complete preemption. In *Ingersoll-Rand Co. v. McClendon,* 498 U.S. 133, 142, 111 S. Ct. 478, 484, 112 L. Ed. 2d 474 (1990), by stating that "state courts, exercising their common law powers, might develop different substantive standards applicable to some employer conduct and that such an outcome is fundamentally at odds with the goal of uniformity that Congress sought to implement." Since this decision, other courts have upheld preemption as well.

In *Jass v. Prudential Health Care Plan Inc.,* 88 F.3d 1482 (7th Cir. 1996), a patient brought action against the HMO, a nurse employed by the HMO, and the treating physician for negligence following knee replacement surgery. The HMO removed the case to federal court, claiming that it was preempted under ERISA. The district court found, and the appellate court affirmed, that the claim fell under the complete preemption provision.

Preemption has been opposed by other jurisdictions, however. *Dukes v. U.S. Healthcare, Inc.,* 57 F.3d 350 (3d Cir. 1995), involved two claims for damages for injuries arising from medical malpractice of HMO-affiliated hospitals and medical personnel. Although the district court ruled in favor of preemption in both cases, the Third Circuit court reversed the decision. This decision was based, in large part, on the fact that the complaints did not involve denial of benefits, but rather negligent care. In other words, the claims involved the quality of the care received, not the quantity of care.

In many cases, state law has not kept up with the growth of managed care. In a 1984 case, *Mitts v. HIP of Greater New York,* 104 A.D.2d 318, 478 N.Y.S.2d 910 (1st Dep't 1984), the court held that a health plan could not be held liable for malpractice committed by its member physicians. This decision was based on the premises that the health plan did not render care and that each provider was an independent contractor. Some courts have not been convinced by the argument that a capitation fee between managed care health plans and medical groups can potentially create incentives to providers to limit care.

Because of the rise in numbers of managed care organizations, there is little doubt that issues surfacing in this area of litigation are very different today than in 1974 when ERISA was enacted. However, because of ERISA's complexity, both the Supreme Court and Congress have been reluctant to change what is perceived to be a statute designed to balance the interests of many powerful competing interests. Insurance companies and employers strongly oppose changes that would broaden legal liability to hold managed care organizations, insurance carriers, and utilization review organizations accountable for decisions that injure patients. New liability would undoubtedly increase the cost of health benefits.

As the number of managed care organizations increases, so will the number of liability claims against them. Legal professionals involved in these cases need to be familiar with appropriate statute and case law affecting this rapidly changing area of litigation.

§ 9.43   —Areas of Litigation Against Managed Care

Managed care organizations are vulnerable to litigation in two main areas: (1) provider selection criteria—establishment and enforcement of selection criteria for all providers in their networks; and (2) utilization review programs—development and administration of benefits and services to members.

§ 9.44   —Provider Selection Criteria

Provider selection criteria are vulnerable through *vicarious* liability and *corporate* liability. *Vicarious liability* sets forth an inherent legal responsibility placed on a person or an entity for the negligent acts or omission of acts of another person because of the relationship between the two parties. Vicarious liability can be alleged under two legal doctrines:

- *Respondeat Superior*—holds that in certain cases, an employer is responsible for the wrongful acts of its employees
- *Ostensible Agency*—holds that a hospital is liable for the actions of an independent contractor if the patient reasonably believes the physician is an employee of a hospital (for example, a physician in the emergency department).

In deciding cases of vicarious liability, the determination of employer-employee relationship is critical as it relates to control of care delivery. If the MCO controls care delivered by their providers, finding of vicarious liability under respondeat superior is likely. Critical issues to determine are:

- right of employer to control work performed
- method of provider payment for work performed
- skill required in specific provider occupation
- determination of whether employer supplies or equipment
- belief of parties as to the nature of the employer-employee relationship.

Corporate liability holds that a hospital owes a duty to the patients it serves. In addition to the responsibility arising from causing patients harm, this doctrine holds organizations liable for failing:

- to properly review and investigate credentials of medical staff requesting privileges.
- to protect patients from malpractice by the medical staff when the organization knew or should have known (through reasonable care) that malpractice was likely.
- in duty to patients by not providing overall surveillance of the equality of care delivered to patients.

One key strategy to minimizing risk of corporate liability is thorough documentation of providers' credentials, including:

- definition of credentialing process in organization bylaws
- development of credentialing processes and procedures
- detailing credentialing requirements in all practitioner contracts.

In *Hughes v. Blue Cross of Northern California* (215 Cal. App. 3d 832) corporate liability for utilization management procedures was at issue in the complaint for breach of good faith and fair dealing from coverage denial for psychiatric hospitalization of plaintiff's son.

The case involved a 21-year-old male who overdosed on aspirin and stabbed himself in the abdomen with a screwdriver. He was admitted to a psychiatric hospital where he received treatment for approximately 6 weeks. During the period of hospitalization, the patient did not respond well to treatment, and expressed grandiose delusions characteristic of schizophrenia to his psychiatrist. Eventually, the patient was discharged to a half way house when his symptoms improved, although his "instability was always apparent." Shortly after his discharge to the half-way house, the patient ran away, returning to his mother's house and repeating overdose attempts that precipitated his first hospitalization. He was readmitted to the psychiatric hospital and again discharged after treatment, but re-hospitalized five times over the next seven-month period because of repeated outpatient treatment failures. He was finally admitted to a long-term psychiatric care facility.

Plaintiff's action concerned two periods of hospitalizations. The insurer paid only a small portion of the submitted costs, disallowing the balance on the grounds that the hospitalizations were not medically necessary. At trial, it was determined that during the utilization review process by the physician reviewer, no attempt was made to secure all pertinent medical information relevant to the claim, nor was there any attempt to communicate with the treating physician before denying the claim. Based on this testimony, the jury could reasonably infer that the insurer employed a standard of medical necessity markedly at variance from that of the psychiatric community in California. Therefore, there was not good faith effort on the part of the insurer to properly investigate the claim.

The court entered judgment in favor of plaintiff. The case was appealed and decision affirmed. The courts held that:

1. Insurer breached covenant by employing a standard of medical necessity that was significantly at variance with community and by failing to properly investigate insured's claim
2. Evidence supported award of punitive damages
3. Insurer waived issue of ERISA preemption by failing to raise it as affirmative defense.

§ 9.45 —Utilization Review Programs

For utilization review/management programs, managed care organizations must establish an effective system to monitor the quality of the treatment given, identify and minimize the use of services, and ensure that the benefits of the program are administered consistently to all members.

The goal of all utilization management programs should be to render quality medical care in a cost effective manner and ensure that all members receive this care in line with their benefit plan. Utilization management programs typically use the following types of review to accomplish these goals:

1. **Prospective.** Requires prior approval before a treatment can be rendered. This type of review has the potential to create liability if the patient believes treatment is denied solely on the basis of cost.

2. **Concurrent.** Monitors hospital length of stay and evaluates the necessity for continued hospitalization.

3. **Retrospective.** Performed after services have been rendered. Usually this review method does not impact actual delivery of service, but may affect provider reimbursement for the service.

    In all cases, utilization management programs must demonstrate that policies, procedures, and practices are in place that protect the right of the patient to receive medically necessary care.

Over the past few years, several common areas of litigation against managed care Utilization Review programs have emerged. Most involve perceived denial of benefits and dissatisfaction with member appeal processes for denials. Some, however, center around health plan policies governing physician-patient communication related to care alternatives, access to specialists, and the right to second opinions. As a result of increased consumer concern, many federal and state governments have passed laws dictating health care behavior in specific areas. Prime areas of focus are denial decisions of coverage made by non-physicians (i.e., health plan administrators), minimum hospital length of stay following certain medical procedures, and informed choice regarding all available options for care. For example, in 1997 New Jersey set up an independent review panel that enabled consumers to appeal decisions by HMOs to suspend or deny care. Included are the following provisions:

• Only physicians can deny or limit coverage.

• No "gag" clauses may bar physicians from discussing all treatment options.

- Disclosure of compensation arrangements with doctors, including financial incentives, must be made.
- There must be an appeals process for patients or doctors who appeal an HMO's decision.
- There must be no retaliation against physicians who appeal.

Legislation regulating minimum maternity length of stay has been passed in several states. Maryland, for example, requires insurers to cover maternity stays in accordance with medical criteria published by American Academy of Pediatrics and the American Academy of Obstetrics and Gynecology. Similarly, legislation has been passed in several states mandating minimum length of stay following mastectomy. Other areas in which a variety of both state and federal laws have been passed or are pending are:

- Limitations on insurers and employers from excluding coverage for preexisting conditions
- "Portable" health care benefits that would allow an individual to retain coverage when changing jobs or when a policy beneficiary becomes ill
- "Any Willing Provider" laws that would require health plans to allow into their network any providers willing to accept the plan's terms and payment rates (Arkansas passed such a law in 1995)
- "Direct Access and Freedom of Choice" bills that would allow patients to visit medical specialists without first obtaining referrals from their primary care provider.
- Establishment of ombudsman programs to help consumers resolve complaints concerning delay or denial of medical care, limits on access to specialists, failure to pay for medical services, problems with HMO grievance systems, and to ban retaliatory action against physicians, patients, or other medical workers who provide information that ensures proper care.

An example of utilization-related litigation can be found in *Wickline v. State of California* (192 Cal. App. 3d 1630). In this case, the plaintiff brought action against her insurer Medi-Cal (State of California) after undergoing amputation of her leg as a result of alleged premature discharge from the hospital. The case involved a female patient admitted to the hospital with severe vascular disease resulting from occlusion of her aorta. This condition was treated surgically with removal of the occluded portion of the aorta and insertion of aortic graft. The patient had a stormy post-operative course requiring two additional operations, one to remove a clot in the graft and a second to relieve spasms in the blood vessels that were impeding blood flow to her lower extremities. After the second surgery, the patient's physicians felt it was medically necessary for the patient to stay in the hospital eight days beyond the number of days initially authorized, and this request was submitted to Medi-Cal. Medi-Cal reviewers authorized four additional days, a decision not questioned by the treating physicians. The patient was discharged four days later, with the agreement of her attending physicians, medically stable.

Within the first few days after discharge to home, the patient began experiencing color changes and increased pain in her right lower extremity. Nine days after discharge, the patient was emergently readmitted to the hospital and found to have wound infection and color changes in her right leg. Eventually, the patient underwent an amputation of her right leg for a clot and infection in her graft.

At the trial court level, the jury verdict in favor of the plaintiff, and the State appealed. The Court of Appeals reversed the lower court's decision, based on the following arguments:

1. Patient who is harmed when care that should have been provided and is not should recover from all responsible, including, when appropriate, health care payor.

2. Third party payors of health care services can be held legally accountable when medically inappropriate decisions result from design or implementation defects in cost containment mechanisms.

3. Physicians who comply without protest with payor decisions cannot escape responsibility for the patient's care.

4. Medi-Cal was not liable for the discharge decision. (The treating physicians did not dispute the four day extension by Medi-Cal.)

In *Wilson v. Blue Cross of Southern California* (222 Cal. App. 3d 660) the mother of a patient brought action against her health insurer and the contractor who performed utilization review. She sought to recover for her son's suicide after he was discharged from a psychiatric hospital following notification that his insurance benefits had been discontinued. The decedent was admitted to the hospital suffering from major depression, drug dependency, and anorexia. His physician determined that three to four weeks of hospitalization were medically indicated. After 10 days of hospitalization, the insurer denied further payment. The patient was discharged and committed suicide shortly thereafter. The *Wickline* case was used by plaintiff's bar as precedent for the insurer's liability.

The trial court entered summary judgment in favor the defendant; this decision was appealed. The appellate court reversed the decision and remanded the case for retrial, holding that:

1. Contractor could be partially liable if their conduct was a substantial factor in bringing about the suicide, and
2. Whether conduct was substantial factor in causing suicide was question of fact precluding summary judgment.

The court ruled that the *Wickline* decision pertained to discharge under Medi-Cal and did not apply to those insured under a policy issued in the private sector. In remanding the case for retrial, the court determined the critical question to answer was whether or not the decision to discharge was a substantial factor in the patient's suicide. The above cases illustrate the liability potential of utilization review programs. Managed Care Organization can however, mitigate this risk potential through development of programs that:

*   allow providers to exercise independent clinical judgment.
*   require providers to document and communicate plan of care (to both patient and UM reviewer) and medical necessity for treatment.
*   encourage patient communication regarding the appeals process when MCO denies care as recommended by the provider.

§ 9.46 Health Care Delivery Organizations Standards

Most states have public agencies that regulate care delivered by health care organizations, much as they do for health plans. However, a private organization critical to setting standards is the Joint Commission on Accreditation of Health Care Organizations (JCAHO). Much as NCQA does for health plans, JCAHO develops standards that encompass multiple areas for healthcare delivery organizations. Originally, JCAHO accredited only acute care hospitals. However, over the years, the scope of its accreditation surveys has expanded and now includes

*   hospitals/critical access hospitals
*   behavioral health care

- long-term care facilities,
- home care organizations
- ambulatory care organizations
- pathology and clinical laboratory services
- health care networks
- assisted living facilities
- office-based surgery settings

Although JCAHO accreditation is voluntary, institutions must be JCAHO-accredited to be eligible for third-party reimbursement.

§ 9.47   —JCAHO Accreditation Process

The JCAHO accreditation process and methodology are currently undergoing significant changes. These changes, first announced in 2002, progressively shift the focus of the surveys from periodic preparation by facilities to continuous systems improvements that will improve quality and safety of patient care. The new methodology, titled Shared-Visions-New Pathways®, is designed to help organizations develop operational systems that will improve the safety and quality of care delivery. *Shared Visions* represents the concept that JCAHO shares with health care organizations, healthcare oversight groups, and the public, that of bridging gaps between current health care delivery and the potential to make changes that will result in better quality care. *New Pathways* encourages new approaches that support the achievement of the shared vision. This support infrastructure will be designed to

- facilitate communication between JCAHO and health care organizations,
- consolidate standards for accreditation,
- reduce paper burden on organizations, and
- make accreditation more of an on-going process through required periodic performance reviews (PPR). See following discussion.

Changes became effective in January 2006. The accreditation process will now have two components: the periodic performance reviews (PPR) and priority focus process (PFP).

Focused on-site reviews, using the *priority focus process* (PFPs) will become unannounced and will utilize a new methodology to evaluate organizational performance. The surveyors will utilize the "Tracer" methodology designed to assess operational systems and processes in relation to *the patient's* care experience. The surveyors will follow a patient's hospital care experience through all departments that provided care during the hospitalization. The new methodology places heavy emphasis on inter-departmental communication during hospitalization and communication with post-discharge care settings, e.g., community agencies and care providers that may provide care after discharge. The organization is in part evaluated in relation to an actual patient care experience.

Periodic Performance Review process requires organizations to conduct a mid-cycle self-assessment against JCAHO standards, identify areas of non-compliance, and identify a correction plan. To support this new process, JCAHO has developed new on-line capabilities that will enable organizations to submit periodic performance reviews electronically.

Additionally, surveyors will draw on the information from a new software application that will utilize data from multiple sources such as ORYX® (see following discussion) and previous accreditation data for the organization. This information will help surveyors identify priority areas and focus on-site surveys.

§ 9.48   —National Patient Safety Goals

In 1999, national concern over patient safety reached new levels with the publication of the National Institute of Medicine (IOM) study, "To Err is Human: Building a Safer Health System." Findings from study included the following:

- Every year, between 44,000 and 98,000 people die in America's hospitals as a result of medical errors.

- Medical mistakes cause more deaths annually than car accidents, breast cancer, and AIDS.

- Medication errors alone, in or out of the hospital, are estimated to account or over 7,000 deaths annually.

The study concluded that a comprehensive approach to patient safety was needed and developed recommendations in four broad areas:

- Establishing a national focus to create leadership, research, tools, and protocols to enhance the knowledge base about safety,
- Identifying and learning from errors through immediate and strong mandatory reporting as well as encouragement of voluntary reporting, both with the aim of making systems safer for patients. The group strongly recommended that peer review protection from disclosure be extended to information in the system.
- Raising standards and expectations for improvements in safety through oversight organizations, group purchasers, and professional groups, and
- Creating safety systems inside health-care organizations through the implementation of safe practices at the delivery level.

These study recommendations created the impetus for organizations such as JCAHO and FACCT to incorporate patient safety into their goals. For JCAHO, the Sentinel Event Alert Advisory Group undertook this work.

The Sentinel Advisory Group was formed February 2002 and charged with conducting thorough review of all past JCAHO Sentinel Event Alert recommendations to assess:

- face validity and evidence for the recommendations, and
- practicality and cost effectiveness of implementing them.

From this assessment, the following framework for patient safety goals was developed:

- No more than six goals established for any given year.
- No more than two recommendations/goals.
- Yearly evaluation of goal effectiveness—some may continue while others may be replaced because of new priorities.

Utilizing this process and their framework cited above, JCAHO finalized six patient safety goals for 2003 accreditation. Since 2003, new goals have been added and existing ones modified. Goals are specific to an organization or site of care. Some goals are common across settings. As of 2006, Patient Safety Goals are as follows:

Goal 1—Improve accuracy of patient identification.

Goal 2—Improve communication effectiveness among caregivers. This goal contains the requirement for standardizing abbreviation, acronyms, and symbols and contains the JACHO list of "Do Not Use" Abbreviations.

Goal 3—Improve safety of using medications.

Goal 4—Eliminate wrong-site, wrong-patient, wrong-procedure surgery.

Goal 5—Improve safety of using infusion pumps.

Goal 6—Improve effectiveness of clinical alarm systems.

Goal 7—Reduce the risk of health care-associated infections

Goal 8—Accurately and completely reconcile medications across the continuum (of care).

Goal 9—Reduce the risk of patient harm resulting from falls.

Goal 10—Reduce the risk of influenza and pneumococcal disease.

Goal 11—Reduce the risk of surgical fires.

Goal 12—Implement applicable National Patient Safety Goals by components and practitioner sites.

Goal 13—Encourage active involvement of patients and their families in tha patient's care.

Goal 14—Prevent health care-associated pressure ulcers

Surveys will include evidence for implementation of the Patient Safety Goals or acceptable alternatives, including specific implementation plans and risk-reduction strategies. If the organization requests an alternative strategy to a specific goal, it must demonstrate that alternatives are at least as effective as published recommendations in achieving the goal. Approval for alternative goal implementation approaches must be requested from JCAHO. Requests are reviewed by the JCAHO Sentinel Event Advisory Group and approved or denied.

§ 9.49   —ORYNX® Quality Indicators

JCAHO also sponsors the ORYNX initiative, a program that integrates outcomes and other performance measurement data into the accreditation process. Introduced in 1997, ORYNX® was designed to implement in phases, ultimately using nationally standardized performance measures that allow for comparative data for outcome measures. In February 2000, JCAHO approved the first core measure sets and continues to add to them over time. As of 2006 the core measures include components of clinical care related to

- acute myocardial infarction, including coronary artery disease
- heart failure
- pneumonia
- surgical procedures and complications
- pregnancy and related conditions, including newborn and maternal care

JCAHO continues its work with ORYNX® data collection and revisions for health-care institution accreditation standards. It complies data received and utilizes it as a component of their quality reports. In addition to ORYNX® data, the quality reports address performance in patient safety goals and patient experience of care measures. The reports compare a specific organization to similar accredited organizations.

§ 9.50   —Office of Quality Monitoring

JCAHO's Office of Quality Monitoring evaluates and tracks complaints and concerns about health-care organizations involving quality-of-care issues. Information about these concerns comes from many sources, including patients, families, public, and an organization's own staff. Concerns may be reported in many ways, including the phone Hot Line (800) 994-6610, email, or written reports.

JCAHO has also implemented the National "Speak Up" program. This effort is a partnership with Centers for Medicare and Medicaid Services (CMS). The program's intent is to provide consumers information that enables them to be active participants in their health care. To accomplish this objective, JCAHO gives consumer information on how to prevent errors in care, how to report a complaint, and how to evaluate health care settings before choosing a care site.

After receiving a concern, JCAHO reviews the organization's most recent accreditation information and depending on nature of the concern, can take any of following actions:

- Incorporate into quality database to track over time (ID trends)
- Ask organization to provide written response
- Review with related standard at time of accreditation
- Conduct unannounced site visit

Regardless of the type of action taken, JCAHO requires that all incident investigation responses submitted by the organization must demonstrate an effective system to address

- identification of errors,
- root cause analysis,
- compilation of data on error frequency,
- dissemination of findings to allow redesign of systems, and
- assessment of effectiveness of actions to reduce errors over time.

Data collection began in July 2002. Over time, results will be used by JCAHO to focus on site survey evaluation.

§ 9.51   —Sentinel Event Identification and Reporting

Ensuring patient safety has always been within the purview of JCAHO accreditation standards. In the 1990s the organization, through its Sentinel Event Policy, began to require in-depth review of cases of medical errors that resulted in severe patient harm or death. Types of Sentinel Events include:

- medicine errors,
- wrong site surgery,
- restraint related deaths,
- blood transfusion errors,
- inpatient suicides,

- infant abductions, and
- fatal falls.

Organizations are required to report all Sentinel Events to JCAHO. The report must include findings of an in-depth case review using root cause analysis methodology on why the incident occurred as well as an action plan designed to prevent similar incidents. Information gained from Sentinel Events is shared with member organizations through JCAHO's "Sentinel Event Alerts" newsletters.

The Joint Commission maintains a robust website that is oriented to both consumers and health care organizations. Be sure to make use of this valuable resource if appropriate to your case issues.

JCAHO can be contacted at
1 Renaissance Blvd.
Oakbrook Terrace, IL 60181
Telephone: (630) 792-5000
Fax: (630) 792-5005
Website address: *http://www.jointcommission.org*

§ 9.52 —Clinical Practice Guidelines

In recent years, *clinical practice guidelines* have become increasingly important in health care delivery. The purpose of clinical practice guidelines is to assist the process of critical thinking, with the goal of improving treatment decisions that will achieve desired outcomes for specific diseases/conditions. Guidelines focus on indications for diagnostic tests and appropriate treatment; many are multidisciplinary in nature. Because guidelines are developed on practices that have demonstrated achievement of desired outcomes (evidence based), they can be used to improve patient care. Guidelines also help contain medical care costs because they focus on treatment elements that are critical to achieving outcomes and eliminate those that are unnecessary. Many sectors are developing clinical practice guidelines, including M.D. and nursing associations, managed care organizations, hospitals, and private companies. However, one of the leaders in this area is the Agency for Health Care Policy and Research (AHCPR).

The AHCPR is a federal agency created in 1989 as an arm of the Public Health Service. Its mission is to enhance quality, appropriateness, and effectiveness of health care services through scientific research. Through research and guideline development, it strives to promote improvements in clinical practice as well as improvements in the organization, financing, and delivery of health care services. Guideline development is carried out by the Office of the Forum for Quality and Effectiveness in Health Care, a division of AHCPR. Specifically, the Forum is responsible for developing, reviewing, and periodically updating clinically relevant guidelines that may be used by physicians, educators, and health care practitioners to assist in diagnosis and treatment of diseases. These are known as *clinical practice guidelines.* Similar responsibilities also exist for developing standards of quality, performance measures, and medical review criteria that can be used as tools to assess health care quality.

From 1992 through 1995, the following AHCPR Clinical Practice guidelines were issued:

1. Acute Pain Management: Operative or Medical Procedures and Trauma (1992)
2. Urinary Incontinence in Adults (1992)
3. Pressure Ulcers in Adults: Prediction and Prevention (1992)
4. Cataract in Adults: Management of Functional Impairment (1993)
5. Depression in Primary Care (1993)
6. Sickle Cell Disease: Screening, Diagnosis, Management, and Counseling in Newborns and Infants (1993)
7. Evaluation and Management of Early HIV Infection (1994)
8. Benign Prostatic Hyperplasia: Diagnosis and Management (1994)
9. Management of Cancer Pain (1994)
10. Unstable Angina: Diagnosis and Management (1994)
11. Heart Failure: Evaluation and Care of Patients with Left Ventricular Systolic Dysfunction (1994)
12. Otitis Media in Young Children (1994)
13. Quality Determinants of Mammography (1995)
14. Treatment of Pressure Ulcers in Adults
15. Acute Low Back Problems in Adults

Although now somewhat dated, copies of these guidelines (hard copy or CD-ROM) are available from:

AHCPR Publications Clearinghouse
P.O. Box 8547

Silver Spring, MD 20907
Telephone: (800) 358-9295
Web: *http://www.nnlm.nlm.nih.gov/*

As of 1996, AHCPR stopped internal development of clinical practice guidelines, but now helps groups in the private sector develop them as evidence-based guidelines.

The Institute of Medicine defines *evidence-based clinical practice guidelines* as follows: "Clinical practice guidelines are systematically developed statements to assist practitioner and patient decisions about appropriate health care for specific clinical conditions." Evidence-based medicine collects information that is patient-reported, clinician observed, and research-derived. This information is synthesized and the strength of the evidence evaluated and used to develop guidelines.

This work occurs at regional evidence-based practice centers around the country.

In 1999 AHCPR launched an Internet-based repository for evidence-based clinical guidelines. Known as the National Guideline Clearinghouse (NGC), this site is operated in partnership with the American Medical Association (AMA) and the American Association of Health Plans (AAHP). The NCG gives clinicians easy access to the latest clinical information on a wide range of diagnoses, including standardized abstracts and tables that allow comparison of different guidelines. It also has discussion groups and annotated bibliographies on guideline development methodologies, implementation, and use. The information is intended primarily for health professionals, but can also be useful to other audiences, including patients. Links to patient resources include, in part:

• Consumer pages for AAHP, AMA, AHCPR
• Consumer magazine of the FDA
• MedlinePlus (U.S. National Library of Medicine)
• PDG—National Cancer Institute database

Consumer information from the National Institutes of Health (NIH).

Consider the utility of the NGC when performing medical research. Its website address is *www.guidelines.gov*.

Case law for failure to follow clinical practice guidelines does exist. In *Lowry v Henry Mayo Newhall Memorial Hospital* (185 Cal. App. 3d 188) a malpractice suit was brought against a physician for treatment administered during CPR. The physician administered atropine instead of epinephrine as recommended under American Heart Association guidelines.

The decedent was admitted to the hospital following an auto accident. While hospitalized, she sustained a cardiac arrest. A Code Blue was called and the defendant physician responded as designated head of the hospital's team. Resuscitation efforts were not successful.

The trial court granted summary judgment to the physician; the decision was appealed and upheld based on the following:

1. Statutory immunity to physicians responding to hospital emergency applied as designated, nonvolunteer, non-Good Samaritan member of the hospital resuscitation team.
2. The physician did not engage in malpractice by administering atropine instead of epinephrine as recommended under American Heart Association guidelines.

As the name implies, these documents are guidelines only and should not be used in a vacuum. The ultimate decision for care rests with the health care professional charged with that responsibility and should be based on the assessment of the individual patient. Thus, deviation from guidelines does not, in and of itself, represent a breach of the standard of care.

§ 9.53   —Critical Paths

Clinical practice guidelines should not be confused with critical paths. Clinical practice guidelines establish goals and expected outcomes for patients, along with optimal timing for outcomes. Critical (care) paths focus on quality and efficiency of care *after* treatment decisions are made. Some purposes of critical paths include reduced rates of patient complications, reduced readmission rates, and reduced resource utilization, as well as enhanced patient education and patient satisfaction. They can be seen as proactive legal instruments. When they are interdisciplinary in nature, care paths are an effective way to communicate variances in the pathway to other team members. They assist with the coordination of care among health care team members, as work can often be compartmentalized with unclear accountabilities and responsibilities. Care paths can be adopted from published documents or developed internally by organizations. To be within the standard of care, the following criteria should be used in development:

- Multidisciplinary in nature
- Based on benchmarking of best practices
- Based on analysis of existing national and local standards
- Based on literature review.

The development of practice guidelines and care paths involves use of benchmarks and best practices. *Benchmarks* are practices that demonstrate the most efficient treatment, with *efficient* defined as optimal treatment without wasting resources along with desired outcomes. They reflect how care is delivered. *Best practices* reflect what is done. Benchmarks and best practices should not be based on financial objectives or volume targets. They should focus on providing the right care, at the right time, in the right setting, with a goal to eliminate waste and inefficiency in the system (e.g., delays that contribute nothing to the quality of care). There is currently tremendous variation in patterns of care delivery in the United States, which suggests that there are opportunities to improve both quality and efficiency of care at lower cost—goals that need not be mutually exclusive. Both practice guidelines and critical paths can be used as objective methods of evaluating performance.

§ 9.54   —Use in Medical Practice

Both practice guidelines and critical paths are often used together in the clinical setting in a complementary manner. However, these tools are only as sound as their design and the judgment of the providers who use them. Deviation from clinical paths may be appropriate; conversely, conforming to them does not result in automatic immunity from liability. Providers are bound to exercise judgment in individualizing care; that is, they are responsible for the care they give whether or not it follows a guideline or pathway. The legal implications of clinical practice guidelines and critical paths remain unclear. It is fairly certain, however, that guidelines will be at least one piece of key evidence in determining a standard of care. Guidelines and pathways are jury-friendly because they can help layper-sons analyze complex medical situations. They can also aid a court's understanding of what actually occurred when, and are more expedient than reading through volumes of medical records.

§ 9.55 Sources of Medical Standards of Care

Most physician and nursing specialties publish standards of care. Information on standards of care for physicians can be obtained from the medical professional organizations listed in § **9.57** *et seq.*

The American Medical Association (535 N. Dearborn St., Chicago, IL 60610) publishes the *Annual Directory of Practice Parameters,* a list of existing practice guidelines, plus information on where to order complete texts. This information is also available on CD-ROM.

The American Nurses Association also has published standards of care and practice for nursing specialties. Inquiries regarding these standards may be addressed to the American Nurses Association at

2420 Pershing Road,
Kansas City, MO 64108.
Website: *http://www.nursingworld.org*

§ 9.56 Sources of Non-medical Standards

In cases involving products liability, toxic exposure, workers' compensation, and personal injury, consultants and experts may rely on other standards to evaluate a case. Such standards will help determine if the cause of the injury involved conditions that were below the standard practiced within a particular industry under similar circumstances. Federal agencies, such as the Occupational Safety and Health Administration (OSHA), the National Institute of Industrial and Occupational Safety (NIOSH), and others publish worker and consumer safety standards. Some of these standards include acceptable levels of exposure to toxic substances and safe work practices for many industries. The Centers for Disease Control and Prevention (CDC) publish guidelines for prevention of exposure to and spread of infectious diseases.

Several federal agencies that may be helpful in providing standards are:

Centers for Disease Control and Prevention (CDC)
Department of Health and Human Services
1600 Clifton Road
Atlanta, GA 30333
Telephone: (404) 639-3311
Website: *http://www.cdc.gov*

Environmental Protection Agency (EPA)
401 M Street SW
Washington, DC 20460
Telephone: (202) 272-0167 (directory assistance)
Website: *http://www.epa.gov*

Federal Drug Administration (FDA)
Department of Health and Human Services
5600 Fishers Lane Rockwell, MD 20857
Telephone: (888) 463-6332
Website: *http://www.fda.gov*

National Institute of Industrial and Occupational Safety (NIOSH)
Department of Health and Human Services
1600 Clifton Road
Atlanta, GA 30333
Telephone: (404) 639-3311
Website: *http://www.cdc.gov/niosh*

Occupational Safety and Health Administration (OSHA)
Department of Labor
200 Constitution Avenue (Domestic inquiries)
Washington, DC 20210
Telephone: (800) 321-6742
Website: *http://www.osha.gov*

Many industries and professions also have established performance standards. Additionally, industrial engineers can be potential resources for evaluation of industrial safety. State and local agencies may also be helpful.

§ 9.57 Medical Specialists

Medical experts can address issues only within their professional realm of expertise. To determine the appropriate medical specialist for a particular case, a good understanding of the types of subspecialties within the various fields of medicine is needed. A list of medical specialists from several fields of expertise are discussed in sections below (**§§ 9.58–9.60**).

§ 9.58   —Medical Specialists: Types and Scopes of Practice

Allergist: treatment of allergies; a pediatric allergist treats allergies in children

Anesthesiologist: administration of anesthesia for surgical procedures; can be either a physician or a nurse anesthetist

Cardiologist: nonsurgical treatment of heart conditions

Dermatologist: treatment of skin diseases

Endocrinologist: treatment of diseases affecting hormone-producing glands of the body

Family practitioner (or general medicine): treatment of general health problems; also promotes wellness

Gastroenterologist: treatment of diseases affecting the digestive tract (stomach and intestines)

Gynecologist: treatment of diseases affecting the female reproductive organs; usually practiced in conjunction with obstetrics

Hematologist: treatment of diseases affecting the blood

Internal medicine (internist): treatment of diseases not requiring surgical intervention

Neonatologist: treatment of diseases and conditions affecting the newborn child

Nephrologist: treatment of kidney disease and direction of kidney dialysis (operation of artificial kidney)

Neurologist: treatment of diseases of the nervous system not requiring surgical intervention

Obstetrician: care of pregnant women and the delivery of babies, usually practiced in conjunction with gynecology

Oncologist: treatment of tumors that cannot be removed by surgery or that require additional treatment after surgery

Ophthalmologist: treatment of eye diseases by surgical, nonsurgical, and optical methods

Orthopedist: treatment of diseases involving muscles, bones, and joints; may subspecialize in treatment of conditions involving a certain part of the body, such as hands, knees, or back

Otorhino-laryngologist: treatment of diseases of the ears, nose, throat, head, and neck; commonly referred to as ENT (ear, nose, throat) specialty

Pathologist: studies causes and nature of disease, examines body tissues microscopically for abnormalities, performs autopsies

Pediatrician: treatment of children, including disease prevention

Physical medicine, physiatry, or rehabilitation: restoration of motion and function of the body affected by events such as stroke, head injury, or spinal cord injury; the goal is to maximize the body's functional ability

Plastic or reconstructive surgeon (cosmetic): repair or restoration of injured, deformed, or damaged body tissues; also performs elective revisions of facial or body characteristics

Proctologist: treatment of diseases of the colon and rectum

Psychiatrist: treatment of mental and emotional diseases, including the use of drugs or surgery to control symptoms

Pulmonist (pulmonary medicine): specializes in the treatment of diseases involving the lungs

Radiologist: interprets X rays and scanning procedures and performs therapeutic procedures requiring the use of X rays (radiation oncology)

Rheumatologist: treatment of arthritis

Surgeon: a physician who performs operations. May subspecialize in the type of surgery performed (neurosurgery, orthopedic surgery, pediatric surgery, cardiac surgery, plastic or reconstructive surgery)

Urologist: treatment of diseases of the urinary tract and of the male reproductive system.

In order to meet the complex needs of health care delivery, registered nursing also offers certification as a means of recognizing and encouraging specialization and advanced practice. In 1991 the American Board of Nursing Specialties (ABNS) was established as a national peer review program for specialty nursing certification bodies. As 2006, the following organizations offered ABNS-accredited certifications, as listed on the ABNS website:

- American Board of Perianesthesia Nursing Certification
- American Board of Occupational Health Nursing
- American Board of Neuroscience Nursing
- American Legal Nurse Consultant Certification Board
- Board of Certification for Emergency Nursing
- Competency and Credentialing Institute (Certification Board Perioperative Nursing)
- Council on Certification of Nurse anesthetists
- National Board of Certification for Hospice and Palliative Nurses
- Nephrology Nursing Certification Commission
- Oncology Nursing Certification Corporation
- Rehabilitation Nursing Certification Board
- Wound, ostomy, Continence Nursing Certification Board
- American Nurses Credentialing Center, offering credentialing for Adult and Family Nurse Practicitioners
- Pediatric Nurse Practitioners
- Acute Care Nurse Practitioners
- Geriatric Nurse Practitioners
- Psychiatric Adult and Child Clinical Nurse Specialists
- Medical/Surgical Clinical Nurse Specialist
- Gerontology Clinical Nurse Specialist
- Pediatric Clinical Nurse Specialist
- Home Health Clinical Nurse Specialist
- Community Health Clinical Nurse Specialist
- Medical/Surgical Nurse
- Gerontology Nurse
- Pediatric Nurse
- Psychiatric Mental Health Nurse
- Cardiac/Vascular Nurse
- Informatics Nurse
- Nursing Administration and Nursing Administration, Advanced Nursing Professional Development

For detailed information, the ABNS website is *http://www.nursing
certification.org.*

In litigation involving standards of care for nursing, a nurse consultant
and/or expert will be needed. The American Association of Legal Nurse
Consultants is an excellent resource for locating nurses with expertise in
specific nursing specialties. Founded in 1989, this association currently
(as of 1998) has over 30 chapters in 21 states. Members work in diverse
practice settings such as law firms, insurance companies, and hospital risk
management departments, and as independent consultants. In addition to
their expertise in nursing standards, nurse consultants can be valuable as
consultants/experts in a wide variety of types of litigation: medical malpractice, personal injury, workers' compensation, toxic exposures, and
product liability. As with any other type of consultant or expert, nurse
consultants should be chosen based on the match of his/her qualifications
to the case type and issues in question. The American Association of Legal
Nurse Consultants can be reached at

4700 W. Lake Avenue
Glenview, IL 60025-1425
Telephone: (847) 375-4713
Fax: (847) 375-4777
Website: *http://www.aalnc.org*

§ 9.59 —Board Certification

The American Board of Medical Specialties, through board certification,
gives formal recognition of a physician's qualifications in a specialty.
To be eligible for board certification, a physician usually completes an
extended residency, demonstrates relevant experience, completes special
studies, and passes extensive written and oral examinations. In addition to
board certification, a physician can also earn certificates for special qualifications, added qualifications, and sub-specialties.

Practice Note: There is a difference between board-eligible and board-
certified. A physician who is board-eligible has completed the prerequi-
sites set forth by the specialty board but has either failed the certification
exam or elected not to take it. When choosing an expert, look for board-
certified status.

§ 9.60   Practice Specialties in Dentistry

General dentist: treats a range of conditions involving the teeth and mouth, including fillings and crowns; also practices preventive dentistry

Endodontist: treatment of diseases of the dental pulp, usually by performing root canals

Oral and maxillofacial surgeon: operations on the face and jaw

Orthodontist: straightening of teeth and application of braces

Periodontist: treatment of gum disease

Prosthodontist: fitting of crowns, bridges, and dentures.

§ 9.61   Locating Consultants or Experts

Information on potential medical consultants can be obtained from various sources, including the following:

Treating physicians. One of the most common sources of expert witnesses includes the plaintiff's treating physicians. However, not all physicians wish to become involved in litigation. Treating physicians who decline to work with an attorney in a consulting or expert capacity can often recommend other medical professionals or provide the names of colleagues for referral purposes.

Colleges and universities. Consultants associated with university teaching hospitals or medical schools are on the cutting edge of medical technology and can be valuable witnesses. Because they make their living as academicians (rather than as professional experts), their credibility is considered to be excellent. These doctors do not rely on fellow physicians for patient referrals and, as result, are more willing to consult with and testify for attorneys. Consulting firms associated with educational institutions are another source of referrals.

Jury verdict services. These publications, usually published on a weekly basis, are very helpful both in determining the value of a claim and in identifying both plaintiff and defense experts used in a case. These services can be utilized to investigate a potential expert's track record at trial and in arbitrations. They are also useful when performing a background check on the opposition's expert. Check your local bar association for the jury verdict publication service in your area. See § **9.63** for a partial directory of jury verdict services.

Other attorneys. Check with attorneys in your area who have tried similar cases or practice in similar fields of law.

Attorney associations. Plaintiff and defense bar associations. (Defense Research Institute, ATLA) often maintain registries of potential expert witnesses.

Professional organizations. Each of the 23 medical specialties has a professional association that can be contacted for referrals. See § **9.48.**

Medical directories. Three resources can be consulted to identify potential experts:

- The *American Board of Medical Specialties (ABMS) Compendium of Certified Medical Specialists* lists most, if not all, of the board-certified physicians in the United States. This publication is updated and published every two years and can be obtained from ABMS at 1007 Church St., Evanston, IL 60201, website: *http://www.abms.org.*
- The *American Medical Directory,* published by the AMA, contains the names of all physicians, not just those who are board-certified. It is available in both hard copy and CD-ROM and can be ordered through their website: *http://www.ama-assn.org.*

Legal publications. Advertisements in legal publications may be a source of potential consultants. However, be wary of using consultants whose major source of income is derived from testifying at trials. These individuals may be portrayed by the opposition and perceived by a jury as hired guns with little or no credibility.

Legal seminars and meetings. Physicians who are speakers at local and national continuing education meetings can be good sources for referrals.

Independent companies whose services include providing expert witness names. Check your local networking resources for companies in your area.

Governmental agencies as listed in § **9.56** often employ researchers knowledgeable in specific areas of litigation, including the latest in research developments.

Before making a final choice for an expert witness, several factors must be considered. In addition to displaying familiarity with the standards of care in the area of litigation, the potential expert's history of past litigation (such as malpractice claims) should be reviewed. Consideration should also be given to unfavorable impressions the expert may make on the jury when testifying, as well as to any evidence of bias. Finally, it is of supreme importance to choose an expert who can take the complicated world of medicine and explain it clearly and succinctly to the layperson.

§ 9.62   —Medical Organizations/Potential Consultants

The following medical organizations are excellent sources for medical consultants and experts. This is a partial list only. If a consultant and/or expert is needed in a field not represented by the disciplines below, search the web using key words. Most recognized medical specialties have professional organizations and websites with contact information.

Accreditation Association for Ambulatory Health Care
3201 Glenview Road, Suite 300
Wilmette, IL 60091
Telephone: (847) 853-6060
Fax: (847) 853-9028
Web: *http://www.aaahc.org*

American Academy of Facial Plastic and Reconstructive Surgery
310 S. Henry St.
Alexendria, VA 22314
Telephone: (703) 2999291
Web: *http://www.aafprs.org*

American Academy of Forensic Sciences
410 N. 21st St.
Colorado Springs, CO 80904-2798
Telephone: (719) 636-1100
Fax: (719) 636-1993
Web: *http://www.aafs.org*

American Academy of Nurse Practitioners
P.O. Box 12846
Austin, TX 78711
Telephone: (512) 442-4262
Fax: (512) 442-6469
Web: *http://www.aanp.org*

American Academy of Pain Management
13947 Mono Way, Suite A
Sonora, CA 95370
Telephone: (209) 533-9744
Fax: (210) 533-9750
Web: *http://www.aapainmanage.org*

American Academy of Physical Medicine and Rehabilitation
330 N. Wabash Avenue, Suite 2500
Chicago, IL 60611-7617
Telephone: (312) 464-9700
Fax: (312) 464-0227
Web: *http://www.aapmr.org*

American Academy of Physician Assistants
950 North Washington Street
Alexandria, VA 22314-1552
Telephone: (703) 836-2272
Fax: (703) 684-1924
Web: *http://www.aapa.org*

American Association for Respiratory Care
9425 N. MacArthur Boulevard, Suite 100
Irving, TX 75063-4706
Telephone: (972) 243-2272
Web: *http://aarc.org*

American Association of Blood Banks
8101 Glenbrook Road
Bethesda, MD 208142749
Telephone: (301) 907-6977
Fax: (301) 907-6895
Web: *http://www.aabb.org*

American Association of Critical Care Nurses
101 Columbia Aliso
Viejo, CA 92656
Telephone: (800) 899-2226
Fax: (714) 362-2020
Web: *http://www.aacn.org*

American Association of Health Plans
1129 20th Street N.W., Suite 600
Washington, DC 20036
Telephone: (202) 778-3200
Fax: (202) 331-7487
Web: *http://www.aahp.org*

American Association of Legal Nurse Consultants
224 West Lake Avenue
Glenview, IL 60025
Telephone: (847) 375-4743
Fax: (847) 375-4777
Web: *http://www.aalnc.org*

American Association of Nurse Anesthetists
222 South Prospect Avenue Park Ridge, IL 60068-4001
Telephone: (847) 692-7050
Fax: (847) 692-6968
Web: *http://www.aana.com*

American Association of Spinal Cord Injury Nurses
75-20 Astoria Boulevard
Jackson Heights, NY 11370-1170
Telephone: (718) 803-3782
Fax: (718) 803-0414
Web: *http://www.aascin.org*

American Association of Peri Anesthesia Nurses
10 Melrose Avenue, Suite 110
Cherry Hill, NJ 08003-3696
Telephone: (856) 616-9600
Fax: (856) 616-9601
Web: *http://aspan.org*

American Board of Allergy and Immunology, Inc.
(a conjoint board of the American Board of Internal Medicine
and the American Board of Pediatrics)
510 Walnut Street, Suite 1701
Philadelphia, PA 19106-3699
Telephone: (866) 264-5568
Fax: (215) 592-9411
Web: *http://www.abai.org*

American Board of Anesthesiology, Inc.
4101 Lake Boone Trail
The Summit Suite 510
Raleigh, NC 27607-7506
Telephone: (919) 881-2570
Fax: (919) 881-2575
Web: *http://www.theaba.org*

American Board of Colon and Rectal Surgery, Inc.
20600 Eureka Road, Ste. 600
Taylor, MI 48180
Telephone: (313) 282-9400
Fax: (313) 282-9402
Web: *http://www.abcrs.org*

American Board of Dermatology, Inc.
Henry Ford Hospital
One Ford Place
Detroit, MI 48202-3450
Telephone: (313) 874-1088
Fax: (313) 872-3221
Web: *http://www.abderm.org*

American Board of Emergency Medicine, Inc.
3000 Coolidge Road East
Lansing, MI 48823
Telephone: (517) 332-4800
Fax: (517) 332-2234
Web: *http://abem.org*

American Board of Family Medicine, Inc.
2228 Young Drive
Lexington, KY 40505-4294
Telephone: (859) 269-5626
Fax: (859) 335-7501
Web: *http://www.abfp.org*

American Board of Internal Medicine, Inc.
510 Walnut Street, Suite 1700
Philadelphia, PA 19106
Telephone: (215) 446-2246
Fax: (215) 446-3633
Web: *http://www.abim.org*

American Board of Medical Genetics, Inc.
9650 Rockville Pike
Bethesda, MD 20814-3998
Telephone: (301) 634-7316
Fax: (301) 634-7320
Web: *http://www.abmg.org*

American Board of Neurological Surgery, Inc.
6550 Fannin Street, Ste. 2139
Houston, TX 77030
Telephone: (713) 441-6015
Web: *http://www.abns.org*

American Board of Nuclear Medicine, Inc.
4555 Forest Park Boulevard
St. Louis, MO 63108
Telephone: (314) 367-2225
Fax: (314) 362-2806
Web: *http://www.annm.org*

American Board of Obstetrics and Gynecology, Inc.
2915 Vine Street
Dallas, TX 75204-1069
Telephone: (214) 871-1619
Fax: (214) 871-1943
Web: *http://www.abog.org*

American Board of Ophthalmology, Inc.
111 Presidential Blvd., Ste.
241 Bala Cynwyd, PA 19004
Telephone: (610) 664-1175
Fax: (610) 664-6503
Web: *http://www.abop.org*

American Board of Orthopaedic Surgery, Inc.
400 Silver Cedar Ct.
Chapel Hill, NC 27514
Telephone: (919) 929-7103
Fax: (919) 942-8988
Web: *http://www.abos.org*

American Board of Otolaryngology, Inc.
5615 Kirby Drive, Suite 600
Houston, TX 77005-2452
Telephone: (850) 850-0399
Fax: (850) 850-1104
Web: *http://www.aboto.org*

American Board of Pathology, Inc.
P.O. Box 25915
Tampa, FL 33622
Telephone: (813) 286-2444
Fax: (813) 289-5279
Web: *http://www.abpath.org*

American Board of Pediatrics, Inc.
111 Silver Cedar Ct.
Chapel Hill, NC 27514-1651
Telephone: (919) 929-0461
Fax: (919) 929-9255
Web: *http://www.abp.org*

American Board of Physical Medicine and Rehabilitation, Inc.
3015 Allegro Park Lane, SW
Rochester, MN 55902
Telephone: (507) 282-1776
Fax: (507) 282-9242
Web: *http://www.abpmr.org*

American Board of Plastic Surgery, Inc.
444 E. Algonquin Road
Arlington Heights, IL 60005
Telephone: (800) 465-2784
Web: *http://www.abplsurg.org*

American Board of Preventive Medicine, Inc.
330 S. Wells Street, Suite 1018
Chicago, IL 60606
Telephone: (312) 939-2276
Fax: (312) 939-2218
Web: *http://www.abprev.org*

American Board of Psychiatry and Neurology, Inc.
500 Lake Cook Road, Ste. 335
Deerfield, IL 60015
Telephone: (708) 945-7900
Fax: (708) 945-1146
Web: *http://www.abpn.org*

American Board of Radiology, Inc.
5441 E. Williams Boulevard, Suite 200
Tucson, AZ 85711
Telephone: (520) 790-2900
Fax: (520) 790-3200
Web: *http://www.theabr.org*

American Board of Surgery, Inc.
1617 John F. Kennedy Blvd., Ste. 860 Philadelphia, PA 19103-1847
Telephone: (215) 568-4000
Fax: (215) 563-5718
Web: *http://www.absurg.org*

American Board of Thoracic Surgery, Inc.
633 N. St. Claire Street, Suite 2320
Chicago, IL 60611
Telephone: (312) 202-5900
Fax: (312) 202-5960
Web: *http://www.abts.org*

American Board of Urology, Inc.
2216 Ivy Road, Suite 210
Charlottesville, VA 22903
Telephone: (434) 979-0059
Fax: (434) 979-0266
Web: *http://abu.org*

American Chiropractic Association
1701 Clarendon Blvd.
Arlington, VA 22209
Telephone: (703) 276-8800
Toll free: (800) 986-4636
Fax: (703) 243-2593
Web: *http://www.amerchiro.org*

American Dental Association
515 N. State Street
Chicago, IL 60610
Telephone: (312) 440-2500
Fax: (312) 440-7494
Web: *http://www.ada.org*

American Medical Association
535 N. Dearborn Street
Chicago, IL 60611
Telephone: (800) 6218335
Web: *http://www.amaassn.org*

American Nurses Association
8515 Georgia Avenue,
Suite 400
Silver Springs, MD 20910
Telephone: (301) 628-5000
Fax: (301) 628-5001
Web: *http://www.nursingworld.org*

American Osteopathic Association
142 E. Ontario Street
Chicago, IL 60611
Telephone: (800) 621-1773
Fax: (312) 202-8200
Web: *http://www.osteopathic.org*

American Psychiatric Association
1000 Wilson Boulevard, Suite 1825
Arlington, VA 22209
Telephone: (703) 907-7300
Web: *http://www.psych.org*

American Psychological Association
750 First St., N.E.
Washington, DC 20002-4242
Telephone: (202) 336-5500
Web: *http://www.apa.org*

**Association for Professionals in Infection
Control and Epidemiology**
1275 K Street N.W., Suite 1000
Washington, DC 20005
Telephone: (202) 789-1890
Fax: (202) 789-1899
Web: *http://www.apic.org*

Association of Child and Adolescent Psychiatric Nurses
2810 Crossroads Drive, Suite 3800
Madison, WI 53718
Telephone: (608) 443-2463
Fax: (608) 443-2474

Association of Operating Room Nurses
2170 Parker Road, Suite 300
Denver, CO 80231
Telephone: (303) 755-6304
Web: *http://www.aorn.org*

Association of Rehabilitation Nurses
4700 West Lake Avenue
Glenview, IL 60025-1485
Telephone: (800) 229-7530
Web: *http://rehabnurse.org*

National Association of Orthopedic Nurses
401 N. Michigan Avenue, Suite 2200
Chicago IL 60611
Telephone: (800) 289-6266
Fax: (312) 527-6658
Web: *http://www.orthonurse.org*

National Association of Pediatric Nurses and Practitioners
20 Brace Road, Suite 200
Telephone: (856) 857-9700
Fax: (856) 857-9700
Web: *http://www.naprap.org*

§ 9.63 —State Jury Verdict Reporters

An additional source for locating consultants and experts can be Jury
Verdict Services. **Table 9–1** includes many of the jury verdict services
operating in the United States.

Table 9–1

Jury Verdict Reporters

State	Reporting Service
Alaska	Jury Verdicts Northwest, Inc. P.O. Box 1165, Seattle, WA 98111 Phone: (425) 774-0530 Fax: (425) 778-4502 *E-mail: jurynw@aol.com*
Arizona	The Trial Reporter of Central and Northern Arizona The Trial Reporter of Southern Arizona Verdict Summaries and Research P.O. Box 8187, Phoenix, AZ 85066-8187 Phone: (800) 266-7773 Fax: (800) 266-3131

State	Reporting Service
California	Trials Digest 1144 65th Street, Suite D, Oakland, CA 94608-2000 Phone: (510) 420-1800 Fax: (510) 420-8006 Web: *http://www.trialsdigest.com* Verdict Search Phone: (800) 832-1900 Web: *http://www.VerdictSearch.com*
Colorado	Jury Verdict Reporter of Colorado 7396 South Garfield Court, Littleton, CO 80122-2201 Phone: (303) 779-4073 Fax: (303) 779-5311 Web: *http://www.jvrc.com*
Connecticut	Metro Verdicts Monthly P.O. Box 709, Crestwood, KY 40014-0709 Phone: (800) 445-3165 Web: *http://www.verdicts.com*
District of Columbia	Metro Verdicts Monthly P.O. Box 709, Crestwood, KY 40014-0709 Phone: (800) 445-3165 Web: *http://www.verdicts.com* Verdict Search Phone: (800) 832-1900 Web: *http://www.VerdictSearch.com*
Florida	Florida Jury Verdict Reporter P.O. Box 3730, Tallahassee, FL 32315-3730 Phone: (800) 446-2998 Web: *http://www.flajury.com* Jury Trials and Tribulations P.O. Box 3730, Tallahassee, FL 32315-3730 Phone: (800) 446-2998 Web: *http://www.floridalegalperiodicals.com*

State	Reporting Service
Georgia	Metro Verdicts Monthly P.O. Box 709, Crestwood, KY 40014-0709 Phone: (800) 445-3165 Web: *http://www.verdicts.com*
Hawaii	Personal Injury Judgments Hawaii 47-378 Hui Koloa Place, Kaneohe, HI 96744 Phone: (808) 239-9639 Fax: (808) 531-0053
Idaho	Jury Verdicts Northwest, Inc. P.O. Box 1165, Seattle, WA 98111 Phone: (425) 774-0530 Fax: (425) 778-4502 E-mail: *jurynw@aol.com*
Illinois	Cook County Jury Verdict Reporter 415 North State Street, Chicago, IL 60610-4674 Phone: (312) 644-7800 Fax: (312) 644-5990 E-mail: *kirkton@lawbulletin.com* Verdict Reporter, Inc. (So. Illinois) 2440 S. Brentwood Blvd., Suite 102 St. Louis, MO 63144-2327 Phone: (314) 962-7500 Fax: (314) 962-6864 Verdict Search Phone: (800) 832-1900 Web: *http://www.VerdictSearch.com*
Kansas	Greater Kansas City Jury Verdict Service 607 Westport Road, Ste. 500, Kansas City, MO 60411 Phone: (816) 931-9400
Lousiana	Verdict Search Texas 8323 Southwest Freeway, Suite 370, Houston, TX 77079 Phone: (800) 783-0313 Web: *http://www.VerdictSearch.com*

State	Reporting Service
Maryland	Metro Verdicts Monthly P.O. Box 709, Crestwood, KY 40014-0709 Phone: (800) 445-3165 Web: *http://www.verdicts.com*
Massachusetts	Metro Verdicts Monthly P.O. Box 709, Crestwood, KY 40014-0709 Phone: (800) 445-3165 Web: *http://www.verdicts.com*
Michigan	Metro Verdicts Monthly P.O. Box 709, Crestwood, KY 40014-0709 Phone: (800) 445-3165 Web: *http://www.verdicts.com*
Missouri	Greater Kansas City Jury Verdict Service 607 Westport Road, Ste. 500, Kansas City, MO 60411 Phone: (816) 931-9400 Verdict Reporting Inc. 2440 S. Brentwood Blvd., Suite 102 St. Louis, MO 63144-2327 Phone: (314) 962-7500 Web: *http://www.verdictreporter.com*
Nebraska	Rocky Mountain Verdicts and Settlements P.O. Box 571261, Murray, UT 84157-1261 Phone: (801) 268-2321 Web: *http://www.rockymtverdicts.com*
New Jersey	Verdict Search Phone: (800) 832-1900 Web: *http://www.VerdictSearch.com*
New Mexico	Verdict Search Texas 8323 Southwest Freeway, Suite 370, Houston, TX 77079 Phone: (800) 783-0313 Web: *http://www.VerdictSearch.com*

State	Reporting Service
New York	New York Jury Verdict Reporter 128 Carleton Avenue, East Islip, N.Y. 11730 Phone: (800) 832-1900 Web: *http://www.VerdictSearch.com*
Ohio	Metro Verdicts Monthly P.O. Box 709, Crestwood, KY 40014-0709 Phone: (800) 445-3165 Web: *http://www.verdicts.com*
Oregon	Jury Verdicts Northwest, Inc. P.O. Box 1165, Seattle, WA 98111 Phone: (425) 774-0530 Pennsylvania Verdict Search Phone: (800) 832-1900 Web: *http://www.VerdictSearch.com*
Rhode Island	Metro Verdicts Monthly P.O. Box 709, Crestwood, KY 40014-0709 Phone: (800) 445-3165 Web: *http://www.verdicts.com*
Tennessee	Tennessee Litigation Reporter 901 Church Street, Nashville, TN 37203-3411 Phone: (615) 255-6288
Texas	East Texas Trial Reports 14027 Memorial Dr., Ste. 436, Houston, TX 77079-6895 Phone: (281) 531-4500 North Texas Reports (Dallas & Tarrant Counties) Litigation Reports Publishing, POB 26960, Phoenix, AZ 85068-6960 Phone: (800) 600-2015 Texas Reporter 16845 Blanco Rd., Suite 190, San Antonio, TX 78232 Phone: (210) 496-1750 Web: *http://www.texasreporter.com*

State	Reporting Service
	Trial Report Service, Inc. 2006 Oak Trail, Rowlett, TX 75088 Phone: (214) 607-9862 Web: *http://www.trialreports.net* Verdict Search Texas Phone: (800) 832-1900 Web: *http://www.VerdictSearch.com*
Utah	Rocky Mountain Verdicts and Settlements P.O. Box 571261, Murray, UT 84157-1261 Phone: (801) 268-2321 Web: *http://www.rockymtverdicts.com*
Virginia	Metro Verdicts Monthly P.O. Box 709, Crestwood, KY 40014-0709 Phone: (800) 445-3165 Web: *http://www.verdicts.com*
Washington	Jury Verdicts Northwest, Inc. P.O. Box 1165, Seattle, WA 98111 Phone: (425) 774-0530
Wisconsin	Wisconsin Jury Verdict 735 S. Main St., Racine, WI 53403 Phone: (414) 635-0400
Wyoming	Rocky Mountain Verdicts and Settlements P.O. Box 571261, Murray, UT 84157-1261 Phone: (801) 268-2321 Web: *http://www.rockymtverdicts.com*

CHAPTER 10

MEDICAL RECORDS IN DISCOVERY AND AT TRIAL

§ 10.1 Introduction

The medical record is among the most basic tools in litigation. From a plaintiff's records, witnesses are identified, experts form opinions, and the case story develops. Stated simply, medical records play a critical role in the prosecution and defense of personal injury and medical malpractice suits. Litigation is propelled by discovery and when discovery is completed, the case is ready either for settlement of the matter through mediation or arbitration, or for trial. After the medical records have been obtained, they are reviewed and summarized for relevant content. After all, a succinct and objective account of the injuries and the events surrounding an act or accident is much simpler to utilize than to wade through potentially thousands of pages of medical documentation in order to relocate the key information needed. In addition to this most obvious purpose, there are other, equally important ones. Because the medical record is the cornerstone in medical malpractice and personal injury cases, it will be used by both the plaintiff and the defense throughout the course of litigation. The plaintiff will use the medical record to gather evidence to substantiate claims of damage and malpractice. The defense will use the same record to refute these claims. The medical record will be reviewed for evidence of prior similar injuries or conditions or to identify alternative causation theories for the plaintiff's injuries. Another significant purpose for a well thought out medical record summary is to educate the reader about the nature of the injuries, the treatment proposed and completed, the residuals of any treatment, and the prognosis or future course of recovery. While specific in-depth discussions of the injury and/or disease, and the potential outcomes are generated by consultants and expert witnesses, the medical record summary is an excellent forum for educating both the attorney who will use the information throughout discovery, and ultimately anyone who takes part in the resolution of the case (e.g., insurance adjustors, mediators, opposing counsel, plaintiff and plaintiff's family, members of the jury, and judges).

§ 10.2 Interrogatories

The initial identity of plaintiff's medical providers can either be provided by counsel, or obtained through the written interrogatory which asks that all medical providers consulted before and after an incident be identified. The records are then either subpoenaed or obtained via medical authorization (See **Chapter 7** for an in depth discussion of this process).

§ 10.3 Depositions

Depositions are taken with two essential purposes in mind. The first is to commit the deponent to a specific set of facts, testified to under oath. The second is to assess the strengths and weaknesses of the deponent as a witness. Unexplained changes in testimony permit trial attorneys to impeach a witness in front of a jury; consistent and well-prepared testimony deters this possibility.

'If It Wasn't Documented, It Didn't Happen'

It has often been stated by litigation counsel that "if it wasn't documented, it didn't happen." While this dogmatic assertion clearly lacks grounding in reality, it appears early and often in litigation in which the medical record is the most important evidence in a case. Realistically, physicians, nurses, and other care providers do not have the time to document every aspect of a visit or a nursing shift. No current technology can capture all of the nuances of patient-provider interactions. However, once a deponent agrees with this suggestion in deposition, testimony regarding events, advice or treatments not specifically documented in the medical record will be revisited many times thereafter. A medical provider can rely on and explain his "custom and practice" of care to explain an apparent deficiency in the record. For example, a physician being deposed can credibly testify that, though she does not specifically recall having a discussion with the plaintiff concerning the risks associated with a prescribed medication, she is reasonably certain that this discussion occurred because it is her custom and practice to discuss such issues when prescribing medications.

Using Medical Records in Deposition

Prior to any deposition involving personal injuries, the attorney taking the deposition will need to be intimately familiar with the medical record. The following are suggestions for using medical records and summaries in depositions:

- Deposition of physician (treating or defendant): complete chronology of the patient's medical record which includes pre and post-incident care; a break-out summary of the deponent's specific entries in the medical record; copies of each record authored and/or signed by the deponent to be attached as exhibits; a copy of the deponent's resume or curriculum vitae.

- Deposition of a plaintiff: complete chronology of the patient's medical record which includes pre and post-incident care; a break-out summary of statements made by the plaintiff as to how the accident occurred, especially if the statements vary.

- Deposition of expert witness: complete chronology of the medical record; copies of any medical journal articles authored by the witness which concern this type of disease or injury; a copy of the deponent's resume or curriculum vitae; the expert's entire file on this case.

- Depositions of other medical professionals (i.e., nurses, pharmacists, physical therapists, etc.): the complete chronology of the patient's medical record which includes pre and post-incident care; a break-out summary of the deponent's specific entries in the medical record; copies of each record authored and/or signed by the deponent to be attached as exhibits.

§ 10.4   Independent Medical Examinations

One of the more important discovery devices is the independent medical examination, a medical (or other) examination performed by a physician chosen by the defendant. This type of examination is commonly referred to as an independent medical examination (IME) or defense medical examination (DME).

§ 10.5   Criteria for Independent Medical Examinations

Federal Rule of Civil Procedure 35 permits the use of a physical or mental examination as a means of discovery. Examinations are appropriate in actions in which the mental or physical condition of a person is in controversy. This can include actions in which an individual's blood group is at issue.

§ 10.6   History

The foundation for the use of medical examinations in litigation in California was laid in *Johnston v. Southern Pacific* (1907) 150 Cal. 535. Plaintiff sued for a skull fracture and brain hemorrhage she sustained when the train from which she was exiting made a sudden, violent movement. The defense asked that she undergo a physical examination by two physicians. The trial court denied the motion because it felt that it lacked the power to make such an order. On review, the California Supreme Court determined that courts did have the power to order examinations of this type and should exercise this power with "sound discretion." The court held that the denial of such power to the trial court would leave the defendant completely at the mercy of the plaintiff's medical witnesses and would constitute an injustice so "gross and intolerable that it must be avoided, even at some cost to the "refined and delicate feelings of the plaintiff."

§ 10.7   When Examinations Are Appropriate

The medical examination as a discovery tool is appropriate only on a showing that the physical or mental condition of the individual is actually *at issue or in controversy* in the case and that *good cause* exists for the examination. Fed. R. Civ. P. 35(a). Often these requirements are interwoven.

In general practice, medical examinations are most frequently used by the defense in personal injury cases. The filing of a personal injury complaint by the plaintiff places his physical condition at issue and provides the defense with good cause to seek a physical examination. A plaintiff who is making a claim for emotional distress or other psychological condition *suffered as a result of the incident* has placed her mental condition at issue. Under these circumstances, the defense is entitled to a mental examination of the plaintiff. However, the mere filing of a claim or action for personal injuries which seeks general damages for pain and suffering does not automatically put the plaintiff's general mental condition at issue, and does not make pre-injury and post-injury records discoverable. (See *Houghton v. M&F Fishing, Inc.* (S.D. Cal. 2001) 198 F.R.D. 666, 669.) Generally speaking, an additional element is required, e.g., a separate cause of action for negligent or intentional infliction of emotional distress or plaintiff's designation of an expert witness to testify to the distress. (See *Turner v. Imperial Stores* (S.D. Cal. 1995) 161 F.R.D. 89, 92–97.)

§ 10.8   Who May Be Examined

Fed. R. Civ. P. 35 and the California Code of Civil Procedure § 2032.220 allow a physical or mental examination of the following categories of individuals:

- Any party to the action.
- A natural person in the "custody or legal control" of a party.

Parties are required to make a "good faith effort" to produce persons over whom they have control, for example, minor children. This may also extend, upon proper showing, to a executor being required to produce the body of a decedent, *In re Certain Asbestos Cases* (N.D. Tex. 1986)

112 F.R.D. 427, 433. See, however, *Holm v. Superior Court* (1986) 187 Cal. App. 3d 1241, 232 Cal. Rptr. 432, in which the court held that even though the physical or mental condition of a decedent may be in controversy, the exhumation of a corpse for an autopsy was not allowed.

Some jurisdictions will allow an agent or employee of a named party to undergo a medical examination by court order. For example, the court may order a defendant corporation, sued as a result of the alleged negligence of its driver, to produce that employee for a compulsory medical examination, even though the driver has not been named as a party. There is no sanction, however, against a nonparty agent or employee who refuses to undergo a court-ordered medical examination. Any sanctions awarded would run against the party who has custody or control of the individual, or who employs the individual whose examination has been ordered. The sanction can be avoided by demonstrating an inability to produce that person for examination (California Code of Civil Procedure § 2032.420).

§ 10.9   Examination of Party

The most obvious candidate for a medical examination is the personal injury plaintiff who is asking the court to resolve issues concerning his medical condition. Some jurisdictions do not limit examination of a "party" solely to the plaintiff, however. California Code of Civil Procedure § 2032.020 allows that the medical examination of a defendant may be obtained where that party's physical or mental condition is the suspected cause of the incident. For example, the plaintiff may allege that the defendant's physical condition (such as poor eyesight) acted, or should have acted, as a bar to operating a vehicle. In this case, an ophthalmologic examination of the defendant may be obtained.

In paternity determination cases, one or both of the parents may be directed to undergo blood tests. Where a libel case is based on defamatory assertions concerning the medical condition of the plaintiff, the defendant is entitled to a medical examination of the plaintiff to aid in the establishment of the affirmative defense of truth. Keep in mind that "good cause" is the benchmark standard. In *Sacramono v. Bridgestone/Firestone, Inc.* (D. Mass. 1993) 152 F.R.D. 428, 431, the court denied a motion to compel the plaintiff to submit to a blood test to determine his HIV status. Defendant argued that plaintiff led a lifestyle exposing him to the risk of contracting HIV. The court held that despite the fact that Plaintiff was seeking future damages and AIDS would shorten his life expectancy, this did not rise to the level of placing his HIV status "in controversy."

In *Reuter v. Superior Court* (1979) 93 Cal. App. 3d 332, 155 Cal. Rptr. 525, the court held that in order to qualify for an examination, the person to be examined must be more than a *nominal* party. The defendant wanted the mother (and guardian ad litem) of a minor plaintiff to undergo a battery of mental tests collateral to those tests to be administered to her son. The court held that the requirement that a minor have an adult representative was no justification for ordering the guardian to submit to the invasion of her body or mental processes. In effect, the mother's mental condition was *not* in controversy and therefore she could not be subjected to an examination.

Practice Note: For purposes of the following sections, it will be assumed that the person to be examined is the plaintiff.

§ 10.10   Number of Examinations

Fed. R. Civ. P. 35(a) does not limit the number of examinations that may be ordered so long as "good cause" is shown for each examination requested, including mental examinations. In *Peters v. Nelson* (N.D. Iowa 1994) 153 F.R.D. 635, 638, the court allowed multiple mental examinations based on the fact that a substantial time lag occurred between the first examination and the trial.

Multiple medical examinations have been allowed under the following circumstances:

- Plaintiff alleges separate injuries requiring examination by different specialists (e.g., orthopedic, neurological, psychological);
- The examining physician requests the assistance of other consultants in making a diagnosis;
- It can be shown that the initial examination was incomplete or inadequate.

In California, the Code of Civil Procedure § 2032.220 allows "any defendant" to demand one physical examination of the plaintiff or cross-complainant in a personal injury case. This would seem to allow each individual defendant and co-defendant the right to demand a separate physical examination on his or her own behalf. This section specifically allows third-party cross-defendants access to this discovery procedure as well.

§ 10.11   The Examiner

A physical examination may be conducted by any "suitably licensed or certified" health care practitioner. Fed. R. Civ. P. 35(a). In the past, only licensed physicians could conduct examinations. However, the definition of licensed health care practitioner has been significantly expanded to include psychologists, chiropractors, dentists, physical therapists, speech pathologists, osteopaths, podiatrists, optometrists, and acupuncturists.

When determining the appropriate individual to perform an examination, the following criteria should be considered.

Professional Qualifications and Experience. The nature and severity of the injury will determine the level of experience required. For example, if the plaintiff is alleging a closed head injury with cognitive and emotional residuals, a board-certified neurologist or neuropsychiatrist would be an appropriate choice. In any case, board-certification in the specialty of choice is an absolute requirement.

Credibility. Medical practitioners who work exclusively for either plaintiff or defendant, or practitioners who do not have an active practice may have less credibility than individuals who are actively engaged in the care and treatment of patients and who have experience "on both sides of the fence."

Ability to Communicate. A medical examiner must be able to formulate his or her ideas on paper and in testimony in a manner that can be easily understood by all persons involved, including members of the jury, because the reality is that the IME physician will probably act as the defense medical expert. In federal practice, the party seeking the medical examination chooses the person who will conduct it and the court generally appoints the examiner requested by the moving party. Trial courts have broad discretion to determine whether good cause exists for refusing to accept the examining party's choice of an examiner. However, a party's unsupported objections to a particular doctor conducting the examination should be given little weight. *Edwards v. Superior Court* (1976) 16 Cal. 3d

905, 913, 130 Cal. Rptr 14.; *Looney v. National Railroad Passenger Corp.* (D. Mass. 1992) 142 F.R.D. 264, 265, in which the court found it "immaterial" that the physician was "prodefendant."

Once the decision is made to require a medical examination, the appropriate specialty for the examiner should be determined. For example, if plaintiff alleges neurological damage resulting from an injury, the defense should choose as examiner, either a neurologist or a neurological surgeon. Many offices have established relationships with physicians and other medical providers. Teaching hospitals and medical school faculty are often excellent sources for an examiner. Jury verdict publications and searches can also identify potential examiners. The next step is to contact the medical provider, obtain an up-to-date curriculum vitae, and make arrangements for the examination, keeping in mind the statutory requirements. Plaintiff's counsel is then notified of the arrangements by letter or demand.

Practice Note: Remember, there is no physician-patient privilege for an IME. The physician is hired solely as a consultant to essentially render a second-opinion. All of the physician's findings should be contained in the IME Report which should only be sent to those parties authorized to receive it. An IME physician should never discuss his findings or recommendations with the patient, family members, treating physicians or opposing counsel; if discussion is required on a certain aspect of the case, it should be done with the firm who hired the examiner.

§ 10.12   Time Frame

Although examinations may be set soon after the first appearance of a defendant, there are reasons to wait to schedule an examination. Most medical professionals who perform medical-legal examinations require a complete set of medical records and x-rays before or during the examination. It is reasonable therefore to wait until after discovery of the plaintiff's medical care or condition has progressed and copies of medical records have been obtained. Because one of the objectives of a medical examination is to determine the extent of residual damage from the initial injury, it may be more appropriate to wait to schedule an examination until the plaintiff has achieved the maximum recovery that can be anticipated. However, if the plaintiff's medical condition is grave, or she is elderly, it may be better to do the examination as soon as possible.

§ 10.13   Obtaining an IME by Stipulation

In cases where the medical condition of the litigant is so obviously and importantly an issue that both sides recognize the need for an examination, Fed. R. Civ. P. 35(b)(c) allows the use of stipulations. More often than not, medical examinations are arranged in this manner between counsel. In fact, local federal rules require that, before moving for a court-ordered examination, the parties must first try to arrange for the examination by agreement. See N.D. Cal. Rule 37-1(a).

Examination by stipulation is most appropriate when:

_____ The case is an action for personal injuries.

_____ The person to be examined is the plaintiff.

_____ The type of examination sought is physical.

_____ No previous examination has been obtained.

_____ The examination will be routine in nature with no diagnostic test or procedure that is painful, protracted, or intrusive.

Examination by stipulation is often arranged informally by telephone between counsel and confirmed by letter. However, confirming the stipulation formally in writing is strongly advised. At this time, counsel can set forth the conditions for the medical examination, including a description of each test or procedure to be done as well as the conditions of the examination. Unless the stipulation expressly states otherwise, however, it will be deemed to incorporate all provisions of FRCP 35, including the requirements concerning the exchange of medical reports and the waiver of privileges. Fed. R. Civ. P. 35; California Code of Civil Procedure § 2032.610; *Grover v. Superior Court* (1958) 161 Cal. App. 2d 644, 327 P. 2d 212. See **Form 10–1**—Correspondence Confirming Stipulation for Medical Examination.

§ 10.14   IME by Noticed Motion

If the initial informal attempts to schedule the examination by stipulation fail, leave of court must be obtained. In federal court, if the parties have been unable to stipulate to the examination, a physical or mental examination may be obtained only by court order on noticed motion showing good cause. Fed. R. Civ. P. 35(a). Pursuant to that rule, the notice of motion must be directed to all parties showing with specificity the following:

- The date, time, place, and location of the examination;
- The manner, conditions, scope, and nature of the examination;
- The identity and specialty, if any, of the physician or other licensed health care provider who will perform the examination.

The showing of "good cause" requires that specific facts be set forth justifying this type of discovery, the need for the examination, and the inability to obtain the information elsewhere. Be prepared to submit declarations in support of the motion indicating that the physical or mental condition to be examined has been placed in controversy, stating the facts constituting good cause, and explaining all attempts made at informal resolution and/or stipulation to the examination. Attach copies of the examiner's curriculum vitae for the court to review. See **Form 10–2** for a Sample Notice of Motion for Physical Examination.

§ 10.15 Scope of IME

In many jurisdictions, leave of court is required if the examination is to include any diagnostic test or procedure that is "painful, protracted, or intrusive." CCP § 2032.220(a)(1); *Klein v. Yellow Cab Co.* (N.D. Ohio 1944) 7 F.R.D. 169, 170, where the court ordered plaintiff to undergo a cystoscopy. If a potentially dangerous or painful procedure is to be part of the examination, the burden of proof is shifted to the plaintiff's attorney to show the danger or pain involved. At the very least, a declaration or affidavit from an expert is required. *Pena v. Troup* (D. Col. 1995) 163 F.R.D. 352, 355.

If counsel for plaintiff wishes to limit the scope of the examination this must be stated at the time of the opposition to the noticed motion. It is not advisable to object to the scope of the exam during the process itself as this might expose the plaintiff and his attorney to sanctions including Oppositions should be succinctly stated, for example:

- If the motion requests that the plaintiff undergo x-rays of the cervical spine, the court should be referred to the specific number of cervical x-rays that have been taken to date and ask that additional x-rays not be taken by the examining physician except by court order for good cause.

- If the plaintiff has specific religious or cultural mores that would argue against disrobing for a physician, request that the examiner respect the plaintiff's wishes and conduct the examination through the individual's clothing.
- Limitation of examination to specific part(s) of the body—e.g., shoulder injury may not require examination of lower extremities.

§ 10.16   Order for Physical Examination

The order granting the motion is subject to the same specificity requirements as the motion. It must specify the designation of the examiner, the time and place of the examination, and the manner, conditions, and scope of the examination. Fed. R. Civ. P. 35(a). An order that does not do so is defective. *Harabedian v. Superior Court* (1961) 195 Cal. App. 2d 26, 15 Cal. Rptr. 420, 89 ALR 2d 994. See **Form 10–3** for a sample Order on Motion for Physical Examination.

§ 10.17   Psychological [Mental] Examination

If a plaintiff stipulates that (1) no claim is being made for psychological [mental] and emotional distress over and above that usually associated with the claimed physical injuries and (2) that no testimony regarding this usual mental and emotional distress will be presented at trial in support of the claim for damages, courts will generally not order a mental examination in the absence of exceptional circumstances.

A defendant cannot place the plaintiff's mental condition in controversy by alleging that the plaintiff's injuries are the result of mental problems. See *Houghton v. M&F Fishing, Inc.* (S.D. Cal. 2001) 198 F.R.D. 666, 669.

Where the injury pleaded is entirely or primarily to an individual's emotional status, these allegations long have been deemed good cause to permit the defendant to obtain a psychological [mental] examination of the plaintiff. *Vinson v. Superior Court* (1987) 43 Cal. 3d 833, 239 Cal. Rptr. 292. This does not mean, however, that the plaintiff forfeits all rights to privacy. The court recognizes that plaintiff is not compelled "as a condition to entering the courtroom, to discard entirely her mantle of privacy." At the same time, plaintiff cannot be allowed to make serious allegations without affording defendants an opportunity to put their truth to the test. *Vinson, supra,* at 840. See **Form 10–4** for sample Notice of Motion for Psychological [Mental] Examination.

§ 10.18   Defense Preparation

Before the examination date, copies of the medical records should be forwarded to the examiner. Many physicians have specific preferences as to how records are sent, either as paper copies or on a CD. Confirm with the physician what her preference is. Additionally, rather than providing full size copies of radiology films, litigation copy services can provide excellent copies of all radiology studies on a CD. Consider also sending copies of the plaintiff's deposition transcript, and any other medical providers who have been deposed, if available.

§ 10.19   Plaintiff Preparation

When the agreement or demand for examination arrives, it is important to perform a background check on the proposed examiner to determine his or her specialty and experience in legal actions. This can be done through various jury verdicts services and other sources.

     The client must be notified immediately of the arrangements for the examination. Close to the date of the examination, the client's attorney should meet with and prepare the client for the examination process. It is important that the client understand who the examiner is and what the purpose of the examination is. The client should be cautioned as to his conduct at the examination.

§ 10.20   Attendance at Physical Examination

Arrangements should be made for the attorney or other representative to attend and record the entire examination by audiotape. Some plaintiff's attorneys feel that allowing a client to attend a medical examination without representation is tantamount to malpractice. The theory is if the plaintiff is without legal representation, the medical examiner is free to inquire into areas of the client's past or present condition unrelated to the subject incident and injuries. However, the majority of federal courts have consistently denied the plaintiff's right to have counsel or other legal representative witness a physical examination. Some federal courts have made an exception and allowed third parties to be present with a *showing of good cause.* See *Vreeland v. Ethan Allen, Inc.* (S.D.N.Y. 1993) 151 F.R.D. 551–552, attorney attended; *Klein v. Yellow Cab Co.* (N.D. Ohio 1944) 7 F.R.D. 169, 170, plaintiff's physician attended. Under these circumstances, it does not seem reasonable that a court would exclude the presence at an examination of a parent or custodian of a minor child, a debilitated elder, or a plaintiff who is developmentally or physically disabled.

California allows observers to attend a physical examination, including the plaintiff's attorney or designated representative, and a court reporter. (California Code of Civil Procedure § 2032.510(a).) It is generally assumed that the term "designated representative" includes a paralegal or an interpreter and could also permit the attorney to be represented by a medical consultant.

Although no California case has dealt directly with the matter, the trial court probably retains discretion to permit a spouse, relative, or friend to attend a physical examination. This is advisable where the plaintiff is a minor or incompetent, and may be appropriate where the examining physician is of the opposite sex.

An examination normally will include detailed questioning of the plaintiff regarding the history of her condition. This questioning poses the possible danger that it will enter into the area of liability, producing statements about the circumstances of the event causing the injury which are or might be construed as harmful to the plaintiff. In a 1955 case, the California Supreme Court held that a lay person "should not be expected to evaluate the propriety of every question at his peril. The plaintiff, therefore, should be permitted to have the assistance and protection of an attorney during the examination." *Scharff v. Superior Court* (1955) 44 Cal. 2d 508, 282 P.2d 896. Thus, the most significant reason for having an observer attend the medical examination is to prevent improper questioning.

A physician conducting a physical examination pursuant to Fed. R. Civ. P. 35(a) may ask the examinee questions which are necessary to reach an opinion about the person's medical condition and the "cause of the alleged injury." See *Romano v. II Morrow, Inc.* (D. Ore. 1997) 173 F.R.D. 271, 273, in which the court refused to limit the physician to questions propounded in advance of the examination.

§ 10.21   Attendance at Psychological [Mental] Examination

In those jurisdictions in which third parties may attend and observe physical examinations, the realm of the psychological [mental] exam remains off limits. In *Vinson v. Superior Court* (1987) 43 Cal. 3d 833, 239 Cal. Rptr. 292, the court denied the plaintiff an unqualified right to the company of counsel during a psychiatric interview. The court reasoned that given the "sensitive" nature of the psychiatric examination itself and the need for a "special and private rapport between examiner and examinee," mental examinations were best conducted on a one-to-one basis. The court found that a psychiatric examination was almost wholly devoted to a "careful probing of the examinee's psyche for the purpose of forming an accurate picture of his mental condition" and the presence of a third party might impair this process.

§ 10.22   Attendance Notification Requirements

In the interests of cooperation, it is advisable to let all involved parties know that an observer will be present. The notification can be made by a letter to the medical examiner with a copy to the opposition attorney, preferably sent beforehand.

Practice Note: While certain jurisdictions allow the presence of third parties, many doctors do not. If the plaintiff has indicated that an observer will be present, ensure that the physician selected to perform the examination knows and agrees. The examining physician may refuse to perform the examination but may bill the attorney for the time anyway.

§ 10.23   Role of Observer at Physical Examination

It is extremely important that any person attending a medical examination be aware of his role as an observer. The attorney's representative often attends the examination to provide emotional support to the client. The representative should:

• Accurately document the information the plaintiff gives the examiner, the type of tests performed, and a description of the examination itself, including the client's verbal and physical responses, in order to allow an objective assessment of the accuracy of the medical report and of the client's version of the examination. An audiotape can provide much of this information.

- Refrain from offering any information to the examiner concerning the plaintiff's history and symptoms, even though the observer may be able to remember more than the client, and even though the examiner may ask the observer questions.

The role of the observer is to monitor the examination, not to participate in or disrupt it. The observer should be sensitive to appropriate and inappropriate areas of questioning by the physician. For example, questions concerning the subject's injury are acceptable, as may be questions concerning prior related injuries. However, questions regarding the use of alcohol or other controlled substances, personal relationships, or unrelated physical conditions may not be appropriate. If, in the opinion of the observer, the examiner becomes abusive to the plaintiff, or tries to perform unauthorized tests or procedures, the examination can be stopped. Plaintiff's counsel can then move for a protective order limiting the scope of any continued IME. On the other hand, if the observer disrupts the examination by directing the plaintiff how to answer a question, for example, the physician may suspend the examination. The party requesting the examination can thereafter move for a protective order and a monetary sanction in order to control the conduct of the plaintiff and observer.

Practice Note: Some medical examiners ask plaintiffs to complete "Client History" forms before the examination. Many plaintiff's attorneys believe it is not appropriate for the client to fill out any papers for the examining physician. At the very least, the attorney should completely review the forms. The reasoning is that the physician can obtain this information from the defense, and medical history forms represent inquiry into inappropriate areas by the examining physician.

§ 10.24   Recording the Physical Examination

In some jurisdictions, due to the intrusive nature of video equipment, an examination may not be videotaped. In *Edmiston v. Superior Court* (1978) 22 Cal. 3d 699, 150 Cal. Rptr. 276, the trial court authorized the videotaping of a discovery physical examination. Its order provided that the operator be a disinterested person, that the taping be conducted in a nondisruptive way, and that the tape itself be made available for viewing by the other side. A divided Supreme Court ruled that the trial court lacked the power to order even such a carefully regulated attempt to obtain a visual record of the examination. The court said that "videotaping with its heavy equipment and necessary additional personnel would unnecessarily create a sideshow atmosphere at which taping was the main attraction."

A federal court has found that videotaping of an examination by a professional videographer (or even an unattended video camera) would give the plaintiff an "unfair advantage" because defendant cannot tape the examination or treatment by the plaintiff's doctors. See *Holland v. United States* (D.S.C. 1998) 182 F.R.D. 493, 495.

However, some jurisdictions do allow a plaintiff to videotape and record the IME. Failure by a physician to allow a videotape or recorder into the examination room could lead to abrupt cancellation of the IME and loss of the defense's chance to have the plaintiff examined. Any taping or form of intimidation will be noted in the IME report. In New York State workers's compensation cases, IMEs can be videotaped by the physician as long notice is given to the claimant. (IME-5, Claimant's Notice of Independent Medical Examination, Section 137 WCL.) Either party may record a medical examination with audiotape. See California Code of Civil Procedure § 2032.510(a). Prior notice of intent to audiotape is not required.

Practice Note: Examinations can last from one to four hours, depending on the complexity of the injuries alleged. Make sure that there are adequate batteries and blank tapes available for a long examination.

§ 10.25   Failure to Appear for IME

If the plaintiff or other person fails to appear for or submit to an examination, monetary sanctions may be imposed on that individual or on the party required to produce her for examination. In addition, the court may preclude the party from introducing expert testimony as a sanction for failure to attend the court-mandated examination. See *Mraovic v. Elgin, Joliet & Eastern Ry. Co.*, 897 F.2d 268, 271 (7th Cir. 1990).

Practice Note: In addition, doctors almost uniformly require payment for the scheduled visit if the examination is not canceled 24 to 48 hours in advance. It may be the case that the examiner is late for the examination. Although no authority appears to address this issue, 45 minutes is an adequate time to wait for the examiner to appear. If, after this length of time, the examiner has still not appeared, the plaintiff may be advised to leave. Always confirm the date and time of the IME 1-2 days prior.

§ 10.26   Exchange of Written Reports

On request, the plaintiff is entitled to receive a copy of any report generated as a result of the examination. The report must be "a detailed written report of the examiner setting out the examiner's findings, including results of all tests made, diagnoses, and conclusions together with like reports of all earlier examinations of the same condition." Fed. R. Civ. P. 35(b)(1); California Code of Civil Procedure § 2032.610(a)(1). See **Form 10–5** for a sample request. A plaintiff's demand for copies of the defense medical report has the following significant consequences:

_____   The defendant is entitled to receive, upon request, copies of all medical reports by the plaintiff's doctors and experts.

_____   The plaintiff must exchange any *future reports* relating to the same condition by the same or any other examiner.

_____   The plaintiff waives any claim of privilege or work product that would otherwise protect such reports from discovery.

   This requirement for the exchange of reports does not apply to consultants who have reviewed the medical records but have not examined the plaintiff personally. These reports are protected by the work product privilege until that consultant is declared an expert witness, at which point all of the expert's reports become discoverable.

Practice Note: Generally speaking, plaintiffs' attorneys should ask any examining doctor they have retained to contact them before preparing a written report. If the results of the examination are to plaintiff's disadvantage, or if the examiner is acting as a consultant only and not an expert, the examiner may be asked not to prepare a written report. The examiner's identity or the unfavorable evaluation remain protected as work product.

If a party fails to make a timely delivery of the reports demanded, the demanding party may move for an order compelling their delivery and for sanctions. If a party then fails to obey the order compelling deliverance of the reports, the court may impose harsher sanctions, including an evidence or terminating sanction. In addition, an examiner whose report has not been provided will not be allowed to testify at trial. Fed. R. Civ. P. 35(b)(1); California Code of Civil Procedure § 2032.620.

§ 10.27   Using Medical Records at Trial

All of the work that has been done in reviewing medical records comes to fruition at this time. One of the more important functions of a legal professional is preparing the documents to be used at trial. This preparation should begin on day one.

§ 10.28   Preparation of Evidence Binder

Ideally, the evidence binder is from the start of litigation, and at the very least, several months prior to the start of trial. It is a convenient method of keeping all of the significant material in one place, making it easily accessible for use during depositions, mediations, and settlement conferences. As new information is obtained (witnesses or treating physicians, additional medical bills), the binder is reviewed and updated. It contains all the investigative and documentary evidence to be used at trial.

The following suggested categories of information should be included:

Witness/Party List. This sheet, located at the front of the binder, contains the phone numbers (office, home, cell) and addresses (home, office, email) of all individuals who are germane to the case and/or who might be called to testify. This includes the trial team members (partner, associate, paralegal, secretary, jury research), client(s), the insurance company claims representative (if a defense case), attorneys for each party, lay witnesses, expert witnesses, investigators, court personnel, and support staff (copy service, attorney services, etc.)

To-Do List. Depending upon the time frame of the case, this list can include such items as depositions to be taken (or summarized), witnesses to be contacted or interviewed, experts to be retained or deposed, tests to be performed, and subpoenas to be issued.

Investigation. This section includes investigative police agency reports, reports made by your private investigator, and photographs of the location of the accident and/or the vehicles involved. (Photographs of injuries to a party would be located in the medical records section.)

Plaintiff(s), Defendant(s), Witnesses. Each individual involved should be assigned a section which contains statements made prior to litigation, documents authored or signed, summaries of deposition testimony, both narrative and page-line, excerpts from applicable answers to interrogatories, responses to requests for production of documents, and requests for admissions and responses.

Expert Witnesses. Designate a separate section for each expert witness. This section includes a copy of the expert's curriculum vitae, any report generated by the expert, a summary of his or her deposition testimony, and copies of any technical articles the expert relied upon in rendering the opinion.

Wage Loss. If the case involves allegations of wage loss or loss of earning capacity, this section will contain information concerning the plaintiff's employment history, including summaries of employment records, W-2 and other tax related information, and statements made by the plaintiff in answers to interrogatories or during deposition that concern wage loss.

Medical Records. All of the summaries that have been prepared throughout the case that document the medical care and treatment received by a party are placed here. Include with the summaries copies of significant records, for example, admission history and physical examinations, operative reports, results of diagnostic tests, discharge summaries, and consultations.

Specific Medical Information. If the medical treatment rendered is complex, additional sections can be added that deal with medical conditions, for example, "Vicodin issue" or "Cervical radiculopathy. These sections include any information that assists in understanding the nature of the disease and/or its treatment, including well-labeled anatomical diagrams, excerpts from medical resource texts explaining a particular injury or surgical procedure, and diagrams illustrating the injury or condition.

Medical Bills. This section contains the itemization of medical bills as illustrated in **§ 8.36,** along with copies of the pertinent medical bills, insurance payments, and notices of lien.

§ 10.29   Preparation of Trial Book

When preparing for trial, one of the most important tools used by the attorney will be the trial book. This book (or books if the case is complex and involves many parties) will present in an organized and easily accessible format the pertinent information needed by the attorney in order to present the case. There is no standard method for preparing a trial book; the format depends entirely upon the size of the case and the attorney's individual needs.

§ 10.30   Working Trial Book

The working trial book contains the informal, formal and procedural legal material needed by the attorney to put on a case. As an example, separate sections pertaining to each of the following categories might be included:

Trial Plan. This section contains the attorney's "road map" for the presentation of the case, i.e., the order of witnesses, exhibits, and so on.

Pleadings. This section contains the basic pleadings—the complaint, any cross-complaints, and answers to them.

Settlement Offers. This section contains written settlement offers including statutorily proposed offers to compromise.

Legal Research. This section should include any research memoranda, plus copies of case law and statutes regarding key questions of law or evidence to be presented or raised at trial.

Motions. A significant portion of any trial can involve motion work, for example, motions to sever or bifurcate certain causes of action or issues, motions in limine regarding evidentiary questions, motions to exclude witnesses or to disclose their identities, and so on.

Voir Dire and Jury Selection. This section will contain the list of voir dire questions to be directed at the jury panel (unless the jurisdiction requires that the judge conduct the voir dire), any notes that have been made regarding particular panel members, and any other information concerning the jury selection process.

Opening Statements. This section will generally include a chronology of significant events in the case, notations regarding points made by opposing counsel in opening remarks, and so on.

Trial Notes. Notes made by the attorney during testimony and following the completion of each day's session are placed here.

Exhibits. This section will contain a list of exhibits offered by all parties as evidence. The actual documentary evidence does not appear in this section, however.

Closing Arguments. This section contains the attorney's notations regarding statements by opposing counsel and her draft of closing arguments.

Jury Instructions. Place copies of jury instructions as given by the court, notations regarding changes and/or additions, and copies of special verdicts utilized in this section.

§ 10.31   Medical Records Allowed at Trial

In personal injury, workers' compensation, and medical malpractice cases, the medical record is crucial to the presentation or defense of a case. Federal Rules of Evidence 101 *et seq.* set the standards for admissibility of medical records as evidence at trial.

—Rule 401 defines *relevant evidence* as that which has "any tendency to make the existence of any fact that is of consequence to the determination of the action more probable or less probable than it would be without the evidence." Accordingly, all relevant evidence is admissible (Rule 402).

—*Hearsay,* defined at Rule 801(c) as "a statement offered in evidence to prove the truth of the matter asserted," is not relevant as evidence. Medical records, however, fall within one of the widely known exceptions to the hearsay rule as defined by Rule 803(6). This exception defines certain records as "a . . . report, record . . . in any form, of acts, events, conditions, opinions, or diagnoses, made at or near the time by, or from information transmitted by, a person with knowledge, if kept in the course of a regularly conducted business activity. . . ." Records kept by hospitals and all medical providers fall within this exception and are admissible as evidence.

§ 10.32   Original Records Versus Duplicates

Federal Rule 1003 states that a duplicate is admissible to the "same extent as an original unless (1) a genuine question is raised as to the authenticity of the original or (2) in the circumstances it would be unfair to admit the duplicate in lieu of the original."

Practice Note: Check applicable state rules regarding use of copies in lieu of original records. If medical records have been obtained by subpoena, these documents will come with a signed affidavit by the custodian of records that they constitute a true and complete copy of the original records in the custody and control of the medical provider. Although notice requirements vary from state to state, generally each party is notified that particular records have been placed under subpoena. Each party is entitled, upon request, to a complete copy of all records provided to the party filing the subpoena. In this manner, subpoenaed records offered as evidence at trial have been made available to all parties. For this reason, and in order to avoid compromising the integrity of the record, no markings should be made on subpoenaed documents.

Practice Note: Copy the subpoenaed documents and use the copies for making markings or notations directly on the records.

§ 10.33   Demonstrative Evidence at Trial

In actions involving medical malpractice, personal injury, or workers' compensation, demonstrative evidence (photographs, models, charts, video or motion pictures) is used to illustrate and supplement the testimony of witnesses. Testimony becomes clearer to the jury when it is accompanied by visual aids.

Visual images, whether photographs or charts, provide jurors with points of reference that tie important concepts together. In short, people remember what they see. Good exhibits must reflect an understanding of all of the processes involved in jury decision-making. Clear, concise graphic communication is required if attorneys are to stimulate the visual imaginations of jurors. Generally speaking, any item that serves to explain or aid the jury in its understanding of an issue is relevant and admissible upon a foundational showing that the item is an accurate portrayal of the matter depicted and that it fairly illustrates the witness testimony.

Most trials utilize some form of demonstrative evidence, from simple copies of documents to enlargements of photographs to sophisticated video reconstructions of accidents. Clearly, anything that will assist a jury in understanding the nature of an injury, its impact on an individual's life, or the manner in which it occurred can be significant.

Enlargements of Chart Entries

At the time the medical records were first reviewed and summarized, certain documents were identified as being of extreme importance to proving or disproving the main issues of the case. These documents are chosen for enlargement and use at trial. For example, in any case in which it appears that the medical record has been altered, an enlargement of the altered records should be prepared. It can then be used by the attorney, by expert physicians, or other individuals who may be called upon to testify about the alterations.

Practice Note: Enlargements of medical record entries must be large enough that details can be clearly seen. Plan to have each page enlarged to poster size (2 × 3 feet).

Still Photographs

Still photographs can be very persuasive exhibits at trial, depicting anything from the plaintiff's injuries to the kinds of medical devices used during rehabilitation (halo braces, full body casts, and so on). In motor vehicle accident cases, photos showing the damage to the vehicles involved can be helpful.

Practice Note: Photographs must also be large enough that details can be clearly seen. Plan to have photographs enlarged to at least an 8 × 10-inch or 11 × 17-inch format. In some cases, it may be valuable to have photos enlarged to poster size.

Videotapes

Videotapes are a dramatic method of demonstrating medical evidence and can have a profound effect at trial. They make the impact of the consequences of a catastrophic event come alive for the jury, especially in a "day in the life" format. Conversely, surveillance films can be used to impeach testimony regarding the effect of injuries on an individual's life.

Practice Note: Make sure that a CD player, video recorder and monitor (or projector and screen) have been obtained for the screening, along with spare batteries and extension cords. Confirm the availability and location of electrical plugs in the courtroom itself, prior to the start of trial, and check with the judge's clerks to determine his particular preferences in use of video equipment.

Prosthetic and Surgical Devices

Often, the most telling piece of evidence will be the actual rod that was placed in a plaintiff's femur, the plate and screws used to stabilize a fracture, the artificial limb worn by the plaintiff, or the halo brace that was anchored into the plaintiff's skull and worn for months. These devices should be retained for potential use at trial.

Anatomical Models, Drawings, or Diagrams

Models are three-dimensional representations used to demonstrate the functioning of a body part or the skeleton as a whole. They are useful in demonstrating the location of an injury. Medical drawings and diagrams are often used in opening remarks and closing arguments and to illustrate the testimony of expert witnesses.

X-Rays

X-rays and scans (MRI, CT, bone scan) are used to illustrate and assist an expert or treating physician in describing the plaintiff's injury.

Practice Note: Make sure that any necessary aids are available to the witness: light screens for viewing x-rays (larger is better than smaller, two to three sections are better than one), laser or collapsible pointers, and so on. Radiology films reproduced onto a CD can easily be enlarged through use of a laptop computer and projecter.

Other Demonstrative Aids

At the time the medical records were first summarized, various formats may have been used in order to present the medical information. These different types of summaries—chronologies, break-out, charts—should now seriously be considered as the basis for demonstrative aids. As with the general, initial summary of the records, the specific issues that must be proven will need to be presented to the jury as well. For example, consider the following potential issues and aids:

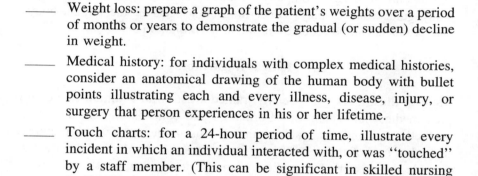

_____ Weight loss: prepare a graph of the patient's weights over a period of months or years to demonstrate the gradual (or sudden) decline in weight.

_____ Medical history: for individuals with complex medical histories, consider an anatomical drawing of the human body with bullet points illustrating each and every illness, disease, injury, or surgery that person experiences in his or her lifetime.

_____ Touch charts: for a 24-hour period of time, illustrate every incident in which an individual interacted with, or was "touched" by a staff member. (This can be significant in skilled nursing facility cases in which plaintiff alleges that their loved one was "abandoned.")

The type of demonstrative aid is limited only by one's imagination and budget.

§ 10.34   —Sources for Demonstrative Aids

Treating physicians and experts often have charts, models, and other teaching aids that can be utilized at trial. Local medical schools and colleges often have models that can be borrowed or rented. Additionally, many demonstrative aids can be downloaded, revised, and printed within the law office itself. Medical images downloaded from the Internet or from purchased software can be integrated into exhibits using Microsoft Power-Point display systems. Many junior or community colleges offer one-day courses in the use of PowerPoint and legal professionals would be well-advised to become proficient in its use. With the use of scanners, laptop computers, and trial software, law firms now have the resources to place their entire trial presentation on a CD for incredible ease of presentation.

§ 10.35 —Guide to Resources and Services

*Life*ART™ is a company that provides quality medical illustrations for various medical content areas, including anatomy, physiology, physical therapy, surgery, pediatrics, 3-D anatomy, neurology, cardiology, and orthopedics. The images can be ordered on-line at *www.Lifeart.com* or *www.mediclip.com.*

Anatomical Chart Company produces charts, models, references, study guides and displays concerning all aspects of the human body. The products can be ordered on line at *www.anatomical.com.*

Medical Illustrators

Medical illustrators are specially trained artists who communicate complex medical and scientific information and concepts in a meaningful, aesthetic and understandable manner. This unique profession requires not only a love of art but an affinity for science as well. Medical illustrators provide the artwork for medical journals, design multimedia websites, produce 3D animated films of cellular processes, and hand craft prosthetic appliances for patients. Advertising agencies and publishers, as well as pharmaceutical and medical product companies, often use medical illustrators for brochures and publications. Attorneys may commission medical illustrators to produce art to be used as demonstrative evidence in complex legal cases. Association of Medical Illustrators, P.O. Box 1897, Lawrence, Kansas, 66004; Telephone (866) 393-4AMI or 393-4264; *www.medical-illustrators.org.*

Medical College of Georgia, Dept. of Medical Illustration, 1120 15th Street CJ1101, Augusta, GA 30912-0300; Telephone: (706) 721-3266; Fax: (706) 721-7855; *www.mcg.edu/medart* The Johns Hopkins School of Medicine, Department of Art as Applied to Medicine, 1830 E. Monument Street, Suite 7000, Baltimore, MD 21205; Telephone: (410) 955-3213; *www.med.jhu.edu/medart.*

Each of these sites has links to other programs and resources for medical illustrators.

FORM 10–1
CORRESPONDENCE CONFIRMING STIPULATION
FOR MEDICAL EXAMINATION

[Date] _____

[Name of Plaintiff's Attorney] _____

[Address] _____

[City, State, Zip] _____

Re: [name of case]

Dear Plaintiff's Attorney:

This letter is in confirmation that your client [name] will appear for a [neurological, identify speciality as required] medical examination to be conducted on [date] at [time] at the medical office of [identity of examiner]. The address and phone of Dr. [name] are [address and phone]. This examination may include the following: taking of oral history by Dr. [name]; physical examination including range of motion, gait and other tests; an electromyogram study [if appropriate].

Thank you for your cooperation in arranging this examination.

Very truly yours,

[Name of attorney]

Practice Note: Whether the examination is arranged by agreement or demand, determine as soon as possible the dates on which the plaintiff is available. Having a list of possible dates is helpful because it is difficult to obtain medical appointments, cancellations can result in significant charges, and most examination have to be set well in advance of the appointment date.

FORM 10–2
NOTICE OF MOTION FOR PHYSICAL EXAMINATION

[CAPTION] Case No. _____

NOTICE OF MOTION FOR PHYSICAL EXAMINATION

To: Plaintiff [name], [his or her or its] attorney, to each other party, and to the attorney of record for each other party in this action:

PLEASE TAKE NOTICE that on [date], at [time], or as soon thereafter as the matter can be heard, in Department_____of the above-entitled Court, located at [address], Defendant [name] will move the Court under, [Fed. R. Civ. P. 35(a); your specific authority] for an order directing Plaintiff, [name], to submit to a physical examination, on [date] and at [time] by Dr. [name], whose specialty is [specify, for example, neurology, pediatric, psychology], at [his or her] office at [address].

This examination will consist of: [state the scope, nature, manner and conditions of the examination, including the diagnostic tests and procedures that will be used].
This motion is made after unsuccessful attempts to arrange for the examination by agreement, and on the ground that the following factors constitute good cause for a physical examination of the Plaintiff conducted at the instance of the Defendant as part of [his or her or its] pretrial discovery:

1. Plaintiff seeks by this action the recovery of damages for personal injuries claimed to have been sustained in the occurrence described in the Complaint.
2. It is anticipated that Plaintiff will offer at trial in support of this claim for damages the testimony of one or more doctors who have had the advantage of conducting a physical examination of the type sought by this motion.
3. Expert opinion on the nature, extent, and duration of the injuries alleged by Plaintiff is essential to a determination of the amount of damages, if any, to which Plaintiff may be entitled for the cause of action alleged in the Complaint.
4. Defendant cannot adequately prepare for trial without having the benefit of an independent medical evaluation of the actual nature, extent, and duration of any physical injuries sustained by Plaintiff.

This motion is based on the attached memorandum of points and authorities, and [specify any documents, exhibits, or declarations that accompany the motion].

Dated: _____

[Named of Attorney]

_____
Attorney for Defendant

Practice Note: This form represents the most common situation in which the examination of the plaintiff is sought by the defendant. It may be adapted to cover more unusual situations in which the plaintiff is a defendant, or a nonparty. It may also be adapted to fit the requirements for any type of medical examination for which a motion is required by statute.

FORM 10–3
ORDER FOR PHYSICAL EXAMINATION

[CAPTION]

Case No. _____

ORDER ON MOTION FOR
PHYSICAL EXAMINATION
TO ALL PARTIES AND TO THEIR ATTORNEYS OF RECORD:

PLEASE TAKE NOTICE that on [date of hearing], the duly noticed motion of [moving party] to compel the physical examination of [plaintiff] came on regularly for hearing, the Honorable [name], judge presiding. [Name of attorney] appeared on behalf of [Defendant or Plaintiff] and [identify moving party], and [attorney] appeared on be half of [Plaintiff or Defendant]. After consideration of the moving papers and oral argument, the court [set forth the court's findings made at the hearing **making sure to fully set forth all rulings made on the scope of the examination, e.g. no further x-rays, plaintiff allowed to remain fully clothed, plaintiff to undergo non-contrast CT scan of spine, etc.**].

Dated: _____   _____
                                    JUDGE OF THE SUPERIOR COURT

FORM 10–4
MOTION FOR PSYCHOLOGICAL [MENTAL] EXAMINATION

[CAPTION]

Case No. _____

MOTION FOR PSYCHOLOGICAL [MENTAL] EXAMINATION

To: Plaintiff [name], [his or her or its] attorney, to each other party, and to the attorney of record for each other party in this action:

PLEASE TAKE NOTICE that on [date], at [time], or as soon thereafter as the matter can be heard, in Department _____ of the above-entitled Court, located at [address], Defendant [name], will move the Court under [cite appropriate authority] for an order directing Plaintiff, [name], to submit to a psychological [mental] examination, on such date and at such time as the Court shall specify, by Dr. [name], whose specialty is [specify], at [his or her] office at [address].

This examination will consist of: [state the scope, nature, manner, and conditions of the examination, including the diagnostic tests and procedures that will be used].

This motion is made after unsuccessful attempts to arrange for the examination by agreement, and on the ground that the following factors constitute good cause for a psychological [mental] examination of the Plaintiff conducted at the instance of the Defendant as part of [his, her, its] pretrial discovery:

　　1. Plaintiff seeks by this action the recovery of damages for psychological [mental] and emotional pain over and above that normally associated with the personal injuries claimed to have been sustained in the occurrence described in the Complaint.

　　2. It is anticipated that Plaintiff will offer at trial in support of this claim for psychological [mental] and emotional damages the testimony of one or more psychiatrists or psychologists who have had the advantage of conducting a psychological [mental] examination of the type sought by this motion.

3. Expert opinion on the nature, extent, and duration of the injuries alleged by Plaintiff is essential to a determination of the amount of damages, if any, to which Plaintiff may be entitled for the cause of action alleged in the Complaint.

4. Defendant cannot adequately prepare for trial without having the benefit of an independent psychological [mental] evaluation of the actual nature, extent, and duration of any psychological [mental] or emotional injuries sustained by Plaintiff.

This motion is based on the attached memorandum of points and authorities, and [specify any documents, exhibits, or declarations that accompany the motion].

Dated: _____   [Name of Attorney]
                      Attorney for Defendant

FORM 10–5
DEMAND FOR MEDICAL REPORTS

[CAPTION]

Case No. _____

DEMAND FOR REPORT OF
MEDICAL EXAMINATION

To: [Defendant or Plaintiff], [his or her or its] attorney, to each other party, and to the attorney of record for each other party in this action:

[Plaintiff or Defendant] demands under [your specific authority] that you furnish to [Plaintiff's or Defendant's] counsel on or before [date no sooner than 30 days after service of demand or, if service is by mail, 35 days], a copy of the written report(s) of the examination of [Plaintiff, Defendant, or non-party plaintiff], [name], conducted by [examiner] on [date], in which [examiner] sets forth [his or her] findings, including the results of all tests made, diagnoses, prognoses, and conclusions, as well as the plaintiff's history and the nature of the examination(s) done.

It is also demanded that you furnish a copy of all reports of earlier examinations by [examiner] or any other [physician or psychiatrist or psychologist or other examiner], relating to the same condition for which [name] was examined by [name].

Dated: _____   [Name of Attorney]
                                 Attorney for [Plaintiff or Defendant]

APPENDIXES

LIST OF ROOT WORDS AND COMBINING FORMS

TERM	PERTAINS TO
ab-	away from
acro-	extremity, end
actin-	ray, radius
aden-	gland
adren-	adrenal gland
aer-	gas, air
alb-	white
alg-	pain
all-	different, another
alve-	trough, channel
ambi-, amphi-	both, both sides
angi-	vessel
ankyl-, ancyl-	crooked, looped
ano-	anus
ante, anter-	before, in front of
arteri-	artery
arthr-	joint
anti-	against
aur-	ear
aux-	increase
ax-	axis
bacill-	small staff, rod
bacteri-	bacteria

<u>TERM</u>	<u>PERTAINS TO</u>
bar-	weight
bi-	life(bios), two
bil-	bile
blep-	look, see
blephar-	eyelid
bol-	ball
brachi-	arm
brachy-	short
brady-	slow
bronch-	windpipe
bry-	full of life
bucc-	cheek
cac-	bad, abnormal
calc-	stone, limestone, heel
calor-	heat
cancer, chancr-	crab, cancer
capit-	head
caps-	container
carbo-	coal, charcoal
carcin-	crab, cancer
cardi-	heart
carp-	wrist
caud-	tail
cav-	hallow
-cele	tumor, hernia
cente-	to puncture
centr-	point, center
cephal-	head
cer-	wax
cerebr-	brain
cervic-	neck
chlor-	green
chol-	bile
chondr-	cartilage

TERM	PERTAINS TO
e-	out from
ec-	out of
ect-	outside
ede-	swell
encephal-	brain
end-	inside
enter-	intestine
ep, epi	upon, after, in addition
erg-	work
erythr-	red
eso-	inside
esophag-	esophagus
esthe-	perceive, feel
eu-	good, normal
ex-	out of
exo-	outside
extra-	outside of, beyond
faci-	face
-facient	make
fasci-	band
febr-	fever
-ferent	bear, carry
fibr-	threadlike, fiber
fil-	thread
fiss-	split
flav-	yellow
-flect-	bend, divert
flu-	flow
for-	door, opening
-form	shape
fract-	break
front-	forehead, front
funct-	perform, serve, function
fund-	pour

TERM	PERTAINS TO
galact-	milk
gangli-	swelling, plexus
gastr-	stomach
gen-	become, be produced
genu-	knee
gest-	bear, carry
gingiv-	gums
gloss-, glott-	tongue
gluc-, glyc(y)-	sweet
gnath-	jaw
gno-	know, discern
grad-	walk, take steps
graph-	scratch, write, record
grav-	heavy
gyn(ec)-	woman
hem(a, o, to)-	blood
hemi-	half
hepat-	liver
hidr-	sweat
hist-	tissue
hom-	common, same
horm-	impetus, impulse
hydat-, hydr-	water
hyper-	above, beyond, extreme
hypn-	sleep
hypo-	under, below, less
hyster-	uterus, womb
iatr-	physician
idi-	peculiar, separate, distinct
ile-	ileum
ili-	lower abdomen, intestines
ilium-	upper hip bone
infra-	beneath
insul-	island
inter-	among

TERM	PERTAINS TO
intra-	within, inside
irid-	rainbow, colored circle
is-	equal
ischi-	hip, haunch
jact-	throw
jejeun-	jejeunum
junct-	yoke, join
kary-	nut, kernal, nucleus
kerat-	cornes, hard tissue, horn
kine-	move
labi-	lip
lact-	milk
lal-	talk, babble
lapar-	loin, flank, abdomen
laryng-	larynx, voice box
lat-	bear, carry
later-	side
lep-	take, seize
leuk-	white
lien-	spleen
lig-	tie, bind
lingu-	tongue
lip-	fat
lith-	stone
loc-	place
log-	speak, give an account
lumb-	loin
lute-	yellow
ly-	loose, dissolve
lymph-	water
macr-	long, large
mal-	bad, abnormal
malac-	soft
mamm-	breast

TERM	PERTAINS TO
man-	hand
mani-	mental aberration
mast-	breast
medi-	middle
mega-, megal-	great, large
mel-	limb, member
melan-	black
men-	month
mening-	membrane
ment-	mind
mes-	middle
meta-	after, beyond
metr-	measure, womb
micr-	small
mne-	remember
mon-	only, sole
morph-	form, shape
mot-	move
my-	muscle
myel-	marrow
myring-	eardrum
myx-	mucus
narc-	numbness
nas-	nose
ne-	new, young
necr-	corpse
nephr-	kidney
neur-	nerve
nutri-	nourish
ocul-	eye
-ode	road, path
odont-	tooth
-odyn	pain, distress
-oid	form
ole-	oil

<u>TERM</u>	<u>PERTAINS TO</u>
olig-	few, small
onc-	bulk, mass
onych-	claw, nail
oo-	egg
oophor-	ovary
-orb	circle
orchi-	testicle
opth-	eye
orth-	straight, right, normal
oss-, ost(e)-	bone
ot-	ear
ov-	egg
oxy-	sharp
pachy(n)-	thicken
pag-	fix, make fast
par(t)-	bear, give birth
para-	beside, beyond
path-	sickness, that which one undergoes
pec-	fix, make fast
ped-	child
pell-	skin
pen-	need, lack
pend-	hang down
peps-, pept	digest
per-	through
peri-	around
pet-	seek, tend toward
pha-	say, speak
phac-	lens
phag-	eat
pharmac-	drug
pharyng-	throat
phen-	show, be seen
pher-	bear, support
phil-	like, have affinity for

TERM	PERTAINS TO
phleb-	vein
phleg-	burn, inflame
phob-	fear, dread
phon-	sound
phot-	light
phrag-	fence, wall off, stop up
phthi-	decay, waste away
phy-	beget, bring forth, produce
phylac-	guard
physe-	blow, inflate
pil-	hair
pituit-	phlegm
plas-	mold, shape
platy-	broad, flat
pleg-	strike
plet-	fill
pleur-	rib, side
plex-	strike
plic-	fold
pne-	breathing
pneum(at)-	breath, air
pneumo(n)-	lung
pod-	foot
poie-	make, produce
pol-	axis of a sphere
poly-	much, many
pont-	bridge
por-	passage
post-	after, behind in time or place
pre-, pro-	before in time or place
proct-	anus
prosop-	face
pseud-	false
psych-	soul, mind
pto-	fall
pub-	adult
pulmo(n)-	lung

TERM	PERTAINS TO
puls-	drive
punct-	prick, pierce
pur-	pus
py-	pus
pyel-	trough, basin
pyl-	door, orifice
pyr-	fire
re-	back, again
ren-	kidney
retro-	backwards
rhag-	break, burst
rhaph-	suture
rhe-	flow
rhex-	break, burst
rhin-	nose
rot-	wheel
rub(r)-	red
sacr-	sacrum
salping-	tube
sanguin-	blood
sarc-	flesh
schis-	split
scler-	hard
scop-	look at, observe
sect-	cut
semi-	half
sens-	perceive, feel
sep-	rot, decay
sept-	fence, wall off, stop off
ser-	whey, watery substance
sial-	saliva
sin-	hollow, fold
sit-	food
solut-	loose, dissolve, set free
somat-	body

TERM	PERTAINS TO
spas-	draw, pull
spectr-	appearance, what is seen
sperm(at)-	seed
spers-	scatter
sphen-	wedge
spher-	ball
sphygm-	pulsation
spin-	spine
spirat-	breathe
splanchn-	entrails, viscera
splen-	spleen
spor-	seed
squam-	scale
sta-	make stand, stop
stal-	send
staphyl-	bunch of grapes, uvula
stear-	fat
sten-	narrow, compressed
ster-	solid
stern-	sternum
stol-	send
stom(at)-	mouth, opening, orifice
strep(h)-	twist
strict-	draw tight, compress, cause pain
stroph-	twist
struct-	pile up against
sub-	under, below
super-	above, beyond, extreme
syn-	with, together
tac-	order, arrange
tachy-	rapid
tact-	touch
tars-	instep of foot, ankle
tect, teg-	cover
tel-	end
tele-	at a distance

TERM	PERTAINS TO
tempor-	time, timely or fatal spot, temple
ten(ont)-	tight stretched band, tendon
tens-	stretch
test-	testicle
the-	put, place
thel-	teat, nipple
therap-	treatment
therm-	heat
thorac-	chest
thromb-	lump, clot
thym-	spirit
thyr-	shield
toc-	childbirth
tom-	cut
ton-	stretch, put under tension
top-	place
tors-	twist
tox-	poison
trache-	windpipe
trachel-	neck
tract-	draw, drag
traumat-	wound
trich-	hair
trip-	rub
trop-	turn, react
troph-	nuture
tuber-	swelling, node
typ-	type
typh-	fog, stupor
typhl-	blind
ur-	urine, urinary
ureter-	ureter
urethr-	urethra
utero-	uterus
vacc-	cow
vagin-	sheath

TERM	PERTAINS TO
vas-	vessel
ven-	vein
ventricul-	ventricle, of heart or brain
ventr-	belly, abdominal
vesic-	bladder
viscer-	viscera
vit-	life
vuls-	pull, twitch
xanth-	yellow, blond
zo-	life
zyg-	yoke, union
zym-	enzyme, ferment

PREFIXES

PREFIX	MEANING
a-, an-	without, absent
ab-	away from
ad-	to, toward
aden-	gland
al-	like, similar
amyl-	starch
angi(o)-	vessel, duct (usually blood vessel)
ankyl-	crooked, looped
ante-	before
anti-	against
arterio-	artery
arthro-	joint
asthen-	weakness, lack
aud-, aur-	ear, hearing
auto-	self
bacter-	bacteria
bar-	weight
bi-	both, two
bi(o)-	life
brachio-	arm
brachy-	short
brady-	slow
bronch(i)(o)-	bronchial
buccal-	cheek

PREFIX	MEANING
carcin-	cancer
cardio-	heart
carpo-	wrist
caud-	tail
centi-	hundred
cephalo-	head
cerebro-	brain
cervic-	neck
chiro-	hand
chole-	bile
cholecyst-	gallbladder
chondro-	cartilage
circum-	around
co-	with, together
col-	colon
colp-	vagina
com-, con-	with, together
contra-	against
cort-	covering
costo-	ribs
cranio-	skull
crypto-	hidden
cubitus-	elbow, forearm
cut-	skin
cyano-	blue
cysto-	bladder, sac
cyt(e)(o)-	cell
de-	away, not
deci-	tenth
demi-	half
dent-	tooth
derma-	skin
dextro-	right
di-, dis-	twice, doubly
diplo-	double
dors-	back
dys-	painful, abdominal

PREFIX	MEANING
e-	out
ecto-	outside
edem-	swelling (fluid)
encephal-	brain
endo-	inside, within
entero-	intestine
epi-	upper, above
erythro-	red
eu-	good, normal
ex-	away from, out
faci-	facies, face
fascia-	band (fibrous)
gastro-	gastro
genu-	knee
gingiva-	gums
gloss-	tongue
glyco-	sugar
gravid-	pregnant
gyn-, gyneco-	female
hemi-	half
hepato-	liver
hetero-	other, different
homeo-	unchanged
homo-	same
hydra-, hydro-	water
hyper-	high
hypo-	low
hyster-	uterus, womb
idio-	peculiar to the individual
ile-	intestine (part)
ili-	hipbone
in-, im-	in, inside, not
inter-	between
intra-	inside

PREFIX	MEANING
ir-	against, into, toward
iri-	iris, eye
iso-	equal, same
kerat-	cornea, scaly
kilo-	thousand
labia-	lip
lacto-	milk
lapar-	abdomen
laryng-	larynx
leuko-	white
lingua-	tongue
lip-	fat
lith-	stone
lymph-	fluid
macro-	large
mal-	bad
mamm-	breast
mast-	breast
mega-	large
melan-	black
mening-	membrane
meno-, mens-	menstruate
meso-	middle
metro-	uterus, womb
micro-	small
milli-	thousand
mono-	one, single
multi-	many
myelo-	bone marrow, spinal cord
myo-	muscle
myx-	mucus
nares-, nas-	nose, nostrils
natus-	birth
neo-	new

PREFIX	MEANING
nephro-	kidney
neuro-	nerve
non-	not
normo-	normal
null(i)-	none
ocul-	eye
odont-	teeth
olig(o)-	little, small, scant
onych-	finger or toenail
oophoro-	ovary
ophthal-	eye
or-	mouth, bone
orchid-	testes
ortho-	straight
osteo-	bone
oto-	ear, hearing
ovario-	ovary
ovi-	egg
pan-	all
para-	beside, along side of
part-	birth, labor
path(o)-	disease
ped-	foot
ped-	child
per-	through
peri-	around
pharyng-	pharynx
phleb-	vein
phrenic-	diaphragm
pleur-	pleura of lung
pneumo-	lung
pod-	foot
poly-	many
post-	behind
pre-	before
pro-	forward, anterior

PREFIX	MEANING
peseudo-	false
psycho-	mind, soul
pulm-	lung
pyelo-	kidney
pyo-	pus
re-	back, again
ren-	kidney
retro-	behind, backward
rhin-	nose
salpingo-	tube
sclero-	hard
semi-	half
semin-	seed
sial-	saliva
sinistro(o)-	left
soma-	body
splen-	spleen
spondyl-	spine
squam-	scaly
steno-	narrow, contracted
stoma-	mouth
stric-	narrowing
sub-	below
super-	above
supra-	above
tachy-	fast
thel-	nipple
therap-	treatment
therm-	heat, warmth
thorac-	thorax
thrombo-	clot
trache-	trachea
trachel-	neck
trans-	across
toxi-	poison
tri-	three

<u>PREFIX</u>	<u>MEANING</u>
uni-	one
vas-	vessel
vesic-	bladder, sac
viscera-	organ

APPENDIX C

SUFFIXES

SUFFIX	MEANING
-ac	pertaining to
-ad	toward, in direction of
-al, -an, -ar(y)	pertaining to
-algia	pain
-ase	enzyme
-atresia	abnormal closure
-cele	swelling, tumor
-centesis	puncture
-cide	killer
-crine	to secrete within
-cyst	bladder-like sac
-dactyl	finger, toe
-dema	swelling (fluid)
-deses	fusion, binding
-desis	surgical fixation
-duct	opening
-dynia	pain
-ectasis	enlargement
-ectomy	excision, cutting out
-ema	swelling, distension
-emia	blood
-form	structure, shape
-ful	full of, characterized by

SUFFIX	MEANING
-gen	production of
-genic	source, origin
-gram, -graphy	act or method of recording, picture
-ia, -iasis	diseased condition
-ic	pertaining to
-ious	capable of, causing
-ism	condition, process of
-itis	inflammation
-less	without, not capable
-lysis	setting free, dissolution
-malacia	softening
-megaly	large, enlarged
-oid	like
-ology	science of, study of
-olysis	breakdown
-oma	tumor
-osis	action, state, condition, disease
-ostomy	surgical opening
-otomy	cutting into, incision
-ous	pertaining to
-pathy	suffering, disease
-penia	deficiency, lack of
-pexy	fixation
-phagia	swallowing
-phasia	speech disorder
-philia	love of
-phobia	fear
-phrenia	mental disorder
-physis	growth (physical)
-plasty	molding, shaping
-plegia	paralysis
-ptosis	drooping

SUFFIX	MEANING
-rraphy	repair or closure of, suture
-rrhage, -rrhagia	hemorrhage
-rrhea	flow, discharge
-rrhexis	rupture
-sarcoma	tumor, cancer
-sclerosis	hardening
-scope, -scopy	look at, examine
-spasm	contraction
-stasis	at a standstill, stoppage
-tonia	stretching, putting under tension
-tripsy	crushing
-uria	urine
-vert	turn

GLOSSARY OF GENERAL MEDICAL AND OBSTETRICAL TERMS

acidosis   increase in hydrogen ion concentration in the blood resulting in a blood pH of <7.35

adnexa   adjacent or accessory parts of a structure. For example, uterine adnexa refers to ovaries and fallopian tubes.

AGA   appropriate (weight) for gestational age

agenesis   failure of an organ to develop

alkalosis   decrease in hydrogen ion concentration in the blood resulting in a blood pH of >7.35

alpha-fetoprotein (AFP)   (blood test) elevated levels may indicate neural tube defects, abortion, multiple pregnancies, and intrauterine death

amnion   innermost of two fetal membranes that form the sac and contain the fetus and amniotic fluid

amnionitis   inflammation of the amnion; occurs frequently with premature rupture of membranes

anomaly   abnormality, anything contrary to general rule

AROM   artificial rupture of membranes

ascities   accumulation of fluid in the abdominal cavity

bimanually   using two hands

bradycardia   slow heart action relative to age: less than 60 in an adult; less than 70 in a child

brain stem   all of the brain except the cerebrum and cerebellum

breech presentation   buttocks or feet nearest the cervical opening that are born first

cephalic presentation   any part of fetal head nearest to cervical opening

cephalopelvic disproportion (CPD)   infant's head is shape, size, or presentation that it cannot pass through the birth canal

chorion   fetal membrane closest to intrauterine wall that eventually forms the placenta

clonus   alternate muscular contraction and relaxation in rapid succession

cor pulmonale   right-sided cardiac failure manifested chiefly by edema, liver congestion, hepatomegaly, ascites, and high venous pressure

cutaneous   pertaining to the skin

dermatitis   inflammation of the skin evidenced by pruritus, erythema, and various skin lesions

diplopia   double vision

dynamic   active

ecchymosis   hemorrhagic spot in the skin or mucous membrane; bruise

eczema   acute or chronic dermatitis with erythema, papules, pustules, vesicles, crusts, or scales alone or in combination; more a symptom than a disease

edema   excessive amount of tissue fluid; fluid within the interstitial fluid compartment of the body; may be localized or generalized

embolus (emboli) moving mass in a blood or lymphatic vessel; may consist of air bubbles or of solids such as tumor cells or blood plaques

emphysema condition in which the alveoli of the lungs are distended, the lungs lose their elasticity, and expiration becomes difficult

empyema pus in a body cavity, especially the pleural cavity

encephalitis inflammation of the brain

endocarditis inflammation of the membrane (endocardium) lining the heart as a result of bacterial invasion

epididymitis inflammation of the epididymis, characterized by local edema, fever, chills, and inguinal pain

epistaxis nosebleed, nasal hemorrhage

erythema redness of the skin produced by congestion of the capillaries from a variety of causes

erythroblastosis fetalis hemolytic disease of the newborn that results from Rh or ABO incompatibility between maternal and fetal blood

excoriation epidermal abrasion caused by heat, moisture, chemicals, trauma, or similar causes

exudate fluid containing cells, protein, and solid material that accumulates in a cavity or oozes through the tissues, usually as the result of an inflammatory condition

fibrillation quivering or spontaneous contraction of muscle fibers, especially atrial or ventricular, when contractions are rapid, tremulous, and ineffectual for adequate functioning

fibroma a fibrous connective tissue tumor that is irregular in shape, firm, and slow-growing

fistula a tubelike passage from one cavity to another or to a free surface (through the surface of the skin)

flaccid   relaxed, flabby, having little or no muscle tone

focal   pertaining to a focus, a specific point or location

frenulum   a fold of mucous membrane connecting two parts; the frenulum of the tongue attaches the lower surface of the tongue to the gum

gait   the manner of walking

gas gangrene   a necrosis or tissue death in a wound infected by a gas bacillus

gastric   pertaining to the stomach

gastroenteritis   inflammation of the gastrointestinal tract (stomach and intestines)

gestational age   the number of completed weeks of a gestation, counting from the first day of the last normal menstrual cycle

glaucoma   a disease of the eye resulting in increased intraocular pressure

glossectomy   removal of the tongue

glycosuria   sugar (glucose) in the urine

goiter   enlargement of the thyroid gland

grand mal seizure   a seizure characterized by unconsciousness, tonic spasm followed by clonic movements, frothing at the mouth, and facial cyanosis; often preceded by an aura

gustatory   pertaining to the sense of taste

hallucination   a false perception lacking any exterior stimuli; may be visual, auditory, or olfactory

heart block   blockage of nerve impulses from the atrium to the ventricles

hemianopsia   blindness of half the field of vision in one or both eyes

hemiparesis   paralysis of one side of the body

hemiplegia   paralysis of one half of the body

hemolytic   referring to the breaking down of red blood cells

hernia   rupture, protrusion, or projection of an organ or part of an organ through the wall of the cavity that normally contains it

hepatic   pertaining to the liver

hepatitis   inflammation of the liver due to a virus or toxin

hepatomegaly   enlargement of the liver

herpes simplex   a cold sore or fever blister caused by herpes simplex virus

herpes zoster   a painful vesicular eruption along the course of a nerve, caused by the varicella-zoster virus (also causes chicken pox)

hydramnios   amniotic fluid

hydrocephalus   increased accumulation of fluid within the ventricles of the brain or within the subdural spaces

hydronephrosis   collection of urine in the renal pelvis due to lower urinary tract obstruction causing nephron destruction and impaired renal function

hydrops fetalis   most severe expression of fetal hemolytic disease

hyperplasia   enlargement of a part as a result of an increase in the number of cells

hyperthermia   unusually high body temperature; treatment of disease by raising body temperature

hypertrophy   enlargement of a part as the result of an increase in the size of the individual cells

hypovolemia   abnormally decreased volume of circulating blood

hypoxia   low oxygen content or tension

ideation   formation of ideas; the process of thinking

incontinence   inability to retain urine, feces, or semen as a result of loss of sphincter control or of cerebral or spinal lesions

induration   an area of hardened tissue

infarction   an area of necrosis within the body

inguinal   pertaining to the groin

insufficiency   inadequate for its purpose

intention tremors   tremors that are initiated upon movement

intraductal   within a duct

ipsilateral   of the same side; affecting the same side of the body

iritis   inflammation of the iris characterized by pain, photophobia, decreased vision, lacrimation, and an irregularly shaped and sluggish pupil

ischemia   local and temporary lack of blood to a body part caused by obstruction of circulation to the part

isoimmune hemolytic disease   breakdown (hemolysis) of fetal/neonatal RBC's because of Rh incompatibility

keratitis   inflammation of the cornea

ketoacidosis   accumulation of ketone bodies resulting from the incomplete metabolism of fatty acids, generally from carbohydrate deficiency or inadequate utilization

kinesthesia   the ability to discriminate the extent, direction, or weight of one's movement

Kussmaul breathing   an extreme rate and depth of respirations

lethargic   drowsy, sluggish, stuporous

leukemia   a usually fatal blood cancer of unknown cause characterized by an elevated leukocyte count and the presence of immature leukocytes

lipoma   a fatty tumor; frequently multiple but not metastatic

lymphadenopathy   disease involvement of the lymph nodes

lymphangitis   inflammation of the lymph system, frequently due to streptococci

maceration   softening process caused by seeping of fluid

mastitis   inflammation of the breast

mastoiditis   inflammation of the air cells of the mastoid process

meconium   first stools of infant

meningitis   inflammation of the membranes of the spinal cord or brain due to bacteria, viruses, or other organisms

meningocele   herniation of the meninges through a defect in the vertebral column or skull; contains CSF but not CNS tissue

metastasis   spread of bacteria or body cells (especially cancer cells) from one part of the body to another; usually describes a secondary malignant growth in a new body location, arising from the primary growth

murmur   a soft blowing or rasping sound heard on auscultation; caused by vibrations produced by movement of blood within the heart and adjacent large blood vessels, does not necessarily indicate pathology

myelomeningocele   neural tube defect; herniation of part of the meninges (containing cerebrospinal fluid and CNS tissue) through a defect in the vertebral column or skull

myocardial   pertaining to the heart muscle

myxedema   hypofunction of the thyroid occurring secondary to anterior pituitary hypofunction, dietary iodine deficiency, atrophy of the thyroid gland, surgical excision of the thyroid gland, or excessive use of antithyroid drugs

necrosis   death of tissue or bone cells surrounded by healthy parts; death of an area; dead mass

neural tube   in developing embryo, the tube from which develops the brain and spinal cord

noncompliance   not participating; nonfunctioning

nonpathologic   not constituting a diseased state

normal range   normative; within the parameter of normalcy

nystagmus   constant involuntary oscillatory movement of the eyeball, in any direction

occlusion   obstruction or closure of a passage; for example, coronary occlusion involves blockage of a coronary artery

oliguria   decreased amount of urine output

opisthotonos   a body position characterized by an arched back, with feet and head on the floor

organomegaly   enlargement of a body organ

osteodystrophy   defective bone development

osteomalacia   softening of the bones so that the bones become flexible and brittle, resulting in deformities

otitis externa   inflammation of the pinna (auricle) of the ear

otitis media   inflammation of the middle ear

otosclerosis   fusion of the stapes and oval window in the middle ear, characterized by chronic progressive deafness

palsy   temporary or permanent loss of ability to move or to control movement

papilledema   edema and inflammation of the optic nerve head due to increased intracranial pressure

paralysis   loss of voluntary motor function

paralytic ileus   paralysis of the intestines, with resulting distention and symptoms of acute obstruction

paraplegia   paralysis of the lower portion of the body and both legs

paresis   partial or incomplete paralysis

paresthesia   abnormal sensation, such as numbness or tingling; a heightened sensitivity

pathologic   constituting a disease or disease process

pericarditis   inflammation of the pericardium (the sac enclosing the heart) characterized by moderate fever, precordial pain, dry cough, dyspnea, palpitations, and a pulse that is initially rapid and forceful, then weak and irregular

peripheral vascular disease   pathologic involvement of the blood vessels in the periphery of the body

peristalsis   an involuntary progressive wavelike movement that occurs in the hollow tubes of the body, especially the alimentary canal

peritonitis   inflammation of the peritoneum (the lining of the abdominal cavity)

phlebitis   inflammation of a vein manifested by pain, erythema, skin warmth, and tenderness along the course of the vein

phonation   the process of uttering vocal sounds

photophobia   inability to tolerate light

pleurisy   inflammation of the pleura (membrane lining the lungs)

pneumonectomy   removal of a lung

pneumothorax   collection of air or gas in the pleural (chest) cavity, causing a severe stabbing pain in the side, marked dyspnea, absence of breath sounds, and unilateral distention of the chest

prostatitis   inflammation of the prostate gland, characterized by frequent urination, discomfort, and pain in the perineal area

pruritus   itching

psychosomatic   pertaining to bodily symptoms suspected to be etiologically related to emotional factors

ptosis   dropping or drooping of an organ or part, especially applied to drooping of the eyelids due to paralysis or muscle weakness

purpura   ecchymotic areas characterized by hemorrhages into the skin

purulent   pertaining to yellow, thick, pus-like fluid

pyloric   pertaining to the opening between the stomach and the duodenum

pyrexia   fever

quadriplegia   paralysis affecting all four limbs

rehabilitative   pertaining to the process that restores a person who has been ill or handicapped to useful life, or that restores a dysfunctional part to usefulness

salpingitis   inflammation of the fallopian tube

scoliosis   lateral curvature of the spine

seizure a   convulsion; a sudden attack of certain symptoms

septicemia   blood poisoning; absorption of septic products or pathogenic bacteria into the blood and tissues

sequelae   conditions following and resulting from a disease

shock   a clinical syndrome of varying degrees of diminished oxygen supply to the tissues and venous return to the heart; manifested by pallor, cyanosis, weak and rapid pulse, increased and shallow respirations, blood pressure decreased and possibly unobtainable, possible dilation of pupils

spastic   pertaining to stiffness and muscular rigidity resembling or of the nature of spasms

spina bifida extrusion of part of the meninges (containing cerebrospinal fluid and CNS tissue) through an opening in the spinal column

splenomegaly enlargement of the spleen

stasis stagnation or pooling of the flow of fluids, such as venous blood, urine, or intestinal contents

symmetrical even; balanced

systemic pertaining to the whole body or a whole system, as in systemic circulation

tachycardia abnormally rapid heart action relative to age

tactile perceptible to the touch

tamponade pathologic compression of an internal organ, especially the heart, by an external agent

tetany intermittent tonic muscular spasms induced by changes in body chemistry

tinnitus a subjective ringing in the ears

tonic characterized by continuous tension (*see* clonus)

tonometry measurement of the tension of a part, such as intraocular tension, using a tonometer

tracheotomy surgical opening into the trachea, usually for insertion of a tube to overcome tracheal obstruction; tracheostomy

trauma an injury (physical or emotional) or wound

tremor quivering; shaking; trembling; may be fine or course, rapid or slow, aggravated or initiated with movement or resting of the part

Trousseau's sign muscular spasm produced when pressure is applied to the nerves and vessels of the upper arm, occurs in osteomalacia

ulcer an open sore or lesion of the skin or of a mucous membrane

uremia   retention of nitrogenous substances normally excreted by the kidneys, producing a toxic state

urticaria   hives

vascular   pertaining to or composed of blood vessels

ventricular   pertaining to a ventricle, especially either of the two lower chambers of the heart

vertex   crown or top of head. In birth process, skull is nearest cervical opening and born first.

viscus (viscera)   any internal organ enclosed within a cavity such as the abdomen or thorax

INDEX TO BRAND NAME & GENERIC DRUGS

BRAND NAME	PURPOSE
ACTH®	Hormone
Achromycin®	Antibiotic
Adalat®	Cardiovascular Drug
Adrenalin®	Respiratory Drug
Advil®	Central Nervous System Drug
Afrin®	Respiratory Drug
Agenerase	Antiviral
Akineton®	Central Nervous System Drug
Aldactone®	Cardiovascular Drug
Aldomet®	Cardiovascular Drug
Alka-Seltzer®	Gastrointestinal System Drug
Allegra®	Respiratory Drug
Allerest®	Respiratory Drug
Alupent®	Respiratory Drug
Amakin®	Antibiotic
Amaryl®	Hormone
Ambien®	Central Nervous System Drug
Aminophyllin®	Respiratory Drug
Amoline®	Respiratory Drug
Amoxicillin®	Antibiotic
Amoxil®	Antibiotic
Amphocin®	Antifungal
Amyl Nitrate®	Cardiovascular Drug
Anabolin®	Hormone

BRAND NAME	PURPOSE
Ancef®	Antibiotic
Android®	Hormone
Antivert®	Gastrointestinal System Drug
Apresoline®	Cardiovascular Drug
Aricept®	Central Nervous System Drug
Asendin®	Central Nervous System Drug
Atarax®	Central Nervous System Drug
Athcar®	Hormone
Ativan®	Central Nervous System Drug
Atrovent®	Respiratory Drug
Avandia®	Central Nervous System Drug
Avelox®	Antibiotic
Aventyl®	Central Nervous System Drug
Axid®	Gastrointestinal System Drug
Axactam®	Antibiotic
Azlin®	Antibiotic
Asulfidine®	Antibiotic
Bactrim®	Antibiotic
Benadryl®	Respiratory Drug
Bicillin®	Antibiotic
Brethaire®	Respiratory Drug
Brethine®	Respiratory Drug
Bretylol®	Cardiovascular Drug
Bricanyl®	Respiratory Drug
Bromoseltzer®	Gastrointestinal System Drug
Bronkaid®	Respiratory Drug
Bronkodyl®	Respiratory Drug
Calan®	Cardiovascular Drug
Capoten®	Cardiovascular Drug
Cardioquin®	Cardiovascular Drug
Cardizem®	Cardiovascular Drug
Cardura®	Cardiovascular Drug
Catapres®	Cardiovascular Drug
Ceclor®	Antibiotic
Cefadyl®	Antibiotic

BRAND NAME	PURPOSE
Cefizox®	Antibiotic
Cefobid®	Antibiotic
Cefotan®	Antibiotic
Cenafed®	Respiratory Drug
Chlor-Trimeton®	Respiratory Drug
Cipro®	Antibiotic
Citrate of Magnesia®	Gastrointestinal System Drug
Claforan®	Antibiotic
Claritin®	Respiratory Drug
Cleocin®	Antibiotic
Clomid®	Hormone
Clopra®	Gastrointestinal System Drug
Clozaril®	Central Nervous System Drug
Cogentin®	Central Nervous System Drug
Cognex®	Central Nervous System Drug
Colestid®	Cardiovascular Drug
Compazine®	Central Nervous System Drug
Combivir®	Antiviral
Coreg®	Cardiovascular Drug
Corgard®	Cardiovascular Drug
Coriciden®	Respiratory Drug
Correctol®	Gastrointestinal System Drug
Cortef®	Hormone
Crestor®	Cardiovascular Drug
Crixivan®	Antiviral
Crysticillin®	Antibiotic
Cytovene®	Antiviral
Dalmane®	Central Nervous System Drug
Dantrium®	Central Nervous System Drug
Darvon®	Central Nervous System Drug
Decadron®	Hormone
Demerol®	Central Nervous System Drug
Dexedrine®	Central Nervous System Drug
Dexitaz®	Central Nervous System Drug
DiaBeta®	Hormone
Diabinese®	Hormone

BRAND NAME	PURPOSE
Diamox®	Cardiovascular Drug
Diflucan®	Antifungal
Digitoxin®	Cardiovascular Drug
Digoxin®	Cardiovascular Drug
Dilantin®	Central Nervous System Drug
Dilaudid®	Central Nervous System Drug
Dimetane®	Respiratory Drug
Diuril®	Cardiovascular Drug
Dobutrex®	Cardiovascular Drug
Dolophine®	Central Nervous System Drug
Dramamine®	Gastrointestinal System Drug
Dristan®	Respiratory Drug
Dulcolax®	Gastrointestinal System Drug
Durabolin®	Hormone
Duricef®	Antibiotic
Dycill®	Antibiotic
Dynocin®	Antibiotic
Dynapen®	Antibiotic
Dyrenium®	Cardiovascular Drug
E-Mycin®	Antibiotic
EES®	Antibiotic
Edecrin®	Cardiovascular Drug
Elavil®	Central Nervous System Drug
Elixophyllin®	Respiratory Drug
Emtriva®	Antiviral
Enduron®	Cardiovascular Drug
Epivir®	Antiviral
Equanil®	Central Nervous System Drug
Ergotrate®	Hormone
Eskalith®	Central Nervous System Drug
Exelon®	Central Nervous System Drug
Ex-Lax®	Gastrointestinal System Drug
Factive®	Antibiotic
Famvir®	Antiviral
Feldene®	Central Nervous System Drug

BRAND NAME	PURPOSE
Fleet Phospho-Soda®	Gastrointestinal System Drug
Flexeril®	Central Nervous System Drug
Flumadine®	Antiviral
Fortaz®	Antibiotic
Fortovase®	Antiviral
Foscavir®	Antiviral
Fulvacin®	Antifungal
Fuzeon®	Antiviral
Gantrisin®	Antibiotic
Garamycin®	Antibiotic
Gaviscon®	Gastrointestinal System Drug
Geopen®	Antibiotic
Glucophage®	Hormone
Glucotrol®	Hormone
Grisactin ®	Antifungal
Halcion®	Central Nervous System Drug
Haldol®	Central Nervous System Drug
Hepsera®	Antiviral
Hivid®	Antiviral
Humulin Insulin®	Hormone
Hydrocortisone®	Hormone
Hydrocortone®	Hormone
Hydrodiuril®	Cardiovascular Drug
Ilosone®	Antibiotic
Imdur®	Cardiovascular Drug
Imitrex®	Central Nervous System Drug
Imodium®	Gastrointestinal System Drug
Inderal®	Cardiovascular Drug
Inocor®	Cardiovascular Drug
Inotropin®	Cardiovascular Drug
Invirase®	Antiviral
ISMO®	Cardiovascular Drug
Isonate®	Cardiovascular Drug
Isoptin®	Cardiovascular Drug
Isordil®	Cardiovascular Drug

BRAND NAME	PURPOSE
Kaletra®	Antiviral
Kaopectate®	Gastrointestinal System Drug
Keflex®	Antibiotic
Keftab®	Antibiotic
Kefurox®	Antibiotic
Kefzol®	Antibiotic
Klonopin®	Central Nervous System Drug
Lamictal®	Central Nervous System Drug
Lamisil®	Antifungal
Lanoxin®	Cardiovascular Drug
Larodopa®	Central Nervous System Drug
Lasix®	Cardiovascular Drug
Levaquin®	Antibiotic
Levophed®	Cardiovascular Drug
Levoxine®	Hormone
Levoxyl®	Hormone
Lexiva®	Antiviral
Librium®	Central Nervous System Drug
Lioresal®	Central Nervous System Drug
Lipitor®	Cardiovascular Drug
Lithane®	Central Nervous System Drug
Lithonate®	Central Nervous System Drug
Lithotabs®	Central Nervous System Drug
Lofene®	Gastrointestinal System Drug
Lomotil®	Gastrointestinal System Drug
Lotensin®	Cardiovascular Drug
Maalox®	Gastrointestinal System Drug
Macrodantin®	Antibiotic
Mandol®	Antibiotic
Medipren®	Central Nervous System Drug
Medrol®	Hormone
Mefoxin®	Antibiotic
Mellaril®	Central Nervous System Drug
Metamucil®	Gastrointestinal System Drug
Metaprel®	Respiratory Drug

BRAND NAME	PURPOSE
Mevacor	Cardiovascular Drug
Mexitil®	Cardiovascular Drug
Mezlin®	Antibiotic
Micronase®	Hormone
Midamor®	Cardiovascular Drug
Midol®	Central Nervous System Drug
Milk of Magnesia®	Gastrointestinal System Drug
Milophene®	Hormone
Miltown®	Central Nervous System Drug
Minocin®	Antibiotic
Minomycin®	Antibiotic
Modane®	Gastrointestinal System Drug
Monocid®	Antibiotic
Monoket®	Cardiovascular Drug
Monopril®	Cardiovascular Drug
Motrin®	Central Nervous System Drug
Moxam®	Antibiotic
Mycostatin®	Antifungal
Mylanta®	Gastrointestinal System Drug
Mysoline®	Central Nervous System Drug
NPH Insulin®	Hormone
Nafcil®	Antibiotic
Namenda®	Central Nervous System Drug
Naprosyn®	Central Nervous System Drug
Nardil®	Central Nervous System Drug
Navane®	Central Nervous System Drug
Nebcin®	Antibiotic
Nembutal®	Central Nervous System Drug
Neosynephrine®	Respiratory Drug
Netromycin®	Antibiotic
Neurontin®	Central Nervous System Drug
Nexium®	Gastrointestinal System Drug
Nitro-Bid®	Cardiovascular Drug
Nitro-Dur®	Cardiovascular Drug
Nitropress®	Cardiovascular Drug
Nitrostat®	Cardiovascular Drug

BRAND NAME	PURPOSE
Nizoral®	Antifungal
No Doz®	Central Nervous System Drug
Noroxin®	Antibiotic
Norpace®	Cardiovascular Drug
Norvasc®	Cardiovascular Drug
Norvir®	Antiviral
Nostril®	Respiratory Drug
Novolin Insulin®	Hormone
Nuprin®	Central Nervous System Drug
Nystat Rx®	Antifungal
Octamide®	Gastrointestinal System Drug
Omnipen®	Antibiotic
Orinase®	Hormone
Osmitrol®	Cardiovascular Drug
Oxycontin®	Central Nervous System Drug
Palladone®	Central Nervous System Drug
Pamprin®	Central Nervous System Drug
Paraflex®	Central Nervous System Drug
Parafon Forte®	Central Nervous System Drug
Paregoric®	Gastrointestinal System Drug
Parnate®	Central Nervous System Drug
Pathocil®	Antibiotic
Paxil®	Central Nervous System Drug
Pen-Vee K®	Antibiotic
Penicillin VK®	Antibiotic
Pentids®	Antibiotic
Pepcid®	Gastrointestinal System Drug
Percocet®	Central Nervous System Drug
Percodan®	Central Nervous System Drug
Pergonal®	Hormone
Phenergan®	Respiratory Drug
Pipracil®	Antibiotic
Pitocin®	Hormone
Pitressin®	Hormone
Placidyl®	Central Nervous System Drug

BRAND NAME	PURPOSE
Plavix®	Cardiovascular Drug
Pravachol®	Cardiovascular Drug
Prednisolone®	Hormone
Prednisone®	Hormone
Prilosec®	Gastrointestinal System Drug
Primacor®	Cardiovascular Drug
Primatene®	Respiratory Drug
Principen®	Antibiotic
Prinivil®	Cardiovascular Drug
Probanthine®	Gastrointestinal System Drug
Procan SR®	Cardiovascular Drug
Procardia®	Cardiovascular Drug
Pronestyl®	Cardiovascular Drug
Prostaphlin®	Antibiotic
Proventil®	Respiratory Drug
Provera®	Hormone
Prozac®	Central Nervous System Drug
Pyopen®	Antibiotic
Questran®	Cardiovascular Drug
Quinidex Extentabs®	Cardiovascular Drug
Quinora®	Cardiovascular Drug
Razadyne®	Central Nervous System Drug
Reglan®	Gastrointestinal System Drug
Regular Insulin®	Hormone
Remeron®	Central Nervous System Drug
Renese®	Cardiovascular Drug
Rescriptor®	Antiviral
Restoril®	Central Nervous System Drug
Retrovir®	Antiviral
Reytaz®	Antiviral
Rhinall®	Respiratory Drug
Riopan®	Gastrointestinal System Drug
Risperdol®	Central Nervous System Drug
Ritalin®	Central Nervous System Drug
Robaxin®	Central Nervous System Drug

BRAND NAME	PURPOSE
Robinul®	Gastrointestinal System Drug
Rocephin®	Antibiotic
Rolaids®	Gastrointestinal System Drug
Seconal®	Central Nervous System Drug
Semilente Insulin®	Hormone
Septra®	Antibiotic
Serophine®	Hormone
Seroquel®	Central Nervous System Drug
Serutan®	Gastrointestinal System Drug
Sinemet®	Central Nervous System Drug
Sinequan®	Central Nervous System Drug
Solu-Cortef®	Hormone
Soma®	Central Nervous System Drug
Somophyllin®	Respiratory Drug
Sorbitrate®	Cardiovascular Drug
SSKI®	Hormone
Stadol®	Central Nervous System Drug
Staphcillin®	Antibiotic
Streptomycin®	Antibiotic
Sublimaze®	Central Nervous System Drug
Sudafed®	Respiratory Drug
Sustiva®	Antiviral
Symmetrel®	Antiviral
Synthroid®	Hormone
Syntocinon®	Hormone
Tagamet®	Gastrointestinal System Drug
Talwin®	Central Nervous System Drug
Tamiflu®	Antiviral
Tazicef®	Antibiotic
Tazidime®	Antibiotic
Tegopen®	Antibiotic
Tegretol®	Central Nervous System Drug
Tenormin®	Cardiovascular Drug
Terramycin®	Antibiotic
Testrid®	Hormone

BRAND NAME   PURPOSE

BRAND NAME	PURPOSE
Tetracap®	Antibiotic
Thorazine®	Central Nervous System Drug
Ticar®	Antibiotic
Ticlid®	Cardiovascular Drug
Tofranil®	Central Nervous System Drug
Tolinase®	Hormone
Tonocard®	Cardiovascular Drug
Toradol®	Central Nervous System Drug
Torecan®	Gastrointestinal System Drug
Tridil®	Cardiovascular Drug
Trimox®	Antibiotic
Tuinal®	Central Nervous System Drug
Tylenol®	Central Nervous System Drug
Ultralente Insulin®	Hormone
Ultram®	Central Nervous System Drug
Unipen®	Antibiotic
V-Cillin®	Antibiotic
Valium®	Central Nervous System Drug
Valtrex®	Antiviral
Vancocin®	Antibiotic
Vasotec®	Cardiovascular Drug
Velosef®	Antibiotic
Ventolin®	Respiratory Drug
Versed®	Central Nervous System Drug
Vibramycin®	Antibiotic
Vicodin®	Central Nervous System Drug
Videx®	Antiviral
Viracept®	Antiviral
Viramune®	Antiviral
Virasol®	Antiviral
Virea®	Antiviral
Vistaril®	Central Nervous System Drug
Vivarin®	Central Nervous System Drug
Wellbutrin®	Central Nervous System Drug
Wycillin®	Antibiotic

BRAND NAME   PURPOSE

Xanax®   Central Nervous System Drug

Zantac®   Gastrointestinal System Drug
Zerit®   Antiviral
Zestril®   Cardiovascular Drug
Ziagen®   Antiviral
Zinacef®   Antibiotic
Zofran®   Gastrointestinal System Drug
Zoloft®   Central Nervous System Drug
Zovirax®   Antiviral
Zoxor®   Cardiovascular Drug
Zyprexa®   Central Nervous System Drug

GENERIC NAME   PURPOSE

GENERIC NAME	PURPOSE
Abacivir sulfate	Antiviral
Acetazolamide	Cardiovascular Drug
Acetominophen	Central Nervous System Drug
Acyclovir sodium	Antiviral
Adefovir dipivoxil	Antiviral
Albuterol	Respiratory Drug
Alprazolam	Central Nervous System Drug
Amakacin	Antibiotic
Amantidine HCL	Antiviral
Amiloride	Cardiovascular Drug
Aminophylline	Respiratory Drug
Amitriptyline HCl	Central Nervous System Drug
Amlodipine besylate	Cardiovascular Drug
Amobarbital	Central Nervous System Drug
Amoxapine	Central Nervous System Drug
Amoxicillin trihydrate	Antibiotic
Amphetamine sulfate	Central Nervous System Drug
Amphotericin B	Antifungal
Ampicillin	Antibiotic
Amprenavir	Antiviral
Amyl nitrate	Cardiovascular Drug
Androgens	Hormone
Aspirin	Central Nervous System Drug
Astemizole	Respiratory Drug
Atenolol	Cardiovascular Drug
Atorvastatin calcium	Cardiovascular Drug
Atropine	Gastrointestinal System Drug
Atropine sulfate	Cardiovascular Drug
Attapulgite	Gastrointestinal System Drug
Atzanavir	Antiviral
Azotrenam	Antibiotic
Baclofen	Central Nervous System Drug
Belladonna Alkaloids	Gastrointestinal System Drug
Benazepril HCl	Cardiovascular Drug
Benztropine mesylate	Central Nervous System Drug
Beperiden HCl	Central Nervous System Drug

GENERIC NAME	PURPOSE
Bisacodyl	Gastrointestinal System Drug
Bretylium tosylate	Cardiovascular Drug
Bupropion HCl	Central Nervous System Drug
Butorphanol tartrate	Central Nervous System Drug
Caffeine	Central Nervous System Drug
Captopril	Cardiovascular Drug
Carbamazepine	Central Nervous System Drug
Carbenicillin	Antibiotic
Carbidopa	Central Nervous System Drug
Carisoprodol	Central Nervous System Drug
Carvedilol	Cardiovascular Drug
Cefaclor	Antibiotic
Cefadroxil	Antibiotic
Cefamandol	Antibiotic
Cefataxime	Antibiotic
Cefazolin	Antibiotic
Cefonicid	Antibiotic
Cefoperazone	Antibiotic
Cefotaxime	Antibiotic
Cefotetan	Antibiotic
Cefoxitin	Antibiotic
Ceftazidime	Antibiotic
Ceftizoxime sodium	Antibiotic
Ceftrioxone	Antibiotic
Cefuroxime	Antibiotic
Cemetidine	Antibiotic
Cephalexin	Antibiotic
Cephapirin	Antibiotic
Cephradine	Antibiotic
Chlordiazepoxide	Central Nervous System Drug
Chlorothiazide	Cardiovascular Drug
Chlorpheniramine	Respiratory Drug
Chlorpromazine	Central Nervous System Drug
Chlorpropamide	Hormone
Chlorzoxazone	Central Nervous System Drug
Cholestyramine	Cardiovascular Drug

GENERIC NAME	PURPOSE
Ciprofloxicin	Antibiotic
Clindamycin HCl	Antibiotic
Clomiphene citrate	Hormone
Clonazepam	Central Nervous System Drug
Clonidine HCl	Cardiovascular Drug
Clopidogrel bisulfate	Cardiovascular Drug
Cloxacillin sodium	Antibiotic
Clozapine	Central Nervous System Drug
Codeine, phosphate and sulfate	Central Nervous System Drug
Colestipol	Cardiovascular Drug
Corticotropin	Hormone
Cortisone	Hormone
Cyclobenzaprine	Central Nervous System Drug
Dantrolene	Central Nervous System Drug
Delavirdine mesylate	Antiviral
Desamethazone	Hormone
Dextroamphetamine sulfate	Central Nervous System Drug
Diazepam	Central Nervous System Drug
Dicloxacillin sodium	Antibiotic
Didanosine	Antiviral
Difenoxin	Gastrointestinal System Drug
Digitalis	Cardiovascular Drug
Diltiazem	Cardiovascular Drug
Dimenhydrinate	Central Nervous System Drug
Diphenhydramine	Respiratory Drug
Disopyramide phosphate	Cardiovascular Drug
Dobutamine	Cardiovascular Drug
Donepezil	Central Nervous System Drug
Dopamine HCl	Cardiovascular Drug
Doxazosin mesylate	Cardiovascular Drug
Doxepin	Central Nervous System Drug
Doxycycline calcium	Antibiotic
Efavirenz	Antiviral
Emtricitabine	Antiviral
Enalaprilat	Cardiovascular Drug

GENERIC NAME	PURPOSE
Enfuvirtide	Antiviral
Epinephrine	Respiratory Drug
Ergonovine maleate	Hormone
Erythromycin	Antibiotic
Esomeprazole	Gastrointestinal System Drug
Estrogens	Hormone
Ethacrynic Acid	Cardiovascular Drug
Ethchlorvynol	Central Nervous System Drug
Famiciclovir	Antiviral
Famotidine	Gastrointestinal System Drug
Fentanyl	Central Nervous System Drug
Fexofenadine HCl	Respiratory Drug
Floconazole	Antifungal
Fluoxetine	Central Nervous System Drug
Flurazepam	Central Nervous System Drug
Fosamprenavir	Antiviral
Foscarnet	Antiviral
Fosinopril	Cardiovascular Drug
Furosemide	Cardiovascular Drug
Gabapentin	Central Nervous System Drug
Galantamine hydrobromide	Central Nervous System Drug
Ganciclovir	Antiviral
Gatifloxicin	Antibiotic
Gemifloxicin	Antibiotic
Gentamicin	Antibiotic
Glimepiride	Hormone
Glipizide	Hormone
Glucagon	Hormone
Grisefulvin	Antifungal
Glyburide	Hormone
Glycopyrralate	Gastrointestinal System Drug
Haloperidol	Central Nervous System Drug
Hydralazine HCl	Cardiovascular Drug
Hydrochlorothiazide	Cardiovascular Drug
Hydrocodone/Acetominophen	Central Nervous System Drug

GENERIC NAME	PURPOSE
Hydrocortisone	Hormone
Hydromorphone HCl	Central Nervous System Drug
Hydroxyzine	Central Nervous System Drug
Ibuprofen	Central Nervous System Drug
Ketoconazole	Antifungal
Ketorolac tromethamine	Central Nervous System Drug
Imipramine	Cardiovascular Drug
Indinavir sulfate	Antiviral
Insulin	Cardiovascular Drug
Ipratropium	Respiratory Drug
Isoproteranol	Central Nervous System Drug
Isosorbide	Central Nervous System Drug
Lamivudine	Antiviral
Lamivudine/zidovudine	Antiviral
Lamotrigine	Central Nervous System Drug
Levodopa	Central Nervous System Drug
Levofloxacin	Antibiotic
Lidocaine	Central Nervous System Drug
Lisinopril	Cardiovascular Drug
Lithium	Central Nervous System Drug
Loperamide	Hormone
Loratadine	Respiratory Drug
Lorazepam	Central Nervous System Drug
Lovastatin	Cardiovascular Drug
Magnesium Sulfate	Central Nervous System Drug
Mannitol	Cardiovascular Drug
Meclizine HCl	Gastrointestinal System Drug
Memanthin HCl	Central Nervous System Drug
Menotropins	Hormone
Meperidine	Central Nervous System Drug
Meprobamate	Central Nervous System Drug
Metaproterenol	Respiratory Drug
Metformin	Hormone

GENERIC NAME	PURPOSE
Methadone HCl	Central Nervous System Drug
Methicillin	Antibiotic
Methocarbamol	Central Nervous System Drug
Methyclothiazide	Cardiovascular Drug
Methyldopa	Cardiovascular Drug
Methylphenidate	Central Nervous System Drug
Methylprednisolone	Hormone
Methyltesterone	Hormone
Metoclopramide	Gastrointestinal System Drug
Mexiletine HCl	Cardiovascular Drug
Mezlocillin	Antibiotic
Midazolam HCl	Central Nervous System Drug
Milrinone lactate	Cardiovascular Drug
Minocycline HCl	Antibiotic
Mirtazapine	Central Nervous System Drug
Morifloxacin	Antibiotic
Morphine Sulfate	Central Nervous System Drug
Moxalactam	Antibiotic
Nadolol	Cardiovascular Drug
Nafcillin	Antibiotic
Naproxen	Central Nervous System Drug
Nilfinavir	Antiviral
Netilmicin	Antibiotic
Nevirapine	Antiviral
Nifedipine	Cardiovascular Drug
Nitrofuradantin	Antibiotic
Nitroglycerin	Cardiovascular Drug
Nitroprusside Na	Cardiovascular Drug
Nizatidine	Gastrointestinal System Drug
Norepinephrine	Cardiovascular Drug
Norfloxacin	Antibiotic
Nortriptyline	Central Nervous System Drug
Olanzapine	Central Nervous System Drug
Omeprazole	Gastrointestinal System Drug
Ondansetron HCl	Gastrointestinal System Drug

GENERIC NAME	PURPOSE
Opium tincture	Gastrointestinal System Drug
Oseltamivir phosphate	Antiviral
Oxacillin	Antibiotic
Oxycodon/ASA	Central Nervous System Drug
Oxycodone/Acetaminophen	Central Nervous System Drug
Oxycodone HCl	Central Nervous System Drug
Oxymetazoline	Respiratory Drug
Oxytetracycline	Antibiotic
Oxytocin	Hormone
Paroxetine HCl	Central Nervous System Drug
Penicillin G	Antibiotic
Penicillin V	Antibiotic
Pentazocine lactate	Central Nervous System Drug
Pentobarbital	Central Nervous System Drug
Phenelzine sulfate	Central Nervous System Drug
Phenobarbital	Central Nervous System Drug
Phenylephrine HCl	Respiratory Drug
Phenytoin	Central Nervous System Drug
Piperacillin	Antibiotic
Piroxicam	Central Nervous System Drug
Polythiazide	Cardiovascular Drug
Potassium iodide	Hormone
Pravastatin sodium	Cardiovascular Drug
Primidone	Central Nervous System Drug
Procainamide	Cardiovascular Drug
Prochlorperazine	Central Nervous System Drug
Progestins	Hormone
Promethazine	Respiratory Drug
Propanolol	Cardiovascular Drug
Propantheline Bromide	Gastrointestinal System Drug
Propoxyphene	Central Nervous System Drug
Pseudoephedrine HCl	Respiratory Drug
Quetiapine fumarate	Central Nervous System Drug
Quinidine	Cardiovascular Drug

GENERIC NAME	PURPOSE
Ranitidine	Gastrointestinal System Drug
Resperidone	Central Nervous System Drug
Ribavirin	Antiviral
Rimantadine HCl	Antiviral
Ritonavir	Antiviral
Rivastigmine tartrate	Central Nervous System Drug
Rosiglitazone/maleate	Hormone
Rosuvastatin calcium	Cardiovascular Drug
Saquinavir	Antiviral
Saquinavir mesylate	Antiviral
Scopolamine	Gastrointestinal System Drug
Secobarbitol	Central Nervous System Drug
Sertraline HCl	Central Nervous System Drug
Simvastatin	Cardiovascular Drug
Sodium Iodine	Hormone
Spironolactone	Cardiovascular Drug
Stavudine	Antiviral
Streptomycin	Antibiotic
Sulfasalazine	Antibiotic
Sulfisoxazole	Antibiotic
Sumatriptan succinate	Central Nervous System Drug
Tacrine HCl	Central Nervous System Drug
Temazepam	Central Nervous System Drug
Tenofovir disoproxil fumarate	Antiviral
Terbutaline	Respiratory Drug
Tetracycline	Antibiotic
Theophylline	Respiratory Drug
Thiethylperazine maleate	Central Nervous System Drug
Thioridazine	Central Nervous System Drug
Thiothixene	Central Nervous System Drug
Thyroid	Hormone
Ticarcillin	Antibiotic
Ticlopidine HCl	Cardiovascular Drug
Tobramycin	Antibiotic
Tocainide HCl	Cardiovascular Drug
Tolazamide	Hormone

GENERIC NAME	PURPOSE
Tolbutamide	Hormone
Tramadol HCl	Central Nervous System Drug
Tranylcypromine sulfate	Central Nervous System Drug
Triamterene	Cardiovascular Drug
Triazolam	Central Nervous System Drug
Trimethoprim/Sulfa	Antibiotic
Valacyclovir HCl	Antiviral
Vancomycin	Antibiotic
Vasopressin	Hormone
Verapamil	Cardiovascular Drug
Xylocaine	Cardiovascular Drug
Zalcitabine	Antiviral
Zidovidine azidothymidine	Antiviral
Zolpidem	Central Nervous System Drug

GLOSSARY OF CHIROPRACTIC TERMS

abduct   to draw away from the midline, from the normal position of a bone or muscle, or from an adjacent part of the limb

acute   coming on suddenly and severely; sharp, as an acute pain

adjustment   in chiropractic, a form of direct, articular manipulation used to correct a subluxation

anatometer   device to measure pelvic and lower extremity symmetry

atlas   first cervical vertebra that supports the head; it articulates with the occipital bone and the axis

auscultation   listening for sounds within the body, either with a stethoscope or with the human ear

autonomic nervous system (ANS)   that part of the nervous system that regulates involuntary actions such as digestive processes, glandular operation, and heart and lung function

axis   second cervical vertebra

Babinski test   stroking the plantar surface of the foot; extension of the great toe upward is normal in infants but abnormal in an adult; used to diagnose spinal cord disease or brain damage

bursa   fluid-containing, membrane-lined cavity located in connecting tissues, usually in the vicinity of joints, where friction would otherwise occur; serves as a lubricating and protecting system

bursitis inflammation of the bursa

capsulitis inflammation of the capsule of an organ or part; if characterized by adhesions, it is known as adhesive bursitis

cervical vertebrae the seven vertebrae in the neck

cervico-occipital neuralgia neuralgia in the upper cervical nerves, especially in the posterior division of the second cervical nerve

chronic long-lasting, frequently recurring

cineroentgenography the production of moving X-ray pictures

congenital existing at (and usually before) birth; may be hereditary or due to some influence during gestation

coccygodynia pain in the coccyx and neighboring region

coccyx tail bone, made up of four rudimentary vertebrae that are fused together

contusion superficial, nonlacerating injury from a blow; a bruise

diathermy use of high-frequency ultrasound or microwaves to raise the temperature of a part of the body; sometimes used to treat deep-seated pain

disc (also disk) a flattened, rounded cushion of cartilage and tissue located between each vertebra

discogenic caused by derangement of an intervertebral disc

discopathogenic abnormal action or function of a vertebral disc, resulting in a disorder or an abnormal condition; caused by disc degeneration

discopathy pathological changes in a disc

dynamometer instrument for measuring the force of muscular contraction; a squeeze (or grip) dynamometer measures the grip of the hand

dysarthrosis deformity or malformation of a joint

dyskinesia impairment of the power of voluntary movement, resulting in fragmentary or incomplete movements

electronic stimulation treatment involving neural stimulation (said to release endorphins), used in the management of pain and stress syndromes

esthesia ability to receive sensory impressions

exacerbation increase in the seriousness of a disease or disorder, usually marked by a worsening of the symptoms

extension stretching; the act of moving two joined parts away from each other

exteroceptor sensory nerve terminal, such as those in the skin and mucous membranes, that is stimulated by the immediate external environment

Fabere sign test for hip-joint dysfunction; derived from the words for the movements tested—*f*lexion, *ab*duction, *e*xternal *r*otation, and *e*xtension; also known as Patrick's test

facet small plane surface on a bone

fasciculus bundle of nerve or muscle fibers having a common function and connection; used in reference to the central nervous system

fibrosis noninflammatory fibrositis

fibrositis inflammatory hyperplasia of fibrous tissue, particularly of the muscle sheaths and fascial layers; also called muscular rheumatism

flexion bending a joint that causes two adjoining bones to come closer together

flexure curved position or the bending of a part

foramen natural opening or passage, especially into or through a bone

foramen magnum large opening in the base of the skull through which the spinal cord passes to join the brain

foramina openings between two vertebrae

functional   the natural or proper action for which a person, office, mechanism, or organ is employed; the assigned duty or activity

funicular   of or pertaining to a cordlike structure or part, usually a bundle of nerve fibers in the nerve trunk

funiculitis   inflammation of a funiculus

galvanotherapy   use of electric current for pain relief and reduction of inflammation; also known as galvanism

ganglion   lesion that resembles a tumor in a tendon sheath or joint capsule

gluteus maximus   the large muscle of the buttocks that involves locomotion

homeostasis   state of physiological equilibrium produced by a balance of functions and of chemical composition within an organism

hydrocollator   preheated silica-gel pack that provides moist heat, relieves pain, increases local blood flow, and relaxes muscle spasms

hypalgesia   diminished sense of pain

hyperactive   overly active

hyperesthesia   increased sensitivity of the skin or sense organs to stimulation

hyperextension   extreme or excessive extension of a limb or part

hyperflexion   forcible overflexion of a limb or part, the reverse of whiplash injury that occurs when the body is in a forward motion and strikes an immovable object

hypermetria   exaggeration of movement giving an excessive range of motion

hypothermy   prolonged, local application of cold, resulting in local anesthesia

intersegmental dysarthria   pain within two or more segments of a joint; acute or chronic

intervertebral disc syndrome   protrusion, herniation or prolapse of intervertebral disc material with resulting neurological findings

intervertebral dysarthria   pain in the intervertebral joint; can be acute or chronic

intervertebral foramen   space between the vertebrae through which spinal nerves branch

kyphosis   abnormal curvature of the spine with posterior convexity; also known as humpback or hunchback

Lasègue's sign   test involving straight-leg raising while lying prone, used to diagnose sciatica and hip disease

lordosis   normal curvature of the cervical and lumbar spine, seen from the side as an anterior concavity

lumbar   lower part of the spine, containing five vertebrae

luxation   misalignment, displacement, or dislocation of an organ or joint

manipulation   hands-on procedure that restores the structural integrity of the body, especially that of the spine, by aligning the vertebrae

massage   manipulation of the soft tissues of the body

meric system   the treatment of visceral conditions through adjustment of vertebrae at the levels of neuromeric innervation to the organs involved

muscle spasm   involuntary contraction of a muscle; persistent spasm is tonic, alternating spasm is clonic

myalgia   muscle pain

myasthenia gravis   syndrome of severe muscle weakness due to a progressive neuromuscular disorder

myofascitis   inflammation of a muscle and its fascia, particularly of the fascial insertion of muscle to bone

myofibrosis   replacement of muscle tissue by fibrous tissue

myositis   inflammation of a voluntary muscle

myospasm   spasm of a muscle

neuralgia   severe, often burning, pain along the course of a nerve

neuritis   inflammation of a nerve, usually of a degenerative nature and usually accompanied by pain, diminished reflexes, and muscular atrophy

neurocalometer   device used to detect temperature variations between two points on the body

neurogenic   originating in the nervous system; any nerve disturbance from intersegmental or intervertebral areas; not a neurological deficit

orthostatic   pertaining to an upright position

osteoarthritis   the most common form of arthritis, characterized by degenerative changes in the joints

osteophytosis   bone disease of bacterial origin

osteoporosis   abnormal rarefaction of bone

palpation   diagnostic technique utilizing manual exploration of the body

parasympathetic nervous system   the part of the autonomic nervous system that slows the heartbeat, decreases blood pressure, stimulates the secretions of most glands and restores digestive activity to normal

paravertebral   alongside the vertebral column

Patrick's test   *see* Fabere sign

plantar   referring to the sole of the foot

plethysmograph   an instrument that determines and registers variations in the size of organs and limbs and the amount of blood passing through them at one time

polyneuritis   inflammation of many nerves at once

popliteal   hollow area behind the knee joint

ptosis   abnormal and permanent lowering of an organ, especially drooping of the upper eyelid caused by muscle failure

radiculalgia   neuralgia of the nerve roots

radiculitis   inflammation of the root of a nerve

radiculoneuritis   inflammation of root and nerve, usually accompanied by paresthesia, paralysis, muscular atrophy, and decreased or lost reflex response

radiculopathy   irritation of a nerve root, usually noninflammatory, nonspecific, and localized; for example, cervical lumbar

receptor   a highly specialized nervous-system information-gathering device

reflex   an involuntary action or response

retracing   the redevelopment, after chiropractic adjustment, of symptoms that had disappeared under previous treatment

rheumatoid arthritis   joint degeneration of unknown etiology, also known as atrophic arthritis

rotation   the process of turning around an axis

sacroiliac   pertaining to the sacrum and the ilium, their articulation or associated ligaments; the joint between the hip bone and the sacrum.

sacrum   spade-shaped portion of the pelvis composed of five fused bony segments

sciatic nerve   nerve running from the lower spine down the thigh to the knee region, where it divides into two nerves that supply the lower leg

sciatica   pain felt in the back and down the back and outer part of the thigh and leg, often associated with degeneration of an intervertebral disc

scoliosis abnormal lateral or sideward curve to the spine

short leg a congenital, pathological, or developmental leg deficiency

skeletal balancing a chiropractic method of balancing leg length and correcting pelvic distortions and abnormalities in the entire spine

SMT spinal manipulative therapy

soft-tissue technique manipulation of the muscles and fascia

somatic of or pertaining to the body, especially as distinguished from a body part, the mind, or the environment

Soto-Hall test test involving flexion of the neck and spine to reproduce back pain or sciatic nerve pain; can be used to help diagnose a herniated disc, tumor of the spinal nerve root, metastatic tumors

spasm sudden, involuntary contraction of a muscle or group of muscles

spina bifida occulta congenital condition in which the neural arch fails to close in the posterior midline with no protrusion of the spinal cord

spinal cord the central nerve cable that runs down the spinal canal inside the chain of vertebrae, sends out 31 pairs of spinal nerves to the body's organs and tissues

spinal inversion therapy chiropractic technique in which the body is turned upside down so the feet are uppermost and the head is nearest the floor

spinography a system of detection of subluxations by geometric analysis of radiographs usually taken in the weight-bearing position

spinous process backward projection of the vertebra that forms, with those of the other vertebrae, the ridge of the back

spondylitis inflammation of a joint of the spinal column, usually characterized by pain and stiffness; may occur after injury or as the result of rheumatoid arthritis or infection

spondylolisthesis forward dislocation of a vertebrae over the one below it, causing pressure on spinal nerves

spondylosis condition in which vertebral joints become fixed or stiff, causing pain and restricted mobility

spondylotherapy therapeutic application of percussion or concussion over the vertebrae

sprain injury to ligaments around a joint, causing pain, swelling, and skin discoloration

strain injury to a muscle, resulting in swelling and pain

structural deviation mechanical displacement of a body part from its normal relationship to another part

subluxation less than a complete dislocation; defines a condition in which a vertebra is out of line, impinges on a nerve, and interferes with the normal flow of nerve energy

synergic doing things in a normal rhythm or acting in harmony with one another

synovitis inflammation of a synovial membrane; for example, tenosynovitis, capsulitis, and bursitis.

tendinitis inflammation of tendons or tendon-muscle attachments

TENS transcutaneous electrical nerve stimulation; through electrodes placed on the skin, a low-voltage current transmits signals that block pain transmissions to higher nerve centers; used to alleviate pain in the neck and lower back, peripheral neuropathies, and so on

thoracic area of the back between the neck and the lower back, composed to 12 vertebrae; also known as dorsal

tonic pertaining to tissue or muscular tension

torticollis contracted state of the cervical muscles, producing twisting of the neck and an unnatural position of the head

traction placing a bone or limb under tension to immobilize the part, align parts in a particular way, or relieve pressure

traumatic degenerative disc changes   narrowing of the disc space as a result of sudden physical injury from destructive bone disease, dehydration, and so on

ultrasound (US)   sound waves of a very high frequency that are projected into the body and reduce nervous system conductivity

unilateral   on or affecting one side

vapo-coolant   a coolant spray used to supercool the skin and employed in the treatment of trigger points; generally ethylchloride or fluoromethane

vertebra   any of the 33 bones of the spinal column, including 7 cervical, 12 thoracic, 5 lumbar, 5 sacral, and 4 coccygeal; plural: vertebrae

viscero-sinal syndrome   physiological changes in the viscera produced by irritation of spinal nerves

whiplash   nonmedical term to describe hyperextension injury to the neck resulting from an indirect force, usually from behind

COMMON ORTHOPEDIC AND NEUROLOGICAL TESTS

Achilles reflex   Achilles tendon is percussed. Increased or decreased response is indicative of S1 nerve root involvement.

Ankle clonus   Foot is forcefully dorsiflexed. Sustained fibrillations are indicative of an upper motor neuron lesion.

Apley's compression   Leg is flexed to 90 degrees, heel is pressed down, and tibia is rotated internally and externally. Pain is positive for torn meniscus on that side.

Apley's distraction   Leg is flexed to 90 degrees and lifted, tibia is rotated internally and externally. Pain indicates ligamentous damage; no pain is positive for meniscus damage.

Apprehension   Arm is abducted and externally rotated. Pain indicates chronic shoulder dislocation.

Adson's maneuver   Pulse is taken, the head is turned and extended, deep breath is held. Cessation or diminishing of pulse indicates compression of the artery by cervical rib.

Babinski's reflex   With a sharp point, the examiner strokes the plantar surface of the foot from heel to the ball and then toward the middle. Extension of the great toe with fanning of the other four is indicative of an upper motor neuron lesion.

Biceps reflex   Crease of elbow is tapped. Increased or decreased reflex response indicates C5 involvement.

Big toe   Examiner holds toe, patient dorsiflexes against resistance. Weakness is indicative of L5 nerve root involvement. Also known as Sicard's test.

Brachioradialis reflex   Forearm is supinated to 90 degrees, radial side is tapped proximal to wrist. Increased or decreased reflex response indicates C6 involvement.

Braggard's   While in supine position, examiner dorsiflexes patient's foot one inch below the point of pain for Lasègue's sign. Pain is indicative of sciatica.

Brudzinski sign   Flexion of the neck that results in flexion of the hip and knee. Indicative of meningitis or meningeal irritation.

Cervical compression   A screening maneuver to localize pain, involves downward pressure by the examiner on various areas of the cervical spine and shoulders.

Cervical distraction   The examiner lifts the patient's head firmly with hands at the base of the skull and underneath the chin. If pain decreases with this movement, the patient is a candidate for traction therapy.

Chaddock's reflexes   Examiner strokes lateral malleolus. Extension of great toe with flexion of other four is indicative of an upper motor neuron lesion.

Chest expansion test   Chest circumference at the nipple line is measured from the point of maximum exhalation to maximum inhalation. A difference of less than $1\frac{1}{2}$ inches is indicative of possible ankylosing spondylitis.

Circumference   Measurements are taken of the extremities. Muscle atrophy indicates nerve, muscle, or vascular damage.

Codman arm drop   Arm is extended, abducted 90 degrees, and struck by examiner downwards. Inability to hold the arm in place indicates a rotator cuff tear.

Collateral ligament   Ankle is stabilized, then internal and external stress is applied to knee. Gapping on internal stress is indicative of medial meniscus instability; gapping on external stress is indicative of lateral meniscus instability.

Dermatome distribution   Sensation is checked in the skin area (dermatome) for a specific spinal nerve. Absence or lessening of sensation can be indicative of specific nerve destruction.

Drawer sign   While supine, the patient's leg is flexed to 90 degrees and the foot is flat on the table; then examiner's hand grasps behind the knee and pushes/pulls. Gapping when pulled is indicative of a torn anterior cruciate ligament, gapping when pushed is indicative of a torn posterior cruciate ligament.

Dynamometer grip   Device that measures grip strength; average test is three tries for each hand. Primary hand will be 10 percent stronger; used as a test for malingering.

Ely   While lying prone, patient's heel is flexed to opposite buttocks and thigh is lifted off of table. Pain is indicative of a lumbosacral or sacroiliac lesion.

Fabere sign   While supine, the thigh and knee are flexed, the external malleolus rests on the patella on the opposite leg, and the knee is depressed. Pain is indicative of hip arthritis or other pathology. Name is taken from the words of the movements necessary to perform the test—flexion, abduction, external rotation, and extension; also known as Patrick's test.

Forced leg lowering   While supine, patient raises extended leg to 30 degrees, examiner applies downward pressure against resistance. Inability to combat pressure is indicative of muscle weakness.

Gastrocnemius muscle   Patient is observed while walking on toes. Inability due to weakness is indicative of possible S1/S2 nerve root involvement.

Heel walk   Patient is observed walking on heels. Inability is indicative of L4/L5 nerve root involvement or femoral neuropathy.

Homan's sign   While in supine position, leg is extended and raised 30 degrees off table while examiner dorsiflexes foot. Calf pain is indicative of thrombophlebitis.

Hoover's sign   The calcaneous of the uninjured leg is stabilized and patient is asked to raise the injured leg. Absence of downward pressure in uninjured leg can be indicative of malingering.

Kemp's   Patient is bent backwards obliquely. Pain is indicative of facet syndrome, fracture, or disc involvement; radiating pain on the side of the test is
indicative of lateral disc protrusion; radiating pain opposite the side of the
test is indicative of medial disc protrusion.

Lasègue's sign   Painful flexion of the hip when the knee is extended, but painless when flexed, is indicative of sciatica, low back problems, tight hamstrings. Also known as the straight leg raising test.

Lhermitte's sign   Forward flexion of the head, resulting in electric shocks
spreading down the body. Indicative of multiple sclerosis, compression of
the spinal cord, or other cervical cord disorders.

Maximum foramina encroachment   The patient moves chin to the shoulder
with extension of the neck. Pain occurring on the side of the motion indicates
nerve root/facet involvement; pain occurring on the side opposite the motion
indicates muscular strain.

McMurray's sign   While supine, the patient's leg is flexed and the examiner
rotates the foot fully outward while extending the knee slowly. A click is
indicative of a tear in the medial meniscus.

Minor's sign   Patient is observed while rising from a sitting position. If weight
is placed on the "good" leg, indicates lumbosacral involvement.

Oppenheim reflex   Examiner runs finger along crest of tibia. Extension of the
great toe with flexion of the other four is indicative of an upper motor neuron
lesion.

Osgood-Schlatter   Tibial tubercle of knee is palpated. Pain or swelling is
indicative of Osgood-Schlatter disease.

Palpation of sciatic nerve   While hip is flexed, the midpoint of the ischial
tuberosity and greater trochanter is palpated. Pain is indicative of disc herniation or space occupying lesion.

Patellar clonus   Leg is extended and patella is forced toward feet. Sustained
fibrillations are indicative of an upper motor neuron lesion.

Patellar reflex   Legs are crossed, patellar tendon of upper leg is tapped. Increased or decreased response indicates L4 nerve involvement.

Patrick's test   While supine, the thigh and knee are flexed, the external malleolus rests on the patella of the opposite leg, and the knee is depressed. Pain is indicative of hip arthritis or other pathology. Also known as Fabere sign.

Phalen's   Wrists are held in a hyperflexed position for 60 seconds. Numbness in fingers indicative of carpal tunnel syndrome or repetitive stress injury.

Piriformis muscle palpation   Area midway between greater trochanter and sacrum is palpated. Contraction of muscle may indicate irritation of the sciatic nerve.

Radial nerve   Patient makes fist, wrist is extended against resistance. Inability to hold wrist indicates radial nerve involvement.

Romberg's sign   Patient observed while standing with feet close together and eyes closed. Swaying of the body or falling is indicative of brain tumor or spinal cord lesion.

Sicard's   Examiner holds toe, patient dorsiflexes against resistance. Weakness is indicative of L5 nerve root involvement. Also known as Big toe test.

Soto-Hall   The examiner's hand is placed on the patient's chest and the head is flexed onto the chest. Pain is indicative of possible vertebral fracture, sprain, or disc lesion.

Straight leg raising   While patient is supine, the leg is raised with knee locked. Pain is indicative of sciatica or tight hamstrings. Also known as the Lasègue's sign.

Supra-spinatous tendonitis   Arm is abducted against resistance. Pain over the head of the supraspinatous area indicates tendonitis.

Tinel sign   Percussion over the site of a divided nerve results in tingling at the distal end of a limb, indicative of a partial lesion or the beginning of nerve regeneration. When palmar surface of wrist is tapped, pain and tingling into all but the little finger is indicative of carpal tunnel syndrome or repetitive stress injury.

Toe walk   Patient is observed walking on toes. Inability is indicative of L5/S1 nerve root involvement or sciatic neuropathy.

Trendelenburg   Patient stands on one leg and flexes opposite thigh and calf. Failure of crest to rise indicative of weak gluteus on opposite side.

Tricep's reflex   Triceps tendon is tapped. Increased or decreased reflex response indicates C7 involvement.

Tripod   While patient is seated, one leg is extended. Pain indicates sciatica, used as a test to determine malingering.

Ulnar nerve   Hands are opened wide and placed palmar side down. Unequal separation of the middle and ring finger indicative of ulnar nerve involvement.

Valsalva's maneuver   The patient crosses arms, head is down, deep breath is taken and held, patient bears down. Pain will appear at the site of the lesion.

Yeoman's femoral stretch   While patient is prone, heel is flexed to same buttocks. Pain is indicative of L3–L5 intervertebral disc syndrome.

GLOSSARY OF DENTAL TERMS AND ABBREVIATIONS

Terms

alveolus   the socket in the jaw that retains the root of a tooth

analgesia   absence of sensibility to pain, while remaining conscious

analgesic   drug or mechanism that can diminish pain

anesthesia   loss of all sensations (touch, temperature, pain), including the loss of consciousness

apical   pertaining to or located at the apex

apicoectomy   excision of the apical portion of a tooth root through an opening made in the overlying labial, buccal, or palatal alveolar bone

basal narcosis   a depression of the central nervous system induced by drugs just short of unconsciousness

bicuspid   having two cusps or points; refers to a premolar tooth

bruxism   rhythmic or spasmodic grinding of the teeth, especially during sleep

bucca (buccae)   the cheek

canine   conical tooth used for tearing food; also known as eyetooth

caries breakdown and death of tooth tissue, resulting in soft and discolored areas; also known as cavities

cementum bonelike connective tissue covering the root of a tooth and assisting in tooth support

cephalometric radiograph X-ray study of the head in profile view, used by orthodontists to analyze a patient's dental-facial form and growth pattern

cervical line area where the crown and root of a tooth join

craniofacial complex face, cranium, and oral cavity (including teeth)

crossbite malocclusion in which the upper incisors bite behind the lower incisors

crown the portion of the tooth that projects into the oral cavity

cusp tapered point, especially on the top of a tooth

dental amalgam an alloy composed of certain metals (silver, tin), used for filling cavities

dentin bonelike major tissue found in a tooth; covers the pulp and is covered by the enamel above the gums

enamel the hard white covering above the gum line of a tooth

endodontics the branch of dentistry that is concerned with the etiology, prevention, diagnosis, and treatment of diseases and injuries that affect the tooth pulp, root, and periapical tissue

exodontics the branch of dentistry that deals with extraction of teeth

gingiva the mucous membrane and fibrous tissue that encircles the neck of each tooth; also known as the gum

gingivitis condition in which the gums are red, swollen, and bleeding

hypnosis depressed state of the central nervous system in which the patient is asleep but conscious

incisors any of eight front teeth, four in each jaw, used for cutting and tearing food

lingual pertaining to the tongue

malocclusion condition in which the teeth of the opposing jaws do not contact or mesh normally; often corrected by orthodontics

mandible the large bone making up the lower jaw, consisting of horizontal part, a horseshoe-shaped body, and two perpendicular branches that connect to the body; contains sockets for the 16 lower teeth.

masseter muscle group of the jaw

mastication process of chewing food in preparation for swallowing and digesting

maxilla one of a pair of large bones that form the upper jaw; consists of a pyramidal body and four processes; contains sockets for the 16 upper teeth; forms part of the structure of the orbits, nasal cavity, and roof of the mouth

molar posterior tooth that is used for grinding food and acts as a major jaw support in the dental arch

obturator device used to close or cover an opening, as a device implanted to cover the opening in the roof of the mouth

occlusion act of closure or state of being closed

odontology study of the anatomy and physiology of teeth and the surrounding structures in the mouth

oral/maxillofacial surgery (OMF) the branch of dentistry that deals with corrective and diagnostic surgery of the mouth and jaws

oral pathology   the branch of dentistry concerned with disease of the mouth, head, and neck

oro-   a combining form pertaining to the mouth

oropharynx   part of the pharynx extending from the soft palate at the back of the mouth to the hyoid bone region; contains the tonsils.

orthodontics   the branch of dentistry concerned with malocclusion and irregularities of the teeth and their correction

orthognathia   the study of the cause and treatment of malposition of the bones of the jaw

overbite   a condition in which the upper teeth extend abnormally over the lower teeth

pain threshold   point at which a stimulus becomes uncomfortable and distinguishable as pain

pain tolerance level   highest level at which an individual can tolerate pain

palate   the structure that is the roof of the mouth and floor of the nasal cavity; separated into hard palate and soft palate

pedodontics   the branch of dentistry concerned with the care and treatment of children's teeth

periodontal disease   disease of the tissues around a tooth, often leading to damage to the bony sockets of the teeth

periodontics   the branch of dentistry concerned with the diagnosis and treatment of diseases of the tissues surrounding the teeth

plaque   deposit of saliva and bacteria found on teeth that encourages the development of caries

preauricular   in front of the ear

premolar   any of eight teeth in adult dentition, two on each side of each jaw, situated behind the canines and in front of the molars; also called bicuspids

prophylaxis use of appropriate procedures and/or techniques to prevent dental and oral disease and malformations

prosthodontics the branch of dentistry concerned with the design and application of dentures

pulp connective tissue containing nerves and blood vessels, located at the center of a tooth under the dentine

root the part of the tooth that is embedded in the gum and firmly attached to a bony encasement or socket

sedation mild depression of the central nervous system in which the individual is still conscious

sublingual gland either of a pair of mucus-secreting salivary glands located on the floor of the mouth below the tongue

submandibular gland either of a pair of salivary glands located near the lower jaw and secreting mucus and serous fluid components of saliva

temporomandibular joint (TMJ) joint between the lower jaw and the rest of the skull

tricuspid having three cusps; also known as molar

Abbreviations

AAA	amalgam
AADS	American Academy of Dental Schools
AAO	American Academy of Orthodontists
AAOP	American Academy of Oral Pathology
AB	axiobuccal
ABC	axiobuccocervical
ABG	axiobuccogingival
ABL	axiobuccolingual
ABS	abscess
AC	axiocervical
ACOMS	American College of Oral and Maxillofacial Surgeons
ACR	acrylic
AD	axiodistal
ADAA	American Dental Assistants Association
Adap B/U	adaptic build-up
ADC	axiodistalcervical
ADG	axiodistogingival
ADHA	American Dental Hygienists Association
ADI	axiodistoincisal
	axiodistoinclusal
ADO	axiodisto-occlusal
ADP	adaptic (dental material)
ADR	acceptable dental remedies
AG	axiogingival
AI	axioincisal
AL	axiolingual
ALA	axiolabial
ALAG	axiolabiogingival
ALAL	axiolabiolingual
ALC	axiolinguocervical
ALCR	aluminum crown
ALG	alginate (dental material)
	axiolinguogingival
ALO	axiolinguo-occlusal
ALVX	alveolectomy
AM	amalgam filling
	axiomesial
AMC	axiomesiocervical

AMD	axiomesiodistal
AMG	axiomesiogingival
AMI	axiomesioincisal
AMO	axiomesio-occlusal
AN	anesthetic
ANUG	acute necrotizing ulcerative gingivitis
AO	axio-occlusal
AP	axiopulpal
ARG	silver
AU	gold
B	bicuspid
	buccal
BA	buccal artery
	buccoaxial
BAC	buccoaxiocervical
BAG	buccoaxiogingival
BC	buccocervical
BD	buccodistal
BDS	Bachelor of Dental Surgery
BDSc	Bachelor of Dental Science
BG	buccogingival
BL	buccolingual
BM	buccomesial
BO	bucco-occlusal
BP	buccopulpal
BR	bridge service
BUC	buccal
BWX	bite-wing X ray
C	canine tooth
CA	cervicoaxial
CaOH	calcium hydroxide
CAV	cavity
CD	complete denture
CDA	certified dental assistant
CDT	certified dental technician
CF	composite filling
CI	central incisor

CLA	cervicolinguoaxial
CN	crown
CO	consultation
COMP	composite
COP	copalite (dental material)
CR	complete restoration
	crown service
CR&BR	crown and bridge
D	deciduous
	denture
DA	dental assistant
DB	distobuccal
DBO	distobucco-occlusal
DC	distocervical
DDS	doctor of dental surgery
DDSc	doctor of dental science
DE	dental examination
DEC	deciduous
DEF	decayed, extracted, filled
DEJ	dental-enamel junction
DENT	dental
	dentistry
	dentition
DF	decayed and filled
DG	distogingival
DI	distoincisal
DL	distolingual
DLA	distolabial
DLAI	distolabioincisal
DLAP	distolabiopulpal
DLI	distolinguoincisal
DLO	distolinguo-occlusal
DLP	distolinguopulpal
DMD	doctor of dental medicine
DMF	decayed, missing, or filled teeth
DMFS	decayed, missing, or filled surfaces
DO	disto-occlusal
DP	distopulpal

DPH	dental public health
DPL	distopulpolingual
DR	denture repair
DS	denture service
DYC	dycal (dental material)
EDENT	edentulous
EN	endodontic
ENDO	endodontist
EUA	examination under anesthesia
EX	examination
FACD	Fellow of the American College of Dentists
FBI	flossing, brushing, irrigation
FD	full dentures
FICD	Fellow of the International College of Dentists
FL	fluoride
FM	first molar
	full mouth
FME	full mouth extraction
FMS	full mouth series
	full mouth surgery
FMX	full mouth X rays
FP	first premolar
	fixed prosthodontics
FX	fracture
G	gingival
GA	gingivoaxial
GBA	gingivobuccoaxial
GLA	gingivolinguoaxial
GPLY	gingivoplasty
GVTY	gingivectomy
HV	hospital visit
HYG	hygiene
i	incisor (deciduous)
I	incisor (permanent)
ICPMM	incisors, canines, premolars, molars

ID	immediate dentures
IEE	inner enamel epithelium
IL	incisolingual
IMP	impression
IMPA	incisor mandibular plane angle
IN	inlay service
INL	inlay
IP	incisoproximal
ITE	initial therapy evaluation
L	lingual
LA	linguoaxial
	local anesthesia
LAG	labiogingival
LAI	labioincisal
LAL	labiolingual
LC	linguocervical
LD	linguodistal
LDDS	local dentist
LG	linguogingival
LI	linguoincisal
LM	linguomesial
LO	linguo-occlusal
LP	linguopulpal
	lower plate
M	mesial
	molar
Malocc	malocclusion
MAND	mandible
	mandibular
MAX	maxilla
	maxillary
MB	mesiobuccal
MBO	mesiobucco-occlusal
MBP	mesiobuccopulpal
MD	mandibular
	mesiodistal
MDS	Master of Dental Surgery

MG	mesiogingival
MI	mesionincisal
MID	mesioincisodistal
ML	mesiolingual
MLA	mesiolabial
MLAI	mesiolabioincisal
MLAP	mesiolabiopulpal
MLI	mesiolinguoincisal
MLO	mesiolinguo-occlusal
MLP	mesiolinguopulpal
MO	mesio-occlusal
MOD	mesio-occlusodistal
MP	mesiopulpal
MPL	mesiopulpolingual
MPLA	mesiopulpolabial
MSD	Master of Science in Dentistry
NIT OX	nitrous oxide
O	occlusal
	oral
OC	occlusocervical
OCC	occlusion
OEE	outer enamel epithelium
OH	oral hygiene
ORTH	orthodontist
OS	mouth
	oral surgery
OV	office visit
OVD	occlusal vertical dimension
PA	pulpoaxial
PAX	periapical X ray
PBA	pulpobuccoaxial
PBW	posterior bite wing X ray
PD	partial denture
PDH	past dental history
PE	periodontic
PEDO	pedodontist
PENT	pentothal

PERIAP	periapical
PERIO	periodontia
	periodontist
PF	porcelain filling
	prophylaxis and fluoride
PFM	porcelain-fused-to-metal crown
PJC	porcelain jacket crown
PL	periodontal ligament
	pulpolingual
PLA	pulpolabical
	pulpolinguoaxial
PM	pulpomesial
PN	pain
PR	prophylaxis
PROPHY	prophylaxis
PROSTH	prosthedontist
PS	preventive service
PX	panoramic X rays
RC	root canal
RCT	root canal treatment
RD	rubber dam
RDFS	ratio of decayed and filled surfaces
RDFT	ratio of decayed and filled teeth
RDH	registered dental hygienist
RE	recementation
RF	root canal filling
RIT	removal of impacted tooth
RP	root planing
SAM	surface amalgam filling
SL	sublingual
SM	second molar
SP	second premolar
SPL	splint
	splinting
SS	stainless steel
SSCR	stainless steel crown
TE	tooth extracted

TM	temporomandibular
	third molar
TMJ	temporomandibular joint
UP	upper plate
XR	X rays
XT	extraction

GLOSSARY OF PODIATRIC TERMS

abnormal compensation an alteration in structure in one area as a result of the tendency of the foot to neutralize an abnormal structure elsewhere

accommodative orthosis generally allows the foot to function in a deformed manner but alleviates some of the patient's pain

arthrodesis surgical fixation of a joint by a procedure designed to accomplish fusion of the joint surfaces by promoting the proliferation of bone cells; also known as artificial ankylosis

biomechanical a term derived from bio- (body) and -mechanics (engineering); the engineering of the body

bunion inflammation and swelling of the bursa at the base of the big toe, with a resultant thickening of the skin

burr drill used for creating openings in bone or similar hard surfaces; also spelled "bur"

bursa a sac situated at a joint

calcaneus irregular quadrangular bone at the back of the tarsus; also known as the heel bone

calcaneal spur bone excrescence on the lower surface of the calcaneus; frequently causes pain on walking

debridement   cutting away dead or contaminated tissue from a wound to prevent infection

diaphysectomy   excision of a portion of the shaft of a long bone

excrescence   normal outgrowth or natural appendage (fingernails, hair, and so on); abnormal or disfiguring outgrowth or addition, as a bunion

exostosectomy digital   removal of an exostosis on a finger

exostosis   abnormal bony growth projecting outward from the surface of a bone

fibroma   nonmalignant tumor composed largely of fibrous tissue

functional orthosis   device designed to realign and help correct the foot, made of a material whose shape will generally not change due to pressure from the patient's weight

Haglund's disease   bursitis in the region of the Achilles tendon

hallux   great toe, or first digit of the foot

hammertoe   condition in which the first joint of a toe is permanently bent downward, resulting in a claw-like deformity

keratosis   horny growth, such as a wart or callosity

metatarsus   the part of the foot, especially the five bones, between the ankle and toes

neuroma   tumor derived from nervous tissue, consisting of nerve cells and fibers

onychectomy   excision of a nail or nail bed

onycho-, onych-   combining form pertaining to the nails

orthosis   any device designed to help straighten, correct, or realign the body through the use of forces (direct, antagonist, or subtle)

osteotomy   surgical cutting of a bone

phalanges digitorum pedis   the 14 bones composing the skeleton of the toes

phalanx (phalanges)   general term for any bone of a finger or toe

plantar   pertaining to the sole of the foot

sesamoid   denotes a small nodular bone embedded in a tendon or joint capsule

spur   a projecting body, as from a bone

verruca   epidermal tumor caused by a virus; also known as wart

GLOSSARY OF PSYCHIATRIC TERMS

acting out   defense mechanism in which one acts without reflection or apparent regard for negative consequences

affect   a pattern of observable behaviors that is the expression of a subjectively experienced emotion (euphoria, anger, sadness); may be broad (normal), inappropriate, labile, or flat

anxiety   apprehension, tension, or uneasiness that stems from the anticipation of danger whose source is largely unknown

catatonia   syndrome in which motor behavior is disturbed, usually characterized by body rigidity and stupor but sometimes by impulsive and purposeless activity

compulsion   repetitive and seemingly purposeful behavior that is in response to an obsession, or performed according to certain rules or in a stereotyped fashion, and designed to produce or prevent some future state

conversion symptom   loss or alteration of physical functioning that suggests a physical disorder, but that is actually a direct expression of a psychological conflict or need

delusion   false belief; continuing irrational idea that cannot be changed by logical argument

depersonalization   alteration in self-perception so that the feeling of one's own reality is temporarily lost

disorientation   confusion about the date or time of day, place, or self-identity

dysthymia   mental depression

echolalia   repetition of the words or phrases of others

flight of ideas   nearly continuous flow of accelerated speech with abrupt changes from topic to topic, usually based on understandable associations, distracting stimuli or plays on words

hallucination   the perception of something that is not actually present; may be visual, auditory, olfactory, gustatory, or tactile

illusion   false impression; wrongful interpretation of what has been perceived by the senses

mood   pervasive and sustained emotion that colors the person's perception of the world

  dysphoric   unpleasant mood, such as depression, anxiety, or irritability

  euphoric   an exaggerated feeling of well-being

  expansive   lack of restraint in expressing one's feelings, frequently with an overevaluation of one's significance or importance

obsession   recurrent, persistent, senseless idea, thought, image, or impulse that is not experienced as voluntarily produced but as an idea that invades consciousness

panic attacks   sudden onset of intense apprehension, fearfulness or terror, often associated with feelings of impending doom

paranoid ideation   ideation involving suspiciousness or the belief that one is being harassed, persecuted, or unfairly treated

passive aggression   defense mechanism in which the person indirectly and unassertively expresses aggression toward others

personality   deeply ingrained patterns of behavior, which include the way one relates to, perceives, and thinks about the environment and oneself

phobia   persistent, irrational fear of a specific object, activity, or situation that results in a compelling desire to avoid the particular stimulus

prodromal   early signs or symptoms of a disorder

psychogenic   originating in the mind, not in the body; refers especially to symptoms or diseases of psychological, not physical, origin

psychomotor agitation   excessive motor activity associated with a feeling of inner tension, usually nonproductive and repetitious

psychomotor retardation   visible, generalized slowing down of physical reactions, movements, and speech

psychotic   gross impairment in reality testing and creation of a new reality

repression   defense mechanism in which one is unable to remember or to be cognitively aware of disturbing wishes, feelings, thoughts, or experiences

schizophrenia   mental disorders characterized by gross distortions of reality, withdrawal from social contacts, and disturbances of thought, language, perception, and emotional response

sign   objective manifestation of a pathological condition as observed by an examiner rather than reported by the individual

somatization   defense mechanism in which one becomes preoccupied with physical symptoms disproportionate to any actual physical disturbances

symptom   manifestation of a pathological condition; includes objective and subjective complaints

syndrome   group of symptoms that occur together and constitute a recognizable condition

APPENDIX K

COMMON MEDICAL ABBREVIATIONS

A2	aortic second sound
A/A	auto accident
AAA	abdominal aortic aneurysm
AAE	active assisted exercises
	acute allergic encephalitis
AAL	anterior axillary line
AAO	awake, alert, and oriented
AAP	air at atmospheric pressure
AB	abnormal
	abortion
	ace bandage
	active bilaterally
	antibody
	asthmatic bronchitis
ABC	air and bone conduction
ABD	abdomen
	abduction
ABE	acute bacterial endocarditis
ABG	arterial blood gases
ABN	abnormal
ABP	arterial blood pressure
ABR	absolute bed rest
ABS	absent
	acute brain syndrome
AC	acromioclavicular
	acute
	adrenal cortex

	air conduction
	anterior chamber (of eye)
	anticoagulant
	before meals
ACA	adenocarcinoma
	anterior cerebral artery
	anterior coronary artery
ACC	accommodation
ACF	accessory clinical findings
ACG	angiocardiography
ACH	adrenal cortical hormone
ACI	acute coronary insufficiency
ACIOL	anterior chamber intraocular lens
ACJT	acromioclavicular joint
ACL	anterior clavicular line
	anterior cruciate ligament
ACO	alert, cooperative, oriented
ACP	acid phosphatase
ACS	acute cervical sprain
	acute cervical strain
ACT	active clotting time
	active motion
	anticoagulant therapy
ACTH	adrenocorticotropic hormone
ACTS	acute cervical trauma syndrome
ACVD	acute cardiovascular disease
AD	admission & discharge
	admitting diagnosis
	adult disease
	alternating days
	right ear
ADA	anterior descending artery
ADD	addiction
	adduct
	adduction
ADH	adhesions
	antidiuretic hormone
ADJ	adjacent
	adjoining

	adjunct
	adjust
ADL	activities of daily living
AD LIB	as desired
ADM	admission
	admit
ADR	adverse drug reaction
ADV	advance
	advised
	arterial deep venous
AE	above the elbow
	active and equal
AER	auditory evoked response
	average evoked response
AF	adult female
	amniotic fluid
	aortic flow
	atrial fibrillation
	atrial flutter
AFL	artificial limb
AFTR	atrophy, fasciculation, tremor, rigidity
AGA	appropriate for gestational age
AGE	acute gastroenteritis
	agreed medical examination
	angle of greatest extension
AGF	angle of greatest flexion
AGG	aggravation
AGL	acute granulocytic leukemia
AGN	acute glomerulonephritis
AGTT	abnormal glucose tolerance test
AH	abdominal hysterectomy
	arterial hypertension
AI	aortic insufficiency
	artificial insemination
AID	acute infectious disease
	artificial insemination by donor
AIDS	acquired immune deficiency syndrome
AIIS	anterior inferior iliac spine
AIT	acute intensive treatment

AJ	ankle jerk
AK	above the knee
AKA	above the knee amputation
AL	left ear
ALB	albumin
ALC	approximate lethal concentration
ALD	alcoholic liver disease
ALK	alkaline
ALK PHOS	alkaline phosphatase
ALL	acute lymphoblastic leukemia
	acute lymphocytic leukemia
	allergy
ALMI	anterior lateral myocardial infarction
ALS	acute lumbar strain
	amytrophic lateral sclerosis
	anterolateral sclerosis
ALT	alternate
	argon laser trabeculoplasty
ALTS	acute lumbar trauma syndrome
ALVF	acute left ventricular failure
AM	adult male
	aerospace medicine
	before noon
AMA	against medical advice
	American Medical Association
AMB	ambulate, ambulatory
AMBL	ambulance
AMI	acute myocardial infarction
AML	acute monocytic leukemia
	acute myeloblastic leukemia
	acute myelocytic leukemia
ANA	anesthesia
	antinuclear antibodies
ANAL	analgesic
ANES	anesthesia
ANG	angle
ANI	acute nerve irritation
ANRI	acute nerve root irritation
ANS	autonomic nervous system

ANT	anterior
ANX	anxiety
AO	angle of aorta
AOB	alcohol on breath
AOD	arteriosclerotic occlusive disease
AOM	acute otitis media
A&P	anterior & posterior
	auscultation & palpation
	auscultation & percussion
AP	after parturition
	angina pectoris
	anteroposterior
APB	atrial premature beat
APC	aspirin, phenacetin, caffeine
APH	anterior pituitary hormone
	aphasia
AP&L	anteroposterior and lateral
APP	appears
	appendix
	appointment
	approximate
AR	active resistance
	admitting room
	apical rate
	artificial respiration
	assisted respiration
	at risk
ARC	AIDS-related complex
ARD	acute respiratory disease
ARDS	adult respiratory distress syndrome
ARE	active-resistance exercise
ARF	acute respiratory failure
	acute rheumatic fever
ARI	anxiety reaction, intense
ARM	anxiety reaction, mild
AROM	active range of motion
ART	Achilles tendon reflex test
	artery

	articulation
	artificial
ARTH	arthritic
AS	anal sphincter
	arteriosclerosis
	astigmatism
	auris sinistra (left ear)
ASA	acetylsalicylic acid, aspirin
ASA I, II, etc.	American Society of Anesthesiology surgery risk assessment
ASAP	as soon as possible
ASC	arteriosclerosis
	ascending
ASCAD	arteriosclerotic coronary artery disease
ASCVD	arteriosclerotic cardiovascular disease
	artherosclerotic coronary artery disease
ASD	atrial septal defect
ASHD	arteriosclerotic heart disease
ASIS	anterior superior iliac spine
ASS	anterior superior spine
AST	astigmatism
AT	anterior tibial
	atlas
ATN	acute tubular necrosis
ATP	attending physician
ATR	Achilles tendon reflex
	atrophy
ATS	anxiety tension state
	arteriosclerosis
AU	both ears
AV	aortic valve
	arteriovenous
	avulsion
AVG	average
AVH	acute viral hepatitis
AW	able to work
	alive and well
AWA	as well as

AX	axial
	axillary
AZT	azidothymidin
BA	backache
	blood alcohol
	bone age
	brachial artery
	brisk and active
	bronchial asthma
BAB	Babinski sign
BAC	blood alcohol concentration
BB	bed board
	blood bank
	both bones
	breakthrough bleeding
	breast biopsy
BBB	blood brain barrier
BB/FS	breast biopsy/frozen section
BBT	basal body temperature
BC	back care
	birth control
	bone conduction
BCC	basal cell carcinoma
BCP	birth control pills
BD	birthdate
BDR	background diabetic retinopathy
BE	barium enema
	below the elbow
	brisk and equal
BF	black female
	blood flow
	bone fragment
BG	bone graft
BGS	balance, gait, station
BGTT	borderline glucose tolerance test
BHP	benign hypertrophic prostate
BHS	beta hemolytic streptococcus
BID	brought in dead
	twice a day

BIL	bilateral
BJ	biceps jerk
	bone and joint
BJE	bones, joints, extremities
BJM	bones, joints, muscles
BK	back
	below the knee
BKA	below the knee amputation
BL	bilateral lower lung fields
	blood loss
BLE	both lower extremities
BLQ	both lower quadrants
BM	basal metabolism
	black male
	body mass
	bone marrow
	bowel movement
BND	barely noticeable difference
BNO	bladder neck obstruction
BOE	bilateral otitis externa
BOM	bilateral otitis media
BOP	blood, ova, parasites
BP	blood pressure
	body part
BPC	blood pressure cuff
BPH	benign prostatic hypertrophy
BPP	blood pressure and pulse
BR	bathroom
	bedrest
BRB	bright red blood
BRBPR	bright red blood per rectum
BRP	bathroom privileges
BRVO	branch retinal vein occlusion
BS	blood sugar
	bowel sounds
	breath sounds
BSA	bowel signs active
BSN	bowel sounds normal
BSP	bilateral salpingo-oophorectomy

BT	bowel tones
BTB	breakthrough bleeding
BTL	bilateral tubal ligation
BTR	biceps tendon reflex
BTW	back to work
BUE	both upper extremities
BUN	blood urea nitrogen
BUQ	both upper quadrants
BUS	Bartholin, urethral, skein's
BV	blood vessel
	blood volume
BW	birth weight
	body weight
	twice per week
BX	biopsy
c	with
C	centigrade
C1–7	cervical vertebrae 1–7
CA	cancer
	cardiac arrest
	Caucasian adult
	chronological age
CABG	coronary artery bypass graft
CAD	coronary artery disease
CAH	chronic active hepatitis
CAL	calorie(s)
CAO	chronic airway obstruction
CAT	cataract
	computerized axial tomography
CB	chest-back
	chronic bronchitis
CBC	complete blood count
CC	chief complaint
	clean catch
	clinical course
	cold and clammy
	color and circulation
	common cold

	costochondral
	craniocervical
	critical condition
	cubic centimeters
	current complaint
	with meals
CCJ	costochondral junction
CCOT	cervical compression overloading test
CCU	coronary care unit
CD	cardiovascular disease
	cause of death
	childhood disease
	cigarettes per day
	communicable disease
	convulsive disorder
CDH	congenital dislocation of the hip
CDS	cervico-dorsal syndrome
CF	compare, refer to
CFNS	chills, fever, night sweats
CH	characteristic
	chest
	chief
	chronic
CHD	coronary heart disease
CHF	congestive heart failure
CHG	change
CHP	child psychiatry
CHR	chronic
	chronological
CI	cardiac insufficiency
	cerebral infarction
CIA	common iliac artery
CIC	crisis intervention clinic
CICU	cardiac intensive care unit
CIM	cortically induced movements
CIRC	circulation
	circumference
CIS	carcinoma in situ
	central inhibitory state

CK	check
CKC	cold knife conization
CL	clavicle
	clean
	closed
	contact lens
CLBB	complete left bundle branch block
CLD	chronic liver disease
	chronic lung disease
CLL	chronic lymphatic leukemia
	chronic lymphocytic leukemia
CM	centimeter(s)
	costal margin
CMC	carpometacarpal
CMG	cystometrogram
CMS	circulation, motion, sensation
CMV	cytomegalovirus
CN	cranial nerve
CNS	central nervous system
CNV	cranial nerve number 5
CNX	cranial nerve number 10
C/O	care of
	complains of
CO	carbon monoxide
	cardiac output
	check out
CO2	carbon dioxide
CO60	radioactive cobalt
COA	condition on admission
COAG	chronic open angle glaucoma
COC	coccygeal
	coccyx
COD	cause of death
	codeine
	condition on discharge
COND	condition
CONT	continue
COPD	chronic obstructive pulmonary disease
COPE	chronic obstructive pulmonary emphysema

CP	cerebral palsy
	chest pain
	constant pressure
	cor pulmonale
CPAP	continuous positive airway pressure
CPD	compound
CPE	chronic pulmonary emphysema
	complete physical examination
CPH	chronic pyelonephritis
CPK	creatine
	creatinine phosphokinase
CPN	chronic pyelonephritis
CPPB	continuous positive pressure breathing
CPR	cardiopulmonary resuscitation
CPT	chest physical therapy
CPX	complete physical examination
CR	clinical records
	closed reduction
CRAO	central retinal arterial occlusion
CRBB	complete right bundle branch block
CR&C	closed reduction and cast
CRD	chronic renal disease
	chronic respiratory disease
CREP	crepitation
CRF	chronic renal failure
CRIT	critical
	hematocrit
CRNA	certified registered nurse anesthetist
CROM	cervical range of motion
CRVO	central retinal vein occlusion
C&S	culture and sensitivity
CS	cervical spine
	cesarean section
CSF	cerebrospinal fluid
CSM	cerebrospinal meningitis
	color, sensation, motion
CSP	cervical spine
CSR	Cheyne-Stokes respiration
	corrected sedimentation rate

CST	convulsive shock therapy
CT	carpal tunnel
	cerebral thrombosis
	cervical-thoracic
	cervical traction
	computerized tomography
CTB	confined to bed
CTL	cervical, thoracic, lumbar
CTS	carpal tunnel syndrome
CU	cause unknown
	clinical unit
	cubic
CUA	complete urinalysis
CUC	chronic ulcerative colitis
CUD	cause undetermined
CUG	cystourethrogram
CV	cardiac volume
	cardiovascular
	cerebrovascular
	cervical vertebra
	color vision
	concentrated volume
	costovertebral
CVA	cerebrovascular accident
	costovertebral angle
CVAT	costovertebral angle tenderness
CVD	cardiovascular disease
	cerebrovascular disease
CVP	central venous pressure
CVR	cardiovascular respiratory
CVS	cardiovascular status
	cardiovascular system
	clean voided specimen
CW	chest wall
	crutch walking
CX	cervix
	chest X ray
	consciousness
CXR	chest X ray
CY	cyanosis

DA	degenerative arthritis
D/A	date of accident
	date of admission
DAT	diet as tolerated
DB	date of birth
	disability
DBP	diastolic blood pressure
DC	damp, cold
	dilation, curettage
	direct current
	discharge
	discontinue
	doctor of chiropractic
DC&B	dilation, curettage, and biopsy
DD	differential diagnosis
	discharge diagnosis
	dry dressing
DDD	degenerative disc disease
D/DW	dextrose in distilled water
D5%DW	dextrose 5% in distilled water
D&E	dilation and evacuation
DEC	deceased
	decrease
DEF	defecation
	deferred
	deficiency
	deficient
	definite
	deformity
DEG	degeneration
DES	describe
DET	determine
DEV	deviation
DF	dorsiflexion
DH	delayed hypersenitivity
DHF	dorsi-hyperflexion
DI	date of injury
	diabetes insipidus
DIC	disseminated intravascular coagulation

DIG	digoxin
DIL	dilated
DIM	diminished
DIP	distal interphalangeal
DIPJ	distal interphalangeal joint
DIS	disabled
	disease
DISI	dorsal intercalary segment instability
DISL	dislocate
	dislocation
DISP	disposition
DIST	distal
	distance
	distended
	distinguish
DJD	degenerative joint disease
DKA	diabetic ketoacidosis
	did not keep appointment
DKB	deep knee bends
DL	date of loss
	deciliter(s)
DL&B	direct laryngoscopy and bronchoscopy
D5LR	dextrose 5% with lactated Ringer's
DM	diabetes mellitus
	diastolic murmur
DME	defense medical examination
DND	died a natural death
DNKA	did not keep appointment
DNR	do not resusitate
	dorsal nerve root
DNS	did not show for appointment
D/NS	dextrose in normal saline
D5%NS	dextrose 5% in normal saline
DOA	date of accident
	day of admission
	dead on arrival
DOB	date of birth
DOC	died of other causes
	documented

DOD	date of death
DOE	date of examination
	dyspnea on exertion
DOI	date of injury
DOS	date of surgery
DOT	date of transfer
DP	deep pulse
	diastolic pressure
	distal phalanx
	dorsalis pedis (pulse)
	dyspnea
DPC	delayed primary closure
DPD	diffuse pulmonary disease
DPT	diphtheria, pertussis, tetanus immunization
DR	diabetic retinopathy
	diagnostic radiology
	dorsal root
	dressing
DSD	discharge summary dictated
	dry sterile dressing
DSG	dressing
	dry sterile gauze
DSP	decreased sensory perception
DT	date and time
	date of treatment
	delirium tremens
	due to
DTP	distal tingling on percussion (Tinel's sign)
DTR	deep tendon reflex
DTS	delirium tremens
DU	diagnosis undetermined
	duodenal ulcer
DUB	dysfunctional uterine bleeding
DVA	distance visual acuity
DVT	deep venous thrombosis
DW	distilled water
	doing well
D5W	dextrose 5% in water

DX	diagnosis
	difficulty
	discharged
	disease
DXD	discontinued
DXR	deep Xray
DYSP	dyspnea
EAB	elective abortion
EAC	external auditory canal
EBL	estimated blood loss
EBV	Epstein-Barr virus
EC	Escherichia coli
	eyes closed
ECC	endocervical curettage
ECCE	extracapsular cataract extraction
ECF	extended care facility
ECG	electrocardiogram
ECHO	echocardiogram
ECT	electroconvulsive shock therapy
ECU	extensor carpi ulnaris
ED	edema
	emergency department
EDC	estimated date of confinement
EEG	electroencephalogram
EENT	eyes, ears, nose, throat
EGD	esophagogastroduodenoscopy
EIB	exercise-induced bronchospasm
EJ	elbow jerk
EKG	electrocardiogram
EL	elbow
ELISA	enzyme-linked immunosorbent assay
EM	ejection murmur
	endometrial
EMB	embolus
EMG	electromyelography
	electromyogram
	electromyography
EMS	electrical muscle stimulation
	eosinophilic myalgia syndrome

EMT	emergency medical technician
ENDO	endoscopy
	endotracheal
ENG	electronystagmogram
ENL	enlarged
ENT	ear, nose, throat
EOM	equal ocular movements
	external otitis media
	extraocular movements
	extraocular muscles
EOMI	extraocular movements intact
EOMM	extraocular movements, muscles
EOS	eosinophils
EP	ectopic pregnancy
EPI	epinephrine
ER	emergency room
	equal and reactive
	equal and regular
	evoked response
	external rotation
ERA	estrogen receptor assay
ERCP	endoscopic retrograde cholangiopancreatography
ERE	external rotation in extension
ERF	external rotation in flexion
ES	electrical stimulation
ESR	erythrocytic sedimentation rate
ESRD	end stage renal disease
ESRF	end stage renal failure
EST	electroshock therapy
ESWL	extracorporeal shockwave lithotripsy
ET	endotracheal
	etiology
	eustachian tube
ETI	endotracheal intubation
ETKM	every test known to man
ETOH	ethyl alcohol
ETT	exercise tolerance test
EUA	examination under anesthetic
EX	exacerbate
	exaggerate

	examination
	example
	excision
EXC	excellent
	except
	exchange
	excise
EXP	expand
	expecting
	expiration
	expired
	explain
EXT	extend
	extension
	extensive
	extensor
	exterior
	external
	extract
	extreme
	extremity

F	Fahrenheit
FA	failed appointment
	forearm
	functional activities
FABERE	flexion, abduction, external rotation, extension
FACP	fellow of the American College of Physicians
FACS	fellow of the American College of Surgeons
FACOG	fellow of the American College of Obstetrics and Gynecology
FADIR	flexion, adduction, internal rotation
FADIRE	flexion, adduction, internal rotation, extension
FB	foreign body
FBD	functional bowel disorder
FBS	fasting blood sugar
FCA	fracture, complete, angulated
FCC	fracture, complete, comminuted
	fracture, compound, comminuted
FCCC	fracture, complete, comminuted, compound

FCD	fracture, complete, deviated
FD	family doctor
FE	female
	iron
FEB	fever
FEF	forced expiratory flow
FEM	femoral
FER	flexion, extension, rotation
FEV	forced expiratory volume
FF	forward flexion
FFC	fixed flexion contracture
FFD	free from disability
FFT	forward flexion: fingertips to toes
FFROM	full, free range of motion
FH	family history
FHX	family history
F/I	fever due to infection
FIB	fibrillation
	fibrous
	fibula
FIF	forced inspiratory flow
FIO2	fraction of inspired oxygen
FJRM	full joint range of motion
FL	flank
	flexion
	fluid
	full liquid
FLEX	flexion
FLK	funny-looking kid
FLX	flexion
FMD	family medical doctor
FNA	fine needle aspiration
FNF	finger-nose-finger test
FPM	full passive movements
FR	fracture
	frequency of respiration
	full range
FRBB	fracture of both bones
FRJM	full range of joint movement

FROM	full range of movement
FS	frozen section
FSC	fracture, simple, comminuted
FSCC	fracture, simple, complete, comminuted
FSH	follicle-stimulating hormone
FT	feet
	foot
	full-term
FTI	free thyroxine index
FTKA	failed to keep appointment
FTSG	full thickness skin graft
F/U	follow up
FUO	fever of unknown origin
FVC	forced vital capacity
FWB	full weightbearing
FX	fracture
FXBB	fracture of both bones
GA	gastric analysis
	general anesthesia
	general appearance
GB	gallbladder
GBD	gallbladder disease
GC	general condition
	gonococcal
	gonococcus
GE	gastroenteritis
GEA	general endotracheal anesthesia
GER	gastroesophageal reflux
GG	gamma globulin
GH	general health
GI	gastrointestinal
GL	glaucoma
GM	gram(s)
	grand mal
GMA	gross motor activity
GOK	God only knows (diagnosis)
GP	general practitioner

GR	gastric resection
	grain
	great, greater
	gross, grossly
	group
GS	gram stain
GSW	gunshot wound
GT	gait training
GTT	glucose tolerance test
GTTS	drops
GU	gastric ulcer
	genitourinary
GXT	graded exercise test
H2O2	hydrogen peroxide
HA	headache
	high anxiety
	hospital admission
HAA	hepatitis-associated antibodies
HAS	hospital ambulatory surgery
HBD	has been drinking
HBF	hepatic blood flow
HBP	high blood pressure
HBSAG	hepatitis B surface antigen
HCG	human chorionic gonadotrophin
HCL	hydrochloric acid
HCT	hematocrit
HCTZ	hydrochlorothiazide
HCVD	hypertensive cardiovascular disease
HD	heart disase
	hemodialysis
	hospital day
HDL	high density lipoprotein
HDS	herniated disc syndrome
HEENT	head, ears, eyes, nose, throat
HEP	heparin lock
	home exercise program
HF	hay fever
	heart failure
HGB	hemoglobin

HH	hard of hearing
	hiatus hernia
HHN	hand-held nebulizer
HIF	higher intellectual functions
HJR	hepatojugular reflex
HL	hearing loss
	heart and lungs
HLA	heart, lungs, abdomen
HLK	heart, liver, kidney
HLV	herpes-like virus
HM	heart murmur
HMO	health maintenance organization
HMP	hot moist packs
HNP	herniated nucleus pulposus
HNV	has not voided
HO	history of
HOB	head of bed
H&P	history and physical
HP	hot pack
HPE	history and physical examination
HPF	high power field
HPI	history of present illness
HR	heart rate
	hospital record
	hour
HS	bedtime
	heart sounds
HSM	hepatosplenomegaly masses
HSV	herpes simplex virus
HT	heart
	height
	hospital treatment
	hypertension
	hyperthyroidism
HTN	hypertension
HV	hepatic vein
	herpes virus
	home visit
	hospital visit
	hyperventilation

HVD	hypertensive vascular disease
HW	healing well
HWP	hot wet pack
HX	history
IA	incurred accidentally
	intra-arterial
	intra-articular
	intra-atrial
IAC	internal acoustic canal
IBW	ideal body weight
IC	between meals
	inspiratory capacity
	intensive care
	intercostal
	intracerebral
	intracutaneous
	irritable colon
ICC	intensive coronary care
ICCU	intensive coronary care unit
ICDA	International Classification of Diseases, Adapted
ICF	intensive care facility
ICFX	intracapsular fracture
ICM	intercostal margin
ICN	intensive care nursery
ICP	intracranial pressure
ICS	intercostal space
ICT	intermittent cervical traction
ICU	intensive care unit
I&D	incision & drainage
ID	during the day
	identification
	idiopathic
	ill-defined
	ineffective dose
	infectious disease
	initial dose
	intradermal
IDA	iron deficiency anemia

IDD	insulin-dependent diabetes
IDK	internal derangement of the knee
IDR	intradermal reaction
IDVC	indwelling venous catheter
I&E	inspiration and expiration
	internal and external
IE	inner ear
	inspiratory-expiratory ratio
IFR	inspiratory flow rate
IgA	immunoglobulin A
IgE	immunoglobulin E
IgG	immunoglobulin G
IgM	immunoglobulin M
IH	infectious hepatitis
	interval history
IHD	ischemic heart disease
IHO	idiopathic hypertrophic osteoarthropathy
IHR	intrinsic heart rate
IL	ilio-lumbar
IM	infectious mononucleosis
	internal malleolus
	internal medicine
	intramuscular
IMBC	indirect maximum breathing capacity
IME	independent medical examination
IMI	intramuscular injection
IMM	immediate
	immobilize
	immunize
IMP	impression
	improved
IN	inch(es)
INC	incomplete
	inconclusive
	increase
IND	independent
	index
	indicated

INF	infant
	infarction
	infected
	inferior
	influenza
ING	inguinal
INJ	inject
	injection
	injury
INK	injury not known
INS	insulin
	insurance
INR	intermittent
	interval
INSP	inspiration
IO	intestinal obstruction
	intraocular
I&O	intake and output
IOFB	intraocular foreign body
IOL	intraocular lens
IOP	intraocular pressure
IOU	intensive therapy observation unit
IP	interphalangeal
	intraperitoneal
IPL	intrapleural
IPPA	inspection, palpation, percussion, auscultation
IPPB	intermittent positive-pressure breathing
IPPO	intermittent positive-pressure inflation with oxygen
IPPR	intermittent positive-pressure respiration
IPPV	intermittent positive-pressure ventilation
IR	internal rotation
IRE	internal rotation in extension
IRF	internal rotation in flexion
IS	in situ
	incentive spirometry
	intercostal space
	interspace
ISL	interscapular line
ISO	isometric
IST	insulin shock therapy

IT	individual therapy
	inhalation therapy
	intensive therapy
	interdermal test
	intermittent traction
	intertrochanteric
	intratracheal tube
ITH	intrathecal
ITT	internal tibial torsion
ITP	idiopathic thrombocytopenic purpura
ITT	internal tibial torsion
IU	immunizing unit
	international unit
	intrauterine
IUD	intrauterine death
	intrauterine device
IUFB	intrauterine foreign body
IUP	intrauterine pregnancy
IUT	intrauterine transfusion
IV	in vitro
	in vivo
	intervertebral
	intravascular
	intravenous
IVC	intravenous cholangiogram
IVD	intervertebral disc
IVJC	intervertebral joint complex
IVP	intravenous push
	intravenous pyelogram
JAMA	*Journal of the American Medical Association*
JCT	junction
JJ	jaw jerk
JND	just noticeable difference
JRA	juvenile rheumatoid arthritis
JT	joint
JUV	juvenile
JV	jugular vein
JVD	jugular venous distension
JVP	jugular venous pulse

K	potassium
KA	ketoacidosis
KB	knee-bearing amputation
KCL	potassium chloride
KFT	kidney function test
KG	kilogram
KI	potassium iodide
KJ	knee jerk
KK	knee kick
KLS	kidney, liver, spleen
KUB	kidney, ureter, and bladder Xray
KVO	keep vein open
L	liter(s)
L1–L5	lumbar vertebrae 1–5
LA	left arm
	local anesthesia
	long action
	long arm
L&A	light and accommodation
	living and active
LAC	laceration
	long arm cast
LAD	left anterior descending
LAE	left atrial enlargement
	long above elbow (cast)
LAHB	left anterior hemiblock
LAM	laminectomy
	laminogram
LANC	long arm navicular cast
LAP	laparotomy
LAPB	long arm plaster bandage
LAR	left arm reclining/recumbent
LAS	left arm sitting
	long arm splint
LASER	light amplification by stimulated emission of radiation
LAT	latent
	lateral

LB	large bowel
	lateral bending
	live birth
	loose body
	low back
L&B	left and below
LBB	low back bend
LBBB	left bundle branch block
LBE	long below elbow
LBH	length, breadth, height
LBP	low back pain
	low blood pressure
LBT	low back tenderness
LBW	low birth weight
LC	left cornea
	lethal concentration
	living children
LCB	left costal border
LCFA	long chain fatty acids
LCM	left costal margin
LD	left deltoid muscle
	lethal dose
	light difference perception
	living donor
LDD	light-dark discrimination
LDL	low density lipoprotein
LDP	lumbo-dorsal pain
LE	laboratory examination
	last examination
	left eye
	lower extremity
	lupus erythematosus
LEVA	left eye visual acuity
LF	left foot
	linear fracture
	low frequency
LFA	left forearm
LFT	liver function test
LG	large
	laryngectomy

	left gluteal muscle
	leg
	long
LH	left hand
L&H	lungs and heart
LHG	left-hand grip
LHS	left-hand side
LIC	left iliac crest
LICM	left intercostal margin
LICS	left intercostal space
LIF	left iliac fossa
	left index finger
LIG	ligament
LIH	left inguinal hernia
LIM	limited
LIO	left inferior oblique
LIQ	left inner quadrant
	liquid
LIR	left iliac region
LK	left kidney
LKS	liver, kidney, spleen
LL	left lateral
	left leg
	left lower
	left lung
	lethal level
	long leg
	lower lobe
LLB	left lateral bending
	long leg brace
LLC	long leg cast
LLCC	long leg cylinder cast
LLD	leg length discrepancy
LLE	left lower extremity
LLF	left lateral flexion
	left little finger
LLL	left lower leg
	left lower lid
	left lower lobe

	left lower lung
LLN	lower limit of normal
LLQ	left lower quadrant
LLR	left lateral rectus
	left lumbar region
LLS	long leg splint
LLWC	long leg walking cast
LLX	left lower extremity
LMF	left middle finger
LML	left middle lobe
LMN	lower motor neuron
LMP	last menstrual period
	lumbar puncture
LMR	left medial rectus
LN	lymph node
LNMP	last normal menstrual period
LOA	leave of absence
LOC	level of consciousness
	loss of consciousness
LOM	left otitis media
	limitation of movement
	loss of movement
LOQ	left lower quadrant
	left outer quadrant
LOS	length of stay
	loss of sight
LP	light perception
	low pressure
	lumbar puncture
LPA	licensed physician's assistant
LPH	left posterior hemiblock
LPI	laser peripheral iridotomy
LPN	licensed practical nurse
LPO	light perception only
LQ	lower quadrant
LR	lactated Ringer's solution
	left rotation
	lethal range
	light reaction

LRF	left ring finger
LRQ	lower right quadrant
LRS	lactated Ringer's solution
LRT	lower respiratory tract
LS	left side
	liver and spleen
	lumbar spine
	lumbosacral
L&S	liver and spleen
LSK	liver, spleen, kidneys
LSO	left superior oblique
LSP	lumbar spine
LT	left
	left thigh
	left thumb
	long-term
LTC	laparoscopic tubal cauterization
LTD	limited
LTP	laser trabeculoplasty
LTS	laparoscopic tubal sterilization
	long tract sign
LU	left upper
LUA	left upper arm
LUE	left upper extremity
LUL	left upper lid
	left upper limb
	left upper lobe
	left upper lung
LUOQ	left upper outer quadrant
LUQ	left upper quadrant
LV	lung volume
LVE	left ventricular enlargement
LVEDP	left ventricular and diastolic pressure
LVH	left ventricular hypertrophy
LVN	licensed vocational nurse
LVR	lumbar ventral nerve root
L&W	living and well
LX	lower extremity

M	meter(s)
MA	medical authorization
	menstrual age
	mental age
	moderately advanced
	muscle activity
MAC	macerated
	maximum allowable concentration
MAJ	major
	majority
MAL	malignant
MAO	monoamine oxidase
MAPS	make a picture story
MAS	manifest anxiety scale
MASS	massage
	massive
MAT	maternal
MAX	maxilla
	maximal
	maximum
MB	muscle balance
MBC	maximal breathing capacity
MBD	minimal brain dysfunction
MBH	maximum benefit from hospitalization
MCL	midclavicular line
MD	medical doctor
	midnight
MDC	minimum detectable concentration
MDV	multiple dose vial
ME	medical examiner
	middle ear
MED	minimum effective dose
	medial
	median
MEDLARS	Medical Literature Analysis and Retrieval System
MEDS	medications
	medicines
MEF	maximal expiratory flow
MEFR	maximal expiratory flow rate

MEH	medical eye history
MEL	melanoma
	melena
M&F	mother and father
MFD	midforceps delivery
	minimum fatal dose
MFT	muscle function test
MFU	medical follow up
MFW	multiple fragment wounds
MG	milligram(s)
	muscle group
MH	marital history
	medical history
	mental health
MHB	maximum hospital benefit
MHR	maximal heart rate
MI	mental illness
	mitral insufficiency
	myocardial infarction
MIC	minimal inhibitory concentration
MICU	mobile intensive care unit
MID	minimum infective dose
MIF	maximal inspiratory flow
MIFR	maximal inspiratory flow rate
MIN	minimal
	minimum
	minor
	minute
MK	marked
MKV	measles, killed vaccine
ML	maximum to left
	middle lobe
	midline
	milliliter(s)
MLC	minimum lethal concentration
MLD	minimum lethal dose
MM	malignant melanoma
	medial malleolus
	millimeter(s)

	movement
	mucous membrane
	murmur
	muscles
MMF	maximal midexpiratory flow
MMFR	maximal midexpiratory flow rate
MMPI	Minnesota Multiphasic Personality Inventory
MMST	muscle strength
MMT	manual muscle test
MOD	medical officer of day
	moderate
MOM	milk of magnesia
MONO	mononucleosis
MP	menstrual period
	metacarpophalangeal
	moist pack
	motor power
	multiparous
MPC	maximum permissible concentration
MPD	maximum permissible dose
	myofascial pain disorder
MPI	multiphasic personality inventory
MR	maximum to right
	mental retardation
MRI	magnetic resonance imaging
MRM	modified radical mastectomy
MS	medical student
	mental status
	minor surgery
	morphine sulfate
	multiple sclerosis
	muscle strength
	muscles
	musculoskeletal
MSTI	multiple soft tissue injuries
MT	manual traction
	maximal therapy
	medical technologist
	more than

	muscle test
	muscles and tendons
MTD	maximum tolerated dose
MTR	masses, tenderness, rebound
MTRG	masses, tenderness, rebound, guarding
MULTIP	multiparous
MUO	myocardiopathy of unknown origin
MUS	muscle
MV	mitral valve
MVA	motor vehicle accident
MVC	maximum vital capacity
MVP	mitral valve prolapse
MVT	movement
MVV	maximum volume ventilation
	maximum voluntary ventilation
MWD	microwave diathermy
NA	no abnormalities
	not admitted
	not applicable
	not available
NAA	no apparent abnormalities
NAD	no active disease
	no acute distress
	normal axis deviation
	nothing abnormal detected
NAG	narrow angle glaucoma
NAI	no acute infection
NAR	narcotic
	no action required
NB	newborn
NBI	no bone injury
NBM	nothing by mouth
NBS	normal bowel sounds
NC	no change
	no complaint
	noncontributory
N&C	nerves and circulation
NCD	not considered disabling
	not considered disqualifying

NCNS	no complications, no sequelae
NCO	no complaints offered
NCS	nerve conduction studies
NCV	nerve conduction velocity
ND	nondisabling
	not dictated
	not done
NE	nerve ending
	neurologic examination
NED	no evidence of disease
NG	nasogastric
NH	nursing home
NIDD	non-insulin dependent diabetes
NIH	National Institutes of Health
NIL	nothing
NIP	no infection present
	no inflammation present
NK	not known
NKA	no known allergies
NKD	no known disease
NL	normal
	normal limits
NLM	National Library of Medicine
NLP	no light perception
	normal light perception
NM	neuromuscular
	not measured
	not mentioned
N&M	nerves and muscles
NMA	neurogenic muscular atrophy
NMI	no middle initial
NMJ	neuromuscular injection
NMN	no middle name
NMP	normal menstrual period
NMTS	neuromuscular tension state
NN	neonatal
	nerves
	nurses' notes
NNR	not necessary to return

NO	number
NOC	night
NOK	next of kin
NOP	no ocular pain
	not otherwise provided for
NOS	not on staff
	not otherwise specified
NP	nasopharynx
	nerve palsy
	neuropathology
	neuropsychiatric
	new patient
	not palpable
	not performed
	nurse practitioner
	nursing procedures
NPC	no previous complaint
	nonproductive cough
NPH	no previous history
NPO	nothing by mouth
NOP MN	nothing by mouth after midnight
NPT	normal pressure and temperature
NR	nerve root
	no report
	no respirations
	no results
	normal range
	normal reaction
	normal report
	not remarkable
NRB	non-rebreathing system
NRI	nerve root involvement
	nerve root irritation
NRM	normal range of motion
NRN	no return necessary
NROM	normal range of motion
NS	nerves
	neurosurgery
	nonspecific

	nonsymptomatic
	normal saline
	no-show
	not significant
	not specified
	not sufficient
NSA	no significant abnormalities
NSAD	no sign of significant disease
NSAID	nonsteroidal anti-inflammatory drug
NSC	no significant change
NSD	no significant defect
	no significant difference
	normal spontaneous delivery
NSF	no significant findings
NSG	nursing
NSI	no sign of infection
	no sign of inflammation
NSR	normal sinus rhythm
NSS	normal saline solution
	normal size and shape
NSU	nonspecific urethritis
NT	nasotracheal
	nerve treatment
	no test
	normal temperature
	not tender
	not tested
N&T	nose and throat
NTG	nitroglycerine
NTP	normal temperature and pressure
NULLIP	nulliparous
NV	neurovascular
N&V	nausea and vomiting
NVD	nausea, vomiting, diarrhea
	neovascularization of disc
NWB	non-weight-bearing
NYD	not yet diagnosed
O	oral
O2	oxygen

OA	osteoarthritis
OAG	open angle glaucoma
OAP	osteoarthropathy
OB	obstetrics
OBD	organic brain disease
OBJ	object
	objective
OBL	oblique
OBP	ova, blood, and parasites
OBS	observer
	obstetrics
	organic brain syndrome
OC	on call
	oral contraceptive
OCC	occasionally
	occiput
	occupation
OCD	osteochondritis dissecans
OCG	oral cholecystogram
OCU	outpatient care unit
OD	occupational disease
	oculus dexter (right eye)
	officer of the day
	once daily
	overdose
OE	on examination
	orthopedic examination
	otitis externa
O&E	observation and examination
OH	occupational history
OI	otitis internal
OM	occupational medicine
	osteopathic manipulation
	otitis media
ON	optic nerve
ONC	oncology
OOB	out of bed
OOP	out of plaster
OP	operation
	outpatient

O&P	ova and parasites
OPC	outpatient clinic
OPP	opposite
OPT	outpatient treatment
OPV	oral polio vaccine
	outpatient visit
OR	open reduction
	operating room
	oriented
ORG	organic
ORIF	open reduction internal fixation
ORT	operating room technician
OS	mouth
	oculus sinister (left eye)
	oral surgery
OT	objective test
	occupational therapy
OTC	over the counter
OU	both eyes
	each eye
	observation unit
OUQ	outer upper quadrant
OV	office visit
OZ	ounce(s)
pO2	partial pressure of oxygen
P1, P2	used with "gravida" to designate the number of pregnancies that resulted in live births
P2	pulmonary second sound
PA	posteroanterior
	pulmonary artery
P&A	percussion & auscultation
PAC	phenacetin, aspirin, codeine
PACU	postanesthesia care unit
PAF	paroxysmal atrial fibrillation
PAP	passive aggressive personality disorder
PAR	postanesthesia recovery
PARA	paraplegic

PAT	paroxysmal atrial tachycardia
	patella
	patient
PB	phenobarbital
	pressure breathing
PBA	pressure breathing assistor
PC	after meals
	phone call
	posterior cervical
	posterior chamber
	present complaint
PCA	patient-controlled anesthesia
PCIOL	posterior chamber intraocular lens
PCN	penicillin
pCO2	partial pressure of carbon dioxide
PCP	pneumocystis carinii pneumonia
PCS	postconcussion syndrome
PCU	progressive care unit
PCV	packed cell volume
PD	partial denture
	per diem
	poorly differentiated
	potential difference
	progression of disease
	pulmonary disease
PDE	paroxysmal dyspnea on exertion
PDH	past dental history
PDR	*Physicians' Desk Reference*
PE	pedal edema
	pelvic examination
	physical evaluation
	physical examination
	point of entry
	present examination
	probable error
	pulmonary embolus
PEEP	positive end-expiratory flow rate
PEF	peak expiratory flow
PEFR	peak expiratory flow rate

PEN	penicillin
PEP	psychiatric evaluation profile
PER OS	by mouth
PERLA	pupils equal, reactive to light & accommodation
PERRLA	pupils equal, round, reactive to light & accommodation
PET	positron emission tomography
PF	past findings
	peak flow
	pertinent findings
	plantar flexion
PFR	peak flow rate
PFT	pulmonary function test
PGP	progressive general paralysis
PH	past history
	personal history
	physical history
	public health
PHN	public health nurse
PHX	past history
PI	personal injury
	present illness
PICU	pulmonary intensive care unit
PID	pelvic inflammatory disease
	post-inertia dyskinesia
	prolapsed intervertebral disc
PIF	peak inspiratory flow
PIFR	peak inspiratory flow rate
PIIS	posterior inferior iliac spine
PIP	peak inspiratory pressure
	probable intrauterine pregnancy
	proximal interphalangeal
PKU	phenylketonuria
PL	plan
	plasma
	plastic surgeon
PLT	pinprick light touch
PM	after noon
	physical medicine
	postmortem
	preventive medicine

PMA	positive mental attitude
	progressive muscular atrophy
PMD	primary medical doctor
	private medical doctor
PMH	past medical history
PMI	past medical illness
	point of maximum impact
PMR	prior menstrual period
PM&R	physical medicine and rehabilitation
PMS	poor miserable soul
	postmenopausal syndrome
	premenstrual syndrome
PMT	premenstrual tension
PN	pain
	peripheral neuropathy
	postnasal
PNB	prostate needle biopsy
PND	paroxysmal nocturnal dyspnea
	postnasal drip
PNF	proprioceptive neuromuscular fasciculation
PNI	peripheral nerve injury
PNPB	positive-negative pressure breathing
PNPR	positive-negative pressure respiration
PNS	parasympathetic nervous system
	peripheral nervous system
PO	by mouth
	parieto-occipital
	period of onset
	postoperative
POAG	progressive open angle glaucoma
POC	products of conception
POD	postoperative day
POMR	problem-oriented medical record
POP	popliteal
PORT	portable
POS	position
	positive
	possible
POST	posterior

POT	potential
POX	point of exit
PP	pedal pulses
	peripheral pulses
	pinpoint pupils
	pinprick
	positive pressure
	postpartum
	presenting problem
	private physician
	private practice
	pulse pressure
PP&A	palpation, percussion, and auscultation
PPB	positive pressure breathing
PPD	packs per day
	permanent partial disability
PPH	past pertinent history
	postpartum hemorrhage
PPV	positive pressure ventilation
PR	partial remission
	peer review
	per rectum
	progress record
	progressive resistance
	pulse rate
PRA	progressive resistance to arms
PRC	packed red cells
PRD	partial reaction of degeneration
PRE	physical reconditioning exercise
	progressive resistance exercise
PRE-OP	pre-operative
PREV	previous
PRH	past relevant history
PRL	passive resistance to leg
PRN	as needed
PROM	passive range of motion
	premature rupture of membranes
PROX	proximal
PRP	psychotic reaction profile

PRRE	pupils round, regular, and equal
PRT	patient refused test
PS	paraspinous
	physical status
	prescription
	present symptoms
P&S	permanent and stationary
PSIS	posterior superior iliac spine
PSP	posterior spinous process
PSR	paranoid schizophrenic reaction
PSV	pressure support ventilation
PSW	psychiatric social worker
PT	patient
	permanent and total
	physical therapy
	pneumothorax
PTA	prior to admission
PTD	permanent total disability
PTH	prior to hospitalization
PTR	patellar tendon reflex
	pelvic traction
PTSD	post-traumatic stress disorder
PTT	partial thromboplastin time
PUD	peptic ulcer disease
	peptic ulcer duodenal
	pulmonary disease
PV	paravertebral
PVC	premature ventricular contraction
PVT	pressure, volume, temperature
	private
PWB	partial weightbearing
PX	physical examination
	pneumothorax
	prescription
	prognosis
Q	every
QD	every day
QH	every hour

QID	4 times a day
QMT	quantitative muscle testing
QN	every night
QNS	quantity not sufficient
QOD	every other day
QOH	every other hour
QON	every other night
QP	as much as desired
	at will
QPM	every afternoon
QS	sufficient quantity
QT	quantity
	quart
	quiet
QUAD	quadriceps
QV	as much as desired
RA	rheumatoid arthritis
	right angle
	right arm
RAD	radiate
	radicular
RAE	right atrial enlargement
RAM	rapid alternating movements
RAR	right arm reclining or recumbent
RAS	right arm sitting
RBBB	right bundle branch block
RBBX	right breast biopsy
RBC	red blood cell
RC	red cell
	respirations ceased
RCM	right costal margin
RD	radial deviation
	Raynaud's disease
	reaction of degeneration
	renal disease
	respiratory disease
	respiratory distress
RDM	readmission

RE	regarding
	resistive exercises
	right eye
REC	rear end collision
	receive
	recommend
	recurrent
RED	reduce
	reduction
REF	refer
REG	regular
RELE	resistive exercises, lower extremities
REM	rapid eye movements
	removal
RESP	respiration
RET	retention
	retired
	returned
REUE	resistive exercises, upper extremities
REV	review
RF	renal failure
RFA	right forearm
RFB	retained foreign body
RFT	renal function test
RH	right hand
RHA	rheumatoid arthritis
RHD	rheumatic heart disease
RHS	right hand side
RI	respiratory illness
	respiratory infection
RIC	right iliac crest
RICM	right intercostal margin
RICU	respiratory intensive care unit
RID	ruptured intervertebral disc
RIF	right iliac fossa
	right index finger
RIH	right inguinal hernia
RIO	right inferior oblique
RIR	right iliac region

RIVD	ruptured intervertebral disc
RL	right leg
	right lobe
	right lower
	right lung
RLA	react to light and accommodation
RLB	right lateral bending
RLC	residual lung capacity
RLE	right lower extremity
RLF	right lateral flexion
RLIPP	resistive intermittent positive pressure
RLL	right lower lateral
	right lower leg
	right lower limb
	right lower lobe
RLQ	right lower quadrant
RLR	right lateral rectus
	right lumbar region
RLX	right lower extremity
RM	radical mastectomy
	respiratory movement
RMF	right middle finger
RN	registered nurse
RND	radical neck dissection
RO	routine order
	rule out
ROM	range of motion
	range of movement
	right otitis media
	Romberg test
	rupture of membranes
ROMCPF	range of motion complete and pain free
ROQ	right outer quadrant
ROS	review of symptoms
	review of systems
ROSS	review of subject systems
ROT	rotation
RP	radial pulse
	referring physician

RPG	retrograde pyelogram
RPT	registered physical therapist
	repeat
	report
RR	recovery room
	regular rhythm
	respiratory rate
RRCT	regular rate, clear tones
RR&E	round, regular, and equal
RRF	right ring finger
RRM	right radical mastectomy
RRR	regular rate and rhythm
	round, reactive, regular
RRT	registered rehabilitation therapist
RS	respiratory system
	review of symptoms
	review of systems
	right side
RSI	repetitive stress injury
RSO	right superior oblique
RSR	regular sinus rhythm
RT	radiotherapy
	reaction time
	recreational therapy
	respiratory therapy
RTC	return to clinic
RTW	return to work
RU	right upper
RUA	right upper arm
RUE	right upper extremity
RUL	right upper lateral
	right upper limb
	right upper lobe
RUOQ	right upper outer quadrant
RUQ	right upper quadrant
RVC	return visit to clinic
RVE	right ventricular enlargement
RX	prescription
	treatment
RXN	reaction

S	without
S1	first heart sound
S1–5	sacral vertebrae 1–5
SAB	spontaneous abortion
SAC	sacral
	sacrum
	short arm cast
SAS	short arm splint
SAT	satisfactory
SB	scleral buckle
	small bowel
	sternal border
S/B	standby
SBA	standby assist
SBD	senile brain disease
SBE	short below elbow
	subacute bacterial endocarditis
SBO	small bowel obstruction
SBR	strict bed rest
SC	sacrococcygeal
	scapula
	self-care
	sternoclavicular
	subcutaneous
S&C	sclera and cornea
SCD	service connected disability
SCFE	slipped capital femoral epiphysis
SCI	spinal cord injury
SCL	scleroderma
	sclerosis
SCM	sternocleidomastoid
SC&M	sensation, circulation, and motion
SD	septal defect
	spontaneous delivery
	sterile dressing
	subdural
	sudden death
SDD	sterile dry dressing
SDS	sudden death syndrome

SEC	second
SED	sedimentation
SEM	scanning electron microscope
	semen
	seminal
	systolic ejection murmur
SENS	sensation
	sensory
SEP	seperate
	separation
SEQ	sequela
SF	spinal fluid
SFD	silver fork deformity
SFP	spinal fluid pressure
SGOT	serum glutamic oxalacete transaminase
SGPT	serum glutamic pyruvic transaminase
SH	self help
	serum hepatitis
	shoulder
	social history
	surgical history
SHO	secondary hypertrophic osteoarthropathy
SI	sacroiliac
	self-inflicted
	stress incontinence
SICU	surgical intensive care unit
SID	once per day
SIDS	sudden infant death syndrome
SIJ	sacroiliac joint
SIQ	self-inflicted wound
SIT	situational
SK	skeletal
SKTR	skeletal traction
SL	slight
	slit lamp
SLB	short leg brace
SLC	short leg cast
SLE	slit lamp examination
	systemic lupus erythematosus

SLR	straight leg raising
SLS	short leg splint
SLT	slight
SLWC	short leg walking cast
SM	simple mastectomy
	small
	systolic murmur
SMA	superior mesenteric artery
SMD	senile macular degeneration
SNB	scalene node biopsy
SNF	skilled nursing facility
SNS	sympathetic nervous system
SNST	sciatic nerve stretch test
SNT	sinuses, nose, and throat
SO	salpingo-oophorectomy
	supraorbital
	sutures out
SOAP	subjective, objective, assessment, plan
SOB	short of breath
SOER	special orthopedic examination and report
SOL	solution
SOM	serous otitis media
SONP	soft organs not palpable
SOP	standard operating procedure
SOS	repeat once if necessary
	stimulation of senses
SP	spinal
	spine
	supra-pubic
SPAS	spasticity
SPD	sociopathic personality disorder
SPL	splint
SPR	sprain
SQ	squamous
	status quo
	subcutaneous
SR	schizophrenic reaction
	sensitization response
	sinus rhythm

	stretch reflex
	systems review
SS	sacrosciatic
	saline soak
	signs and symptoms
	sitting and standing
	soapsuds
SSC	size, shape, and consistency
SSE	soapsuds enema
SSN	severely subnormal
ST	shock therapy
	slight trace
	speech therapy
	sphincter tone
	stomach
STAT	immediately
STD	sexually transmitted disease
	skin test dose
STG	split thickness skin graft
STL	swelling, tenderness, limitation
STLOM	swelling, tenderness, limitation of motion
STM	soft tissue massage
STN	sphincter tone normal
STP	standard temperature and pulse
STR	straight
	strain
	strength
STS	serological test for syphilis
STSAG	split thickness skin graft
SUBq	subcutaneous
SUD	sudden unexpected or unexplained death
SUDI	suddent unexpected death, infant
SUP	superior
	supination
	supine
SVD	spontaneous vaginal delivery
SW	stab wound
	swelling
	swollen

SWD	short wave diathermy
SX	symptoms
SYM	symmetric
	symptom(s)
SYS	system(s)
	systemic
	systolic
SZ	schizophrenia
	seizure
T1–T12	thoracic vertebrae 1–12
TA	traffic accident
T&A	tonsillectomy and adenoidectomy
	tonsils and adenoids
TAB	therapeutic abortion
TACH	tachycardia
TAH	total abdominal hysterectomy
TAL	tendon Achilles lengthening
TAT	tetanus antitoxin
	thematic apperception test
TB	total body
	tuberculosis
TBA	to be arranged
TBF	total body fat
TBLC	term birth, living child
TBV	total blood volume
TBW	total body weight
TC	throat culture
	tissue culture
	total cholesterol
T&C	turn and cough
	type and crossmatch
TCI	transient cerebral ischemia
TCN	tetracycline
TCU	transitional care unit
TD	total disability
TDWB	touch down weightbearing
TE	therapeutic exercises
TEN	tension

TEND	tender
TENS	transelectrical nerve stimulator
TF	tube feeding
TH	thoracic
THC	tetrahydrocortisone
THOR	thoracic
THR	total hip replacement
TIA	transient ischemia attack
TIB	tibia
TID	three times a day
TIN	three times a night
TIW	three times a week
TJ	triceps jerk
TKO	to keep open
TL	tubal ligation
TLC	total lung capacity
TM	temperature by mouth
	temporomandibular
	tender midline
	tympanic membrane
TMAS	Taylor Manifest Anxiety Scale
TMJ	temporomandibular joint
TML	tender midline
	tongue in midline
TMT	tarso-metatarsal joint
TNC	too numerous to count
TND	test not done
TNS	tension
TOPV	trivalent oral polio vaccine
TOS	thoracic outlet syndrome
TOT	total
TOW	transfer off ward
TP	transverse process
TPD	temporary partial disability
TPN	total parenteral nutrition
TPR	temperature, pulse, respiration
TQ	tourniquet
TR	temperature, rectal
	therapeutic radiology
	total resistance

	total response
	trace
	traction
	trauma
	treatment
	tremor
T&R	tenderness and rebound
TRO	to return to office
TRT	treatment
TS	thoracic spine
TSD	Tay-Sachs disease
TSH	thyroid stimulating hormone
TSP	thoracic spine
TT	tactile tension
	total time
TTD	temporary total disability
TTP	thrombotic thrombocytopenia purpura
TUR	transurethral resection
TURB	transurethral resection of bladder
	turbinate
TURP	transurethral resection of prostate gland
TV	tinea versicolor
	total volume
	trichomonas vaginalis
TVC	timed vital capacity
TVH	total vaginal hysterectomy
TVR	thoracic ventral root
TWHW	toe walking, heel walking
TX	traction
	transplant
	treatment
TYP	typical
U	unit(s)
UA	umbilical artery
	uric acid
	urinalysis
UC	ulcerative colitis
	unchanged
	unconscious

UCD	usual childhood diseases
UCG	urinary chorionic gonadotrophin
UCR	unconditioned reflex response
UCS	unconditioned stimulus
	unconscious
UD	ulnar deviation
	underdeveloped
	urethral discharge
	urethral drainage
UE	undetermined etiology
	upper extremity
UGA	under general anesthesia
UGI	upper gastrointestinal
UIQ	upper inner quadrant
UK	unknown
UL	upper lobe
U&L	upper and lower
ULN	upper limits of normal
ULOQ	upper left outer quadrant
ULQ	upper left quadrant
UMN	upper motor neuron
UMNL	upper motor neuron lesion
U&MNP	ulnar and median nerve palsy
UN	ulnar nerve
UNC	uncertain
	unchanged
	uncomplicated
	unconscious
	uncooperative
UND	undetermined
UNG	ointment
UNK	unknown
UO	undetermined origin
	ureteral orifice
	urinary output
U/O	under observation for
UOQ	upper outer quadrant
UPOR	usual place of residence
UQ	upper quadrant

UR	unconditioned response
	upper respiratory
	urinary retention
	utilization review
URD	upper respiratory disease
URI	upper respiratory infection
UROQ	upper right outer quadrant
URQ	upper right quadrant
US	ultrasound
UT	urinary tract
	uterus
UTI	urinary tract infection
UTOC	upper thoracic outlet compression syndrome
UV	ultraviolet
	umbilical vein
	urinary volume
U/WB	unit of whole blood
V	vision
VA	vacuum aspiration
	vertebral artery
	visual acuity
VAG	vaginal
VAH	Veteran's Administration hospital
VALE	visual acuity, left eye
VAOD	visual acuity, right eye
VAOS	visual acuity, left eye
VAOU	visual acuity, both eyes
VAR	variation
	variety
VARE	visual acuity, right eye
VBP	venous blood pressure
VC	ventricular contraction
	vital capacity
	vocal cord
VD	veneral disease
	venous dilation
	ventrodorsal
VDA	visual discriminatory acuity

VE	vaginal examination
VERT	vertebra
	vertical
	vertigo
VF	ventricular fibrillation
	visual field
VFI	visual fields intact
VH	vaginal hysterectomy
VI	vaginal infection
	viral infection
VIT	vitamin(s)
VM	vasomotor
VMO	vastus medialis oblique
VMR	vasomotor rhinitis
VMS	visual memory span
VMT	vasomotor tone
VNA	Visiting Nurse's Association
VNR	ventral nerve root
VO	verbal order
VOC	vocal
	vocational
VOL	volatile
	volume
	voluntary
VP	venipuncture
	venous pressure
VPB	ventricular premature beats
VPC	ventricular premature contractions
	volume packed cells
VPS	vibrations per second
V&PS	vibration and peripheral sensation
VQ	voice quality
VR	ventilation rate
	ventral root
	ventricular rate
	vocational rehabilitation
VRC	ventral root, cervical
VRL	ventral root, lumbar
VRT	ventral root, thoracic

VS	vesicular sounds
	vital signs
VSBE	very short below elbow (cast)
VSD	ventral septal defect
VSO	vital signs normal
VSS	vital signs stable
VSTT	ventral spinothalamic tract
VT	ventricular tachycardia
VV	varicose veins
	veins
W/	with
W/A	weakness atrophy
WA	while awake
WAIS	Wechsler's adult intelligence scale
WB	weight-bearing
	whole blood
	whole body
WBC	well baby care
	well baby clinic
	white blood cell
WC	wheelchair
	will call
	work capacity
	worker's compensation
	wound check
WD	well-developed
	wound
W&D	warm and dry
WDWN	well-developed, well-nourished
W/E	wound of entry
WF	white female
WFO	will follow in office
WH	walking heel cast
	well-healed
	well-hydrated
WHP	whirlpool
WK	weak
	week
	work

WL	work load
WM	white male
WMF	white middle-aged female
WMM	white middle-aged male
WN	well-nourished
WNL	within normal limits
WO	written order
WOE	wound of entry
WOX	wound of exit
WP	wet pack
	whirlpool
WPD	whirlpool bath
WPK	wet pack
WR	weak response
	wrist
WT	weight
WTB	weight-bearing
W/U	workup
XIP	X ray in plaster
XOOP	X ray out of plaster
XOP	X ray out of plaster
XR	X ray
XT	exotropia
XYL	xylocaine
Y/A	years of age
YAG	yttrium aluminum garnet laser
YD	yard
YO	years old
YOB	year of birth
YR	year
Z	zero
ZD	zero defects
Z-PLASTY	plastic surgery skin repair technique
ZYG	zygoma

COMMON MEDICAL SYMBOLS

$-$	absent, negative
$\pm$	equivocal
$+$	plus, present

Reflexes	
$+$	just present
$++$	moderately reactive
$+++$	very reactive
$++++$	maximum reactivity

♂	male
♀	female
$\|\|$	parallel bars (physical therapy symbol)
$=$	equals
$\neq$	not equal
$\leq$	less than or equal to
$<$	less than
$\geq$	greater than or equal to
$>$	greater than
$\downarrow$	decreased, below

↑	above, increased
▲	change
√	observed
↓↓	down bilaterally
↑↑	up bilaterally
c̄	with
s̄	without
~	about, approximately equal to
∞	infinity
%	percent
∅	none, absent
1°, 2°	1 hour, 2 hours
1°	primary
2°	secondary
2 × 2	gauze pad dressing measuring 2 inches by 2 inches
4 × 4	gauze pad dressing measuring 4 inches by 4 inches
I, II	one, two
#	fracture; pound
?	questionable
ℨ	dram, teaspoon
℥	ounce
Ψ	psychology, psychiatric
μ	micro, micron
γ	gamma
α	alpha
β	beta

APPENDIX M

SURVEY OF STATE-SPECIFIC HIV/AIDS CITATIONS

Authors' Note: This survey of state-specific codes and cases regarding the confidentiality of HIV- and AIDS-related information is necessarily incomplete. The language in the cited statutes and cases has been edited for clarity and brevity, and is meant to be used as a reference only. The reader is advised to consult the original legal sources for the complete statute and references, and for other related statutes.

Alabama

Voluntary informed consent required for HIV test. A general consent form signed for medical or surgical treatment which specifies testing for HIV may be considered as meeting the standard of informed consent. Ala. Code § 22-11A-51.

When a written consent for HIV testing has not been obtained, consent shall be implied when an individual presents himself to a physician for diagnostic treatment or other medical services, and the physician shall determine that a test for HIV is necessary for any of the following reasons: said individual is, based upon reasonable medical judgment, at high risk for HIV infection; said individual's medical care may be modified by the presence or absence of HIV infection; knowledge of the HIV status of the individual is necessary to protect health care personnel from infection. Ala. Code § 22-11A-52.

Individuals shall be notified of positive test results; notification shall include face-to-face post-test counseling, information regarding health and mental health care, and explanation of the benefits of locating, testing, and counseling any individual who may have been exposed to HIV. Ala. Code § 22-11A-53.

HIV test results are confidential. Ala. Code § 22-11A-54.

Any health care worker infected with HIV or HBV who performs invasive procedures, as defined in 22-11A-60, shall notify the State Health Officer of the infection; any physician providing care to an infected health care worker shall notify the State Health Officer about the presence of the infection. Ala. Code § 22-11A-61.

No health care worker with knowledge that he or she is infected with either HIV or HBV shall perform or assist in the performance of an invasive procedure unless and until the State Health Officer has been notified and the health care worker has agreed to cooperate with any authorized investigation and any necessary practice modifications. Ala. Code § 22-11A-62.

Such a health care worker's practice will be reviewed not less than annually by an expert review panel. It shall be grounds for the revocation, suspension, or restriction of the professional license of any health care worker who fails to cooperate with the review. Ala. Code § 22-11A-63 to 22-11A-65.

Alaska

Persons charged with sexual offenses shall be tested for HIV and other sexually transmitted diseases; test results are confidential but may be released to the victim and the victim's parents or legal guardian if the victim is a minor. Health care providers are immune from civil liability for disclosing results of an HIV test unless the release was negligent or intentional. Alaska Stat. § 18.15.310.

Arizona

Oral or written consent required for testing; oral consent shall be documented in the medical record. Informed consent includes a discussion of the meaning of the test, the nature of the disease, confidentiality aspect, and the voluntary nature of the consent. Informed consent is not required under the following circumstances: in the procuring of human body parts for transplant; for statistical purposes only; during an autopsy to determine the cause of death; if necessary in providing emergency medical treatment to a person who lacks the capacity to consent; if the existence of an emergency medical condition necessitates an HIV test to diagnose and treat the emergency condition and the patient lacks the capacity to consent. Ariz. Rev. Stat. § 36-663.

Information is confidential but may be released to the following individuals or entities: the person who is the subject of the test or that individual's authorized representative; anyone authorized in a disclosure; the department of health as mandated by law; to quality assurance committees; under court order; to facilities engaged in the procuring of human body parts for transplant; for statistical purposes. Ariz. Rev. Stat. § 36-664.

Physician-to-medical-team disclosure permitted. Ariz. Rev. Stat. § 36-664(3-4).

A release of confidential communicable disease-related information shall be signed by the protected person, or if the protected person lacks the capacity to consent, a person authorized pursuant to law to consent to health care for the person. The release must be dated, specify to whom the disclosure is authorized, the purpose of the release, and the time period during which it is valid. A general authorization for the release of medical records is not valid for release of HIV-related information unless the authorization specifically indicates its purpose both as a general authorization and as a release for the confidential HIV-related information. Ariz. Rev. Stat. § 36-664(e).

AIDS, an HIV-related disease, or HIV infection can be listed on a death certificate, autopsy report, or related documents. Ariz. Rev. Stat. § 36-664(j).

Arkansas

Mandatory reporting of AIDS diagnosis or HIV positive status; information is confidential. Ark. Code Ann. § 20-15-904.

Informed consent for HIV test not required when a health care provider has direct skin or mucous membrane contact with the blood or bodily fluids of an individual; results of the test shall be provided to the affected health care individual. Ark. Code Ann. § 20-15-905(b).

Informed consent is not required for the performance of an HIV test when, in the judgment of a physician, such testing is medically indicated to provide an appropriate diagnosis and treatment to the subject of the test, provided that the subject has otherwise provided his or her consent to such a physician for medical treatment. Any patient so tested shall be informed of any HIV-positive results. Ark. Code Ann. § 20-15-905(c).

Blood donors to be informed that their blood will be tested for HIV and, if positive, their name shall be made available to the Department of Health for partner notification and contact tracing. Ark. Code Ann. § 20-27-302(1).

Prior to receiving any health care services from a physician or dentist, any HIV-positive individual shall advise such physician or dentist of their HIV status; misdemeanor for failure to notify. Ark. Code Ann. § 20-15-903(a).

Persons charged with sexual offenses shall be tested for HIV; test results may be released to the victim. Ark. Code Ann. § 16-82-101.

California

Informed and written consent required for testing. Consent not required under the following circumstances: to detect antibodies to the probable causative agent of AIDS on a cadaver when an autopsy is performed or body parts are donated; when blood is tested as part of a scientific investigation conducted either by medical researchers operating under institutional review board approval or by the department in accordance with a protocol for unlinked testing. Cal. Health & Safety Code § 120990.

Written authorization required for the disclosure of test results by a person responsible for the care and treatment of the person subject to the test; required for each separate disclosure of the test results, and shall include to whom the disclosure would be made. Cal. Health & Safety Code § 120980(g).

The results of an HIV test can be included in the medical record of the patient who is the subject of the test; the inclusion does not authorize further disclosure. Cal. Health & Safety Code §§ 120980(1), 120985.

Physician-to-medical-team disclosure of HIV status is allowed. Cal. Health & Safety Code § 121010 (b)-(c).

No physician or surgeon shall disclose information concerning an individual's HIV status unless the following has occurred: the physician has first discussed the test results with the patient and has offered the patient appropriate educational and psychological counseling; has attempted to obtain the patient's voluntary consent for notification of his or her contacts; and the physician has notified the patient of his or her intent to notify the patient's contacts prior to doing so. No identifying information about the individual believed to be infected shall be disclosed. Cal. Health & Safety Code § 121015.

Colorado

Mandatory reporting of HIV-positive status, diagnosis of AIDS, or HIV-related illness; report will contain name, date of birth, sex, and address of the individual; physicians immune for good faith disclosure in compliance with law. Colo. Rev. Stat. § 25-14-1402.

Information regarding AIDS and HIV infection in medical records held by a facility that provided ongoing health care is considered medical information, not public health reports, and is protected from unauthorized disclosure. Colo. Rev. Stat. § 18-4-412.

Informed consent required for HIV test except in the following circumstances: when a health care provider has been exposed to blood or other bodily fluids; when a patient's medical condition is such that knowledge and consent cannot be obtained; for statistical surveys; when the individual is sentenced to or in the custody of the department of corrections; when an individual is bound over for trial of a sexual offense. Colo. Rev. Stat. § 25-14-1405(8).

Privacy protection afforded to individuals who are tested for HIV with limited exception for HIV-positive individual engaging in reckless behavior. Colo. Rev. Stat. §§ 25-4-1401 to 25-4-1410.

Connecticut

Informed consent required for HIV testing (written is preferable); consent to be documented in the medical record. Informed consent not required in the following circumstances: when the subject is unable to grant or withhold consent, and no other person authorized to grant consent is available; in the procuring of human body parts for transplant; for statistical purposes only; during an autopsy to determine the cause of death; when a health care worker has had significant exposure to blood or body fluids; in correctional facilities when needed for diagnosis or treatment, or under circumstances in which the individual's behavior exposes others; under court order; when conducted by insurer for purposes of assessing an applicant for insurance. Conn. Gen. Stat. Ann. § 19a-582.

Any insurer that requests an application for coverage to take an HIV test shall obtain written informed consent for the test; disclosure of HIV-positive results by the insurer to industry organizations that assemble or collect information about insurance applicants is not prohibited as long as the test cannot be identified as an HIV-related test. Conn. Gen. Stat. Ann. §§ 19a-586 and 19a-587.

Physician-to-medical-team disclosure of HIV status is allowed. Conn. Gen. Stat. Ann. § 19a-583(4).

A physician or public health officer may disclose confidential HIV information to an individual's partner if certain conditions are met: the physician or officer reasonably believes there is a significant risk of transmission to the partner; the physician or officer has counseled the individual and reasonably believes that the individual will not inform the partner; and the physician or officer informs the individual of his or her intent to make the disclosure to the partner. The physician or officer is not required to identify or locate a partner. Referrals for appropriate medical advice and counseling shall also be made. Conn. Gen. Stat. Ann. § 19a-584.

Any disclosure of HIV-related information should include the following or substantially similar language: "This information has been disclosed to you from records whose confidentiality is protected by state law. State law prohibits you from making any further disclosure of it without the specific written consent of the person to whom it pertains, or as otherwise permitted by said law. A general authorization for the release of medical or other information is NOT sufficient for this purpose." Conn. Gen. Stat. Ann. § 19a-585.

Written authorization specifying release of HIV-related information required—general authorization is not sufficient. The authorization must be signed by the individual or person authorized to consent to health care for the individual, dated, specify to whom disclosure is authorized, the purpose of the disclosure, and the applicable time period. Conn. Gen. Stat. Ann. § 19a-581(9).

Delaware

Informed consent required for HIV testing. If the consent is oral, all facts pertaining to this agreement must be documented in the medical record. The consent process must contain the following: an explanation of the test, including its purpose, potential uses, limitations, and the meaning of its results; an explanation of the procedure to be followed, including that the test is voluntary, that consent may be withdrawn, and the extent and limitations of the manner in which the results will be confidential; an explanation of the nature of AIDS and other manifestations of HIV infection and the relationship between the test result and those diseases; and information about behaviors known to pose risks for transmission of HIV infection. Del. Code Ann. tit. 16, § 1201.

Consent is not required in the following circumstances: knowledge of such test results is necessary for medical diagnostic purposes to provide appropriate emergency care or treatment, and the subject of the test is unable to grant or withhold consent; the testing is done for the purposes of research in a manner by which the identity of the test subject is not known and may not be retrieved by the researcher; a health care provider or health care facility procures, processes, distributes, or uses human body organs or fluids; the health of a health care worker has been threatened during the course of a health care worker's duties, as a result of exposure to blood or body fluids of the patient in a manner known to transmit HIV; necessary to control the transmission of HIV infection as may be allowed pursuant to Chapter 7 or § 6523(b) of Title 11; when testing is court ordered within the confines of civil or criminal litigation where the results of an HIV-related test of a party, or a person in the custody or under the legal control of another party, are relevant to the ultimate issue of culpability and/or liability, and upon a showing of compelling need for such test results which cannot be accommodated by other means. Del. Code Ann. tit. 16, § 1202.

A release of HIV test results requires a written authorization for disclosure of HIV-related test results which is signed, dated, specifies to whom disclosure is authorized, and the time period during which the release is to be effective. Del. Code Ann. tit. 16, § 1201(9).

A minor 12 years of age or older may consent or refuse consent to be a subject of HIV-related testing and to counseling relevant to the test. The consent or refusal of the minor shall be valid and binding as if the minor had achieved majority, and shall not be voidable, nor subject to later disaffirmance, because of minority. Del. Code Ann. tit. 16, § 1202(6d).

No insurer shall request or require that an applicant submit to an HIV test unless the insurer first: obtains the applicant's prior written informed consent; reveals to the applicant the use to which the HIV test results may be put and entities to whom test results may be disclosed pursuant to §§ 7404 and 7405 of this title; and provides the applicant with written information approved by the Department of Health and Social Services. Del. Code Ann. tit. 18, § 7403.

Florida

Mandatory reporting requirements: when any attending health care practitioner who diagnoses or suspects the existence of a disease of public health significance, he or she shall immediately report the fact to the Department of Health and Rehabilitative Services; this information is confidential and shall be made public only when necessary to protect public health. Fla. Stat. Ann. § 381.231(1), (4).

Informed consent required for HIV testing, to be preceded by an explanation of the test, its purpose, potential uses and limitations, the meaning
of its results, and the right to withdraw consent at any time prior to the test;
consent need not be in writing provided there is documentation in the
medical records that the test has been explained and consent obtained.
Fla. Stat. Ann. § 381.609(3a). Post-test counseling is required. Fla. Sta.
Ann. § 381.609(3c).

Informed consent is not required under the following circumstances:
when testing is required by state or federal law; when testing persons
convicted of prostitution or procuring another to commit prostitution;
HIV testing by a medical examiner or as part of an autopsy; in bona
fide medical emergencies when the test results are necessary for medical
diagnostic purposes to provide appropriate emergency care or treatment,
and the person is unable to consent as supported by documentation in
the medical record; when, in the opinion of the attending physician,
informed consent would be detrimental to the patient as supported by
documentation in the medical record, and the test results are necessary
for medical diagnostic purposes; when a victim requests the test in a
prosecution for any type of sexual battery; when mandated by court
order; for epidemiological research; when medical personnel experience
significant exposure during the course and scope of their duties. Fla. Stat.
Ann. § 381.609(i).

The identity of any person who is tested for HIV and the results of such
testing are confidential. No person who has obtained or has knowledge of a
test result may disclose or be compelled to disclose the identity of the
person or the results, except as follows: the subject of the test or the
subject's legal representative; any person so designated in a legally
effective release executed prior to or after the test by the subject of the
test or the subject's legal representative, a general release without such
prior written authorization is not sufficient to release HIV test results;
a health facility or health care provider which procures, processes, distributes, or uses human body parts or fluids; for epidemiological, statistical, and quality assurance purposes; by court order, pursuant to compelling
need, and possible in camera review; to individuals working in child protective and child-related agencies on a need-to-know basis; medical
personnel who have been subject to a significant exposure during the
course of medical practice or in the performance of professional duties;
or individuals who are the subject of the significant exposure. Fla. Stat.
Ann. § 381.609(f).

Physician-to-medical-team disclosure of HIV status is allowed. Fla. Stat. Ann. § 381.609(f)(3)-(4).

Disclosure of the identity of a blood donor who may have AIDS is barred; blood donors' rights of privacy are protected by the state and federal constitutions. *Rasmussen v. South Florida Blood Service,* 500 So. 2d 533 (Fla. 1987).

Georgia

Mandatory reporting of HIV-positive status. Ga. Code Ann. § 24-9-47.

Physician-to-medical-team disclosure of HIV status is allowed. Ga. Code Ann. § 24-9-47(i).

Confidential information concerning AIDS may be disclosed to any person or legal entity designated to receive that information when that designation is made in writing by the person identified by that information or, if that person is a minor or incompetent person, by that person's parent or legal guardian. Ga. Code Ann. § 24-9-47(d).

When an individual has been determined to be infected with HIV and that patient's physician reasonably believes that the spouse or sexual partner or any child of the patient, spouse, or sexual partner is a person at risk of being infected with HIV by that patient, the physician may disclose to that spouse, sexual partner, or child that the patient has been determined to be infected with HIV, after first attempting to notify the patient that such disclosure is going to be made. Ga. Code Ann. § 24-9-47(g).

When exposure of a health care provider to any body fluids of a patient occurs in such a manner as to create any risk that such provider might become HIV-infected, a health care provider otherwise authorized to order an HIV test shall be authorized to order any HIV test on such patient and obtain the results thereof. If the patient or representative refuses the test, it can be compelled if at least one other health care provider who is otherwise authorized to order an HIV test concurs in writing to the testing. The patient must be informed of the results of the test and provided counseling with regard to those results. Ga. Code Ann. § 24-9-47(g2).

Hawaii

Mandatory reporting of HIV-positive status. Haw. Rev. Stat. § 325-2.

The medical records of any person that indicate that a person is HIV-positive, has ARC or AIDS, and are held or maintained by any state agency, health care provider, facility, physician, laboratory, etc., shall be strictly confidential. "Records" shall be broadly construed to include all communications that identify any individual as having AIDS or ARC or being HIV-positive. Information shall not be released or be made public pursuant to subpoena or any other method of discovery. Release is permitted as follows: to the department of health to comply with federal reporting requirements, all personal identification information to be protected from disclosure; with prior written consent; to medical personnel in a medical emergency only to the extent necessary to protect the health, life, or well-being of a party; by a physician to the department of health to protect sexual or needle-sharing contacts; to any child protective agencies; to a health care insurer. Haw. Rev. Stat. § 325-101.

Physician-to-medical-team disclosure of HIV status is allowed. Haw. Rev. Stat. § 325-101(10).

The recording or maintaining of protected information in a separate portion of an individual's file which is clearly designated as confidential shall not be construed as a breach per se of that individual's confidentiality. Haw. Rev. Stat. § 325-101(b).

Idaho

AIDS, ARC, and HIV are contagious, infectious, communicable, and dangerous to the public health. Idaho Code § 39-601.

Mandatory reporting of HIV-positive status; information is confidential; health care team disclosure is allowed. Idaho Code § 39-609.

Illinois

Illinois Aids Confidentiality Act (IACA) found at 410 I.L.C.S. 305 *et seq.*

Mandatory reporting of AIDS and ARC; information is confidential. 410 I.L.C.S. 310/1, 4.

Written informed consent required for HIV test with specific requirements for counseling. 410 I.L.C.S. 305/4.

In a case in which plaintiffs were tested for HIV without their knowledge and consent, and for which no counseling was provided, the court held that the IACA imposes various duties on physicians conducting HIV testing. The plaintiffs asserted that IACA violations caused them emotional distress and that this distress resulted from a breach of a duty imposed by law; accordingly plaintiffs' claim for negligent infliction of emotion distress could not be dismissed. *Doe v. City of Chicago,* 883 F. Supp. 1126 (N.D. Ill. 1994).

Informed consent is not required under the following circumstances: in the procuring, processing, etc., of human body parts for transplant; when a health care provider, law enforcement officer, or emergency services personnel is involved in an accident in which there is direct skin or mucous membrane contact with blood or bodily fluids; for research purposes; when in the judgment of a physician such testing is medically indicated to provide appropriate diagnosis and treatment to the subject of the test, provided that the subject of the test has otherwise provided his or her consent to such physician for medical treatment. 40 I.L.C.S. 205/7-8.

Results of such testing are confidential except to the following: the test subject or to his or her legal representative; the spouse of the test subject, provided that the physician has first sought unsuccessfully to persuade the patient to notify the spouse, or when, a reasonable time after the patient has agreed to notify his or her spouse, the physician has reason to believe that it has not been done. The physician is not obligated to notify the spouse; no civil liability for disclosing or not disclosing the results; any person designated in a legally effective release or that person's legal representative; a health facility or health care provider which procures, processes, distributes, or uses human body parts or fluids; for epidemiological, statistical, and quality assurance purposes. 410 I.L.C.S. 305/9.

Physician-to-medical-team disclosure is allowed. 410 I.L.C.S. 305/9(c).

This act is not applicable to the publication of information already contained in open and public court files and does not prevent the dissemination of information available in open and public court files. *Doe v. Alton Telephone,* 805 F. Supp. 30 (C.D. Ill. 1992). *See also In re Multimedia KSDK, Inc.,* 221 Ill. App. 3d 199, 163 Ill. Dec. 757, 581 N.E.2d 911 (1991).

Sections 1-15 of this Act do not apply to a health maintenance organization, insurance company, fraternal benefit society, or other insurer. 410 I.L.C.S. 305/15.1.

Indiana

Mandatory reporting of HIV-positive status including each confirmed case of AIDS; but report may not include the name or other identifying characteristics of the individual tested. Ind. Code § 16-1-9.5-2.

Informed consent required for HIV testing, including the right to anonymous testing; consent required unless physician has obtained a health care consent under Ind. Code § 16-8-12 or an implied consent under emergency circumstances and the test is medically necessary to diagnose or treat the patient's condition; under court order based on clear and convincing evidence of a serious and present health threat to others; on blood collected anonymously as part of an epidemiological study. Ind. Code §§ 16-1-9.5-2(c), 35-38-1-10.5(a), 35-38-2-2(a)(15).

Iowa

Mandatory reporting of HIV-positive status. Iowa Code § 141.23(e).

Informed consent required for HIV testing; testing is voluntary, can be anonymous; pre- and post-test counseling required. Iowa Code § 141.22.

Informed consent not required under the following circumstances: when a health care provider or health facility procures, processes, distributes, or uses a donated human body part or fluid; by licensed medical personnel in medical emergencies when the subject of the test is unable to grant or withhold consent, and the test results are necessary for medical diagnostic purposes to provide appropriate emergency care or treatment, except that post-test counseling shall be required; by a person engaged in the business of insurance who is subject to section 505.16; when the subject of the test is deceased, a significant exposure has occurred, and written consent is obtained from certain identified parties. Iowa Code § 141.22(5).

Physician-to-medical-team disclosure of HIV status is allowed. Iowa Code § 141.23(c)-(d).

Records concerning HIV-related tests are confidential and may not be released except to the following: the subject of the test or the subject's legal guardian; any person who secures a written release of test results executed by the subject of the test or the subject's legal guardian; a health facility or health care provider that procures, processes, distributes, or uses a human body part from a deceased person; a person allowed access to a record by a court order which is issued upon a showing of a compelling need for the test results. Iowa Code § 141.23.

Written release for records: Any person who secures a written release of test results shall not disclose the test results to another person except as authorized; the disclosure shall be accompanied by a statement in writing which includes the following or substantially similar language: "This information has been disclosed to you from records whose confidentiality is protected by state law. State law prohibits you from making any further disclosure of the information without the specific written consent of the person to whom it pertains, or as otherwise permitted by law. A general authorization for the release of medical or other information is not sufficient for this purpose." An oral disclosure shall be accompanied or followed by such a notice within 10 days. Iowa Code § 141.23(k).

Kansas

Physician-to-medical-team disclosure of HIV status is allowed. Kan. Stat. Ann. § 65-6004.

Mandatory reporting of HIV-positive status and AIDS diagnosis; but report may not include name or address for an HIV-positive status. Kan. Stat. Ann. § 65-6002(a).

Information is confidential and cannot be released upon subpoena or otherwise except for the following: statistical purposes; upon presentation of a written release; in a medical emergency to health care personnel only to the extent necessary to protect the life and health of the patient. Kan. Stat. Ann. § 65-6002(c).

A physician performing medical or surgical procedures on a patient known to the physician to be HIV-positive or to have AIDS may disclose this information to others who have or will be in contact with the patient's bodily fluids. Kan. Stat. Ann. § 65-6004(a).

A physician may inform the spouse of an individual known to the physician to be HIV-positive of the risk of exposure; the physician has no duty to warn and is immune to liability for the disclosure or nondisclosure. Kan. Stat. Ann. § 65-6004(b).

Kentucky

HIV and AIDS defined as sexually transmitted diseases. Ky. Rev. Stat. Ann. § 214.410.

Mandatory reporting of HIV status; records are confidential. Ky. Rev. Stat. Ann. § 214.420.

Written consent required for release of medical information concerning HIV and AIDS except in the following circumstances: to the physician retained by the test subject; for epidemiological or statistical purposes in a manner so that no individual person can be identified; as necessary to enforce the provision of the rules and regulations relating to the control and treatment of sexually transmitted disease; and release of information made to medical personnel in a medical emergency to the extent necessary to protect the health or life of the named party. Ky. Rev. Stat. Ann. § 214.420(3).

Louisiana

Written informed consent required for HIV test; patient shall be provided with the opportunity for anonymous testing. La. Rev. Stat. Ann. § 1300.13.

Physician-to-medical-team disclosure of HIV status is allowed. La. Rev. Stat. Ann. § 1300.14.

A physician may disclose confidential HIV information to a patient's contact if certain conditions are met: the physician reasonably believes disclosure is medically appropriate and there is a significant risk of infection to the contact; the physician has counseled the patient regarding the need to notify the contact, and the physician reasonably believes that the patient will not inform the contact; and the physician informs the patient of his or her intent to make the disclosure to the contact and gives the patient the opportunity to express a preference as to whether the disclosure should be made by the physician directly or by a public health officer. The physician must provide or make referrals for the provision of appropriate medical advice and counseling for the contact. Disclosure does not include information concerning the identity of the patient or any other contact. The physician is not required to identify or locate a contact. La. Rev. Stat. Ann. § 1300.14(E).

HIV test results can be disclosed pursuant to court order. La. Rev. Stat. Ann. § 1300.15.

Maine

Informed consent required for HIV test; requires understanding that the test is being performed, the nature of the test, the persons to whom the results of that test may be disclosed, the purpose for which the test results may be used, any reasonably foreseeable risks and benefits of the test, and that the consent is given wholly voluntary and free from express or implied coercion. Me. Rev. Stat. Ann. tit. 5, § 19201(5-A).

Written consent required for disclosure.

Physician-to-medical-team disclosure of HIV status is allowed.

Maryland

Mandatory reporting of HIV and AIDS; reports concerning asymptomatic HIV contain the age, sex, race, and zip code of residence of the patient and a patient identifying number that does not disclose the identity of the patient; reports are confidential, not open to public inspection, and subject to subpoena or discovery in any criminal or civil proceeding only pursuant to a court order sealing the court record. Md. Health-Gen. Code Ann. §§ 18-201, 18-202, 18-205.

Massachusetts

No health care facility, physician, or health care provider shall test any person for the presence of the HTLV-III antibody or antigen without first obtaining the person's written informed consent; the results of such test may not be disclosed to any person other than the subject thereof without first obtaining the subject's written informed consent; the subject of such tests may not be identified to any person without first obtaining the subject's written informed consent. Mass. Ann. Laws ch. 111, § 70F.

"Written informed consent" means a written consent form for each requested release of the results of an individual's HTLV-III antibody or antigen test, or for the release of medical records containing such information; the purpose for which the information is being requested and shall be distinguished from written consent for the release of any other medical information. Mass. Ann. Laws ch. 111, § 70F.

AIDS testing may not be performed without written informed consent of the person being tested. *Langton v. Commissioner of Correction,* 34 Mass. App. Ct. 564, 614 N.E.2d 1002, *review denied,* 416 Mass. 1101, 618 N.E.2d 71 (1993).

No employer shall require HTLV-III antibody or antigen tests as a condition for employment. Mass. Ann. Laws ch. 111, § 70F.

Privacy protection is afforded to individuals who are tested for HIV. Mass. Gen. Laws Ann., ch. 111, § 70F.

Michigan

Mandatory reporting of HIV-positive status within seven days after obtaining the test result, including all of the following information: name, address, and telephone number of the test subject; name and address of the person/entity that submits the report; age, race, sex, and county of residence of the test subject; date on which the test was performed; whether or not the test subject has tested positive for the presence of HIV or an antibody to HIV on a previous occasion; probable method of transmission; purpose of the test. Mich. Stat. Ann. § 14.15(5114).

HIV-positive individuals must be referred to the local health department for sexual or hypodermic needle-sharing partner notification; notification to take place within 35 days of interview with test subject. Mich. Stat. Ann. § 14.15(5114a)(5b).

Mississippi

Mandatory reporting of HIV and AIDS status, including mandatory reporting to a hospital or health care facility; failure to report by a physician can be grounds for suspension of the physician's license. Miss. Code Ann. § 41-23-1.

HIV- and AIDS-related information is confidential. Miss. Code Ann. § 41-23-1(9).

A hospital or physician, and employees of such hospital or physician, may conduct an HIV antibody test without specific consent for such tests if the hospital or physician determines that the test is necessary for diagnostic purposes to provide appropriate care or treatment to the person to be tested, or in order to protect the health and safety of other patients or persons providing care and treatment to the person to be tested. The person who is to be tested shall be informed of the nature of the test that is to be conducted. Miss. Code Ann. § 41-41-16.

Missouri

Mandatory reporting of HIV-positive status. Mo. Rev. Stat. § 191.653.

All information and records containing any information held or maintained by any person, or by any agency, department, or political subdivision of the state, concerning an individual's HIV infection status or the results of any individual's HIV testing shall be strictly confidential and shall not be disclosed except to the following: pursuant to the written authorization of the subject of the test result or results; to the spouse of the subject of the test result or results; to the subject of the test result or results; to the parent or legal guardian or custodian of the subject of the testing, if the subject is an unemancipated minor; to the victim of any sexual offense defined in [Mo. Rev. Stat.] chapter 566 which includes sexual intercourse as an element of the crime; to employees of a state licensing board in the execution of their duties; to public employees within an agency, department, or political subdivision who need to know to perform their public duties; to persons other than public employees who are entrusted with the regular care of those under the care and custody of a state agency, including but not limited to operators of day care facilities, group homes, residential care facilities and adoptive or foster parents. Mo. Rev. Stat. § 191.656.

Physician-to-medical-team disclosure of HIV status is allowed. Mo. Rev. Stat. § 191.656.

Seropositive individuals must disclose status to health care professionals from whom they receive care. Mo. Rev. Stat. § 191.656.

No liability for health care workers who report in good faith the names of persons suspected of being HIV-positive. Mo. Rev. Stat. § 191.656.

When the results of HIV testing are included in the medical records of the patient, this does not constitute a disclosure so long as such medical records are afforded the same confidentiality protection afforded other medical records. Mo. Rev. Stat. § 191.656(4).

Montana

HIV is a sexually transmitted disease that is contagious, infectious, communicable, and dangerous to public health. Mont. Code Ann. § 50-18-101.

A health care facility may not refuse to admit a person solely because the person has an HIV-related condition. Mont. Code Ann. § 50-5-105.

No civil liability for disclosure of an HIV-related test result in accordance with any reporting requirement for a diagnosed case of AIDS or an HIV-related condition by the health department or the CDC. Mont. Code Ann. § 50-16-1013(d5).

Nevada

Test and medical information is confidential medical information and must not be disclosed to any person under any circumstances, including pursuant to any subpoena, search warrant, or discovery proceeding, except as follows: for statistical purposes, provided that the identity of the person is not discernible from the information disclosed; if the person who is the subject of the information consents in writing to the disclosure; if the disclosure is made to the welfare division of the department of human resources and the person about whom the disclosure is made has been diagnosed as having AIDS or an illness related to HIV and is a recipient of or an applicant for assistance to the medically indigent. Nev. Rev. Stat. tit. 36, § 441A.220.

Physician-to-medical-team disclosure of HIV status is allowed. Nev. Rev. Stat. tit. 36, § 441A.220(5).

Mandatory HIV test of person detained for commission of sexual offense; disclosure of results to victim. Nev. Rev. Stat. tit. 36, § 441A.320.

New Hampshire

Informed consent required for HIV testing. N.H. Rev. Stat. Ann. § 141-F:5.

Informed consent not required under the following circumstances: when testing is done by any blood bank, blood center, plasma center, or agency that purchases or receives donated whole blood, blood plasma, a blood product, or a blood derivative; any health care practitioner who procures, processes, distributes, or uses a human body part, tissue, or fluid; for purposes of medical research; on individuals convicted and confined to a correctional facility; when the person being tested is incapable of giving informed consent and when a test for the presence of an antibody or antigen to a human immunodeficiency virus is immediately necessary to protect the health of the person. N.H. Rev. Stat. Ann. § 141-F:5(I-V).

Test results are confidential; may not be released except as follows: to the physician who ordered the test; to the health department; in response to a written request if such person has given written authorization for such disclosure (such written request shall state the reasons for the request and shall contain only the identity of the infected person); to a blood bank, blood center, plasma center, or other agency that receives blood donations. N.H. Rev. Stat. Ann. § 141-F:7, 8.

Physician-to-medical-team disclosure of HIV status is allowed. N.H. Rev. Stat. Ann. § 141-F:8(IV).

Contact referral of any persons who may be or have been infected; identity of the individual found serologically positive shall not be disclosed. N.H. Rev. Stat. Ann. § 141-F:9(III).

No health care worker who is knowingly infected with the human immunodeficiency virus or communicable hepatitis B virus shall perform or participate in the performance of any exposure prone invasive procedure unless the health care worker has filed a letter of application to engage in such procedures. N.H. Rev. Stat. Ann. § 141-F:9-b.

New Jersey

Mandatory reporting of all diagnosed cases of AIDS and all diagnosed cases of HIV infection along with identifying information for the person diagnosed. N.J. Stat. Ann. § 26:5C-6.

No action for damages based upon personal injury, survivorship, or wrongful death brought against a proprietary manufacturer of blood products based on infusion of a blood product resulting in contracting HIV or AIDS shall be deemed to accrue prior to July 13, 1995. N.J. Stat. Ann. § 2A:14-26.1(b).

The content of an HIV-related record may be disclosed in accordance with the prior written informed consent of the person who is the subject of the record. N.J. Stat. Ann. § 26:5C-8.

Written consent is not required under the following conditions: for the purpose of conducting scientific research; to qualified personnel for the purpose of conducting management audits, financial audits, or program evaluation; to qualified personnel involved in medical education. N.J. Stat. Ann. § 26:5C-8.

Physician-to-medical-team disclosure is allowed but limited to only personnel directly involved in the diagnosis and treatment of the person. N.J. Stat. Ann. § 26:5C-8.

The record of a person who has or is suspected of having AIDS or HIV infection may be disclosed by an order of a court of competent jurisdiction which is granted pursuant to an application showing good cause therefor. N.J. Stat. Ann. § 26:5C-9.

When consent is required for disclosure of the record of a minor who has or is suspected of having AIDS or HIV infection, consent shall be obtained from the parent, guardian, or other individual authorized under state law to act for the minor. N.J. Stat. Ann. § 26:5C-13.

New Mexico

Informed consent for HIV test required, preceded by an explanation of the test, including its purpose, potential uses and limitations, and the meaning of its results. Consent need not be in writing provided there is documentation in the medical record that the test has been explained and the consent has been obtained. N.M. Stat. Ann. § 24-2B-2.

Informed consent not required under the following circumstances: in the procuring of human body parts for transplant; for statistical purposes only; if the existence of an emergency medical condition necessitates an HIV test to diagnose and treat the emergency condition and the patient lacks the capacity to consent; for the purpose of research if the testing is performed in a manner by which the identity of the test subject is not known and may not be retrieved by the researcher; the performance of a test is required in order to provide appropriate care or treatment to a health care worker who may have been exposed to excessive amounts of blood or bodily fluids when the subject of the test is unable to grant or withhold consent and the test results are necessary for medical diagnostic purposes. N.M. Stat. Ann. § 24-2B-5.

Mandatory counseling required with positive test result and shall include the meaning of the test results, the possible need for additional testing, the availability of appropriate health care services, including mental health care, social and support services, and the benefits of locating and counseling any individual by whom the infected person may have been exposed to the human immunodeficiency virus and any individual whom the infected person may have exposed to the human immunodeficiency virus. N.M. Stat. Ann. § 24-2B-4.

Physician-to-medical-team disclosure of HIV status is allowed. N.M. Stat. Ann. § 24-2B-6.

New York

Written authorization specifying release of HIV-related information required; general authorization is not sufficient. Authorization must be dated, specify to whom disclosure is authorized, the purpose of the disclosure, and the applicable time period. N.Y. Pub. Health Law § 2780(9).

Physician-to-medical-team disclosure of HIV status is allowed; need-to-know basis only, penalties for intentional violation of confidentiality. N.Y. Pub. Health Law § 2782.

Written informed consent for HIV testing required, with exceptions (procuring human tissue or body parts for transplantation, research, or in the process of an autopsy). Explanation of confidentiality protections must be given as part of the informed consent; subject shall be given the option to remain anonymous or be given a referral to a test site that does anonymous testing. N.Y. Comp. Codes R. & Regs. tit. 10, § 58-1.1; N.Y. Pub. Health Law §§ 2611, 2781.

A physician may disclose confidential HIV information to a patient's contact if certain conditions are met: the physician reasonably believes disclosure is medically appropriate, and there is a significant risk of infection to the contact; the physician reasonably believes that the patient will not inform the contact; the physician informs the patient of his or her intent to make the disclosure to the contact. Disclosure does not include information concerning the identity of the patient or any other contact. The physician is not required to identify or locate a contact, and is not subject to criminal sanctions or civil liability for failing to disclose HIV-related information to a contact. N.Y. Pub. Health Law § 2782(4).

Unauthorized disclosure of HIV status can be grounds for a civil action for damages, including punitive damages. An HIV-positive person has a legal duty to disclose that fact to a health care provider before undergoing any intrusive care. *Doe v. Roe,* 599 N.Y.S.2d 350 (App. Div. 1993).

Confidential HIV-related information shall be recorded in the medical record of the individual, including a death certificate or autopsy report. N.Y. Pub. Health Law § 2782(8).

North Carolina

Physician-to-medical-team disclosure of HIV status is allowed. N.C. Gen. Stat. § 130A-143(3).

All information and records, whether publicly or privately maintained, that identify a person who has AIDS or who has or may have a disease or condition required to be reported pursuant to this Article shall be strictly confidential. This information shall not be released or made public except under the following circumstances: for statistical or research purposes in a way that no person can be identified; with written consent of the patient or his or her guardian; as necessary to protect the public health; pursuant to subpoena or court order with in camera review of the records at the request of the patient. N.C. Gen. Stat. § 130A-143.

Informed consent is required for an HIV test. If informed consent is not obtained, the test may not be performed. If the patient is incapable of providing consent or incompetent to do so and if others authorized to give consent are not available, the test may be performed if necessary for the appropriate diagnosis or care of the person. N.C. Gen. Stat. § 130A-148(h).

No test for the AIDS virus shall be required, performed, or used to determine suitability for continued employment, housing, or public services. It is unlawful to discriminate against any person having HIV or AIDS because of that infection. However, employers are not prohibited from the following: requiring an HIV test for job applicants in pre-employment medical exams; denying employment to a job applicant based solely on an HIV-positive test; including an HIV test in the course of a routine annual and required medical exam; taking appropriate employment action (e.g., reassignment or termination) if the continued employment of the employee who is HIV-positive or has AIDS would pose a significant risk to the health of the employee, co-workers, or the public, or if the employee is unable to perform the normally assigned job duties. N.C. Gen. Stat. § 130A-148(i).

North Dakota

Mandatory reporting of HIV-positive status. N.D. Cent. Code § 23-07-02.1.

Written informed consent for testing or disclosure of HIV results; specifics of form detailed; requires signature of individual to be tested. N.D. Cent. Code § 23-07.5-02.

Reports are strictly confidential information and may not be released, shared with any agency or institution, or made public, upon subpoena, search warrant, discovery proceedings, or otherwise, except under the following circumstances: to the test subject or his or her parent, guardian, or custodian; for statistical or research purposes in a manner such that no individual person can be identified; to the test subject's health care provider, including those instances in which a health care provider provides emergency care to the subject; to an agent or employee of the test subject's health care provider who provides patient care or handles or processes specimens of body fluids or tissues; to a licensed embalmer; to health care facility staff committees for accreditation or quality assurance review; anyone to whom the test subject has authorized to obtain the results. N.D. Cent. Code § 23-07.5-05.

An individual who is tested for HIV, that individual's parent or legal guardian or custodian in the case of a minor, or that individual's legal guardian in the case of an incapacitated individual, may authorize in writing a health care provider, blood bank, blood center, or plasma center to disclose the test results to any person at any time after providing informed consent for disclosure. A record of this consent must be maintained by the health care provider, blood bank, blood center, or plasma center authorized to disclose test results. N.D. Cent. Code § 23-07.5-03.

Ohio

Mandatory reporting of HIV-positive status. Information is confidential and may be released only with written consent of the patient, with exceptions. Ohio Rev. Code Ann. § 3701.24(C).

Oral or written informed consent is required for test; anonymous testing available; counseling shall be provided. Ohio Rev. Code Ann. § 3701.242.

Physician-to-medical-team disclosure of HIV status is allowed. Ohio Rev. Code Ann. § 3701.243.

Results of HIV tests may be disclosed to the following: the person who was tested, his or her legal guardian, spouse, or any sexual partner; anyone authorized by a written release executed by the individual tested or his or her legal guardian and specifying to whom disclosure is authorized, the time period during which the release is effective; the individual's physician; department of health; health care facility that procures or distributes human body parts; peer review committees; health care workers with significant exposure; law enforcement officials pursuant to a search warrant or subpoena. Ohio Rev. Code Ann. § 3701.243(B).

A plaintiff who received HIV-infected blood from blood bank was entitled to the medical records of the now-deceased donor, but not to the identity of the donor. Under Ohio Rev. Code Ann. § 3701.243, any discovery order compelling disclosure of identifying information concerning a voluntary donor of allegedly infected blood would be an order affecting a substantial right made in a special proceeding. The plaintiff failed to show a compelling reason for disclosure of this private information. *Arnold v. National Red Cross,* 93 Ohio App. 3d 564, 639 N.E.2d 484 (1994).

Oklahoma

Mandatory reporting of HIV-positive status. Okla. Stat. tit. 63, § 1-534.2.

Written consent for release of records required. Okla. Stat. tit. 63, § 1-525.

Results of HIV test to be provided to the victim of assault along with pre- and post-test counseling. Okla. Stat. tit. 63, § 1-525.

Oregon

Informed consent required for HIV test. Or. Rev. Stat. § 433.075.

HIV test can be requested when a worker has experienced an occupational exposure, or while in the course of administering health care has experienced a substantial exposure; court procedure defined when consent for test is refused. Or. Rev. Stat. § 433.080.

Pennsylvania

Written informed consent required for HIV test with exceptions. Pa. Stat. Ann. tit. 35, § 7605. Exception for a health care provider with significant exposure who has submitted to an HIV test, and the patient refuses to consent to testing or cannot be located. HIV test can be performed on any of the patient's blood that may still be available. If the health care provider's HIV test was negative, he or she will be informed of the results of any test on the patient's blood. Pa. Stat. Ann. tit. 35, §§ 7606 to 7608.

HIV results can be released to the following: the patient; the physician who ordered the test or the physician's designee; any person specifically designated in a written consent; medical personnel involved in the care of the patient; peer review committees; insurers; or persons authorized to receive information for statistical purposes. Pa. Stat. Ann. tit. 35, § 6707.

HIV information can be included in the medical record. Pa. Stat. Ann. tit. 35, § 6707.

Written consent specifying release of HIV-related information required and must include the following: specific name or general designation of the person permitted to make the disclosure; name or title of the individual or organization to whom the disclosure is to be made; name of the patient; purpose of the disclosure; how much and what kind of information is to be disclosed; the patient's signature; date on which the consent is signed; statement that the consent is subject to revocation at any time; date, event, or condition upon which the consent will expire. Pa. Stat. Ann. tit. 35, § 6707.

A trial court did not err in ordering a limited disclosure of the fact that a hospital surgeon was HIV-positive; compelling need within the meaning of 35 Pa. Cons. Stat. § 7608(a)(2) existed to disclose the surgeon's real name to patients on whom the surgeon had operated and that a "resident physician" who had participated in their procedures had tested positive, and to selected physicians who had worked with the surgeon or had been authorized by affected patients. *In re Milton S. Hershey Medical Center,* 634 A.2d 159 (Pa. 1993).

Rhode Island

Physician can enter test results in medical record and disclose HIV status to medical team. R.I. Gen. Laws § 23-6-17(2).

Physician may inform third parties with whom an AIDS-infected patient is in close and continuous contact, including but not limited to a spouse, if the nature of the contact, in the physician's opinion, poses a clear and present danger of AIDS transmission to the third party; and if the physician has reason to believe that the patient, despite the physician's strong encouragement, has not warned and will not warn the third party. R.I. Gen. Laws § 23-6-17(2).

Written informed consent for HIV testing is required. R.I. Gen. Laws § 23-6-11(3v).

Informed consent is not required under the following circumstances: when the person to be tested is under one year of age; when the person to be tested is between one and thirteen years of age and appears to be symptomatic for AIDS; when the person to be tested is a minor under the care and authority of the department of children, youth, and families, and the director of that department certifies that an AIDS test is necessary to secure health or human services for that person. R.I. Gen. Laws § 23-6-14.

Informed consent is not required when a person (the complainant) can document significant exposure to blood or other bodily fluids of another person (the individual to be tested), during performance of the complainant's occupation (including health care), providing that the complainant completes an incident report within 48 hours of the exposure, identifying the parties to the exposure, witnesses, time, place, and nature of the event; and the complainant submits to a baseline AIDS test and is negative on that test for the presence of the AIDS virus, within 72 hours of the exposure and there has been a significant percutaneous or mucous membrane exposure (i.e., needlestick; bite; splash over open wound, broken skin, or mucous membrane) by blood or bodily fluids of the person to be tested of a type and in sufficient concentration to permit transmission of the AIDS virus, if present in those fluids. If a sample of the patient's blood is not otherwise available and the patient refuses to grant informed consent, then the health care worker may petition the superior court for a court order mandating that the test be performed. R.I. Gen. Laws § 23-6-14(4)-(5).

Mandatory testing for HIV of persons convicted of sexual offense; release of test results to victim by the court. R.I. Gen. Laws § 11-37-17.

South Carolina

Mandatory reporting of HIV-positive status. S.C. Code Ann. § 44-29-70.

Records concerning sexually transmitted diseases, including HIV, are confidential and may not be released or made public, except under the following circumstances: medical and epidemiological information released for statistical purposes with no patient identifiers included; with consent of the person tested; to the extent necessary to enforce public health's control and treatment of the disease; in the case of a minor with HIV or AIDS, this information must be released to the superintendent of the school district and other school health professionals. S.C. Code Ann. § 44-29-135.

Physician-to-medical-team disclosure of HIV status is allowed to the extent necessary to protect the health or life of any person. S.C. Code Ann. § 44-29-135(d).

When an individual tests positive for HIV, his or her known sexual or intravenous drug contacts must be notified; the identity of the infected person is not revealed. S.C. Code Ann. § 44-29-90. Physicians and state agencies that identify and notify known contacts of a person with HIV are immune from damages for disclosure of this information. S.C. Code Ann. § 44-29-146.

If a health care worker is involved in an incident resulting in possible exposure to HIV and a medical professional has probable cause to believe that the incident may have caused infection, a patient may be required to be tested; test results must be given to the patient and the health care worker. S.C. Code Ann. § 44-29-230.

For individuals who know they are infected with HIV, it is a felony with a monetary fine and imprisonment to engage in behavior that exposes another to the virus. S.C. Code Ann. § 44-29-145.

South Dakota

No HIV- or AIDS-related statutes found concerning informed consent, testing, or disclosure issues.

Tennessee

Mandatory reporting of HIV-positive status; whenever any health care practitioner knows or suspects that any person is infected with any communicable disease, the practitioner shall immediately notify the health authorities of the town or county where the diseased person is found. Tenn. Code Ann. §§ 39-13-521, 68-10-101.

HIV test results are confidential and inaccessible to the public. Tenn. Code Ann. §§ 68-11-222, 14-1-41(2).

Mandatory HIV test for persons convicted of sexual offenses; results are released to the victim; peace officer can request an HIV test. Tenn. Code Ann. §§ 39-13-521, 68-10-116.

Texas

A patient may be required to submit to an HIV test preceding a medical procedure involving potential exposure to health care workers; as a bona fide occupational qualification when there is not a less discriminatory means of satisfying the occupational qualification. Tex. Health & Safety Code § 81.102.

HIV test results are confidential; results may not be released or disclosed except as follows: health authorities as required; the physician or other person authorized by law who ordered the test; the person tested or a person legally authorized to consent to the test on the person's behalf; the spouse of the person tested if the person tests positive for AIDS or HIV infection, antibodies to HIV, or infection with any other probable causative agent of AIDS; for statistical purposes. A person legally authorized to consent to disclosure of that person's test results to any other person may authorize the release or disclosure of the test results; authorization under this subsection must be in writing and signed by the person tested or the person legally authorized to consent to the test on the person's behalf, must state the person or class of persons to whom the test results may be released or disclosed. Tex. Health & Safety Code § 81.103.

Physician-to-medical-team disclosure of HIV status is allowed. Tex. Health & Safety Code § 81.103.

Utah

Mandatory reporting of HIV-positive status; AIDS is a communicable and infectious disease. A positive HIV test or diagnosis of AIDS requires that the Public Health Department initiate contact tracing and identification. Utah Code Ann. §§ 26-6-3.5, 26-6-6.

Vermont

No specific statutes located concerning HIV or AIDS; *see* Vt. Stat. Ann. tit. 19, § 1093, for statutes concerning communicable and venereal diseases generally.

Virginia

Informed consent, either oral or written, shall be obtained prior to performing any test to determine infection with HIV. Va. Code Ann. § 32.1-37.2(a).

Mandatory reporting of HIV-positive status; no duty on the part of the physician to notify any third party other than the local health department of such test result, and a cause of action shall not arise from any failure to notify any other third party; patient's identity and disease state shall be confidential. Va. Code Ann. § 32.1-36(c), (d).

Upon investigation by the local health department of a patient reported to be HIV-positive, the Commissioner may, to the extent permitted by law, disclose the patient's identity and disease to the patient's employer if the Commissioner determines that (i) the patient's employment responsibilities require contact with the public and (ii) the nature of the patient's disease and nature of contact with the public constitutes a threat to the public health. Va. Code Ann. § 32.1-37.2(d).

The results of every test to determine HIV infection shall be confidential. Such information may be released only to the following persons: the subject of the test or his or her legally authorized representative; any person designated in a release signed by the subject of the test or his or her legally authorized representative; the Department of Health; health care facility staff committees providing quality assurance services; for epidemiological or statistical use; to any person allowed access to such information by a court order; to any facility that procures, processes, distributes, or uses blood, other body fluids, tissues, or organs; to any person authorized by law to receive such information; to the parents or other legal custodian of the subject of the test if the subject is a minor; and to the spouse of the subject of the test. Va. Code Ann. § 32.1-36.1.

Physician-to-medical-team disclosure of HIV status is allowed. Va. Code Ann. § 32.1-36.1.

Washington

Consent required for HIV test except under the following circumstances: pursuant to Wash. Rev. Code § 7.70.065 for incompetent persons; for research purposes when neither the persons whose blood is being tested know the test results nor the persons conducting the tests know who is undergoing testing; if the department of labor and industries determines that it is relevant, in which case payments made under Wash. Rev. Code tit. 51 may be conditioned on the taking of an HIV antibody test; or as otherwise expressly authorized by this chapter. Wash. Rev. Code § 70.24.330.

Physician-to-medical-team disclosure of HIV status is allowed. Wash. Rev. Code § 70.24.105(6).

No person may disclose or be compelled to disclose the identity of any person upon whom an HIV antibody test is performed, or the results of such a test, nor may the result of a test for any other sexually transmitted disease when it is positive be disclosed. This protection against disclosure of test subject, diagnosis, or treatment also applies to any information relating to diagnosis of or treatment for HIV infection. Wash. Rev. Code § 70.24.105(2).

Test results may be released to the following persons: the subject of the test or the subject's legal representative for health care decisions in accordance with Wash. Rev. Code § 7.70.065; any person who secures a specific release of test results or information relating to HIV; public health officers; a health care facility or provider that procures or processes human body parts, etc.; any state or local public health officer conducting an investigation provided that the record was obtained by means of court-ordered HIV testing; pursuant to a court order upon a showing of good cause; contacts of the individual who may have been placed at risk for acquisition of HIV if the health officer believes that the exposed person was unaware that a risk of exposure existed; any health care worker or law enforcement personnel who has had substantial exposure to the blood or bodily fluids of an individual; claims management personnel associated with an insurer, etc., when such disclosure is to be used solely for the prompt and accurate evaluation and payment of medical or related claims; and individuals making decisions/recommendations concerning a minor child. Wash. Rev. Code § 70.24.105(2).

Disclosures shall be accompanied by a statement in writing that includes the following or substantially similar language: "This information has been disclosed to you from records whose confidentiality is protected by state law. State law prohibits you from making any further disclosure of it without the specific written consent of the person to whom it pertains, or as otherwise permitted by state law. A general authorization for the release of medical or other information is NOT sufficient for this purpose." An oral disclosure shall be accompanied or followed by such a notice within 10 days. Wash. Rev. Code § 70.24.105(5).

West Virginia

Physician-to-medical-team disclosure of HIV status is allowed; HIV status can be entered into the medical record and is not a breach of confidentiality. W. Va. Code § 16-3C-3(4)-(5).

A written authorization is required for the release of HIV test results and must be signed, dated, specify to whom the disclosure is to be made, and the time period the release is effective. W. Va. Code § 16-3C-1(p).

An HIV test can be requested by any physician, dentist, or the commissioner under the following circumstances: when there is cause to believe test could be positive; when there is cause to believe that the test could provide information important in the care of the patient; and with the patient's voluntary consent. Informed consent can be oral or in writing and requires counseling before and after the test. No informed consent is required under the following circumstances: test is for research purposes; in the procuring and processing of human body parts or fluids; in a medical emergency when the individual is unable to give consent. W. Va. Code § 16-3C-2.

Mandatory HIV test for persons convicted of prostitution, sexual abuse, or sexual assault; consent not required but counseling is. W. Va. Code § 16-3C-2(f).

Wisconsin

Mandatory reporting of HIV-positive status to include subject's name, address, date of birth, and ethnicity; information concerning sexual orientation or contacts not included. Wis. Stat. Ann. § 146.025(7).

Written informed consent required for HIV test. Wis. Stat. Ann. § 146.025(d), (e).

Privacy protection afforded to individuals who are tested for HIV. Wis. Stat. Ann. § 631.90.

Insurer may not require or request directly or indirectly of any individual to reveal whether the individual has been tested for HIV; condition the provision of insurance coverage on whether or not an individual has obtained an HIV test; or consider the determination of rates based on whether or not an individual has obtained an HIV test. Wis. Stat. Ann. § 631.90.

Wyoming

Sexually transmitted diseases are contagious and dangerous to public health. Wyo. Stat. § 35-4-130.

In the event of a significant exposure (e.g., needle stick, sexual contact, dental treatment, etc.) to blood or other bodily fluids, contact with third parties is required; identification of the infected person is not released. Wyo. Stat. § 35-4-133(b).

In the case of exposure of a health care worker to the blood or body fluids of a patient, where exposure could lead to a communicable disease infection, a heath care provider may order, with the patient's consent, the necessary testing. Absent the patient's consent, a court order is required. Wyo. Stat. § 35-4-133(4).

INTERNET RESOURCES

This Appendix consists of all Internet Web sites and resources referenced in the body of the text. The following addresses have been verified as of the date of publication. However, readers are cautioned that addresses and individual Web sites on the Internet change frequently.

Accreditation/Regulation of Health Care Organizations and Health Plans

Joint Commission on Accreditation of Health Care Organizations (JCAHO). *www.jointcommission.org*

National Committee for Quality Assurance (NCQA). *www.ncqa.org*

Utilization Review Accreditation Committee/American Accreditation Healthcare Commission. *www.urac.org*

Federal Government Sites

Centers for Disease Control. *www.cdc.gov*

Environmental Protection Agency (EPA). *www.epa.gov*

FirstGov for Consumers—*www.consumer.gov*

Food & Drug Administration. *www.fda.gov*

Health & Human Services—*www.hhs.gov*

Human Genome Project (including workplace discrimination). *www.ornl.gov/hgmis* and *www.nhgri.nih.gov*. Also see: National Conference of State Legislatures for laws related to genetics. *www.ncsl.org*

MediCare—*www.medicare.gov*

MediCare Skilled Nursing Home information—*www.medicare.gov/nursing/home.asp*

Medwatch: *www.fda.gov/medwatch*

National Cancer Institute—*www.cancer.gov*

National Center for Complementary and Alternative Medicine (NCCAM). *www.nccam.nih.gov*
National Institute for Occupational Safety and Health (NIOSH). *www.cdc.gov.niosh*
National Institute of Mental Health—*www.nimh.nih.gov*
National Institutes of Health—*www.nih.gov*
National Library of Medicine—*www.nlm.nih.gov*
Occupational Health and Safety Administration (OSHA). *www.osha.gov*

Health Care Plans
American Association of Health Plans. *www.aahp.org*

HIPAA
The Privacy Rule—*www.hhs.gov/ocr/hipaa*
Sample Business Associate Contract—*www.hhs.gov/ocr/hipaa/contractprov.html*

Information Databases
Medical Information Bureau—*www.mib.com*
National Practitioner Data Bank (NPDB)—*www.npdb-hipdb.gov*
Healthcare Integrity and Protection Data Bank (HIPDB)—*www.npdb-hipdb.gov*
Federation of State Medical Boards—*www.fsmb.org*; *www.Docinfo.org*
National Council of State Boards of Nursing, Inc.—*www.ncsbn.org*

Jury Verdict Reporters
(See **Chapter 9, § 9.63**)

Litigation
American Society of Questioned Document Examiners—*www.asqde.org*
Anatomical Chart Company—*www.anatomical.com*
Association of Forensic Document Examiners—*www.afde.org*
Daubert case law and explanation—*www.DaubertOnTheWeb.com*
EMTALA Online—*www.medlaw.com*

Federation of State Medical Boards—*www.fsmb.org*
Judicial Statistical Inquiry Form—*www.healthfinder.gov*
Legal Resource Network—*www.witness.net*
LifeArt™ Professional Medical Computer Illustrations—*www.lifeart.com*;
    www.mediclip.com
The Medical Malpractice Home Page—*www.vcilp.org/~sand/medmal/*
    open.html
The Medical School for Trial Lawyers—*www.seak.com*
Medi-Net—*www.healthfinder.gov*
National Council of State Boards of Nursing, Inc.—*www.ncsbn.org*

Medical Illustration

LifeArt™ Professional Medical Computer Illustrations. *www.lifeart.com*
    (or) *www.mediclip.com*
Association of Medical Illustrators—*www.medical-illustrators.org*
Medical College of Georgia, Dept. of Medical Illustration—*www.mcg*
    .edu/medart
The Johns Hopkins School of Medicine, Department of Art as Applied to
    Medicine—*www.med.jhu.edu/medart*

Medical Research

Advances Medical Technology Association—*www.himanet.com*
AIDS.Com—*www.aids.com*
Alzheimer's Disease. *www.Alz.org*
American Cancer Society—*www.cancer.org*
American Heart Association—*www.americanheart.org*
American Spinal Injury Association (ASIA). *www.asia-spinalinjury.org*
Anesthesia Doc—*www.anesthesiadoc.net*
Association of Cancer Online Resources—*www.acor.org*
eMedicine—*www.emedicine.com*
Entrez PubMed—*www.ncbi.nlm.nih.gov/entrez*
EurekAlert!—*www.eurekalert.org*
Greater Midwest Regional Library—*www.nnlm.nlm.nih.gov/gmr/*
Guide to Clinical Laboratory Testing—*www.arup-lab.com*
Hardin MD—*www.lib.uiowa.edu*
Health Industry Manufacturers Association—*www.himanet.com*
Health on the Net Foundation—*www.hon.ch*

Healthfinder—*www.healthfinder.org*
HealthGate—*www.healthgate.com*
HealthWorld—*www.healthworld.com/library/search/medline.htm*
HIV InSite—*www.hivinsite.org*
Human Anatomy On-Line—*www.innerbody.com*
Infotrieve—*www.infotrieve.com*
Institute for Safe Medication Practices (ISPM). *www.ispm.org*
Internet Literacy Consultants™—*www.matisse.net/files/glossary.html*
Internet Mental Health—*www.mentalhealth.com*
Lab Tests On Line—*www.labtestsonline.org*
Mayo Clinic Health Oasis—*www.mayoclinic.org*
MedGate—*www.healthgate.com*
MEDguide—*www.medguide.net/index.asp*
Medi-Net—*www.healthfinder.gov*
Medical Abbreviations—*www.neilmdavis.com*
The Medical List—*www.kumc.edu:80/mmatrix*
Medical Matrix—*www.medmatrix.org*
The Medical School for Trial Lawyers—*www.seak.com*
Medicine Net, Inc.—*www.medicinenet.com*
MEDLINE®. *www.medlineplus.gov* or *www.nlm.nih.gov/medlineplus*
    www.nlm.nih.gov
    www.ncbi.nlm.nih.gov/entrez
Medscape—*www.medscape.com*
MEDTropolis (Virtual Body_)—*www.medtropolis.com*
MedWeb—*www.cc.emory.edu/WHSCL/medweb.html*
Merck Manuals—*www.merck.com/pubs*
Merck Source (medical dictionary)—*www.mercksource.com*
Midcontinental Regional Library—*www.nnlm.nlm.nih.gov/mcr/*
Middle Atlantic Regional Library—*www.nnlm.nlm.nih.gov/mar/*
National Cancer Institute—*www.cancer.gov*
National Library of Medicine—*www.nlm.nih.gov*
National Spinal Cord Injury Association (NSCIA). *www.spinalcord.org*
New England Journal of Medicine—*www.nejm.org*
New England Regional Library—*www.nnlm.nlm.nih.gov/ner/*
OncoLink—*www.oncolink.upenn.edu*
Orthopaedic Web Links (OWL)—*www.orthopaedicweblinks.com*
Pacific Northwest Regional Library—*www.nnlm.nlm.nih.gov/pnr/*
Pacific Southwest Regional Library—*www.nnlm.nlm.nih.gov/psr/*
PaperChase—*www.paperchase.com*

Pharmaceutical Research and Manufacturers of America—
www.phrma.org
PharmInfo Net—*www.pharminfo.com*
PharmWeb—*www.mcc.ac.uk/pharmacy*
PubMed—*www.pubmed.gov*
Physicians Online—*www.po.com*
RadiologyInfo—*www.radiologyinfo.org*
South Central Regional Library—*www.nnlm.nlm.nih.gov/scr/*
Southeastern Atlantic Regional Library—*www.nnlm.nlm.nih.gov/sar/*
Thrive@pathfinder—*www.pathfinder.com/thrive*
Virtual Body_ at MEDTropolis—*www.medtropolis.com*
Virtual Hospital®—*www.vh.org*
The Visible Human Project®—*www.nlm.nih.gov*
Whiplash. *www.spinalinjuryfoundation.org*

Medical and Allied Professional Specialties and Organizations
(Refer to **Chapter 9, § 9.62** for websites)
Also: American Board of Nursing Specialties (ABNS) for nursing specialty certification. *www.nursingcertification.org*

Pharmacology
Internet Drug Index—*www.rxlist.com*
Pharmaceutical Research and Manufacturers of America—
www.phrma.org
Pharmaceutical Information Network—*www.pharmweb.net*
Also see: Drug Internet Resources, **Chapter 5, § 5.14**

Quality Assurance & Clinical Standards
Agency for Healthcare Research and Policy (AHQR) formerly Agency for Health Care Policy and Research (AHCPR). *www.ahcpr.gov* or *www.ahrq.gov/clinic*
American Pain Society. *www.ampainsoc.org*
Clinical Practice Guidelines for Chronic Pain Management (American Association of Anesthesiologists). *www.asahg.com*
Foundation for Accountability (FACCT). *www.facct.org*

International Association for Study of Pain. *www.iasp-pain.org*
Leapfrog Group. *www.leapfrog.org*
National Guideline Clearinghouse. *www.guidelines.gov*

Regional Medical Libraries
Middle Atlantic Region—*www.nnlm.gov/mar/*
Southeastern Atlantic Region—*www.nnlm.gov/sar/*
Greater Midwest Region—*www.nnlm.nih.gov/gmr/*
Midcontinental Region—*www.nnlm.nih.gov/mcr/*
South Central Region—*www.nnlm.nih.gov/scr/*
Pacific Northwest Region—*www.nih.gov/pnr/*
Pacific Southwest Region—*www.nnlm.nih.gov/psr/*
New England Region—*www.nnlm.nih.gov/ner/*

Skilled Nursing Facilities
COBRA Online—*www.medlaw.com*
MediCare site for SNF information—*www.medicare.gov/nursing/home.asp*
CarePathways—*www.carepathways.com*

BIBLIOGRAPHY

AACN Clinical Reference for Critical Care Nursing. 4th ed. Marguerite Kinney, Editor-in-Chief, St. Louis: C.V. Mosby Co., 1998.

Anatomy Coloring Book. 3rd ed. Wynn Kapit and Lawrence M. Elson. New York: Pearson Education, 2001.

Chiropractic Standards of Practice and Quality of Care. Herbert J. Vear. Gaithersburg, Md.: Aspen Publishers, Inc., 1992.

Current Medical Diagnosis and Treatment. 46th ed. Lawrence J. Tierney, Jr., Stephen J. McPhee, and Maxine A. Papadakis. Norwalk, Conn.: Appleton & Lange, 2007. [See also Current Pediatric Diagnosis and Treatment, Current Obstetric and Gynecological Diagnosis and Treatment.]

Diagnostic and Statistical Manual of Mental Disorders DSM IV-R-TR and *Quick Reference to the Diagnostic Criteria from DSM-IV-TR.* 4th ed. Washington, D.C.: American Psychiatric Association, 2000.

Dorland's Illustrated Medical Dictionary and *Dorland's Pocket Medical Dictionary.* 30th ed. Philadelphia: W.B. Saunders, 2003.

Drug Facts and Comparisons. 60th ed. St. Louis, Miss; Facts and Comparisons, 2005.

2005 *Health Devices Sourcebook.* Plymouth Meeting, Pa.: Emergency Care Research Institute, 2004.

Hospital Law Manual. Cynthia Conner, ed.-in-chief. Gaithersburg, Md.: Aspen Publishers, 1998.

Hospital Phone Book 2005–2006. Finn & Grabois, Eds. Douglas Publications, 2005.

ICD-9-CM International Classification of Diseases, Clinical Modification. 9th rev. Salt Lake City, Utah: Practice Management Information Corporation, 2004.

Law Every Nurse Should Know. 5th ed. Helen Creighton, R.N., J.D. Philadelphia, Pa.: W.B. Saunders, 2006.

Legal Nurse Consulting Principles and Practice. 2nd ed. Patricia Iyer, Ed., American Association of Legal Nurse Consultants. Glenview, Il.: CRC Press, 2002.

Long-Term Care Nursing Desk Reference. Barbara Acello. HCPro, Inc., 2005.

Luckman and Sorenson's Medical Surgical Nursing: A Psychophysiologic Approach. 4th ed. Joyce M. Black and Esther Matassarin-Jacobs, eds. Philadelphia, Pa: W.B. Saunders, 1993.

Medical Abbreviations: 26,000 Conveniences at the Expense of Communications & Safety. 12th ed. Neil M. Davis. Huntingdon Valley, Pa.: Neil M. Davis Associates, 1997.

Medical-Surgical Nursing: Assessment and Management of Clinical Problems. Sharon Mantik Lewis, Margaret McLean Heitkemper, and Shannon Ruff Dirksen, 2004. St. Louis, Mo. Mosby.

Mosby's Diagnostic and Laboratory Test Reference. 8th ed. Kathleen Pagana and Timothy Pagana. St. Louis, Mo.: C.V. Mosby, 2006.

Merck Manual of Diagnosis and Therapy. 17th ed. John Wiley & Sons, 2006.

Merck Manual of Geriatrics. 3d ed. Mark Beers, ed. John Wiley & Sons, 2000.

Musculoskeletal Primary Care. Sharon A. Gates and Pekka A. Mooar, 1999. Philadelphia PA: Lippincott.

2006 Comprehensive Accreditation Manual for Hospitals: The Official Handbook. Joint Commission for Accreditation of Health Care Organizations. Oakbrook Terrace, Ill.: JCAHCO, 2006.

Nurse's Drug Looseleaf, Blanchard & Loeb Publishers, LLC, updated annually, 2002.

Nursing Care of the Elderly. 4th ed. John Lanz ed. Brockton, Mass. Western Schools Press 1999.

Nursing 2006 Drug Handbook. 26th ed., Springhouse, Pa.: Lippincott Williams & Wilkins, 2005.

The Official ABMS Directory of Board Certified Medical Specialists. 37th ed., W.B. Saunders, 2005.

Orthopedic and Sports Medicine for Nurses. Sharon A. Gates and Pekka
   A. Mooar. Baltimore, Md.: Williams & Wilkins, Co., 1989.

Physician's Desk Reference. 60th ed. Thomson Healthcare, 2006.

Principles and Practice of Chiropractic. 3rd ed. Scott Haldeman, Editor-
   in-Chief, McGraw-Hill Companies, 2005.

Quick Medical Terminology: A Self-Teaching Guide. 4th ed. Shirley
   Soltesz Steiner. STG Guides.

Taber's Cyclopedic Medical Dictionary. 20th ed. F.A. Davis Company,
   2005.

INDEX

References are to section, appendix, or form number.